# DIAGNOSTIC AND
# REMEDIAL TEACHING

## LEO J. BRUECKNER
*Professor of Elementary Education*
*University of Minnesota*

AND

## ERNEST O. MELBY
*Dean, School of Education*
*New York University*

## HOUGHTON MIFFLIN COMPANY

BOSTON · NEW YORK · CHICAGO · DALLAS
ATLANTA · SAN FRANCISCO

**The Riverside Press Cambridge**

TEXAS SOUTHMOST COLLEGE LIBRARY
1825 MAY STREET, FT. BROWN
BROWNSVILLE, TEXAS. 78520

5782

The Riverside Press
CAMBRIDGE · MASSACHUSETTS
PRINTED IN THE U.S.A.

# EDITOR'S INTRODUCTION

A QUARTER of a century ago both teachers and principals paid but little attention to any individual differences that may have been evident in the learning ability of children under their control. Semi-annual promotions and an occasional special advancement of a capable pupil constituted practically all that was attempted by way of adjusting instruction to individual needs. The vast differences in pupil abilities which we now know to exist, and make some attempts to adjust our instruction to meet, were then largely ignored or entirely unknown. The coming of the test and measurement movement after about 1908, which revealed the wide differences in accomplishment of pupils, and the development of intelligence testing since 1911, which has made us aware of the vast differences in ability to learn, have in time changed the whole aspect of both school instruction and school supervision. What before had been but dimly sensed by a few now stands revealed to all, and it is seen that school work must be changed from guesswork to scientific accuracy, and school supervision from a managerial type of job for which little or no professional preparation is needed to an expert professional service for which careful preparation is required.

Since the beginning of the test and measurement movement we have traveled far. From one standardized test in 1908 we today have around six hundred standardized measuring instruments, in many school subjects and for many different educational purposes. Besides tests for intelligence and achievement, there are analytical subject tests, general survey tests, diagnostic tests, prognostic tests, rate tests, accuracy tests, and personal-trait tests, to mention the more important types, and the problem now is how and when and for what purposes should these different types be used, how the results obtained from their use are to be interpreted in the light of pupil needs, and how teaching adjustments that will be effective are to be made. Stated another way, how can these new tools best be used as guides in adapting the instruction of the schoolroom to that wide range of individual differences which we now recognize that children possess?

The authors of the present volume have taken this problem for their theme, and have offered us a treatise dealing with diagnostic procedure and remedial treatment as applied to the work of the elementary school. After setting forth the nature and function of standardized educational tests, the aspects of intellectual progress that are to be measured, and the nature and the technique of educational diagnosis, they proceed, in some detail, to deal with diagnostic and remedial procedures for each of the elementary school subjects. For each subject considered they first set forth the agreed-upon objectives in instruction, the levels of attainment, and the specific skills that need to be developed. They next describe and illustrate the different standardized tests that may be used for different diagnostic purposes, explain how to measure progress and how to diagnose peculiar difficulties, for both individuals and groups, and finally they describe the different remedial techniques that have been developed.

A helpful book of this type, covering the elementary school field, has been needed for some time, and a study of the procedures here presented should be enlightening to both teachers and supervisory officers. The volume at the same time contains materials that make it an important classroom textbook in the use of tests and measurements, and an

exceedingly useful reference work on both diagnostic procedures and remedial techniques in the instructional work of
the elementary school.   It is a noteworthy contribution to
our educational literature.

ELLWOOD P. CUBBERLEY

# PREFACE

THE development of the measurement movement in education has influenced instruction in many ways. It has provided techniques whereby the individual differences of children have been determined quantitatively and portrayed in such a striking manner that the schools can no longer ignore them. More recently, efforts have been made to develop methods for the utilization of measuring devices in the adaptation of instruction to the needs, interests, and capacities of children. This book gives primary consideration to the ways in which test procedures have modified classroom teaching, the techniques that may be used to diagnose the nature and causes of pupil difficulties, and the methods by which remedial adjustments of various kinds may be made.

The discussion is directed to the teacher rather than to the specialist. Emphasis is placed on the techniques of diagnostic and remedial teaching which experience has shown can be effectively employed by the average teacher. In a number of places devices in early and imperfect stages of development have been included in the belief that they may be suggestive to teachers in their work of developing new techniques. A definite attempt has been made to show how teaching procedures related to the skill subjects may be based on test methods or other objective devices in such a way that the traditional mass instruction found in many of our schools may be broken down. Methods of adapting instruction to individual differences are described and evaluated. The typical causes of difficulty in the several school subjects are discussed, and types of remedial work that experimentation has found helpful are summarized. An effort has been made to indicate to teachers how practice may be made purposeful and more effective through the use of self-diagnostic methods which enable the pupil to measure his progress and to determine the points at which his work is deficient or below standard. In this way much of the routine practice which has so frequently characterized the drill work in our elementary schools may be eliminated. Emphasis is given to the point of view that teachers who are conscious of the types of difficulty pupils encounter in their school work can do much to avert their development by "preventive teaching." The authors believe that the use of tests that is emphasized in this book is in accord with progressive educational theory and practice.

In the discussion of tests and other illustrative materials no effort has been made to mention all tests and materials available, those included having been selected because they illustrate various procedures that are presented. Much of the discussion involves the results of original research by the authors and their students, as well as of other workers. The names of these investigators appear in footnote references and bibliographies. The authors wish to express their appreciation for permission to quote from numerous studies. The authors also wish to acknowledge their indebtedness to the many publishers who have granted permission to quote copyrighted materials.

LEO J. BRUECKNER
ERNEST O. MELBY

# CONTENTS

# LIST OF TABLES

# CHAPTER I

## EVIDENCES AND CAUSES OF MALADJUSTMENT IN OUR SCHOOLS

### I. EVIDENCES OF MALADJUSTMENT

DURING the past three decades a large amount of information has been assembled showing that the schools have failed in many cases to adapt the curriculum and methods of teaching to the differences in ability, interests, and needs of individual pupils. The most significant sources of such information have been age-grade studies, studies of pupil progress, and the results of standard achievement tests. Age-grade studies have shown, in practically every case, that a large proportion of the pupils are over-age for their grade. The studies of rates of promotion and progress have shown that in many schools there is a very high percentage of pupil failure, which obviously results in an increased amount of over-ageness. The results of achievement tests have shown not only that many pupils fail to make satisfactory progress in their school work, but that there is also a wide overlapping in the abilities of pupils in the different grades. In an attempt to remedy the conditions revealed by these studies, many schools have conducted investigations to determine the causes of this maladjustment, and have made certain modifications which have in many cases greatly improved the situation.

**Age-grade and progress.** The first striking statistical presentation of data which brought to the attention of American educators the serious maladjustment in the schools of the United States was the age-grade table of Superintendent Maxwell, showing the extent of over-ageness

in the schools of New York.   Similar age-grade studies have
been made in many of our cities, and in most cases a serious
condition has been revealed.   Table 1 contains a typical
age-grade table showing the ranges in the ages of the pupils
enrolled in the same grade.

TABLE 1.  AGE-GRADE TABLE SHOWING NUMBER AND PER CENT
OF OVER-AGE PUPILS FOR AURORA, ILLINOIS, FOR
THE YEAR 1929–30

| GRADE / AGE | 1 | 2 | 3 | 4 | 5 | 6 | 7 | 8 | TOTALS |
|---|---|---|---|---|---|---|---|---|---|
| 6 | 353 | 41 | 1 | | | | | | 395 |
| 7 | 130 | 192 | 38 | | | | | | 360 |
| 8 | 32 | 100 | 207 | 44 | 2 | | | | 385 |
| 9 | 7 | 41 | 115 | 159 | 36 | 1 | | | 359 |
| 10 | 5 | 14 | 39 | 104 | 138 | 49 | 13 | | 362 |
| 11 | 1 | 2 | 9 | 42 | 112 | 145 | 51 | 2 | 364 |
| 12 | | 1 | 4 | 12 | 45 | 93 | 119 | 57 | 331 |
| 13 | | | | 5 | 17 | 60 | 96 | 117 | 295 |
| 14 | | | 1 | 2 | 12 | 26 | 33 | 83 | 157 |
| 15 | | | | 2 | 3 | 3 | 27 | 52 | 87 |
| 16 | | | | | | | 3 | 3 | 6 |
| Totals | 528 | 391 | 414 | 370 | 365 | 377 | 342 | 314 | 3101 |
| Number over-age | 45 | 58 | 53 | 63 | 77 | 89 | 63 | 55 | 503 |
| Per cent over-age | 9 | 15 | 13 | 17 | 21 | 24 | 18 | 18 | 16 |

Many problems are raised by the data contained in the
table.  Note, for example, the range in age from 8 to 15 in
grade 4.  Similar variations may be noted for each of the
grades.  The per cents of pupils over-age increase grade by
grade from grade 1 to 6, when a falling-off occurs, showing
that over-age pupils probably are being eliminated by
leaving school.  What readjustments can the school make
to alleviate this condition?

The facts revealed by an age-grade table for an entire city
conceal the variations that may be found among the several
schools.   In a recent report Superintendent Weet, of
Rochester, New York, presented some striking information,

as shown in Table 2, regarding age-grade and progress conditions in twelve schools of that city.

TABLE 2. SUMMARY OF AGE-GRADE AND PROGRESS OF PUPILS
IN TWELVE ROCHESTER SCHOOLS (1928) *

| | TOTAL (per cent) | RANGE (per cent) | | TOTAL (per cent) |
|---|---|---|---|---|
| Under-age.... | 6.5 | 2.4–15 | Rapid Progress | 7 |
| Normal age... | 54.1 | 44.1–78.3 | Normal Progress | 45.5 |
| Over-age..... | 39.4 | 12.1–53.6 | Slow progress | 47.5 |

* From *The Work of the Public Schools.* Board of Education, Rochester, New York, 1928.

In all twelve schools 6.5 per cent of the pupils enrolled were under-age, 54.1 per cent normal age, and 39.4 per cent were over-age. The range in per cents of pupils under-age in the twelve schools was from 2.4 per cent in one school to 15 per cent in another. The range in per cents of pupils over-age was from 12.1 to 53.6 per cent. Clearly the problems of administration and teaching in these schools must differ greatly. Any attempt to require all schools in a system to cover the same amount of subject-matter must result in serious maladjustments. The fact that 47.5 per cent of all pupils had not progressed at normal rates indicates that many of them had encountered such difficulty in their school work that they were not promoted at the end of the semester.

**The extent of non-promotion.** The amount of non-promotion in a school system is an indication of the extent to which attempts have been made to adjust instruction so as to eliminate pupil failure. Table 3 shows the variation in the per cents of failure in the schools of three cities.

The per cents of failure in Denver are lower in all grades than in either New York or Rochester. It will be noted also that the per cents of failure in New York were much lower in 1927 than in 1917. Records are available which show that in a single school system the per cents will vary as much as from less than 1 per cent of failure in one school to as much

TABLE 3. PER CENTS OF NON-PROMOTION IN THREE TYPICAL CITIES

| GRADES | DENVER (1929) | ROCHESTER (1928) | NEW YORK (1927) | NEW YORK (1917) |
|---|---|---|---|---|
| 1B..... | 10.2 | 21.9 | 16.4 | 22.8 |
| 1A..... |  | 12.2 | 9.1 | 11.7 |
| 2B..... | 6.2 | 12.0 | 8.9 | 11.8 |
| 2A..... |  | 10.1 | 7.1 | 9.2 |
| 3B..... | 4.4 | 8.2 | 7.6 | 10.2 |
| 3A..... |  | 7.9 | 6.6 | 9.4 |
| 4B..... | 3.8 | 8.5 | 7.7 | 10.1 |
| 4A..... |  | 10.8 | 7.1 | 10.3 |
| 5B..... | 3.3 | 10.9 | 7.9 | 12.0 |
| 5A..... |  | 8.9 | 7.1 | 11.5 |
| 6B..... | 2.2 | 8.7 | 7.7 | 12.5 |
| 6A..... |  | 7.9 | 6.5 | 11.5 |

TABLE 4. CAUSES OF NON-PROMOTION, ROCHESTER, NEW YORK *
* From *The Work of the Public Schools.* Board of Education, Rochester, New York, 1928.

|  | NUMBER OF CASES |
|---|---|
| *Mental condition* | |
| Immaturity................... | 284 |
| Slowness.................... | 1094 |
| Backwardness............... | 313 |
| Subnormality............... | 33 |
| Poor memory............... | 45 |
| Lack of attention........... | 106 |
| Lack of application.......... | 289 |
| Lack of perseverance........ | 20 |
| Special reading disability..... | 61 |
| Special number disability..... | 92 |
| | |
| *Wrong attitude* | |
| Dislike of school............. | 3 |
| Indifference................. | 82 |
| Carelessness................ | 14 |
| Incorrigibility............... | 8 |
| Overconfidence.............. | 7 |
| Lack of confidence.......... | 6 |
| Day-dreaming............... | 15 |

|  | NUMBER OF CASES |
|---|---|
| *Irregular attendance* | |
| Personal illness.............. | 159 |
| Illness in family............. | 10 |
| Illegal absence.............. | 20 |
| Late start.................. | 53 |
| | |
| *Physical condition* | |
| General ill health........... | 47 |
| Specific ill health........... | 26 |
| Speech impediment.......... | 15 |
| Defective hearing or vision... | 16 |
| | |
| *Environment* | |
| Change of schools........... | 62 |
| Change of school systems..... | 54 |
| Home environment.......... | 19 |
| Foreign environment......... | 38 |
| Outside interests............ | 10 |
| | |
| *Administrative* | |
| Half-day sessions............ | 12 |
| Unwise promotions.......... | 9 |
| Wrong classification......... | 25 |

as 56 per cent in another. The per cents of failure are usually greatest in the lower primary grades, as was the case in the cities listed above, although the amount of failure in some schools has been found to be larger in the upper grades than in the lower. Failure of pupils unduly and unnecessarily increases the cost of the schools. Steps taken by many cities have greatly reduced the extent of failure.

**The causes of non-promotion.** The causes of non-promotion have been classified by the schools of Rochester, New York, as shown in Table 4.

## II. CONTRIBUTORY FACTORS LEADING TO MALADJUSTMENT

Some of the factors that contribute to maladjustment are of a permanent kind; others are temporary in character and can be easily obviated. These contributing factors vary widely from pupil to pupil, and may be classified as follows: *a.* Mental; *b.* Physical; *c.* Pedagogical; *d.* Emotional; *e.* Volitional; *f.* Social; *g.* Moral.

**The mental factor.** Probably the greatest single cause of maladjustment of pupils and failure to make satisfactory progress in their school work is lack of native intelligence. Inability to learn is a symptom of subnormality. Therefore an essential fact to be considered in making a diagnosis of the cause of maladjustment in individual cases is the mental level of the pupil. This may be determined by a standard intelligence test, preferably an individual test. However, the level of mentality alone may not be the only factor to be considered. It has been found,[1] for example, that pupils markedly deficient in arithmetic ability have a range in I.Q. of from 75 to 135, which shows that pupils of relatively high mental ability may encounter serious difficulty in some

[1] Souba, A. *Diagnosis of Pupil Difficulties in Arithmetic.* Master's dissertation (unpublished), University of Minnesota, 1924.

subject, owing to other factors which must be determined by systematic inquiry into other causes, such as are included in the list above.

In some cases pupils of otherwise normal mentality have specific mental deficiencies, such as inability to learn to read or to spell. This condition may be present whenever a pupil fails to profit from the work done in these subjects. Such cases present unusual problems and should, if possible, be referred to a specialist for diagnosis.

**The physical factor.** Many pupils fail to make satisfactory progress due to various physical defects; their vision may be so far below normal that they cannot see the printed pages clearly or read the work written on the blackboard; they may be undernourished, anemic, fatigued; because of previous serious illnesses their health may be undermined, and hence they may not be capable of the sustained effort that successful school work requires. Therefore, the teacher should consult the school physician or nurse as to the pupil's physical condition whenever a study is being made of the failure of a pupil to progress satisfactorily in his school work. Many a pupil has been labeled as stupid, or has been thought by his teacher to be inattentive, when as a matter of fact he could neither hear what was being said nor see the written assignments on the blackboards. In most schools provision is now made for systematic physical examinations and the segregation in special classes of pupils with marked physical deficiencies. Deficiencies due to physical conditions can in most cases be greatly alleviated and even removed by the right kind of medical attention. Teachers must learn to recognize the symptoms of the most common types of physical deficiencies which may interfere with satisfactory school progress.

**The pedagogical factor.** Many deficiencies in the work of pupils are due to factors over which the school has control. Failure of the pupil to make satisfactory progress may be due to the inadequacy of the instructional materials which may not have been scientifically constructed. In them little attention may have been given to the learning difficulties which careful investigations have demonstrated that the subject presents. Hence in the initial presentation of a topic textbooks may plunge the pupil at once into a step involving many difficult points that have not been previously presented, and consequently the pupils fail to master the subject. The textbooks may also be too difficult for the pupils, as well as uninteresting and unattractive.

Instruction in the classroom may be by mass methods in which little consideration is given to the needs of individuals. As a consequence, pupils through trial and error during undirected practice may acquire faulty, roundabout, inefficient methods of work. Because of lack of care in teaching the pupil efficient procedures to follow in the application of the skills involved in various subjects, he may acquire faulty habits of work which seriously interfere with the efficiency of his performances. For example, inability of the pupil to solve arithmetic problems or to understand the discussion in textbooks in the social studies may be due to faulty reading habits. Similarly, failure in long division may be due wholly to weakness in the subtraction steps involved in the solution of the example, rather than to a general deficiency in the process. These difficulties must be diagnosed before remedial work is undertaken to eliminate the deficiencies. Many pupils whose scores on tests are up to the standard for their grade are performing at a level considerably below that which they could attain if they used more efficient, economical methods of work.

Because of the continued absence of the pupil when certain topics in such subjects as arithmetic are being considered, there may be serious gaps in his training which under conventional teaching procedure are not eliminated, and which subsequently cause difficulty whenever a situation involving the use of the particular skills arises. These gaps can of course be avoided through well-planned individual work when the pupil returns to his classes after his absence. The transfer of pupils from school to school also often results in serious gaps in the pupil's training due to differences in the curricula of the two schools.

**The emotional factor.** Emotional disturbances often have an important relation to the failure of the pupil to make satisfactory progress. Fear of the teacher or principal may inhibit his responses to a marked degree. Because of ridicule he may have developed a violent dislike for the teacher which is reflected in his attitude toward all of his school work. Some pupils feel keenly the little unpleasantnesses that arise in the activities of daily life. Some pupils develop strong anti-social tendencies which result in lying, cheating, and malingering. The nervousness exhibited by pupils under test conditions is often due to emotional instability.

A healthy social and personal relationship between the teacher and pupil is vitally necessary in the classroom. This may be assured if the teacher has a strong, rich, sympathetic personality and deals with the emotional problems of both herself and the pupils objectively, just as the physician deals with problems of health. The teacher must inform herself concerning the personalities under her care. She should study their likes and dislikes, their interest in play, their relations with their classmates, their reaction to praise and reproof, their behavior in difficult situations. Every effort should be made by the teacher to take the needs of the various personalities into consideration in the planning of the instructional activities. Constructive measures should be taken to develop a strong positive attitude toward the school work, and to eliminate all factors that may tend to develop undesirable negative reactions.

Pupils with undesirable emotional traits should be made to see themselves as others view them, and should be led to realize that their uninhibited tendencies lead only to trouble and failure.

The importance of a consideration of the influence of the home life of the pupil in connection with his emotional re-actions is of course self-evident. A happy home life reduces the likelihood of serious emotional disturbances. Sympathetic conferences with parents of pupils who are problem cases can do much to bring about an improvement in home conditions which may be the direct cause of the emotional difficulty. In such cases the school should make use of every organized social agency available. In serious cases the psychologist or the psychiatrist should be consulted.

**The volitional factor.** Some pupils fail to progress because of a lack of effort on their part. Sometimes this is the result of lack of interest in the subject, and sometimes sheer laziness. They may lack confidence in their ability to master the topic. They may lack initiative, or may not be able to adapt themselves to new situations presented in the activities being engaged in by the class. Such pupils are often unwilling to ask the teacher for assistance, and as a consequence flounder helplessly and usually hopelessly. They dislike to ask questions before the class, and are often shy and diffident. They fail to stick to the task until it is finished. Their attention is easily distracted by minor interruptions, and they are incapable of periods of sustained attention such as are necessary in the intensive study of a difficult topic.

To overcome volitional weaknesses the teacher must provide interesting situations in which the pupil will be impelled to activity through the urge from within to participate.  Many such occasions arise on the playground, in the gymnasium, and in the regular school work.   Through charts, progress graphs, merit schemes, and other devices the teacher may stimulate the pupil to activity by appealing to his desire for self-improvement and growth.   Every effort must be made to vitalize the work in the various subjects through excursions, projects, and activity of various kinds in which the subject-matter may function in a normal, natural way.   If the right attitude between the pupil and teacher exists, the pupil will regard the teacher as a counsellor and helper in rich educative experiences, rather than as a taskmaster whose job it is to "put the pupil through his paces."   It is the obligation of every teacher to lead the pupil to see that the teacher is there to assist him in the acquisition of skills, attitudes, controls, and abilities that society deems valuable and essential, and to help him to overcome any difficulties that may arise in the process.

**The social factor.**   Faulty attitudes of the pupil are often the direct result of unsatisfactory environmental conditions.   The parents of the child may be indifferent to his success in the schoolroom, and in some cases they have been known deliberately to counteract the constructive work being done in the school.   The attitude of the social group toward the value of an education may determine the amount of effort the pupil will make.   The individual may possess certain personality traits that determine the character of his social relationships.   He may be untrustworthy, selfish, solitary, overbearing, stubborn, or argumentative.  Under such conditions his contacts with the individuals in his group are socially undesirable and corrective measures should be undertaken.   It is one of the major functions of the school to provide a social environment in which undesirable and anti-social traits will be nipped in the bud and worthwhile qualities developed.   The recognition of this obligation by the schools is the direct cause of the strong trend toward such socialized forms of school work as socialized recitations, provision for group work, projects, and excursions.

**A school history blank.** A school history blank [1] suitable for recording various data concerning a pupil's social traits and status is given on pages 12 and 13.

**The moral factor.** In making a diagnosis in a general problem case some consideration must be given to the moral qualities of the individual. Moral qualities refer to those aspects of personality which produce "in varying degrees adaptation and conformity to social custom." These include honesty, trustworthiness, personal habits, religious attitudes, and similar component parts of character. Definite provisions for moral education grow out of the hope that something can be done by the school to improve the moral qualities of the pupil. A good beginning has been made by Hartshorne and May [2] to develop test techniques by which to measure various character traits. There seems to be no good reason why the clinical examiner should not ultimately have as definite objective information regarding the pupil's moral qualities as he now has for his pedagogical performances. A detailed discussion of techniques for measuring character traits is given in the chapter on character education.

## III. THE SCOPE OF DIAGNOSTIC AND REMEDIAL TEACHING

The purpose of this book is to assemble a body of material that will assist teachers and supervisors to reduce the amount

[1] Cornell, E. L., "Why are More Boys than Girls Retarded in School?"; in *Elementary School Journal*, vol. 29, pp. 96–106.

[2] Hartshorne, L., and May, M. *Studies in Deceit*. New York, The Macmillan Company, 1928.

FORM 1. SCHOOL AND PERSONAL HISTORY BLANK

Name _____ Date _____

Place _____ School _____ Grade _____

Address _____ Sex _____ Color _____ Age _____

Birthplace _____ Date of birth _____ Parent's name _____

Age at entering school _____ Grades repeated _____

Is he doing satisfactory work in present grade? _____ Communities in
which child has attended school _____

Age and causes of any prolonged absences _____

_____

Daily attendance regular or irregular _____ If regular, cause _____

_____

*School work.* (Place check on part of line where you estimate child's
position.)

*Industry*

I ———————————— I ———————————— I

| Marked persistence | Ordinary effort | Extreme laziness |

*Attention*

I ———————————— I ———————————— I

| Excellent concentration when studying | Ordinary concentration | Extreme inability to put attention on task |

*Interest*

I ———————————— I ———————————— I

| Marked indifference to work | Ordinary degree of interest in study. Needs stimulation | Absorbed and genuine interest in work |

*Memory*

I ———————————— I ———————————— I

| Excellent memory | Average ability to retain lesson | Marked inability to remember facts apparently learned |

*Comprehension*

I ——————— I ——————— I ——————— I

| Complete inability to comprehend work of the difficulty of his grade. | Slow to grasp but understands with effort | Follows explanation with ordinary ease | Marked ability to anticipate explanation, to grasp work of greater difficulty |

## FORM 1 (*continued*)

Mention any special aptitudes or disabilities or subjects or activities in which child shows particular interest or lack of interest _____

_____

Date of last physical examination _____ Defects found _____

_____

*Personality.* (Underline the words that describe the child.)
   Over-quiet, quiet, talkative, active, over-active, restless, energetic, leader, ringleader.
   Impulsive, nervous, excitable, easily discouraged, hot-tempered, irritable, "goes to pieces easily."
   Cheerful, depressed, changeable, stolid.
   Easily led, suggestible, shy, timid, unambitious, lacking self-confidence, self-conscious.
   Selfish, conceited, self-centered, overconfident, unable to conform to group.
   Distant, seclusive, oversensitive, suspicious, unsociable, evasive.
   Social, friendly, responsive, popular, adaptable, quarrelsome, unfriendly.

*Conduct.* Describe any abnormal tendencies shown by child such as lying, stealing, bullying, truancy, outbursts of temper, abnormal sex tendencies, abnormal fear, anti-social activities.

*Personal history.* (If further information about family of child's development can be given, attach extra sheet.)

Birthplace of father _____ of mother _____

Occupation of father _____ of mother _____

If parents are dead, with whom is child living? _____

Language spoken at home _____ Do parents read and write English? _____ native language? _____ General repute of family as to economic and moral status _____

Peculiarities in environment or family conditions which may be detrimental to child _____

_____

Names and ages of brothers and sisters and school grades of those in school

_____

(Signed) _____ History obtained from _____
                Position

of maladjustment in our schools due to the causes described in the preceding pages, and to increase the effectiveness with which the schools can deal with the individual differences of pupils. To this end the following chapters will deal in detail with the points below:

1. The techniques, both administrative and instructional, that may be used to adapt instruction to the individual differences of pupils.

2. The use of standard tests and of other types of objective devices as a means (a) of surveying the achievements and ability of pupils, (b) of determining and diagnosing their instructional deficiencies, and (c) of improving teaching techniques.

3. Procedures other than test techniques that must be used to diagnose the nature and causes of difficulty in the various school subjects, especially in the skill phases, in so far as these faults are not revealed by test scores.

4. Corrective and remedial exercises, based, in so far as is possible, on experimentation, that may be used to eliminate the faults revealed by diagnostic study.

To facilitate the work of diagnosis, the most common faults revealed by systematic studies of the work of pupils are presented and illustrated. The authors believe that teachers who are aware of these sources of difficulty can prevent their incidence in the work of pupils by taking steps to avert them when the subject-matter is first presented. This may be accomplished by the use of well-organized instructional materials in the construction of which due consideration has been given to the steps in the learning process and the results of diagnostic studies. The amount of remedial instruction required after the initial presentation of the subject should thereby be greatly reduced.

## QUESTIONS FOR STUDY, DISCUSSION, AND REPORT

1. What is meant by maladjustment?
2. What might a school do to improve the situation described in the age-grade table on page 2?
3. How many pupils in your class are doing failing work? Examine the records for promotion for the past semester or year, and if possible for several years. What steps may be taken to improve the situation?
4. If possible make an age-grade study of some school, and suggest measures for improvement.
5. Prepare a blank that would guide the teacher in collecting information that might help her to determine the reasons for lack of progress in the case of given pupils.
6. Make a careful case study of some problem case.
7. Discuss the psychological effect on the pupil of continued failure in his school work.
8. Which of the causes of maladjustment described in this chapter do you think it would be most difficult to eliminate or counteract?
9. Name local agencies that might help the school to deal with problem cases.
10. In some schools the policy of not failing any pupils has been adopted. Can you justify such a policy? What arguments can you raise against it?

## SELECTED REFERENCES

Blanchard, Phyllis, and Paynter, R. H. *Educational Achievement of Problem Children.* New York, Commonwealth Fund, 1929.

Bronner, A. *Psychology of Special Abilities and Disabilities.* Boston, Little, Brown and Company, 1917.

Burt, C. *The Young Delinquent.* New York, D. Appleton and Company, 1925.

"Education of Gifted Children," in *Twenty-Third Yearbook of the National Society for the Study of Education*, Part I. Bloomington, Illinois, Public School Publishing Company, 1924.

Goddard, H. H. *School Training of Defective Children.* Yonkers-on-Hudson, New York, World Book Company, 1914.

Goddard, H. H.   *School Training of Gifted Children*.   Yonkers-on-Hudson, New York, World Book Company, 1928.

Hollingsworth, L. S.   *Gifted Children; Their Nature and Nurture*. New York, The Macmillan Company, 1926.

Hollingsworth, L. S.   *Special Talents and Defects*.   New York, The Macmillan Company, 1923.

Hollingsworth, L. S.   *The Psychology of Subnormal Children*. New York, The Macmillan Company, 1920.

Horn, J. L.   *The Education of the Exceptional Child*.   New York, Century Company, 1924.

Mateer, F.   *The Unstable Child*.   New York, D. Appleton and Company, 1924.

Morgan, J. J. B.   *The Psychology of the Unadjusted School Child*. New York, The Macmillan Company, 1924.

Peppard, H. M.   *The Correction of Speech Defects*.   New York, The Macmillan Company, 1925.

Pressey, L. C. and S. L.   *Mental Abnormality and Deficiency*. New York, The Macmillan Company, 1926.

Reavis, W. C.   *Pupil Adjustment in Junior and Senior High Schools*. Boston, D. C. Heath and Company, 1926.

Thomas, W. I.   *The Unadjusted Girl*.   Boston, Little, Brown and Company, 1923.

Tredgold, A. F.   *Mental Deficiency*.   New York, Wm. Wood and Company, 1924.

Wallin, J. E. W.   *The Education of Handicapped Children*.   Boston, Houghton Mifflin Company, 1924.

Woodrow, H. W.   *Brightness and Dullness in Children*.   Philadelphia, J. B. Lippincott Company, 1919.

Wickman, E. K.   *Children's Behavior and Teachers' Attitudes* New York, Commonwealth Fund, 1928.

# CHAPTER II

## ADAPTING INSTRUCTION TO THE INDIVIDUAL DIFFERENCES OF PUPILS

### I. THE PROBLEM OF INDIVIDUAL DIFFERENCES

**Early attitude.** While individual differences of pupils have no doubt been recognized for centuries, their import for teaching has only recently been realized. The traditional attitude of the school prevented a careful consideration of the problem. School was looked upon as preparation for adult life. Its curriculum was determined by traditional concepts of what would be valuable in adult life. In case a child was unable to master satisfactorily the work prescribed by the school this fact was immediately pronounced to be the fault of the child. Had not the school existed for centuries? In it revered subjects were taught by scholarly and consecrated teachers. The school was *there*. The child came to it. He must meet its demands. If he failed, his failure was evidence of deficiency or perhaps laziness on his part. To vary the program of instruction for this child would have been unthinkable. It would have been considered as a "lowering of standards." In fact the school often prided itself on the fact that its work was difficult and that many failed. Incidentally, there are probably schools today which have the same attitude, judging from the large numbers of pupils who are not promoted at the end of each term.

Since the school attributed failure on the part of the child to shortcomings on the part of the child, it was prevented from focussing its attention on any possible shortcomings of its own. The total effect of the situation was to perpetuate the traditional school practices. More than that, the current educational philosophy supported the attitude of the school. Learning, after all, was not for the masses.

It was only to be expected that a large proportion of individuals would be unable to master the work of the schools. The number of persons who even attempted such mastery was relatively small. It seems likely that those who continued for any length of time in the schools were highly selected individuals. The school came to look upon itself as an agency which ministered to a mental aristocracy.

**Early studies.** In our own country education for the masses has seen a development never before approached. By 1900 it was expected that every individual should have a common-school education, and by 1925 a high-school education was coming to be looked upon as the right of every boy and girl. The result of this great extension of educational privileges (to say nothing of legal requirements) was to confront the school with a problem it had never before really faced, the problem of educating all types and abilities of children. While many educational leaders no doubt influenced the school to give more attention to the child and his needs, it is nevertheless probably true that the attention which has been given to the problem of individual differences has in large measure been due to the fact that when the traditional school machinery undertook to educate *all* of the children it broke down. Evidences of this breakdown are found in the studies of Ayres,[1] Maxwell, and Thorndike. According to these studies, large numbers of children were unable to progress regularly through the grades of the schools. Large numbers of children not only repeated grades, but finally dropped out of school. Other studies, especially the school surveys, have shown that the early studies pointed to real problems. Attention has been given not only to retardation and elimination, but also to their probable causes in school organization and instructional practices.

[1] Ayres, Leonard P. *Laggards in Our Schools.* New York, Russell Sage Foundation, 1909.

**Early attempts at adaptation.**  Partly as a result of the early studies mentioned above, and partly as a result of a growing recognition of the problem on the part of educational leaders, a number of attempts were made to solve the problem of adapting the schools to the needs of the children. Perhaps more important than any of the various plans developed was the growing feeling, both in and out of the school, that the school was *for the child*.  When the school began to make modifications for different children it took a distinct step in advance.  It may be true that many of the modifications were superficial.  The mere fact, however, that the school was scrutinizing itself was far-reaching in effect.  It was beginning to question the desirability of many of its time-honored practices.  Here and there an experimental project was launched.

**The influence of tests.**  This early experimentation and interest in the problem of individual differences was greatly stimulated by developments in the field of educational measurements which took place at about the same time.  The development of individual and later of practicable group tests of intelligence stimulated the study of individual differences in the mental levels of pupils in ways that before were impossible.  No longer could children be classified into types as normal and abnormal.  Intelligence was found to be distributed as are other human traits.  Moreover, the range of intelligence within a typical schoolroom was found to be very large.  For example, the nature of the ranges of scores on intelligence tests by pupils in various grades is shown in Table 5.  While these data are drawn from a particular school system, they nevertheless serve to illustrate the character of the facts which became available to teachers through the use of intelligence tests.

Continued study of the results of intelligence tests made it readily apparent that mass methods of instruction could never provide adequately for children whose needs varied as widely as was shown by the tests. The result was a great stimulus to the further study of children. The tests served to focus the attention of teachers upon the characteristics and needs of the child.

TABLE 5. DISTRIBUTION OF MENTAL AGES BY GRADES, ELEMENTARY SCHOOL, AURORA, MINNESOTA, NOVEMBER, 1926 *

| MENTAL AGES | GRADES | | | | | | | | TOTAL |
| | Third | | Fourth | | Fifth | | Sixth | | |
| | B | A | B | A | B | A | B | A | |
|---|---|---|---|---|---|---|---|---|---|
| Below 7–3 . . . . . . . . . | 9 | 1 | 1 | | | | | | 11 |
| 7–3 to 7–8 † . . . . . . | 12 | | 6 | 1 | | | | | 19 |
| 7–9 to 8–2 . . . . . . . . | 14 | 2 | 9 | 2 | 3 | 3 | | | 33 |
| 8–3 to 8–8 . . . . . . . . | 10 | 5 | 14 | 4 | 4 | 2 | | | 39 |
| 8–9 to 9–2 . . . . . . . . | 3 | 4 | 9 | 8 | 6 | 2 | 4 | | 36 |
| 9–3 to 9–8 . . . . . . . . | 3 | 3 | 6 | | 10 | 5 | 3 | | 30 |
| 9–9 to 10–2 . . . . . . . | | 4 | 7 | | 7 | 4 | 6 | 1 | 29 |
| 10–3 to 10–8 . . . . . . . | 1 | 1 | 3 | 1 | 11 | 1 | 8 | 2 | 28 |
| 10–9 to 11–2 . . . . . . . | | 1 | | | 6 | | 13 | 4 | 24 |
| 11–3 to 11–8 . . . . . . . | | | | | 3 | | 5 | 1 | 9 |
| 11–9 to 12–2 . . . . . . . | | | | | 4 | 1 | 7 | 1 | 13 |
| 12–3 to 12–8 . . . . . . . | | | | | | | 5 | 1 | 6 |
| 12–9 to 13–2 . . . . . . . | | | | | 1 | | 3 | 2 | 6 |
| 13–3 to 13–8 . . . . . . . | | | | | | | 3 | 1 | 4 |
| 13–9 and over . . . . . . . | | | | | 1 | | 2 | 1 | 4 |
| Total . . . . . . . . . . . . | 52 | 21 | 55 | 16 | 56 | 18 | 59 | 14 | 291 |
| Median mental age | 8–0 | 9–0 | 8–6 | 9–0 | 10–0 | 9–6 | 11–0 | 11–3 | |

* Taken from Fred Engelhardt. Survey Report, Aurora Public Schools, Aurora, Minnesota. University of Minnesota Press, Minneapolis, 1928.
† Read: Seven years, three months, to seven years, eight months, and so on.

**Achievement tests.** The development of achievement tests preceded the development of group measures of intelligence. From the results of achievement tests teachers learned that pupils vary as much in their achievement in school subjects as they vary in mental development. Pupils within a grade vary more than the average for a grade varies from that of the next grade. In fact, the variation within a grade is sometimes several times the

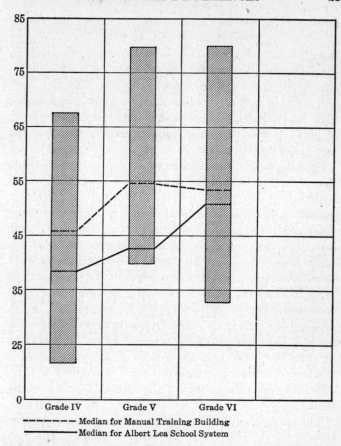

FIG. 1

From Fred Engelhardt and Ernest O. Melby, *The Supervisory Organization and the Instructional Program*, Albert Lea, Minnesota. University of Minnesota Press, Minneapolis, Minnesota.

difference between the averages for two grades. As an example, Figure 1 shows the range of scores on the Thorndike–McCall Reading List in a certain school in grades four to six, as well as the medians for that school and for all schools in the system. It will be noted that the range from lowest to highest score in the fourth grade is 47, in the fifth grade 41, and for the sixth grade 49. The difference between the median scores for grades four and six is only 6.3. In fact the median score for grade five is higher than for grade six. Likewise it is found that the majority of pupils in this particular building score higher than the median for the city as a whole.

**Specific nature of differences.**   Not only have tests shown that children differ in mental development and in achievement in school subjects, but also that the differences extend to detailed aspects of learning. Inventory and diagnostic tests have brought out the fact that a child may do well in some kinds of reading, for example, but poorly in other kinds. Similarly, he may be doing satisfactory work in addition, but fail in problem solving. The exact nature of all these differences is not known. By means of various tests many of the differences can be determined for individual children, as well as for groups. Recently attention has also been given to detailed studies of the various character traits of children. Differences are also pronounced in the field of emotional characteristics. The effect of these differences upon the school work of the child is only partially known.

The modern school thus faces a serious problem in relationship to the individual differences of pupils. The facts in regard to these differences cannot be questioned. The differences are there. At the same time society demands that the school provide education for *all* children. It is only to be expected that the efforts to solve the problem have taken many forms. While the merits of the various plans devised to meet individual differences are not easily determined, the various devices are suggestive and will therefore be briefly discussed.

## II. TYPICAL PLANS FOR MEETING INDIVIDUAL DIFFERENCES

**Classification of plans.** On an *a-priori* basis it may be said that there are three principal ways in which the school may provide for the individual differences among its pupils. The school may: (1) allow for such differences by varying the time in which pupils are to complete their work; (2) vary the amount of work required according to pupil ability; or (3) vary the methods of teaching used. Combinations of these methods might also be found. For example, a school might expect all pupils to complete their work in a given time, but vary both the content and the method to suit pupil needs.

Another way to describe the three methods given above is to classify them as administrative, curricular, and method devices.

Probably no one of these devices is a solution for the problem of individual differences. As an illustration, the attempt to give slow pupils more time to complete their work than is allowed brighter pupils may be ineffective because the slow pupils need a different content, as well as different methods of instruction. Since the various classes of devices have taken different forms it is necessary to discuss some of the more significant plans.

### A. ADMINISTRATIVE DEVICES FOR HANDLING INDIVIDUAL DIFFERENCES

#### 1. *Flexible promotion plans*

**Semi-annual and quarterly promotions.** One of the earliest ways of providing for individual differences was the tendency toward more flexibility in promotions. If a child failed of promotion under an annual promotion system, repetition of the grade would cause a year of retardation. Semi-annual promotions and quarter-annual promotions tend to reduce

this loss.   However, flexibility in promotions is no assurance
that any real variations will be made in other phases of
school work.   Generally no attempt is made to make adjustments in curriculum or method.   All pupils take the
same course and are taught by the same methods.

These promotion schemes, like the methods of varying
the time for pupils of different abilities, are unsound.   It is
absurd to say that pupils require either one year or two
years, one half year or one year to complete the work of a
grade or of a given subject.   In fact some require four
months and some twelve months, with all sorts of variations
in special fields.   The time required may be distributed like
the characteristics of pupils.   At best, therefore, the various
promotion schemes are makeshifts in the process of adapting
instruction to individual differences.   The practice of semi-
annual promotions is almost universally followed in the
large city systems.   In the smaller systems semi-annual
promotions do not seem to have operated to the benefit of
the schools.   For example, Table 6 shows the enrollments

TABLE 6. ENROLLMENTS OF ELEMENTARY SCHOOL PUPILS BY
GRADE GROUPS, AURORA, MINNESOTA, SEPTEMBER, 1926*

| Group † | NUMBER OF PUPILS IN GRADES | | | | | |
|---|---|---|---|---|---|---|
| | 1 | 2 | 3 | 4 | 5 | 6 |
| Bx.......... | 20 | 22 | 22 | 26 | 26 | 29 |
| Bw.......... | 27 | 25 | 32 | 30 | 34 | 31 |
| A.......... | 21 | 22 | 23 | 17 | 18 | 11 |
| Total...... | 68 | 69 | 77 | 73 | 78 | 71 |

* Fred Engelhardt, loc. cit.
† The Bx indicates the less advanced section of the grade, while the Bw designates the
more advanced.

in the various grades of a small school system operating on
the semi-annual promotion plan.   Note that the A grades
made up of pupils entering at the middle of the school year

are only about half as large as the B grades which are made up of pupils entering in September. Table 7 shows the

TABLE 7. MEDIAN SCORES IN ARITHMETIC, AURORA, MINNESOTA, ELEMENTARY GRADES FOUR, FIVE, AND SIX, COMPARED WITH STANDARDS, NOVEMBER, 1926 *

(Courtis Supervisory Test)

| GRADE | STANDARD | AURORA | | |
|---|---|---|---|---|
| | | A | Bw | Bx |
| 4.............. | 372 | 44 | 76 | 0 |
| 5.............. | 778 | 372 | 665 | 148 |
| 6.............. | 660 | 321 | 636 | 311 |

* Fred Engelhardt, *loc. cit.*

median scores for these grades in arithmetic. The A grades, which are supposedly one year in advance of the B grades, actually show lower achievements than the B grades. If teachers in the A grades in this school were actually trying to teach the content which the course of study set up for A grades, the pupils in these grades were facing greater difficulties than they would face under a system of annual promotions.

**The semi-annual plan in practice.** No thoroughgoing studies of the relative effectiveness of semi-annual promotion plans in large and small cities are available. Traditional practices of having pupils enter the first grade in September rather than in January may be responsible for the small groups usually found in the grades which are classified as A during the first semester. It is also likely that the pupils entering the first grade in September who at the end of the first semester have a more or less doubtful achievement status are asked to repeat the first semester. Such pupils then fall into the first semester A groups. If throughout the school teachers ask pupils to repeat the first rather than the second semester, a study of such a school during the first semester of any year would probably show that the A grades have collected a large proportion of the failing pupils. Especially will this be true if the B grades are large and the A grades are small.

If the school desires to group pupils according to ability, the semi-annual promotion plan will be a hindrance rather than a help in the small school. If in the case of the school from which data are given in Table 6 there had existed a system of annual promotions, three ability groups might have been formed in each grade. As it is no such grouping is possible in A grades, and only two groups can be formed in each B grade. In a large school this difficulty may not be of any serious consequence.

## 2. Double-track plans

**The new Cambridge plan.** This plan is illustrative of the various double-track schemes which have been devised. The plan is based upon the principle of rapid and slow progress groups covering the same curricular content. As will be seen from Diagram 2, each of the first seven grades is divided into three groups and grade eight has two groups in the basal course, which requires eight years. In the parallel course of six years each grade also has three groups. It will be noticed that pupils can shift from one group to the other at certain points where the grade divisions coincide. The plan really meets the needs of bright or specially gifted children better than it does the needs of children who are having general difficulty. No special slow-moving group or other form of special adjustment is provided, while there is special provision for the bright pupils.

There is no assurance that with plans, such as the Cambridge plan, there will be any modifications of the methods of the work for pupils of varying abilities. Although such changes are essential to the success of the plan in small schools, the plan is difficult to administer because of the number of groups required. In fact the problems of individual differences of pupils are probably too complex to be solved by any such mechanical device for shifting pupils from one group to the other.

| A Basal Course 8 Years | 1 | | 2 | | 3 | | 4 | | 5 | | 6 | | 7 | | 8 | |
|---|---|---|---|---|---|---|---|---|---|---|---|---|---|---|---|---|
| | 1 | 2 | 3 | 4 | 5 | 6 | 7 | 8 | 9 | 10 11 | 12 | 13 14 15 | 16 17 18 | 19 20 21 | 22 | 23 |

| B Parallel Course 6 Years | 1 | 2 | 3 | 4 | 5 | 6 | 7 | 8 | 9 | 10 | 11 | 12 | 13 | 14 | 15 | 16 | 17 |
|---|---|---|---|---|---|---|---|---|---|---|---|---|---|---|---|---|---|
| | **1** | | | **2** | | | **3** | | | **4** | | | **5** | | | **6** | |

FIG. 2. THE NEW CAMBRIDGE PLAN
From Cubberley's *Public School Administration*, p. 452.

### 3. *Ability grouping*

**A widely used plan.** A vast amount of attention and effort has been devoted to ability grouping as a means of adapting instruction to individual differences. A study of ability grouping made by the United States Bureau of Education in December, 1926, brings out the fact that 36 out of 40 cities of 100,000 population or more employ ability grouping in some schools; of 90 cities of 30,000 to 100,000, 66 employ ability grouping. Not only has ability grouping been widely used but its merits have been the subject of a great deal of controversy.[1] While it is impossible accurately to evaluate ability grouping at the present time, its operation, nevertheless, suggests some problems which deserve consideration.

**Theoretical considerations.** Ability grouping is really a

[1] Miller, W. S., and Otto, Henry J. "Analysis of Experimental Studies in Homogeneous Grouping"; in *Journal of Educational Research*, vol. 21, pp. 95–103. (February, 1930.)

mass production method for adapting instruction to individual differences. It is based upon the assumption that if we can bring together pupils who are very nearly alike in instructional needs it will be practicable to maintain group instruction. The proponents of ability grouping therefore acknowledge that variations must be made in methods of instruction for pupils of different abilities or characteristics. It would appear, therefore, that the success of ability grouping as a means of adapting instruction to individual differences would depend upon the extent to which we can accomplish two purposes, namely, an accurate grouping and a proper adjustment of instruction to the needs and abilities of the groups.

**The problem of securing homogeneity.** The advent of mental tests provided a great stimulus for ability grouping, since the tests appeared to be a solution to the problem of effecting real homogeneity. It is not surprising to find, therefore, that mental tests have been used as a basis for ability grouping in a number of ways. In fact mental test scores (treated in various ways) have been the most widely used basis for grouping in the reported experimental studies.[1] Achievement tests have also been widely used as a basis for grouping, as have school marks and various combinations of the different bases. Judging from present data in regard to the effectiveness of the various plans for grouping, it does not appear that a method has yet been found which actually does make groups homogeneous.

The difficulties involved in effecting homogeneity become more apparent from the examination of concrete procedures. For example, if I.Q.'s are used as a basis for grouping no account will be taken of mental maturity. Certainly mental maturity is a factor in achievement. If grouping is by mental age, pupils of widely varying I.Q.'s and supposedly

[1] Miller and Otto, *loc. cit.*

## TABLE 8. SCORES ON STANFORD ACHIEVEMENT TEST

*For six pupils with educational ages which do not vary more than two months. Expressed in specific subject ages*

| PUPIL | BOY OR GIRL | AGE Years | AGE Months | TESTS 1 Par. Mean. | TESTS 2 Word Mean. | TOTAL READING | 3 Spell. | 4 Lang. Usage | 5 Lit. | 6 Hist. & Civ. | 7 Geog. | 8 Phys. & Hyg. | TESTS 9 Arith. Reas. | TESTS 10 Arith. Comp. | TOTAL ARITHMETIC | EDUCATIONAL AGE |
|---|---|---|---|---|---|---|---|---|---|---|---|---|---|---|---|---|
| A............ | B | 14 | 2 | 12- 8 | 13-9 | 13-8 | 12- | 12-7 | 9-10 | 12-11 | 11-8 | 12-8 | 12-3 | 11-0 | 11- 7 | 12 |
| B............ | B | 13 | 3 | 10-10 | 11-5 | 11-2 | 11-8 | 13-3 | 11-6 | 11-9 | 10-10 | 12-11 | 12-3 | 12-7 | 12-6 | 11-10 |
| C............ | B | 14 | 4 | 11-10 | 13-9 | 12-8 | 14-10 | 16-5 | 10-6 | 12-7 | 12-2 | 15- | 13-5 | 12-7 | 12-11 | 11-11 |
| D............ | G | 13 | 10 | 12-2 | 12-6 | 12-3 | 12-7 | 12-3 | 10-6 | 12-10 | 11-11 | 11-5 | 12-3 | 11-3 | 11-8 | 11-11 |
| E............ | B | 14 | 7 | 10-10 | 12- | 11-5 | 12-6 | 12-8 | 11-6 | 11-8 | 11-1 | 11-1 | 12-3 | 13-3 | 12-8 | 11-10 |
| F............ | B | 15 | 11 | 10-9 | 10-0 | 10-9 | 11-9 | 9-10 | 11-6 | 13-1 | 12-7 | 12-6 | 13-5 | 13-7 | 13-7 | 11-10 |
| Range in months.......... | .... | ...... | 32 | 23 | 36 | 42 | 26 | 79 | 20 | 15 | 21 | 47 | 14 | 31 | 24 | 2 |

varying rates of learning will be grouped together. Even where attempts have been made to combine I.Q. and M.A. as a basis the results have not been entirely satisfactory. The difficulties encountered with the use of achievement tests as a basis for grouping seem equally serious. When pupils are grouped according to achievement no account is taken of rate of learning or of social characteristics of children. If pupils are grouped by some battery of tests, such as the Stanford Achievement Test, on the basis of educational age, we may secure groups with similar educational ages, but the members of the group will be very different in achievement in any particular subject.

Table 8 shows the range of scores in various subjects for a group of pupils whose educational ages do not vary more than two months. These six pupils were selected at random from a group of more than one hundred pupils, the only criterion for selection being nearness to an exact educational age of twelve years. The pupils included were the only ones in the group who met this criterion for selection. There seems no reason to believe that the variations found in these cases are not typical of the group as a whole. While the variation in educational age is only 2 months, the variation in specific subject ages ranges from 14 months to 79 months. There is a range of 42 months in total reading age, and 24 months in arithmetic age. It must be obvious that pupils C and F, who differ by only one month in educational age, present greatly different problems in language usage in which subject they differ by more than six and one half years.

If the school were large enough so that pupils could be grouped in such a way that there would be only a month variation in educational age within the group, it is evident that there would still be large differences in the various subjects and parts of subjects. At the same time it must be kept in mind that even this refinement in classification would not be possible in most schools.

**The nature of individual differences.** It is evident from a study of the characteristics of groups of children that they present an endless variety of traits and abilities. The number of different pupil characteristics which affect instruction is very large. Pupil interests, emotional factors, home environment, health, and many other influences are at work. It is a well-known fact that pupils of equal intelligence do not present the same instructional problems. Even if it were possible to control a large proportion of the factors and bring together children who are shown to be nearly equal in I.Q., M.A., achievement, and chronological age, it is likely that in each subject there would still be a wide range of achievement and large individual differences to be met. In fact it is probably true that individual differences of pupils are of such a kind and variety that true homogeneous grouping is an impossibility; that is, if its purpose is to bring together children who present the same instructional problems.

**Adapting instruction to ability groups.** One of the unfortunate aspects of the work which has been done in ability grouping in our schools is the small degree to which instruction has been varied in groups of different abilities. One of the authors interviewed a teacher for employment in his school. He was told that this teacher in her previous position taught five sections of algebra, and that these sections were based upon a scheme of ability grouping. The teacher then made the remark that she had liked her position very much, especially because she only needed to make one preparation. Cases of this kind have been all too common where pupils have been grouped ostensibly according to ability, and instruction of nearly the same sort has been provided for all groups. Likewise, no changes may have been made in the materials used.

In many instances the use of ability grouping has probably caused the teacher to relax her attention to the problems of individual differences. Have not the pupils been grouped according to ability? Should not a class method of teaching suffice under these conditions? Was not ability grouping established for the express purpose of solving the difficulties which arose because of the differences within heterogeneous groups? The seriousness of this situation becomes more apparent when it is realized that rarely is ability grouping completely carried out. Teachers and principals point out that because of program difficulties and for other administrative reasons certain children could not be placed in the section in which their ability would have placed them. This fact, taken together with the variations which would be bound to exist even under the most careful attempts at ability grouping, emphasizes the dangers which would arise from complacency on the part of the teacher growing out of a feeling that ability grouping has solved the problem of individual differences.

**Advantages of ability grouping.** Evidently homogeneous grouping is not actually attainable. Differences will exist between members of a group of pupils in spite of our best efforts. At the same time only moderate progress has been made in adapting instruction to the needs of any groups we may set up. Since ability grouping cannot accomplish its real purpose, the question is, do any benefits come from it? Do children achieve more in the groups which on one basis or another are homogeneous than they do in the more or less fortuitously organized groups of the school? Thus far the evidence is conflicting. In those instances in which pupils in homogeneous groups do excel in achievement the differences are so small as to raise doubts about their statistical significance.[1]

[1] Miller, W. S., and Otto, Henry J. "Analysis of Experimental Studies

On this point Miller and Otto say:

Before presenting an analysis of the outcomes of the seven which represent varying degrees of acceptability, it may be desirable to raise a few pertinent questions. What shall we accept as a good basis for classification? If grouping is made by mental age, raw score on intelligence tests, or percentile rank on intelligence tests, the same group contains pupils whose mental maturity is somewhat the same, but whose rate of learning, as manifest by the I.Q., varies greatly. If classification within a grade is secured by grouping together pupils of like I.Q., then wide ranges in mental ages may be found. Is either situation desirable? Some teachers use school marks, either in the same subject or a composite of marks, as the basis for forming ability groups. Where a composite score representing marks over an extended period is used, it has been found rather satisfactory.[1]

Scores of objective achievement tests are also used in some instances as a basis for grouping. This brings together pupils of approximately the same achievement, but of varying mental age and I.Q. Kelley [2] suggests that a comprehensive achievement test measures essentially the same capacities as a good intelligence test, which would suggest the efficacy of this method of grouping. Where pupils are grouped, however, for instruction in one subject only, such as algebra, the technique may need to be altered.

Another problem which needs consideration is the basis on which the merit of homogeneous classification is to be judged. If the relative number of A, B, C, or D grades, or the number of failures, or the per cent of promotions is used, it seems apparent that the experiment is foredoomed. This raises the question as to the extent to which teachers' marks are an index of achievement. Van Wagenen, in comparing the objective achievement scores of pupils in the thought and information phases of American history, says, "It is clear that many of the pupils with the highest scores receive only average marks, while many with average scores receive the

in Homogeneous Grouping"; in *Journal of Educational Research*, vol. 21, pp. 95–103. (February, 1930.) Public School Publishing Company.

[1] Brooks, F. D. "Sectioning Junior High-School Pupils by Tests and School Marks"; in *Journal of Educational Research*, vol. 12, pp. 359–69. (December, 1925.)

[2] Kelley, Truman L. *Interpretation of Educational Measurements*, p. 21. New York, World Book Company, 1927.

highest marks.  Surely the relation between attainment and teach ers' marks is far from being a close one." [1]

Where a project in homogeneous grouping has been introduced to reduce failures, it would be quite absurd to evaluate an experi ment in terms of reduction in the number of failures.  Equally ridiculous is the notion that ability grouping can be justified be cause the achievement of groups of high ability is greater than those of low ability.  Experimentation is hardly necessary to demonstrate that.  The nature of the problem assumes that pupils in segregated sections are to be compared with pupils of corre sponding ability in mixed groups.

It seems, then, that the only acceptable measure of the effective ness of grouping is in achievement of comparable groups, but even this measure is not devoid of controversy.  Shall the gains be ex pressed in terms of raw-score units, T-score or C-score units, the per cent of initial score, the per cent of possible gain, or in some other way?  Several writers have discussed certain aspects of this problem.[2]

In the light of the above discussion it is difficult to formulate a summary of the outcomes of the studies of ability grouping. Burt *et al.* note no significant differences in the correlations between intelligence and achievement when all groups, segregated as well as controls, were taught by the same method and at the same rate. During the second semester, when the high and medium groups and their controls were "pushed," covering the work in thirty hours in stead of thirty-seven, there was a distinct advantage for the high and medium segregated groups.  The use of final marks as a measure of success in the course makes one question the value of the study.

Van Wagenen studied the effects of segregation upon the achieve ment of superior pupils in grades seven and eight.  The results showed small differences; in some cases the mixed groups were ahead.  Apparently, homogeneous grouping has been of no ad vantage to these pupils.

---

[1] Van Wagenen, M. J.  *A Teacher's Manual in the Use of Educational Scales*, p. 59.  Bloomington, Illinois, Public School Publishing Company, 1928.

[2] Kincaid, Margaret.  "A Study of Individual Differences in Learning"; in *Psychological Review*, vol. 32, pp. 34–53.  (January, 1925.)

Stoddard, G. D.  "The Problem of Individual Differences in Learning"; in *Psychological Review*, vol. 32, pp. 479–85.  (November, 1925.)

Dvorak and Rae studied the achievement of a group of superior segregated first-grade children. Objective tests were used throughout the study. They conclude that mere segregation of bright pupils into homogeneous groups without proper adaptation of methods and materials produces negative or indifferent results.

The most extensive study in this field has been conducted by Billett. This study included, during the first year, 109 pupils in ninth-grade English. His data show that in four cases out of five the difference of the mean gains is in favor of the slow homogeneous group. In three cases out of five the difference of the mean gains is in favor of the average homogeneous group. In four cases out of five the difference of the mean gains is in favor of the fast heterogeneous group. Only two of the ratios are above 1.0; ten out of fifteen of the critical ratios are less than 0.50. The differences in gains are probably not significant, and do not warrant his conclusions that homogeneous grouping is advantageous to pupils of low and average ability. The fact that a repetition of the experiment the second year corroborated the conclusions of the first year is, however, of some importance.

While the evidence is contradictory, at least two of the studies suggest that ability grouping is quite ineffective unless accompanied by proper changes in method. Unless adaptation of methods and materials is a necessary correlate to ability grouping, one of the purposes of the project is defeated. Homogeneous classification makes possible but does not insure such adaptation.[1] The tendency, all too often, is to use exactly the same method for the different sections. Unfortunately, we do not yet know enough about differences between methods of instruction for the different levels of ability to make proper adaptations. If it is true that in the conventional school today the achievement of the slow pupils corresponds much more closely with their mental level than does that of bright pupils, then our present methods must be quite efficacious for the dull pupil.[2] Possibly the future may bring equally efficient instructions for the bright pupil.

Of course, none of the studies has attempted to measure any outcomes except pure achievement. It may be that the social and

[1] Miller, W. S. "The Administrative Use of Intelligence Tests in the High School"; in *Twenty-First Yearbook of the National Society for the Study of Education*, Part I, pp. 189–223.

[2] Wilson, W. R. "The Misleading Accomplishment Quotient"; in *Journal of Educational Research*, vol. 17, pp. 1–11. (January, 1928.)

psychological advantages coming out of homogeneous classification will justify the practice, even though there is no significant difference in achievement.

If one were to make a final summary statement about the studies of ability grouping, one would have to say that, so far as achievement is concerned, there is no clear-cut evidence that homogeneous grouping is either advantageous or disadvantageous. The studies seem to indicate that homogeneous classification may be effective if accompanied by proper adaptation in methods and materials.[1]

One of the difficulties which complicates the problem is that in experiments thus far carried on it has been possible to measure only those skills and abilities for which tests are available. It is generally admitted that there are many outcomes of instruction for which there are no tests. Even if ability grouping showed no better results in achievement than the regular grouping it might be possible to defend it on other grounds. For example, if it could be shown that pupils would be happier in their school experience when grouped with pupils of approximately their own mental level, this fact would constitute a valid argument for ability grouping. Unfortunately no facts are available concerning the effect of ability grouping on pupil attitude and interest. In any case it appears that ability grouping can never be a solution in full of the problems of instruction growing out of individual differences of pupils. Even under the most careful and scientific grouping, large differences will exist which must be provided for in teaching. The work of the teacher in making provision for such differences may not be greatly different from that of the teacher who has the usual class of ungrouped pupils. In other words, individual differences will exist no matter how pupils are grouped. This fact has given powerful impetus to methods of individual instruction which will next be discussed.

[1] Purdom, T. L. *The Value of Homogeneous Grouping.* Baltimore, Warwick and York, 1929.

#### 4. *Individual instruction*

The individual-instruction movement had its origin in the work of Frederick Burk at the San Francisco State Normal School. Since that time it has been further developed by several persons, notably Carleton Washburne [1] of Winnetka and James E. McDade, Assistant Superintendent of Schools in Chicago. While other examples might be mentioned, their work will be used for illustrative purposes.

**Theoretical considerations.** Those who advocate individual instruction base their demands largely upon two contentions. The first of these is that pupils differ from one another so markedly and in so many ways that any attempt to teach them by mass procedure is certain to be ineffective. The second contention is that only under individual instruction is education under modern educational philosophy actually possible. It is maintained that as long as a child must do the same thing which other children are doing he cannot purpose for himself. He is always carrying out either the teacher's purposes or those of the group.

**Individual instruction and adaptation of instruction to individual differences.** Unfortunately, in the thinking of many people, individual instruction and adaptation of instruction to pupil needs have become more or less synonymous. As matter of fact there is no factual basis for this belief. The establishment of individual instruction in a school is no guarantee that instruction in that school will meet the needs of pupils. It is readily apparent that merely teaching one pupil at a time does not mean that that pupil will be properly taught. It is entirely possible that the wrong type of content may be employed, or it may be that proper attention is not given the child's particular difficulties. With-

[1] *Twenty-Fourth Yearbook of the National Society for the Study of Education*, p. 59. Bloomington, Illinois, Public School Publishing Company, 1925.

out doubt the failure to make this distinction has resulted in much harm not only to the individual-instruction movement, but to the whole tendency toward a better adaptation of instruction to individual differences of pupils. Individual instruction has without doubt been tried and discarded in instances where no real attempt has been made to adjust either materials or methods to pupil needs. At best all individual instruction can do is to make possible a better adaptation of instruction to individual interests, abilities, and rates of learning of pupils.

A second misconception is the belief that individual instruction is the only method whereby instruction can be adapted to pupil needs. The fallacy of this notion is evident in the fact that the Winnetka plan, the best known of the individual-instruction plans, does provide for group work in the socialized aspects of the child's work. Probably it would be admitted by even most extreme individual-instruction enthusiasts that there are some school activities which can best be conducted on a group basis. Perhaps it would also have to be admitted that instruction in some class groups may actually be better adapted to the needs of the pupils in those groups than is the instruction in some types of individual instruction. The harm growing out of the fallacy just discussed is that it causes teachers to relax in their efforts to make adaptations simply because they cannot have individual instruction.

While the great differences existing in the abilities of any group of children can readily be established and will perhaps not be argued, there are those who feel that the greatest advantage of individual instruction lies in the fact that it makes possible education in harmony with that extreme branch of modern educational philosophy which stresses freedom and regard for individuality as the only sound basis for truly educative experiences.

**How teacher differences modify instruction.** In order to illustrate the point of view, two descriptions of teaching procedures are given below. Teacher A utilizes children's purposes for motivation. She believes that learning takes place most effectively when it grows out of the felt needs of children. Teacher B is concerned largely with assigned tasks. Pupils are motivated to study because, if they do not, punishment or other undesirable consequences follow. In the case of Teacher A pupils study because they feel a need for participating in the activities. It seems reasonable to assume that in this case teaching is most effective when *all* of the children in the group are participating because they desire to participate.

*Teacher A* began to prepare for the lesson several days in advance. Pictures and newsclippings were pasted on the class bulletin and each day some children inquired about the points raised. Few of these questions were answered outright by the teacher and usually the references looked up led to further questions and problems. About the time the topic was scheduled for class work by the teacher, a group of children came to the teacher and asked if the geography lesson couldn't be devoted to the given topic. The teacher demanded reasons and raised objections until good reasons had been advanced. She then graciously yielded to the demands of the class on the condition that the class submit a good plan of work and take charge of their study and discussions themselves. The class accepted, organized itself into committees, and carried on a series of discussions and debates. The teacher took no part except to ask for information when the class discussion touched on points of which she was ignorant and in which she was interested, or when the discussions tended to wander too far afield. There was no questioning to find out what was learned and no testing of any kind except that the children themselves selected certain facts as worth remembering, and learned them by heart by playing games with them. Nevertheless, every point in the textbook was more than covered, all the children were interested in the subject and the class as a whole had worked itself into the next topic in the course of study without realizing it. For the most part the children talked freely and moved about the room to consult each other at will.    Occasional outbursts of fooling or roughness were promptly checked by the children themselves.

*Teacher B* assigned the children paragraphs 85–6–7 on page 57 of the textbook and directed them to be prepared to answer the first seven questions on page 64.    She pointed out unusual words whose meanings should be looked up and whose spelling should be learned. In class the next day, the recitation consisted of rapid fire questions in regard to the facts stated in the text, answers to the questions in the text, spelling, etc.    Only answers in the exact words of the text were accepted as correct.    The three paragraphs assigned for the lesson were covered three times and by the end of the hour every child had answered many questions.    Rigid order and perfect outward attention were maintained by force.    Children who proved to be unprepared were kept after school for extra drill.    At the end of the first lesson most of the children could have passed well a test based on facts or memory questions.

Now it is contended that if *all* children are to do the same things, it is very likely that *some* children will be submitting to the will of the majority.    For these children the activities engaged in will not grow out of their own felt needs, even though for other children this may be true.    The contention, in other words, is that only under individual instruction can instruction be completely motivated through felt needs.    If each child can do the thing which he wants to do his learning activities will be more effectively motivated.

**The Winnetka plan.**    Under the Winnetka plan the curriculum is divided into two parts.    One part is concerned with the skills, such as the fundamental operations in arithmetic, spelling, writing, reading skills, and certain facts in history and geography.    It is maintained that all children must master these skills, therefore the work in these skills is individualized.    The other part includes a number of socialized activities.    These are maintained for the purpose of providing opportunities for self-expression on the part of pupils.    They are largely group activities.    No attempt is made at a common mastery of facts.    It may be that each child will come away from the work with outcomes different from those of other children. The school day is divided about equally between the two lines of work.[1]

It is evident that the Winnetka plan affects the teaching of the skills more than the teaching of other activities, since the skills are the only part of the instruction which is individualized. It is maintained, however, that the plan does affect even the socialized activities by effecting economy of time resulting in more time for socialized activities.

Under the Winnetka plan there are no recitations in the drill phases of the various subjects. Each child works in the practice exercises at his own rate. A child progresses as rapidly as he can in each subject. He may be in one grade in reading and in another in arithmetic. When a unit is completed the child tests himself. If his test shows 100 per cent mastery he goes on to the next unit. If not he receives further assistance from the teacher. The units are grouped together and are called "goals." For example, a goal may be the ability to work a given number of addition examples in a certain length of time with a certain percentage of accuracy. As the child reaches each goal he undertakes work leading to the next goal. No child is allowed to "fail" or skip a grade. If at the end of the year a child has not completed the work for his grade he takes it up in the fall at the point where he left off in the spring. All the pupil's work in the skills is on a piece-work basis. The socialized studies are not used as a basis for pupil advancement. A considerable variety of activities is carried on in which a large proportion of the children participate.

**Kilpatrick on the plan.** The Winnetka plan has provoked some interesting discussions in educational philosophy. To quote Kilpatrick: [2]

[1] Reprinted by permission from *Twenty-Fourth Yearbook, National Society for the Study of Education*, Part II, p. 77. Bloomington, Illinois, Public School Publishing Co., 1925.

[2] *Ibid.*, pp. 280–81, and 284–85.

The term "the common essentials" is used at Winnetka to refer to the subject-matter content assigned for learning by "goals." By this Mr. Washburne means "certain knowledges and skills... needed by every child." That there are certain knowledges and skills which are needed by each child need not be disputed; but there are decided difficulties with the implications. First, it is implied that such an "essential" can be learned in isolation from its "natural setting" (to use Charters's term). This, it would seem certain, is only partially true. Second, it is implied that so large a body of such "essentials" can be definitely named. The more definitely this is tried, the further off does agreement seem to betake itself. Third, it is implied that "*the* common essentials" should consist exclusively of "knowledges" ("facts" were perhaps a better term) and skills. Surely this cannot be true. To leave out common honesty and truthfulness from any list of "common essentials" is at once to queer the list. Why are they omitted? Is it that they are not needed? Certainly not. The reason they are omitted is that they do not lend themselves to assignment by "goals." In other words, the phrase "the common essentials" carried with it just a shade of rationalization. The content is chosen on one basis; a name that implies a better basis is then given. Not "the common essentials," but "some common essentials that lend themselves to self-teaching assignment" — these constitute the content of the first part of the Winnetka scheme.

And what now is the conclusion regarding Winnetka's plan of learning by goals? First and foremost, it tends to break the child's learning into two disconnected parts. One part, highly mechanical, belongs to the system of goals — a system too nearly complete in itself, too little connected with life. Stated psychologically, the danger is that the learning will not transfer. Stated in terms of life, the danger is a divided self — that the child will look on learning as something apart from life, something to be "learned" and then put behind him. If it be rejoined that the freer classwork at Winnetka counteracts this danger, the answer comes that the freer work does seem to be in far greater degree continuous with life, but the gap still remains between the individual drill work and the freer group work. The two parts of school do not connect. And unfortunately, in the whole discussion at Winnetka, learning by goals seems to be counted as the essential. The chosen term implies it, and it is only the time saved from the goal work that is available for the other. If further rejoinder be made that the children are happy, that they like not only the freer group work but quite as well to work for goals, then we have to say that present happiness, though a good, can never be taken by itself as final. The question of long run effect must decide. That the Winnetka plan of goals is a better way of doing many of the things the ordinary school tries less successfully to do, may well be admitted. But unless the danger of little transfer and the danger of the divided self can be better safeguarded, the present writer, for one, does not believe that learning by goals will continue to hold its present prominence at Winnetka.

**Results of the Winnetka plan.** It is noteworthy that the Winnetka plan has remained in successful operation in Winnetka for a number of years. Mr. Washburne and his associates have carried on a vast amount of research in an effort to evaluate the plan.[1] While the pupils in Winnetka schools show a slight superiority in some respects, it would probably be premature to attempt any far-reaching evaluation of the plan. The following quotation and Table 9 are taken from the Winnetka Survey:

The graphs show clearly that Winnetka is doing a distinctly good job in reading; that in spelling ability Winnetka runs slightly below the other schools; that Winnetka excels in formal language and in arithmetical speed and accuracy, as shown by the Winnetka

TABLE 9. PER CENT THAT WINNETKA SCORES ARE OF THE
AVERAGE SCORE OF SCHOOLS STUDIED

("Test" and "Supplementary" Winnetka groups are here combined)

| TEST | M.A. 8–9 | M.A. 9–10 | M.A. 10–11 | M.A. 11–12 | M.A. 12–13 | M.A. 13–14 |
|---|---|---|---|---|---|---|
| Burgess Silent Reading....... | 113 | 106 | 103 | 102 | 102 | .... |
| Spelling..................... | 99 | 98 | 99 | 97 | 96 | 98 |
| Language..................... | .... | .... | .... | 123 | 113 | 116 |
| Cleveland Arithmetic......... | 127 | 108 | 111 | 116 | 98 | 100 |
| Winnetka Arithmetic (Speed).. | .... | 108 | 160 | 135 | 111 | 106 |
| Winnetka Arithmetic (Accuracy)................... | .... | 110 | 120 | 106 | 98 | 106 |

[1] Gray, W. S., Washburne, C., and Vogel, M. *Survey of the Winnetka Schools.* Public School Publishing Company, Bloomington, Illinois.

tests, and is at least equal to the other schools in arithmetical ability, as shown by the Cleveland Survey tests.

The variation that exists among classes in Winnetka is clearly shown by the wide differences that sometimes exist between "test" and "supplementary" groups. These differences must be attributed to differences among teachers, and differences among the children themselves.

The survey in general, then, shows that in grades and subjects tested the Winnetka schools are doing distinctly effective work — work which on the whole is more efficient, as measured by the various tests which were used, than that done by comparable schools which use class methods of instructions.

**The McDade plan of individual instruction.** The plan developed by Assistant Superintendent McDade of Chicago has much in common with the Winnetka scheme. Both Mr. Washburne and Mr. McDade stress the importance of special materials for successful individual instruction. The McDade plan, however, is made up of shorter units. It is McDade's view that instructional materials should be organized in units of such a size that they can readily be fitted into the program of teaching for any child. The lack of flexibility in large textbooks has frequently been emphasized. When materials are organized in short units it becomes possible to select for any pupil only those which he should use. Such materials can also be easily filed and cared for by the teacher. In the work of distributing the drill materials and replacing them provision is definitely made for pupil participation.

The McDade plan is being used in a considerable number of schools in the city of Chicago. The claim is made that it meets the needs of schools which have large classes and which cannot effect a complete reorganization of their work. Many of the materials used have been published,[1] and individual units are being used in several school systems.

[1] Plymouth Press, Chicago, Illinois.

### B. CURRICULAR DEVICES FOR HANDLING INDIVIDUAL DIFFERENCES

One method of providing for individual differences is to retain the group organization of the school, but to provide for pupil differences through variations in the curriculum. In a general way this plan has been worked out in two different methods. The first method is based upon variations in assignments within classes. The second calls for different subjects to be pursued by pupils of differing abilities.

**Variable assignments.** Under this plan the slower pupils are asked to do less work. Sometimes the teacher provides minimum, average, and maximum assignments. The pupil may choose which assignment he is to undertake. In other instances the teacher may decide that, because of a pupil's mental-test score or achievement record, he should undertake a particular assignment. It should be noted that this method varies the amount and nature as well as the difficulty of the work undertaken. The "contract plan" is also a curricular device in that the "contract" may call for large or small amounts of work, according to the abilities of the pupils.

**The Morrison Mastery Technique.** While Morrison's plan is not purely a plan for meeting the individual differences of pupils, it nevertheless deserves consideration in any discussion of the problem.[1] Under this plan the subject-matter is organized into large units, requiring perhaps twenty days to complete. The instructional procedure is divided into five steps:

1. The exploration, devoted to discovering what children already know about the unit and also to the stimulation of interest in the new unit.
2. The presentation, a discussion of the unit by the teacher with an attempt to give an over-view of the unit.

[1] Morrison, H. C. *The Practice of Teaching in Secondary Schools* (revised ed.), 1931. Reprinted by permission of the University of Chicago Press.

3. The assimilation, reading and study by pupils, with such assistance from the teacher as they may need. This step may take from 12 to 15 days.
4. Organization, a period during which pupils without the help of books, magazines, or notebooks, write out an organized outline of the unit. This step constitutes a rather severe examination.
5. Recitation, a period or two in which pupils present from three to five minutes talks before the class on some aspect of the unit.

Teachers who use this plan find it desirable to outline the units carefully, with working instructions for pupils.

In the organization of these units there is opportunity to allow for pupil differences. Variations may be made in the amount of material read, in the difficulty of the material, or in the extensiveness of the field to be covered. The method literally places the course of study in the hands of the pupils. One effect of the use of the method is to give teachers a striking illustration of the extent and nature of the individual differences of pupils. One teacher assigned a unit with the thought that it would keep the pupils at work for fifteen days. This teacher found, to his surprise, that at the end of the fourth day two pupils had completed the assimilation step. Other pupils required twenty days.

A number of problems result from an attempt to follow the plan of variable assignments. If all pupils are to be kept at a uniform rate of progress through the curriculum, the slower pupils may have to omit material which is highly important. Whole sections of content may have to be omitted if the pupil is to "keep up with his grade." For the brighter or more rapid pupils the problem is also serious. In order to keep such pupils occupied teachers may feel it necessary to include in so-called maximum assignments material which is difficult but perhaps of doubtful value. With pupils of all abilities there is always the problem of seeing to it that they are working at maximum capacity.

Some teachers feel that bright pupils sometimes select the minimum assignments merely to escape work.

It should also be kept in mind that we have no assurance that the problems growing out of the individual differences of pupils can be solved merely by making variations in *amount* of work. Pupils may need specialized methods of teaching or variations in the amount of time allotted to a project, or even changes in the nature of the material or the courses to be covered.

**Multiple curricula.** This device has been used widely, especially in the secondary schools. The assumption underlying the plan of setting up several different courses of study has been that pupils of differing abilities should take different subjects. Often the working out of the plan has been to set up curricula of an academic nature for bright pupils, and curricula of industrial or manual work for slower pupils.

In junior high schools especially these curricular variations have been employed in two ways. In the first place, so-called try-out courses have been set up whereby pupils have opportunity to pursue several different courses for short periods of time, largely for the purpose of determining pupil aptitudes and abilities. In the second place, the schools have been organized with several parallel curricula which could be pursued by pupils of differing interests and abilities.

While there is no doubt much merit in these procedures, it should be remembered that even when such variable curricula are provided they will not bring together pupils who are homogeneous from the point of view of instruction. Probably it will be found that within any one curriculum there will be wide differences in ability which may be very serious. Certainly the choice of curricula even under the most careful guidance will not result in groups of equal ability. It may result only in groups of somewhat similar interests.

### C. METHOD DEVICES FOR HANDLING INDIVIDUAL
### DIFFERENCES

**Factors in the situation.**  In one sense the use of the word "method" in this connection may not be accurate.  There are those who include under the method the "total learning situation." [1]  In this usage the term method would include curriculum, materials, and teaching devices.  The problem may be clarified by a consideration of some of the basic principles upon which schools may be adapted to pupil needs.

On an *a-priori* basis one might say there are three principal factors in the situation.  They are the time allowed, the amount or difficulty of content, and the methods of teaching.  Attempts to adapt instruction to pupil differences might be made by bringing about variations in any one or all of these factors.  For example, one might assume that all pupils will be taught the same content and by the same methods, but the time for different pupils will vary.  In a similar way variations may be made in content, but time and method will be constant for all pupils.  Or it may be that time and content will be constant, and variations will be made in methods of teaching.  Another plan would be to assume that variations would take place in all of the three factors.  In other words, different pupils need different content, different time allotments, and different learning methods.

If a broad concept of method is accepted no doubt the term "method devices" would include all of the variations referred to above.  However, if one thinks of method largely as teaching devices or procedures, "method devices" would include principally variations of a relatively narrow sort.  Mention will be made here of only a few such devices.

**Teaching procedures.**  Do dull pupils learn by different

[1] Kilpatrick, W. H.  *Foundations of Method.*  New York, The Macmillan Company, 1925.

procedures than do bright pupils?  Or, to put the question in another form, Do different pupils learn in different ways? At the present time there are different teaching procedures in almost every subject, but little is known about the extent to which each method is adapted to the needs of different pupils.  For example, in reading, one can teach by the alphabet method, the word method, or the sentence method. Which of these methods is best adapted to dull pupils?  In a given group of dull pupils can we be assured that all of them will learn most effectively by a given method, or by a combination of methods?

In spelling there are test-study methods, and study-test methods.  Shall it be assumed that there is one best method for all pupils, or may it be that some pupils learn to spell most rapidly and accurately by one method and other pupils by a different method?  In arithmetic many drill devices have been developed.  By some it is assumed that if a child is taught how to add 5 and 6 he must also be taught how to add 6 and 5.  Does this hold true for all pupils?  There is suggestion in recent studies that it does not.

Even if it were found that a particular method seems best for most pupils, there can be no assurance that it is best for all pupils.  The teacher must therefore constantly face the necessity of individualizing her methods.  Since the chapters dealing with the several school subjects discuss methods of teaching designed to adapt instruction to individual differences, no effort will be made at this point to describe them.  The reader is referred to these chapters for detailed descriptions of such procedures.

**Individuality as a factor of method.**  The adaptation of instruction to individual differences involves certain educational theory which is well expressed by Dewey [1] in the following statement:

---

[1] Quoted by Ratner, J., in *Philosophy of John Dewey*, p. 398.  New York, Henry Holt and Company, 1928.

Individuality as a factor to be respected in education has a double meaning. In the first place, one is mentally an individual only as he has his own purpose and problem, and does his own thinking. Unless one does it for himself, it isn't thinking. Only by a pupil's own observations, reflections, framing, and testing of suggestions can what he already knows be amplified and rectified. Thinking is as much an individual matter as is the digestion of food. In the second place, there are variations of points of view, of appeal of objects, and of modes of attack, from person to person. When these variations are suppressed in the alleged interests of uniformity, and an attempt is made to have a single mode or method of study and recitation, mental confusion and artificiality inevitably result. Originality is gradually destroyed, confidence in one's own quality of mental operation is undermined, and a docile subjection to the opinions of others is inculcated, or else ideas run wild.... That systematic advance in scientific discovery began when individuals were allowed, and then encouraged, to utilize their own peculiarities of response to subject matter, no one will deny.

The essence of the demand for freedom is the need of conditions which will enable an individual to make his own special contribution to a group interest, and to partake of its activities in such ways that social guidance shall be a matter of his own mental attitude, and not a mere authoritative dictation of his acts. Freedom means essentially the part played by thinking — which is personal — in learning: it means intellectual initiative, independence in observation, judicious invention, foresight of consequences, and ingenuity of adaptation to them.

That individualization of instruction involves more than the grouping of the pupils into ability groups or administrative adjustments of various kinds is clearly indicated by the following statement,[1] from Dewey himself:

Individual activity has sometimes been taken as meaning leaving a pupil to work by himself or alone. Relief from attending to what anyone else is doing is truly required to secure calm and concentration. Children, like grown persons, require a judicious amount of being let alone. But the time, place and amount of such separate

[1] Quoted by Ratner, J., in *Philosophy of John Dewey*, p. 399. New York, Henry Holt and Company, 1928.

work is a matter of detail, not principle. There is no inherent opposition between working with others and working as an individual. On the contrary, certain capacities of the individual are not brought out except under the stimulus of association with others. That a child must work alone and not engage in group activities in order to be free and let his individuality develop, is a notion which measures individuality by spatial distance and makes a physical thing out of it.

If the teacher is really a teacher, and not just a master or "authority," he should know enough about his pupils, their needs, experiences, degrees of skill, and knowledge, etc., to be able not to dictate aims and plans but to share in a discussion regarding what is to be done and be free to make suggestions as anyone else. And his contribution, given the conditions stated, will presumably do more to getting something started which will really secure and increase the development of strictly individual capacities than will suggestions springing from uncontrolled haphazard sources.... The fuller and richer the experience of the teacher, the more adequate his own knowledge of "traditions" the more likely is he, given the attitude of participator instead of that of master, to use them in a liberating way.

**Method and curriculum integrated.** The problems involved in providing a rich series of socializing activities and integrating them with the drill on essential skills and concepts, which must be individualized in order to allow for individual differences in rates of learning, are well expressed by Courtis [1] in the following statement:

The work already done has revealed certain difficulties and defects and suggested desirable modifications. For one thing, it is apparent that an ideal course of study would consist of two parts: (1) a series of social projects in which there would be need for the use of fundamental skills in meaningful situations, and (2), a series of self-instructive, self-appraising practice exercises, so closely correlated with the project work that children could avail themselves of drill exercises as they become conscious of the need. The danger of the completely organized drill system, however per-

[1] In the *Twenty-Fourth Yearbook of the National Society for the Study of Education*, Part II, pp. 112–13. Bloomington, Illinois, Public School Publishing Company, 1925.

fectly individualized, is that both teachers and children will come to consider skills as ends in themselves. Under such conditions, the transfer value of the skill developed is small. While the danger is negligible for competent teachers who neither overemphasize the drill work, nor permit the use of drill exercises by children except in response to a felt need, it is a very real danger for teachers without vision. In many ways the problem is not "How to individualize school work?" but "How to secure teachers with the right points of view?" On the other hand, the unit-task idea, democratically administered by a competent teacher, solves very many of the distressing problems caused by individual differences and greatly increases the efficiency of teaching.

## QUESTIONS FOR STUDY, DISCUSSION, AND REPORT

1. Compare the Winnetka and the Dalton plans. Which seems best adapted to elementary schools?

2. What objections are there to classification of pupils on the basis of I.Q.? M.A.?

3. Set forth the advantages and disadvantages of the semi-annual promotion plan.

4. Summarize the evidence in regard to the effectiveness of ability grouping in providing for the individual differences of pupils.

5. What is the relationship between educational philosophy and the methods used for adapting instruction to individual differences?

6. Trace the principal influences which have led to a more complete recognition of the nature of the individual differences of children.

## SELECTED REFERENCES

Ayres, L. P. *Laggards in Our Schools.* 236 pp. New York, Charities Publication Committee, 1909.

Cubberley, E. P. *Public School Administration.* Revised and Enlarged Edition. Boston, Houghton Mifflin Company, 1929.

Miller, W. S., and Otto, H. J. "Analysis of Experimental Studies in Homogeneous Grouping"; in *Journal of Educational Research,* vol. 21, pp. 95–103. (February, 1930.)

Mort, Paul R. *The Individual Child in Class and School.* New York, American Book Company, 1928.

Otto, Henry J. *The Organization and Administration of Elementary Schools.* Northwestern University Contributions to Education. Bloomington, Illinois, Public School Publishing Company, 1931.

*Twenty-Third Yearbook, National Society for the Study of Education,* Part I. Bloomington, Illinois, Public School Publishing Company, 1924.

*Twenty-Fourth Yearbook, National Society for the Study of Education,* Part II. Adaptation of Instruction to Individual Differences. Bloomington, Illinois, Public School Publishing Company, 1925.

Wallin, E. W. *The Education of Handicapped Children.* Boston, Houghton Mifflin Company, 1924.

Washburne, Carleton, Vogel, Mabel, and Gray, William S. *A Survey of the Winnetka Public Schools.* Bloomington, Illinois, Public School Publishing Company, 1926.

# CHAPTER III

## THE NATURE AND FUNCTIONS OF STANDARD EDUCATIONAL TESTS

### I. CHARACTERISTICS OF INTELLECT TO BE CONSIDERED IN MEASUREMENT AND DIAGNOSIS

To determine general ability in any particular subject there are at least five aspects or characteristics of intellect that must be considered. They are: (1) rate of response; (2) accuracy or quality of work; (3) altitude or level of development of power; (4) area or range of ability at given levels and in general; (5) methods of work in exercising the element being considered.

Each of these will be considered in the order stated.

### 1. *Rate of response*

**Standard rates of work.** It is commonly recognized that rate of work is a valuable index of skill and control of a particular function. Other things being equal, the person who can respond rapidly has a greater skill than the individual whose rate of response is slow. We recognize this fact particularly in the field of motor skills, such as in speed of running, rate of writing, and in labor at machines.

One purpose of drill in school subjects is to increase the speed of responses in such elements as rate of reading and rate of computation. The enthusiasm for drill has often resulted in excessive stress on speed of work, and in the development of a rate of response far beyond that which should normally be required of pupils of a given level of maturity. This stress on speed of work has often resulted in the breakdown of accuracy of work, and in some cases in the development of serious nervous disorders.

To overcome the tendency on the part of some teachers to place undue emphasis on excessive speed of work, standard rates of work have been suggested for various important skills, such as rate of writing, rate of reading, rate of adding columns of a given difficulty, and the like. Pupils whose rate of work is up to the established standards for their grade are considered to be working at a rate that is satisfactory. Pupils working at a lower rate are expected to try to increase their rate of work. Many standard tests in reading, writing, and arithmetic have standards for rate of work.

**Measuring rate of work.** Rate of work is readily measured by determining the number of items in a given exercise an individual can complete in a unit of time, such as a minute. For example, rate of reading may be measured by finding the number of words an individual can read in a given time; rate of writing by finding the number of letters or words he can write in a specified time; rate of computation in a certain process by finding the number of a given type of examples he can work in a specified time.

Rate of work may also be determined by finding how long it takes a pupil to complete a given unit of work. To accomplish this purpose the test should consist of items to which the pupil can respond and with which he is familiar. Otherwise no valid measurement of rate of response can be secured.

**Factors affecting rate of work.** Many factors may affect the rate at which an individual works. Maturity is an important consideration, since psychology has shown that speed of work increases in children as they grow older. Their interest in the task, the zeal with which the task is undertaken, and their mental attitude obviously are reflected in their rate of work. The directions for work on the test may be so stated that the pupil may hurry unduly in his work, and his test score hence may give a false and exaggerated index of his real ability. In the primary grades, lack of control over the motor skills involved makes it difficult to secure a true measure of the pupil's knowledge of arithmetic combinations by means of a timed written exercise. What such a test measures is a complex composed of his speed in computation and his speed and ability to write figures. His control over the physical skills involved in writing may be so inadequate that he cannot write down the answers as rapidly as he can think of them. The result is that two pupils who in fact have equal ability in addition may make widely different scores in a timed test, due to differences in their rates of writing. Such factors, and others of a similar nature, must always be considered in making an interpretation of scores purporting to express the pupil's rate of work.

## 2. Accuracy or quality of work

The term "accuracy" refers to freedom from error. Certain types of performance in arithmetic, spelling, and reading can be classified as either correct or incorrect. Many types of performance in handwriting, composition, and drawing cannot be so classified. In such cases the quality or general merit of the item is determined by comparing the sample with standard samples of known merit.

**Rate and accuracy.** Accuracy of work probably is a more important factor to be considered in the evaluation of any general or specific ability than is the rate of work. If the work of an individual shows a low degree of accuracy it has relatively little merit.

Rate and accuracy may be found in various combinations, as follows: (1) superior speed and accuracy; (2) average speed and a high degree of accuracy; (3) low speed and a high degree of accuracy; (4) superior speed and average accuracy;

(5) average speed and average accuracy; (6) low speed and average accuracy; (7) high speed and a low degree of accuracy; (8) average speed and a low degree of accuracy; (9) low speed and a low degree of accuracy.

Pupils of types 1, 2, and 3 represent a high class educational product; types 4, 5, and 6 represent instructional problems of some significance; types 7 and 8 probably are the product of inferior instruction. Type 9 may be either the result of lack of ability or mentality, or may be the product of a low level of teaching.

Some tests have standards expressed only in terms of the number of correct responses. Such standards disregard wholly the factor of speed of work as related to the degree of accuracy. Test scores based on the number of correct responses do not give as valuable a body of information to the teacher as is supplied by tests having standards for both rate and accuracy. For example, two pupils may each have answered 40 items of a test correctly. Suppose that this score indicates an ability equal to the average for their grade. However, one of the pupils may have attempted 80 items, and the other only 40 items. The first pupil, a very rapid worker, would have had only 50 per cent of the items attempted correct; the second would have had 100 per cent correct. Clearly there is a marked difference in the quality of the work of these two pupils. This point would have been overlooked if their rates of work had not been considered. The evaluation of the work of pupils on tests designed to measure accuracy of work should therefore take into consideration the pupil's rate of work. On the other hand, if a pupil is a very slow but accurate worker his performances are also not satisfactory. Thus it becomes evident that both rate of work and accuracy of work must be considered in evaluating the ability of an individual.

### 3. *Altitude or level of development*

**Wide variations.** The level of the development of a general ability constitutes a third characteristic that must be considered in measurement or diagnosis. "We measure the level of the altitude of an intellect by the difficulty of the intellectual tasks which it can perform successfully, or, more exactly, by the difficulty of the tasks a certain per cent of which it can perform successfully." [1] The tasks that the pupils undertake in school, the skills they are to acquire, and the abilities that are to be developed cover a wide range of difficulty. The pupil in the primary grades usually acquires only the simplest, least difficult of these elements. As he progresses through the school he should acquire elements of greater difficulty. The higher on the scale of difficulty a pupil can perform satisfactorily, the more superior his general development may be considered to be. Pupils of relatively inferior ability can assimilate only those elements low on the scale of difficulty. It is obvious to every wide-awake teacher that the range in the levels of development of the abilities of pupils in any class is very large. This wide variation in ability presents many teaching problems, and has been the direct cause of the development of various plans for grouping pupils into classes of approximately the same level of development.

**The concept illustrated.** The concept of the altitude of intellect or ability may be illustrated by an example from the field of spelling. To measure the altitude of the pupil's general ability to spell, he may be given a test consisting of words of increasing spelling difficulty, such as the Starch Spelling Scales. The pupil who can spell only the easy words on the list obviously has a much lower development of general spelling ability than the pupil who can spell al-

---

[1] Thorndike, E. L. *The Measurement of Intelligence*, p. 159. New York, Bureau of Publications, Columbia University, 1928.

most all of the words in the list; that is, the altitude of the general ability to spell of the former does not reach as high a level as that of the latter. In the same way the altitude of development of ability in arithmetic, algebra, reading, and other skills may be determined. Likewise the level of the development of general intelligence may be determined by the ways in which the individual responds to items of increasing difficulty.

In such factors as the quality of writing, or the general merit or quality of compositions, the general altitude of ability is determined by comparing a particular specimen with others of known value, ranging in merit or value from very inferior to very superior. The higher on the scale of values the value of the item which the specimen most nearly resembles, the greater is the altitude of the ability or skill included. Here altitude of development is determined by quality and merit, rather than by the ability of the pupil to perform tasks of increasing difficulty.

#### 4. *Area or range of ability at given levels*

**Area or range.** Thorndike [1] has suggested the necessity of considering the extent to which the intellect of an individual has been developed at each level of difficulty. He has demonstrated that at any single level of difficulty there are many different constituent elements. Thorndike believes that the intellect of an individual can only be adequately measured by evaluating his performance on a wide range of items at each level of difficulty. For this purpose he has developed the C.A.V.D. Tests.

Area may also be thought of as consisting of the whole range of skills and specific abilities that constitute various

[1] Thorndike, E. L. *The Measurement of Intelligence*, p. 24. New York, Bureau of Publications, Columbia University, 1928.

phases of a subject, such as the addition of whole numbers, the subtraction of fractions, or the use of marks of punctuation. For example, the Brueckner Diagnostic Test in Subtraction of Fractions (see page 183) contains 53 different types of examples in that process, the combination of skills in each example differing in some way from the skills that are required in the solution of each of the other examples in the test. By means of this test the teacher can determine whether the pupil knows how to manipulate each of the combinations of skills presented in the test.

**Importance of this concept.** The concept of area must be borne in mind in making any generalizations concerning general ability in a particular field on the basis of the results of a single test, such as the Thorndike–McCall Test in Reading. This test consists of a series of exercises in silent reading of increasing difficulty in which the pupils' comprehension is tested by their ability to answer questions based on the paragraphs included in the test. As will be shown in Chapter VIII, this specific ability is only one of a large number of reading abilities which should be developed through careful instruction. The conclusion that a class with a score considerably above the standard on this one test has superior general reading ability is obviously not based on adequate information, and is a misconception of the function of the test. Before a conclusion as to the general reading ability of the pupils can be reached, the other major abilities, which constitute the area of reading, must be evaluated.

In addition to specific skills and abilities, the concept of area also includes reference to such outcomes of instruction as attitudes, appreciation, purposes, insight, and interpretations. No teacher should evaluate ability wholly in terms of specific knowledge and skills, acquired by pupils, since the mere possession of these tools without the proper appreciation of their use and significance, or the ability and disposition to apply them in socially useful ways, means that they may be of little value to the individual or to society. Positive, desirable attitudes of pupils are reflected in their ways of responding, in their interest in the subject, and in their intensity of application to the task at hand. The teacher who wishes to appraise the efficiency of instruction must therefore consider the whole range of instructional outcomes; not only the relatively simple outcomes in terms of knowledges and skills, but also the important associated learnings which may be thought of as attitudes, purposes, ways of responding, appreciation, and ideals.

### 5. Methods of work

**Importance of efficient methods.** Obviously an important factor in estimating ability is the methods of work of the individual while using particular skills in test exercises or in other activities. Efficient methods of work insure much better results than can be achieved when the pupil uses faulty, uneconomical procedures. Under such conditions his potential ability cannot function at optimum levels.

Faulty habits of work cannot be discovered by direct measurement, although their presence may be suspected in cases where the pupil's performance is clearly inferior to that which may be expected of a pupil of his general mental level. Faulty habits of work may often be detected by observation of the pupil's activities while, for example, he is taking a test, or preparing an assignment. An analysis of the written work often reveals the causes of the difficulties. It is very difficult to discover faulty mental procedures, although much progress has been made in developing techniques by means of which this may be done.

**An illustrative case.** The following case, described by

Gray,[1] will make clear what is involved in considering a pupil's methods of work in reading:

*Detailed diagnosis.* In the Jones Vocabulary Test, she made a score of 90 on the sight list and 74 on the phonetic list. Whenever errors occurred, the words which were pronounced usually differed very slightly from the printed word, as big for dig and ship for skip. Many errors were due to carelessness, as shown by the fact that she was able to correct them without assistance when her attention was called to them. Other errors were due to the fact that she did not know some of the simple phonetic elements. In the visual memory test, she made five slight errors. The fact that she was able to correct the error in most cases, when told that her first attempt was incorrect, supplied further evidence that she did not see details accurately, due very largely to carelessness.

Informal tests in oral reading revealed several significant facts: (1) She frequently mispronounced words in context which she recognized accurately when isolated. (2) Many substitutions, such as trust for taste, and rob for rub, indicated that she did not direct her attention to the content. (3) She had difficulty in distinguishing different forms of the same word, such as come, came, and coming, or work, worked, and working. (4) She repeated frequently either because the thought was not clear or to correct errors. (5) She had some knowledge of phonetics as shown by her ability to recognize certain word elements, but she failed to use her knowledge effectively. (6) She read very haltingly because of word difficulties and because she recognized individual words rather than groups of words at each fixation.

Informal tests in silent reading revealed evidence of a limited background of experience and inadequate meaning vocabulary. Furthermore, her difficulties in the pronunciation of polysyllabic words interfered with the interpretation of the thought of more difficult passages. In simple selections her weakness in interpretation was due largely to the fact that she had not formed the habit of directing her attention to the content. She was satisfied with a general impression of the story and was unable to answer specific questions concerning the content or to think independently about it. When told beforehand that she would be asked to retell a story, she reproduced the points satisfactorily.

[1] Gray, W. S. *Remedial Cases in Reading; Their Diagnosis and Treatment,* Supplementary Educational Monographs, no. 22. University of Chicago. (June, 1922.)

## II. THE TRADITIONAL EXAMINATION AND THE STANDARD TEST

**The essay-type examination.** The typical procedure that has been used by the teacher to determine the achievement of the pupils has been the traditional written examination of the essay type. Teachers have long felt that these tests are a most unsatisfactory means of making an accurate appraisal of the pupil's achievements. Kelly,[1] Ruch,[2] Lang,[3] and many others have shown that teachers' marks based on such tests are wholly unreliable. The marks are influenced by many uncontrollable factors, such as undue stress on unimportant details, lack of definite rules to guide the rater, variations in standards of estimate, and personal prejudices. It has been found that the marks given to a single paper by a number of investigators vary all the way from 20 to 90 per cent. Such wide variations show that the ability of the pupil has not been measured at all. The fact that his work is graded as superior by one teacher and inferior by another proves this.

**Principal characteristics of standard tests.** To overcome the weaknesses of the essay-type examination the standard test and the new type of objective examination have been devised. The principal characteristics of standard tests are as follows:

1. The conditions under which the standard test is to be given with respect to directions, time allowances, and method of responding are standardized to insure uniform procedures in the administration of the test.

[1] Kelly, F. *Teachers' Marks.* Teachers College Contributions to Education, no. 66. New York, Columbia University, 144. The pioneer report in this field.

[2] Ruch, G. M. *The Objective or New Type Examination.* Chicago, Scott, Foresman and Company, 1929. A complete summary of critical investigations of the reliability of the teachers' marks.

[3] Lang, A. R. *Modern Methods in Written Examinations.* Boston, Houghton Mifflin Company, 1930. Contains a very good discussion of marks and marking.

2. The method of scoring is so definite and objective that the personal equation is almost completely eliminated in the marking of the test paper.

3. Norms or standards based on the performances of large numbers of typical pupils on the same tasks are provided. These norms or standards make it possible to evaluate and interpret the scores of individual pupils.

It is estimated that at present there are approximately five hundred standardized tests available. Estimates of the number of standardized tests sold each year vary from fifteen million to twenty-five million. In one or two cases as many as two million copies of a single standard test are sold each year.

**The objective or new-type examination.** The necessity of supplementing the standard test by exercises more closely adapted to the local curriculum has resulted in the development in many school systems of informal objective tests quite similar in form to the exercises found in standard tests. The principles that should underlie their construction will be considered in Chapter VI. For the present it will be sufficient to illustrate several of the important types.

1. (Simple recall.)   When was America discovered?. . . . . . . . . . .
2. (Multiple choice.)   America was discovered in
    1492,   1200,   1508,   1609
3. (Completion.)   America was discovered in. . . . . . . . . . . . . . . . .
4. (True-false.)   America was discovered in 1492.

The objective test exercises have certain values as well as certain limitations. They can be prepared easily and cheaply by any teacher who understands the principles underlying their construction. The scoring is objective, and papers may be quickly and accurately rated. The elimination of the personal equation in the marking of test papers insures less dissatisfaction with the marks on the part of the pupils than is the case with the traditional essay type of examination. Such test exercises afford an economical and effective basis for checking up quickly the extent to which pupils have mastered a wide range of subject-matter. The chief limitations of such exercises are the lack of norms or standards by which to interpret individual scores, and the crudities that are likely to be found because the tests were not subjected to careful standardization and experimental study.

**Measuring aspects of ability.** Four of the five characteristics of ability that have been discussed may be evaluated by direct measurement, namely, rate of work, accuracy or quality of response, altitude, and area. The fifth characteristic, methods of work, cannot be determined directly by measurement. Methods of work must be evaluated after an analysis of the nature of the pupil's responses to test items, answers he gives to questions, and by means of other suitable diagnostic devices which may reveal inefficient and uneconomical procedures, skills, and habits.

**Rate tests.** To measure the rate of a pupil's work, rate tests have been devised. Such tests usually consist of a number of relatively easy items of approximately the same degree of difficulty. The pupil's rate of work in such a test is determined by the number of items he can complete per unit of time or in a given time. The time allowed is such that ordinarily no pupil is able to finish the test. If the items of a test are of varying degrees of difficulty the pupil's rate of work is likely to be reduced, because of the greater amount of work required for the difficult exercises. If the pupil is unfamiliar with the test exercise and hence does very little actual work on the test, it is obvious that his true rate of work is not measured. For example, if a teacher who wishes to measure rate of writing has the pupil write from memory a short poem that has not been well memorized, it is obvious that the results will not yield a true index of the pupil's rate of writing.

Rate tests are also used to measure accuracy of work on tasks of a single level of difficulty. Standards for accuracy are usually expressed as the number of items worked correctly in a given time. Sometimes standards are expressed as per cents of accuracy. Such standards have little meaning unless they are associated with the number of items attempted.

Some of the most widely used rate tests are the following: Cleveland Survey Arithmetic Tests; Courtis Standard Research Tests in Arithmetic, Series B; Chapman Cook Speed of Reading Test; Burgess Picture Supplement Scale of Measuring Ability in Silent Reading; and the Courtis Silent Reading Test, No. 2.

**Scales.** Three different kinds of scales are used in educational measurement, namely, scaled tests, quality scales, and product scales. The nature and purpose of each kind of scale will now be briefly considered.

(*a*) *Scaled tests.* To measure altitude or power, scaled tests are used. Scaled tests are often called "power tests." Such scales consist of a series of tasks arranged in order of increasing difficulty from very easy to very difficult. The difficulty of the items in the scale is usually determined by first giving a number of exercises of varying form and complexity to a large group of children. Then on the basis of the responses of the children the items are arranged in order of difficulty. Theoretically the differences in the difficulty of the successive steps of a scale are all equal. This arrangement can be accomplished by a somewhat technical statistical procedure.

In order to get a measure of altitude of ability by means of a scale the difficulty of the most difficult item or group of items on the scale that the pupil can solve or answer with a specified degree of accuracy is determined. The scoring procedure involved in getting a rating on some of the scales is quite complicated. It is therefore a more common practice to use simply the number of correct items in a test exercise to represent the pupil's score. By comparing his score with standards, the altitude or level of the pupil's ability as compared with others of the same general level of development may be determined.

Scaled tests do not provide a measure of the pupil's rates of work, because the amount of time allowed for the test is long enough to permit every subject to complete as many of the test exercises as he is able to do. The purpose of scaled tests is to measure power, not rate of work. A few of the most common measuring instruments of this type are:

> Henmon Latin Tests
> Hotz Algebra Scales
> Thorndike–McCall Reading Scales
> Van Wagenen American History Scales
> Woody–McCall Mixed Fundamentals in Arithmetic

The nature of scaled tests is illustrated in the reproduction of the Woody McCall Scale in Mixed Fundamentals (page 170).

(b) *Quality scales.* Quality scales are used as a means of measuring the quality of a pupil's work in such abilities as those involved in composition, writing, and art. Quality scales consist of a series of samples arranged in the ascending order of their quality or general merit from very inferior to superior. The order of merit is usually determined by securing the rankings of a large number of samples by a group of competent judges, and applying a technical, statistical procedure to these data. As in scaled tests, theoretically the successive steps between pairs of samples on a quality scale are equal. Samples of the pupil's work are evaluated by comparing them with the scaled items, and then assigning each of the samples value corresponding to that of the scaled item which in the judgment of the rater it most nearly resembles. Widely used quality scales are the

Hudelson English Composition Scale, the Ayres Handwriting Scale, and the Thorndike Handwriting Scale. In many school systems scales for various subjects have been developed locally. Specimens which will make clear the nature of quality scales are included in the illustrative materials in various chapters of this book.

(c) *Product scales.* A product scale consists of a series of groups of items, arranged on a scale of difficulty. The items in each group are of approximately equal difficulty or value. The steps between the several groups of items are equally spaced on a scale. In theory there is no known limit to the number of items that may be found in any single group. Usually the number of items to be included in a product scale is determined by some such standard as the merit of the particular items, their frequency of use in everyday life, or their social value. Typical product scales are the Ayres Spelling Scale, the Iowa Spelling Scales, and the Hahn–Lackey Geography Scales.

Product scales represent excellent sources of material to be used in the construction of rate or scaled tests. A rate test may be constructed from the items in any single difficulty group. The breadth or area of an individual's general ability, say in spelling, may be determined by his scores on tests composed of items selected at each level of difficulty. Scaled tests may be made by selecting one or more items from each level of difficulty, thus affording a means of securing an index of the altitude of the pupil's general ability by determining the difficulty of the most difficult items he is able to solve.

Considerable use has been made of product scales in the preparation of the textbooks in such subjects as spelling and arithmetic.

**Combination type of test.** At the present time there are being used many standard tests which are neither rate tests nor scales. Such tests consist of groups of items in a single subject of varying degrees of difficulty, and the items are not scaled. They may be limited to one phase of a subject, such as addition of fractions, the use of punctuation marks, or history information. There is usually a time limit for these tests. Such tests are valuable for survey purposes, but they are not tools for exact measurement. Informal tests of this type may be prepared for survey purposes by local school systems. Typical tests of this kind are the Courtis Supervisory Tests in Geography, the Compass Survey Test in Arithmetic, and the Wilson Language Error Test. The Courtis Supervisory Test in Arithmetic, presented on page 173, is also a good illustration of this kind of test.

## III. STANDARD TESTS CLASSIFIED ACCORDING TO PURPOSES

**Types.** Standard tests may be classified according to their purposes or functions. The basis for selecting any particular test should be the specific purpose the teacher or supervisor has in mind in giving the test. A convenient basis of classification of tests according to their purposes is as follows: (1) intelligence test; (2) general survey test; (3) subject achievement test; (4) analytical subject test; (5) diagnostic test; (6) curriculum test; (7) prognostic or aptitude test.

The nature and uses of each of these types of tests will now be considered in the order given.

1. **Intelligence tests.** Teachers have always noted wide variations in the mental ability of pupils in their classes. These differences were expressed by teachers vaguely by such terms as bright, dull, stupid, dunce, or superior. Such evaluations are subject to the same kinds of errors that have made teachers' marks on the essay type of examination

unreliable and inaccurate.   For instance, pupils of pleasing appearance may be rated as of higher mentality than pupils of less attractive personal qualities, a condition that can be easily explained.   Similarly, the quiet child of good intellect but with little initiative may be rated as of lower mentality than pupils of lower intelligence who are aggressive, and therefore more in the limelight in class discussions.

In order to measure the variations in intelligence definitely and with precision two types of intelligence tests have been devised, namely, those that may be given to a whole group of individuals at one time, and those that are to be given to individual pupils.   Group tests afford an excellent means of arriving at an approximate measurement of mentality of the pupils of a group, sufficiently accurate for practical purposes.   Great economy of time results from the use of group tests.

The results of group tests provide a fairly reliable basis for isolating pupils of inferior or superior mentality, whose mental ratings, when necessary, may be determined more accurately by means of a complete individual examination.

Some of the best-known group intelligence tests are: Dearborn Group Test of Intelligence, Detroit First Grade Intelligence Test, Haggerty Intelligence Examinations, Illinois General Intelligence Scale, Kuhlmann–Anderson Intelligence Test, Otis Self-Administering Test of Mental Ability, Pressey Classification Test, Terman Group Test of Mental Ability.

For individual testing various revisions of the Binet–Simon Test are widely used, the best known being the Stanford Revision, Kuhlmann's Extension, and the Herring Revision.

General intelligence, which may be defined as the capacity to learn, is measured indirectly by measuring what the individual has learned. The assumption is that the more the individual has learned as compared with a group of individuals who have had approximately equal opportunity for acquiring the particular achievement measured, the greater is his intelligence as compared with the rest of the group. Relatively low mentality may be inferred from a performance considerably below the average of a typical group of individuals. Mental ages are used to describe levels of intelligence. A pupil whose performance on an intelligence test is equal to that of the average of children having a chronological age of fourteen is said to have a mental age of fourteen; that is, mentality equal to that of average fourteen-year-old children.

2. General survey tests. General survey tests are used to measure in only a superficial way the achievement of a group of pupils in a number of separate subjects, or in general. Such tests should be used to make a survey of the general achievements of classes in an entire school system. The data thus secured may serve as the basis on which to establish administrative and supervisory practices and policies, and to make necessary instructional adjustments.

There are several kinds of survey tests. One kind consists of a series of tests in specific subjects, such as reading, geography, history, language, and literature. The New Stanford Achievement Test is an example. Another kind of survey test is constructed on the "cycle" plan. The pupil is first tested on easy items in all the subjects, then on items of medium difficulty, then on the difficult items. The Otis Classification Test is an illustration. This test combines the measurement of both intelligence and achievement. While it is designed principally as an aid in classification, the results of the test on the several subjects will give an index of the educational status of the school.

3. Subject achievement tests. Subject achievement

tests are used to measure achievement in a specific school subject, such as reading, arithmetic, or spelling. Such tests give more exact information concerning the ability of pupils in a narrow field than is supplied by a general survey test. Several of these subject achievement tests may be used together as a battery of tests to make a survey of instruction.

Subject achievement tests afford information as to the general status of pupils in some subject, rather than as to their ability in various aspects of the subject. For example, the Woody–McCall Mixed Fundamentals in Arithmetic Scales afford a general measure of the pupil's abilities in all phases of arithmetic processes, including whole numbers, fractions, decimals, per cents, and denominate numbers. The scores on these tests enable the teacher to determine how the general level of activity of the pupils in a particular class compares with published standards or norms. The results do not show the teacher whether the class is superior or deficient in any of the one or more phases of arithmetic included in the test. Therefore these subject achievement tests must be supplemented by others which provide a more definite means of diagnosis.

4. **Analytical subject tests.** Analytical subject tests make it possible to secure information as to the ability of pupils in major subdivisions of a school subject, and hence are of considerable value for diagnostic purposes. Such tests consist of several parts. Each part deals with a particular phase of the subject. For example, the Sangren–Woody Reading Test has separate tests on vocabulary, rate of reading, comprehension of facts read, total meaning, central thought, following directions, and organization.

The Courtis Standard Research Test, Series B, consists of four tests in arithmetic process in whole numbers, one each for addition, subtraction, multiplication, and long division. The results of this series of tests show the teacher in what phase of arithmetic processes with whole numbers the pupil's performance is normal, or above or below standard. Similar analytical tests are available for grammar, history, geography, and subjects at the high-school level.

5. **Diagnostic tests and devices.** Diagnostic tests are used to determine the elements in a subject in which there are specific weaknesses, and to provide a means of discovering the causes of the deficiencies.

There are several types of diagnostic tests. Some tests, such as the Compass Arithmetic Tests, seek to locate deficiencies by means of an exact measurement of the ability of pupils with respect to the various elements that constitute the total process. A comparison of the achievements of pupils on different parts of the test with standard scores enables the teacher to determine the step in the process at which a general skill, such as addition of whole numbers, breaks down. Other tests, such as the Brueckner Diagnostic Tests in Fractions and Decimals, or the Buswell–John Diagnostic Test in Arithmetic, might be better described as comprehensive inventory exercises by means of which the teacher can locate the particular type of example or process that may be difficult for a whole group or for individual pupils.

The Gates Silent Reading Tests and the Sangren–Woody Silent Reading Tests provide a means of locating a few of the specific phases of reading ability in which a pupil's performance may be below standard. The Freeman Handwriting Scale is a device that may be used to locate the causes of inferior quality of writing. The various diagnostic tests and exercises will be considered in detail in discussion of the application of diagnostic procedures in the different school subjects.

In a sense almost any test may be called diagnostic. However, many of the tests that are labeled "diagnostic" by their authors are in fact survey tests of general achievement, since the results of the tests do not supply the teacher with specific information regarding pupil achievement that may be used for diagnostic purposes. To be truly diagnostic a test must be based on a detailed analysis that permits the exact location of the spot in the work at which there is difficulty, or of the phase of general ability in which there is a deficiency.

To facilitate the diagnosis of pupil difficulties by means of diagnostic tests, individual record blanks are often provided upon which the teachers' analysis of the pupil's faults may be recorded. Such blanks list the types of difficulties that have been found by investigators to occur most frequently. Part of a typical blank (Form 2) is given on pages 78, 79.

**6. Curriculum tests.** To enable the teacher to determine from time to time throughout the year how well pupils have mastered the work that has been covered, standardized curriculum tests have been prepared. These tests parallel closely the work that is being taken up in the classroom. In constructing such tests the subject-matter that is being studied is first analyzed into items, skills, and topics. This list is divided into units — which constitute the basis of the work in a given period of time, such as a month. From this list for each unit of time a number of elements are selected, and a test containing them is constructed. When the work on the part of the curriculum contained in the test is completed, this test is then given to a representative sampling of pupils following the curriculum from which the items were selected. On the basis of these results standards and norms are established. By means of progress charts and class graphs, showing graphically the results of curriculum tests, any teacher can show her pupils how well the test scores of the class compare with the results of the same test given to other pupils who have in former years completed the same curriculum.

The results of periodic curriculum tests furnish valuable information for the supervisor and teacher. On the basis of the available data, educational and administrative adjustments of various kinds may be made. The supervisor can readily locate classes in which satisfactory progress is not being made. The teacher can make an analysis of the work of the pupils on specific items in the test. On the basis of this information, necessary remedial work may be undertaken. Pupils whose ratings on such tests are unsatisfactory may be selected for careful individual examination and diagnosis.

Curriculum tests have been prepared for several of the school subjects; chiefly arithmetic, mathematics, and spelling. Sometimes these tests appear in textbooks, and sometimes they appear in separate test pamphlets or in a teacher's manual. When they are included in the textbook it is likely that an accurate measurement of achievement cannot be obtained, since there is too much opportunity for the pupils to study the test items before the time the test is to be given. The result is that pupils make much higher scores than should normally be expected without previous preparation on the test. A much more satisfactory method of securing a reliable and valid measurement is to administer the curriculum tests in such a way that pupils do not have access to them prior to the time of taking the test. This is insured if a separate test pamphlet is used, and if the tests are filed in some inaccessible place until they are to be used. The nature of curriculum tests is illustrated in the specimen of the Brueckner Curriculum Tests in Arithmetic Processes, presented on page 175. These tests consist of a series of ten

# Form 2. BRUECKNER DIAGNOSTIC TEST IN FRACTIONS

## INDIVIDUAL DIAGNOSTIC RECORD SHEET — ADDITION

Name............................................

School...........................................

Grade........... Room...........

Date...........

| Diagnosis | Summary |
|---|---|
| I. Lack of Comprehension of Process | |
| a. Adds numerators and denominators.... | |
| b. Adds numerators, multiplies denominators | |
| c. Numerator added without changing to common denominator. Either denominator used in sum... | |
| II. Reduction to Lowest Terms.......... | |
| a. Fraction not reduced............. | |
| b. Denominator divided by numerator...... | |
| c. Denominator and numerator divided by different numbers........ | |
| III. Difficulties with Improper Fractions...... | |
| a. Not changed to mixed numbers......... | |
| b. Changed but not added to whole number | |

| Diagnosis | Summary |
|---|---|
| IV. Computation Errors | |
| a. Addition......................... | |
| b. Subtraction....................... | |
| c. Division.......................... | |
| V. Omitted.......................... | |
| VI. Wrong Operation.................. | |
| VII. Partial Operation | |
| a. In adding mixed numbers adds only fractions............................. | |
| VIII. Changing to Common Denominator...... | |
| IX. Other Difficulties.................. | |

First indicate by number opposite each row the types of errors made on each example that was missed. For example, Ia means that the pupil adds numerators and denominators.

Then summarize under "Summary" the total number of times each difficulty was found.

Copyright, 1926, by L. J. Brueckner, Minneapolis, Minn.

*Examples*

| Row | 1 | 2 | 3 | 4 | 5 |
|---|---|---|---|---|---|
| I | | | | | |
| II | | | | | |
| III | | | | | |
| IV | | | | | |
| V | | | | | |
| VI | | | | | |
| VII | | | | | |
| VIII | | | | | |
| IX | | | | | |

standardized monthly tests for each grade, from three through eight. These tests will be discussed in detail in Chapter VII.

**7. Prognostic or aptitude tests.** Prognostic or aptitude tests are used to measure potential aptitude or ability in a subject. Such tests have been developed for a number of subjects at the high school and college levels, among them languages and industrial work. Prognostic tests for particular purposes, such as to determine aptitude for work on the college level, have been devised and are widely used in the universities of the country. Aptitude tests are designed to measure not specific achievement in a particular field, but underlying ability essential to success in that field. The following are some of the well-known prognostic and aptitude tests: The Orleans–Solomon Latin Prognosis Test, The Rogers Test of Mathematical Abilities, The Seashore Musical Talent Tests, The Stenquist Mechanical Aptitude Test, The Minnesota Placement Examination, The Nelson–Denny Reading Test.

## IV. CONSTRUCTION OF ACHIEVEMENT TESTS

In constructing standardized tests one should follow generally recognized methods of procedure. The various steps in such a procedure are given here. Certain tests or scales may not include all of the steps listed. Most of these steps, however, are necessary in the scientific construction of standardized tests or scales of measurement.

1. To determine what is to be measured. This includes not only a definition of the outcomes of instruction or learning in any particular subject, but also a definition of the grade or grades and ages with which the measure is to be used.

2. To determine the criteria of success in the lines of work or the outcomes of instruction to be measured.

3. To select the items. In the light of the outcomes to be meas-

ured select a large number of items that would probably be associated with success in the desired outcomes.

4. To organize the items according to the technique best suited for testing, determining
    a. The type of question or exercise that is best suited to each item that is to be included.
    b. The organization of various types of questions for the purpose of testing. This last step will include some preliminary editing of the try-out test.

5. To give the experimental preliminary try-out of this large number of items in the form worked out under No. 4.

6. To analyze the statements and pupil responses, and to study the results statistically to determine difficulty of items and per cent passing the successive grade levels.

7. To scale and weight the items of the test if this step is desirable. That is, to give more value to more difficult or important questions or items.

8. To break the items into equivalent and duplicate forms if these are desired.

9. To determine the equivalence of the duplicate forms.

10. To determine uniform methods of giving, timing, and scoring the test and of tabulating results.

11. To derive norms and standards.

12. To determine the reliability of the test as a measure of groups and of individuals.

13. To determine the validity of the test by correlating results obtained from its use with the results of other measures of the same type.

14. To edit the forms, giving due cognizance to cost in time, money, and ease of use.

15. To provide and edit a manual of directions.

16. To provide adequate keys.


## V. CRITERIA FOR SELECTING TESTS

**The purpose of giving the test.** In selecting a test to be given to a class or to an individual pupil, the teacher and supervisor must have clearly in mind the purpose of giving the test. If only general information regarding the present educational status of a class is desired, a general survey test may be selected. If the purpose of a test is to determine the specific nature of pupil difficulty in some phase of reading or arithmetic, a detailed diagnostic test or exercise suitable for the purpose should be selected. Such exact information cannot be secured through the use of general survey tests. If a careful measurement is to be made of the results of an experimental study, reliable tests which will provide an accurate measurement of the educational outcomes should be selected. If tests are always given for some definite purpose, the random "blunderbus" testing in which tests were given out of curiosity and without careful consideration of the use to be made of the results, which characterized much of the testing of the past generation, will be eliminated.

**The value and nature of the contents of the test.** The value and nature of the contents of the test should be considered before it is finally selected for use. If the material in the test does not involve important and desirable outcomes of instruction, the teacher should be skeptical of the significance of the test results. For example, primary arithmetic tests involving long examples in difficult column addition may test power in that process, but the abilities involved are of little educational significance in the primary grades, since they cannot be mastered by the little pupils in these grades without undue effort and expenditure of time in tedious drill. Similarly, to measure the achievements of pupils in spelling, words selected from the curriculum that has been taught, rather than words selected at random from a standard list of words should be used to measure the ability of the pupils to spell or to determine the effectiveness of the current curriculum in spelling. Tests which contain items of little social value are being severely criticized by many curriculum makers, who point out that in schools in which stress is placed on the ability of pupils to pass tests teachers are likely to stress the types of information and skills contained in the test, regardless of their social significance or value.

**Validity.** The validity of a test is an expression of the degrees to which the test measures the knowledges, skills, abilities, and qualities which it is designed and supposed to measure. Ruch[1] suggests that the nearest synonyms for validity are "goodness," "general merit," and "worthwhileness." The principal methods of validating tests are given by Ruch, as follows:

1. By judgments of competent persons.
2. By analysis of courses of study of textbooks.
3. By harmonizing with the recommendations of national educational committees or other recognized bodies on curricula, courses of study, minimum essentials, etc.
4. By experimental studies of social utility (such as the Horn and Thorndike studies of the most frequently used words, the Ashbaugh and Horn studies of spelling lists, the studies of Wilson, Woody, *et al.*, on the arithmetic needs of business, etc.)
5. By studies of the most frequently recurring errors.
6. By the computation of the percentages of pupils answering each item correctly at each successive age or grade level.
7. By correlation against an outside criterion.
8. By combination of the above methods.

The first three techniques involve the selection of the content in accordance with its value as judged by expert opinion, national committees, and the best of current practice. Methods 4, 5, and 6 involve experimental studies on the

[1] Ruch, G. M. *The Objective or New-Type Examination*, p. 29. Chicago, Scott, Foresman and Company, 1929.

basis of which to determine scientifically the value as well as the difficulty of items to be used in test construction. The seventh method involves the determination of the extent to which test results agree with some outside criterion; for example, the validity of the first intelligence tests was determined by finding the extent to which they agreed with the ranking of pupils according to intelligence by their teachers and other competent individuals. The validity of a test may also be established by various combinations of the first seven methods; for example, any teacher may validate a test exercise by determining the extent to which it parallels the local course of study, an analysis of the textbooks in use, and her judgment of the relative value of the contents selected. The validity of a test is increased if it contains a large enough number of items to represent an extensive sampling of the curriculum, if the items in the test range in difficulty from very easy to very difficult, and if the explanations to pupils are clear and adequate.

**Reliability.** The reliability of a test refers to the extent to which it consistently and accurately measures the elements which it does measure. A valid test is necessarily a reliable one, since a valid test measures what it is claimed to measure. A test may be reliable, but is not necessarily a valid measure of what it is claimed to measure. A test is reliable to the extent to which the pupil's scores on repeated trials of the same test, or on duplicate forms of the tests, do not have large fluctuations from one form to the next.

The reliability of a test may be guaranteed by the character of the sampling of the items included in it. It is obviously not possible to measure the abilities of pupils by means of tests containing every item of the curriculum. Therefore the method of sampling is employed, that is, testing on items selected according to some plan from the total curriculum. The smaller the sampling of items, the less complete is the picture of the ability of the individual; conversely, the larger and better selected the number of items, the more reliable will be the measurement secured. The teacher, therefore, must bear in mind the fact that a test is always based on a sampling, and consequently involves a certain amount of error in measurement. The greater the error in measurement, the greater is the unreliability of the test. One method of reducing this error is to increase the length of the test. The use of the new type of objective examination makes it possible to secure a measure of a much more complete sampling of the curriculum than is possible by means of the traditional essay type of examination, which contained questions dealing with only a small part of the subject-matter covered by the class.

Increased reliability is also guaranteed by the extent to which the scoring of the test and the evaluating of the results are made objective. Objectivity of scoring refers to the extent to which the opinion of the scorer has been eliminated in the scoring. This means greater accuracy in scoring and therefore greater reliability of the results of tests. The lack of objectivity in scoring the essay type of examination is probably the most serious weakness of that type of test. In the new type of examination, objectivity of scoring has been secured by changing the form in which test items are stated, and by the use of mechanical methods of scoring the exercises. In most well-constructed tests only one answer satisfies the requirements of the test item. Well-trained clerks can easily score most of our modern standardized tests by following a few clearly stated directions. An easy way to measure the objectivity of scoring is to determine the differences between the scores assigned to a set of test papers by the same person at different times. Perfect objectivity is indicated if there is perfect agreement between the several sets of ratings; errors in scoring tend of course to reduce the possibility of perfect correspondence in the several ratings.

**Ease of administration and scoring.** In general the ease of administering a test is an important characteristic to be considered. Tests, such as those in spelling, are relatively easy for the teacher to administer; other more complicated types, such as intelligence tests, should probably be administered only by special examiners. In introducing the use of tests into any school system those should be selected that are easy to give, score, and interpret. The directions for giving any test should be complete and specific. For most tests the authors provide teachers' manuals containing detailed statements as to the purpose of the test, its validity and reliability, and the methods of giving, scoring, summarizing, and interpreting the test results. For some of the tests simple mechanical scoring devices and answer keys are provided to reduce the labor involved in scoring. The scoring of some tests involves quite complicated statistical procedures. This point should be carefully considered, especially in the selection of tests to be given by relatively inexperienced teachers, untrained in the use of tests. Tabulation sheets are sometimes provided which automatically sort pupils into groups according to their needs, and thus enable the teacher to determine in general the type of instruction needed by each individual. The class record sheet for the Courtis Supervisory Test, for instance, automatically divides the pupils into five groups, each of which requires a certain kind of instruction. Some tests for measuring progress throughout the year, as, for example, the Brueckner Curriculum Test in Arithmetic Processes, also provides individual record blanks and individual as well as class progress charts which are valuable instructional tools.

**Self-marking tests.**
The scoring of tests is greatly facilitated when they are printed in such a way as to employ the self-marking device invented by Clapp and Young. The technique is illustrated in Figures X and Y, which show how any test may be put up and scored.

The figures represent the marking device applied to a multiple-choice test in each item of which there are five numbered choices. Each group of squares in Figure X is associated with a question in the test. The student decides which one of the five choices represents the correct answer, then notes the number of this answer and marks in the square bearing the same number. The first square in Figure Y is printed directly back of square Number 4 in the first group of squares in Figure X. In the same way each of the remaining squares in Figure Y is printed opposite some one

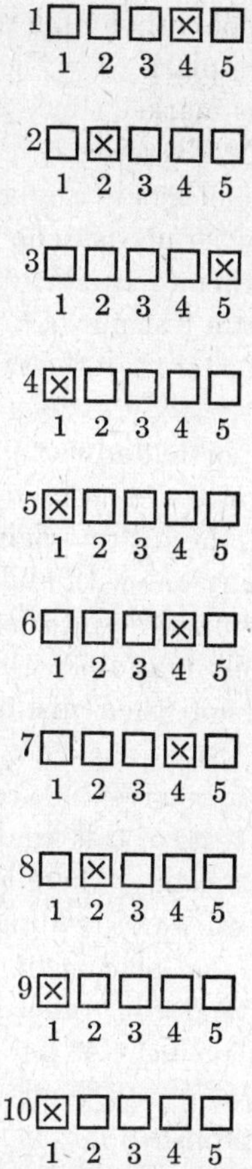

FIG. X
Showing how pupil indicates his answers on the Clapp–Young Self-Marking device.

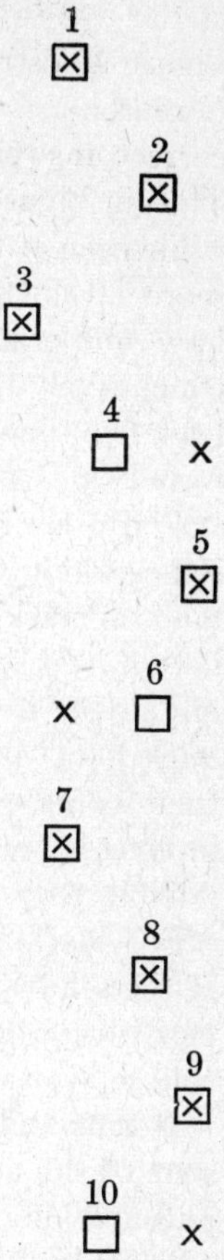

FIG. Y
Showing how correct and incorrect answers are automatically recorded by the Clapp–Young Self-Marking device.

of the five squares in Figure X. As the student marks in Figure X a strip of carbon underneath the squares in Figure Y reproduces his mark — *in* the square in Figure Y if the correct answer is marked, but *outside* the square otherwise. Thus in Figure Y, Exercises 1, 2, 3, 5, 7, 8, and 9 are correct, while each of the others is wrong. In determining a pupil's score, all the teacher needs to do is to count the squares that have marks in them. Studies thus far made have proved conclusively that a test put up in this form can be scored at least five times faster than the same test put up in any other form.

Five other important advantages resulting from use of the self-marking device are as follows: (1) no mistake can be made in marking the answers right or wrong; (2) scores can be determined by any one with ability to count, or (3) no scoring key or stencil and no intricate scoring directions are required; (4) pupils may open their own test folders, count their scores, and note their mistakes immediately, while their interest is keen; (3) more comprehensive and therefore more reliable tests can be given.

Self-marking tests of this kind are available for a number of the school subjects. There have been published tests in English, arithmetic, and reading as well as high school and college aptitude and placement tests.[1]

**Norms and standards.** If it is desired to make comparisons of the achievement of pupils in the local schools with nation-wide norms, tests should of course be selected which provide well-established norms based on a wide sampling of pupils from all parts of the country. Many teachers' manuals include test scores from a variety of communities of all sizes with which comparisons may be made. Comparison of results secured from different sets of tests must be

[1] The *Clapp–Young Self-Marking Tests*, published by Houghton Mifflin Company, Boston.

made cautiously, since investigations have shown that the norms for many of the tests are highly unreliable. For example, Ruch [1] reports the results of a series of seven different survey tests in arithmetic, suitable for grades seven and eight, which were given to a group of slightly over-age pupils, as given in Table 10.

TABLE 10. COMPARISON OF TEST SCORES ON SEVEN STANDARD ARITHMETIC TESTS

| TEST* | AVERAGE SCORE | AVERAGE SCORE IN TERMS GRADE EQUIVALENTS (NORMS) | |
|---|---|---|---|
| A | 224.3 | 8.5 | |
| B | 70.8 | H 6 | |
| C | 32.0 | H 7 | |
| D | 26.8 | H 5 | |
| E | 30.1 | 9 | (Estimated: above H 8) |
| F | 38.0 | H 6 | |
| G | 56.1 | 11 | |

\* The names of these tests will be supplied to responsible persons by personal letter upon request to G. M. Ruch.

Ruch comments on these results, as follows:

When seven standard tests rate the same pupils all the way from fifth to eleventh grade abilities, surely there is little value in such norms, not to mention standards. The moral seems to be "pay your money and pick the test that will give the showing you wish to make."

**Provision for equivalent forms.** In order to be able to measure progress several times during the year, or several successive years, tests should be selected for which there are several equivalent forms. In doubtful cases it may be desirable to retest the pupils by means of a different form of the test. A record of the scores made by the pupils for a number of years in the same tests furnishes valuable information for educational guidance. A summary of such cumulative data for a large number of pupils for several years is of great value in appraising supervisory and administrative programs and practices.

[1] *Twenty-Ninth Yearbook of the National Society for the Study of Education*, p. 699. Bloomington, Illinois, Public School Publishing Company, 1930.

## QUESTIONS FOR STUDY, DISCUSSION, AND REPORT

1. What is meant by altitude of ability or power in reading? In spelling?

2. What is meant by area of intellect in the field of arithmetic or social science?

3. In what ways are methods of work to be associated with ability?

4. How do we measure each of the aspects of intellect described in this chapter?

5. Why are teachers' marks of pupils' performances not reliable?

6. Name some deficiencies of the traditional type of essay examination.

7. How have these deficiencies been overcome to a large extent by the new type of objective examination?

8. Differentiate between scaled tests, quality scales, and product scales. Give illustrations of each type.

9. If possible discuss the results of a mental test given to the pupils of a school, and the implications of the data.

10. Under what conditions should individual mental tests be given?

11. For what purposes would you give survey tests? Analytical subject tests? Diagnostic tests? Curriculum tests? Aptitude tests?

12. What is meant by validity? How can one determine the validity of a test?

13. Describe methods of determining the reliability of a test.

14. Examine test manuals for data concerning the factors described in this chapter that should guide the teacher in selecting tests.

15. Select a series of tests which you feel should be given to secure essential information for the teacher, on the basis of which to organize the program of instruction. Justify your selection.

16. Do you think that standard tests should be given by the teacher of the class or by some special examiner? Who should score the tests?

17. Collect graphs of test scores that are on display. Which of them do you think most effective?

## SELECTED REFERENCES

Dearborn, W. F. *Intelligence Tests*. Boston, Houghton Mifflin Company, 1928.

Dickson, V. E. *Mental Tests and the Classroom Teacher*. Yonkers-on-Hudson, New York, World Book Company, 1923.

Freeman, F. N. *Mental Tests*. Boston, Houghton Mifflin Company, 1926.

Gilliland, A. R., and Jordan, R. H. *Educational Measurements and the Classroom Teacher*. New York, Century Company, 1925.

Greene, H. A., and Jorgensen, A. N. *Use and Interpretation of Educational Tests*. New York, Longmans, Green Company, 1929.

Kelley, T. L. *Interpretation of Educational Measurements*. Yonkers-on-Hudson, New York, World Book Company, 1927.

*Kuhlmann–Anderson Intelligence Tests; Manual of Instructions*. Published by Educational Tests Bureau, Minneapolis, 1927.

Lang, A. R. *Modern Methods in Written Examinations*. Boston, Houghton Mifflin Company, 1930.

McCall, W. A. *How to Measure in Education*. New York, The Macmillan Company, 1922.

May, M., and Hartshorne, L. *Studies in Deceit*. New York, The Macmillan Company, 1928.

Monroe, W. S., De Voss, J. C., and Kelly, F. J. *Educational Tests and Measurements*. Boston, Houghton Mifflin Company. Revised and enlarged edition, 1924.

Ruch, G. M. *The Objective a New Type of Examination*. Chicago, Scott, Foresman Company, 1930.

Seashore, C. F. *The Measurement of Musical Talent*. New York, Silver, Burdett and Company, 1919.

Smith, H. L., and Wright, W. W. *Tests and Measurements*. New York, Silver, Burdett and Company, 1928.

Stenquist, J. L. *Measurement of Mechanical Ability*. Teachers College Contributions to Education, no. 130. New York, Columbia University, 1923.

Terman, L. M. *The Measurement of Intelligence*. Boston, Houghton Mifflin Company, 1916.

Thorndike, E. L. *The Measurement of Intelligence*. New York, Teachers College, Columbia University, 1927.

Trabue, M. R. *Measuring Results in Education*. New York, American Book Company, 1924.

Wilson, G. M., and Hoke, K. J. *How to Measure*. New York, The Macmillan Company, 1928. Revised edition.

# CHAPTER IV

## THE INTERPRETATION AND USE OF TEST RESULTS

### I. INTERPRETING TEST SCORES

#### 1. *The need of norms and standards*

**Lack of meaning of school marks.** Many different methods are used by teachers to "mark" the work of pupils. Such marks as A, B, C, D, E; 80%, 60%, 40%; and "Excellent," "Good," "Fair," or "Poor," supposedly indicate the relative merits of the work being appraised. The difficulty with such ratings is that they have little meaning, since they are merely the expression of personal judgments, which are not guided by any standard basis of comparison. Numerous investigations of teachers' marks have shown their unreliability because of their subjective character.

The introduction of the modern test procedure has resulted in a great change in this condition. Tests have been given to thousands of pupils, and the consolidation and interpretation of these test scores have given teachers a reliable basis on which to evaluate the performances of individual pupils. Without such comparative information the results of tests have little meaning. For example, the following scores were made by a sixth-grade pupil on the Courtis Arithmetic Test, Series B:

| | ADDITION | SUBTRACTION | MULTIPLICATION | DIVISION |
|---|---|---|---|---|
| Tried.................. | 8 | 12 | 8 | 6 |
| Per cent correct......... | 75 | 83 | 63 | 67 |

**Value of norms.** The teacher cannot evaluate these scores without having some basis on which to determine how they compare with the usual performances of typical sixth-grade pupils. Is a score of 8 tried and 75 per cent correct in the addition test a satisfactory score for a sixth-grade pupil? How do the other scores compare with the results of similar tests given to pupils in the same grade? The norms based on tests given to thousands of pupils in each grade help the teacher to answer these questions. The norms for the Courtis Tests for grade 6 are as follows:

|  | ADDITION | SUBTRACTION | MULTIPLI- CATION | DIVISION |
|---|---|---|---|---|
| Tried............. | 9.8 | 10.3 | 9.1 | 8.2 |
| Per cent correct...... | 75 | 85 | 78 | 87 |

A comparison of the scores of the above pupil and the test norms shows that his rate of work in addition, 8 examples tried, was less than the norm, 9.8, while his accuracy, 75 per cent, was slightly above the norm, 73 per cent. In subtraction his rate was above the norm, while his accuracy was slightly below the norm. In multiplication and division both his rate of work and his accuracy were considerably below the norms. Similar detailed information for other subjects enables the teacher to determine in what phases of the subject the pupil's work is inferior to that of the average pupil of his grade. On the basis of these facts necessary modifications and adaptations of instruction may be intelligently made.

## 2. *Kinds of norms*

In order to help teachers and pupils to interpret the scores made on standard tests, authors have supplied norms based on the results of tests administered to a representative sampling of pupils from all parts of the country, and in all kinds of schools and communities. The three chief ways of expressing these test norms are as follows: (1) grade norms; (2) age norms; (3) percentiles.

The derivation and usefulness of each of these will next be set forth.

**Grade norms.** Grade norms are based on the average or median scores made by pupils in each grade. A pupil whose score on a test is equal to that of the norm for his grade has ability, in so far as it is measured by the test, equal to that of the typical pupil in that grade. Grade norms are easily derived and because the grade concept is familiar to teachers and school officers in all parts of the country, such norms are easily understood. The chief problem involved in establishing grade norms arises from the task of selecting a representative sampling of pupils for each grade.

The first grade norms that were published were for whole grades, and in a few cases for half grades. No provision was made for differentiating the value of the scores that fell in the interval that represented the grade norm. If the grade norm for grade 4 was 12 items correct, and for grade 5 18 items correct, on the basis of grade norms scores of 12 items or 17 items would each be given the same rating, namely, grade 4 ability. McCall inaugurated a new plan for overcoming this objection by dividing the increment between grades into tenths. By means of this plan the pupil's score can be translated into tenths of a grade. Instead of expressing a score as equal to grade 4, it can be expressed in such units as 4.2, 4.8, etc., depending on how closely it approximates the norm for grade 5. This use of grade norms is called the *B-score*.

The chief difficulty with grade norms and B-scores is that they do not offer easy comparisons with mental-test results, since they are not expressed in the same units. The use of grade norms, however, does make it possible to make direct comparisons between test scores which otherwise would be difficult to compare.  This can easily be shown by the following scores in four different subjects, made by a fourth-grade pupil:

|  | RAW SCORE | GRADE EQUIVALENT |
|---|---|---|
| Courtis Silent Reading Test — Rate | 147 | 4 |
| Quality of Handwriting (Ayres Scale) | 55 | 5 |
| Composition (Hudelson) | 4.0 | 5 |
| Woody Arithmetic — Addition | 29 | 6 |

The numerical scores listed range from 4 to 147.  When the several scores are interpreted and expressed as grade norms it is found that the pupil's rate of reading is equivalent to grade 4 ability; his quality of writing is equal to the norm for grade 5; his composition ability is also equal to the norm of grade 5; his score on the Woody Arithmetic Test in Addition is equal to the norm for grade 6.  These results show that the pupil's scores are above the norms for his grade in quality of handwriting, in composition, and in addition, while his rate of reading is approximately equal to the norm for his grade.  The comparison of these grade norms is much more meaningful and definite than the comparison of the raw scores.

**Age norms.**  Age norms which are used to establish the educational age, or E.A., of the pupil, are based on the average or median scores made by unselected pupils in chronological age groups found in all grades.  Unless otherwise stated an age norm is usually based on scores made by all pupils ranging from the designated age up to the next.  For example, a score given as a norm for nine-year-old children is ordinarily understood to be for children who are at least nine years of age, but not yet ten.  For many tests, tables of scores are provided which make it possible to translate a raw score into years and months.  The procedure used to establish age norms is illustrated by Ruch and Stoddard [1] by data for the Stanford Achievement Test, as follows:

| Age group | 9 | 10 | 11 | 12 | 13 | 14 |
|---|---|---|---|---|---|---|
| Mental score | 23 | 33 | 46 | 57 | 66 | 72 |

Since the 9-year-old group will average 9–6 (9 years, 6 months) in age because it includes pupils 9, but not yet 10, years old, the raw score, 23, is the age equivalent of 9–6. The score, 33, is the age equivalent for 10–6.

The method of finding the intermediate months of E.A. (educational age) is that of interpolation between the experimentally-determined values for successive ages, thus:

| Raw score | 23 | 24 | 25 | 26 | 27 | 28 | 29 | 30 | 31 | 32 | 33 |
|---|---|---|---|---|---|---|---|---|---|---|---|
| Educational age | 9–6 | 9–7 | 9–8 | 9–10 | 9–11 | 10–0 | 10–1 | 10–2 | 10–4 | 10–5 | 10–6 |

The values in bold-faced type are those found by examination; those in light-faced type were found by interpolation.

A pupil's educational age is determined by finding his average standing in a number of school subjects expressed in terms of an age score. The term *subject age* is synonymous with educational age, except that the term is used only in connection with single subjects.

Table 11 shows how T-scores on Forms I and II of the Thorndike–McCall Reading Test can be converted into reading ages. Similar tables are provided by various authors for tests in other subjects. According to Table 11 a pupil whose T-score is 21 has a reading age of 67 months.

The chief advantage of age norms is that they permit easy comparisons with mental ages and chronological ages, especially in the elementary grades, and thus enable the teacher to interpret test scores more satisfactorily and adequately. Because of the additional clerical and experimental work involved the expense of establishing age norms is much greater than for grade norms.

[1] Ruch, G. M., and Stoddard, G. D.  *Tests and Measurements in High School Instruction*, p. 346.  Copyright, 1927, by World Book Company, publishers, Yonkers-on-Hudson, New York.

TABLE 11. TABLE FOR CONVERTING T-SCORES IN THORNDIKE–
McCALL READING TEST, FORMS I AND II, INTO READING AGES
IN MONTHS

| T-Score | Reading Age | T-Score | Reading Age | T-Score | Reading Age |
|---------|-------------|---------|-------------|---------|-------------|
| 21 | 67 | 41 | 124 | 61 | 181 |
| 22 | 70 | 42 | 127 | 62 | 184 |
| 23 | 73 | 43 | 130 | 63 | 186 |
| 24 | 76 | 44 | 133 | 64 | 189 |
| 25 | 79 | 45 | 135 | 65 | 192 |
| 26 | 82 | 46 | 138 | 66 | 195 |
| 27 | 84 | 47 | 141 | 67 | 198 |
| 28 | 87 | 48 | 144 | 68 | 201 |
| 29 | 90 | 49 | 147 | 69 | 203 |
| 30 | 93 | 50 | 150 | 70 | 206 |
| 31 | 96 | 51 | 152 | 71 | 209 |
| 32 | 99 | 52 | 154 | 72 | 212 |
| 33 | 101 | 53 | 158 | 73 | 215 |
| 34 | 104 | 54 | 161 | 74 | 218 |
| 35 | 107 | 55 | 164 | 75 | 220 |
| 36 | 110 | 56 | 167 | 76 | 223 |
| 37 | 113 | 57 | 169 | 77 | 226 |
| 38 | 116 | 58 | 172 | 78 | 229 |
| 39 | 118 | 59 | 175 | 79 | 232 |
| 40 | 121 | 60 | 178 | 80 | 235 |

**Percentiles.**  Percentiles are the points in a distribution
of scores which divide the total number of cases contained
in it into 100 equal parts, each of which contains the same
number of cases.  Norms for standard tests, based on
*medians*, represent scores found at the fiftieth percentile in a
distribution; fifty per cent of the scores of the pupils made or
excelled this score, and fifty per cent made either this score
or a lower one.  The median is thus a special case of a percentile.  For some tests, especially those of the high-school
field, the scores corresponding to the tenth, twentieth, and
every successive tenth percentile, called *deciles*, are given.
Sometimes the seventy-fifth percentile and the twenty-fifth
percentile, called *quartiles*, are included, thus breaking the
distributing of scores into quarters.

The value of such percentile norms is that one can com-

pare the median or average achievement of a class and the
scores of individuals with the complete range of scores in the
representative sampling of pupils on whom the test was
standardized. The teacher who finds that a pupil's score
falls at the fifth percentile knows that his score is equal to or
better than the scores made by five per cent of the pupils,
and also that ninety-five per cent of the pupils either
equaled or exceeded that score. Likewise a pupil whose
score falls at the ninetieth percentile has a score at or below
which ninety per cent of the scores made by the other pupils
fell, and which was equaled or exceeded by ten per cent of
the pupils.

Percentiles may be found by a teacher for the distribution
of the scores made by a class or group of classes on any
standard or informal test. Because of the value of such percentile ratings the procedure to be followed in finding the
percentiles (deciles) for a typical set of scores will be explained in detail, as shown by the calculations in Table
12.

In Table 12 the scores are distributed in class intervals of
5. The column headed "$f$" gives the number of pupils
whose scores fell in each of the group intervals.

The column headed "Cumulative Frequency" shows the
number of scores that fell at or below each class interval.
The figure opposite each class interval is the sum of the frequencies as we move up the column through the class intervals; for example, 3 opposite the 30–34 interval is the
sum of 1 and 2; 4 opposite the 35–39 interval is the
sum of 1, 2, and 1; and so on for the other cumulative
frequencies.

The calculation at the right of the table shows in detail
the exact computations used in figuring every tenth percentile in the distribution. The detail given in the table for
the 10–percentile is explained on page 98.

| CLASS INTERVAL | f | CUMULATIVE FREQUENCY | CALCULATION OF DECILES |
|---|---|---|---|
| 125–129 | 1 | 262 | 90 percentile = $95 + \dfrac{(235.8 - 222)\,(5)}{18} = 98.83$ |
| 120–124 | 1 | 261 | |
| 115–119 | 0 | 260 | 80 percentile = $90 + \dfrac{(209.6 - 201)\,(5)}{21} = 92.04$ |
| 110–114 | 2 | 260 | |
| 105–109 | 6 | 258 | 70 percentile = $85 + \dfrac{(183.4 - 171)\,(5)}{30} = 87.09$ |
| 100–104 | 12 | 252 | |
| 95– 99 | 18 | 240 | 60 percentile = $80 + \dfrac{(157.2 - 145)\,(5)}{26} = 82.34$ |
| 90– 94 | 21 | 222 | |
| 85– 89 | 30 | 201 | 50 percentile = $75 + \dfrac{(131 - 103)\,(5)}{42} = 78.3$ |
| 80– 84 | 26 | 171 | |
| 75– 79 | 42 | 145 | 40 percentile = $75 + \dfrac{(104.8 - 103)\,(5)}{42} = 75.21$ |
| 70– 74 | 30 | 103 | |
| 65– 69 | 21 | 73 | 30 percentile = $70 + \dfrac{(78.6 - 23)\,(5)}{30} = 70.96$ |
| 60– 64 | 18 | 52 | |
| 55– 59 | 12 | 34 | 20 percentile = $65 + \dfrac{(52.4 - 52)\,(5)}{21} = 65.9$ |
| 50– 54 | 8 | 22 | |
| 45– 49 | 9 | 14 | 10 percentile = $55 + \dfrac{(26.2 - 22)\,(5)}{12} = 56.75$ |
| 40– 44 | 1 | 5 | |
| 35– 39 | 1 | 4 | |
| 30– 34 | 2 | 3 | |
| 25– 29 | 0 | 1 | |
| 20– 24 | 0 | 1 | |
| 15– 19 | 1 | 1 | |
| | 262 | | |

26.2 is 262 ÷ 10, the number of cases below the 10–percentile.

22 is the cumulative frequency below the interval containing the 10–percentile.

55 is the lower limit of the class interval containing the 10–percentile.  There are 22 cases below this interval.

5 is the range of the class interval.

12 is the frequency of the interval containing the 10–percentile.

## The procedure may be expressed in words as follows:

We wish to find the point below which ten per cent of the cases fall.  Ten per cent or one tenth of the cases, 262, is equal to 26.2. To find the interval in which the 10–percentile falls we must move up the column of cumulative frequencies and decide in which class interval the 26.2 case falls.  This we find to be in the 55–59 group, since there are only 22 cases up to this point.  We must therefore move up with the 55–59 interval $26.2 - 22$, or $4.2$ frequencies. Since 4.2 frequencies is only a fraction of the frequency of cases, 12 at this interval, we must find what fraction of the distance across the interval (5 points) $26.2 - 22$ is.  The answer is found by the following computation:

$$\frac{(26.2 - 22) \times (5)}{12} = \frac{4.2 \times 5}{12} = 1.75 \text{ units.}$$

The last step is to add 1.75 to 55 the lower limit of the interval in which the 10–percentile falls, which gives us $55 + 1.75$ or $56.75$ as the value of the 10–percentile.

## The other percentiles are found in the same way.[1]  The reader should try to explain each of the numbers found in the calculations of the other percentiles before proceeding to the next topic.

Practice finding the deciles in the following distribution of scores:

---

[1] Tables for expressing rankings in groups of less than 100 as percentiles have been published by the World Book Company in a pamphlet by F. and O. Buros, *Expressing Educational Measures as Percentile Ranks.*

| Class Interval | f | Cumulative Frequency | |
|---|---|---|---|
| 120–129 | 3 | | |
| 110–119 | 7 | | |
| 100–109 | 14 | | |
| 90– 99 | 16 | | |
| 80– 89 | 18 | | |
| 70– 79 | 14 | | |
| 60– 69 | 25 | | |
| 50– 59 | 16 | | |
| 40– 49 | 7 | | |
| 30– 39 | 8 | | |
| 20– 29 | 4 | | |
| 10– 19 | 2 | | |
| 0– 9 Total | 1 | | |

In the above table find the 2-, 9-, 25-, 75-, 91-, 98-percentiles.

### 3. *Expressing relationships between scores on tests*

**Three relationship quotients.** The development of age norms for intelligence and for achievement tests has made it possible to express relationships between the pupil's chronological age and his subject and mental ages. These relationships may be expressed numerically by quotients. There are three important kinds of quotients:

       1. Intelligence quotients
       2. Educational quotients
       3. Accomplishment quotients

**Intelligence quotients.** The intelligence quotient (**I.Q.**)

makes it possible to express the relationship between a pupil's mental age and his chronological age, thus supplying an index of his brightness. The intelligence quotient is determined by dividing the pupil's mental age in months by his chronological age in months. The I.Q. of a pupil whose mental age is 132 months and whose chronological age is 120 months is found as follows:

$$\frac{\text{M.A.}}{\text{C.A.}} = \frac{132}{120} = 1.10, \text{ commonly expressed as } 110.$$

Investigations have shown that there is a wide range in I.Q.'s in any single age group. The I.Q. is thus an index of relative mental development, but in itself is no indication of the level of mental ability. For example, two pupils, one having a chronological age of 9 and the other one of 12, may each have an I.Q. of 125. The mental level of the 12-year-old is manifestly higher than that of the 9-year-old with the same I.Q., because of the difference in their chronological ages.

The nature of intelligence indicated by the intelligence quotient is given by Terman as follows:

| INTELLIGENCE QUOTIENT | SIGNIFICANCE |
|---|---|
| Above 140 | Genius or near genius |
| 120–140 | Very superior intelligence |
| 110–120 | Superior intelligence |
| 90–110 | Normal or average intelligence |
| 80– 90 | Dullness |
| 70– 80 | Borderline deficiency |
| Below 70 | Definitely feeble-minded |

A knowledge of the individual's I.Q. is valuable information for the teacher. Such knowledge aids in the adaptation of instruction to the ability of the pupil, in the classification and grouping of pupils, and in dealing with various problems of behavior and conduct. A low I.Q. affords a valuable index of the possible cause of the failure of a pupil to make satisfactory progress in the classroom.

It is obvious that a teacher can place greater reliance on the results of an individual test administered by a trained examiner than on the results of a group test. The ratings from group tests, valuable as they are, are too unreliable to be considered as final in the case of any single individual. In case only group tests can be used to determine the mental age or I.Q. of an individual, at least two forms of the same test or two different tests should be given. Even this procedure may result in conclusions regarding the mental level of a pupil that in some cases may be incorrect. In the future this weakness of group tests will probably be obviated to some extent by the development of more accurate and refined methods of group testing.

**Educational quotients.** When scores on achievement tests can be converted into subject or educational ages, it is possible to express numerically the relationship between the pupil's subject or educational age and his chronological age by means of the educational quotient.

The method of determining the educational quotient is similar to that used in finding the intelligence quotient; the pupil's educational age is divided by his chronological age, the quotient being his educational quotient. The data in Table 13, based on results of the Thorndike–McCall Reading Test, may be used to make clear the procedure.

TABLE 13.  DETERMINING PUPILS' READING QUOTIENTS

| PUPIL | T-SCORE | READING AGE (months) | CHRONOLOGICAL AGE (months) | READING QUOTIENT |
|-------|---------|----------------------|----------------------------|------------------|
| 1 | 59 | 175 | 175 | 100 |
| 2 | 57 | 169 | 130 | 130 |
| 3 | 41 | 124 | 155 | 80 |

Pupil 1 had a T-score of 59, which represents a reading age of 175 months. This pupil is 175 months old chronologically. His reading and his chronological ages are equal; his reading quotient is equal to

$$\frac{\text{E.A.}}{\text{C.A.}} = \frac{175}{175} \text{ (or 1.00, commonly expressed as 100).}$$

This shows that his reading ability has been developed to as high a level as might normally be expected of a pupil of his chronological age. Pupil 2 has a reading quotient of 130, which indicates that his reading ability is considerably above the normal accomplishment for pupils of his chronological age. Pupil 3, whose educational quotient is only 80, has reading ability that is considerably less than normal for his age. A knowledge of the educational quotient of this pupil is obviously of considerable value to the teacher.

The chief weakness of the educational-quotient technique is its unreliability, due to the unreliability of the test used to determine educational age. This is shown by the educational quotients in Table 14, based on the results of four equivalent forms of the Woody–McCall Arithmetic Tests given on four successive days to pupils in grade 5.[1]

An analysis of the table reveals interesting but disturbing variations in the educational quotient of the ten pupils. The variations for pupils 1, 7, and 10 are relatively slight; the variations for pupils 4, 6, 8, and 9 are very large. The teacher has no way of knowing definitely the factors that may have caused such wide variations. In the cases of pupils 8 and 9 the quotients on the first day were much higher than on the other days; in the case of pupil 6 the quotient on the fourth trial was the highest. Woody points out that it is possible that on some days certain pupils have a much higher educational efficiency than on other days. Woody believes, however, that the wide variations in the

[1] Woody, C. "Results from Successive Repetitions of Certain Arithmetic Tests"; in *Bulletin of Educational Reference and Research*, no. 73, p. 19. (November, 1924.) Ann Arbor, Michigan, University of Michigan.

TABLE 14. EDUCATIONAL QUOTIENTS * BASED UPON SCORES IN
GRADE 5 ON THE WOODY–MCCALL ARITHMETIC TEST

(After Woody)

TESTS

| PUPIL | 1 | 2 | 3 | 4 |
|-------|-----|-----|-----|-----|
| 1 | 111 | 127 | 125 | 127 |
| 2 | 89 | 104 | 117 | 100 |
| 3 | 111 | 137 | 137 | 113 |
| 4 | 97 | 106 | 125 | 105 |
| 5 | 133 | 116 | 132 | 116 |
| 6 | 113 | 133 | 127 | 157 |
| 7 | 151 | 157 | 157 | 157 |
| 8 | 122 | 85 | 77 | 87 |
| 9 | 137 | 92 | 96 | 91 |
| 10 | 79 | 91 | 82 | 88 |

* Selected cases.

quotients were chiefly due to the fact that the tests were not
sufficiently reliable to serve as an adequate measure of an
individual pupil.  He concluded that the variations in the
educational quotients were so great that it seems folly to
apply the technique until the reliability of the original
measures has been more thoroughly established.  This
recommendation should always be borne in mind in interpreting a pupil's educational or subject quotient.

**Accomplishment quotient.**  When the teacher knows the
pupil's educational and mental ages, the question may be
raised as to whether he is making the progress that he is
capable of making.  In order to express this relationship
between the pupil's educational age and his mental age,
Franzen [1] and others have suggested the use of the accomplishment ratio or quotient.  The accomplishment quotient
(A.Q.) is the ratio between the pupil's relative educational
development (E.Q.) and his relative brightness (I.Q.).  The
simplest way to find the A.Q. is to divide the pupil's educational age by his mental age.  The method may be illus-

[1] Franzen, R. S.  *The Accomplishment Ratio.*  Teachers College Contributions to Education, no. 125.  New York, Columbia University, 1922.

trated by means of the data in Table 15, based on the
Thorndike–McCall Reading Test.

TABLE 15.    READING ACCOMPLISHMENT QUOTIENTS OF PUPILS,
BASED ON THE THORNDIKE–McCALL READING TEST

| PUPIL | T-SCORE | READING AGE (months) | MENTAL AGE (months) | ACCOMPLISHMENT QUOTIENT |
|-------|---------|----------------------|---------------------|-------------------------|
| 1 | 59 | 175 | 175 | 100 |
| 2 | 57 | 169 | 195 | 83 |
| 3 | 41 | 124 | 120 | 103 |

Pupil 1 has a reading age of 175, and a mental age of 175.
His reading accomplishment quotient is the ratio of 175 and
175, or $\frac{175}{175}$, or 1.00. The other ratios are found in the same
way. The reading ability of pupil 1 is developed to the
same level as his general mental ability; the relative reading
ability of pupil 2 is less than may be expected of pupils of
his mental level; the level of the reading ability of the third
pupil is somewhat higher than may normally be expected of
pupils of his mental level.

In theory, a pupil cannot be expected to develop the
relative level of a specific skill or ability higher than the level
of his general mental ability, and hence theoretically accomplishment quotients of more than 100 are impossible.
Investigations, however, show that accomplishment quotients of more than 100 are often found, especially in the
measurement of the achievements of pupils of inferior mentality. The data in Table 16, adapted from a study of the
achievement quotients of pupils in the Minneapolis junior
high schools, illustrate this point.

Sorenson [1] found the median accomplishment quotients
for the subjects listed in the table for pupils in each of the
five ability groups used in classifying pupils into homogene-

[1] Sorenson, H. "Validation of Ability Grouping of 6–A Pupils." Unpublished master's thesis, College of Education, University of Minnesota.

TABLE 16. ACCOMPLISHMENT QUOTIENTS OF PUPILS IN FOUR
MINNEAPOLIS JUNIOR HIGH SCHOOLS ACCORDING TO FIVE
ABILITY GROUPS

(After Sorenson)

| Subject | ABILITY GROUPING | | | | | |
|---------|------|------|-------|-------|-------|-----|
|         | A    | B    | C     | D     | E     | n   |
| Reading...... | 92.9 | 99.0 | 102.7 | 105.3 | 112.5 | 507 |
| Arithmetic.... | 85.8 | 89.0 | 96.7 | 104.7 | 117.1 | 441 |
| Geography.... | 87.8 | 89.0 | 93.0 | 102.3 | 106.0 | 497 |

Tests used: Haggerty Intelligence Examination, Delta II; Thorndike–McCall Reading
Scale; Buckingham Scales for Problems in Arithmetic; Posey–Van Wagenen Geography
Scales.

ous groups in the Minneapolis junior high schools. In the
A group are the pupils of superior mentality, in the B group,
pupils of good mentality, in the C group, pupils of average
mentality, and in the D and E groups, pupils of relatively
inferior mentality, the E group being the lowest. As can be
seen from the facts in Table 16, in the three subjects reading,
arithmetic, and geography, the median A.Q.'s of pupils in
the A and B groups for all subjects are less than 100; in the
C group the median A.Q.'s are less than 100 in arithmetic
and geography, and above 100 in reading; in all subjects the
median A.Q.'s, of the pupils in D and E groups are more than
100. In all groups Sorenson found wide variations in A.Q.'s,
the range, for example, for the A group in reading being from
72 to 112, in the B group from 60 to 126, in the C group from
70 to 160, in the D group from 86 to 142, and in the E group
from 75 to 146. Sorenson believes that the relatively low
A.Q.'s of the A group and the relatively high A.Q.'s of the
E group may be due to the fact that pupils of superior ability
have not been required to work up to their maximum capacity, and therefore do not have the ability that should be
expected of pupils of their intellectual level. He points out
that pupils of inferior ability possibly have been so inten-

sively taught that their achievement is greater than would normally be expected of them.   The results revealed by this investigation suggest the need of further study of the problems involved in ability grouping, and of developing methods of grading the work of inferior and superior pupils in which due consideration is given to the relation between ability and performance.

### 4. *The inadequacy of present norms*

**How norms are obtained.**   To establish norms, makers of tests usually give them to large numbers of pupils in schools in all parts of the country.   The test scores are then summarized by grade or other homogeneous group, and the average or median score is determined.   These scores, called norms, represent the typical performance of pupils under conditions as they existed at the time the tests were given. These norms may be much inferior to results that should be expected under more ideal conditions, or that are demanded in life outside the school.   For example, the Courtis norm for accuracy in addition in grade 6 is 73 per cent.   This represents a degree of accuracy much below the high degree of accuracy that is demanded by industry and business. Courtis has therefore proposed that the standard to be set by the schools should be 100 per cent accuracy.   A standard is thus a goal of attainment.   In some cases, as in determining satisfactory rates of writing, standards are based on norms.   In other cases standards, as in quality of handwriting, have been determined not by the performance of pupils on tests but by the demands of life outside the school.

It is evident from the foregoing discussions that present test standards may in some cases be too high, and in others too low.   Such standards should therefore be subject to revision, from time to time.   In general, however, standards should guide the teacher in determining the emphasis to be placed on a subject. If the scores of an individual compare favorably with the standard for his grade, obviously there is no need of further intensive work on the skills involved. Further practice may well be omitted or at least greatly reduced, and the time thus saved may be used to greater advantage in other ways. This procedure would obviate a common practice of teachers of spending an undue amount of time on drill work and thus bringing the performances of the pupils up to a point considerably above reasonable standards, at the same time neglecting other important phases of instruction for which measurements are lacking.

## II. USES OF EDUCATIONAL AND MENTAL MEASUREMENTS

### 1. *Administrative and supervisory uses*

**Use in city-wide testing programs.** Standardized educational tests are of great value to administrative and supervisory officers. By means of a city-wide testing program the relative status of the achievements of the several schools may be determined, and the weak spots in the system located. Intensive studies may be undertaken to determine if possible the causes of the deficiencies. Instructional needs, due to inadequacy of materials, possibly inferior teaching, and similar causes, may be discovered; supervisory and instructional policies can be adapted in the light of conditions revealed by the survey.

The results of these tests may be used in classifying pupils into homogeneous groups. Investigations have revealed the wide range in the mentality of pupils in almost every class. To obviate the teaching difficulties due to such a condition, in many systems pupils are being grouped roughly according to their mental level. In various ways attempts have been made to adapt instruction to the abilities and needs of each group. (See Chapter II.)

The information revealed by measurements is also of distinct value in educational and vocational guidance. On the basis of these facts attempts can be made to improve the gradation of pupils who are manifestly not properly graded. The cumulative record of the test results for individual pupils supplies valuable information for guidance in particular cases.

**Attempted use in teacher rating.** In some school systems attempts have been made to use the test results as a basis for teacher rating. The assumption has been that the ability of the teacher can be measured by determining the growth in pupil achievement during a year in such subjects as reading, spelling, and arithmetic. The results of such attempts have on the whole been unsatisfactory because of the difficulty of interpreting the data secured in this way. Superior teachers having classes of inferior mentality obviously cannot be expected to secure as good results, as measured by mere growth in the achievement of pupils, as can be secured by less skillful teachers with superior pupils. Numerous other factors, such as the previous training of the pupils, the adequacy of the instructional materials, the social background of the community, and the attitude of the home toward the school are such vital contributing elements in the situation that it is almost impossible to measure the effect of teaching skill as a separate item in such a complex situation.

With the aid of standard tests the supervisor has been better able to carry on the necessary research work he must undertake in order to evaluate experimentally the effectiveness of instruction. Standard tests have made it possible to measure the results of experimental adaptations of the curriculum, or the relative superiority of having two forms of school organization, such as the traditional as contrasted with the platoon school. The value of various supervisory devices and methods, the effectiveness of instructional materials of different kinds, and the value of such special forms of teaching procedures as excursions, projects, and the contract plan, can all be determined in part by the measurement of the growth that takes place in both teachers and pupils.

Recently a supervisor stated, "The most valuable tool I have is the standard test. It enables me to secure quickly a much more accurate picture of instruction in the schools than I could secure through weeks of visitation. It points out the weak spots for me, and helps me to arrive at a sound basis for planning a program of all of my supervisory activities."

## 2. Uses in measurement in teaching

Although educational measurements are of great value to the supervisor and administrator, their most valuable contributions have been made in the improvement of teaching.

**In setting up standards.** The objective techniques used in educational measurement have made it possible for the teacher to set up standards of attainment that are definite and meaningful for the pupils. For example, the attempts to measure the general merit of handwriting have yielded information on the basis of which definite standards for both rate and quality of writing may be set up by the teacher. As a result of the measurement of the skills involved the teacher now has definite standards for rate of reading for each grade, for rate of computation for various purposes, for ability to spell, and for many other specific items. These standards enable the teacher to determine with precision how well the pupils in the class compare with pupils of the same level of advancement in other parts of the country. A comparison of the class results with standards for the country yields definite information as to the points at which the instruction has been inadequate, and at which additional teaching and practice are necessary.

Objective standards also serve as an excellent means of motivating the pupils to attack the problem of improving their work, and help to develop in them a definite feeling of responsibility for raising their various skills to satisfactory levels. By repeated measurement the pupil can measure his progress. In this way the dull routine drill of the past has been replaced by vitalized purposeful practice with definite objectives to be reached.

**In pre-tests and re-tests.** The use of techniques similar to those employed in the tests has simplified and made more effective many teaching procedures. For example, in spelling, by means of a pre-test on the list of words for the week the teacher now helps the pupil to discover the words he does not already know how to spell. Pre-tests, often called inventory tests, are found in many of the modern textbooks in such subjects as spelling and arithmetic. They are to be given at the beginning of the year to enable the teacher to determine the needs of the pupils in the class, and to supply information on the basis of which to do the necessary teaching. Pre-tests often are given by teachers before teaching any unit of work, since they afford an excellent means by which the teacher can discover the knowledge or skill the pupils in the class already possess. On the basis of this information the teacher can adjust the instruction to the needs, interests, and attitudes of the group.

Similar test procedures may be used at the end of a unit of work as re-tests, to determine what the pupils have learned as a result of the instruction. Such methods are much more effective than the typical question and answer recitations, in which individual pupils recite and in which ordinarily no method of checking the information or the accomplishments of the other pupils in the class is used. Pre-tests and re-tests in such subjects as history, geography, nature study, and health may take the form of the new type of objective examinations, based on essentials in the unit of work.  The test items can be dictated one at a time to the class, and all of the pupils can be required to write the answers on their papers.  An analysis of the test papers yields the desired information relative to the items included.

**In individualizing teaching.**  The test procedure serves as a sound basis for individualizing the instruction in the various skill phases of such subjects as arithmetic, writing, geography, and reading.  In its extremest form the test procedure is applied in the Winnetka schools.  In these schools the entire course in the skill phases of instruction is divided into units.  As rapidly as the pupil is able to pass a satisfactory test on a unit in any subject he may proceed to the next unit in that subject.  The rates at which pupils progress in various subjects under this plan vary greatly.

The following statement of principles by Washburne [1] explains the organization and means for administering individual work in the Winnetka schools:

The general plan of the system is to permit the promotion of each individual pupil in each subject whenever he completes the work of his grade in that subject.  He may complete fourth-grade arithmetic in February, fourth-grade language in June, and fourth-grade spelling the next October.  Other members of his class will complete the same subjects at widely different times, but each one, when he finishes one grade's work in a certain subject, either proceeds to the next grade's work in that subject, or uses the time to bring up other subjects in which he is behind.  In order that such a system may be administered without confusion, without too much work on the part of the teacher, and without loss of the social elements of school, certain general principles must be adhered to.

1. The most important of these principles is that the goals of a grade's work in a subject must be absolutely definite, must be

[1] Washburne, C. W.  "The Individual System in Winnetka"; in *The Elementary School Journal*, vol. 21, pp. 52–68.

known to pupils as well as to teachers, and must be attainable by the slowest, normal, diligent pupil. The big goals of the grade must be subdivided so that a child's progress is obvious to himself. Goals must be in terms of concrete facts to be known, habits to be acquired, or skills to be developed. This is in contrast to the usual outline type of course of study in which nothing is set forth but pages to be covered, or general aims to be achieved.

2. The plan requires the establishment of tests which are complete and diagnostic. These tests must show whether or not a pupil has attained all of the goals and must show his specific weaknesses. For under the individual system each pupil must achieve 100 per cent efficiency in the work he undertakes. Eighty per cent on a test does not mean passing; it means that there is 20 per cent of the work yet to be done before the pupil goes on. The results of the test must indicate exactly what the pupil has yet to accomplish.

3. The plan requires the preparation of practice material for the pupil's use, such material to correspond with each weakness shown in a test. This practice material must be self-corrective, so that the pupil may correct his own daily work. The fact that marks and promotions are based upon the test and not upon the practice material eliminates any temptation for the pupil to cheat himself in the correction of his daily practice work.

4. There must be sufficient social work to counteract the individual work and to give flesh and blood to a course of study which without it would be a mere skeleton.

Less extreme plans of individualizing instruction in the various subjects are provided by various methods which will be described in the following chapters. In general, the plans that will be described provide various methods of adapting the drill in any class to the particular needs of each individual, without emphasizing the rapid progress on completely individualized units which characterizes the Winnetka plan. Most of the plans provide for the self-scoring of practice exercises by the pupils, the use of objective devices by which the pupil can determine his own deficiencies, and the assignment of remedial work on the basis of diagnostic tests.

**In the improvement of instructional materials.** In order to construct valid tests, those interested in their development have either had to assume that the present curriculum is satisfactory, or else they have been forced to make scientific studies on the basis of which to select a body of valid materials to be used in constructing the test or scale. The emphasis that has been placed on measurement of the educational outcomes has obligated test makers to include in their tests a body of subject-matter of demonstrated social utility and value. For example, the thousand words in the Ayres Spelling Scale contain the words that occur most frequently in written speech. Hence tests based on this scale consist of words that pupils ought to know. Similar scientific studies of curricular content have influenced the selection of the items included in tests of arithmetic, history, geography, and language. This tendency has definitely contributed to the improvement of curricular content.

The necessity of preparing valid individualized practice exercises in the various subjects has required a searching analysis of the steps in the learning process. Practice exercises in arithmetic, for example, based on such detailed analyses, lead the pupil gradually through the various steps that must be learned before the processes are mastered. Instead of plunging the pupil at once into a complex situation involving many difficulties, the process has been simplified and is now presented in a much better series of graded exercises. From time to time standardized tests are included in these materials by means of which the teacher can repeatedly check up on the progress being made by pupils, and at the same time discover difficulties and places at which normal progress is not being made by the class as a whole or by individuals. The careful analysis of the unit skills in various subjects has been reflected in the care with which textbooks are being constructed with due regard for the learning process.

By means of the test procedure, curriculum-makers have been able to determine the difficulty of units in the curriculum. This information has proved of great value in the gradation of the subject-matter. It is possible by the test technique to determine the difficulty of reading matter included in textbooks, and to make necessary adjustments to adapt the material to the grade for which it is intended. By means of the test procedure it has been possible to determine the difficulty of specific items for pupils in each grade, such as the spelling difficulty of words, or the grade at which pupils can master certain topics in arithmetic. The information revealed by such studies has made it possible to take definite steps to prevent many of the difficulties pupils encounter in various phases of school work. Special exercises to prevent the development of specific difficulties are now provided. Study helps to guide the pupils over known crucial steps in the learning process reduce the likelihood of failure to master the step.

The use of charts and other means of helping the pupil to visualize correct forms or procedures, and to determine the nature and causes of faults and deviations from satisfactory standards, is a direct contribution to teaching that grew out of the attempts to study the classroom product objectively. Diagnostic charts in handwriting, neatness scales in arithmetic work, scales of compositions which contain analyses of the deficiencies in the specimens, and pupil progress charts and graphs all have developed since the testing movement began. These devices help the pupils to measure their progress and diagnose the nature of their deficiencies and they serve as valuable means of vitalizing and motivating the necessary practice that must be done to bring about an improvement. This drill is purposeful because definite objectives and standards are before the pupil at all times. To achieve those objectives he does the necessary work to eliminate deficiencies and undesirable qualities that detract from the general merit of his performances.

The necessity of doing something to remedy the conditions revealed by measurements has resulted in many intensive studies of the causes of pupil difficulties, and has brought about the preparation of carefully constructed remedial exercises designed to obviate and prevent the most common faults of pupils. The story is told of a well-known director of research in a city school system who for several years had been reporting the results of survey tests to his superintendent. The conditions revealed by these tests were on the whole quite disturbing. Early one autumn the usual report of the test results was made to the superintendent. Near the close of the conference, at which the data were discussed, the superintendent said, "I wonder what we ought to do about it?" This same question has been asked by thousands of teachers when the results of tests, given at the end of the year, revealed an unsatisfactory condition. There are at least two constructive things to do; the first is not to delay the measurement of abilities until the end of the year or the end of the school term, but to provide for the continuous systematic testing of pupils at regular intervals throughout the year; the other is to adapt the instruction to the needs of the individual as revealed by these periodic tests. If this procedure is followed, unsatisfactory performances will be discovered at an early date and steps can be taken to remedy the weaknesses.

### III. CASE STUDIES ON USES OF TESTS

The following cases illustrate certain uses of tests which have obvious merits, as well as limitations. Consider each case in detail, and be prepared to point out the merits and limitations of each. What changes or additions would you make in each case?

## Case 1

The principal of School X (1200 pupils, grades 1 to 6) planned to group the pupils in grades 4 to 6 on the basis of the results of the Stanford Achievement Test, which had been expressed as subject ages. Data were available for reading, arithmetic problem-solving and computation, nature study, history, and language, all expressed as subject ages. The complete school records for all pupils were also available.

## Case 2

The results of the Thorndike–McCall Reading Test, given in May near the close of the school, showed that the class rating was considerably below the standard for the country. Similar results were found for arithmetic, geography, and spelling. No similar tests had been given at the beginning of the year. On the basis of the results the principal recommended the dismissal of the teacher on the ground of inefficiency.

## Case 3

The administration of a certain large city school system was inclined to favor the adoption of the platoon school type of organization as the organization policy of the system. However, before this action was recommended, the superintendent asked for an investigation of the efficiency of instruction in schools of the traditional type and in schools in the system which had been organized on the basis of the platoon plan. A direct comparison was made between the scores of comparable groups of pupils, in both types of schools, on a comprehensive series of well-selected standard achievement tests. The test results were slightly in favor of the pupils in the platoon schools. The superintendent therefore recommended the adoption of the platoon school type of organization as the organization policy for the city.

## Case 4

Courtis and Barns conducted an investigation to evaluate the effectiveness of four types of supervisory activities. Schools were divided into equated groups, one criterion being the scores made on a standard test in locational geography. Each group was supervised in a manner differing from that used in the other groups, one group being used as control and being entirely unsupervised. At the end of the period of the investigation a second test in locational geography was given. It was found that the average score of classes in the unsupervised schools was lower than in the supervised schools. Courtis has held that this experiment showed that supervision paid.

## Case 5

In a certain city a new superintendent inaugurated a city-wide testing program in the fundamental subjects, in which he required all schools to participate. The tests were selected, with the advice of the Director of Tests and Measurements, by the superintendent himself. Teachers in the system had not been accustomed to the giving of tests. Meetings of principals were held at which they were given instructions on the giving of the tests. In turn the principal instructed the teachers. The test papers were sent to the office of the Research Department for scoring and for tabulation of the results. The tests were given in November. A general report of the results was sent to the schools in March. In this report the schools were listed by name. Comparative data were given regarding other school systems.  A general interpretation of the results was included in the report.  No systematic program was organized on the basis of the results of this investigation, the superintendent apparently being satisfied with the knowledge that the city as a whole was practically up to the standard in all subjects in which tests were given.  Each school received graphs of the test results for its pupils, but the test papers were filed in the office of the Research Bureau and were not returned to the schools.

## QUESTIONS FOR STUDY, DISCUSSION, AND REPORT

1. Find the I.Q.'s of the following:

| CHRONOLOGICAL AGE | MENTAL AGE |
|---|---|
| a. 12 years | 9 years |
| b. 11 years 6 months | 12 years 9 months |
| c. 145 months | 132 months |

2. Find the E.Q.'s of the following

| CHRONOLOGICAL AGE | SUBJECT AGE |
|---|---|
| a. 9 years | 8 years 6 months |
| b. 13 years 2 months | 14 years 4 months |
| c. 132 months | 168 months |

3. Find the A.Q.'s of the following:

| MENTAL AGE | SUBJECT AGE |
|---|---|
| a. 140 months | 130 months |
| b. 7 years 2 months | 8 years |

4. Is the A.Q. of a pupil having an I.Q. of 120 likely to be above 100?

5. How is a test score converted into age norms?

6. How does an age norm differ from a grade norm?

7. Why are standards expressed as grade norms, instead of ages, often unsatisfactory?

8. Give a test to the pupils in a class, and compute the percentile rankings.

9. What is the value of a percentile graph?

10. What is the median, and how is it computed?

11. Describe a simple way of finding the class average score.

12. What is a distribution table?   What is meant by frequency?

13. What is meant when we say that a person's rating on a test was the 95–percentile?

14. Why are educational and accomplishment quotients at present quite unreliable?

15. Why are test results an unsatisfactory basis for teacher rating?

16. What are some of the educational outcomes that are at present not measurable with the tools that have been devised?

17. Is it reasonable to assume that we may devise methods of measuring what some people call the "intangible" outcomes of instruction?

18. Be prepared to report on some educational experiment in which standard tests have been an essential tool.

19. List ways in which standard tests have been used in schools in which you have taught.

20. Describe ways in which tests have helped teachers to establish reasonable norms of pupil achievement.

21. If possible, secure illustrative Winnetka lessons and discuss the principles involved.

22. What standardized practice materials are available in which the test technique is an essential element?   Consider especially the fields of arithmetic, language, reading, and social science.

23. Name some test that you feel includes a type of subject-matter that you feel the pupils should not be held responsible for.

24. Describe cases in which you feel an excellent use has been made of the results of standard tests.

25. Describe cases in which you feel an unwise or faulty use has been made of test results.

26. Who should select tests to be given to pupils?

27. Should the giving of standard tests be voluntary or compulsory?

28. How should a supervisor or superintendent introduce the use of tests in a school in which they have never been given, and in which there are teachers who do not understand their use or value?

## SELECTED REFERENCES

Franzen, R.  *The Accomplishment Quotient.*  Teachers College Contributions to Education, no. 125.  New York, Teachers College, Columbia University, 1922.

Garrett, H. E.  *Statistics in Pyschology and Education.*  New York, Longmans, Green and Company, 1926.

Greene, H. A., and Jorgensen, A. N.  *Use and Interpretation of Educational Measurements.*  New York, Longmans, Green and Company, 1929.

Greene, H. A.  *Workbook in Educational Measurements, Forms A and B.*  New York, Longmans, Green and Company, 1929.

Holzinger, K. J.  *Statistical Methods for Students of Education.*  Boston, Ginn and Company, 1928.

Kelley, T. L.  *Statistical Method.*  New York, The Macmillan Company, 1923.

McDonald, M.  *Practical Statistics for Teachers.*  New York, The Macmillan Company, 1930.

Otis, A. L.  *Statistical Method in Educational Measurement.*  Yonkers-on-Hudson, New York, World Book Company, 1925.

Rugg, H. O.  *A Primer of Graphics and Statistics.*  Boston, Houghton Mifflin Company, 1925.

Rugg, H. O.  *Statistical Methods Applied to Education.*  Boston, Houghton Mifflin Company, 1925.

Terman, L. M.  *Measurement of Intelligence.*  Boston, Houghton Mifflin Company, 1916.

Tiegs, E. J., and Crawford, C. C.  *Statistics for Teachers.*  Boston, Houghton Mifflin Company, 1930.

# CHAPTER V

## THE NATURE AND TECHNIQUES OF EDUCATIONAL DIAGNOSIS

### 1. *Importance of proper diagnostic procedures*

**The need of diagnosis.** In every classroom there are pupils who at some stage of their work encounter difficulty and fail to make satisfactory progress. Some of them do not seem to be able to compute with speed and accuracy; some of them fail to show growth in ability to read; the written work of others is full of misspellings; some pupils encounter difficulty in only some single phase of a subject, others are unable to do satisfactory work in any subject. Formerly, in many cases, these pupils were labeled "lazy," "stupid," or "indifferent" by their teachers. This was due to the fact that little was done by the school to determine the causes of the difficulties. Under the traditional "lock-step" system pupils, regardless of their needs, were all given the same treatment. The situation was quite similar to what would be the case if a physician prescribed the same remedy for all ailments.

Such "blunderbuss" random diagnosis of educational ills, or rather failure to diagnose them, has been the cause of much waste in our whole scheme of education. The facts concerning the large per cent of failure, the large amount of retardation, and the elimination of pupils from our schools that have been revealed by surveys of various school systems describe a condition that was in large part the result of failure on the part of teachers to make adequate provision for diagnosis of pupil difficulties, and on the basis of the results of the information thus secured to do the necessary remedial work.

Just as the modern physician makes use of such scientific instruments as the test tube, the microscope, the stethoscope, and the clinical thermometer in making a diagnosis of a physical ailment, the modern teacher has learned to use scientific tools and devices for making a diagnosis of educational ailments, such as standard diagnostic tests in the various subjects, diagnostic charts which help the teacher to visualize deficiencies, charts for measuring vision, apparatus for measuring hearing, and any other means that may be of assistance in determining the specific or general nature of the difficulty.

**The approach to diagnosis.**  The approach to diagnosis may be either through general observation and measurement, or through more refined and specialized clinical methods.  By measurement with standard educational tests the teacher can determine with precision the present status of the pupil's general ability in a subject, as compared with that of pupils of his mental and chronological level of development.  Such information helps the teacher to locate the phases of educational achievement in which the pupils are above or below standard, and the point at which the clinical procedures needed to locate the causes of the difficulties should be applied.  The clinical methods used in educational diagnosis have been borrowed from various fields of science, in so far as they have enabled the teacher or the clinician to study the child from different angles.  From psychology the teacher has taken the techniques of the individual clinical examination, the methods of observing and analyzing the pupil's ways of responding, and the test technique.  In making a diagnosis the teacher likewise uses the findings of the school physician, the facts concerning the home environment secured by the visiting teacher or social worker, and any other pertinent information that may be of value in a particular case.  In short, the approach to diagnosis involves the application by the school of the tools and techniques devised by any allied science which may help the teacher to make the necessary educational adjustments. The specialized tools of diagnosis devised by technical workers in the field of education are in themselves an essential part of the teaching process, but the information they reveal must be supplemented by any additional facts that may help the teacher to diagnose correctly and completely the nature and cause of the difficulty.

While the teacher in the classroom should be familiar with diagnostic techniques and the most common faults of pupils in the several subjects, as well as with the means of overcoming these difficulties, in many cases more specialized training may be needed to locate subtle forms of interferences. The essential qualities of such an examiner in the field of reading are well stated by Sangren,[1] as follows:

(1) Training and experience to observe and interpret certain types of behavior as evidence of the influence of underlying causes of reading ability: (2) a thorough control over some technique of diagnosis which brings to the surface facts concerning the nature of the pupil's reading ability which otherwise would go unobserved; (3) a thorough knowledge of the causes underlying the development of reading ability and the way in which they operate; (4) a knowledge of the specific habits and skills essential to effective reading; (5) a knowledge of what remedial measures to employ when the diagnosis has been completed.

## 2. Kinds of diagnosis

By diagnosis we mean the procedure used to identify or to determine the nature of a deficiency or weakness. In education the term has had a wide variety of applications, some of them quite inconsistent with its accepted specific meaning. For purposes of discussion three kinds of diag-

[1] Sangren, Paul V. "Methods of Diagnosis in Reading"; in *Elementary English Review*, vol. 7, p. 105. (April, 1930.)

nosis may be differentiated: (1) general diagnosis; (2) analytical diagnosis; (3) psychological diagnosis.

Procedures under each of these types will now be described.

**General diagnosis.** By general diagnosis we mean any procedure that may be used to secure general information regarding the educational status of a pupil or of a class. A superintendent of schools may wish to secure information regarding the general status of the achievements of the pupils throughout the system. For this purpose a test of general achievement, such as the Stanford Achievement Test, may be given. The information thus secured will show the superintendent how the schools compare with the established test norms. Comparisons between classes can be made and weak spots located. The score of an individual pupil on such a test will enable the teacher to determine his relative educational status.

The chief limitation of this kind of diagnosis is that it does not give the teacher any facts on the basis of which to determine the specific causes of superiority or inferiority. This same limitation is present in the use of the results of such subject tests as the Woody Arithmetic Scales, or the Thorndike–McCall Reading Tests. These tests serve admirably as a means of securing a general measure of the pupil's present status in arithmetic and reading, but they do not supply the kind of detailed information needed to make a diagnosis of a particular pupil's deficiency; nor can the teacher determine on the basis of the test results the particular phases of the subject in which deficiencies exist. However, these tests do help the teacher to select those pupils whose performances are not up to standard, and whose work should be more carefully studied to determine what steps should be taken to remedy the condition.

**Analytical diagnosis.** The purpose of analytical diagnosis is to determine the specific phases of such fields as reading, arithmetic, writing, and language in which the pupil is deficient. The basis of an analytical diagnosis is the pupil's performances on a series of standard tests, or carefully constructed diagnostic exercises, based on a detailed analysis of the several skills which constitute the general ability under consideration. For example, arithmetic is made up of a large number of skills which have been listed by various investigators. To make a diagnosis of difficulty in subtraction of fractions, the teacher must determine whether the pupil has mastered such specific skills as reducing unlike fractions to a common denominator, the procedure to use in subtracting fractions when borrowing is involved or when borrowing is not involved, the ability to reduce fractions to lowest terms, and the other specific skills that constitute the ability to subtract fractions. By means of separate exercises involving each of these skills the teacher can readily locate the particular phases of the ability to subtract which the pupil has not mastered. It should be pointed out that the mere location of the points at which difficulty exists by means of those analytical methods is only a partial diagnosis, since the teacher must in addition determine the causes of the difficulty.

Standard tests in arithmetic best exemplify the procedures by means of which these analytical diagnoses may be made. The tests range in the detailed information they yield from such tests as the Courtis Standard Research Tests, Series B, which enable the teacher to measure the ability of pupils to work only one type of example in each of the four fundamental processes with whole numbers, to such detailed analytical exercises as the Buswell–John Diagnostic Test in Arithmetic, and the Brueckner Diagnostic Tests in Fractions, which contain a wide variety of types of examples based on complete analysis of the specific skills that constitute the abilities involved. By means of the Brueckner tests the teacher can determine the specific types of examples in each of the four processes in fractions that each individual pupil cannot solve. This detailed specific information helps the teacher to determine the points at which additional instruction is needed. Other excellent tests for analytical diagnosis in arithmetic are the Compass Diagnostic Test, the Clapp–Young Self-Marking Tests in Arithmetic, and the Monroe Diagnostic Tests.

In the field of reading the Gates Silent Reading Tests, Sangren–Woody Silent Reading Tests, and the Nelson Reading Tests are excellent illustrations of analytical diagnostic tests. In language the Charters Diagnostic Language and Grammar Tests, the Briggs English Form Tests and the Clapp–Young Self-Marking English Tests are instruments of analytical diagnosis. The Freeman Scale for Handwriting, and the Self-Corrective Handwriting Charts devised by Miss Nystrom, may be used to make an analytical diagnosis of defects in writing. The application of these and similar diagnostic devices will be discussed in detail in the chapters which follow dealing with the several subjects.

**Psychological diagnosis.** As has been pointed out, the techniques of analytical diagnosis enable the teacher to determine the location of a difficulty, or the particular condition because of which a deficiency may exist. These techniques, however, do not reveal the causes of the faults. It is to discover the *why* of the pupil difficulty that the psychological method of diagnosis has been devised. This method includes all techniques that can be used by the teacher to discover the more subtle hidden causes of faults and deficiencies in the responses of pupils. To be able to make a satisfactory psychological diagnosis the teacher must know the possible causes or symptoms of maladjustment of all kinds, the most common faults that have been found to exist in the performance of pupils, and the various methods by which a diagnosis of these faults may be made. The teacher must also appreciate the value of any available pertinent information that may help to explain the deficiency, and must take the necessary steps to assemble these facts from school records and reports by special workers, such as the school nurse or social worker.

Any diagnosis may be incorrect because of the inability of the examiner to recognize the signs or symptoms of the deficiency, or because of ignorance of fundamental facts revealed by scientific inquiry; the techniques used by the examiner may be inadequate, careless, and unscientific; the conditions under which the examination is made may be unfavorable, and hence the responses by the pupil may not be those he ordinarily makes; or the basis on which the diagnosis is made may be inadequate, due to the fact that important items are overlooked. Training of teachers in the use of precise objective techniques of diagnosis and in accurate observation of cases will do much to insure reliable diagnosis.

**Necessity of knowledge by the teacher of the most common faults and symptoms of deficiency.** Just as the physician must have a well-classified knowledge of the characteristic symptoms of physical and mental ailments as a basis for diagnosis, the teacher should have a systematic knowledge of the most common pedagogical faults and their symptoms in making a diagnosis of an educational difficulty. If such precise organized information is lacking, the diagnosis by the teacher is not penetrating and is empirical. The reliability of any diagnosis is conditioned by the previous training and experience of the examiner. The systematic studies that have been made in recent years by various investigators to determine the most common faults of pupils in the several subjects of the curriculum have supplied a

wealth of information of great value in educational diagnosis. A teacher who is familiar with the findings of these
investigations, and the techniques that were used to discover the faults as well as their causes, can apply the same
procedures in the study of individual cases in her own
classes. Familiarity with the causes and the symptoms of
various faults will make the teacher conscious of the wide
variety of factors that may be at the basis of the failure of
pupils to make satisfactory progress. Furthermore, a
knowledge of the most common faults and difficulties will
show the teacher the need of taking positive steps to prevent
their occurrence. For example, faulty methods of work can
be prevented by teaching efficient procedures at the time the
skills and abilities involved are first presented, and by special
practice exercises on difficult points.

Pupils can readily appraise their work in various school
subjects. The scoring of papers in arithmetic is quite simple, since answers are either correct or incorrect. The use
of standard practice exercises involves in most cases provision for pupils to mark their own work. Pupils can readily
locate the causes of errors in computation, or indicate the
step at which difficulties arise. Similarly, pupils can rate
their compositions by the standard composition scales;
and careful proofreading of written work provides a check
on punctuation, spelling, and grammatical errors due to
carelessness. Pupils can also be trained to evaluate their
work in the light of accepted standards of composition.
Diagnostic charts in handwriting make it possible for pupils
to analyze the causes of lack of merit of their own writings,
and at the same time make them conscious of good standards. There is no question but that teachers must systematically train pupils to appraise their own work in all subjects. This practice is wholly in accord with progressive
educational theory.

Investigators have endeavored to discover how well pupils can appraise their own work for errors. In the report of one of these studies, Lull [1] presented data to show that a group of fifth-grade pupils "doubted correctly" 83 per cent of their misspellings in a test-rated exercise; sixth-grade pupils, 61 per cent; seventh-grade pupils, 67 per cent; and eighth-grade pupils, 67 per cent. Children in grades five through eight were positive that they had misspelled 16 to 38 per cent of the words they actually misspelled. These data indicate that a pupil very often does not know whether or not he has spelled a word correctly. In spite of this fact, teachers should realize that the establishment of a spelling conscience through pupil appraisal of the spelling on their written work is more significant than the usual valueless marking of misspellings by the teacher.

In the chapters for each school subject which follow, summaries of investigations of pupil faults and deficiencies in the several subjects are presented. These summaries, as well as the descriptions of methods of teacher diagnosis, and of self-diagnosis by the pupils there given, should be carefully studied by the teacher.

### 3. *The techniques of psychological diagnosis*

Various techniques have been devised by investigators to determine the causes of the failure of pupils to make satisfactory progress.

**Observation.** Through observation of the behavior of the pupil on the playground and in the schoolroom the teacher can secure much information concerning his general methods of responding, his social attitudes, and his moral and volitional qualities. While he is at work in the classroom preparing his lessons, his methods of work, his application to

[1] Lull, H. G. "A Plan for Developing a Spelling Consciousness"; in *Elementary School Journal*, vol. 17, pp. 355–61. (January, 1917.)

the task at hand, his study habits, and similar obvious traits can be studied without giving the pupil any notion that his behavior is being observed. An analysis of the individual pupil's reactions in some single situation, such as taking a test in arithmetic, enables the teacher to locate such faults as counting, faulty nervous or muscular reactions, and faulty handling of materials, such as the way in which a pencil is held or the position of the paper on which the pupil is writing.

In special cases much more controlled forms of observation than those indicated in the preceding case may be utilized. A good illustration is the use of the Morrison Attention Profile technique, by means of which the teacher can chart on a prepared form the attention of the pupil during a certain time, such as a study period. The technique is described in detail in Morrison's book, *Practice of Teaching in the Secondary School*. In making the attention profile the observer takes a position where he can observe clearly the actions of the pupil without attracting his attention. On the prepared record blank, which is divided into minute spaces and further subdivided into ten-second intervals, a record is made of the pupil's attention by ten-second intervals. Other time intervals, such as half minutes, can be used. Portion of an analytical record is given on the opposite page.[1]

In Figure 3, the record, it will be noted, is divided into two parts by a heavy vertical line. To the right of the line application is recorded, to the left distraction; the former indicates attention, the latter lack of attention. The observer notes the shifting of attention by placing a dot at the nearest ten second interval on the proper side of the

[1] Blume, C. E. "Measuring Pupil Attention"; in "Scientific Method in Supervision." *Second Yearbook of the National Conference of Supervisors and Directors of Instruction*, New York, Bureau of Publications, Columbia University, 1929.

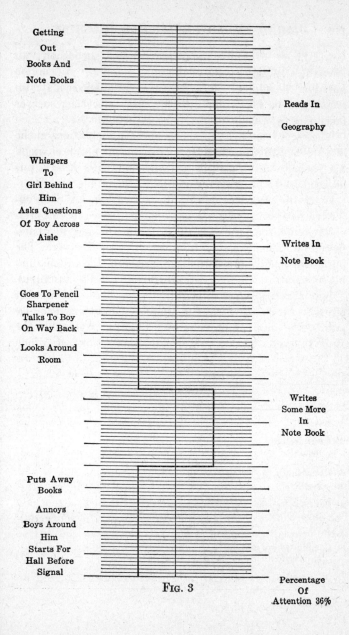

Getting
Out
Books And
Note Books

Reads In
Geography

Whispers
To
Girl Behind
Him
Asks Questions
Of Boy Across
Aisle

Writes In
Note Book

Goes To Pencil
Sharpener
Talks To Boy
On Way Back

Looks Around
Room

Writes
Some More
In
Note Book

Puts Away
Books

Annoys
Boys Around
Him
Starts For
Hall Before
Signal

Fig. 3

Percentage
Of
Attention 36%

vertical line. By connecting these points in succession with lines the attention-profile of the pupil is found. As may be noted on the pupil blank on page 131, the observer may also record on the blank opposite the time intervals whatever facts may be of value in interpreting the profile.

The record on page 131 shows marked fluctuations in the attention of this pupil.[1] He was shown the profile chart by his teacher and it was discussed with him. His interest was aroused, and a program for improving the profile was undertaken with very satisfying results. (See Fig. 4.) Such objective records are of great value in conferences with pupils and parents, since the data they contain are impersonal and picture graphically a condition viewed by an observer. The pupil can readily grasp the significance of the profile, and his coöperation in a remedial program can easily be secured.

Similar records may be kept by the teacher of the number of errors in oral English, the number of blunders made by pupils, the number of voluntary reports they make, the kinds of questions they ask, or any other set of facts which

TABLE 17. SURVEY OF FAULTY HABITS IN READING

|  | 1C | 1B | 1A | 2C | 2B | 2A | 3C | 3B | 3A | 4B | 4A | 5C | 5A | 6A | TOTAL |
|---|---|---|---|---|---|---|---|---|---|---|---|---|---|---|---|
| 1. Lip readers | 19 | 6 | 19 | 5 | 9 | 6 | 3 | 4 | 9 | 6 | 3 | 4 | 2 | 2 | 97 |
| 2. Excessive head movements | 4 | 2 | 5 | 2 | 2 | 2 | 2 | 4 | 0 | 0 | 1 | 3 | 0 | 0 | 27 |
| 3. Use of finger to keep place | 0 | 0 | 4 | 0 | 0 | 0 | 0 | 1 | 0 | 0 | 0 | 0 | 0 | 0 | 5 |
| 4. Position of books | | | | | | | | | | | | | | | |
| (a) Holding off desk | 3 | 0 | 0 | 1 | 0 | 3 | 0 | 2 | 2 | 0 | 0 | 0 | 0 | 0 | 11 |
| (b) Close to eyes | 2 | 0 | 3 | | 1 | 0 | 0 | 3 | 3 | 0 | 0 | 0 | 0 | 0 | 12 |
| 5. Combined head and lip movement | 3 | 3 | 3 | 3 | 1 | 0 | 0 | 0 | 1 | 0 | 0 | 0 | 0 | 0 | 14 |
| Grade enrollment | 27 | 9 | 38 | 21 | 23 | 21 | 18 | 23 | 13 | 26 | 14 | 27 | 24 | 15 | |

[1] Op. cit.

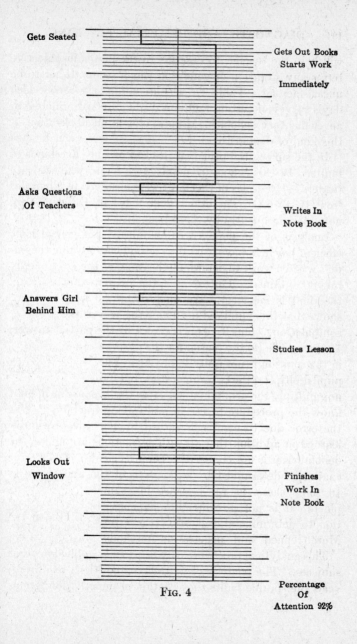

Gets Seated

Gets Out Books
Starts Work

Immediately

Asks Questions
Of Teachers

Writes In
Note Book

Answers Girl
Behind Him

Studies Lesson

Looks Out
Window

Finishes
Work In
Note Book

Fig. 4

Percentage
Of
Attention 92%

will help the teacher to describe to the pupils in objective terms any situation or condition which seems to her to be unsatisfactory. Table 17, which contains the record of a day's survey of certain faults in reading by the principal of an elementary school in Minneapolis, is an illustration of this kind of diagnosis.

In the survey the principal checked on only five kinds of faults. In this school 97 pupils were found who were lip readers. Examples of this fault were observed in all grades from 1C to 6A. The other faults listed in Table 17 were noted less frequently by the principal.

**Analysis of the pupil's written work.** For generations, efficient teachers have used the method of analyzing the pupil's written work to determine the cause of the errors it contained. For example, the answer (a) at the right is incorrect. An analysis of the work shows that this pupil did not know the sum of the combination, 5 plus 3. This is shown by the partial answer, 7. In sample (b) the reason for the mistake in the solution is not quite so obvious. The pupil multiplied the two numerators, but did

$$(a) \quad \begin{array}{r} 75 \\ 43 \\ \hline 117 \end{array}$$

$$(b) \quad \frac{1}{8} \times \frac{3}{8} = \frac{3}{8}$$

not multiply the denominators. Was this because he did not know the procedure to use in multiplying fractions? Was the error due to confusion caused by the rule previously learned in addition that when like fractions are added the denominator is not changed? The exact cause of the error cannot be determined by an analysis of the written work. In some cases, as for instance in example (c), it is not possible through inspection to determine the cause of the error.

$$(c) \quad \frac{4}{5} + \frac{1}{2} = \frac{7}{9}$$

More refined and penetrating methods must be used.

This analytical procedure may be usefully applied in other subjects. The analysis of written compositions readily reveals the specific faults they contain in punctuation, grammar, and spelling. On the basis of the results the teacher can plan group and individual remedial work. Unsatisfactory characteristics of handwriting can be discovered by a careful analysis of these written compositions. An analysis of the results of a test in locational geography helps the pupils and the teacher to determine the locations that are not known or have actually been mislearned. The responses that pupils make to questions in informal reading exercises based on the several studies may be analyzed to determine in a general way whether the pupils have mastered such skills as are involved in the use of the index, the ability to outline, the ability to remember what was read, or the ability to summarize what was read.

The chief weakness of the technique of diagnosis based on an analysis of the pupil's written responses is the lack of reliability of the diagnosis. In many doubtful cases the examiner is forced to make inferences as to the nature of the difficulty which may be incorrect. For instance, in example (d) the diagnosis may be made by inspection of the written work that the pupil forgot to carry. Clearly there are at least two other possibilities; he may have carried the 1 to the 6, and then made an error in giving the sum of 7 and 7. Similarly he may have made an error in giving the sum of 8 and 6.

$$(d) \quad \begin{array}{r} 78 \\ + 64 \\ \hline 132 \end{array}$$

**An illustration of analytical diagnosis.** An interesting illustration of the use of the method of analytical diagnosis is reported by Wilson.[1] Wilson had given the Woody–McCall Mixed Fundamental Arithmetic Test to the pupils in his schools. In scoring the papers he noticed that in the lower grades a group of the easier examples was consistently solved incorrectly because the pupils failed to note the process to

[1] Wilson, W. K. "The Woody–McCall Arithmetic Test as a Test in Reading"; in *Educational Research Bulletin*, vol. 3, no. 15, pp. 327–29. (November, 1924.) Ohio State University, Columbus, Ohio.

be used in the solution of the examples. Examples in addition were solved as examples in multiplication or subtraction, and *vice versa*. This was possible because the process to be used in the solution was in most cases printed directly above the example, thus:

| (5)<br>MULTIPLY | (6)<br>SUBTRACT | (7)<br>ADD |
|---|---|---|
| 23 | 13 | 17 |
| 3 | 8 | 2 |

In form these three examples are identical. The solution in each case depends on the use of the process indicated in each example. Wilson analyzed the kinds of errors made in 124 papers, in grades three through six, with the results given in Table 18.

TABLE 18. SHOWING FREQUENCY OF MISREADING DIRECTIONS IN THE WOODY–MCCALL MIXED FUNDAMENTALS TEST

(After Wilson)

| RESPONSE | GRADES | | | AVERAGE |
|---|---|---|---|---|
| | III and IV | V | VI | |
| Per cent misread.................... | 39 | 35 | 27 | 37 |
| Per cent of examples misread in which operation was done incorrectly....... | 73 | 95 | 100 | 85 |

The results show that in grades three and four 39 per cent of the "misreadable" problems were misread, and that in 73 per cent of all those misread the process used was worked correctly. Similar results were found for the other grades. This analysis of the pupil's written work showed that many of the incorrect answers were due to confusion caused by the form in which the test is set up, rather than to inability to use the process indicated.

**Analyzing the oral responses of the pupil.** In order to overcome the difficulty present in the method of diagnosis based on the analysis of the pupil's written responses, various investigators, especially in arithmetic, have required the pupils to give orally the steps in the solution of the example worked incorrectly. Some of the peculiar, round-about mental processes used by pupils in the solution of arithmetic examples are listed in detail in the chapter on arithmetic. These inefficient forms of response cannot be determined by a mere analysis of the written work. The teacher who is aware of the results of the investigations that have been made of the mental processes of pupils will not be satisfied to use test scores alone as a means of diagnosis, or to attempt to determine the cause of difficulty wholly by an analysis of the errors in the written work. The teacher with the deeper insight growing out of an appreciation of the information supplied by these more far-reaching and pene-trating methods of diagnosis will wish to make careful studies of the mental processes of at least those pupils whose work is not up to the standard for the grade.

The analysis of the oral reading of pupils is also a valuable basis of diagnosis. Inability of the pupil to pronounce the words in the reading exercises may be due to lack of ability in phonics or phonetics, or a failure to recognize the word. Jerky reading shows that the pupil is probably reading separate words, rather than phrases or groups of words. Omission of small words, insertion of words, substitution of words, and repetition of words are all symptoms of difficulties in reading, which in turn may be the cause of failure to make satisfactory progress in the subjects in which reading is involved.

The method of diagnosis based on an analysis of oral re-sponses and mental processes requires the examination of individual pupils. Various record blanks, containing lists of the most common faults of pupils, and indicating the types of supplementary uniform items to be secured by the examiner, have been devised to facilitate this kind of individual diagnosis. See pages 185 and 318 for illustrative blanks. These lists of faults help teachers to recognize the faults in the work of the pupils. In many schools such record blanks are filed for future reference. These blanks when properly used prevent oversight of the crucial factors in the examination, aid in the careful observation of individual cases, and provide a valuable source of information in the future study of similar cases. These detailed blanks are especially necessary in schools in which problem cases are referred to specialists for diagnosis, and the findings must be reported back to the teachers with recommendations.

**The method of testimony.** In the absence of more accurate scientific procedures, some investigators have attempted to secure various kinds of information from pupils regarding such factors as their general methods of study, their procedures in studying lists of words in spelling, their methods of memorizing material, and their methods of determining the processes to use in solving problems in arithmetic. Such information may be secured either by interviewing the pupils directly or through a questionnaire, or by asking them to write a composition in which the facts desired are presented for analysis by the investigator. An illustration of the use of the interview technique to secure testimony from the pupils as to their method of studying spelling is reported in the chapter on spelling in the discussion of Atkin's investigation.

The report of Hathaway and French [1] on the nature of study activities by pupils is an excellent example of the use of the written composition as a basis for diagnosis.

In this report are given the results of an analysis of compositions written by 465 children in grades three through to

[1] Hathaway, G. M., and French, H. H., "Study Activities of Children"; in *School of Education Journal*, vol. 3, no. 5, pp. 94–100. University of Pittsburgh.

eight, on the topic, "What I do when I study." The main findings for the reading activities that were reported by the pupils are given in Table 19.

TABLE 19. READING ACTIVITIES AS REVEALED BY A STUDY OF PUPILS' COMPOSITIONS

(Hathaway and French)

| ACTIVITIES RELATING TO READING | NUMBER OF MENTIONS BY GRADES * | | | | | | TOTAL |
|---|---|---|---|---|---|---|---|
| | 3 (19) | 4 (68) | 5 (115) | 6 (81) | 7 (106) | 8 (76) | (465) |
| 1. Reading (no specific activity named) | 16 | 7 | 32 | 10 | 30 | 38 | 133 |
| 2. Read to find subject of lesson | | 1 | | | 5 | 33 | 39 |
| 3. Read the lesson twice | | | 12 | 10 | 13 | | 35 |
| 4. Read with mouth closed | 2 | 7 | 7 | 6 | 5 | | 27 |
| 5. Re-read (number of times not stated) | | | | | | 26 | 26 |
| 6. Read questions | | | | | | 12 | 12 |
| 7. Read the lesson three times | | | | 2 | 8 | | 10 |
| 8. Read the lesson several times | | | | | 4 | | 4 |
| 9. Read fast | | | 1 | 2 | 1 | | 4 |
| 10. Learn to read | | 4 | | | | | 4 |
| 11. Read to understand problem | | | | | | 3 | 3 |
| 12. Read a book when I am through | | | | | 3 | | 3 |
| 13. Make sure of pronunciation | | | 2 | | 1 | | 3 |
| 14. Read with my lips | | | 3 | | | | 3 |
| 15. Read carefully | | | | | 1 | 1 | 2 |
| 16. Read to get interesting facts | | | 1 | | 1 | | 2 |
| 17. Read attentively | | 1 | 1 | | | | 2 |
| 18. Read to follow directions | | | | | 1 | | 1 |
| 19. Read the heading | | | | 1 | | | 1 |
| 20. Read slowly | | | | 1 | | | 1 |
| 21. Read without skipping words | | | 1 | | | | 1 |
| 22. "Sometimes I do not get anything out of it after all" | | | 1 | | | | 1 |
| Total | 18 | 19 | 62 | 32 | 73 | 115 | 319 |

* The number of pupils in each grade is placed in parenthesis below the number of the grade.

## Testimony by the checking method.

In the opinion of many authorities the data secured from groups of children by means of such methods is of doubtful reliability, since the children have had no training in introspective techniques and hence cannot analyze clearly the methods they use in studying their lessons. However, there is undoubtedly much of value in such attempts to study a pupil's methods of work. To increase the reliability of their report, several investigators have made efforts to aid pupils to describe their habits of work by checking the description of procedures.

listed in questionnaires, which most nearly described their own. Similar questionnaire methods have been used in studying the interests of pupils through association-tests, and other devices. Form 3 contains part of a blank of this kind, used by Eurich to study the work habits of senior high-school and college pupils.

FORM 3. STUDIOUSNESS RATING SCALE[1]

A number of activities are listed below which are involved in reading and study situations. You are to rate yourself on each one of these activities with respect to your habits of study. If you *never* follow the procedure which any item describes place an (X) in Column 1. If you have *very rarely* followed this procedure, place an (X) in Column 2 which is labeled "seldom." If you occasionally follow this procedure while reading or studying, place an (X) in Column 3. If you *usually* follow this procedure, place an (X) in Column 4. If the activity is a fixed habit so that you always follow it, place an (X) in Column 5.

|  | 1 NEVER | 2 SELDOM | 3 OCCASIONALLY | 4 USUALLY | 5 ALWAYS |
|---|---|---|---|---|---|
| 1. Looks up any new word in dictionary which is not clear in meaning. | | | | | |
| 2. Skims over printed material before reading it in detail. | | | | | |
| 3. Reviews the ideas and facts secured from the printed pages immediately after reading them. | | | | | |
| 4. Analyzes in detail the tables which appear as part of the content of the material read. | | | | | |
| 5. Grasps the meaning of a chart or table without difficulty. | | | | | |
| 6. Reads silently without moving the lips. | | | | | |
| 7. Comprehends the author's ideas in the first reading. | | | | | |
| 8. Searches for the most important points while reading. | | | | | |
| 9. Thinks about the materials while reading and constantly tries to relate new ideas and facts to previous experience. | | | | | |
| 10. Has a definite purpose for reading. | | | | | |
| 11. Seeks to weigh evidence carefully while reading. | | | | | |
| 12. Attempts to make use of ideas secured from reading. | | | | | |

[1] Eurich, A. E., *Journal of Applied Psychology.*

Information concerning phases of the past history of any case may be secured from teachers of earlier grades, or through interviews with parents, friends, and other acquaintances. These facts, if secured by trained social workers, may be of great value in studying the volitional, emotional, and social behavior of the individual under varying conditions.

**The use of more refined laboratory methods.** Where the facilities are available, much more refined techniques of studying the responses of individual pupils than those described in the preceding pages may be used. For example, the mechanical apparatus invented by Buswell and Judd may be used to study the reading eye-movements of pupils. Special types of tests, such as the Downey Will Temperament Test, may be given by competent clinical psychologists. The psychiatrist may be consulted in the cases of pupils with marked abnormal or undesirable personality traits or emotional disturbances. Glandular disorders can be diagnosed in the medical clinic. The trained social worker, through careful investigation, can secure information concerning social and environmental factors that may be of vital importance in making a complete diagnosis. The rapid development of psychological clinics, educational clinics, child-guidance clinics, and similar specialized units insures the availability for teachers of trained technical workers [1] to whom special problem cases may be referred. Where such facilities are not available, individual teachers have often taken it upon themselves to specialize in the diagnosis of difficulties in particular subjects. To these persons other teachers have referred cases which presented unusual pedagogical problems. The educational value of such a practice is undoubtedly large.

[1] A summary of the present status of this movement is given in Gertrude Hildreth's *Psychological Service for School Problems*. Yonkers-on-Hudson, New York, World Book Company, 1930.

## QUESTIONS FOR STUDY, DISCUSSION, AND REPORT

1. What is meant by "blunderbuss" diagnostic procedures? Give an example.
2. Differentiate between general and analytical diagnosis.
3. What is meant by the method of psychological diagnosis?
4. What is the place of educational measurement in diagnosis?
5. Why is it necessary to supplement the results of tests by more refined clinical methods?
6. Name some of the conditions that might be revealed by psychology, medical analysis, and social workers that would aid the teacher in making a diagnosis.
7. In what ways would a knowledge of the most common faults of pupils in the several subjects be of help to the teacher?
8. Make an attention profile of some problem case, preferably of a pupil who does not appear to have good study habits.
9. Make a list of faulty pupil habits that an observer might detect in an arithmetic classroom.
10. Describe briefly the techniques of psychological diagnosis described in this chapter. Name conditions under which each should be applied.
11. Describe cases which you feel present problems that should be referred to specialists for study.

## SELECTED REFERENCES

Brueckner, L. J. *Diagnostic and Remedial Teaching in Arithmetic*, chapters 2, 3, and 7. Philadelphia, John C. Winston Company, 1930.

Buswell, G. T., in coöperation with L. John. *Diagnostic Studies in Arithmetic*. Supplementary Educational Monograph, no. 30. Chicago, University of Chicago Press, 1926.

Gray, W. S. *Remedial Cases in Reading: Their Diagnosis and Treatment*. Supplementary Educational Monograph, no. 22. Chicago, University of Chicago Press, 1922.

Lyman, R. L. *Summary of Investigations Relating to Grammar, Language, and Composition*, chapters 3 and 4. Supplementary Educational Monograph, no. 36. Chicago, University of Chicago Press, 1929.

Monroe, W. S. *Measuring the Results of Teaching.* Boston, Houghton Mifflin Company, 1918.

*Twentieth Yearbook of the National Society for the Study of Education*, Part I, chapter 10. Report of the Society's Committee on Reading. Bloomington, Illinois, Public School Publishing Company, 1921.

*Twenty-Ninth Yearbook of the National Society for the Study of Education*, Part I, chapters 4 and 5. Bloomington, Illinois, Public School Publishing Company, 1930.

# CHAPTER VI

## THE NATURE AND USE OF OBJECTIVE TEST EXERCISES

### 1. *The need of new types of examinations*

**Why teachers should be familiar with these.** There are several important reasons *why* teachers should be familiar with the principles of construction and the value of the new type of objective examination. In the first place, because of the lack of standardized exercises and tests for measuring many of the specific skills involved in the teaching of such subjects as reading, arithmetic, and the social studies, teachers must prepare informal types of objective exercises similar in structure to the standard test to aid in the careful study of the extent to which pupils have mastered the skills involved.

The following reading test is an illustration of an exercise made by a teacher to test the ability of the pupils to comprehend the main ideas of a paragraph:

### INFORMAL SILENT READING TEST

Aim: To test the ability to comprehend the main ideas in a paragraph.

A. A shepherd had a faithful dog called Sultan who had grown very old and had lost all his teeth. One day when the shepherd and his wife were standing together before the house, the shepherd said, "I will shoot old Sultan tomorrow morning, for he is of no use now."

   1. Underline the word which best describes the old shepherd:
      kind — cruel — thoughtful — old.

   2. Underline the word which best describes the dog: angry —
      sly — faithful — mean.

B. Once upon a time there was a poor man who had an only son.

The child was born under a lucky star and it was prophesied that when he grew up he should marry the King's daughter.

1. Underline the words which tell where the child was born: in a house — under a tree — in a hut — under a lucky star.

2. Underline the word which tells whom the child should marry: King's daughter — miller's daughter — poor man's daughter — parson's daughter.

C. Walter made up his mind that he should like some kind of pet that he would be able to manage. At last when his birthday came, he went down to see Uncle Robert, who had always given him a birthday present. His Uncle had a goat for him.

1. Underline the word which tells what Walter wanted: sled — watch — pet — knife.

2. Underline the word which tells the name of the person who always gave Walter a present: grandfather — Uncle Robert — sister — brother.

D. Matti had cheeks as red and round as an apple, clear blue eyes, and hair as yellow as gold — the only gold to be found in the cabin. It was Matti's face that often filled the cabin window when anything passed on the road.

1. Underline the words which tell the color of Matti's hair; black — red — yellow — brown.

2. Underline the words which tell what kind of a house Matti lived in: cabin — palace — hut — castle.

E. A hunter went out hunting every day, but each night he came home empty handed. Each night the wife looked at the empty bag with a frown and said, "Have you forgotten that you are a hunter and that you must bring home some game to show for your day's work?"

1. Which of these words describe the hunter's wife when he came home empty handed? lazy — scolding — kind — happy.

2. Which of these words tell what kind of a hunter he was? good — clever — poor — cruel.

Similar objective test exercises may be devised by the teacher to test many of the other specific abilities in reading.

Such exercises may also be used for practice lessons on specific abilities. Their need and their place in the reading program will be discussed in detail in the chapter on reading.

In many of the newer textbooks in such subjects as arithmetic, history, reading, and language, exercises of the objective type are included. Sometimes such informal test exercises are given in manuals or workbooks which supplement the textbooks. To make the most effective use of these exercises, teachers should understand how they are constructed and what their functions are.

**New-type test *vs.* traditional examination.** The new type of objective examination should replace the traditional type of essay examination, which has serious limitations. The marking of the essay type is wholly subjective, the subjectivity varying with the nature of the subject. For example, with the guidance of a few simple rules teachers should be expected to assign approximately the same mark to an examination in spelling except for accidental errors, while there is greater likelihood of wide variations in marking history papers because of the many factors that are involved. The items in the traditional examination are not equal in difficulty, and they have not been weighted in value. Because of the way in which the tests are constructed they usually contain an inadequate sampling of the subject-matter that has been covered, and hence do not offer the pupil an adequate opportunity to demonstrate his ability.

The traditional essay type of examination also neglects rate of work. Because of difficulty in expressing their ideas in writing, many pupils are seriously handicapped in tests of the essay type. After any test paper of this type has been marked, the teacher must evaluate the rating. This implies the existence of subjective norms in the mind of the teacher. The inadequacy of such norms has been repeatedly demonstrated. For instance, Hudelson [1] has shown that teachers' norms for the various grades for English composition are in many cases much too high, and as a whole are unreliable. To demonstrate this point, he asked teachers of English to indicate the school grade for which a certain composition would be accepted by them as satisfactory. The results, for two themes, appear in Table 20.

TABLE 20. JUDGMENTS OF TEACHERS AS TO GRADE PLACEMENT ON THE BASIS OF ONE THEME *

| SCHOOL YEAR | THEME 1 | | THEME 2 | |
|---|---|---|---|---|
| | Number of Judges | Percentage of Judgments | Number of Judges | Percentage of Judgments |
| XIV......... | | | 1 | 0.52 |
| XIII........ | | | 2 | 1.04 |
| XII......... | 4 | 2.07 | 9 | 4.69 |
| XI.......... | 17 | 8.81 | 4 | 2.08 |
| X........... | 57 | 29.53 | 21 | 10.94 |
| IX.......... | 49 | 25.39 | 55 | 28.65 |
| VIII........ | 39 | 20.21 | 53 | 27.60 |
| VII......... | 26 | 13.47 | 30 | 15.63 |
| VI.......... | 1 | 0.52 | 12 | 6.25 |
| V........... | | | 5 | 2.60 |

* From his monograph. Rearranged, from author's data, by Lyman.

Theme 1 was rated by one judge as satisfactory for grade VI; twenty-six judges rated the same theme as satisfactory for grade VII; four of the judges would not have accepted the theme as satisfactory below the twelfth school grade. Similar results for theme 2 demonstrate clearly the inadequacy of the grade standards of teachers of composition.

## 2. Characteristics of the objective exercise

**Type of response required.** In the new type of objective exercise, the form of the question and the required response

[1] Hudelson, Earl. "Diversity of Judgment upon Standards of Content and Achievement in English"; in *Teachers College Record*, vol. 27, pp. 33–51. (September, 1925.)

are the distinguishing characteristics which differentiate it from the old type of essay examination. Instead of requiring an answer of a paragraph or more in which the student gives the information called for by the question, in the new type of test short answer questions are asked which can be answered by the pupil by writing a word, by underlining one of a group of words, by checking one of a given group of answers, or by some other short-cut method which reduces the amount of writing to a minimum.

The new type of examination is generally composed of a much larger number of items than are found in the essay type of examination. Instead of the five to fifteen questions usually given in the essay type, the new type of examination may have as many as three hundred items for a two-hour examination, the usual number of items in a one-hour examination averaging between fifty and one hundred.

The new type of examination is essentially a test of the knowledge that is acquired, the assumption being that correct answers to specific fact questions are symptomatic of organized knowledge in the field covered. An analysis of the errors made in marking the items of the test paper will often reveal to the teacher the places at which instruction has been inadequate.

The simplicity of the scoring of most types of objective exercises is another important feature. In carefully constructed tests the scoring is wholly objective, since the correct answer to each item is known, and the personal judgment of the rater as to the value of the answer does not enter into the marking of the paper. Increased accuracy of scoring insures greater reliability of marks based on objective examinations.

The efficiency of teaching can be greatly improved by means of the new type of objective examination. Short objective exercises enable the teacher to check up quickly on the extent to which the pupils as a whole have retained the work of previous lessons. By means of a preliminary objective exercise the teacher can discover what the pupils already know about a given subject. Such diagnostic exercises can be prepared to help the teacher to locate specific weaknesses in the work of the pupils; and the points at which reteaching may be necessary. In many schools a wide variety of objective test and practice exercises, similar to the standard practice materials in various subjects, have been assembled.

### 3. *Varieties of new-type or objective exercises*

**Two main types.** The new types of objective exercise may be divided into two general classes: (*a*) the *recall* type, and (*b*) the *recognition* type. By the recall type are meant all exercises in which the pupil supplies the answer; the recognition type includes all forms of response in which two or more answers to an item are given and the pupil is required to indicate the correct answer by choosing from among the given alternatives. There are many variations in the forms in which these two types of objective exercises may be cast. Since it is beyond the scope of this discussion to consider all of these variations, only a few of the more widely used forms will be described and evaluated.

**Recall types.** Two widely used forms of objective exercises of the recall type are: (1) Recall exercises or questions with single correct answers, usually of one word; and (2) completion exercises.

Suppose that we wish to test a pupil's knowledge of arithmetic vocabulary. The usual form of question used to find out if the pupil knows the meaning of "sum" would be to ask the question, "What is the meaning of 'sum'?" The answer would be stated as a sentence. In the new type of exercise the question would be stated, "What is the answer of an addition example called?" When stated in this form, the only correct answer is the single word, sum. The question may be stated in a different form as a completion exercise. "The answer of an addition example is called the ......" Here the pupil must supply the answer by inserting the missing word.

### ILLUSTRATIONS OF RECALL TYPES OF EXERCISES IN OTHER SUBJECTS

*Reading.* The story of Heidi begins on page ..

*History.* Who was President of the United States during the Civil War?

*Geography.* The ...... River drains the middle portion of the United States.

*Arithmetic.* Give the name for each part of the example at the right.

$$3\overline{\smash{)}76}^{\,25-1}$$

*Grammar.* What part of speech is the word *he*?......

The chief difficulty in devising recall tests is due to the fact that in some subjects it is difficult to frame questions which call for only a single possible answer. To overcome this the answers in recall exercises may be controlled or suggested by various devices. Consider the following items:

1. The answer of a multiplication example is called the p......
2. The battle of ......(7) ended the Revolutionary War.
3. The largest city in Minnesota is ...........

In exercise 1 the letter p is the first letter of the missing item. In exercise 2 the number (7) indicates the number of letters in the word that is the correct answer. In exercise 3 each of the dots stands for a letter.

The following exercise illustrates another method of controlling the response or recall types:

Complete the following statements by inserting in each blank space the number of the correct word written in the list at the left of the page. Do not write any number more than once.

| | |
|---|---|
| 1. Civil War | 1. The battle of Manila Bay was fought in the . . |
| 2. Spanish-American War | 2. The battle of Saratoga was fought in the . . |
| 3. Revolutionary War | 3. The battle of Gettysburg was fought in the . . |

**Advantages and disadvantages of recall exercises.** The advantages of the simple recall type of exercise are that guessing or chance scores are almost negligible, the scoring is almost entirely objective, and is easily and rapidly done, and the responses are quite similar to those called for on the fact questions to which the pupils are accustomed. The chief criticisms that have been made of these exercises are that they test factual content only, and that the scoring is somewhat more laborious than in the case of the recognition types. If the exercises of the completion type are not carefully constructed several answers to a question may be possible, and this tends to introduce the factor of subjectivity in scoring.

**Recognition types.** The most commonly used types of recognition exercises are as follows: (1) true-false exercises; (2) matching exercises; (3) multiple choice given alternative answers; (4) association exercises.

**(1) True-false exercises.** True-false exercises consist either of separate sentences which are either true or false, or of questions that are answered by Yes or No. Items in which there is a choice between two given answers are really true-false exercises. The correct answer in true-false exercises may be indicated by checking or underlining the correct word, by using the symbol + for true and − for false, or by writing the word, true or false, or Yes or No, as illustrated in the following exercises:

I. Georgia is in the western part of the United States.  False

II. Georgia is in the western part of the United States.  T  F

III. All apples are red    —

IV. Is Georgia in the western part of the United States?  No

V. Is Georgia in the Western part of the United States?  Yes No

VI. Underline the correct items in the following:

This boy $\dfrac{\text{don't}}{\text{doesn't}}$ know where his cap is.

Mary $\dfrac{\text{may}}{\text{can}}$ go with you.

The advantages claimed for the true-false tests are that they are purely objective, are easily and rapidly scored, and can be applied in almost any field of subject-matter.  Furthermore, the rapidity with which pupils can answer makes it possible for the teacher to use an extensive sampling of items for a test exercise.  True-false questions can be made to measure reasoning ability as well as the retention of factual information.

**Limitations for the true-false test.**  One of the chief limitations of tests composed of true-false questions is that guessing by the examinee is too large a factor in the marking of answers, since the pupil has a "50–50" chance of guessing the correct answer.  To overcome this objection various writers recommend the use of a large number of true-false statements, the minimum number suggested varying from 75 to 100.  In a study of true-false statements in each examination, Wood[1] found that 100 items did not yield sufficiently reliable results, and hence recommended the use of two hundred questions as a minimum for such examinations.

To counteract the effects of guessing in true-false, yes-no,

[1] Wood, B. D. "Studies of Achievement Tests"; in *Journal of Educational Psychology*, vol. 17, pp. 1–22, 125–129, 263–269.  (1926.)

and other forms of tests having but two alternative answers, a method of scoring commonly known as the "right minus wrong" is sometimes used. If in a test of 50 items the pupil has 25 "right" and 25 "wrong" his score is 25 − 25, or 0. The score of 0 in such a case may be assumed to be a correct measure or index of the pupil's knowledge, since on the basis of pure chance the pupil would guess the correct answers of half of the items and the incorrect answers of the other half. His actual knowledge of the test items on the basis of 25 "right" and 25 "wrong" is therefore correctly expressed by 0.

Another limitation of the true-false exercise is the difficulty of constructing questions of this kind which are not ambiguous or partly true and partly false. This objection applies particularly in such fields as history and civics, in which there are controversial questions to which the answers are neither absolutely true nor false.

(2) **Matching exercises.** Matching exercises consist of two parallel sets of facts that are related in some way. In one column one set of facts is numbered or lettered in succession; in the other column the related facts are in random order and are not numbered. The pupils are required to match or pair the two sets of items by writing before or after the unnumbered item the number of the related item. The following exercise is an illustration:

Match the dates in column II with the events in column I.

| Column I | Column II | |
| --- | --- | --- |
| 1. Discovery of America | 3 | 1776 |
| 2. Settling of Jamestown | 4 | 1781 |
| 3. Signing of the Declaration of Independence | 1 | 1492 |
| 4. Capture of Yorktown | 5 | 1861 |
| 5. Beginning of the Civil War | 2 | 1607 |

Matching tests are purely objective, easily constructed, and rapidly scorable. While there is a slight element of chance success in matching related items in short matching exercises, of three or four pairs, Ruch [1] points out that this may be avoided by using ten or more pairs in an exercise. On the other hand, there is the danger in tests consisting of long matching exercises of twenty or more pairs that the pupils may spend an inordinate amount of time in searching out the pairs of related items. This may be avoided by dividing pairs of related items into groups of ten or fifteen.

(3) **Multiple-choice exercises.** This type of exercises consists of statements with several alternative answers — usually from three to five — only one of which is correct. The pupil is to choose the correct answer. For example, "*Evangeline* was written by Whittier, Longfellow, Tennyson, Guest." If the pupil underlines the word Longfellow, the assumption is that he in fact knows who wrote *Evangeline*. If he does not know, it is assumed that the pupil will consider the other answers to be equally or more likely correct and will therefore underline the incorrect answer. There is thus a one to four chance of guessing correctly. Paterson [2] suggests that to overcome the likelihood of guessing correctly, the examiner should include in the alternative answers those "which seem plausible and yet are unequivocally wrong." For example:

The author of *Lady of the Lake* was
Scott   Irving   Shakespeare   Tennyson

In multiple-choice exercises the pupil can indicate the correct answer by underlining it, by checking it, or by placing the number of the correct answer in parentheses at the right-hand margin of the paper. The last procedure is

[1] Ruch, G. M. *The Objective or New-Type Examination*, p. 276. Chicago, Scott, Foresman and Company, 1929.

[2] Paterson, D. G. *Preparation and Use of New Type of Examinations*, p. 22. Yonkers, World Book Company, 1925.

probably on the whole the most satisfactory, since the listing of answers in a single column simplifies the scoring with a key. Otis, in his General Intelligence Examination, uses the device of having the pupil both underline the correct answer and indicate the number of the correct answer. This plan makes it possible to check the scoring when the written numbers in the margin are illegible.

The following are illustrations of various kinds of multiple-choice exercises.

I. Normal temperature of the human body is
68°   92.4°   <u>98.6°</u>   104°

II. Fulton invented the
(1) cotton gin   (2) the steam engine   (3) the steamboat   <u>3</u>
(4) the radio

III. The answer in a division example is called
(a) the quotient   (b) the divisor   (c) the remainder   <u>a</u>
(d) the sum

In some multiple-choice exercises there is a plural choice of answers.

I. Underline the names of famous generals in the following:
<u>Grant</u>, Edison, <u>Lee</u>, <u>Jackson</u>, <u>Greene</u>, Seward.

II. Check the sentences below that best describe Chicago
———— 1. Chicago is a mining center.
—X— 2. Chicago is noted for its stockyards.
—X— 3. Chicago is a railroad center.
—X— 4. Chicago is a rapidly growing city.

III. Check the two best answers.
The early settlements in Oregon were made by
...... fur traders
...... farmers
...... soldiers
...... missionaries.

**Advantages and disadvantages of multiple-choice exercises.** The chief advantages of the multiple-choice type of exercise are that they are easy to construct and to score, are purely objective, and are more reliable than true-false tests. The objection to the element of guessing and chance methods in choosing answers can be to a large extent overcome by increasing the number of statements in the test. In selecting the alternative responses care must be taken to select various possible answers of reasonable plausibility. Otherwise the choice may be so obvious that neither the pupil's specific knowledge of the subject nor his ability to reason with the facts is tested — rather his common-sense and good judgment.

(4) **Association exercises.** Association tests of various kinds have been invented. The following illustrate the most common types:

OPPOSITES EXERCISES

I. White — black                        Same — opposite
   Boy — girl                           Same — opposite
   Short — brief                        Same — opposite

II. Analogies.
   *a.* Boy is to girl as man is to
       (1) youth   (2) woman   (3) large   (4) jump      2

   *b.* Automobile is to motorcycle as carriage is to
       (1) horse   (2) bicycle   (3) train   (4) buggy      2

   *c.* Circle is to square as sphere is to (1) curve
       (2) pyramid   (3) circumference   (4) triangle      1

Questions of the analogy form are particularly useful in the upper grades. They enable the teacher to test a pupil's knowledge of relationship existing between the facts, principles, and concepts in the several courses. The ability to think in terms of the relationships between the various aspects of the courses depends to a large extent on a thorough mastery of the subject-matter, and the ability of the pupil to perceive similarities and differences in various phases of the course. Analogies tests therefore are a valuable means of testing the ability of the pupil to think in terms of the subject. The chief drawback to the analogy form of questions is the difficulty of preparing them.

### 4. *The criteria of a good informal test*

The criteria by which to judge the merits of an objective examination prepared by the teacher are the same as those that were given for evaluating standard tests. The items selected for the test should be worth while, and they should be based on a careful analysis of the objectives of the course. To insure a valid content the teacher should make use of the information resulting from the pertinent scientific investigations in the field under consideration, and in related fields. To aid teachers in the preparation of worth-while examinations an adequate course of study containing a summary of such studies should be available. To insure reliability of the test, the test items should be carefully constructed, the scoring should be objective, the sampling should be adequate, and the directions to the pupils should be definite and clear. If a record is kept of test scores and the same test is given to classes in subsequent years, it is possible to develop fairly satisfactory norms on the basis of these cumulative results.

## QUESTIONS FOR STUDY, DISCUSSION, AND REPORT

1. Show how informal tests of the new objective type have improved instructional practices.
2. Examine textbooks in reading, arithmetic, geography, etc., to determine the extent to which exercises of the objective type are included in them, and what their apparent function is.
3. Criticize an objective test that you have prepared, or that has been used by some other person.

4. Collect specimens of objective tests, and appraise them.

5. List specific uses that could be made of objective test exercises by the classroom teacher.

6. How can a teacher determine the marks to give a pupil on the basis of the results of an informal objective test?

7. Why is an objective test of the completion type often difficult to score?

8. Short true-false tests are very unreliable. Why?

9. Suggest a plan by which the teachers of a building might assemble a large number and variety of objective test exercises, and secure norms by which to measure pupil achievement.

## SELECTED REFERENCES

Many books on objective examinations are being published at the present time. Most of them contain large numbers of illustrative types of exercises in the various subjects. The following references will be found especially helpful and suggestive for teachers who wish to make a more intensive study of the new type of examination:

Lang, A. R. *Modern Methods in Written Examinations.* Boston, Houghton Mifflin Company, 1930.

Monroe, W. S., DeVoss, J. C., and Kelly, F. J. *Educational Tests and Measurements* (revised edition). Boston, Houghton Mifflin Company, 1924.

Odell, C. *Traditional Examinations and New-Type Tests.* New York, Century Company, 1928.

Orleans, J. S., and Sealy, G. A. *Objective Tests.* Yonkers-on-Hudson, World Book Company, 1928.

Paterson, D. G. *The Preparation and Use of New Type Examinations.* Yonkers-on-Hudson, World Book Company, 1925.

Ruch, G. M. *The Objective or New Type Examination.* Chicago, Scott, Foresman and Company, 1929.

Ruch, G. M., *et al.* *Objective Examination Methods in the Social Studies.* Chicago, Scott, Foresman and Company, 1926.

Ruch, G. M., and Rice, G. A. *Specimen Objective Examinations.* Chicago, Scott, Foresman and Company, 1929.

Russell, Chas. *Class Room Tests.* Boston, Ginn and Company. 1926.

# CHAPTER VII

## DIAGNOSTIC AND REMEDIAL TEACHING IN ARITHMETIC

### I. OBJECTIVES AND LEVELS IN INSTRUCTION

**The objectives of arithmetic instruction.** Efficiency of instruction in arithmetic may be measured by the ability of pupils: (1) to think intelligently regarding quantitative aspects of the environment; (2) to apply number and to appreciate its significance and functions in the activities of daily life; and (3) to perform the necessary computations with facility and accuracy. From these points of view instruction in arithmetic has much broader objectives than those that determine the nature of the work in that subject in many schools, in which the major portion of time is devoted to mere practice or drill in computation and little attention is given to the informational and sociological functions of arithmetic.

Number may be thought of as a mode of thinking. In his reading the individual constantly is confronted by quantitative terms and relationships of various kinds which he must understand to be able to read intelligently. Instruction in arithmetic must make certain that the necessary vocabulary and quantitative concepts are learned. As a result of his work in arithmetic, and its application in all subjects of the curriculum, the pupil should acquire an appreciation of the value of precise and accurate information. He should learn to appreciate the value of number as a method of thinking by means of which man has brought order, arrangement, and precision to quantitative aspects of the environment. He should learn to read simple graphs, charts, tables, diagrams, and other types of materials in which quantitative data are arranged in a systematic, orderly manner.

**Use in the activities of daily life.**  The ability of the pupil to apply number in various ways in the activities of daily life, rather than his ability to solve verbal textbook problems, is another valid measure of the efficiency of instruction.  Verbal problems may give him practice in recognizing situations in which processes are used; however, the teacher must not have too much faith that these skills will transfer directly to life situations.  For example, the pupils in a sixth-grade class were able to solve readily verbal problems involving the finding of the area of a surface, but were not able to perform the simple tasks involved in finding the area of the floor and walls of their classroom; they knew the process to use to find areas in verbal problems, but they did not know how to apply the formula in a particular concrete situation.  Hence the importance of projects, excursions, and similar activities in which the pupil may apply number functionally.

The development of the ability of the pupil to compute in the several processes in whole numbers, fractions, decimals, and per cent has always been one of the major objectives in arithmetic.  The present tendency is clearly in the direction of a reduction of the stress placed on mere computation, and toward an increased emphasis on the informational and sociological functions of arithmetic.

**Specific abilities involved.**  Ability in arithmetic should be thought of in a broad sense.  Bobbitt [1] suggests that, among others, such matters as the following are involved in a specific ability, such as the ability to compute:

1. *Interest* in the thing involved.
2. Right *valuation* of the thing involved.

[1] Bobbitt, F.  *Curriculum-Making in Los Angeles*, pp. 34–36.

3. *Desire for the practical results* that come from exercise of the ability.
4. *Delight* in the experiences involved.
5. An effective *desire* to avoid error.
6. *Disposition to be active* in all matters that involve action.
7. *Confidence* in one's ability to achieve the desired results.
8. *Ability to coöperate fully* with one's associates.

The teacher of arithmetic should, therefore, strive to develop power to use number, bearing in mind the general elements that constitute an ability. The outcomes of arithmetic instruction other than ability to compute are certain desirable attitudes, ideals, appreciations, powers, and social qualities, as well as the ability to think in quantitative terms in situations where this is essential.

**The levels of instruction.** Various levels of instruction in arithmetic may be differentiated, ranging from teaching which has a very narrow vision of the possibilities and functions of the subject to teaching which is enriched, socialized, vitalized, and significant. The following statements include descriptions of seven levels in the teaching of arithmetic, in which the methods of achieving the functions of the subject are briefly described, and the place of diagnostic and remedial teaching is made clear: [1]

LEVELS IN THE TEACHING OF ARITHMETIC — GRADES 3 to 6

*Level* 1. The teacher emphasizes the skills involved in computation in the fundamental operations and their application in isolated problems found in the textbook. The objectives of the teaching are to develop the ability of the pupil to perform the computations with speed and accuracy. The teacher has an inadequate conception of the variety of skills involved in each operation and frequently omits important skills and steps in the learning process. There are no adequate standards of achievement. The only tests of achievement used are those prepared by the teacher, none being included in the textbook that is used. The content of the material

[1] Brueckner, Leo J. "A Chart for the Analysis of the Teaching of Arithmetic"; in *Educational Method*, vol. 9, pp. 130–37. (December, 1929.)

used in the arithmetic period is mostly limited to that given in a formal textbook. The text makes a minimum use of pupil interests and stresses the formal application of the processes in verbal problems largely on the adult level. The class is dealt with as a unit, no attempt being made to adapt instruction to the individual differences existing among the pupils. No attempt is made to diagnose pupil difficulties. Sometimes the teacher supplements the drill material in the textbook with cards containing sets of examples prepared by the teacher. No use is made of graphs, games, or other devices to create interest in the work. There is no discussion of the social applications of the processes other than the material in the textbook. No attempt is made to consider the application of arithmetic in the other subjects of the curriculum. Work in arithmetic is limited strictly to the time assigned to that subject on the daily schedule of classes. Tables of measures are memorized, but no concrete work in their application is undertaken.

*Level 2.* At this level the major objectives of the work in arithmetic are to develop in the pupils the ability to perform the operations in arithmetic with speed and accuracy and to develop an interest in the subject by various devices. The teacher has a good grasp of the basic skills in the various operations and of the steps in the learning process, and presents them logically and clearly. The text used by the class contains many problems on the level of the pupil's interests and within their range of experiences. Most of the problems are in isolated sets, one problem being unrelated to another. The class is taught as a unit, no definite provision being made for individual differences. Pupils having serious difficulty are given special help. The teacher often supplements the drill material given in the text with well organized exercises on difficult points. Games, charts, graphs, and other devices are used to stimulate interest in the drill work. The pupils are required to give original problems showing the application of the processes that are being learned. As the occasion arises the teacher points out instances of the application of arithmetic in the other subjects of the curriculum. However, no specific provision is made to show the application of what is learned in social situations. Tables of measure are memorized but little is done to make their use concrete and meaningful. Standard tests in the fundamental processes are rarely given to determine the level of pupil achievement.

*Level 3.* The activities at this level are in general similar to those of the second level, the objectives of the work being to develop speed and accuracy in the fundamental operations, and in interest in arithmetic. The presentation of new processes is logical and adequate. The practice exercises needed to establish new skills are satisfactory. The review work on processes previously taught is individualized by the use of such standard practice exercises as those of Studebaker, Courtis, Brueckner, and others. However, these exercises are used mechanically, the teacher not recognizing the fact that they must often be supplemented by diagnostic work with pupils who are not making satisfactory progress. The applications of the processes are largely limited to the problems given in the textbook, although as occasion arises the teacher may suggest other applications without giving any exercises dealing with them. The work in denominate numbers is made concrete by means of class exercises involving their application, such as measuring the height or weight of pupils, the area of the floor of the classroom, and similar exercises. Games, charts, graphs, and records of progress on the practice tests are used to stimulate and maintain interest in the subject.

*Level* 4. The objectives of the work in arithmetic are somewhat broader than those of level 3, since the teacher recognizes that in addition to the ability to perform computations speedily and accurately the activities of the class period can result in the development of desirable social qualities, such as initiative, self-control, self-appraisal, self-direction, and ability to work effectively as a member of the group. To this end the work in the practice periods is so organized that the pupils are led to attack purposefully the problem of improving their ability to compute. Pupil leaders are taught to direct the activities of the class during the practice period. Pupils are taught to locate their difficulties, to appraise their work by comparison of their achievements with standards, to correct their own papers, to record their results, and to construct individual graphs of progress. The review work in processes is individualized by use of the standard practice exercises in arithmetic used in level 3. The teacher pays special attention to the diagnosis of pupil difficulties and organizes the class work in such a way that a major portion of the teacher's time is given to diagnostic and remedial work. In the development of new processes the presentation is logical and complete. Pupils who need more help than it was possible to give during the class presentation are grouped for special work on their weaknesses. Often they are assigned to superior pupils for assistance. At this level the teacher still stresses the computational aspects of arithmetic. The problem work is limited to the solution of verbal problems contained in the textbook in which the operations are applied. Considerable attention is given to the development of ability to solve these verbal problems. Special exercises on problem solving are used to give the pupils a systematic method of attack in solving a problem. Diagnosis of pupil difficulties in problem solving is used to determine the needs of individuals. The applications of arithmetic in social situations are not stressed except as they are given in the textbook. No attempt is made in any way to relate the work in the arithmetic class to the work in the other subjects, although the teacher takes the occasion to suggest the applications that may arise incidentally. No use is made of reference materials, local situations, or pupil experiences to enrich the applications of the processes that are taught. No attempt is made to provide opportunities for pupils to explore aspects of arithmetic in which they have particular interest, such as the historical development of measurement, banking practices, etc.

*Level 5.* The distinguishing characteristic of the fourth level is the excellent type of work done in the processes and the attempt to develop desirable social qualities in pupils, relatively little stress being placed on the possibilities of enriching the work by making clear to pupils the social applications of the processes that are taught. At level 5 the drill phases of the subject are taught in the same way as in level 4. The review work is individualized and new processes are carefully presented. Diagnostic and remedial work are also stressed in both problem solving and in processes. Stress is given to the development of desirable social qualities. At this level special consideration is given to the enrichment of the work in arithmetic through a consideration of the applications of the processes in social situations. The teacher uses the school bank, playstores, the purchase of school supplies, and similar natural situations in the life of the school to show the applications of arithmetic. Verbal problems of the traditional type are used much less than at the other levels, since the teacher believes that pupils will learn to apply arithmetic processes in life situations by practice in applying them in life situations. Pupils are encouraged to suggest local applications of arithmetic. Special assignments such as the preparation of reports or the collection of illustrative data and materials are frequently made. At this level the teacher is still consciously emphasizing the development of speed and accuracy in computation and does not fully appreciate the real social significance of arithmetic. Whatever does not contribute directly to the development of ability in computation is rejected. The processes that are being taught rather than the situations in which they are used are the basis of the classwork. The informational function of arithmetic is therefore not stressed, nor is number thought of as an invention by man by means of which he has brought order, arrangement, and precision into the quantitative aspects of the environment.

*Level 6.* At level 6 the drill aspects of arithmetic are given a subordinate position, although the work in this phase of the subject is carefully provided for by means of well standardized, individualized practice exercises and systematic diagnostic and remedial work.

The main stress is placed on the function and uses of number, that is, the consideration of the quantitative aspects of life and the methods which man has devised to bring "order, arrangement, and precision" to the environment. The teaching of arithmetic is organized on the basis of large units of study, prepared in detail by the teacher, or prescribed by the course of study. The purpose of the teacher is to systematize the content of the material that is related to the topic being studied and to develop the associated skills, habits, attitudes and appreciations in their natural setting. The tendency is clearly to break down the compartmentalized subject organization and to show the applications of a particular phase of number in important social situations. Under the teacher's direction a large variety of activities is carried on, much as is now done in the social studies, since arithmetic when taught as it is on this level is a social study of great importance. Excursions are planned; reports are made; situations are dramatized; related material in reference books is assigned and read; the significance and development of such concepts as the measurement of quantity, distance, time, value, area, weight, and volume are considered. The work is all done under the immediate direction of the teacher. While a definite attempt is made to socialize the work, the socialization is often not real since it is too much in the hands of the teacher and the pupils have almost no part in the selection and planning of the activities.

It is obvious that at this level the concept that the arithmetic period should be used to develop skill in computation and in solving verbal textbook problems breaks down. Under the teacher's direction the pupils consider number as a method of thinking which has been one of the chief factors in the rapid social progress of the past few centuries. They see how number has helped men to systematize quantitative aspects of the environment which otherwise would be chaotic and unorganized. Problem work at this level consists largely in the selection and performance of the computations that would be needed in a particular situation in which the pupil would need to locate and select the essential data himself instead of having it presented to him in an organized manner as is now done in verbal problems.

*Level* 7. At level 7 provision is made for active pupil participation in the selection of the content of the work in arithmetic and in the organization of the subject-matter to be covered. The major units of the work are prescribed by the curriculum on the basis of careful experimental work to determine the most valuable topics or activities from the point of view of society suited to each grade and through a consideration of which the pupils will grow in socially desirable ways. The order in which the topics are taken up is left to the teacher who guides the activities according to the interests and abilities of the class. Other topics of marked social value which may arise in the course of the daily work may also be made the basis of the class activities.

Pupils and teacher together coöperate in determining the character of the activities to be engaged in by the class. The teacher uses the veto power very rarely and seeks to guide the work toward socially valuable objectives. The teacher believes that this method of organizing the material will result in the systematic consideration of problems, topics, and subject-matter that will be within the experience and interests of the pupils. The method of teaching is based on the belief that pupils should learn in natural situations such as they encounter in life itself and should have an active part in the planning and execution of such activities to the end that they may develop those social qualities which are needed in a democracy. Special provision is made for group work under pupil leaders on phases of a subject which are of particular interest to individuals. Much use is made of excursions, projects, construction work and similar activities selected by the pupils under the guidance of the teacher. Little attention is paid to time allotment or subject organization since the work on any topic usually involves the application of the other subjects in many important and significant ways.

Ideally, new processes are taught to pupils as their need arises in carrying out the activities involved in the topic under consideration, rather than according to a systematic plan set up in advance as is done in level 6.   Pupils strive wholeheartedly to acquire skills and to learn new processes because they are needed in the class activities.

From a practical point of view it may often be necessary for the review of processes previously taught and the development of the new processes to be carried on independently of the work in applied arithmetic, using the individualized exercises described in level 6.   However, it is clearly desirable that the drill on processes should not be completely isolated as might be necessary under such a plan but should be made to function in the activities in which the pupils are engaged.

At this level the teacher stresses the informational function of arithmetic and the significance of the uses of the number system as a method of dealing with the quantitative aspects of the environment.   The materials used in the class are chosen primarily because of what they contribute to these objectives, not because of the computations involved.   Arithmetic is considered to be a social subject of major importance rather than a "tool" subject.

## II.  STANDARD TESTS IN ARITHMETIC

The standardized educational tests in arithmetic that are available at the present time are limited to the measurement of skill and power in computation and in solving verbal problems.   Practically nothing has been done to develop methods of measuring ability to understand the uses of number in reading materials involving quantitative generalizations or concepts, in interpreting graphic information, or in applying number in concrete situations such as are found in the activities of daily life.

### 1.  *Survey tests*

Survey tests may be considered under four main headings: (1) rate tests, (2) scales, (3) general survey tests, and (4) curriculum tests.   We shall consider each of these types of survey tests, in the above order.

(1) **Rate tests.** Rate of work is an important component of ability in arithmetic. Rate may be interpreted either as the number of exercises attempted, or as the number of examples correct. The number of exercises attempted gives a measure of the speed of work; the number of examples correct gives the speed of correct work. The Courtis Standard Research Tests in Arithmetic — Series B, which consist of four tests, one for each of the four fundamental processes, contain examples of only one type in each test. (See pages 169 and 170.) There are standards for both rate and accuracy. The grade norms for these tests are given in Table 21.

TABLE 21. GRADE NORMS IN COURTIS STANDARD RESEARCH
TESTS — SERIES B

| GRADE | ADDITION | | SUBTRACTION | | MULTIPLICATION | | DIVISION | |
|---|---|---|---|---|---|---|---|---|
| | Rate | Accuracy | Rate | Accuracy | Rate | Accuracy | Rate | Accuracy |
| 4 | 7.4 | 64 | 7.4 | 80 | 6.2 | 67 | 4.6 | 57 |
| 5 | 8.6 | 70 | 9.0 | 83 | 7.5 | 75 | 6.1 | 77 |
| 6 | 9.8 | 73 | 10.3 | 85 | 9.1 | 78 | 8.2 | 87 |
| 7 | 10.9 | 75 | 11.6 | 86 | 10.2 | 80 | 9.6 | 90 |
| 8 | 11.6 | 76 | 12.9 | 87 | 11.5 | 81 | 10.7 | 91 |

TYPE EXAMPLES IN COURTIS STANDARD RESEARCH TESTS —
SERIES B

*Addition*

| 127 | 996 | 237 | 386 | 186 | 474 | 877 | 537 |
| 375 | 320 | 949 | 463 | 775 | 787 | 845 | 685 |
| 953 | 778 | 486 | 827 | 684 | 591 | 981 | 452 |
| 333 | 886 | 987 | 240 | 260 | 106 | 693 | 904 |
| 325 | 913 | 354 | 616 | 372 | 869 | 184 | 511 |
| 911 | 164 | 600 | 261 | 846 | 451 | 772 | 988 |
| 554 | 897 | 744 | 755 | 595 | 336 | 749 | 559 |
| 167 | 972 | 195 | 833 | 254 | 820 | 256 | 127 |
| 554 | 119 | 234 | 959 | 137 | 533 | 258 | 323 |

*Subtraction*

| 146246252 | 80630266 | 124485018 | 107419373 |
| 52160891 | 68164329 | 73098624 | 65348405 |

*Multiplication*

| 2964 | 8357 | 6249 | 3785 | 4965 |
|------|------|------|------|------|
| 94   | 87   | 78   | 35   | 19   |

*Division*

29)24679     57)51642     38)32300     64)61504

The relative level of ability of the class for each of the four processes is determined by comparing the class median score with the standard for the grade.   The scores made by individual pupils aid the teacher to locate their weaknesses.

(2) **Scales.**   Scales for measuring the altitude or level of the pupil's development in arithmetic computation and problem solving have been devised.   Several of the most widely used scales are as follows: (1) Woody–McCall Mixed Fundamentals; (2) Los Angeles Diagnostic Arithmetic Tests; (3) Stanford Achievement Test (Processes and Problems); (4) Woody–Van Wagenen Mixed Fundamentals; (5) Buckingham Scale for Problems in Arithmetic.

In each of these tests the items are arranged in the order of their difficulty, as determined by the results secured when they were worked by large numbers of children.   The more difficult the examples or problems in the test the pupil is able to work, the higher is the level of the development of his ability in the phases of arithmetic tested.   These scales are especially adapted for survey purposes.   They do not yield information on the basis of which the teacher can either determine the specific nature of a pupil's difficulty, or in what phases of the general subject the pupil may be performing at a relatively low level of efficiency.   Such power tests must be supplemented by more comprehensive diagnostic exercises.

(3) **General survey tests.**   Several general survey tests are available that are neither pure rate tests nor scales. They usually contain examples in several processes, and are

# Woody–McCall Mixed Fundamentals: Form IV [1]

Name.................... Age.......... Grade........ Building............... City...............

Get the right answer to as many examples as you can in 20 minutes. Do all work on the front or back of this sheet.

(1) ADD
4
1
3

(2)
$5 \times 1 =$

(3)
$8 \overline{) 24}$

(4) SUBTRACT
9
3

(5)
$4 \times 9 =$

(6) SUBTRACT
11
8

(7) ADD
62
27

(8) ADD
21
23
34

(9) SUBTRACT
89
47

(10) MULTIPLY
60
3

(11)
$8 \overline{) 0}$

(12)
$26 + 52 =$

(13) SUBTRACT
50
35

(14)
$7 \overline{) 4494}$

(15) MULTIPLY
1027
8

(16) SUBTRACT
475362
204383

(17) ADD
$ .65
2.35
.88

(18) MULTIPLY
8976
9

(19)
$60 \div 7 =$

(20) ADD
$6.00
2.49
6.32
5.57
.99
4.61

(21) MULTIPLY
26
242

(22)
$24 \overline{) 487}$

(23) SUBTRACT
$9\frac{5}{6}$
$5\frac{3}{4}$

(24)
$\frac{1}{3} + \frac{1}{3} =$

(25) MULTIPLY
24
$2\frac{1}{2}$

[1] Published by Teachers College, Columbia University. Copyright, 1923, By Teachers College.

(26)

.003 ) .0968

(27)
ADD
$4\frac{1}{2}$
$5\frac{5}{6}$
$7\frac{1}{3}$

(28)
MULTIPLY
7.15
2.3

(29)

$75.25 \div 1\frac{1}{3} =$

(30)

$5\frac{7}{8} - 2\frac{3}{8} =$

(31)

$3\frac{1}{3} \times 5\frac{1}{3} =$

(32)
SUBTRACT
10 yds. 2 ft. 3 in.
6 yds. 2 ft. 9 in.

(33)
ADD
2 ft. 6 in.
3 ft. 5 in.
4 ft. 9 in.
6 ft. 11 in.
15 ft. 6 in.

(34)

$3\frac{1}{4} \times 5\frac{1}{2} \times 2\frac{1}{2} =$

used to secure a general measure of the level of achievement of a school. They do not provide information which enables the teacher to locate the cause or the nature of the deficiency if the school or class is below standard. Examples of this type of test are the Courtis Supervisory Tests, A and B (see page 173); the Compass Survey Tests; the Cleveland Survey Tests; and the Pittsburgh Tests. A school graph of the Courtis Supervisory Test, for instance, might show that in all grades a particular school was below the standard in arithmetic. It would not, however, indicate the specific reason for the deficiency.

For surveying ability in problem solving such tests as Monroe's Standardized Reasoning Tests in Arithmetic, Stevenson Problem Analysis Tests, and the Stone Reasoning Test (revised) may be used. Several of the newer textbooks in arithmetic include standardized problem tests to be used for survey purposes.

(4) **Curriculum tests in arithmetic processes.** Survey tests designed to measure achievement in a number of grades are usually available in two or three forms of equivalent difficulty. Each test contains sets of examples that have a wide range of difficulty, ranging in the scales from examples that are easy enough for pupils in the primary grades to others that are so difficult that few pupils in the upper grades can work them correctly. Because it is necessary to keep the length of these tests within reasonable limits it is obvious that they cannot contain an adequate sampling of each process, and that they afford an unsatisfactory measure for many of the skills that constitute the total curriculum in arithmetic processes. The small number of equivalent forms of these tests results in the practice of giving the tests only once or twice a year, or even only once in two or three years in order to obtain a measure of general growth. The consequence is that until recently teachers have had no basis for

## COURTIS STANDARD SUPERVISORY TESTS

*Test B*                                *Form 2*

*Instructions:* Work as many of these examples as you can in the time allowed.   You will be marked for both speed and accuracy, but it is more important to have your answers right than to try a great many examples.

### Add

| 61 | 43 | 44 | 88 | 87 | 43 | 22 | 34 |
|----|----|----|----|----|----|----|----|
| 82 | 69 | 66 | 96 | 92 | 76 | 86 | 83 |
| 79 | 75 | 62 | 53 | 79 | 47 | 95 | 22 |
| 88 | 95 | 47 | 74 | 86 | 65 | 66 | 97 |
| 62 | 43 | 54 | 65 | 76 | 87 | 98 | 29 |

### Subtract

| 7758 | 13684 | 16397 | 17168 |
|------|-------|-------|-------|
| 2709 | 5096 | 7134 | 9024 |

| 4827 | 7525 | 5562 | 6653 |
|------|------|------|------|
| 3516 | 3145 | 3768 | 5878 |

### Multiply

| 47 | 76 | 63 | 85 | 38 |
|----|----|----|----|----|
| 94 | 57 | 86 | 48 | 76 |

### Divide

62)3348        36)1908        74)7252        45)3690

Name_____Grade_____

SCORES       Number of Examples Tried_____Examples Right_____ measuring the progress made by their pupils month by month during the school year, and hence have been obliged to "work in the dark."

**Brueckner's Curriculum Tests.**[1] To obviate this deficiency the Brueckner Curriculum Tests in Arithmetic Processes have been devised. They consist of six sets of ten standardized monthly tests each, a set for each grade from three to eight. The tests have been standardized month by month for the school year. The content of the tests for each of the ten months consists of a careful sampling of the new processes or portion of the curriculum taught during the corresponding month. Each test therefore affords a measure of the pupil's relative achievement in a much narrower range of difficulty in processes, and hence a much more complete measure of the progress made in the arithmetic curriculum than is afforded by any other series of tests that may be used for survey purposes.

The standards for each test are given at the foot of the test, as shown on page 175.

The standard ratings are based on the results of over 60,000 tests, given to pupils in a wide variety of rural and urban schools.

The ratings secured by an evaluation of the pupil's scores are to be interpreted as follows:

| RATING | INTERPRETATION | CUMULATIVE PER CENT |
|---|---|---|
| 1 | Scores made by lowest 2% of pupils tested.............. | 2 |
| 2 | Scores made by next 7% of pupils tested................ | 9 |
| 3 | Scores made by next 16% of pupils tested............... | 25 |
| 4 | Scores made by next 25% of pupils tested............... | 50 |
| 5 | Scores made by next 25% of pupils tested............... | 75 |
| 6 | Scores made by next 16% of pupils tested............... | 91 |
| 7 | Scores made by next 7% of pupils tested................ | 98 |
| 8 | Scores made by next 2% of pupils tested................ | 100 |

[1] The basis of these tests is explained in the author's *Manual for Curriculum Tests.*

## BRUECKNER CURRICULUM TEST IN ARITHMETIC PROCESSES, III [1]

Name........................ Grade.......... Room...

## CURRICULUM TEST III

*Directions:* You will be allowed 10 minutes to work the examples below. Do your work on the paper in the space for each example. Work rapidly, but try to have every example correct. Begin to work when your teacher says "Start." Find your rating and continue your *Progress Chart.*

| Number correct... | ... |
| Rating........... | ... |

1.  162
    360
    407

2.  16,575
    − 6,778

3.  $\frac{4}{5} + \frac{2}{5} =$

4.  412
    × 301

5.  $\frac{5}{8} - \frac{1}{8} =$

6.  $6.54
    − 5.79

7.  808
    507
    808

8.  936
    × 78

9.  $2\frac{2}{8}$
    $+ 7\frac{5}{6}$

10.  $\frac{2}{3} + 7 =$

11.  $2\frac{1}{8}$
     $- \frac{1}{8}$

12.  73)42,632

13.  $4\frac{3}{5}$
     $- 2\frac{1}{5}$

14.  78)55,224

15.  413
     × 659

16.  249
     787
     456
     865
     798
     839

## STANDARDS

| Rating | 1 | 2 | 3 | 4 | 5 | 6 | 7 | 8 |
|---|---|---|---|---|---|---|---|---|
| Number correct | 0–2 | 3–4 | 5–6 | 7–8 | 9–10 | 11–12 | 13–14 | 15–16 |

[1] Copyright by The John C. Winston Company.

Pupils whose scores give them a rating of 1 make scores equivalent to those made by approximately the lowest 2 per cent of the pupils tested; pupils receiving a rating of 2 make scores equivalent to those made by the next 7 per cent of the pupils, etc. The median, which may be used as the norm for each test, is the first score in the group of scores which gives the pupil a rating of 5. Fifty per cent of the pupils on whom these tests were standardized made scores which give them ratings of less than 5. A pupil who consistently makes a rating of 5 in the series of ten tests for the year maintains his same relative position in the distribution of scores made by the pupils on whom the tests were standardized. An individual pupil-progress chart and a class-progress chart are provided, which help the teacher to visualize the progress of each pupil and of the class as a whole. (See page 177.) These graphs serve as useful devices for motivating the class work. Results of instruction have shown marked improvement where such progress graphs have been used, due undoubtedly to the greater efforts made by pupils to improve their ratings on the tests.

Several kinds of analytical records are provided that enable the teacher to make an analysis of the work of the class to locate points at which reteaching is necessary. This analysis may be made by determining the frequency of error in each example in the test, and the nature of the errors made by the class on the examples in the test.

These test pamphlets containing the curriculum tests should be filed in some convenient place after the class summary sheet has been given to the principal, the progress chart constructed, and the analysis of errors completed. This insures a reliable measurement, since no previous preparation on the examples in the test will be possible.

## Brueckner Pupil–Progress Chart for Arithmetic [1]

Name...................... Grade.......... Room.........

### Curriculum Tests in Arithmetic

#### Record of Test Results

Enter the results of the tests in the spaces below. Keep your record up to date. Write neatly and clearly.

| NUMBER OF TEST | DATE TAKEN | NUMBER CORRECT | RATING |
|---|---|---|---|
| | | | |
| | | | |
| | | | |
| | | | |
| | | | |
| | | | |
| | | | |
| | | | |
| | | | |
| | | | |

### Progress Chart

Use this chart to graph your scores. Watch your progress. Your teacher will show you how to make your graph.

| RATING | TEST | | | | | | | | | | |
|---|---|---|---|---|---|---|---|---|---|---|---|
| | I | II | III | IV | V | VI | VII | VIII | IX | X | |
| 8 | | | | | | | | | | | Excellent |
| 7 | | | | | | | | | | | |
| 6 | | | | | | | | | | | } Very Good |
| 5 | | | | | | | | | | | Median |
| 4 | | | | | | | | | | | Danger Line |
| 3 | | | | | | | | | | | |
| 2 | | | | | | | | | | | |
| 1 | | | | | | | | | | | |

[1] Copyright by The John C. Winston Company.

## 2. *Diagnostic tests*

Diagnostic tests in arithmetic vary widely in the theories underlying their construction and use. Three different types will be discussed.

**The Monroe Diagnostic Tests.** The Monroe Diagnostic Tests contain a series of test exercises in various elements of four processes. Typical examples from each test are given on page 179. Each part of the test is a rate test. The scores on the individual tests enable the teacher to determine on what phases of the subject the pupil may be deficient, in so far as the tests contain examples dealing with all phases of the process. It can be seen, through an analysis of the types given on page 179, that there are many important types of examples missing from the standard list of types on page 173, for example, in types of examples in processes in mixed numbers. The scores made by a pupil on each test may be graphed, thus giving a profile revealing the pupil's strengths and deficiencies.

**The Compass Diagnostic Tests.** The Compass Diagnostic Tests consist of a series of twenty tests, each dealing with some one of the processes or with problem solving.

The method of diagnosis in this case is to give a test in a single process to determine the *level* at which the skill of the pupil in an element of the process breaks down, and thus to make it possible for the teacher to locate the apparent cause of weakness in the process. The method may be illustrated

TEST RECORD OF JOHN JACKSON, GRADE 4A

*Compass Test I, Addition of Whole Numbers*

|  | NORM | PUPIL SCORE |
|---|---|---|
| Part 1. Basic Addition Facts | 62 | 65 |
| Part 2. Higher Decade Addition | 60 | 61 |
| Part 3. Column Addition | 40 | 26 |
| Part 4. Carrying in Column Addition | 80 | 41 |
| Part 5. Checking Answers in Addition | 31 | 22 |

## Monroe Diagnostic Test — Typical Examples from Each Test[1]

### Addition

| Test I | Test II | Test VII | Test XII | Test XV |
|---|---|---|---|---|
| 4 | 7862 | 7 | $\dfrac{1}{6}+\dfrac{1}{3}=$ | $\dfrac{1}{6}+\dfrac{3}{5}=$ |
| 7 | 5013 | 6 | | |
| 2 | 1761 | 6 | $\dfrac{5}{6}+\dfrac{1}{2}=$ | $\dfrac{3}{12}+\dfrac{5}{8}=$ |
| | 5872 | 5 | | |
| | 3739 | 0 | $\dfrac{3}{10}+\dfrac{3}{5}=$ | |
| | | 5 | | |
| | | 1 | $\dfrac{5}{9}+\dfrac{2}{3}=$ | |
| | | 8 | | |
| | | 5 | | |
| | | 3 | | |

### Subtraction

| Test II | | Test IX | | Test XIII |
|---|---|---|---|---|
| 37 | 94 | 739 | 1853 | $\dfrac{3}{4}-\dfrac{2}{5}=$ |
| 5 | 8 | 367 | 948 | |
| | | | | $\dfrac{5}{6}-\dfrac{3}{4}=$ |

### Multiplication

| Test III | Test VIII | | | Test X | |
|---|---|---|---|---|---|
| 6572 | 4857 | 560 | 807 | 617 | 840 |
| 6 | 36 | 37 | 59 | 508 | 80 |

| Test XIV | Test XVIII | | Test XX | |
|---|---|---|---|---|
| $\dfrac{2}{3}\times\dfrac{3}{4}=$ | 657.2 | 67.50 | 487.5 | 57.28 |
| | .7 | .03 | .62 | 9.5 |
| $\dfrac{2}{5}\times\dfrac{3}{7}=$ | 46004 | 20250 | 302250 | 544160 |

### Division

| Test IV | Test VI | Test XI | Test XVI |
|---|---|---|---|
| $8\overline{)3840}$ | $82\overline{)3854}$ | $47\overline{)27589}$ | $\dfrac{2}{5}\div\dfrac{1}{3}=$ |

| Test XIX | Test XVII | Test XXI |
|---|---|---|
| $.4\overline{)148}$  Ans.: 37 | $.03\overline{)16.2}$  Ans.: 54 | $.47\overline{)2758.9}$  Ans.: 587 |
| $.9\overline{)65.7}$  Ans.: 73 | $.07\overline{)1.82}$  Ans.: 26 | $8.2\overline{)38.54}$  Ans.: 47 |

(In Tests XVII, XIX, and XXI pupils write in answers and place decimal points.
Pupils insert decimal points in Tests XVIII and XX.)

[1] Public School Publishing Company, Bloomington, Illinois.

by means of the analysis of the results in the test in addition
of whole numbers, given on page 186.  The data given on
page 178 are the scores made by a pupil, considerably below
standard in addition of whole numbers, on each of the five
parts into which the test is divided, each of which involves a
basic skill in the total process.

An analysis of the data shows that the pupil's score
on Part 1, Basic Addition Facts, was 65, or 3 above the
norm for his grade.  On Part 2 of the test, Higher Decade
Addition, his score was again above the norm for his grade.
His difficulty is not revealed by the scores on the first two
parts of the test.  His weakness, however, is located by his
score on Part 3 of the test, since his score is 26 as compared
with the grade norm of 40.  Although his knowledge of the
facts in higher decade addition is satisfactory, he does not
seem to have the power to use these facts in either single-
column addition or in column addition involving carrying.
This apparent weakness also is present in checking answers
in addition.  This pupil did inferior work on tests in addition, because he was slow and inaccurate due to his inability
to use the facts in higher decade addition.

Such a specific analysis of the pupil's ability in addition is
possible only when highly detailed diagnostic instruments of
this kind are available.  The Compass Diagnostic Tests are
to be used for group measurement and diagnosis.  An
analysis of the scores made by the individual pupils furnishes
a reliable basis for diagnosis, much more complete and definite than is possible by most diagnostic tests now available.
Remedial exercises may be assigned to overcome the weaknesses revealed by the tests.

**Limitations of the Compass tests.**  The chief limitations
of this excellent series of tests are the failure to consider
speed of work in interpreting the test scores, and the incomplete sampling of skills in each process.  For example, consider the following scores on Part 1 of the addition test.

This portion of the test contains only 70 of the 100 simple addition combinations, and hence the test results do not give the teacher any information as to the pupil's knowledge of the missing combinations, thus making an incomplete diagnosis. A few examples will illustrate these defects.

| Pupil | Attempted | Correct | Standard Number Correct |
|-------|-----------|---------|-------------------------|
| P. T. | 70 | 54 | 48 |
| A. R. | 50 | 50 | 48 |
| A. T. | 50 | 36 | 48 |
| P. C. | 58 | 48 | 48 |
| C. R. | 47 | 27 | 48 |
| O. V. | 34 | 34 | 48 |

According to these test results, as expressed by the number of answers correct, pupils P. T., A. R., and P. C. would all be rated as up to standard and pupils A. T., C. R., and O. V. as below standard. Pupils P. T., A. R., and P. C., would therefore be considered, according to the directions for interpreting test results given in the Manual, as not needing any additional practice on the addition combinations. An analysis of the test results in terms of both speed and accuracy makes such a conclusion a questionable one. For example, pupil P. T., with a score of 70 attempted and 54 correct, is a rapid but inaccurate worker since he had 16 incorrect answers in the test, although his score for number correct on the test is considerably above standard. Pupil A. R., with a score of 50 attempted and 50 correct is an accurate worker whose speed of work is well adjusted to efficiency in computation. Pupil P. C. does not work as rapidly as pupil P. T.; he is inaccurate in his work, but his score is exactly the same as the standard for his grade. Pupils A. T. and C. R. are fairly rapid but inaccurate workers, whose ratings on the test show that they are below the standard for the grade. Pupil O. V. is a slow but accurate worker. Since the Compass Tests are essentially speed tests it is possible that pupil O. V. was handicapped by a slow speed of writing which means that the test did not give a true measure of his ability in addition.

Courtis and Thorndike [1] have shown that speed of writing is a factor that should be taken into consideration in the interpretation of test scores on speed tests, especially in the lower grades when pupils have not mastered the mechanics of writing. The point is that scores expressed in terms of number of examples correct, and that disregard the factor of speed, often give an incorrect index of the real ability of the pupil. As has been shown, a pupil's score for number of examples correct may be above the standard for his grade, thus indicating a satisfactory status, when as a matter of fact the pupil may be inaccurate but because of a very rapid rate of work he may be able to give enough correct answers so that his score is above the standard.

The teacher must also be aware of the fact that these tests merely point out the general levels or phases of the process at which the pupil's ability breaks. The Compass Tests are therefore not instruments for specific detailed diagnosis, and do not indicate *why* the skill breaks down. The teacher must discover the causes of the deficiency by a supplementary examination, since test scores are only symptoms that help the teacher to locate the possible places where faulty habits of work, roundabout procedures, and lack of comprehension of the process involved are likely to exist.

**The Brueckner Diagnostic Tests.**[2] The Brueckner Diagnostic Tests in whole numbers, fractions, decimals, and per cent enable the teacher to inventory the ability of the pupils to work a large variety of types of examples in each process. These tests are especially designed for use during the learning process. They were constructed on the basis of a careful

---

[1] Courtis, S. A., and Thorndike, E. L. "Correction Formulæ for Addition Tests"; in *Teachers College Record*, vol. 21, pp. 1–24.

[2] The John C. Winston Company.

## BRUECKNER TEST IN FRACTIONS [1]

Date........................ School........................

Name........................ Grade......... Age....... Sex.......

Find the answers to the following subtraction examples:

| | a | b | c | d | e | f | g |
|---|---|---|---|---|---|---|---|
| 1. | $\frac{5}{4}$ $\frac{4}{4}$ $\frac{3}{4}$ | $\frac{3}{8}$ $\frac{2}{8}$ $\frac{1}{8}$ | $\frac{2}{8}$ $\frac{2}{8}$ $\frac{1}{8}$ | $\frac{5}{8}$ $\frac{3}{8}$ | $4\frac{2}{3}$ $\frac{1}{3}$ | $4\frac{2}{3}$ $\frac{2}{3}$ | $7\frac{5}{6}$ $\frac{1}{6}$ |
| 2. | $5\frac{1}{4}$ $3$ | $4\frac{3}{5}$ $2\frac{1}{5}$ | $3\frac{3}{4}$ $2\frac{3}{4}$ | $7\frac{7}{8}$ $2\frac{1}{8}$ | $1\frac{5}{8}$ $1\frac{1}{8}$ | $9$ $\frac{1}{2}$ | $5$ $1\frac{1}{3}$ |
| 3. | $3$ $2\frac{5}{12}$ | $6\frac{1}{2}$ $\frac{2}{3}$ | $7\frac{1}{2}$ $\frac{5}{8}$ | $10\frac{1}{3}$ $4\frac{2}{3}$ | $9\frac{3}{5}$ $8\frac{4}{5}$ | $4\frac{1}{8}$ $1\frac{1}{2}$ | $\frac{1}{2}$ $\frac{1}{4}$ |
| 4. | $\frac{1}{2}$ $\frac{1}{6}$ | $1\frac{1}{3}$ $\frac{2}{3}$ | $3\frac{3}{4}$ $\frac{1}{2}$ | $4\frac{5}{6}$ $\frac{1}{3}$ | $3\frac{3}{8}$ $1\frac{1}{2}$ | $7\frac{3}{4}$ $1\frac{1}{10}$ | $4\frac{1}{3}$ $\frac{2}{3}$ |
| 5. | $7\frac{1}{2}$ $2\frac{3}{4}$ | $3\frac{1}{6}$ $1\frac{2}{3}$ | $\frac{1}{2}$ $\frac{1}{4}$ | $1$ $\frac{1}{2}$ | $2\frac{1}{4}$ $2\frac{1}{2}$ | $2\frac{3}{8}$ $1\frac{1}{3}$ | $1\frac{1}{10}$ $\frac{4}{5}$ |
| 6. | $1\frac{1}{2}$ $\frac{5}{6}$ | $1\frac{5}{6}$ $1\frac{1}{2}$ | $3\frac{1}{4}$ $2\frac{5}{8}$ | $2\frac{1}{6}$ $\frac{2}{3}$ | $3\frac{1}{2}$ $1\frac{1}{3}$ | $6\frac{1}{4}$ $6\frac{2}{5}$ | $\frac{1}{4}$ $\frac{3}{4}$ |
| 7. | $\frac{9}{15}$ $\frac{1}{3}$ | $2\frac{3}{8}$ $\frac{1}{3}$ | $8\frac{1}{2}$ $\frac{2}{3}$ | $4\frac{5}{6}$ $1\frac{2}{5}$ | $14\frac{3}{4}$ $14\frac{1}{2}$ | $1\frac{1}{3}$ $\frac{5}{8}$ | $6\frac{1}{4}$ $5\frac{2}{3}$ |
| 8. | $1\frac{1}{3}$ $\frac{1}{2}$ | $10\frac{1}{2}$ $10$ | $2\frac{1}{2}$ $1\frac{3}{4}$ | $9\frac{1}{10}$ $8\frac{1}{2}$ | | | |

[1] Brueckner, L. J. *Diagnostic and Remedial Teaching of Arithmetic*, p. 168. John C. Winston Company.

analysis of the skills in each process, and of the different combinations in which these skills appear in various types of examples.   For example, the Diagnostic Test in Subtraction of Fractions reproduced on page 183 contains 53 examples, each of which differs from the others because of a difference in the skills involved in its solution.   These differences may be easily discovered by solving the examples and noting the differences in procedure.   Similar tests containing a wide sampling of types of examples in each process in whole numbers, fractions, and decimals are also available.

The Brueckner Diagnostic Tests are essentially inventory exercises, as may be seen from the sample page for subtraction here reproduced.   The pupils are allowed as much time as they need to complete the examples in each part of the test; hence speed of work is not a factor.   It is the purpose of the tests to enable the teacher to discover the types of examples that the pupils have most difficulty in solving or cannot solve.   This is especially necessary in the initial learning stages, where the pupil is likely to be confused by slight differences in the processes involved in solutions of particular types of examples.   A teacher who is conscious of the many varied types of examples in each process can use these diagnostic tests as a guide in instruction, and can thus make certain that the pupils practice on the numerous types of examples represented in the tests.

There are no standard scores for the Brueckner Diagnostic Tests.   On the class tabulation sheet the teacher records the number of times each example was solved incorrectly by the class, as shown in the sample tabulation sheet on page 186. An analysis of the record shows the points at which additional help is needed.   For pupils whose work is inferior a special individual record blank is provided.   On this blank are listed the type of difficulties and errors most frequently found in the written work of pupils.   This information enables the teacher to make a careful analysis of the pupil's work, and on the basis of the diagnosis to do whatever re-teaching is necessary and to prescribe the necessary remedial work.   (See below.)

The Buswell–John Diagnostic Chart for Individual Difficulties in Fundamental Processes in Arithmetic is another

## BRUECKNER DIAGNOSTIC TEST IN ARITHMETIC
### Record of Individual Diagnosis—Whole Numbers
### ADDITION DIFFICULTIES

Name_____Grade_____Room_____Date_____

AGES: Chronological_____Mental_____I. Q._____Test Used_____

General Rating by Teacher:  Scholarship_____Effort_____Intelligence_____

| Classification of Difficulties | Row | *Diagnosis and Remarks |
|---|---|---|
| 1. Weakness in combinations. | 1 | |
| 2. Counting. | 2 | |
| 3. Vocalizes his work. | 3 | |
| 5. Bridging the tens. | 4 | |
| 6. Zero difficulty. | 5 | |
| 7. Breaks up combinations. | 6 | |
| 8. Roundabout methods. | 7 | |
| 9. Carrying difficulty: | 8 | |

*Under "Diagnosis" indicate by number the types of difficulties found in each row.

(1) Forgets to carry.

(2) Adds carried number irregularly.

(3) Carries wrong number.

Difficulties:—

10. Column addition:

   a. Major

(1) Adds large numbers first.

(2) Trouble with second addition in column.

(3) Forgets sum and repeats work.

(4) Adds by tens.

(5) Loses place in column.

   b. Minor

(6) Inspects example to find starting point.

11. Others.

comprehensive diagnostic test, similar in type to the Brueckner Diagnostic Tests.

### BRUECKNER DIAGNOSTIC TEST IN WHOLE NUMBERS

**Class Summary Sheet**

SCHOOL_____GRADE_____ROOM_____

CITY_____STATE_____DATE_____

PROCESS_____

| No. of Pupils Missing (Use tally marks): | |
|---|---|
| 20 or more | |
| 19 | |
| 18 | |
| 17 | |
| 16 | |
| 15 | |
| 14 | |
| 13 | |
| 12 | |
| 11 | |
| 10 | |
| 9 | |
| 8 | |
| 7 | |
| 6 | |
| 5 | |
| 4 | |
| 3 | |
| 2 | |
| 1 | |
| 0 | |
| Total No. of Pupils | |
| Median No. of Errors | |

DIRECTIONS: Use tally marks to record the number of errors on the first paper in each row. Then take the next paper and so on until all are recorded. For example, 2 examples wrong in row 1 is to be recorded by a tally mark in the column headed 2.

| Row | Number of Examples Missed | | | | | | |
|---|---|---|---|---|---|---|---|
| | 0 | 1 | 2 | 3 | 4 | 5 | 6 OR MORE |
| 1 | | | | | | | |
| 2 | | | | | | | |
| 3 | | | | | | | |
| 4 | | | | | | | |
| 5 | | | | | | | |
| 6 | | | | | | | |
| 7 | | | | | | | |
| 8 | | | | | | | |
| 9 | | | | | | | |
| 10 | | | | | | | |

CLASS DIAGNOSIS

Major Difficulties

1_____

2_____

3_____

4_____

Minor Difficulties

1_____

2_____

3_____

4_____

SIGNED_____

**Overman on transfer of training.** The necessity of considering the wide variety of types of examples in each process is clearly demonstrated by the results of a study by Overman[1]

[1] Overman, J. R. "An Experimental Study of Certain Factors Affecting Transfer of Training in Arithmetic," pp. 124–125. Baltimore, Warwick and York, 1931.

of the extent to which training on a few specific types of examples transfers to other types on which no training is given. He says:

1. The results indicate that, while transfer from one type of example to a related type may occur in large amounts and may be complete in the case of some individuals, it is seldom complete for a group as a whole. This fact means that instruction and practice in the fundamentals of arithmetic must be based on full analyses of the fundamental processes. In view of the fact that transfer is seldom complete, all the essential facts and all the essential steps in the processes should be taught.

2. Although transfer from one type of example to other related types is possibly never complete, the results of this experiment show that it occurs in useful amounts — in amounts that we cannot afford to ignore.

3. The effectiveness of a given method of teaching in securing the immediate end sought is not the sole test of its worth. The methods of teaching the fundamentals of arithmetic should be those which will secure the maximum transfer to related types as well as the best mastery of the specific types taught. When the results of this experiment are considered, this fact means that, in addition to teaching any given type of example, we should help the pupils to use it as a basis for generalizing the process.

### 3. Teaching tests

One way in which the testing technique has greatly influenced teaching practices in arithmetic is through the improvement of instructional materials. The necessity of adapting instructions to the individual differences in rates of learning and difficulties in computation revealed by test scores has resulted in the development of instructional techniques which have greatly increased the efficiency of teaching. Some of these are discussed below.

**Practice Tests.** Teaching tests such as the Courtis Practice Tests in Arithmetic and the Studebaker Economy Practice Exercises in Arithmetic provide an excellent type of individualized drill on previously learned processes in whole numbers, in which each pupil progresses as rapidly as his proficiency reaches a standard set up by the authors. The work on these practice exercises may be scored by the pupils, thus greatly reducing the labor of the teacher.

**Keyed Remedial Exercises.** Several of the new types of diagnostic tests provide keyed remedial exercises which are geared into the tests. Provision is made in the Brueckner Diagnostic Tests for direct reference to suitable remedial exercises containing types of examples on which the pupil has difficulty. For example, the page references at the left of each row of examples in the diagnostic test on page 189 refers to the pages of the Brueckner, Anderson, Banting, Merton, Diagnostic Tests and Practice Exercises, which have a Workbook for each grade from three to eight, on which the remedial and practice exercises may be found that should be used to overcome the apparent deficiency. Each pupil may practice on those examples which the diagnostic test shows are difficult for him. Hence these materials are admirably adapted for the individualization of instruction. The teacher must do the reteaching that may be needed if pupils whose work is fairly satisfactory do not show improvement during a period of practice. Reteaching should probably always precede practice in the case of pupils whose work on closer inspection contains evidences of lack of comprehension of the process involved or faulty habits of work. The Economy Remedial Exercise Cards are geared in with the Compass Diagnostic Tests, and furnish another source of excellent material for remedial work.

**Using the test technique in teaching new processes.** The Courtis and the Studebaker practice test are not intended for use when pupils are first being taught a new process. A much more careful grading of steps in learning is necessary in the presentation of processes than is provided in these practice materials, which are intended chiefly for review

## DIAGNOSTIC TEST IN MULTIPLICATION OF FRACTIONS [1]

Change improper fractions in answers to mixed numbers and common fractions to lowest terms

| Row | a | b | c | d | e |
|---|---|---|---|---|---|
| 1. (A-73) | $\frac{1}{4} \times 12 =$ | $1\frac{1}{2}$ of $3 =$ | $\frac{8}{7} \times 2 =$ | $\frac{2}{3} \times 17 =$ | $\frac{5}{6} \times 16 =$ |
| 2. (A-73) | $2 \times \frac{2}{5} =$ | $5 \times \frac{1}{5} =$ | $6 \times \frac{1}{2} =$ | $14 \times \frac{1}{5} =$ | $14 \times \frac{1}{6} =$ |
| 3. (B-76) | $\frac{1}{2}$ of $\frac{1}{3} =$ | $\frac{1}{4} \times \frac{8}{15} =$ | $\frac{1}{2} \times \frac{5}{9} =$ | $\frac{5}{8} \times \frac{2}{7} =$ | $\frac{5}{6} \times \frac{18}{25} \times \frac{1}{3} =$ |
| 4. (C-77) | $4 \times 2\frac{1}{2} =$ | $9 \times 3\frac{1}{2} =$ | $10 \times 3\frac{5}{6} =$ | $2 \times 5\frac{1}{8} =$ | $4\frac{3}{8} \times 6 \times 2\frac{4}{5} =$ |
| 5. (D-78) | $1\frac{3}{5} \times \frac{1}{4} =$ | $4\frac{1}{5} \times 3 =$ | $6\frac{1}{8} \times 6 =$ | $5\frac{2}{5} \times 7 =$ | $2\frac{1}{3} \times 5\frac{3}{8} \times 6 =$ |
| 6. (D-78) | $\frac{1}{5} \times 2\frac{1}{8} =$ | $\frac{1}{2}$ of $1\frac{1}{3} =$ | $\frac{5}{6} \times 7\frac{1}{5} =$ | $\frac{3}{4} \times 3\frac{2}{3} =$ | $4\frac{3}{4} \times \frac{2}{3} \times 2\frac{2}{3} =$ |
| 7. (D-78) | $6\frac{2}{3} \times \frac{2}{9} =$ | $6\frac{2}{3} \times \frac{1}{8} =$ | $12\frac{1}{2} \times \frac{2}{5} =$ | $7\frac{3}{5} \times \frac{4}{7} =$ | $\frac{8}{9} \times \frac{3}{8} \times 3\frac{1}{5} =$ |
| 8. (E-80) | $2\frac{1}{8} \times 2\frac{1}{8} =$ | $3\frac{3}{4} \times 6\frac{2}{3} =$ | $5\frac{2}{5} \times 4\frac{1}{6} =$ | $2\frac{1}{7} \times 2\frac{2}{3} =$ | $2\frac{6}{7} \times 4\frac{3}{8} \times 1\frac{4}{5} =$ |
| 9. (E-80) | $16$   $3\frac{1}{8}$ | $36\frac{3}{4}$   $12$ | $16$   $15\frac{5}{8}$ | $15\frac{1}{4}$   $7$ | $12$   $18\frac{8}{5}$ |

[1] This diagnostic test is one of a series of such tests found in L. J. Brueckner, C. J. Anderson, G. O. Banting, E. Merton, *Diagnostic Tests and Practice Exercises*, Grades 3, 4, 5, 6, 7, 8, published by The John C. Winston Company, Philadelphia.

purposes or for bringing previously acquired skills to a satisfactory level. For example, in the Minneapolis schools a number of kinds of well graded instructional practice tests have been devised for the arithmetic work in the primary and intermediate grades. After a step in a process has been developed by the teacher, each pupil is given a card (see page 191) containing similar examples, and he then tests himself to discover whether he has learned how to work them. The pupils score their work on these exercises by means of answers printed on the back of the card. On the basis of this work the teacher groups the pupils according to their needs. Those who apparently have learned the step, practice for speed; those who did not learn the step at the initial presentation are then retaught, retested, and again retaught until all have learned the process. It has been found that pupils in the primary grades, who have not been taught formal arithmetic, already know a great many of the number combinations. They have learned these facts incidentally in their everyday activities. A simple pre-test by means of a card containing a set of number facts will readily point out the combinations that are not known by individuals, and indicate the facts that should be studied.

## III. THE TECHNIQUES OF DIAGNOSIS APPLIED TO ARITHMETIC PROCESSES

In order to make a diagnosis of the causes of a pupil's deficiency in arithmetic the teacher should have a grasp of the skills that constitute the processes, an appreciation of how complex the processes must appear to the learner, and a knowledge of the most common causes and kinds of difficulties revealed by the study of the work of the pupils in the grades. Test scores aid the teacher to locate possible places where difficulty exists, but they do not locate the causes of the difficulty.

SPECIMEN OF BRUECKNER PRACTICE TESTS IN FRACTIONS
(This Shows a Part of One of the Drill Card Forms Used in
Minneapolis)

## SUBTRACTION DRILL CARD 1—FRACTIONS

| | | | |
|---|---|---|---|
| $\frac{2}{3}$ $\frac{1}{3}$ | $\frac{3}{6}$ $\frac{2}{6}$ | $\frac{7}{8}$ $\frac{4}{8}$ | $\frac{1}{4}$ $\frac{1}{4}$ |
| (a) | | | |
| $\frac{3}{5}$ $\frac{2}{5}$ | $\frac{5}{6}$ $\frac{5}{6}$ | $\frac{4}{5}$ $\frac{2}{5}$ | $\frac{5}{12}$ $\frac{4}{12}$ |
| (b) | | | |

*Answers — Reverse side of card*

| | | | |
|---|---|---|---|
| $\frac{1}{3}$ | $\frac{1}{6}$ | $\frac{3}{8}$ | 0 |
| (c) | | | |
| $\frac{1}{5}$ | 0 | $\frac{2}{5}$ | $\frac{1}{12}$ |
| (d) | | | |

Copyright 1926 — L. J. Brueckner for the Board of Education, Minneapolis

## 1. *The basic number facts in arithmetic*

**Stone's early study.** The complexity of arithmetic processes has been demonstrated by many investigators. One of the first significant studies, that of Stone,[1] showed that arithmetic is not one general ability, but that it is made up of a large number of specific abilities and skills, which may be thought of as a hierarchy of habits in which each new skill is based in part on simpler skills previously developed. The solution of an example in long division, for example, involves a large number of specific skills in addition, subtraction, multiplication, and division, each of which must be developed before the long-division process can be effectively taught.

**Osburn's study.** Many teachers think of 45 basic addition facts as constituting the sum total of facts that should be automatized in order that the child may be able to add. Investigations by Osburn [2] and others have shown that there are many more than 45 addition facts that must be learned. In the first place, the "45 combinations" usually thought of do not contain the reverse forms of combinations; that is,

$$\frac{7}{+3}$$ is not regarded as different from the combination $$\frac{3}{+7}$$

and hence is not included in the practice exercises. Nor do the "45 combinations" include facts involving zero, such as

$$\frac{5}{+0}\ \frac{0}{6}$$, etc. If all of these zero and reverse facts are counted

as addition combinations there are in all 100 addition combinations. The writer has often seen sets of blank cards in use in classrooms in which neither reverse forms of combinations nor zero combinations were included.

---

[1] Stone, C. W.  *Arithmetic Abilities and Some Factors Conditioning Them.*  Teachers College Contributions to Education, no. 19.  New York, Columbia University, 1908.

[2] Osburn, W. J.  *Corrective Arithmetic*, p. 11.  Boston, Houghton Mifflin Company, 1924.

Addition facts are also used in column addition.    87
For example, in solving the example at the right the    64
pupil must have knowledge of the following com-    59
binations:    77
                                                    ——

7 + 9 = 16        (2) + 7 = 9        (20) + 8 = 28.
(16) + 4 = 20     (9) + 5 = 14       *Note.* Numbers in parentheses
(20) + 7 = 27     (14) + 6 = 20      are "thought of," not "seen."

Some authorities think that the pupil must be given special practice on the combinations involved in adding by endings, as illustrated above. The alternative is to assume that there is complete transfer from such a combination 7 + 9 to the combination 7 + 29 — an assumption that hardly seems justifiable. If it is assumed that pupils should be given practice on the adding by endings involved in column addition, a large number of addition facts must be added to the 100 basic combinations. Osburn maintains that adding by endings of numbers greater than 39 need not be drilled upon, since the sums of columns of figures in examples found in life rarely exceed 39.

Addition is also used in carrying in multiplication. For example, in multiplying 46 by 5, the pupil must carry the 3 from 5 × 6 = 30 to the 20. This skill in-    46
volves an extremely difficult mental activity, which    × 5
can be made much easier by giving direct practice    ———
on the addition facts involved in carrying in multi-    230
plication examples, or in the carrying in the multiplication involved in uneven division.

The number of addition facts involved in carrying in multiplication is easily found. For example, the only number that is ever carried in multiplying by 2 is 1. In multiplying by 3 the numbers 1 or 2 are the only ones ever carried; in multiplying by 4, the numbers carried may be 1, 2, or 3; and so forth for all multipliers through 9.

The combinations involving carrying in multiplication by 2 are

| | | | |
|---|---|---|---|
| $0 + 1$ | $6 + 1$ | $12 + 1$ | $18 + 1$ |
| $2 + 1$ | $8 + 1$ | $14 + 1$ | 10 combinations |
| $4 + 1$ | $10 + 1$ | $16 + 1$ | |

In multiplying by 3 the combinations involving carrying are:

| | | | |
|---|---|---|---|
| $0 + 1$ | $9 + 1$ | $18 + 1$ | $27 + 1$ |
| $0 + 2$ | $9 + 2$ | $18 + 2$ | $27 + 2$ |
| $3 + 1$ | $12 + 1$ | $21 + 1$ | 20 combinations |
| $3 + 2$ | $12 + 2$ | $21 + 2$ | in all |
| $6 + 1$ | $15 + 1$ | $24 + 1$ | |
| $6 + 2$ | $15 + 2$ | $24 + 2$ | |

**Total number of addition facts.** Similarly it is possible to list all combinations involved in carrying in multiplication by the other numbers. Eliminating duplicate combinations, such as $21 + 1$, which would appear in carrying when multiplying by 3 or 7, there are in all 175 addition combinations that may appear in multiplication. It should be clear to the teacher that practice on a combination such as $27 + 4$ does not involve the same mental processes that arise in using this combination in solving the example $35 \times 9$, where the number 4 must be carried "in mind" while the combination $9 \times 3$ is thought out; the pupil must then add two "thought of" numbers, 27 and 4 — a process much more difficult than adding 27 and 4 when the figures are on the paper before the pupil.

$$\begin{array}{r} 35 \\ \times 9 \\ \hline 315 \end{array}$$

Addition facts are also used in a different way in the checking of subtraction examples, where the difficulty consists chiefly in a knowledge of how to use the ability to add in checking the work. Here the pupil in checking the example at the right adds 9 and com-

$$\begin{array}{r} 786 \\ -459 \\ \hline 327 \\ \hline 7 \end{array}$$

pares the sum with the 6 in the minuend before carrying the 1 to the 2 to check the second figure. The extra step of comparison here involved is an element that undoubtedly causes confusion.

**Total number facts.** Similar analyses can be made for the basic facts in each of the processes. For example, the teacher must not overlook the subtraction facts involved in uneven short division. It thus becomes clear that the number of basic number facts that must be taught is much greater than has usually been recognized. Osburn [1] classifies the facts to be learned as follows:

Group 1. The 100 facts in simple addition.
Group 2. The 225 addition facts which are prerequisite for the most important column addition.
Group 3. The 175 addition facts which are prerequisite for carrying in multiplication.
Group 4. The 100 facts in simple subtraction.
Group 5. The 175 subtraction facts which are prerequisite for short division.
Group 6. The 100 facts in simple multiplication.
Group 7. The 90 facts in division without remainders.
Group 8. The 300 facts in division with remainders.
Group 9. The character of practice in long division.

It thus becomes evident that the failure of a pupil in multiplication may be due to weakness in addition by endings, either because of lack of knowledge of the addition facts or because of lack of ability to carry in mind the "carried" number and to add it to the next product, rather than to a lack of knowledge of the multiplication facts as such or to lack of understanding of the multiplication process itself.

[1] Osburn, W. J. *Improvement in the Fundamentals of Arithmetic.* (Mimeographed statement, issued by the State Department of Education, Madison, Wisconsin, 1923.)

## 2. *The basic skills in arithmetic processes*

**Basic skills in subtraction.** If a teacher could take the time to attempt to make a clean-cut analysis of the basic skills involved in a single process the results would be most enlightening. The complexity of the processes that a pupil must learn to perform with facility is clearly revealed by such an analysis. An illustration of such a classification of skills is the following list of the basic elements, prepared by Miss Merton, [1] that may be considered to make up the general ability to subtract whole numbers:

### KNOWLEDGE REQUIRED FOR SUBTRACTION

#### (Subtraction Method)

1. The 100 subtraction combinations
2. Three ideas in one's subtraction concept:
    Taking away idea: 15–7, 7 and 15.
    Adding idea: What number added to 7 equals 15?
    Difference idea: 15 is how many more than 7?
3. The meaning of the following terms: Minus, less, subtrahend, minuend, borrowing, difference, remainder
4. The meaning of the subtraction sign
5. That the complete minuend must never be smaller than the complete subtrahend
6. That in writing the example, units must be placed under units, tens under tens, etc.
7. That one must begin at the right and work to the left
8. That the order of units in the subtrahend must be subtracted from the same order in the minuend
9. How to proceed when the first number to be subtracted in the minuend is larger than the corresponding number in the subtrahend
10. That one must not borrow unless the number in the subtrahend is larger than the corresponding number in the minuend
11. How to proceed when a number of the subtrahend is larger than the corresponding number of minuend; i.e., borrowing

[1] Merton, Elda, in *Second Yearbook of the Department of Elementary School Principals*, pp. 395–410.

12. What it means to place a 1 in front of a number when necessary:

$$423$$
$$-219$$

1 adds in terms of 10

13. What it does to the next number in the minuend when a 1 has been placed before the following number
14. Must be able to remember the new number made through borrowing

$$628$$
$$-239$$

After subtracting 9 from 18, the child is dealing with 11, not 12.

15. How to proceed when the need for borrowing and no borrowing are met alternately in the example
16. How to borrow when two or more successive digits in the subtrahend are larger than the corresponding digits in the minuend
17. How to proceed when there are fewer figures in the subtrahend than in the minuend
18. How to proceed when the last subtraction takes place with the subtrahend and minuend the same:

$$649$$
$$-623$$

(The zero must not be placed in the remainder.)

19. Ability to handle a zero or a succession of zeros in the subtrahend
20. Ability to handle a zero or a succession of zeros in the minuend
21. How to check for correct answers

These basic skills are used in many different ways in the solution of examples in subtraction. The chief concern of the teacher should be to see to it that the steps in which these skills are taught present to the pupil only one new difficulty at a time. The following set of examples suggests a suitable arrangement for the step by step introduction of these skills.

| (1) | (2) | (3) | (4) | (5) | (6) |
|-----|-----|-----|-----|-----|-----|
| 8   | 75  | 14  | 47  | 27  | 128 |
| 6   | 12  | 6   | 3   | 24  | 75  |

| (7) | (8) | (9) | (10) | (11) |
|-----|-----|-----|------|------|
| 95  | 60  | 73  | 962  | 708  |
| 28  | 47  | 64  | 138  | 495  |

| (12) | (13) | (14) | (15) | (16) |
|------|------|------|------|------|
| 845  | 43   | 435  | 600  | 5276 |
| 269  | 8    | 86   | 497  | 1427 |

| (17) | (18) | (19) | (20) | (21) |
|------|------|------|------|------|
| 8764 | 9362 | 6001 | 8070 | 8100 |
| 5278 | 7698 | 2746 | 5042 | 7263 |

The techniques used for analyzing skills in fractions are quite similar to those used for whole numbers.

**Knight's basis for analysis.** A suggested basis for analyzing the skills included in such a process as subtraction of fractions has been proposed by Knight [1] and his co-workers. Their list of skills for that process is as follows:

ANALYSIS OF SUBTRACTION OF FRACTIONS IN TERMS OF THE LEARNING PROCESS

(According to Knight-Luse-Ruch)

|  | UNITS OF SKILL No. |
|---|---|
| I. AS TO THE FORM OF STAGING THE EXAMPLE | |
| A. When the numbers are written with figures | |
| 1. Indicated subtraction, as 1/2 — 1/4 | 1 |
| 2. Column subtraction, as 7 2/3 — 1/2 | 2 |
| 3. Words as "minus," "less," "subtract —— from ——," "from —— subtract ——," "from —— take ——," "take —— from ——," as from 5/12 take 1/3 | 3 |
| B. When numbers are written in words | |
| 1. Indicated subtraction, as two sevenths — one sixth | 4 |
| 2. Words as I.A. 3 above, as seven and two thirds minus one fourth | 5 |
| II. AS TO PROCEDURE | |
| A. Nature of the minuends and subtrahends | |
| 1. When both are proper fractions | |
| a. Similar fractions, as 7/9 — 2/9 | 6 |
| b. When one given denominator is common denominator, as 8/9 — 2/3 | 7 |
| c. When denominators have no common factor, as 3/4 — 2/7 | 8 |

[1] Knight, F. B., Luse, E. M., and Ruch, G. M.  *Problems in the Teaching of Arithmetic.*  Iowa Supply Store, Iowa City, Iowa.

These basic skills, similar lists of which are available for each process, can be found in many different combinations in examples in fractions. The diagnostic test in subtraction of fractions on page 183 contains a large sampling of examples, each of which contains a different combination of the skills. For example, the solution of the example $\frac{4\frac{1}{8}}{2\frac{1}{4}}$ involves the following five skills listed in the above table:

| UNIT SKILL | |
|---|---|
| 2 | Column subtraction |
| 18 | Minuend and subtrahend mixed numbers, one given denominator the common denominator |
| 25 | Subtraction of fractions, then integers |
| 32 | Borrowing — fraction in minuend smaller than in subtrahend |
| 43 | Answer a mixed number, fraction irreducible |

Similar analysis of the unit skills in each example in a diagnosis test may be made by the teacher.[1] A little practice in making analysis will do much to make clear the complexity of skills in each example, and should aid the teacher in the presentation of the steps by which the example is solved. Inability of the pupil to learn how to solve an example may be due to weakness in one or more of the skills involved. This difficulty must be removed before the process can be thoroughly mastered.

**Analysis of skills in fractions.** A suggestive technique proposed by Osburn [2] for analyzing the skills in fractions is to list the processes that must be used in succession in each step in the solution of an example. For example, there are two steps in solving the example $\frac{1}{4} + \frac{3}{4} = 1$. The first step is to add 1 and 3; the next step is to reduce the fraction by dividing the numerator 4 by 4, the denominator. The steps in solving such an example as $1\frac{1}{3} + 4\frac{8}{9} = 6\frac{2}{9}$ are (1) to divide 9 x 3, (2) multiply 3 by 1, (3) add 3 and 8, (4) divide

[1] A somewhat different analysis of skills involved in fractions is given in L. J. Brueckner's *Diagnostic and Remedial Teaching of Arithmetic.*

[2] Osburn, W. J. *Corrective Arithmetic*, vol. 2, pp. 38–45. Boston, Houghton Mifflin Company, 1929.

11 by 9, (5) subtract 9 from 11, and (6) to add the 1, the 4, and the 1 carried. Such an analysis makes clear the complexity of the process involved in solving apparently simple examples in fractions. It is no wonder that many pupils find the work in fractions very difficult. Illustrations of the complexity of skills in the other processes are given in the following cases in which each letter represents a step in the solution, M standing for multiplication, D for division, etc.

$$3\frac{1}{3} - 2\frac{1}{2} \qquad \text{M D M D M A A S S}$$
$$3\frac{1}{3} \times \frac{3}{5} \qquad \text{M A D D M M D}$$
$$7\frac{1}{2} \div 5\frac{1}{3} \qquad \text{M A M A D M M D S}$$

## 3. The most common difficulties of pupils

Careful studies of the work of pupils whose scores in achievement tests were unsatisfactory have shown that test scores alone furnish a wholly inadequate picture of the character and quality of their work. Test scores show where a difficulty exists, but do not give any direct help in locating its causes.

**Techniques of analysis to determine causes.** Several significant studies have been made of pupils' methods of work on the basis of which it has been possible to arrive at a fairly definite statement of the kinds of faulty, peculiar methods of procedure that are to be found in the work of pupils not making satisfactory progress. Buswell,[1] Brueckner,[2] and others have applied the techniques of analysis of the oral and written responses of pupils as a method of discovering faults in arithmetic processes. Educational literature contains many interesting descriptions of the peculiar

[1] Buswell, G. T., and John, Lenore. *Diagnostic Studies in Arithmetic.* Supplementary Educational Monograph, No. 27. University of Chicago Press, 1926.

[2] Brueckner, Leo J. *Diagnostic and Remedial Teaching in Arithmetic.* Philadelphia, 1930. John C. Winston Company. Contains a comprehensive study of diagnostic and remedial procedures in all phases of arithmetic.

methods of work that have been revealed by analytical studies. The teacher should be familiar with the results of these investigations in order that she may more readily perceive the faults in the work of pupils.

Table 22 contains the list of difficulties in addition of whole numbers, discovered by Buswell and John [1] through the observation and analysis of the oral responses of pupils in working examples with which they had difficulty.

The most common fault in addition reported by Buswell and John was errors in simple number combinations. This was true for all grades from three through six. The next most common fault was counting, which was found in all grades. Buswell and John report that pupils count with their fingers, toes, nods of the head, taps of the pencil, and in many other ways that interfere seriously with efficiency in computation. Special attention should be directed to the large variety of faults due to inability in carrying, to faulty procedures, and to lapses of various kinds; a person who has never attempted to analyse the oral responses of pupils in solving arithmetic examples can hardly realize the peculiar methods of work that some pupils have invented.

To demonstrate to herself that the findings by Buswell and John are typical of the conditions in any school system, the teacher should make a diagnosis of the work of any pupil whose achievement in arithmetic is unsatisfactory. Difficulties such as those listed in the table, and others of a different nature that may be found by the teacher, have been consistently discovered in the analysis of the oral responses of pupils who fail to make satisfactory progress in arithmetic. The use of comprehensive diagnostic-test exercises and record blanks, such as are provided by Brueck-

---

[1] The table from Buswell and John's monograph has been rearranged, as given in the table on page 203, to show a classified arrangement of faults. In the original they are listed in order of frequency.

## TABLE 22. FREQUENCY OF FAULTY HABITS IN ADDITION

### After Buswell and John

| | III | IV | V | VI | TOTAL |
|---|---|---|---|---|---|
| 1. Errors in combination.............. | 81 | 103 | 78 | 58 | 320 |
| 2. Counting........................ | 61 | 83 | 54 | 17 | 215 |
| 3. Carrying | | | | | |
| (a) Added carried number last........ | 39 | 45 | 45 | 26 | 155 |
| (b) Forgot to add carried number..... | 37 | 38 | 34 | 17 | 126 |
| (c) Added carried number irregularly.. | 26 | 30 | 28 | 18 | 102 |
| (d) Wrote number to be carried....... | 34 | 25 | 18 | 12 | 89 |
| (e) Carried wrong number........... | 28 | 19 | 26 | 14 | 87 |
| (f) Carried when nothing to carry..... | 6 | 9 | 9 | 5 | 29 |
| (g) Wrote carried number in answer... | 10 | 2 | 2 | 1 | 15 |
| (h) Added carried number twice....... | 0 | 1 | 0 | 0 | 1 |
| (i) Subtracted carried number........ | 0 | 0 | 0 | 1 | 1 |
| 4. Faulty procedure | | | | | |
| (a) Retraced work partly done........ | 26 | 34 | 39 | 22 | 121 |
| (b) Irregular procedure.............. | 16 | 29 | 23 | 18 | 86 |
| (c) Grouped numbers................ | 25 | 22 | 21 | 16 | 84 |
| (d) Split numbers................... | 12 | 29 | 25 | 14 | 80 |
| (e) Lost place in column............. | 17 | 17 | 17 | 14 | 65 |
| (f) Disregards column............... | 34 | 11 | 9 | 1 | 55 |
| (g) Omits digits.................... | 13 | 21 | 13 | 5 | 52 |
| (h) Disregarded one column.......... | 15 | 11 | 8 | 2 | 36 |
| (i) Error in writing answer........... | 12 | 3 | 14 | 5 | 34 |
| (j) Added in pairs.................. | 6 | 6 | 6 | 2 | 20 |
| (k) Added same digit in two columns.. | 10 | 6 | 1 | 1 | 18 |
| (l) Began with left column.......... | 1 | 1 | 1 | 0 | 3 |
| 5. Lapses, and other miscellaneous faults | | | | | |
| (a) Used wrong operation............ | 23 | 25 | 20 | 11 | 79 |
| (b) Depended upon visualization...... | 24 | 8 | 27 | 2 | 61 |
| (c) Errors in reading numbers........ | 14 | 10 | 21 | 7 | 52 |
| (d) Dropped back one or more tens.... | 13 | 12 | 17 | 5 | 47 |
| (e) Derived unknown from known.... | 13 | 7 | 11 | 11 | 42 |
| (f) Skipped decades................. | 11 | 7 | 9 | 5 | 32 |
| (g) Confused columns............... | 1 | 0 | 0 | 0 | 1 |
| (h) Added imaginary numbers........ | 0 | 0 | 1 | 0 | 1 |
| 6. Used scratch paper................. | 7 | 5 | 9 | 0 | 21 |
| Total...................... | 96 | 124 | 116 | 78 | 414 |

ner and by Buswell and John, will facilitate the diagnosis. Buswell and John give many detailed case studies that show the peculiar kind of responses and habits of work that may be discovered by this method of diagnosis.

**A diagnostic study of forty-five pupils.**  The following statement summarizes the findings of a diagnostic study of forty-five pupils, in a Minneapolis elementary school, who were considerably below standard in arithmetic: [1]

The types of difficulty disclosed were most interesting.  The most common fault proved to be the habit of counting.  The teachers had worked faithfully, to secure automatization of all combinations, but in spite of their efforts, twenty-three counters slipped through.  They counted in the most amazing ways — with lips, tongue, toes and fingers.  Sometimes the counting was scarcely perceptible.  Fourteen had a short attention span.  They could readily add a column of four or five figures, but beyond that they were lost.  Fourteen moved lips constantly, vocalizing every step, ten had a bad habit of guessing, eight failed because of faulty procedure, and six failed because of slowness.

*Addition difficulties.*  Twenty-two skipped around, selecting combinations that seemed easy to them, eighteen hunted about for addends of 10, eighteen inspected the example to find a starting point, eleven had trouble with carrying, five added all the large numbers first to get them out of the way, and nine used curious roundabout methods.

*Subtraction difficulties.*  Fifteen showed weakness in the fundamentals, fourteen had trouble with borrowing, twelve used roundabout methods, three always subtracted the smaller numbers from the larger, whether it was in the minuend or subtrahend, four added to obtain results, and three counted backwards, using the fingers to keep track of the count.

*Multiplication difficulties.*  Ten showed weakness in fundamentals, seven had carrying difficulties, nine used the multiplicand and the multiplier, and two had zero difficulties.

*Division difficulties.*  Nineteen had trouble with uneven divisions, twelve had zero difficulties, eleven repeated the tables to secure results, eight used roundabout methods, twelve had diffi-

[1] Reported by Ella M. Probst, in *Proceedings of Second Annual Conference of Minnesota Society for the Study of Education*, pp. 33–34.

culty with trial division, and six couldn't remember what to carry in the multiplication involved.

It took from forty-five to ninety minutes to complete an individual diagnosis, the time depending upon the number and kind of difficulties encountered. We were fortunate in having the assistance of student examiners, but if we had not had their help, we could readily have made our own diagnoses. Any one who is supplied with the necessary diagnostic material can do the work. As a matter of fact, it is a distinct advantage for a teacher to make her own diagnosis, and some of our teachers preferred to do so.

The children, themselves, were keenly interested in the analysis, and coöperated willingly with the teachers in their effort to improve the situation. It sometimes happened that a child had only one or two special difficulties. When these were known it was a comparatively easy matter to clear up the trouble. On the other hand, one boy in the 5A grade had a total of twenty-three separate kinds of trouble. No wonder his teachers considered him extremely "careless" in the handling of figures!

Certain subtle, less apparent causes of difficulty are often overlooked by the inexperienced examiner. Some of these causes, such as the length of the attention-span of the pupil, are revealed by rather definite symptoms, which have been described as follows: [1]

Irregular speed up the column may be due to either of two factors: lack of control of attention, or lack of knowledge of the combinations. Attention will be considered here.

There is a limit to the length of time that a person can carry on any mental activity continuously. As time goes on, the mind tends to respond more and more readily to any new mental stimulus than it does to the old. The mind "wanders," as it is said. The attention span for many children is six additions, for some only three or four, for others, eight, or ten, and so on. That is, a child whose attention span is limited to six figures may add rapidly, smoothly, and accurately, for the first five figures in the column, giving its attention wholly to the work. As the limit of its attention span is reached, however, it becomes increasingly difficult for

[1] Courtis, S. A. *Standard Practice Tests in Arithmetic, Manual.* Yonkers, World Book Company, 1916.

TABLE 23. ANALYSIS OF ERRORS IN THE SUBTRACTION OF FRACTIONS

| | GRADE V A | GRADE VI B | GRADE VI A | TOTAL | PER CENT |
|---|---|---|---|---|---|
| 1. Difficulty in borrowing.................. | 769 | 414 | 645 | 1,828 | 24.3 |
| a) Disregarded having borrowed from whole number: 10 1/4 − 3 2/4 = 7 3/4........ | 333 | 195 | 239 | 767 | ..... |
| b) Prefixed number borrowed to numerator: 3 1/8 − 6/8 = 2 11/8 − 6/8 = 2 5/8..... | 116 | 97 | 260 | 473 | ..... |
| c) Added number borrowed to numerator without changing it to a fraction: 9 3/5 − 8 4/5 = 8 4/5 − 8 4/5 = 0.............. | 177 | 5 | 9 | 191 | ..... |
| d) Borrowed unnecessarily and left improper fraction in remainder: 4 2/3 − 2/3 = 3 5/3 − 2/3 = 3 3/3............. | 53 | 58 | 47 | 158 | ..... |
| e) Borrowed but disregarded fraction in minuend: 7 1/8 − 5/8 = 6 8/8 − 5/8 = 6 3/8 | 52 | 28 | 53 | 133 | ..... |
| f) Borrowed but did not change fraction in minuend to same denominator: 3 1/4 − 6/8 = 2 9/8 − 6/8 = 2 3/8.................. | 12 | 10 | 39 | 17 | ..... |
| g) Considered 1 borrowed where no borrowing was involved: 3 3/4 − 1/2 = 2 1/4....... | 16 | 21 | 2 | 39 | ..... |
| h) Borrowed as much as was needed to make numerator in minuend larger than numerator in subtrahend: 7 1/8 − 1/4 = 5 3/8 − 2/8 = 5 1/8............................ | 10 | 0 | 18 | 28 | ..... |
| 2. Used wrong process................... | 774 | 414 | 333 | 1,521 | 20.3 |
| a) Addition: 5/8 − 1/8 = 6/8 = 3/4....... | 503 | 267 | 224 | 994 | ..... |
| b) Multiplication: 1/2 − 2/8 = 2/16 = 1/8.. | ..... | 2 | ....... | 2 | ..... |
| c) Subtracted whole numbers and added fractions: 10 1/4 − 3 2/4 = 7 3/4....... | 153 | 87 | 46 | 286 | ..... |
| d) Subtracted fractions and added whole numbers: 7 3/5 − 1 1/10 = 8 5/10 = 8 1/2... | 106 | 48 | 55 | 209 | ..... |
| e) Added fractions and disregarded whole numbers: 9 3/5 − 8 4/5 = 7/5 = 1 2/5... | 6 | 5 | 4 | 15 | ..... |
| f) Added whole numbers and disregarded fractions: 3 5/6 − 1 3/12 = 4........ | 6 | 5 | 4 | 15 | ..... |
| 3. Difficulty in reducing fractions to lowest terms ................................ | 625 | 311 | 158 | 1,094 | 14.6 |
| a) Did not reduce fraction: 7 1/5 − 3 3/6 = 3 21/30............................ | 581 | 248 | 118 | 947. | ..... |
| b) Divided numerator and denominator by different numbers: 3 7/12 − 2/8 = 3 8/24 = 3 2/3.............................. | 28 | 44 | 11 | 83 | ..... |
| c) Divided denominator by numerator: 1/2 − 2/8 = 2/8 = 4.................. | 16 | 19 | 29 | 64 | ..... |
| 4. Lack of comprehension of process involved... | 497 | 330 | 267 | 1,094 | 14.6 |
| a) Subtracted numerators and multiplied denominators: 5/8 − 1/8 = 4/64 = 1/16.... | 25 | 43 | 31 | 99 | ..... |
| b) Added numerators and subtracted denominators: 2/4 − 1/2 = 3/2 = 1 1/2....... | 2 | 4 | 3 | 9 | ..... |
| c) Subtracted numerators and added denominators: 3/5 − 2/3 = 1/8.............. | 10 | 12 | 6 | 28 | ..... |
| d) Multiplied numerators and subtracted denominators: 3/5 − 2/4 = 6/1 = 6........ | ...... | 4 | ...... | 4 | ..... |
| e) Multiplied numerators and added denominators: 1/2 − 2/8 = 2/10 = 1/5........ | 28 | 5 | 11 | 44 | ..... |
| f) Subtracted numerators and denominators: 2/4 − 1/2 = 1/2...................... | ...... | 30 | 7 | 37 | ..... |
| g) Called common denominator answer where remainder was zero: 2/4 − 1/2 = 4....... | 2 | 2 | 2 | 6 | ..... |
| h) In subtracting two equal fractions, expressed remainder by same fraction: 4 2/3 − 4/6 = 4 4/6 − 4/6 = 4 4/6 = 4 2/3.......... | 16 | 8 | 12 | 36 | ..... |

## TABLE 23 (continued)

| | GRADE V A | GRADE VI B | GRADE VI A | TOTAL | PER CENT |
|---|---|---|---|---|---|
| **4. Lack of comprehension of process involved —** *Continued* | | | | | |
| *i)* In subtracting two equal fractions, called the remainder 1: $2/4 - 1/2 = 2/4 - 2/4 = 1$ ............................ | 12 | 15 | 14 | 41 | .... |
| *j)* In subtracting mixed numbers with equal fractions, placed common denominator under difference between whole numbers: $7\ 1/2 - 4\ 2/4 = 3/4$ ................ | ...... | 6 | 5 | 11 | ..... |
| *k)* Subtracted fraction in minuend from fraction in subtrahend: $2\ 1/3 - 3/6 = 2\ 1/6$ | 62 | 29 | 23 | 114 | .... |
| *l)* Added the two numerators and from that sum subtracted numerator in subtrahend: $7\ 1/8 - 5/8 = 7\ 6/8 - 5/8 = 7\ 1/8$ ...... | 5 | 5 | 26 | 36 | ..... |
| *m)* Added denominators and numerators and used the sum as numerator in minuend: $10\ 1/4 - 3\ 2/4 = 10\ 11/4 - 3\ 2/4 = 7\ 9/4 = 9\ 1/4$ ................ | 8 | ....... | 2 | 10 | ..... |
| *n)* In subtracting mixed number from whole number, subtracted whole numbers and placed same fraction in result: $3 - 1\ 2/3 = 2\ 2/3$ ............................ | 270 | 164 | 115 | 549 | ..... |
| *o)* When numerator in minuend was smaller than numerator in subtrahend, called remainder zero: $9\ 3/5 - 8\ 4/5 = 1\ 0/5$ .... | 56 | 1 | 8 | 65 | ..... |
| *p)* Did not express denominator: $5/8 - 1/8 = 4$ ................................ | 1 | 2 | 2 | 5 | .... |
| **5. Difficulty in changing fractions to common denominator** ........................... | 288 | 147 | 191 | 626 | 8.3 |
| *a)* Subtracted without changing fractions to common denominator and used one of the given denominators for denominator in result: $4\ 6/8 - 1/4 = 4\ 5/8$ ............... | 229 | 110 | 160 | 499 | ..... |
| *b)* Changed fractions to wrong denominator: $3\ 5/8 - 2\ 3/6 = 3\ 10/12 = 2\ 6/12 = 1\ 4/12 = 1\ 1/3$ ........................ | 33 | 27 | 8 | 68 | ..... |
| *c)* Disregarded numerator being more than 1: $7\ 1/5 - 3\ 3/6 = 7\ 6/30 - 3\ 5/30 = 4\ 1/30$ | 13 | 3 | 17 | 33 | ..... |
| *d)* Changed fraction in minuend only to common denominator: $3/5 - 2/4 = 12/20 - 2/4 = 10/20 = 1/2$ .................. | 13 | 7 | 6 | 26 | ..... |
| **6. Computation errors** ...................... | 230 | 216 | 168 | 614 | 8.2 |
| *a)* Unknown: $4\ 5/6 - 1\ 2/5 = 4\ 25/30 - 1\ 12/30 = 3\ 3/5$ .................... | 129 | 100 | 53 | 282 | ..... |
| *b)* Subtraction: $6\ 2/4 - 5\ 1/6 = 6\ 6/12 - 5\ 2/12 = 1\ 5/12$ ....... | 87 | 102 | 105 | 294 | ..... |
| *c)* Addition: $9\ 3/5 - 8\ 4/5 = 8\ 7/5 - 8\ 4/5 = 3/5$ ........................ | 14 | 14 | 10 | 38 | ..... |
| **7. Omitted example (no attempt)** ............ | 291 | 81 | 47 | 419 | 5.6 |
| **8. Partial operation** ........................ | 138 | 53 | 110 | 301 | 4.0 |
| *a)* Subtracted fractions but disregarded whole numbers: $4\ 6/8 - 1/4 = 4/8 = 1/2$ | 56 | 46 | 47 | 149 | ..... |
| *b)* Subtracted whole numbers but disregarded fractions: $3\ 6/8 - 1\ 1/4 = 2$ ............ | 82 | 7 | 63 | 152 | ..... |
| **9. Errors in copying:** $3\ 5/6 - 1\ 3/12 = 3\ 10/12 - 1\ 2/12 = 2\ 8/12 = 2\ 2/3$ ............... | 1 | 12 | 1 | 14 | 0.2 |
| Total ........................ | 3613 | 1978 | 1920 | 7511 | 100.1 |

it to concentrate its attention. The child suddenly becomes conscious of its own physical fatigue, of the sights and sounds around it. The mind balks at the next addition; it may be a simple combination, as adding 2 to the partial sum, 27, held in mind. It finally becomes imperative that the child momentarily interrupt its adding activity and attend to something else. If this is done for a small fraction of a second, the mind clears and the adding activity will go on smoothly for a second group of six figures, when the inattention must be repeated.

It should be evident that these periods of inattention are critical periods. If the sum to be held in mind is 27, there is great danger that it will be remembered as 17, 37, 26, or some other amount, as the attention returns to the work of adding. The child must, therefore, learn to "bridge" its attention span successfully. It must learn to recognize the critical period when it occurs, consciously to divert its attention while giving its mind to remembering accurately the sum of the figures already added. This is probably best done by mechanically repeating to one's self mentally, "twenty-seven, twenty-seven, twenty-seven," or whatever the sum may be, during the whole interval of inattention. Little is known about the different methods of bridging the attention span, and it may well be that other methods would prove more effective. The use of the device suggested above, however, is common.

Giving up in the middle of a column and commencing again at the beginning is almost a certain symptom of lack of control of the attention. On the other hand, mere inaccuracy of addition (as 27 plus 2 equals 29) may be due to lack of control over the combinations. If the errors occur at more or less regular points in a column, and if, further, the combinations missed vary slightly when the column is re-added, the difficulty is pretty sure to be one of attention and not one of knowledge.

**Analysis of errors made by pupils.** Table 23 contains a detailed analysis of the wide variety of errors made by pupils in subtraction of fractions, as reported by Brueckner.[1] Similar lists of errors for each of the other processes in fractions are available, Brueckner has also published similar

[1] This summary first appeared in an article by the author entitled "Analysis of Errors in Fractions," in *Elementary School Journal*, vol. 28, pp. 760–70.

lists of the kinds of errors and faults most frequently found in processes with decimals and per cent.

**Analysis of most common faults.** Table 24 gives Brueckner's summary of the investigation of the most common kinds of faults in addition, subtraction, multiplication, and division of fractions:

### TABLE 24. CAUSES OF ERRORS IN COMPUTATION

1. Errors in computation are one of the major causes of mistakes in work with fractions, the per cent of error due to computation in addition being 13.8 per cent, for subtraction 8.1 per cent, for multiplication 28.7 per cent, and for division 13.8 per cent.

2. The major causes of errors in each process are as follows:

*Addition:*

|  | PER CENT OF TOTAL |
|---|---|
| (a) Lack of comprehension of process involved | 20.2 |
| (b) Difficulty in reducing fractions to lowest terms | 17.5 |
| (c) Difficulty with improper fractions | 17.1 |
| (d) Computation | 13.8 |
| Per cent due to these four causes | 68.6 |

Per cent unknown was 20.4

*Subtraction:*

| | |
|---|---|
| (a) Difficulty in borrowing | 24.4 |
| (b) Use of the wrong process | 20.3 |
| (c) Difficulty in reducing to lowest terms | 14.6 |
| (d) Lack of comprehension of process | 14.6 |
| (e) Computation | 8.1 |
| (f) Difficulty in changing to common denominator | 8.3 |
| Per cent due to these causes | 90.3 |

*Multiplication:*

| | |
|---|---|
| (a) Computation | 28.7 |
| (b) Lack of comprehension of process | 17.3 |
| (c) Difficulty in simple reduction | 17.2 |
| (d) Omitted (Probably lack of comprehension) | 11.3 |
| (e) Failure to change improper fractions to mixed numbers | 8.8 |
| (f) Difficulty in changing mixed numbers to improper fractions | 2.8 |
| Per cent of total | 86.1 |

TABLE 24 (*continued*)

| *Division:* | PER CENT OF TOTAL |
|---|---|
| (a) Wrong operation, failure to invert | 31.1 |
| (b) Computation | 13.8 |
| (c) Lack of comprehension or processes involved | 12.1 |
| (d) Difficulty in reducing to lowest terms | 8.9 |
| (e) Difficulty in changing mixed numbers to improper fractions | 8.6 |
| (f) Omitted (Lack of comprehension of process?) | 8.3 |
| (g) Failure to reduce improper fractions to mixed numbers | 7.1 |
| Per cent of total | 89.9 |

3. Major difficulties in all processes are:
   (a) Lack of comprehension of process involved
   (b) Difficulty in simple reduction
   (c) Difficulty in reducing improper fractions to lowest terms

4. Difficulty of changing fractions to a common denominator is a cause of relatively little error in addition of fractions, but a significant cause of error in subtraction.

5. Changing mixed numbers to improper fractions is a major cause of difficulty in both multiplication and division of fractions.

6. There is clear evidence that the kinds of errors that have been analyzed exist in each of the grades which were investigated. Supplementary investigations show that they are also found in large number in the upper grades.

7. The analysis of errors here given is based as a detailed study of the written work of pupils. It should be supplemented by an individual study of the work of pupils who have special difficulties in much the same way that Buswell and John and the writers have analyzed the work of pupils in the fundamentals. The many peculiar types of errors listed in the tables clearly show the need of special attention to individual difficulties. This is especially true in the addition of fractions, since it was not possible to analyze the causes of the errors in 20.4 per cent of the cases.

8. Special attention should be given to the preparation of special exercises whose purpose it is to remove the types of difficulty listed under (2). These exercises should recognize the different types of examples in each of the processes, as well as the apparent major causes of error.

The discussion for subtraction gives some notion of

the wide variety of faults that may be found in any of the processes in fractions.[1]

### 4. *The techniques of detailed diagnosis*

The techniques for making a detailed diagnosis of specific causes of difficulty in arithmetic are: (1) observation of the pupil's methods of work under normal conditions; (2) analysis of the pupil's written work; and (3) observation of the pupil's habits of work at the time of a clinical examination.

**Observation of the pupil's daily work.** Such faults as tapping, counting, dawdling, erratic behavior, inattention, lack of interest or effort, and similar obvious traits may be readily observed while the pupils are at work on the daily assignment.

**Analysis of the pupil's written work.** Efficient teachers have always used the technique of analyzing the written work of the pupil, and have in that way in many cases located the source of the difficulty. It is quite a simple matter to locate the error in such an incorrect example as $\frac{3}{8} \times \frac{1}{8} = \frac{4}{8} = \frac{1}{2}$, a very common error due to faulty transfer of skills previously acquired in addition of fractions. It is quite a different matter to be certain, as the result of an examination of the written work above, what the exact causes of error were in working the example at the right. The error may have been due to failure to allow for borrowing or to incorrect subtraction in the

$$\begin{array}{r} 942 \\ 795 \\ \hline 157 \end{array}$$

combination $13 - 9$. It is practically impossible to locate the exact cause of error in the work given at the right by analyzing the written work. The error in column 1 may have been due to inability to add $8 + 5$, or $13 + 8$; the error in column 2 may have been due to failure to carry, to incorrect sums in combinations,

$$\begin{array}{r} 78 \\ 165 \\ 198 \\ \hline 230 \end{array}$$

---

[1] Similar lists of faults for decimals and percentage may be found, by those interested in making a more detailed study of arithmetic difficulties, in Brueckner's *Diagnostic and Remedial Teaching in Arithmetic.*

or to other similar causes. In spite of its obvious short-comings, the method of diagnosis based on an analysis of the pupil's written work should always be used at first before the more careful methods of the clinical examinations are employed, since a large per cent of the errors can thus be located by an analysis of the pupil's written work.

**The clinical examination.** In almost every class there are pupils whose work is so far below desirable standards in one or more exercises or phases of a process that a more careful study of their work is necessary if the difficulty is to be located. A simple technique to use, especially in the lower grades, is to observe the pupil's responses and reactions as he works an example aloud. The following statement by Uhl [1] describes the results of such an analysis of the work of a pupil.

A pupil from the fifth grade presented a quite different method of adding. In adding 4, 9, and 6, she explained: "Take the 6, then add 3 out of the 4. Then 9 and 9 are 18, and 1 are 19." Other problems were worked out similarly; one containing 3, 9, and 8 was solved as follows: "8 and 8 are 16 and 3 are 19 and 1 are 20"; 5, 6, and 9 as follows: "6, 7, 8, 9, and 9 are 18 and 2 are 20." This tendency to build up combinations of 8's or 9's continued in the case of another problem: 6, 5, and 8 were added thus: "6, 7, 8, and 8 are 16 and 3 are 19." Probably her first problem was worked similarly, but I had to have her dictate her method twice before I understood; she then gave it as quoted.

**Procedure to follow in selecting pupils, and a clinical examination.** The following procedure may be followed in making a diagnosis of difficulties in arithmetic:

1. The teacher should give a survey test to secure an initial picture as to the status of the class as a whole.

2. The teacher should make a careful analysis of the work on

[1] Uhl, W. L. "The Use of Standardized Materials in Arithmetic for Diagnosing Pupils' Methods of Work"; in *Elementary School Journal*, vol. 18, pp. 215–18.

the test to locate obvious deficiencies or the types of exercises most frequently solved incorrectly by the class as a whole.

3. The teacher should then select for careful study those pupils whose work was considerably below the standard in one or more of the processes. Usually not more than ten per cent of the pupils in a class will need much study. The class should be given the ordinary assignment of work to be done at their seats, so that all may be profitably occupied.

4. After the class has begun to work on the assignment, one pupil who has been selected for special study should be called to the teacher's desk, or to a table conveniently located in the room. The pupil should be told that the purpose of the teacher is to help him to determine the cause and nature of his arithmetic difficulties, and he should be encouraged to assume a coöperative attitude in the undertaking. The teacher should think of his part of the examination as being like that of a physician who is making a clinical diagnosis of the cause of the illness of an individual. The purpose of the diagnosis by the teacher should be the location of faulty methods of work, lack of knowledge on the part of the pupil, and other possible causes of inefficiency of work. At this step the teacher should not attempt to remedy the situation by teaching correct procedures.

5. The teacher should next select a standardized diagnostic test in the process to be investigated, such as the Buswell–John or Brueckner tests, or, if they are not available, should use some similar set of examples prepared for the purpose. Usually not more than one process at a time should be studied, to avoid fatigue on the part of the pupil.

6. The teacher should explain to the pupil that he will make it easier to diagnose his difficulties if he will do his work aloud, so that the teacher may observe his procedure. The teacher should illustrate the method by working one or two typical examples. Pupils readily respond to these directions and demonstrations, especially if the teacher has created the right attitude, and if the examination is conducted in a friendly, helpful spirit.

7. As the pupil works the teacher should make notes of the types of faults that are discovered. Such a record is facilitated by the use of the record blanks that are prepared on certain of the standard diagnostic tests. These blanks contain lists of the most common types of faults revealed by extended clinical studies of the work of pupils deficient in arithmetic. It is obvious that the

teacher must have a first-hand appreciation of the various kinds of errors that may be discovered and of their symptoms. Sometimes the pupil stops in the middle of an example and apparently is blocked by some difficulty. By careful questioning the teacher should make an effort to get the pupil to tell what his mental processes are during the period of apparent inactivity. While the method of securing the pupil's testimony as to his mental processes may not be a wholly reliable one, due to his inability to describe them accurately, nevertheless an observing teacher with insight can usually secure quite a vivid picture of what mental activity takes place. The length of the time required for a diagnosis will of course vary according to the extent and nature of the faults discovered in the pupil's work. The average time required for a single process is between fifteen and thirty minutes.

8. When the work of the test has been completed the teacher should carefully analyze the notes taken during the examination, and summarize the findings of the diagnosis. These may be recorded on the standardized blank, on the pages of a notebook in which records of a diagnosis are kept, or may be filed in some other convenient form for reference.

9. The necessary reteaching and remedial work should then be undertaken in the light of the findings of the diagnosis.

## IV. REMEDIAL WORK IN ARITHMETIC PROCESSES

Remedial work in arithmetic may be considered from both the preventive and the corrective points of view. On the one hand the school must see to it that faults in the work of the pupils are not due to inadequacy of instructional materials, lack of insight in teaching procedures, or failure to teach efficient methods of work. On the other hand, the necessary corrective work must be undertaken to remedy the faults revealed by a diagnostic study.

**Necessary instructional materials.** A primary requisite for effective teaching of arithmetic is the provision of instructional materials, constructed according to specifications based on the available body of scientific information. Such facts as the relative difficulty of number facts, the difficult points in the development of a process, the learning steps in the analysis of a process, the variety of skills that constitute a process, and the combinations in which these skills may occur in varying types of examples in the process must be considered in the selection of instructional materials. The use of teaching tools which have been constructed without careful consideration of the results of important research studies or the nature of the arithmetic processes is almost certain to result in the development of faults that could have been prevented by the use of more carefully constructed instructional material.

The essential teaching tools for instruction in the processes of arithmetic are:

1. Survey tests to provide a picture of the status of the class from time to time, preferably given at regular intervals during the year rather than only at the beginning or the end of the year. Graphs and progress charts of these scores provide an excellent basis for motivation of the work in arithmetic.

2. Diagnostic tests for locating the steps in processes in which pupils may be deficient, or the places at which difficulties may exist.

3. Diagnostic devices for determining the causes of the deficiencies and faults.

4. Carefully constructed remedial exercises and instructional units, to be used to overcome the weaknesses revealed by the diagnosis.

5. Tests for measuring the effectiveness of the remedial work.

6. Exercises and drills for cumulative practice, to insure retention of the acquired skills.

7. Carefully graded exercises in which there is a step by step development of the processes new to the grade, and through which the pupil acquires correct concepts and ideas.

8. Ample problem material in which the need of such process is illustrated when it is presented, and in which the pupil is given practice in solving problems that are based on situations such as arise in life in which the process is used.

**The adaptation of instruction to individual differences.** The most significant fact revealed by the use of tests is the wide differences in the individuals in a class, from whatever angle the group may be considered. Pupils learn at different rates; they do not all have difficulty on the same phase of a process; they exhibit different kinds of faults in their work; the amounts of practice required to develop a specific ability to a desirable level vary among a group of individuals. These differences are ignored in classes where the whole group is dealt with as a unit and the same exercises are prescribed for all. The "lock-step" system violates all of the principles of instruction that have been established through the findings of educational science.

The attempt of the schools to provide for the differences in individuals has resulted in many interesting modifications of methods of teaching and in the development of new types of instructional materials. Courtis and Studebaker have devised drill exercises in arithmetic processes in whole numbers which make it possible to individualize the review work on processes previously taught. The exercises provide a fairly adequate basis for remedial work, although they are not as well graded in the steps of each process as, for example, the Economy Remedial Exercises.

The record below shows how widely the pupils in a fourth-grade class were distributed on lessons in the Courtis Practice Tests, at the end of the second month:

> 1 pupil  on Lesson  1 — Addition — single column
> 2 pupils on Lesson  2 — Easy subtraction
> 3 pupils on Lesson  3 — Easy multiplication
> 2 pupils on Lesson  4 — Easy short division
> 1 pupil  on Lesson  5 — Addition by endings
> 3 pupils on Lesson  6
> 2 pupils on Lesson  7
> 4 pupils on Lesson  8
> 2 pupils on Lesson  9
> 3 pupils on Lesson 10
> 1 pupil  on Lesson 11
> 2 pupils on Lesson 12
> 1 pupil  on Lesson 14
> 1 pupil  on Lesson 17

Some of the pupils made very rapid progress, while others made relatively little improvement. If all pupils had been assigned work according to the needs of the average or the least able pupil in the class, a large decrease in efficiency would have resulted. As a consequence of the modified class procedure, pupils of superior ability progressed rapidly through the series of exercises without any special help from the teacher; the teacher used the time thus made available to help the pupils whose work did not show any improvement due to practice, as shown by their inability to complete the easier exercises. Careful diagnosis of their difficulties was followed by the use of suitable remedial exercises, and such reteaching as each case seemed to require.

In some schools, notably Winnetka, an attempt has been made to individualize instruction in the new as well as the review phases of arithmetic.

**The prevention of faults at the time of learning.** Many possible faults can be prevented at the time a process is first presented. Methods of work that are judged by competent individuals to be efficient should be taught from the beginning. The procedures should be practiced under careful supervision until they have been learned. While it must be admitted that at present little is known as to what the best methods of work are for individual pupils, it is self-evident that the faulty, roundabout procedures used by some pupils should not be allowed to become established habits. When such a faulty habit is discovered in the work of pupils not making satisfactory progress the teacher should at once teach a simpler method of work. Pupils usually can be shown the desirability of a simpler procedure, and in most cases can learn it quickly. As a general rule, it is best not to interfere with established methods of work in the case of pupils whose work is at a satisfactory level, as measured by test results, even if minor faults are apparent.

In some cases it has been discovered that the pupil is bewildered by the differences in procedures taught by teachers of successive grades; as, for example, in the statements to be used in subtraction of whole numbers. This situation usually exists in schools in which there has not been a common acceptance by all teachers of a uniform procedure to be taught in all grades. Some teach the "borrowing" method; others the Austrian method. Some teachers demand a short, simple statement of procedure; others require a lengthy, involved statement. It is important that the teachers in a system agree on a basic plan, after due consideration of any pertinent scientific evidence, and then teach it uniformly. When pupils new to the city enter the school, teachers should not require the pupil to unlearn methods of work he has already been taught until they are certain that it would be for the best interests of the pupil if he learned the methods used locally.

The knowledge that certain kinds of errors tend to persist in the upper grades should be considered at the time the process is being taught. For example, the error in $\frac{3}{8} \times \frac{1}{8} = \frac{3}{8}$ occurs frequently in examples of that type. The difficulty probably is due to the transfer of skills learned in addition and subtraction of fractions, which require that the pupils write the denominator without changing it when the common denominator is present. Such difficulties can probably be eliminated if the likelihood that this fault will subsequently arise is guarded against by the use of exercises, at the time of learning the step, that are likely to prevent its subsequent occurrence.

**The necessity of drill to insure retention of acquired skills.** Skill in arithmetic rapidly deteriorates, due to disuse. This is best shown by the loss in skill revealed by tests given before and after the summer vacation; a time when there is relatively little practice on many of the arithmetic processes taught in school. To insure retention of the new skills that are taught from time to time and mastery of processes previously taught, the teacher must provide for the systematic cumulative review of old and new processes. This may be accomplished by means of mixed drills, in which samplings of various kinds of examples are included. Care must be exercised in the preparation of these drills to make certain that the practice is well distributed over the whole process, and is not limited to a few of the many types of examples that constitute the "area" of the subject. The following exercise is a typical mixed drill for grade 5:

### Mixed Drill 16

1. 756
   878
   964
   759
   127

2. 9764
   − 1793

3. $\frac{1}{3} + \frac{1}{6} =$

4. $4 - \frac{1}{2} =$

5. 768
   × 309

6. $375\overline{)89600}$

7. $\frac{4}{5} \times \frac{10}{13} =$

8. Express 4 feet 6 inches as feet.
9. Change $\frac{7}{8}$ yard to inches.
10. Add $6\frac{2}{3}$, $7\frac{1}{6}$, and $4\frac{7}{12}$.

**Reduction in the requirements of the course of study.** More pupils have failed in the subject of arithmetic than in any other subject of the curriculum. This failure has been due in part to the improper grade placement of the topics presented, and in part to the inclusion in the course of much subject-matter of little social value. This has been clearly demonstrated by curriculum studies, such as those of Wilson,[1] Bobbitt, Woody, and others. Much of this driftwood and deadweight has been eliminated and does not appear in the newer courses of study. Studies of the grade placement of topics, such as fractions, long division, and decimals, reveal

[1] An excellent summary of curriculum studies in arithmetic is given in the *Third* and *Fourth Yearbooks of the Department of Superintendence.*

wide variations in practice. Recent investigations, such as those of Washburne,[1] show that in many schools these topics are being taught to pupils who do not have the mentality to grasp them and therefore fail to profit from the instruction. Relatively little is known at present as to where topics can be taught with some assurance that they will be mastered by the pupils. Undoubtedly the teaching of arithmetic would be much more efficient if teachers were required to teach a body of subject-matter which experiments have shown is not too difficult for the pupils.

## V. THE POSSIBILITY OF IMPROVING ABILITY TO SOLVE ARITHMETIC PROBLEMS

**The nature of problem-solving.** According to psychological principles a problem arises out of some "felt need or difficulty" in a particular situation. The consequence of this "felt need" is that a series of mental or motor activities is begun, leading to a possible solution of the problem. For example, an individual may wish to find the relative merits of two different automobiles of the same price. His first procedure is to collect the necessary data regarding depreciation, durability, gasoline consumption, the ease of riding, and all other pertinent information. This information may be arranged in some systematic manner. Then by a process of selection, balancing one set of data against the other, and a consideration of the relative importance of differences found, finally a choice is made. Another situation of a similar type may involve such a question as the determination of the profit derived from a farm club project. Here the individual must compile the information from a whole series of records that have been kept more or less carefully, selecting the data to list as expenses and as receipts; he must

[1] Washburne, C. W., in *Twenty-Ninth Yearbook of the National Society for the Study of Education*, Part II, pp. 641–71.

array these facts systematically, checking his work at each stage; and finally, he can find the profit, if any, by a series of computations.

In life, problems involving number arise, as has been described above. When the problem has been formulated in the mind of the individual, he must decide on a method of solving it. This involves setting up the objective, the assembling of pertinent data and methods of solution, the selecting tentatively of the most desirable method of solution, and then the carrying out and appraisal of the selected solution. In life situations of this kind the data needed are not presented to an individual in a systematic fashion; the individual must select from a mass of facts those that are pertinent to the situation; he must be able to set forth clearly his objective, and then to direct his activities in such a way that a satisfactory solution may be reached.

**Problems in school.** In school the pupil is constantly placed in natural problematic situations in which the need of arithmetic arises. The quantitative thinking may involve merely informational aspects of number, such as knowing what 1000 is, or what 25 degrees means, or it may involve actual computation, such as finding the cost of a dozen apples at 5 cents each, or the cost of refreshments for a school party for a class of 40 individuals. A whole series of social activities arise in connection with a school party in which number has a functional application. Other illustrations of natural problematic situations in which the pupils will encounter the need for number will readily occur to the teacher. These occasions arise in the daily activities of the school and are therefore in the immediate experiences of the pupils. In these problematic situations, the pupil will need to assemble the pertinent facts from a variety of sources, array them in systematic manner, and then perform the necessary computations in order to arrive at a solution.

The following illustrate some of the types of problematic situations that frequently arise; they are meaningful to the child, and he is vitally interested in their solution:

1. Finding the cost of an education.
2. The school bank deposits.
3. Balancing a personal account.
4. Finding the cost of a week's automobile trip.
5. The relative cost of articles bought in bulk and in **packages.**
6. The cost of the school milk.
7. The cost of playground equipment.
8. The area of the school playground.
9. Finding the amount each pupil is under-weight or over-weight.
10. Finding distances on a road map.

Under present conditions most of the problem work in arithmetic classes is of a quite different character from that which has just been described. Textbooks contain large numbers of verbal "problems" for pupils to solve. In these problems the pupils are given all the information needed to arrive at a solution. It is apparently assumed that the pupils will learn to apply processes in the natural situations of life by learning to solve verbal problems of the type found in textbooks. While there is undoubtedly some justification for this assumption, it is clearly desirable that more attention be given to the use of the many natural situations that arise in the activities of the school to show the pupils the concrete applications of the arithmetic processes.

**The elements in problem-solving.** The solution of verbal problems found in textbooks involves four major factors: (1) the ability to comprehend the meaning of the statements in the problem and the situation that is presented; (2) the knowledge of essential facts and principles needed to arrive at the solution; (3) the ability to select the processes to be used in solving the problem; (4) and the ability of the pupil to perform the necessary computations accurately.

Investigations have shown that from 20 to 40 per cent of the errors in problem-solving are due to errors in computation. Lutes [1] has shown that a large increase in scores on problem tests results from preliminary practice on computations similar to those involved in the problems. If, therefore, efficiency in computation is increased, a large improvement in scores on problem tests should result. This fact suggests the need of carefully constructed instructional materials in which special attention is given to the prevention of the errors that are made because of lack of understanding of the process involved, or because of some special unit of unusual difficulty in the process.

**Experimental evidence on improving ability to solve verbal problems.** Most of the experiments on the possibility of improving the ability of pupils to solve verbal problems have dealt with the effectiveness of the use of various types of reading exercises in problem-solving. In general it may be said that a marked growth in problem-solving ability has resulted from the use of such exercises.

Newcomb [2] found that teaching the pupils a systematic method of attacking the solution of a problem yielded excellent results. The method he taught was as follows:

Reading problems over carefully and thoughtfully before attempting a solution, looking up the meaning of any unfamiliar word, analyzing and arranging data given in an orderly manner, determining the precise data required, selecting in the proper order the various processes necessary to effect a solution, deciding beforehand a reasonable result to expect, and carefully checking or evaluating the final result secured.

[1] Lutes, O. S. *An Evaluation of Three Techniques for Improving Ability to Solve Problems.* University Monograph in Education, no. 6; University of Iowa, 1926.

[2] Newcomb, R. S. "Teaching Pupils How to Solve Problems in Arithmetic"; in *Elementary School Journal*, vol. 23, pp. 183–89.

Wilson [1] found that a marked improvement resulted from the use of the following types of exercises:

1. Estimating answers and judging absurdities. One exercise asked pupils to judge whether answers were reasonable or absurd. These problems were all selected from the Buckingham scale and the absurd answers were actually given by pupils taking the test.

2. Another exercise asked the pupils to restate sentences using other words than those which were underlined. For example, in the following statement, "I can buy pencils at the rate of two for five cents," the pupils were asked to substitute words for the three words, "at the rate." This was done in order to find out how much of the difficulty is due to such arithmetical phrases as "at the rate of," "total," and "average." An attempt was also made to discover how many of the difficulties were due to incomplete comprehension or to the skipping of words which are crucial to the solution of the problems correctly.

3. A third exercise asked pupils to read the problem and to indicate the processes necessary to its solution.

Stevenson [2] reports an experiment in improving problem-solving ability by the use of the following types of reading exercises which yielded excellent results, especially with dull pupils. It is interesting to note that this study is one of the few in which the results were interpreted in terms of the mental levels of the pupils:

1. Telling what facts are given, what questions are asked, what processes to use, and what the approximate answer would be.

2. Solving problems without number, such as, "If you knew the cost of an apple how would you find the cost of several apples?"

3. Vocabulary exercises on difficult words.

4. A large variety of problems arising out of immediate life needs.

Washburne and Osborne [3] report an experiment to evalu-

[1] Wilson, Estaline. "Improving the Ability to Solve Problems"; in *Elementary School Journal*, vol. 22, pp. 380–86.

[2] Stevenson, P. R. *Report of a Nation-Wide Testing Survey in Problem-Solving*. Public School Publishing Company, 1926.

[3] Washburne, C. W., and Osborne, R. "Solving Arithmetic Problems"; in *Elementary School Journal*, vol. 25, pp. 219–26, 296–305.

ate the effectiveness of various types of exercises in problem-solving, as follows:

Training in the seeing of analogies (stating a problem in simpler terms or with simpler number) appears to be equal or slightly superior to training in formal analysis for the superior half of the children; analysis appears to be decidedly superior to analogy for the lower half; but merely giving many problems, without any special technique of analysis or the seeing of analogies, appears to be decidedly the most effective method of all.

The general recommendations, then, growing out of the investigation are as follows: Problems should be so constructed as to present real situations familiar to the child. Children should be given many such problems to solve without special training in any generalized, formal technique of analyzing problems. Concentration on practice in solving practical problems will yield gratifying results.

The results of these and other similar experiments show that large returns result from a systematic attack on work in problem-solving. The use of such exercises as have been listed may yield better results with inferior pupils than with superior pupils. This is suggested by the results of the experiments reported by Stevenson and Washburne. Modern arithmetic textbooks contain many exercises in problem-solving similar to those that have been used in these investigations. Others can easily be prepared by the teacher.

**Reading exercises in problem-solving.** Instructional materials to be used in improving instruction in problem-solving are similar in form to the various types of standard tests that are widely used to improve the quality of the written examination. Illustrations of the most important of these types of exercises are as follows:

1. Multiple choice
    a. In one foot there are 2   8   12   16   inches.
    b. Draw a line around the number which is most likely to be the correct product of $18 \times 27$

   256  366  486  594  1006

2. Completion
   a. The answer of an.......... example is called the sum.
   b. $\frac{1}{4}$ and $\frac{3}{4}$ are called.......... fractions.
3. True-false
   a. Mark the sentences that are true ($c$).  Mark those that are
      false ($x$).
      (1) In a yard there are 3 feet.
      (2) The formula for finding the area of a circle is $2\ r$.
      (3) Interest is the same as amount.
      (4) Six per cent is equal to .06.
4. Simple recall
   a. How many square rods are there to an acre? .........
   b. What is the formula for finding the area of a rectangle?...
   c. What is the answer of a multiplication example called? .....
5. Recognition
   a. What process would you use in solving each of the following
      problems?  Write $a$ for addition, $s$ for subtraction, $m$ for
      multiplication, and $d$ for division.
      (1) What is the cost of two apples at 5 cents each? .........
      (2) What is the cost of butter a pound if 6 pounds cost
          $3.24? .............
6. Yes — no.
   a. Is a mile equal to 160 rods?  yes  no
   b. Is an ounce less than a pound?  yes  no
   c. Is the formula for interest, i = $prt$?  yes  no
7. Matching exercises
   a. Before each item at the left write the number of the correct
      formula in the list at the right.

| .............. Area of a square | 1. $p = 4s$ |
| .............. Volume of a rectangular solid | 2. $v = lwd$ |
| .............. Perimeter of a square | 3. $a = s^2$ |

8. Selection
   a. Draw a line around the numbers of the statements below the
      problem which are not true.
      (1) Jack bought 7 apples at 3 cents apiece.  What change
          should he receive from a quarter?
          1. Jack bought 7 apples.
          2. Jack paid 5 cents apiece for the apples.
          3. He gave the clerk 15 cents.
          4. He would receive no change.
          5. Jack sold 7 apples.

Objective exercises constructed in the manner that has been described can easily be prepared. They can be used to develop or to detect weakness of pupils in such important skills involved in problem-solving as the following:

1. Ability to tell what facts are given.
2. Ability to tell what question the problem asks.
3. Ability to select essential facts.
4. Ability to estimate answers.
5. Ability to tell how to check answers.
6. Ability to name the process to use in solving one-step problems.
7. Ability to name process in order used to solve two-step problems.
8. Knowledge of vocabulary.
9. Knowledge of essential denominate numbers and units of measure.
10. Knowledge of essential principles and concepts.
11. Ability to judge absurdities.
12. Ability to check true and false statements.
13. Ability to assemble essential data.
14. Ability to read accurately and exactly.
15. Ability to follow directions.
16. Ability to attack the solution of a problem in a systematic manner.
17. Ability to apply processes in local situations.
18. Ability to interpret tables found in reference books.
19. Ability to use the index, table of contents, etc., as aids in studying.
20. Ability to understand quantitative concepts in map reading.
21. Range of information in application of arithmetic.
22. Ability to make analogies.
23. Ability to answer specific questions about problems.
24. Ability to formulate problems from given data.
25. Ability to illustrate uses of processes.
26. Ability to detect cues in solving problems.
27. Knowledge of historical background.
28. Ability to restate a problem in the words of the pupil.

**Verbal problems analyzed as to type.** Ability to analyze situations, and then to select the correct method of solution, depends to some extent on the provisions that have been made in the instructional material. Provision should be made to give the pupil experience in solving problems involving the important basal types of solutions found in arithmetic. An analysis of arithmetic situations shows that these basal types of solutions can be classified as eleven different kinds of patterns. Each type may occur in isolation in one-step problems, or in combination with others in two- or three-step problems. The eleven types and examples of each are as follows:[1]

1. The addition problem. (One type.)
    *Example.* Jack has 4 cents, Mary has 5 cents, and Alice has 7 cents. How many cents do they have in all?
2. Subtraction problem. (Three types.)
    (*a*) Type 1. Taking away.
        *Example.* Jack had 10 cents. He spent 5 cents. How much did he have left?
    (*b*) Type 2. Comparing.
        *Example.* Harry has 15 cents. Jane has 10 cents. How much more than Jane has Harry?
    (*c*) Type 3. Increasing.
        *Example.* Jack has 5 cents. How much more must he have before he can buy a 15-cent top?
3. Multiplication. (Two types.)
    (*a*) Type 1. Told about one; asked about many.
        *Example.* An apple costs 5 cents. How much do 5 apples cost?
    (*b*) Type 2. Finding a part of a number.
        *Example 1.* Find the cost of $\frac{3}{4}$ pound of butter at 40 cents a pound.
        *Example 2.* How much is 15% of $400?
4. Division. (Five types.)
    (*a*) Type 1. Told about many; asked about one.
        *Example.* If 5 apples cost 15 cents, how much does one apple cost?
    (*b*) Type 2. Finding a number of equal groups.
        *Example.* How many apples at 5 cents each can I buy for 50 cents?

[1] In Brueckner's *Diagnostic and Remedial Teaching in Arithmetic*, p. 327. Philadelphia, John C. Winston Company, 1930.

(c) Type 3. Finding what part one number is of another.

*Example 1.* What part of 50 is 25?

*Example 2.* At a sale I bought a $4.50 pair of skates for $1.50 less than the regular price. What was the per cent of savings?

(d) Type 4. Finding the whole with a part given.

*Example 1.* If ¾ pound of butter costs 30 cents, how much does one pound cost?

*Example 2.* Frank received $3.00 interest at the end of the year on money deposited in his savings account. The bank pays 3 per cent interest a year. How much money did Frank have on deposit in the bank?

(e) Type 5. Finding a missing factor.

*Example.* Find the width of a field containing 4,000 square rods if its length is 80 rods.

## VI. DIAGNOSIS OF PUPIL DIFFICULTY IN PROBLEM-SOLVING

**The techniques of diagnosis.** The techniques of diagnosis of pupil difficulty in problem-solving are similar to those used for diagnosing difficulties in processes. The testing approach enables the teacher to measure the ability of the pupils to solve problems, and to locate those individuals who are not able to solve problems as well as pupils of their level of development should be able to solve them. The testing approach helps the teacher to locate the places where difficulty exists, but does not indicate the causes. Analysis of the written work on the test will reveal such obvious faults as inaccuracy in computation, inability to select the correct process, and lack of knowledge of essential facts. Osburn [1] suggests that the answer to the problem often indicates the nature of the difficulty, but not its cause. For example, in solving the problem, "How much do 10 apples cost at 5 cents each?" such answers as 5, 15, or 2 would in-

[1] Osburn, W. J. *Corrective Arithmetic*, pp. 55–58. Boston, Houghton Mifflin Company, 1924.

dicate that the faulty process was used; such answers as 45
or 55 might be due to errors in computation, and not to use
of the incorrect process; such errors as 19, 65, etc., give no
indication of the cause of the difficulty. Further study is
needed before the exact cause can be determined. This
method of diagnosis based on pupil's answers is quite useful
in the study of causes of inability to solve one-step problems, but is of doubtful value in analyzing difficulties in
problems of more than one step.

TRIAL TEST IN STEVENSON'S ARITHMETIC READING TEST

On May 5th, Alice deposited $0.50 in the school bank; on the
10th, she deposited $1.50; on the 15th, she put in $0.50; and on the
20th, she deposited $1.00. How much did she deposit altogether
during May?

A. WHICH OF THE FOLLOWING FACTS ARE GIVEN IN THE
   PROBLEM?
   1. The different amounts deposited.
   2. The total amount deposited.
   3. The interest paid by the bank.
   4. The time when money was withdrawn.

B. WHICH OF THE FOLLOWING THINGS ARE YOU ASKED TO FIND
   OUT IN THE PROBLEM?
   1. The profit gained on the deposits.
   2. The number of times that she deposited money.
   3. The total amount deposited.
   4. The amount of each deposit.

C. WHICH OF THE FOLLOWING IS THE MOST REASONABLE
   ANSWER?

   | 1 | 2 | 3 | 4 |
   |---|---|---|---|
   | $22.00 | $15.50 | $1.00 | $3.50 |

D. WHICH PROCESS SHOULD BE USED IN SOLVING THE PROBLEM?

   | 1 | 2 | 3 | 4 |
   |---|---|---|---|
   | Addition | Subtraction | Multiplication | Division |

**The causes of difficulty in problem-solving.** Banting's [1]

[1] Banting, G. O., in *Second Yearbook of the Department of Elementary
School Principals*, pp. 411–21. Another excellent analysis of faults in
problem-solving is Lenore John's study reported in the *Elementary School
Journal*, October, 1930.

study of pupil difficulties in problem-solving is one of the most comprehensive that has been undertaken. It contains information concerning the faults revealed by a careful scrutiny of the pupil's daily work and by questioning boys and girls as to their difficulties in problem-solving. Banting's list of causes of inability to solve problems is as follows:

I. Failure to comprehend the problem in whole or in part. This may be due to any one of the following:
   a. Lack of general ability in silent reading.
   b. Lack of knowledge of the technical terms used, i.e., inability to read the language of arithmetic.
   c. Carelessness in reading. The child may know how to read the problem but yet fail to comprehend it because of lack of care and attention. This often results in a partial solution of the problem.
   d. Lack of the necessary experiences to reproduce mentally the concrete situation of the problem.

II. Lack of the ability to perform accurately and readily the fundamental operations.

III. Lack of the knowledge of facts essential to the solution of a problem. For example, lack of knowledge of the tables of weights and measures, etc.

IV. Lack of the ability to identify the proper process or processes with the situations indicated in the problem. One may understand the processes very well and yet not know which to choose to solve a particular concrete problem. The lack of this ability, not to know whether to add, subtract, multiply, or divide in a concrete case is characteristic of so-called dull pupils in arithmetic, and is the chief cause of the painful stabbing, the mere juggling with figures that is the despair of the teacher in the middle and upper grades.

V. Lack of sufficient interest in the problem to inspire the required mental effort.

VI. Failure to form the habit of verifying the results. Pupils who are able to read the problem and to identify the proper process often make snap judgments, which are easily apparent if an attempt is made to verify the partial and the total results.

VII. The habit of focusing the attention upon the numbers and being guided by them instead of by the conditions of the problem. For example, in a problem in which the essential fact was that a man received $18 for 24 hours' work, a number of children divided 24 by 18 to find the hourly wage, because 18 is a smaller number than 24. It will be noted that the correct process was identified. Another example is the fact that many children feel that they must use every number stated in a problem in its solution.

VIII. Akin to the foregoing, pupils are sometimes completely nonplussed by large numbers. Though they can read the problem and identify the process when smaller numbers are used, they are perplexed by numbers larger than those of everyday experience.

IX. The habit of being guided by some verbal sign instead of making an analysis of the problem. For example, in the problem from Buckingham's test, "A boy had 210 marbles, and lost one-third of them. How many had he left?" A bright boy whose answer was 70, explained his mistake as follows: "Miss —— (his teacher) told us that if we saw 'of' after a fraction in a problem we were to multiply." Other examples are rules given based not on an analysis but upon some verbal expression. For example, in the problem, "What part of 36 is 9?" teachers frequently tell pupils that the number after "of" is always the base and we must divide the other number by it.

X. Lack of ability or care to properly arrange the written work in orderly, logical form. In longer problems this is a fruitful source of error.

XI. The failure to recognize the mathematical similarity to type problems which the pupils understand, because of some unusual situation in the problem in question. For example, the pupil who readily solved problems dealing with the purchase and sale of familiar things, failed when given a problem dealing with the purchase and sale of a farm.

XII. Lack of ability to understand quantitative relations such as:
   a. Cost, loss or gain, selling price.
   b. Income, expenditures, amount saved.
   c. Interest, rate, time, principal, amount.
   d. Time, distance, rate.
        In order to solve problems containing such quantities one must know not only their meaning but the relations existing between them.

XIII. The pupil may fail because the problem requires exertion beyond his span of attention.

XIV. The pupil may fail because of absolute inability to do reflective thinking.

**Specific remedial exercises in problem-solving.** Little is known on the basis of experiment as to what may be done to overcome specific or general difficulties in problem-solving. Banting [1] has suggested a series of remedial exercises for each of the difficulties listed on page 231. The Roman numerals of the exercises below correspond to the numbers of the difficulties in Banting's list. The exercises given under each numeral suggest the kinds of remedial work that have been used with success in a typical school situation.

I. *a* (1) Give special drill in silent reading to the pupils in any grade who show lack of general ability to comprehend problems.

(2) Introduce the written or printed problem to the child in the first grade, not as an exercise in numbers, but as an exercise in silent reading. *Example:* A first-grade exercise in silent reading for seat work.

### PICTURE I

Draw a tree
Put five little birds in the tree

### PICTURE II

Draw the tree again
Two of the little birds are flying away
Draw them
How many little birds are left in the tree?
Draw them

Such exercises are invaluable for seat work and hundreds of them should be given to children in the first and second grades. The language used should gradually approach the ordinary form of the arithmetic problem.

Problems of this kind are also excellent for dramatization and for graphic illustration. In one of the second grades of the city,

[1] Banting, G. O., in *Second Yearbook of the Department of Elementary School Principals*, pp. 411–21.

pupils have produced dozens of original devices in paper cutting, drawing, and dramatizations to illustrate problems in which they have become interested.

The important thing to consider is that the skill required to read a problem should be developed, not in the arithmetic class, but in the silent reading lessons. As Thorndike well says, "The pupil should not be given elaborate drill in reading during the time devoted to the treatment of quantitative facts and relations." It is the business of the reading class to prepare the pupil to read the problem in Arithmetic.

I. *b* (1) In teaching the fundamentals, acquaint pupils with the proper arithmetical terms at the outset. Give drills upon the vocabulary of arithmetic used in the stating of problems. Such terms and phrases as: total amount, how many are left? how much remains? gained, lost, sold, bought, etc., should be thoroughly understood by the child and be to him a cue to the process required for solution.

(2) Give drill upon the common abbreviations used in arithmetic.

(3) Avoid needless verbal difficulties. Select only such problems as are expressed in words which ought to be familiar to the pupils.

(4) Pupils confined to one text become accustomed to the language and form used by one writer in the stating of problems and are unable to solve the same problems when stated somewhat differently in another text. For this reason teachers should be supplied with copies of a number of arithmetic texts so that they may select problems from various sources and give their pupils a richer experience in problem-solving.

I. *c.* "Carelessness" in reading problems is a phase of lack of ability in silent reading and should be corrected in the reading class.

Exercises like those listed under IV and VI are, however, very valuable and insure against carelessness.

(1) From the outset put a premium upon accuracy in reading and in copying the figures of a problem.

(2) Let every problem contain such a challenge to effort that the pupil is alert and attentive.

I. *d* (1) In the first, second, and third grades pupils should be given a wealth of experience in situations which involve number relations, number games of many kinds, playing post office, store, etc. Every opportunity should be embraced which introduces an element that helps to form a foundation of experience for problem work.

(2) If the pupil has not had the experience that enables him to reproduce mentally the concrete experience necessary to the solution of some particular problem, there are two things which the teacher may do.

Produce in the schoolroom the conditions of the problem, or similar conditions, in order to give the pupil the required experience. If a pupil fails in a problem give another problem dealing with familiar situations involving the use of the same process or processes in the same order. If the child solves II and fails to solve I he needs further practice.

II. (1) For remedial suggestions in fundamental operations see Part I of this article.

(2) It must be remembered that accuracy does not come by repetition alone. Pupils should be impressed with the one hundred per cent accuracy standards demanded by the business world.

(3) Pupils (in the fifth and sixth grade) should be given practical methods of checking and of proving the work. The modern adaptation of the old method of casting out nines is valuable for multiplication and long division.

III. (1) Pupils should not be given problems which require for solution facts which they do not know and cannot secure. However, problems which do not state all the facts necessary for their solution are especially valuable. For example, problems which require reference to price lists, market prices, etc.

(2) Pupils should be taught to analyze a problem and be able to state what they need to know in order to solve it. The following principles given to slow pupils and memorized by them proved very helpful in determining a process:

(a) When we know the price of a number of miscellaneous articles of different prices, we find their total cost by adding.

(b) When we know that one thing has greater value than another, we find how much greater one is than the other by subtracting.

(c) When we know the value of one thing, we find the value of many similar things by multiplying.

(d) When we know the value of many similar things, we find the cost of one of these things by dividing.

(3) If the pupil finds the need of a piece of knowledge in order to solve a problem and knows where to get it, he is acquiring information under the best conditions and is very liable to retain it.

IV. This is the most important consideration of the whole subject. The success of the pupil in problem-solving depends very largely upon the strength and permanency of the bonds formed in the mind of the child between a specific concrete situation and the proper arithmetical process to apply. The forming of these bonds is the all-important work of the lower grades. If the pupil does not acquire this ability there, he is a helpless failure in upper-grade arithmetic and frequently in algebra as well.

The child must first comprehend the concrete situation of the problem. That he may do so and yet not know the proper process to apply is shown by the following attempts at the solution of one of Buckingham's problems by 3B pupils who had not yet been taught to divide by 9. "If an electric car runs 9 miles an hour, how many hours will it take to travel from one city to another, a distance of 117 miles away?"

| SOLUTION BY HAROLD S. | SOLUTION BY FRANK B. | SOLUTION BY RAY K. |
|---|---|---|
| 9 | 9    108 | 12   13 |
| 9 | 12    9 | 12   13    13 |
| 9 | 108   117 | 12   13   × 9 |
| 9 | | 12   13    117 |
| 9   Answer 13 hrs. | Answer 13 hrs. | 12   13 |
| 9 | | 12   13 |
| 9 | | 12   13   Answer 13 hrs. |
| 9 | | 12   13 |
| 9 | | 12   13 |
| 9 | | 108   117 |
| 9 | | |
| 9 | | |

The pupil is ready for the process when he understands the situation.

As a means of aiding pupils in problem-solving the following suggestions will be found helpful:

(1) Teach no isolated fact in arithmetic, but every fact in connection with some practical situation.

(2) Have the pupils make up one-step problems, giving them specific directions, as:

Make up a problem in which you add.
Make up a problem in which you multiply, etc.

(3) Give the pupils one-step problems and have them indicate

the process by writing the word or giving the sign of the operation. Later have them specify the number to be added or multiplied, subtracted or divided.

(4) Give the pupils a number of problems and have them make up problems from their own experience different in condition but similar in solution.

(5) From lists of review problems in textbooks, have pupils select problems in which the same process must be applied. In checking a page in the text a list of one-step problems may be divided into four classes in some such form as the following:

| PROCESS | NUMBER OF PROBLEMS |
|---------|--------------------|
| Add | 1, 8, 7, 3 |
| Multiply | 2, 4, 6 |
| Subtract | 5, 9 |
| Divide | 10 |

A bright child should be given a number of arithmetics from which to select problems for assignments of this nature.

(6) There are fifteen kinds of two-step problems which should be studied intensively:

| | |
|---|---|
| Add and subtract | Multiply and subtract |
| Add and multiply | Multiply and multiply |
| Add and divide | Multiply and divide |
| Subtract and subtract | Divide and add |
| Subtract and add | Divide and subtract |
| Subtract and multiply | Divide and multiply |
| Subtract and divide | Divide and divide |
| Multiply and add | |

Collect problems which cover all of these and see that pupils are able to meet any of these situations by solving any such problem. They should be asked to make up problems in which these steps are required for solution, as, "Make up a problem in which you add and multiply, in which you subtract and divide, etc."

(7) Give problems without numbers for which the pupils will give the processes, for example: "If I know all the items of a bill and the amount I give in payment is greater than the amount of the bill, how do I find what change I am to receive?"

(8) Teachers should avoid assigning lists of problems in any particular process as review work. Such work has little or no value as a reasoning exercise. Unless problems require a variety of response so that the child must think in every case, they are valuable merely as an exercise in mechanics.

(9) When giving a problem similar in process to the one which has preceded it, teachers should not tell pupils, "this is another problem just like it." Pupils must be required to discover for themselves the similarity of the situations involved.

V. (1) The cause of lack of interest is mainly lack of motivation. Discard the bookish problem. Give to the pupil the practical problem of daily life.

(2) Let every problem be a challenge to the pupils to do something that is worth while.

(3) Have pupils bring actual problems from the home.

(4) Correlate with situations in geography, history, or reading which involve situations requiring the use of numbers.

(5) Appeal to the interests of pupils. Boys are interested in batting averages, basket-ball scores, the laying out and measurement of a baseball diamond, etc. On pages 9 to 23 of his *Psychology of Arithmetic*, Thorndike gives an excellent discussion on this subject, which every teacher should read.

VI. Lead the pupil to form the habit of doing the following: After reading the problem, as aids to the solution: (1) Label your answer. (Will the answer be in dollars, yards, days, etc.?) (2) Estimate the answer in numbers — Will it be larger or smaller than some number in the problem, and why? (3) After solving the problem check all your work, and if possible prove your answer; and (4) If it is impossible to prove the answer, its reasonableness should be tested.

VII. Secure a careful analysis of the problem by such devices as the following:

(1) Have the pupils specify what each number in the problem represents.

(2) Give the pupils a similar problem, but with the numbers of such character that they will not lead to error, for example: A man received $24 for 6 hours' work.

(3) Give a similar problem without numbers and have pupils tell the solution in general terms. For example, in problem under discussion, divide the total amount received by the number of hours the man worked.

VIII. (1) Have the pupils make up a problem just like the one given, but with smaller numbers. After he has solved it let him again try the original problem.

(2) In teaching a new principle use only simple numbers.

IX. (1) In this case the teacher is generally responsible for the failure. There is a constant tendency to give the pupils some rule or guide (like the examples given in the list of Causes of Failure under IX) by which they can arrive at a solution without reflective thought. This is, of course, the very reverse of what ought to be done.

(2) It is true, however, that some dull pupils who can never be led to reason effectively can be taught to solve problems of some degree of difficulty by giving them rules and cues to solution; but care must be taken to select only cues which have no exceptions which will at some later time lead a pupil into error.

(3) Require oral analyses of pupils who are failing to do satisfactory work in reasoning. This will enable the teacher to find the exact spot where a pupil is erring in his reasoning.

X. (1) Pupils must be impressed with the importance of neatness, care, and logical order in all written work in arithmetic.

(2) Partial results should always be labeled.

(3) A premium should be put upon good written solutions to problems by displaying them upon the bulletin board.

(4) Pupils should keep arithmetic note-books in which, from time to time, are inserted neat, orderly solutions of type problems and of such others as have proved difficult to them.

XI. Training in the solution of problems by means of type problems is of value. Suggestions already given, listed below, will be found helpful. See IV, 2, 3, 4, 5, and 6; X, 4. When an important and difficult type problem is taught, an effective method will consist of omitting the mechanical operations and merely discussing the solution.

XII. Special care should be taken in a study of the relations between various quantities like those cited. The algebraic form may be used. For example:

$$Amount = Principal + Interest$$
$$Distance = Rate \times Time$$
$$Cost + Gain = Selling\ Price$$
$$Area = Length \times Width$$

XIII. (1) Pupils should not be given problems beyond their powers of comprehension and span of attention. Two-step problems should not be given until the pupils have displayed a complete mastery of one-step problems; three- or more-step problems until there is mastery of the two-step problem.

(2) Care must be taken that the situation described in the

problem be not unnecessarily complicated or the statement too wordy.

XIV. Teachers should have the intelligence quotients of all their pupils, and must realize that it will be impossible to train those whose rank is below that of the dull normal to do much reflective thinking in arithmetic. Such pupils may often be proficient in mechanical work, to which the attention in such cases should be largely confined.

## Characteristics of a group of pupils low in problem-solving ability.

The following is a summary of Martin's [1] study of the social, intellectual, and educational characteristics of fifty-six pupils who were one and one half years or more below standard in their ability to solve problems:

1. The pupils attended sixteen different grade schools during the preceding year.

2. There are two pupils in the subnormal level of intelligence, eleven in the borderline, ten in the dull, fourteen in the average and nineteen in the bright.

3. The average number of grades repeated for the *entire* group is .54 *full* grades.

4. The average number of schools attended for the *entire group* is 2.1.

5. Two thirds of the pupils in the study were over-age for their respective grades. The amount of over-ageness varies from a few months to nearly three and one half years.

6. The teachers' intelligence ratings are below those of the Haggerty Delta 2 Intelligence Examination.

7. The group is low in general scholarship according to the estimates of the teachers.

8. The group is slightly above normal in industry as judged by the teachers' ratings.

9. The pupils, as a whole, have a decidedly good attitude toward school work according to the teachers' estimates.

10. The pupils of this group have a rather poor attitude toward problem-solving.

11. This group was, according to teachers' estimates, exception-

[1] Martin, Curtis.  *An Analysis of the Difficulties in Arithmetical Reasoning of Fourth-, Fifth-, and Sixth-Grade Pupils*.  Unpublished master's thesis, University of Minnesota, 1927.

ally well-behaved, over 76 per cent of the pupils being rated either "A" or "B" in deportment.

12. The pupils in the upper two intelligence levels were in better physical condition than those in the lower levels.

13. The group, as a whole, was estimated by the teachers to be usually composed, meek, usually dependent, light-hearted, docile, usually confident, usually deliberate, coöperative, usually industrious, usually careful, and usually attentive.

14. The predominating nationality of the fathers of the children in this group is American.

15. The principal types of occupations of the fathers of the children in this group are: common labor, commercial service, miscellaneous trades, and building trades.

16. The pupils of the higher levels of intelligence attend school more regularly than those of the lower levels.

17. Fifty-one of the fifty-six pupils were reported by their teachers of the previous year as being weak in some phase of arithmetic.

18. Thirty-two of the pupils were reported to be having difficulty in either "all phases of arithmetic" or in problem and thought work.

19. The 4B and 4A pupils were, on the average, 6.3 and 3.9 months, respectively, below standard in the Stevenson Problem Analysis Test, 12.8 and 7.5 months below standard in the Stanford Reasoning Test, and from .3 to 12.8 months below standard in the various fundamental tests.

20. The 5B and 5A pupils were, on the average, 16.2 and 3.5 months, respectively, below standard in the Stevenson Problem Analysis Test, 3.8 and 8 months below standard in the Stanford Reasoning Test, and from 1.8 to 11.4 months below standard in the several fundamental tests.

21. The 6B and 6A pupils were, on the average, 1.3 and 3.9 months, respectively, below standard in the Stevenson Problem Analysis Test, 3.8 and 9.2 months below standard in the Stanford Reasoning Test and from 5.7 months below standard to 6.2 months above standard in the fundamental tests.

22. As a whole, the group was normal in intelligence, above standard in reading, and below standard in arithmetic reasoning and fundamentals.

**The essential elements of a program to improve ability to solve problems.** The essential elements of a training program for increasing ability in solving problems are well presented in the following quotation from a report of a special study by Stevenson,[1] which describes a procedure that has been successfully used after a preliminary survey of ability in problem-solving has revealed an unsatisfactory condition. Many of the types of exercises he suggests were used in the experiments on improving problem-solving that have been reported.

### A Twelve-Week Remedial Program

*The program.* All sane testing programs should involve the following procedure: (1) give tests, (2) locate individual difficulties, (3) apply remedial instruction, (4) give tests again to see if remedial instruction was effective. The following project has been tried out several times and has proved successful in increasing pupils' ability to solve problems.

The remedial instruction is planned to cover a period of twelve weeks. All the work is to be done in the recitation period. Three fifteen-minute periods each week are to be devoted to special remedial work. This makes a total of nine hours.

*First, second, and third weeks.* During these three weeks the pupils should be taught to read and analyze problems. The pupils should be directed to open their books to a page containing a list of problems. Before solving a problem, drill should be given in finding what facts are given in the problem, what is asked, the process or different processes which should be used in solving the problem, and the answer in round numbers. (Some of the problems should be worked to see if the estimated answers are approximately correct.)

A list of problems should also be written on the board and pupils instructed to answer the above types of questions either orally or in writing. The teacher should study the results of the analysis test, and see that each pupil gets practice in the exercises upon which he failed. Pupils having the same difficulties may be given instruction in groups.

*Fourth, fifth, and sixth weeks.* The pupils should work a large variety of problems during these three weeks. The problems should contain data from actual life situations.

---

[1] Stevenson, P. R. *Remedial and Follow-Up Work Bulletin in Problem Solving.* The complete bulletin published by Public School Publishing Company, Bloomington, Illinois,

The teacher should ask the pupils to submit lists of problems in addition, subtraction, multiplication, and division. These problems should be similar to those which the pupils and their parents have occasion to solve.

The teacher should try to arouse pupils' interest in solving different types of problems.

*Seventh, eighth, and ninth weeks.* During this time have pupils solve problems without the use of numbers. These problems will, of necessity, have to be made up by the teacher and should be adapted to each grade. The following examples will furnish suggestions:

1. If you knew the amount of cloth needed to make a dress, how could you find the amount necessary for three dresses?
2. If you knew the cost of one dozen oranges, how would you find the cost of six oranges?
3. If you knew the height of each pupil in your class, how could you find the average height?
4. If you knew the amount paid for a house and the rate of commission, how could you find the commission?
5. If you knew the present population of your town and the population five years ago, how could you find the amount of gain? The per cent of gain?

*Tenth, eleventh, and twelfth weeks.* During these weeks teach pupils to read problems and have them study their vocabulary. Devices which will be of assistance are:

1. Have pupils state problems in their own words. Have each problem stated in as many different ways as possible.
2. In various problems, study words which might cause difficulty. Have the children explain the meanings or define such words. Some words with which children have difficulty are: area, average, dealer, retail, commission, salary, rent, broker, wages, merchant, debt, expenses, acre, income, profit, loss, and insurance. Whenever possible, concrete explanations should be made by the teacher or the pupils.

## QUESTIONS FOR STUDY, DISCUSSION, AND REPORT

1. Show that arithmetic consists of a large number of specific skills and abilities.
2. Why is rate of work an important factor in ability to perform arithmetic operations? What provision is made in textbooks

and standard drill materials for giving standards for rate of work?

3. Select a series of tests for measuring achievement in arithmetic processes and problem-solving.

4. Examine arithmetic textbooks to find out what provision is made for survey tests, diagnostic tests, and practice exercises. How are the standards stated?

5. Secure a set of test papers and make an analysis of the examples worked incorrectly, and try to determine the causes of each error. What difficulties do you encounter in making such a diagnosis? Are you sure that your diagnosis is correct?

6. How do you account for the round-about methods of work that have been discovered in pupils' procedures in solving examples?

7. Suggest some things that a teacher might do to prevent the development of faulty methods of work.

8. Describe methods of class organization that would give the teacher time to do special work with pupils having difficulty.

9. How would you teach the pupil to find the quotient in the following examples?   16)76   25)93

10. Why might continued practice by a pupil on exercises on which he has difficulty fail to produce an improvement?

11. What is the difference between a curriculum test and a diagnostic test?

12. How could you find out whether or not your pupils are deficient in arithmetic vocabulary?

13. Describe techniques you could use to diagnose difficulties in problem-solving.

14. Make a careful case-study of some pupil considerably below standard in problem-solving.

15. Outline a diagnostic and remedial program in arithmetic.

## SELECTED REFERENCES

Brown, J. C., and Coffman, L. D.   *The Teaching of Arithmetic.* Chicago, Row, Peterson and Company, 1924.

Brueckner, L. J.   *Diagnostic and Remedial Teaching in Arithmetic.* Philadelphia, John C. Winston Company, 1930.

Brueckner, L. J., and Hanson, E.   *Curriculum Tests in Problem Solving*, Grades 3–8.   Philadelphia, John C. Winston Company.

Buswell, G. T., in coöperation with John, L.   *Diagnostic Studies in Arithmetic*, Supplementary Educational Monograph, no. 30. University of Chicago Press, 1926.

Buswell, G. T., and Judd, Chas. H. *Summary of Educational Investigations Related to Arithmetic.* Supplementary Educational Monograph, no. 27. University of Chicago Press, 1926.

Burton, W. H. *Supervision of Elementary Subjects*, Chapter 2. New York, D. Appleton and Company, 1929.

Morton, R. L. *Teaching Arithmetic in the Primary Grades.* New York, Silver, Burdett and Company, 1926.

Morton, R. L. *Teaching Arithmetic in the Intermediate Grades.* New York, Silver, Burdett and Company, 1926.

Osburn, W. F. *Corrective Arithmetic*, vols. 1 and 2. Boston, Houghton Mifflin Company, 1924 and 1929.

Thorndike, E. L. *Psychology of Arithmetic.* New York, The Macmillan Company, 1922.

*Twenty-Ninth Yearbook of the National Society for the Study of Education.* Bloomington, Illinois, Public School Publishing Company, 1930.

## ARITHMETIC TESTS CITED IN CHAPTER VII

| Test | Grades or Ages | Publisher |
|---|---|---|
| Brueckner Diagnostic Tests in Fractions | 3–5 | Educational Test Bureau, Minneapolis, Minn. |
| Brueckner Curriculum Tests in Arithmetic Processes | 3–8 | John C. Winston Company, Philadelphia, Pa. |
| Brueckner Diagnostic Test in Whole Numbers | 3–5 | Educational Test Bureau, Minneapolis, Minn. |
| Buckingham Scale for Problems in Arithmetic | 3–8 | Public School Publishing Co., Bloomington, Ill. |
| Buswell-John Diagnostic Tests for Fundamental Processes in Arithmetic (Individual) | Elementary | Public School Publishing Co., Bloomington, Ill. |
| Clapp–Young Self-Marking Arithmetic Test | 5–8 | Houghton Mifflin Company, Boston |
| Compass Diagnostic Tests in Arithmetic (Ruch and others) | Elementary | Scott, Foresman & Co., Chicago |
| Compass Survey Tests in Arithmetic | Elementary | Scott, Foresman & Co., Chicago |
| Courtis Standard Research Tests: Series A and Series B | 3–8 | S. A. Courtis, Detroit, Mich. |
| Courtis Supervisory Tests in Arithmetic | 4–8 | S. A. Courtis, Detroit, Mich. |
| Los Angeles Diagnostic Test | Elementary | Research Service Company, Los Angeles, Cal. |
| Monroe Diagnostic Tests in Arithmetic | Elementary | Public School Publishing Co., Bloomington, Ill. |
| Monroe Standardized Reasoning Tests in Arithmetic | 4–8 | Public School Publishing Co., Bloomington, Ill. |
| New Stone Reasoning Test in Arithmetic | 4–9 | Bureau of Publications, Teachers College, Columbia University, N.Y. |
| Pittsburgh Arithmetic Scale (Guy) | 3–9 | Public School Publishing Co., Bloomington, Ill. |
| Stanford Achievement Test: Arithmetic Examination | 2–8 | World Book Company, Yonkers-on-Hudson, N. Y. |
| Stevenson Arithmetic Problem Analysis Test | 4–9 | Public School Publishing Co., Bloomington, Ill. |
| Woody Arithmetic Scales: Series A and Series B | 2–8 | Bureau of Publications, Teachers College, Columbia University, N.Y. |
| Woody–McCall Mixed Fundamentals in Arithmetic | 3–8 | Bureau of Publications, Teachers College, Columbia University, N.Y. |
| Woody–Van Wagenen Scales in Arithmetic | 3–8 | Bureau of Publications, Teachers College, Columbia University, N.Y. |

# CHAPTER VIII

## DIAGNOSTIC AND REMEDIAL TEACHING IN READING

**Rapid recent development.** Probably no subject in the elementary schools has undergone more development in recent years than has reading. Many reasons may be suggested to account for this fact. In the first place, the relationship of reading ability to achievement of pupils in other subjects has no doubt focused attention upon reading. The result has been a series of research activities probably unmatched in any other field.[1] In the second place, there has been a growing recognition of the importance of the rôle played by reading in the cultural, vocational, and recreational life of the nation. Modern social, economic, and political developments have forced the individual to depend more and more upon reading as a source of information and guidance.[2] The amount of reading material has also increased very rapidly in recent years.[3] The great amounts of material which adults in modern society today feel called upon to read make high levels of reading skill and rate a necessity.

**The responsibility of the school.** Because of the importance of reading the schools are charged with the responsibility of making effective readers of all pupils. The task of the schools is made especially difficult in two ways. The modern demands upon reading proficiency are very great, as has already been indicated. At the same time the

[1] Gray, W. S. *Summary of Reading Investigations.* Supplementary Educational Monographs, no. 28. Chicago, University of Chicago Press, 1925.

[2] Gray, W. S. "Importance of Intelligent Silent Reading"; in *Elementary School Journal*, vol. 24, pp. 348–56. (January, 1924.)

[3] Judd, Charles H. "Relation of School Expansion to Reading"; in *Elementary School Journal*, vol. 23, pp. 253–55. (December, 1922.)

individual differences among pupils confront the teacher with serious problems. In spite of the great variations in the pupil interests and abilities, society demands the attainment of superior reading ability on the part of practically all individuals.

## I. DEVELOPMENTS IN READING INSTRUCTION

### 1. *Kinds and types of reading*

**Kinds of reading.** There was rather early recognition of the fact that oral and silent reading are different processes psychologically.[1] Oral-reading methods had been traditionally employed in the schools. However, it was found that oral-reading methods were not effective in developing silent-reading ability. The wider use of silent reading in school, and in adult life as well, created urgent need for effective silent-reading instruction. The result was a period of development when considerable attention was given to the methods of teaching in silent reading.[2] When attention was given to oral reading there was a tendency to emphasize the "audience situation." The special needs of the two kinds of reading, oral and silent, came to be recognized.

**Types of reading.** Both pupils in school and adults in everyday life are called upon to use their reading ability in a wide variety of situations. Probably no complete check has ever been made of the many different types of reading. For instructional purposes, however, it is desirable to group reading activities into two types — *work type*, and *recreational type* reading.[3] The basis for making this distinction is that the reading abilities or skills required are affected by the purpose of the reader.

[1] Brooks, Fowler D.  *The Applied Psychology of Reading*, chap. 3,  New York, D. Appleton and Company, 1926.  278 pp.

[2] Smith, Nila Banton.  *One Hundred Ways of Teaching Silent Reading.*

[3] *Twenty-Fourth Yearbook of the National Society for the Study of Education,* pp. 4–5.  Bloomington, Illinois, Public School Publishing Company.

*Work-type reading.* Under work-type reading can be classified those types of reading connected with our vocations and various aspects of daily life. Reading to prepare a history lesson, reading the directions for assembling a radio, and studying a legal document are examples. It is obvious that pupils in school are called upon to do a large amount of this type of reading, whether or not they are given specific training in its use.

*Recreational reading.* Recreational reading has for its main purpose the proper use of leisure time. Here the emphasis is perhaps not so much upon exactness of detail. The individual reads for enjoyment. While commonly the material is of a narrative type, perhaps fiction, it is not necessarily so. One may read *The Art of Thinking*, or *Why We Behave Like Human Beings*, guided by much the same purpose as if one reads the latest novel. In either case the purpose of the reading may be enjoyment. In either case a natural and useful curiosity may be the motivating influence.

The last illustration suggests that no absolutely hard-and-fast lines can be drawn between the two types of reading. No doubt some of the skills used in *work-type reading* are also employed in *recreational reading*. Nevertheless, the two types are sufficiently distinct to demand specialized types of learning activities, and definite recognition of each in the school reading program.

## 2. Inventory of specific skills and abilities

**Specific skills and abilities.** Among the many studies made in reading have been several attempts to subject the wider abilities in reading to analysis. As an example, in silent reading both rate and degree of comprehension were recognized. However, comprehension is made up of, or at least is dependent upon, a large number of abilities. Not all of the skills involved in the two major types of reading have been isolated. In addition there is probably not complete agreement upon the exact nature of the abilities and skills required. There is, however, no question but that a large number of specific skills and abilities play a part in reading. The list given in Table 25 is submitted for illustrative purposes.

TABLE 25. AN INVENTORY OF SKILLS, KNOWLEDGES, ATTITUDES, AND ABILITIES IN WORK-TYPE AND RECREATIONAL-TYPE READING, WITH SUGGESTIVE ACTIVITIES [1]

WORK-TYPE READING

I. In which silent reading predominates:
  A. Ability to locate material quickly required:
    1. Knowledge of and an ability to use an index, which suggests:
      a. Learning the alphabet
      b. Finding words in alphabetical arrangement
      c. Arranging words alphabetically
      d. Finding answers to questions by use of an index
      e. Making an index for a book which has none, etc.
    2. Ability to use a table of contents, which suggests:
      a. Finding lessons in the table of contents
      b. Finding authors in the table of contents
      c. Finding all the stories written by a single author
      d. Finding all the stories on a certain topic
    3. Ability to use the dictionary, which suggests:
      a. Practice in locating words rapidly
      b. Practice in selecting definitions pertinent to the material being read
    4. Ability to use a library file, which suggests:
      a. Responsibility for the care of classroom files
      b. Excursions to a near-by library
    5. Ability to use reference material, which suggests:
      a. Practice lessons in using reference sets of informational readers in school
      b. Stimulate interest — locating material at home
    6. Ability to use maps, tables, graphs, which suggests:
      a. Practice in interpreting maps, tables, graphs, and diagrams
      b. Practice in making simple graphs to illustrate a topic or point
      c. Answering questions based on maps, graphs, etc.
    7. Ability to skim, which suggests:
      a. Skimming to find material on a certain topic
      b. Skimming to find the answer to a given question

---

[1] This list is taken from *The Technics and Evaluation of a Supervisory Program in Work Reading.* Minneapolis Educational Bulletin, no. 12. Minneapolis Board of Education.

## TABLE 25 (*continued*)

    *c.* Skimming to find a sentence which proves or disproves a certain point

    *d.* Skimming to find suitable material for a school program

    *e.* Skimming to find different types of information in the daily paper

**B.** Ability to comprehend quickly what is read requires:

  8. The establishment of rhythmic and rapid eye-movement, which suggests:

    *a.* Practice from the beginning in reading groups of words instead of single words

    *b.* Practice in rapid reading

    *c.* Flash card exercises using phrases and sentences

    *d.* Rapid reading of interesting material

  9. The elimination of lip reading and vocalization, which suggests:

    *a.* Establishing the habit of eye reading from the beginning

    *b.* Practice in reading under time pressure

    *c.* Short exposure exercises (flash cards)

    *d.* Rapid reading of interesting material

 10. Acquiring a vocabulary of accurate meanings, which suggests:

    *a.* Wide reading which gives an acquaintance with new words

    *b.* Conscious acquisition of new words in oral and reading vocabulary

    *c.* Answering questions to check comprehension

    *d.* Checking true and false statements

    *e.* Completion exercises

 11. The habit of vigorous reading, which suggests:

    *a.* Practice in seeing how much can be accomplished in a limited time

    *b.* A knowledge and an acceptance of good study habits

**C.** Ability to select and evaluate material needed requires:

 12. Judging the validity of information, which suggests:

    *a.* Practice in noticing the date of publication

    *b.* Practice in noting the author's name and position

 13. Choosing ideas from different sources which explain or supplement one another, which suggests:

    *a.* Finding like statements in two articles upon the same topic

 14. Discovering different ideas in different sources, which suggests:

    *a.* Reading two articles upon the same topic to discover points of differences

 15. Deciding whether a given question is answered, which suggests:

    *a.* Answering a series of *Yes-No, Didn't Say* questions

    *b.* Skimming an article to determine whether a particular question is answered

 16. Ability to sort essential and non-essential statements:

    *a.* Classifying as to major and minor importance of statements chosen by the teacher from a given selection

 17. Telling what questions are answered by material, which suggests:

    *a.* Making a list of questions that are answered

TABLE 25 (continued)

b. Reading to determine what questions in a proposed list, prepared by the teacher, are answered by a given article
18. Finding the solution of a problem, which suggests:
a. Locating material which will help to solve this problem
b. Reading an article to solve a problem

D. Ability to organize what is read requires:
19. Practice in picking out central idea, which suggests:
a. Reading an article and telling in one sentence what it is about
b. Reading an article and giving it a title
20. Practice in selecting main topics, which suggests:
a. Reading a series of paragraphs and giving a topic sentence for each paragraph (informational material)
b. Selecting everything that bears upon a certain topic
21. Practice in outlining, which suggests:
a. Arranging in proper sequence a series of topics selected by the teacher from a given lesson
b. Outlining a short thought unit or an entire lesson
22. Practice in summarizing, which suggests:
a. Reading articles of varying length and telling in one or more sentences what each is about

E. Ability to remember what is read requires:
23. Practice in selecting things to remember (see ability to organize)
24. An understanding of the best way to memorize
a. Acquaint pupils with rules for memorization
25. An understanding of the necessity of overlearning
26. Practice in remembering

F. A knowledge of the best sources of materials requires:
27. Practice in selecting the proper reference books to gain an answer to a given problem. (Use reference books which are accessible to the child.)

II. Oral reading
A. A knowledge of what makes oral reading of the work type effective
28. Pupils formulate a statement of the things which make oral reading effective
29. Pupils discuss why the oral reading of certain directions or announcements was not effective
30. Pupils practice to make their oral reading more effective

B. Ability to select material which is pertinent to a given oral reading situation
31. Selecting and reading to the group material to prove a point under discussion

C. Skimming in preparation for oral reading
32. Children discuss and illustrate the difference between reading unfamiliar and familiar material orally

D. An understanding of the purpose to be served by the reading
33. Practice in reading material to serve different purposes

## Table 25 (continued)

E. Ability to recognize and pronounce all the words in a selection
    34. Phonics
    35. Word analysis
    36. Drill on lists of words commonly mispronounced
    37. Using the dictionary to secure the correct pronunciation of a word

F. Ability to use the voice in a pleasing and effective way
    38. The habit of noting the effect of a pleasing voice upon an audience

G. Ability to interpret the thought of a selection accurately
    39. Practice in reading selections to give different interpretations

H. Proper attitude toward an audience
    40. Practice in reading announcements
    41. Practice in reading directions for making things
    42. Practice in reading informational material which the rest of the group wants to know.

*Note:* Subsidiary to the above abilities are such skills as, skill in adjusting the rate of reading to the purpose, clear enunciation, correct pronunciation, ability to recognize new words independently, and skill in using punctuation marks as an aid in accurate interpretation.

### Recreational Reading

I. These activities involve both oral and silent reading.

  A. Ability to comprehend what is read
    1. Technical skills involved here should be gained in silent reading and oral reading of the work type.

  B. An appreciation of well-written material, including pure literature
    1. Listening to the reading of a group of poems by a certain poet to arouse interest in finding other poems by the same poet.
    2. Listening to the reading of a group of poems illustrating a certain type, as the story-poem, to stimulate an interest in collecting other illustrations of story-poems
    3. Listening to reading for some purpose, as for rhythm or for delightful pictures
    4. Ability to take an active part in the discussion of a selection
      *a.* Locating and discussing the pictures
      *b.* Locating and discussing the funny parts
      *c.* Locating and discussing the parts which give a knowledge of characters
      *d.* Locating and discussing the interesting episodes in a selection

  C. Acquiring vicarious experience through reading
    1. Silent reading of a story, book, or article to extend the child's experience
      *a.* Extending the child's experience to other lands
      *b.* Extending the child's experience to other peoples
      *c.* Extending the child's experience to other periods in history
      *d.* Extending the child's experience to unfamiliar industries

TABLE 25 (*continued*)

  *e.* Extending the child's experience to inventions
  *f.* Extending the child's experience to pertinent civic situations
 2. Formulating and using a list of readings which will extend a child's knowledge of a certain subject or problem; as "The Importance of the Panama Canal"
 3. The ability to locate interesting reading material pertaining to individual interests
  *a.* Readings on gardening
  *b.* Readings on the care of dogs
  *c.* Readings on the history of various musical instruments

D. Appreciation of desirable social traits and attitudes
 1. Reading selections, prose or poetry, to determine the citizenship traits of the characters in the selection and to stimulate an interest in noting the traits of characters found in other selections
  *a.* Recalling characters which portray honesty, unselfishness, and patriotism
 2. Identifying and comparing personal experiences which are related to reading experiences in the field of literature, history, geography, or citizenship
  *a.* Recalling personal experiences comparable to those related in the selection read

E. A knowledge of interesting, enjoyable materials to read
 1. Familiarity with a list of good books which may be obtained at the library
 2. A knowledge of attractive, enjoyable books and magazines
  *a.* Pupils read good books and magazines made available in the classroom or school library
  *b.* Pupils prepare a book display during Children's Book Week
  *c.* Pupils read a book in which the teacher aroused an interest through the reading of an interesting incident

F. Developing a desire to read
 1. An appreciation and enjoyment of the teacher's reading of books, stories, poems, and plays
  (These selections should be chosen because of literary merit. They should be well read and may be slightly above the child's own reading ability.)
  *a.* Listening to poems read by the teacher with only running comments
  *b.* Listening to a story read by the teacher, followed by an informal but purposeful discussion
 2. Dramatizing scenes from suitable material
  (If the literary value of the selection lies in its highly imaginative quality, it should not be used for dramatization.)
  *a.* Pupils read the story silently and locate the best episodes for dramatization
  *b.* Groups of pupils work out their own interpretation of certain selections chosen for dramatization

Table 25 (continued)

3. The ability to recommend a good book in such a manner that the class will wish to read it
   a. Pupils may tell of books which they have read and have found interesting
   b. Pupils may read selections from interesting books
   c. Pupils may dramatize
   d. Pupils may put on a puppet show
   e. Pupils may make posters advertising books
4. The experience of "losing one's self" in an interesting book
   a. The teacher should encourage and stimulate an interest in wide reading
      (Studies of individual interests must be made if the teacher would put the child in touch with the books which may lead him to a permanent interest in reading)
5. Reading merely for fun
   a. Reading just to find how a story ends
   b. Reading jokes or nonsense rhymes
   c. Reading and learning to sing ballads

G. Reading various types of material for the purpose of entertaining others
   1. Reading to entertain the school assembly
   2. Reading to entertain the members of the child's own class or group
      a. Members of the class locate interesting short stories to be read to their group
      b. Members of the class read a group of poems
      c. Members of the class read a play

### 3. *Skills and Enrichment*

Even the specific abilities mentioned in the above list may be analyzed into narrower skills. The list of skills involved in the use of the table of contents given below is illustrative of the specificity of the abilities involved in reading. Each of the abilities listed in the above inventory could no doubt be subjected to a similar analysis.

## SKILLS INVOLVED IN THE USE OF THE TABLE OF CONTENTS [1]

I. Knowledge of the structure of tables of contents:
   A. Need for table of contents:
      1. To furnish in concise, summary form the main topics of a book,

---

[1] Abbreviated from list in Minneapolis Bulletin, no. 12, *The Technics and Evaluation of a Supervisory Program in Work Reading.*

permitting the reader to determine at a glance whether there are matters of information or interest for him.

2. As a matter of economy of time to quickly locate information if index is not provided in text.

B. Study of different types of tables involves:

1. Text having table of contents in which title and pages of a specific unit are listed

2. Text having table of contents in which titles and pages of chapter division are listed

3. Text having table of contents in which titles and pages are grouped under a central theme

4. Text having table of contents in which main topics, sub-topics, or both are listed

5. Text having table of contents which lists the aids in the text, such as appendix, maps and illustrations

II. Skills involved:

A. Mechanical skills

1. Ability to recognize title

2. Ability to recognize numbers

3. Ability to recognize author or sources of a given selection

B. Uses of the table of contents

Locate information when title and pages of a unit in table of contents are stated

1. To locate the title of a story in the table of contents

2. Titles listed in table of contents, class reads them

3. Titles read by teacher, class locates same and pages in table of contents

4. Locate materials in table of contents when information sought is not specifically stated

5. Locate information in table of contents when name of author only is specifically stated

6. Locate information when chapter divisions are given

7. Locate information when title is specifically listed under a central theme grouping

8. Locate information when title is not specifically stated, involving the use of more than one book

9. Determine whether or not a text has certain aids

**Developments in philosophy of method.**    Attention given to skills in reading should not lead to the erroneous conclusion that the only purpose of reading instruction is the acquisition of skills.    In fact, the tendency in modern reading instruction is ever in the direction of a richer program of instruction, and this enrichment is taking place largely as a result of a development in our educational philosophy.

Such developments are, of course, not confined to reading, but include other subjects as well.

**The wider concept of method.** Kilpatrick and others have emphasized the fact that learning never occurs singly.[1] Accordingly, the teacher must be concerned with a wide variety of associate and concomitant learnings. Many teachers also believe that learning takes place most effectively when it grows out of the felt needs of pupils. The result is a much greater emphasis upon children's purposes as motivation in teaching. The influence of this "wider concept of method" is plainly evident in the objectives of reading instruction as they are currently expressed. The *Twenty-Fourth Yearbook of the National Society for the Study of Education* gives the following as the major objectives of reading instruction:

1. Rich and varied experience through reading
2. Strong motives for and permanent interests in reading
3. Desirable attitudes and economical and effective habits and skills

**The tendency toward a richer program.** It is evident from the objectives mentioned above that skills are looked upon merely as means to an end and not as ends in themselves. The teacher wants children to learn to read, but she is even more interested in providing rich experiences through reading, and in so conducting the work in reading that children will *enjoy* reading and *desire* to read. There is thus a constant effort on the part of teachers to promote classroom activities which provide opportunities for rich reading experiences.

### 4. *Levels of teaching in reading*

The nature of the development of a richer program in

[1] Kilpatrick, William Heard. *Foundations of Method.*

reading is well illustrated by the series of levels of teaching of reading suggested by Gray.[1]

## LEVELS OF TEACHING READING

### Level 1

The teacher emphasizes the mechanics of oral and silent reading by having the pupils read aloud or silently and testing their comprehension of what is read. The objectives of the teaching are to develop the ability to read at a desirable rate, to pronounce the words correctly, and to understand what is read during the reading period. The content of the material read is limited to the textbook. The more scientifically the test is organized, the greater is the possibility that the teacher is securing valuable results.

### Level 2

The teacher has a broader concept of objectives than the teachers in Level 1. In addition to developing the ability to read aloud in a satisfactory way and to comprehend what is read orally or silently, the teacher stresses the development of the abilities and skills involved in work reading. This broader concept of objectives includes the ability to locate material quickly, to organize what is read, and to summarize what is read. Some attention is given to dramatization and to various methods of enriching the mechanical phases of the work. The class is dealt with as a whole and no specific attention is given to remedial and diagnostic work. No attempt is made to create interests in reading in other subjects, but there is a definite effort to bring the pupil into contact with a variety of reading material in textbooks which contain both literary and factual selections.

### Level 31

The activities are in general similar to those on the second level. However, in addition to these the teacher makes definite provision for diagnostic and remedial work for pupils who are encountering difficulties. There are many adjustments of the work to provide for individual differences. The subject-matter used in the reading period is limited to the regular textbooks in reading and in content subjects which may contain both factual and literary material.

---

[1] Taken from unpublished material. The descriptions of the levels as they appear below have been prepared by L. J. Brueckner.

No definite attempts are made to broaden the pupil's reading interests, and recreational reading is neglected.

### Level 4

This teacher has in mind the broader concept of reading objectives of the teacher at Level 3 and also provides for diagnostic and remedial work. The teacher differentiates the work according to the capacities of the pupils. In addition to this, a definite attempt is made to correlate the work of the reading period with the work in other subjects and to develop the necessary abilities required to carry them on satisfactorily. This teacher believes that the teaching of reading should not be limited to the regular reading period and does not hesitate to teach reading in other periods when the need arises. Stress is placed chiefly on the abilities needed in the work type of reading, and pupils are given some training in reading literary material through the directed study of selections from suitable books. No attempt is made to encourage voluntary reading of a recreatory type, either in or out of school.

### Level 5

This teacher carries on all of the activities of the teacher at Level 4, but in addition stresses recreatory reading. No attempt is made to relate the recreatory reading to the content subjects. A definite effort is made to arouse an interest in free, unassigned reading outside of school. This teacher believes that pupils should be encouraged to read whatever they may wish, regardless of the contribution that may be made to the work being done in the school in any other subject. This results in a diffusion of interests and effort rather than in a focusing of attention on organized fields of subject-matter.

### Level 6

This teacher develops an enriched program of oral and silent reading activities of the work type, makes adequate provision for remedial work, and in addition to this makes a definite attempt to relate the recreatory reading to the work in the content subjects. The teacher believes that organizing the reading in such a way is an economical procedure, since the child's recreational reading contributes to the achieving of the purpose of the school. Provision is also made to encourage reading of unassigned material outside of school and to develop broad reading interests.

### Level 7

At this level the teaching of reading is organized on the basis of large units of study, prepared in detail by the teacher or prescribed by the course of study. Stress is placed on directed study, the development of necessary study habits, the correlation of work and recreatory reading, and the systematic consideration of large bodies of subject-matter. The purpose of the teacher is to systematize the content of the material the pupil is to read and to develop the necessary skills, habits, attitudes, and appreciations in their natural setting. Provision is made for diagnostic and remedial work. Provision is also made for free reading of unassigned material to be read voluntarily by the pupil either in or out of school. The tendency clearly is to break down the compartmentalized subject-organization. However, the stress is primarily upon the acquisition of a body of subject-matter, and the development of attitudes, ideals, and desirable types of behavior is subsidiary. The latter may be an expected outcome of the former, but no attempt is made to provide for this directly.

### Level 8

On Level 7 the organization of the subject-matter is controlled by the teacher and all pupil activity is directed by the teacher. On Level 8 provision is made for active pupil participation in the selection of the content of the reading work and in the organization of the subject-matter to be covered. Pupils and teachers coöperate in determining the character of the reading activities to be engaged in by the class. Little attention is paid to the traditional subjects of the curriculum. The basis of the organization of subject-matter is the belief that problems, topics, and subject-matter of all kinds should be within the interest of pupils. The basis of the method is the belief that pupils should learn in natural situations such as they encounter in life itself, so that self-control, self-direction, self-appraisal, and the ability to coöperate in groups may be a natural outgrowth of the work that is done.

Examination of the descriptions of the levels will suggest that in Level 1 the emphasis is largely, if not entirely, on the skills in reading. With each succeeding level a form of enrichment occurs. It is significant to note that there is not only enrichment, but also a definite effort to relate reading to other subjects. Finally, in Level 8 the emphasis is upon the purposes and activities of children. Children in this level of the teaching of reading participate in the selection of the materials and activities in which reading instruction takes place. It may of course be that no single school passes through each of these levels, yet in the main the levels probably describe the general development which has taken place.

**The reading materials.** The widespread acceptance of a philosophy of method which considers the child and his interests and activities has profoundly influenced the character of the reading materials desired for the schools. Since it is one of the fundamental objectives of reading instruction to provide wide experiences for children through reading, it follows that a great increase in the amount and variety of reading material has been necessary. At the same time there has been a greater and greater tendency to consider the preferences of children in selecting materials. Studies have been made which throw light on the nature of children's preferences as to types of material, and the mechanical make-up of books. Among the results have been great improvements in the selection of materials in children's books, as well as improvement in the make-up of texts. The tabulation on page 262 (Table 26), taken from Zirbes, shows the development which has taken place.

## II. DIAGNOSIS IN READING

The foregoing discussion has served to indicate the complex character of the reading work in the schools. The classroom teacher is faced with the problem of providing effective instruction in reading for pupils of widely varying abilities and interests. It is highly important that the teacher be possessed of techniques whereby she may de-

TABLE 26. READING MATERIAL AND AMOUNT READ IN A PROGRESSIVE CITY SCHOOL SYSTEM [1]

| GRADE | KINDERGARTEN | FIRST | SECOND |
|---|---|---|---|
| Total No. of Separate Titles Available for Reading | 9 | 33 | 32 |
| Total No. of Pages | 1064 | 4012 | 4953 |
| Variety Rating | Very high | Very high | Very high |
| Quality Rating | + | + | + |
| Additional Material | A. Book table | A. Book table | A. Class library |
| | B. Picture books | B. Picture books | B Bulletin board |
| | C. Illustrated story books | C. Illustrated story books | C. Illustrated collections of stories |
| | D. Illustrated rhymes, labels | D. Illustrated rhymes | D. Books of rhymes |
| | | E. Borrowed library books | E. Books borrowed from public library |
| | | F. Blackboard reading matter | F. Blackboard reading matter |
| | | G. Charts | G. Phrase cards, sentence cards |
| | | H. Phrase cards, sentence cards | H. Class newspaper |
| | | I. Class records of experience | |

[1] Laura Zirbes. *Comparative Studies of Current Practice in Reading.* By permission of Teachers College, Columbia University.

TABLE 26. READING MATERIAL AND AMOUNT READ IN A PRO-
GRESSIVE CITY SCHOOL SYSTEM (*continued*)

| THIRD | FOURTH | FIFTH | SIXTH | ALL GRADES |
|---|---|---|---|---|
| 31<br>5702<br>Very high<br>+ | 25<br>6554<br>Very high<br>+ | 23<br>5986<br>Very high<br>+ | 26<br>6828<br>Very high<br>+ | 179<br>34099 |
| A. Class library | A. Class library | A. Class library | A. Large circulating classroom library | |
| B. Incidental reading matter | B. Incidental reading matter | B. Incidental reading matter | B. Collections of poems | |
| C. Bulletin board | C. Collections of poems | C. Collections of poems | C. Story books | |
| D. Collections of poems | D. Books borrowed from public library | D. Books borrowed from public library | D. Class subscriptions to magazines | |
| E. Books borrowed from public library | E. Collections of stories | E. Current magazines | E. Other current magazines | |
| F. Collections of stories | F. Story books | F. Reference books | F. Reference books in class | |
| G. Informational books | G. Informational books on history and geography | G. Individual borrowers' card from public library | G. Individual borrowers' card from public library | |
| H. Blackboard work | H. Geography text | H. Geography text | H. Geography text | |
| I. Access to school library | I. Other texts | I. History text, other texts | I. History text | |
| J. Sentence cards, phrase cards | J. Access to school library for reference books and home reading | J. Informational materials related to geography and history work, hygiene books | J. Informational materials related to geography and history work | |
| K. Riddle cards | | K. Use of school library for home and school reading | K. Health books | |
| L. Arithmetic text | | | L. Science books | |
| | | | M. Nature books | |
| | | | N. Arithmetic text | |

termine the instructional needs of such individual children, as well as techniques whereby suitable remedial instruction may be supplied. In modern reading instruction, testing or measuring for diagnostic purposes is not an appendage of reading instruction but a vital and integral part of the whole process of teaching. It is thus difficult to discuss tests and measurements in reading, for example, without discussing them as parts of the wider teaching process.

**Meaningful tests and drills.** If teaching is so organized that the needs of pupils are revealed to them and to the teacher in carrying on activities which are in and of themselves worth while, there need be no fear that tests and drills will become isolated and unmotivated. The teacher who seeks to provide proper motive for drills will first assure herself that worthwhile activities are provided for children. She will so guide these activities that needs for specific skills of various kinds will arise. As children become aware of their needs the teacher will provide the means whereby the needed skills may be developed. Under such conditions, tests and drills may become just as significant for children as many other activities.

**The emergence of needs.** A group of pupils in the fifth grade was studying the Indians. After having read about Indians in one or two school books, the question arose: Where can we find out more about the Indians? The teacher suggested that perhaps some of the books in the library might have information about Indians. How can we tell whether a book has anything in it about the Indians? Accordingly, the pupils learned how to use the Index and Table of Contents of books. This was an actual case in a real classroom where needs for learning certain specific reading skills emerged from an activity in which children were engaged. Many other examples, doubtless, could be given.

Another example of emergence of needs is taken from the Work Reading Program in Minneapolis,[1] and concerns itself with the development of felt needs on the part of children for learning how to make an outline:

### ILLUSTRATIVE LESSON 1

PURPOSE:

To create a problematic situation in order that the children might feel a need for developing some skill in outlining.

The reading materials used in this lesson were selected from the *Learn to Study Reader*, Book III.

DESCRIPTION OF THE LESSON:

The children read silently the story of Soap-Making in Pioneer Days, after which the teacher asked them to tell how soap was made. The children encountered great difficulty in recounting the information. After they had struggled with the problem for a time the teacher asked who could tell the cause of the difficulty. Several children said it was because they did not have a plan. Finally one child said that an outline would help them. The teacher then told the class something of the uses of outlines. She closed the lesson by saying that she would give them an outline on Soap-Making for the next lesson.

This lesson was taught four days before the teacher gave her illustrative lesson. Many fourth grade children know little or nothing about outlines, nor have they any experience to show them that an outline is of value in recalling material read.

**Effectively meeting needs.** There are times when it may not be readily apparent to teachers that pupils lack certain specific abilities. Again, the teacher may not be sure of the extent to which various skills have been taught. In these cases the various tests become very helpful. The teacher gives tests to find out what assistance pupils need, to help pupils discover their deficiencies, and to ascertain where to place the emphasis in teaching. She is also able to use the tests for the purpose of checking the effectiveness of her teaching.

[1] Taken from Minneapolis Educational Bulletin, no. 12, *The Technics and Evaluation of a Supervisory Program in Work Reading*.

**Diagnosis needed by all pupils.** The impression is current in some quarters that diagnosis and remedial work is necessary only with the slower pupils. Study of the achievements of pupils with specific tests shows that even pupils who rate high in intelligence and general achievement often have difficulties with specific phases of reading. Even high-school and college students lack many simple reading skills which should supposedly have been learned in the elementary schools. Diagnostic and remedial teaching should therefore be thought of as the normal teaching procedure, and not a special plan designed for "pathological" cases.

**Steps in diagnosis.** The *Twenty-Fourth Yearbook* suggests the following steps as typical of well-conceived work with remedial cases:

1. Discovery of deficiency in the course of classroom activities.
2. More intensive observation and study of the exact nature of the difficulties encountered in regular classroom work.
3. Individual examination by means of personal interview and selected standardized and informal tests with a view to revealing fundamental attitudes and causes of deficiency.
4. Formulation of specific remedial measures which attack the cause of the deficiency.
5. Initiation of regular remedial work in a manner to enlist pupil coöperation and effort.
6. Measurement with records, notes on pupil reactions, and study of progress.
7. Adjustment of work to changing needs until deficiency is removed.

**A comprehensive program.** As can be seen from the above statement, diagnosis is not purely a matter of tests. It involves securing information of a wide variety of types concerning the child and his abilities. Some of this information can best be secured by observation, some by tests, and some by interviews with the child, his parents, or his teachers. For the purposes of this discussion, however, it is desirable to discuss the various diagnostic techniques separately. It will also be possible to supply a number of case studies in which a variety of techniques have been employed with an individual child or group of children.

## III. DIAGNOSIS BY GROUP MEASUREMENTS

Presumably if diagnosis were to be carried on in its entirety by tests it would be desirable and necessary to have tests measuring every reading skill and ability. In this case it would be possible through tests to locate the exact needs of every pupil.

However, tests have not been prepared covering all of the specific reading skills and abilities that have been singled out by study and analysis. At the same time there are doubtless large numbers of narrower skills which play an effective part in reading which have not been isolated. Many of the factors in reading can probably not be measured at all by tests. Some factors, such as eye movements, require complicated laboratory equipment for measurement.[1] Reading is affected likewise by a large number of physical factors, such as vision, breathing habits, or illumination.

Complete diagnosis in reading will not be accomplished merely through the use of tests. On the other hand, diagnosis to be comprehensive will probably involve rather extended case study, including results of reading tests, mental tests, and data in regard to the pupil's age, home environment, interests and attitudes, and many other factors. The classroom teacher, however, need not employ all available diagnostic procedures, at least at any one time or perhaps for any one pupil. Certain of the more important diagnostic techniques will now be classified and discussed separately.

No attempt is made to describe all available tests in the field of reading, nor to include all types. Such tests as are

[1] Buswell, G. T. *Fundamental Reading Habits. A Study of Their Development.* Supplementary Educational Monograph, no. 20. University of Chicago.

included are offered merely as examples. Many useful tests have not been included because obviously they were not intended for diagnostic purposes.

### 1. *Tests for general diagnosis*

A great many reading tests can be described as diagnostic only in a very general way. They give a measure of levels of achievement in reading, but do not reveal in any detail what the nature of the achievement is. Commonly they measure some rather large composite ability, the detailed nature of which is only partially known.

**The Thorndike–McCall Reading Scale.** This scale has been widely used, and is therefore well known; hence only an illustrative paragraph is offered here.

THORNDIKE–McCALL READING SCALE
For the Understanding of Sentences

*Form* 1

*Read this and then write the answers. Read it again if you need to.*

Both before and after Christmas, Bob Adams worked harder than he did in the spring, summer, or fall. Only very rarely did he reach home before eleven o'clock; and on every morning except Sunday he was up at six, dressed and done with breakfast by quarter of seven, left the house at ten minutes of seven and reached Mr. Clark's store at ten minutes of eight. In spite of the long hours and hard work, he was happy because his pay had been raised twice.

14. What was the cause of Bob's pleasant feelings? . . . . . . . . . . . . . .

. . . . . . . . . . . . . . . . . . . . . . . . . . . . . . . . . . . . . . . . . . . . . . . . .

15. What other person besides Bob is mentioned in the paragraph?

. . . . . . . . . . . . . . . . . . . . . . . . . . . . . . . . . . . . . . . . . . . . . . . . .

16. How often did Bob reach home before eleven o'clock? . . . . . . .

. . . . . . . . . . . . . . . . . . . . . . . . . . . . . . . . . . . . . . . . . . . . . . . . .

This test is probably a measure of power in comprehension. It seeks to answer the question, "How difficult a paragraph can you read and answer questions about?" It singles out poor readers and good readers, but does not tell us why they are good or poor. Since the time limit for the test is thirty minutes, this test gives no measure of rate. The scoring is somewhat subjective and is also time consuming.

**Monroe Silent Reading Tests.** The Monroe Standardized Silent Reading Tests provide separate scores for rate and comprehension. They thus afford a measure of two aspects of reading. They are made up almost wholly of narrative material. Since the pupil reads the paragraph and then must stop to underline the words in following the directions, the pupil's score cannot be said to be an adequate measure of rate. In reality the test measures the rate at which the pupil can read the paragraphs and indicate answers to questions about them. The tests require only four minutes to give, and are easily scored. They are available in three levels of tests, covering grades 3 to 12 inclusive. Since there are three equivalent forms, the tests can be used to measure pupil progress during the school year.

While the Monroe tests provide measures of both rate and comprehension, they give no specific measure of the narrower skills which are involved, as, for example, in comprehension. Some teachers have attempted to use the results of the tests for the purpose of grouping children into six groups, on the basis of the test scores. Such grouping, however, must necessarily be very rough, and does not provide the detailed information concerning the child's learning difficulties in reading which is essential to proper adaptation of instruction to individual differences.

Test I
For Grades 3, 4 and 5     { Published by the     { Rate...............
Form 1                    Public School Publishing Co.    Comprehension......
                          Bloomington, Ill.
                          Printed in U.S.A.

### MONROE'S STANDARDIZED SILENT READING TEST REVISED

94     3. Nowhere in the world do the children have so many
105    good times as in Japan.  They are allowed to play anywhere, and
117    there are all sorts of toys and games for their amusement.
127        Draw a line under the word which best describes the chil-
138    dren of Japan.
140            cross     happy     fretful     good     contented

---

145    4. The mother stork sat in her nest with her four little
157    ones.  At a little distance, on the roof, stood the father stork.
170    He held one leg up and stood on the other.
178        Where does this paragraph say the father stork was standing?
188            chimney     roof     tree     nest     ground

---

Below is given a sample grouping scheme based upon results of the Monroe Silent Reading Test.  If a group of
pupils show high rate of reading and low comprehension
scores, we have no assurance that they are similar in instructional needs.  It may be that the causes for the low
comprehension scores are different in every case.

TABLE 27.  ILLUSTRATION OF CLASSROOM CHART BASED ON
RESULTS OF MONROE SILENT READING TEST

| I. Rate High–Comp. High | IV. Rate Average–Comp. Average |
|---|---|
| II. Rate High–Comp. Average | V. Rate Average–Comp. Low |
| III. Rate High–Comp. Low | VI. Rate Low–Comp. Low |

If the plan of grading pupils according to these scores is
followed, the likelihood is that groups formed on this basis
will show wide variations in the specific skills listed on page
250.  These conditions will obtain with all tests of this type,
and the Monroe test has been used here for illustrative purposes only.

TABLE 28. READING SCORES BASED ON MONROE SILENT READING
TEST [1]

| GRADE | RATE | | | COMPREHENSION | | |
|---|---|---|---|---|---|---|
| | High | Average | Low | High | Average | Low |
| | Above | From | Below | Above | From | Below |
| 3a | 113 | 75–113 | 75 | 8.7 | 4.5– 8.7 | 4.5 |
| 4b | 132 | 85–132 | 85 | 10.7 | 5.0–10.7 | 5 |
| 4a | 146 | 94–146 | 94 | 11.3 | 6.3–11.3 | 6.3 |
| 5b | 152 | 104–152 | 104 | 11.8 | 7.7–11.8 | 7.7 |
| 5a | 163 | 113–163 | 113 | 12.8 | 8.7–12.8 | 8.7 |
| 6b | 170 | 132–170 | 132 | 13.8 | 10.7–13.8 | 10.7 |
| 6a | 173 | 146–173 | 146 | 14.1 | 11.3–14.1 | 11.3 |
| 7b | 182 | 152–182 | 152 | 15.0 | 11.8–15.0 | 11.8 |
| 7a | 186 | 163–186 | 163 | 15.6 | 12.8–15.6 | 12.8 |
| 8b | 195 | 170–195 | 170 | 16.2 | 13.8–16.2 | 13.8 |
| 8a | 200 | 173–200 | 173 | 16.8 | 14.1–16.8 | 14.1 |

## 2. *Tests for analytical diagnosis*

According to a classification set forth in an earlier chapter, tests for analytical diagnosis not only locate the subject weaknesses of the pupil, but also indicate the specific abilities and the specialized fields of subject-matter in which such weaknesses exist.

**The Gates Primary Reading Tests.** As an example of such analytical diagnostic tests might be mentioned the Gates Primary Reading Tests. These tests are available in three types, each measuring a separate phase of primary reading. Type 1 is a test of word recognition. Illustrations are given below which indicate the construction of the test and the manner of pupil response. Type 2 measures word, phrase, and sentence meaning. Type 3 is designed to test the ability to read directions.

The Gates Primary Reading Tests are made more helpful in a diagnostic way through the Manual of Directions which accompanies the tests. This Manual lists causes for failure

[1] From Gist's *Elementary School Supervision.* Charles Scribner's Sons.

in reading, and indicates some remedial instruction. In addition to listing the causes for failure, the Manual also includes suggestions for types of practice material which will be helpful. The list of causes for failure, together with suggested practice exercises for one section of the test, are given below.[1]

## SAMPLE OF THE GATES OUTLINE

CAUSES OF DISABILITY OF TYPE II. The causes of difficulties in comprehending phrases and higher reading units are many. Omitting such causes as inferior native intellectual capacity and nervous or organic defects resulting in inadequate management of attention, the following are frequent sources of difficulty:

1. Overemphasis on word study due to the mistaken idea that pupils must have a large vocabulary before they should read sentences. Excessive zeal in teaching, testing, and drilling on isolated words is a related cause.

2. Overemphasis on phonetic drill or other analytic exercises designed to help the pupil recognize new words. When excessive, this type of drill makes certain pupils "word-conscious"; they must, for example, see *cat* as made up of the sounds *ku-aa-tt*; and perhaps have a fleeting recollection of *rat, sat, bat, hat*, etc., during the act of perception. As a man giving too much attention to his steps is likely not only to see little else, but also to stumble, so the word-conscious child not only is absorbed in the form of the word, but also often fails, or fears he may fail, on a word that would come easily if perceived with less concern. Such pupils are likely to neglect the thought and be slow to grasp the larger units.

3. Overemphasis on correct oral reading. Whether phonetics are used or not, pupils may become "word-conscious" if the teacher places great emphasis on correct articulation and pronunciation in oral reading. Reading may become a motor rather than a thinking exercise.

4. Overemphasis on reading by large (sentence or story) units in the beginning stages. Paradoxical as it may seem, failure to comprehend phrase and larger units may be the result of stren-

---

[1] By permission of Teachers College, Columbia University.

# GATES PRIMARY READING TEST [1]

## Type 1. Word Recognition

Grades 1 and 2            **FORM 2**

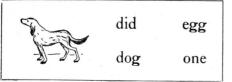

| did | egg |
| dog | one |

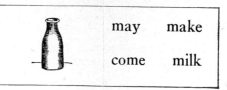

| may | make |
| come | milk |

## Type 2. Word, Phrase and Sentence Reading

Grades 1 and 2            **FORM 1**

### 1. A bed.

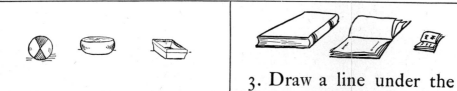

## Type 3.    Reading of Directions

Grades 1 and 2            **FORM 1**

1. Put an X on the ball.

3. Draw a line under the little book.

[1] By permission of Teacher's College, Columbia University.

uous efforts on part of the teacher to develop comprehension
of larger units from the start.  The pupil, on the teacher's
insistence that he do the impossible, may resort to memorizing
passages by rote and to other subterfuges which later interfere
with the necessarily gradual development of the hierarchies
of comprehension.

5. Lack of training at some critical period due to illness, etc.,
   after which the pupil, finding it impossible to bridge the gap
   to a higher level, may continue as a word-by-word reader.

6. Confusion due to varied and conflicting methods.

7. Lack of training in the utilization of punctuation marks.

8. Lack of training in the identification of natural units —
   "phrasing" as it is often called.

9. Lack of encouragement in depending on the context — rather
   than upon phonetics or other analysis — to recognize unfamiliar words.

10. Lack of reading primarily for the thought, inadequate use of
    practice material with comprehension exercises, of oral ques-
    tions and the like.

REMEDIAL MEASURES.  When the test reveals good word
recognition coupled with deficiency in comprehension of the
phrase, sentence, or paragraph units, it is advisable first of all for
the teacher to run over the ten common causes of these deficiencies, just listed, to see whether one or more of them are now
operating to the pupil's disadvantage.  If so, the causes should be
promptly removed, and a type of instruction of a more favorable
sort substituted.  Particular methods of accomplishing these ends
will be found in various good books on reading that are now available.  Judicious use of flash cards, phrasing exercises, etc., will be
helpful in some cases.  Space permits us here to mention but a
few types of practice material that will be helpful for difficulties in
phrase, sentence, and paragraph comprehension, however caused.

SOME TYPES OF PRACTICE MATERIAL.  The tests results should
indicate the approximate level of the pupil's present skill.  Give
materials that begin a little below this level and extend somewhat
above it.  The following indicate types:

1. *Story-making.*  A picture on the back of an envelope, which
   contains word, phrase, or sentence cards of familiar and

relevant material. The pupil builds up sentences or stories about the picture by arranging the cards.

2. *Story-illustrating.* Phrases, sentences, and paragraphs to be read and comprehension indicated by selection (or drawing) of illustrations.

3. *Directions as to color, draw, cut, make, find, do,* etc., may be graded from very easy to harder and longer.

4. *Yes-No exercises* like the following:

| Do cats sing? | Yes | No |
| Is milk white? | Yes | No |

5. *Selection exercises.*

corn

Dogs like to eat meat or (corn, meat, soap)

soap

What does a bird do?

It sings
It swims
It talks

6. *Reasoning choices.*

Where does the sun set?

In the east
In the morning
In the west

7. *Observation choices.* A picture mimeographed at the top of a page. Beneath are 12 questions to be answered by reference to the picture. A sample question is —

What are under the trees?

children   the fire   the dogs   the birds

8. *Exercises on the order of Test 2.*

Exercises of these types should not be used to the exclusion of those applied to longer stories or other contexts, or to unitary paragraphs. The use of various comprehension exercises such as those mentioned above, made up for pages in school readers, and other such material is highly desirable. Some of the publishing houses have ready-made comprehension materials of these sorts. The main purpose of these exercises is to encourage the pupils to read primarily to get not merely the word but the thought of the phrase or sentence as a whole and to lead them gradually to increase the range, fluency, and breadth of comprehension.

The judicious use of flash cards to encourage getting whole phrases and short sentences in a single span of comprehension, and of phrasing exercises to assist the pupil in detecting natural thought division; the explanation of punctuation marks; the use of oral reading followed by explanations by the pupil; the use of oral questioning following silent reading, etc., may all be employed to assist pupils deficient in comprehension. Since comprehension is not everywhere one and the same skill, there is merit in the use of a variety of exercise and test devices. A good reader is also a versatile reader. Versatility, alertness, and interest are all encouraged by the sagacious use of many such thought-provoking exercises.

The abilities measured by the test are, however, quite complex. Just what narrower skills are involved in "reading to follow directions" probably is not known. A large number of specific skills are necessary in order to read directions accurately. For example, any one or several of these narrow skills, such as vocabulary or ability to remember, might be the cause of a child's failure to secure a satisfactory score. As a result it is difficult for the teacher to determine the exact type of remedial work needed for any pupil.

If reading tests are to meet the criteria for diagnostic tests given in Chapter V (see page 121), they must not only tell the teacher the level of achievement of the pupil in reading but must also reveal the causes for the pupil's failure, if any. Efforts have been made to make reading tests more specific in order that they might be better adapted for diagnostic purposes. In the main these efforts have been directed along two lines. In the first place, investigators have sought to build tests around a larger classification of reading abilities involved in reading for certain purposes. In the second place, efforts have been made to analyze the composite reading abilities into narrower skills, such as those listed on page 250.

**The Gates Silent Reading Tests.** These tests have been constructed in four types. Type A is entitled "Reading to Appreciate the General Significance of a Paragraph"; Type B, "Reading to Predict the Outcome of Given Events"; Type C, "Reading to Understand Precise Direction," and Type D, "Reading to Note Details." An illustrative paragraph from each of the four tests is given below.[1]

GATES SILENT READING TEST

*Type A.   Reading to Appreciate the General Significance of a Paragraph*

Grades 3–8                                    FORM 1

4. With an anxious look in her brown eyes, Jane hurried to the telephone. "Central, will you give me Dr. Brown's office, please?" she said. Then, after a pause — "Is this you, Dr. Brown? Well, the puppy dragged doll baby from her bed and chewed her until she's torn to pieces. I'm afraid there won't be a chance to save her if you don't come at once."

Draw a line under the word that best tells how Jane felt.

weary   naughty   happy   worried   lonesome

8. Carefully Sue parted the leaves and looked down into the nest. Six baby robins greeted her with shrill cries for food. "John," she called down to her playmate below, "guess what I've found. A nest of baby robins! What fun we'll have putting food out for them. Oh, I can hardly wait until they are old enough to leave the nest."

Draw a line under the word that tells best how Sue felt.

happy   frightened   angry   worried   sad

*Type B.   Reading to Predict the Outcome of Given Events*

Grades 3–8                                    FORM 1

9. Johnny had been told not to eat any of the cherries before they were ripe, because they would make him sick. He had been watching a certain cherry tree for days and days. They were not ripe yet, although they looked so juicy and fine. Johnny could wait no longer. He climbed the tree and ate as many of the juicy balls as he could.

[1] By permission of Teacher's College, Columbia University.

Johnny ate another pailful of cherries
Johnny's mother said he was a good boy
Johnny went home sick
Johnny went home hungry

13. A black cat used to watch a bright goldfish in its bowl. His eyes followed its every motion. Sometimes he would put his paw into the bowl, but the water would make him draw it back. One afternoon as he watched the goldfish it swam near the surface. It made too big a flop and fell out of the bowl. It lay at the cat's feet.

The goldfish swam away
The cat got into the bowl
The cat ate the goldfish
The hungry cat went to sleep

*Type C.  Reading to Understand Precise Directions*

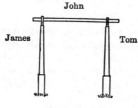

John

James          Tom

Grades 3-8                           FORM 1

10. This pole is in Tom's back yard. John, James and Tom try to see which can chin it best. All three boys are the same size, but James can chin it best. Maybe it is because he is stronger than John or Tom. Draw a line under the name of the boy who can chin the pole best.

14. The Eskimos live in a summer home much like an Indian tent. It is made of seal skins, and the poles are of whale bones. Sometimes the Eskimos find bits of wood. These, too, are used for

poles in the tents. Draw a line under what the Eskimos sometimes use for tent poles.

*Type D. Reading to Note Details*

Grades 3–8 FORM 1

7. One day a toad and a frog talked. Said the frog, "Why, certainly, I was once a tadpole, and every frog is a tadpole before he is full-grown. I had a tail, but when my legs began to grow my tail went away. Now I have no tail, but I have four strong legs. I am now a real frog. I use my legs when I swim and when I hop."

What was the frog once?

fish worm tadpole turtle

What went away?

legs tail head eyes

What does the frog use when he swims?

hop tail legs tadpole

10. In the mountains we find many pretty flowers. Among those that can be found in the early fall are the golden rod and purple aster. Think of the color they give to the sides of the hills. A story tells that these two flowers were once two little girls who wanted to make every one happy. So a fairy changed them into golden rod and asters.

When are golden rod and asters found?

spring summer fall winter

What does a story say these flowers were once upon a time?

stars girls sunbeams boys

How did they want to make every one feel?

gay excited young happy

**How the tests were secured.** This team of tests has been planned for diagnostic purposes on the assumption that each of the four tests measures a group of important reading skills. To quote the author:

Although there are many types of reading techniques, it does not follow that it is necessary to measure every one for purposes of diagnosis. It is probable that a certain small number of tests may be found which indicate the significant strengths and weaknesses sufficiently well for practical purposes. To ascertain whether this was the case and to find the most useful team tests for diagnosis, considerable research has been performed. It will be unnecessary here to review all of these studies which have appeared or will appear in the technical journals. The types of studies conducted may, however, be indicated briefly as follows:

1. Preliminary studies with various types of test units, mostly in mimeographed form.

2. Judgments of about thirty experts on defects and merits of a series of sample test-unit type.

3. Certain studies of the effects of practice on reading of the types represented by the test units.

4. Study of correlation obtained between various types of reading tests.

As a result of these studies six types of tests were finally selected and two forms of each printed. With each of these types approximately 1,600 children have been tested and the results analyzed. Data of the following sorts have been studied for the purposes of finding the best team of tests.

1. The self-correlations of each test.

2. The intercorrelations of each test with all others.

3. The percentages of errors in the comprehension exercises of each test at each grade level.

4. The nature of errors made.

5. The way selected types of readers work on the material during the test period.

6. The effects of giving the tests repeatedly.

7. Further studies of particular pupils who vary greatly in achievements in the different tests and children who are uniformly good or poor in all the tests.

On the basis of the evidence from these different sources, a team of four tests was finally selected as serving most adequately, within limits of practicality, the purposes sought, namely, to secure by objective means a diagnostic picture of the most significant feature of a pupil's reading ability.[1]

## Testing for narrower skills and abilities. The second method of diagnosis assumes that the various narrow read-

[1] Gates, Arthur I. *The Improvement of Reading*, pp. 181–83. By permission of The Macmillan Company, publishers, New York, 1929.

ing skills and abilities are specific.   Those who would follow this method believe that the first step in developing effective methods of diagnosis is to analyze the composite reading abilities into narrower skills in some manner similar to the Inventory of Skills in Work-Type Reading, found on page 250 in this chapter.   Having determined what the various reading skills and abilities are, the next step is to construct tests which measure these skills.   Since in most cases there are no standardized tests to measure the several narrow skills, it is incumbent upon the teacher to construct informal tests to be used for diagnostic purposes.

The problem of preparing the necessary tests is further complicated by rapid developments in the study of the reading process.   There is not complete agreement on what the essential reading skills are.   Any series of tests, designed to be more or less comprehensive for the moment may become obsolete as new skills are revealed by continued study and analysis.   It may be that standardized tests can only partially fill the need for diagnostic measurement in reading. There are those who hold that the classroom teacher should be trained in methods of test construction so as to be able to prepare the tests needed to meet specific situations.   For illustrative purposes, a number of tests designed by a teacher to measure specific reading skills are included.   In most cases only a single item or two of the test is shown.   If the tests are used, additional similar items may be added.   The illustrative informal tests are not to be used as models, but are intended rather to be suggestive to teachers.

**The Iowa Silent Reading Tests.**   Among the few attempts that have been made to prepare reading tests measuring specific skills in reading, the Iowa Silent Reading Tests may be mentioned.   While these tests do not of course measure every reading skill found in the Inventory of Reading Skills given on pages 250–56, they do attempt to measure a considerable number of specific skills, as can be seen from the list given below.

## IOWA SILENT READING TESTS

*Comprehension*

1. Paragraph Meaning
    A. Social Science
    B. Literature
    C. Science
2. Word meaning: Subject-matter vocabulary
    A. Social Science
    B. Science
    C. Mathematics
    D. English
3. Sentence comprehension

*Organization*

4. Sentence
5. Paragraph
    A. Selection of central idea
    B. Outlining
    C. Organization of paragraph

*Location*

6. Ability to use the Index
    A. Use of the index
    B. Selection of key words
    C. Alphabetizing

*Total Comprehension Score*

*Rate*

7. Silent Reading Rate

The Iowa tests are also unique in that the various abilities are measured in terms of different types of subject matter. Thus, paragraph meaning is measured in social-science material, literature, and science material. Four major aspects of reading are measured: comprehension, organization, location, and rate. In comprehension, paragraph

# IOWA SILENT READING TESTS [1]

## TEST 1. PARAGRAPH COMPREHENSION

### Part A. (Time allowance: 8 minutes)

*Directions to the Pupil:* This is a test of paragraph comprehension. There are three parts to the test. Read the paragraphs in Part A carefully. You will be immediately asked to answer questions on what you have read. *You are to answer these questions by writing on the dotted line after each question the number of the bracketed passage in the test which contains the correct answer.* The first question is answered correctly. Answer the other questions in the same manner.

When the services of representatives are persistently unsatisfactory there are two —1— methods of remedy. The people can elect different officers or they can take away —2— their powers. Dissatisfaction with state legislatures and city councils, and a belief —3— —4— —5— that the people have a right to express an opinion on many matters, have been respon- sible for the introduction of the initiative and the referendum — examples of direct —6— —7— —8— legislation.

The initiative is a plan by which citizens may draw up a law and by filing with a —9— —10— state or local officer a petition signed by a certain percentage of the voters may cause —11— —12— —13— —14— —15— it to be submitted to popular vote at a regular or special election. —16—

1. What definition is given for the power of initiative? ......9.

2. What current belief was largely respon- sible for the introduction of direct legislation? ........

3. What definition is given for the right of referendum? ........

4. May the people deprive an officer of his powers after he is elected? ........

5. How many remedies do the voters have if dissatisfied with representative service? ........

[1] From *Iowa Silent Reading Tests*. Copyright, 1931, by World Book Company, publishers. Yonkers-on-Hudson, New York.

# TEST 2. WORD MEANING

## Subject-Matter Vocabulary

*Directions to the Pupil:* Study the sample below. Each of the following exercises consists of a statement which is correctly completed by one of the numbered words or phrases. *Write the number of the proper word or phrase on the line at the right as shown in the sample.*

*Sample:* To toil is to (1) *read*, (2) *play*, (3) *work*, (4) *fall*, (5) *believe.*  .....3....

### Part A. Social Science Vocabulary
#### (Time allowance: 2 minutes)

1 To make a treaty means to (1) *make war*, (2) *trespass*, (3) *make an agreement*, (4) *become violent*, (5) *restrict.*  ........

2 Suffrage means (1) *women's voting*, (2) *representation*, (3) *the right to vote*, (4) *intrigue*, (5) *suffering.*  ........

3 A statute means (1) *statuary*, (2) *a legislative act*, (3) *by-laws*, (4) *legal procedure*, (5) *height.*  ........

4 Sedition means (1) *passion*, (2) *treason*, (3) *confidence*, (4) *certainty*, (5) *secret.*  ........

5 Revenue is the same as (1) *a retreat*, (2) *an appeal*, (3) *a revolt*, (4) *a reunion*, (5) *a collection of funds for public use.*  ........

6 Ratification means (1) *appraisal*, (2) *taxation*, (3) *treason*, (4) *majority*, (5) *public sanction.*  ........

7 Naturalization means (1) *nationalism*, (2) *nationalization*, (3) *international*, (4) *receiving immigrants*, (5) *receiving the rights and privileges of a citizen.*

8 Jurisdiction means (1) *vindication*, (2) *legality*, (3) *administration of law*, (4) *sphere of authority*, (5) *judicial decision.*  ........

9 Legislation means (1) *passing laws*, (2) *lawful*, (3) *legal*, (4) *diplomacy*, (5) *law enforcement.*  ........

10 Initiative means (1) *iniquity*, (2) *prohibition*, (3) *inheritance tax*, (4) *the right of the people to introduce a new course of action*, (5) *an injunction.*  ........

11 Indemnity means (1) *insurance*, (2) *pension*, (3) *compensation for loss*, (4) *indenture*, (5) *income.*  ........

# TEST 6. USE OF THE INDEX

## Part A. (Time allowance: 2 minutes)

*Directions to the Pupil:* This is a sample index. It is needed in connection with the following exercises on the use of the index.

## INDEX

*Study the following samples:*

1 Where (on what page as shown in the above index) will you find information on coal mining in Indiana?  ..*145*..

2 Can you find information regarding oil in Indiana?  ..*Yes*..

*Answer the remaining exercises in a similar manner.*

1 Next to what page can you find a map of Alaska? .................

2 On what pages does the longest continued discussion occur about corn? .................

3 What is the number of the figure which shows something about the export of corn by the United States? ....

4 Under what topic can you find additional references to gas? .................

5 On what page can a definition be found for citizenship? .................

6 (*The original Test contains also five additional questions not quoted here*) .................

7 .................

8 .................

9 .................

10 .................

Score = number right.......... × 2 = ..........

(*Total possible score = 20 points*)

meaning, word meaning, and sentence meaning are included. Under organization, sentence and paragraph organization are measured. In the case of paragraph organization there are included three abilities; selection of the central idea, outlining, and paragraph organization. Location includes use of the index, selection of key words, and alphabetizing.

**Sample sections from the Iowa tests.** The Iowa tests are suggestive of a type of measurement in reading which should prove very helpful in diagnosis. More tests, measuring still other skills, would be desirable. Because of the comprehensive character of these tests only a few sample sections are reproduced on the preceding pages.

### 3. *Measurement of rate of reading*

The measurement of rate of reading presents some problems which demand that this type of measurement be given special attention. One of the earliest tests which attempted to measure rate of reading was that by Starch. The pupil was given a paragraph to read. He was told to read it as rapidly as he could, consistent with his getting the thought of the selection. He was told to draw a circle around the last word read when the time signal was given. The speed of reading was then determined by counting the number of words read. It will be readily apparent that this method of measurement introduces some difficulties that may affect the reliability and validity of the test scores. The pupil may merely skim the selection, and in this way show a high rate of reading, or he may be inaccurate or dishonest in marking the last word read.

Test makers have sought to prepare rate tests in such a way as to insure at least a degree of careful reading. The Monroe Test already illustrated requires that the pupil answer questions about the materials he reads. It must be remembered, however, that the measure of rate which is secured is in reality a relative measure, since the test measures the rate at which the pupil can read paragraphs and answer questions about them.

**The Chapman-Cook Speed-of-Reading Test.** This test is an example of the ingenious efforts made to construct a "pure rate" test. In each of the paragraphs included in the test a word is inserted which has no place and which spoils the meaning. The pupil is asked to read the paragraphs and cross out in each paragraph the word which spoils the meaning. Since the word cannot well be found without reading the paragraph, the scores of pupils actually represent rates at which the pupils read the selections. It should perhaps be mentioned that we do not know the effect of the organization of the test on the pupil's rate. When a pupil reads a paragraph looking for an irrelevant word is his rate the same as when he reads under ordinary conditions? Probably we do not know the answer to this question. Nevertheless the technique employed in this test is interesting and suggestive.

From the above it is clear that the construction of a test of rate of reading must include some provision for making sure that the pupil actually reads the material. At the same time such provisions should require as little time as possible so as not to affect the rate score. Many questions arise in connection with the various tests. For example, in the Chapman–Cook Test the paragraphs are very short. It is possible that the rate for reading a large number of short paragraphs is different from that for reading a few long paragraphs. It is also likely that the purpose of the reader materially affects his rate of reading. For example if the reader is reading to memorize or to get exact directions or details, he may read at a slower rate than if he is merely seeking the general ideas brought out in the material. Therefore rate must be measured in terms of the purpose of the reader.

# CHAPMAN–COOK SPEED OF READING TEST (GRADES IV TO VIII)

## FORM A

Cross out, in the second part of each paragraph, the one word which spoils the meaning. (2⅓ minutes allowed.)

8. John did his work so well, and got such good marks during the whole of the year, that his teacher thought he would be sure to fail in the examination.

9. When one goes on a picnic, and takes along a big pail of lemonade, it is very provoking to find someone has forgotten the forks, and left them at home.

10. The old schoolmaster was very harsh and cruel to the boys, and beat them when they made mistakes, so, when he left all the boys were sorry.

11. When my mother saw the marks of muddy shoes on the floor, and all over the nice clean beds, she was surprised to see how careful the children had been.

23. Frank hopes to be a great baseball player when he grows up. He plays all the time, and never goes out in the afternoon without taking his cane with him.

24. On rainy afternoons, we amuse ourselves by cutting things out of paper and cardboard; dolls, and soldiers, and even playhouses can all be easily made with a pair of pinchers.

25. There was a great deal of rain and dampness in that country, so the poor people who lived there could raise no corn, because of the dryness of the soil.

26. In order to make our garden in the front of the house more beautiful, we were careful to plant a number of potatoes, as early in the Spring as possible.

Copyright J. C. Chapman, 1923. Published by the Educational Test Bureau, Inc., Minneapolis, Minn.

# Standards of Achievement for the various levels of the various grades, (Midyear smoothed results)

| Levels of Achievement | | Grade IV | Grade V | Grade VI | Grade VII | Grade VIII |
|---|---|---|---|---|---|---|
| Indeterminate ........ | 9+ | | | | | |
| Highest ............ | 95 | 15.4 | 18.3 | 20.7 | 22.4 | 23.9 |
| Very High.......... | 88 | 13.4 | 16.3 | 18.7 | 20.4 | 21.9 |
| High.............. | 79 | 11.5 | 14.4 | 16.8 | 18.5 | 20.0 |
| Medium High...... | 66 | 9.5 | 12.4 | 14.8 | 16.5 | 18.0 |
| MEDIAN.......... | 50 | 7.5 | 10.4 | 12.8 | 14.5 | 16.0 |
| Medium Low ...... | 34 | 5.5 | 8.4 | 10.8 | 12.5 | 14.0 |
| Low .............. | 21 | 3.5 | 6.4 | 8.8 | 10.5 | 12.0 |
| Very Low.......... | 12 | 1.6 | 4.5 | 6.9 | 8.6 | 10.1 |
| Lowest............ | 5 | 0 | 2.5 | 4.9 | 6.6 | 8.1 |
| Indeterminate...... | 1– | | | | | |

Score is the number right

Score of pupil

The table given shows the achievement of the various levels of each grade. Thus a pupil of Grade VII, scoring 14, is a Median pupil, while a pupil scoring 20 is a Very High pupil for that grade. By placing on each pupil's sheet a small cross at the point of achievement which he reached, a picture of the pupil's relative standing in his grade is obtained. Thus for a pupil of Grade VI, scoring 13, a cross should be placed slightly above **12.8**.

#### 4. *Measurement of appreciation*

**Appreciation a vital factor.**   Brooks points out that "to appreciate means to estimate properly, to set a just value on.   Appreciation implies the use of wise judgment or delicate perception, and is a vital factor in the promotion of reading interests.   It also implies enjoyment, satisfaction, or a feeling of pleasure."   It seems reasonable to assume that persons possessed of proper appreciation will by that fact be motivated to read.

The importance of appreciation as an aim in the teaching of reading is also argued on other grounds.   "It provides a highly elevating, impersonal recreation which broadens the sympathies and increases the range of desirable interests — and helps in forming high ideals of conduct."

The problems in relationship to teaching appreciation are especially difficult for the teacher.   In the first place, there is not complete agreement upon what is meant by appreciation.[1]   To some it implies enjoyment, to others it suggests discrimination or recognition of merits.[2]

No doubt true appreciation involves a complex array of psychological elements.   Langfeld maintains that when one appreciates he "participates completely in the object of beauty.   One lives in the object, in the sense that one allows oneself to be entirely swayed by the laws of the object without any opposition on one's own part."   Langfeld points out also that "it is the depth of the appeal to the deep-lying fundamental reactions of the race which has caused the simple folk lore and folk-music to endure, and it is the same factor which has preserved certain compositions which technically are inferior art."

**Types of appreciation.**   Brooks lists three important areas

---

[1] Brooks, F. D.   *The Applied Psychology of Reading*, chap. 16.

[2] Speer, Robert K.   *The Measurement of Appreciation in Poetry, Prose, and Art.*   Columbia University Contributions to Education, no. 360, 1929.

of appreciation.[1] They are enjoyment of humor, appreciation of social values, and appreciation of intellectual elements. An extended discussion of the problem is impractical at this point. The foregoing materials have been presented merely to indicate the complexity of the problem facing the teacher. The problem is aggravated by a lack of means whereby the teacher can measure the growth of pupils in appreciation. This absence of measuring devices makes it difficult for the teacher to determine either the effectiveness of her teaching devices or the instructional needs of her pupils. Diagnosis in the sense that it is used in this volume is thus especially difficult in the field of appreciation.

**Speer's method of measuring appreciation.** One of the most interesting attempts to measure appreciation is that by Speer. Speer does not presume to measure appreciation directly. He maintains that recognition of merit is basic to appreciation, and accordingly sets out to measure recognition of merit. To quote the author:

It may be maintained that appreciation is an emotional expression and that our inability to measure the emotional exhaust makes it impossible for us to measure the degrees of appreciation. If this were true, our measurement of appreciation would seem, indeed, to be most difficult, if not an altogether hopeless task.

If, however, we can find the indices of appreciation which we may measure, we have moved toward the solution of the problem.

Recognition of merit does not guarantee appreciation but it is basically essential to appreciation on the higher levels. One may recognize merit in a poem, a bit of prose, a landscape, or a symphony without appreciating it in an emotional sense; but proper appreciation of a poem, a bit of prose, a landscape, or a symphony is based upon one's recognition of merit in it. If, then, we measure an individual's recognition of merit, we have measured an index which is basic and essential to appreciation.[2]

[1] Brooks, F. D. *The Applied Psychology of Reading.*
[2] Speer, Robert K. *The Measurement of Appreciation in Poetry, Prose, and Art,* pp. 2–3. Columbia University Contributions to Education, no. 362, 1929. Reprinted by permission.

As an illustration, Speer's method in measuring recognition of merit in poetry will be described. By an elaborate plan of securing expert judgments a scale was developed. With the help of this scale a new set of judges was asked to rate 250 specimens. From these specimens as rated a test was constructed by arranging the material in thirty-six items, each item being a couplet, made up of one poor specimen and one good specimen. The items were arranged in order of the differences between the qualities of the specimens; the difference between the quality of the two specimens in the first item being large, the difference between the next two items slightly smaller, while the difference between the qualities of the specimens in the last item was quite small. The aim was to get a test which would measure "nicety of discrimination." The directions to pupils are given below:

### DIRECTIONS FOR THE SPEER TEST OF RECOGNITION OF MERIT IN POETRY

*(Examiner reads aloud. Pupils read silently.)*

Read the two samples of poetry below and then check the one which you think is the better. If you think "A" is the better poem, put a check mark on the little line near the letter "A." If you think "B" is the better poem, put a check mark on the little line near "B." You may read the two samples of poetry now. (The two samples of poetry were entered here.)

*(Examiner reads.)*

Which one did you think was the better sample of poetry? **(B.)** Yes, I think so too. There should be a little check on the little line near "B." (See that this is done.)

There are thirty-six (36) more sets just like this one. When I tell you to do so, you are to turn to set one which is on the next page. Having finished set one, go on to set two, and then to set three, etc., until you have finished the thirty-six sets.

Do not hurry, you will have plenty of time, but do not waste it. Be careful not to skip a set. Each time you turn over a page, look at the number at the top and see that it is the next one to be done.

Speer states that the effort to measure nicety of discrimination was unsuccessful. It is difficult to appraise the value of Speer's tests in actually measuring appreciation, but his study is a record of one of the most suggestive attempts thus far made to measure this elusive outcome.

It will be apparent to the reader that the method used by Speer is similar to that widely used in penmanship, namely, comparing specimens. It would appear that measurement of recognition of merit is a feasible undertaking. What other factors are involved in appreciation is not known. Inadequate as they are the tests bring out some interesting facts. It is found that the correlation between recognition of merit in prose and ability in English composition is very low. Likewise there is a low correlation between ability to draw and recognition of merit in art. There is thus a small relationship between "doing" and "judging." The further suggestion is that since the two abilities are more or less specific they must be developed by specific teaching methods.

Without doubt much of the work in all of the arts has been based upon the assumption that the development of skill in doing or performance is also accompanied by better appreciation. Judged by Speer's data, teachers cannot be too sure about the soundness of this assumption. As the author points out, teachers have difficulty in the determination of methods of teaching since objective measures of appreciation are lacking. If such measures can be provided it will be possible to determine the extent to which methods supposedly designed for teaching appreciation actually do function.

**Literature tests; the Van Wagenen Scale.** Several tests have been prepared in the field of literature. No doubt many teachers have hailed these tests as measures of appreciation. In many cases, however, it is difficult to determine the extent to which these tests measure appreciation.

One of the most carefully prepared examples of such tests is the Van Wagenen English Literature Scale. A sample paragraph follows:[1]

### VAN WAGENEN ENGLISH LITERATURE SCALE

#### Paragraph 7

There was never a leaf on bush or tree,
The bare boughs rattled shudderingly;
The river was dumb and could not speak,
    For the weaver Winter its shroud had spun;
A single crow on the tree-top bleak
    From his shining feathers shed off the cold sun;
Again it was morning, but shrunk and cold,
As if her veins were sapless and old,
And she rose up decrepitly
For a last dim look at earth and sea.

Sir Launfal turned from his own hard gate,
For another heir in his earldom sate;
An old, bent man, worn out and frail,
He came back from seeking the Holy Grail;
Little he recked of his earldom's loss,
No more on his surcoat was blazoned the cross,
But deep in his soul the sign he wore,
The badge of the suffering and the poor.

Sir Launfal's raiment thin and spare
Was idle mail 'gainst the barbed air,
For it was just at the Christmas time;
So he mused, as he sat, of a sunnier clime,
And sought for a shelter from cold and snow
In the light and warmth of long-ago.

12. (79) Draw a line under the word or words which describe Sir Launfal.

    stealthy    wavering    troublesome    noble    bitter

---

[1] From Van Wagenen's *English Composition Scales*. Copyright, 1923, by World Book Company, publishers, Yonkers-on-Hudson, New York.

13. (80) **Draw a line under the word or words which describe the scene.**

      shocking   cheerless   comfortless   stirring   desolate

14. (84) **Draw a line under the word or words which describe the feelings of Sir Launfal.**

      frightened   angered   gay   gleeful   pensive

While it is true that in order to answer the questions pupils must engage in generalizations of a character involving appreciation, it is also true that the ability of pupils to answer the questions is largely a measure of ability to comprehend meaning. It is possible, therefore, that these tests may be better measures of ability to comprehend the meaning of literature than of appreciation. It should be admitted that ability to comprehend meaning is involved in appreciation. The various factors are, however, so complex as to make it difficult to isolate them.

### 5. *Measurement of reading attitudes and interests*

**Permanent interests in reading.** One of the three essential elements of a progressive reading program is "The establishment of strong motives for and permanent interests in reading." [1] Another way to express this principle is that the teacher not only wishes to teach the pupil how to read, but she desires to assure herself that he will read. Without doubt there are individuals who *can* read but who *do not* read. Such persons lack the interest or motive for reading. Among other things it is possible that the methods by which they have been taught were such that a distaste for or an indifference toward reading resulted. The progressive teacher of reading would therefore like to teach in such a way that pupils will acquire a genuine interest in reading, and in fact will continue to read throughout life.

[1] *Twenty-fourth Yearbook, National Society for the Study of Education,* Part I, chap. 2.

Unfortunately, little is known about the methods by which permanent interests in reading are developed. Books on reading usually contain suggestions for "developing interest in reading." Most of these, however, are largely opinion. There are practically no studies which indicate their relative effectiveness. One of the reasons, perhaps, why such studies are lacking is that it is so difficult to measure the extent to which interests in reading have been developed. Generally we have no methods for determining the amount of reading which children do after they leave school. Thus little is known concerning the effectiveness of our methods in "developing permanent interests in reading." It is a difficult matter even to secure a record of the reading which pupils do while they are in school.

**Cutright and Brueckner's study of library cards.** Efforts on the part of teachers to reward extra reading do not always lead to accurate data concerning the amounts read. At the same time the amount of "free" reading done by children is difficult to determine. Perhaps the most suggestive method for measuring the amount of such reading is the study of library cards. Cutright and Brueckner divided Minneapolis schools into three groups.[1] Group I included schools which had libraries in the school building, Group II those which, while they did not have libraries in the building did have libraries within five blocks, and Group III those schools which were six blocks or more from the library. The average percentage of pupils in Grades 3, 4, 5, and 6 with library cards was 76.8 for Group I, 66.7 for Group II, and 60.7 for Group III. It is apparent that availability of materials is an important factor in the amount of reading done by children. To quote the authors:

[1] Cutright, Prudence, and Brueckner, L. J.   "A Measurement of the Effect of the Teaching of Recreational Reading"; in *The Elementary School Journal*, vol. 29, pp. 132–37.  (October, 1928.)

There is no question but that the availability of books is an important factor in determining the extent to which books are read. However, the data presented suggest the fact the teacher can do much to influence the outside reading of pupils. Many different methods are being used to develop interest in free, extensive reading, but the effectiveness of these methods is not definitely known. The mere fact that the library station is located in a school is not an indication that the pupils are engaging in extensive reading.

**Periodical reading.** The great increase in the circulation of magazines suggests that the form of the reading material employed by both children and adults may be undergoing a change. If it should be found that an increasingly large proportion of the reading done out of school is in the form of magazines, this fact should be taken into account in studying the relative effects of methods. It is possible that studies of book reading only may overlook important aspects of the reading of both children and adults.

Studies made thus far of the periodical reading of pupils give no data concerning the relative popularity of materials in book and magazine form. Elder and Carpenter studied the reading interests of high-school girls, both in book and magazine form. The study indicates the nature of the material which girls prefer, but throws no light on the rôles played by book and magazine materials in the reading of high-school girls.[1]

## 6. *Preparation of informal diagnostic tests in reading*

A discussion of the nature and construction of diagnostic tests is given in another chapter. A brief discussion of the preparation of informal diagnostic tests in reading may be helpful to teachers. Generally the rules and suggestions

---

[1] Elder, Vera, and Carpenter, Helen S., "Reading Interests of High-School Children"; in *Journal of Educational Research*, vol. 19, pp. 276–82. (April, 1929.)

for the preparation of tests usually given in books on tests deal largely with standardized testing. Frequently they are more concerned with reliability and standards for large groups of children than with diagnosis. Nevertheless a few suggestions of this type may be helpful, even if they are not all employed in the construction of any one test. Smith and Wright list the following steps in the preparation of a "new type" examination:[1]

1. Determine what is to be measured or tested
2. Determine detailed aspects to be covered
3. Determine best type of test for measuring selected outcomes
4. Preparing the questions or items
5. Determine the rules for giving
6. Giving the test
7. Scoring the test
8. Diagnostic analysis of the results

In a general way tests may be classified into recognition and recall types. In reading the recall type is not very applicable, since the purpose is to determine whether the reader can get the thought from the page, and not whether he can recall facts once he has read them. For this reason nearly all reading tests are so constructed that the pupil may, if he desires, re-read the material in order to answer the questions. The selection read is constantly before him. If from the time he reads a paragraph to the time he attempts to answer a question he forgets the content of the paragraph, he can go back and secure the desired information. It is true that in the case of tests with time limits this process of re-reading greatly interferes with reading rate, but it is always possible for the student to do it. Usually, therefore, the responses in reading tests are in the form of recognition rather than recall. The Monroe and Thorndike–McCall tests already described are examples in point.

[1] Smith, Henry Lester, and Wright, Wendell William. *Tests and Measurements*, chap. 21. Silver Burdett, 1928.

**The Los Angeles Primary Reading Test.** The type of response must be determined somewhat by the maturity and ability of the children. For example, it would be futile to ask children in the first half of the first grade to write out the answers to questions, since many of them can neither spell nor write. Consequently in this case children are asked to perform some action of which they are capable to show whether or not they comprehend the material. The performance of this act is evidence of their comprehension of the materials. The following extract from the Los Angeles Primary Reading Test illustrates the procedure involved. If a child "puts a ring on the line" it is assumed that he is able to comprehend the sentence.

### Los Angeles Primary Reading Test — Form 2
#### Department of Psychology and Educational Research
#### Los Angeles City School District
#### Devised by Jessie E. Ingraham

#### Form 2
(Time, 10 minutes)

1. Make a ring, like this, O, on the line:..................
2. Make a × after soon: did   soon

The Minneapolis Second Grade Reading Test below is another example. In the case of the Los Angeles test only comprehension of instructions is measured. In the Minneapolis test the pupil reads a sentence. He is then called upon to perform an action to indicate whether or not he understood the sentence.

### Minneapolis Second Grade Reading Test

One day when John was in the woods, he caught a little squirrel.
Draw a line around the word below which tells where John caught the squirrel

House   woods   river   tree

**The Indiana Recall Test.** Occasionally measure of recall is attempted. The pupil is asked to read a story. He then turns his paper over and is asked to answer yes or no to questions about the story. He indicates his response by placing a check mark below the correct answer. The Second Grade Reading Test, published by the State Normal School of Indiana, Pennsylvania, from which the following extract was taken, is an example of this type of recall test.

INDIANA, PENNSYLVANIA, RECALL TEST

RETENTION – REPRODUCTION TEST

*Directions*

(Children should now turn the booklet this side up. Read the following to them.)

Below are questions on the story you have just read. The answer to each question is either "yes" or "no." After each question, at the end of the line, are the words "yes" and "no." If the answer to the question is "yes," put a line under the word "yes." If the answer is "no" put a line under the word "no."

(Repeat directions until all know what to do. Have them do the first two for practice. Allow five minutes to finish.

## PROUD DUCK

Once upon a time a duck was proud.
So she was called "Proud Duck."

One day Proud Duck was in a pond.
She said, "I am a fine duck!
I can swim! I can fly! I can run!"
Then she began to swim.

---

1. Could Proud Duck swim?........................Yes...No
2. Could she run and fly?..........................Yes...No
3. Did she swim in a pond?.......................Yes...No
4. Did she see a fish?.............................Yes...No
5. Could the fish run, or fly?.....................Yes...No
6. Did this make the duck feel proud?............Yes...No
7. Could the dog run and swim and fly?..........Yes...No
8. Could Proud Duck run and swim and fly?........Yes...No

**The Los Angeles Elementary Reading Test.** Some tests have different types of responses for the different items included. In the judgment of some authorities this is undesirable, since the differences in type of response from item to item tend to confuse the pupil. The Los Angeles Elementary Reading Test is an illustration.

## Los Angeles Elementary Reading Test

### Form 1
#### (Time 30 minutes)

"Oh! Here comes a wave! I'll just run away!" cried James.

Put one word on the line to make the sentence right:

1. James saw a...........................coming.

---

At half-past eight, Bobby went upstairs to bed. Mother tucked him in and told him a good night story.

When she came down, father was reading the paper, John sat reading a book, and Sue was playing the piano.

2. At what time, by the clock, did Bobby go to bed?
.................................................................

3. What was father reading?..............................

4. Who went to bed first?................................

---

A few days after mother came home, they were all gathered in the sitting room after supper. In the stove a fire was burning. On the table a big lamp sent a bright light through the room. Mother was putting baby Betty to bed. Father was reading, and Bobby and James were playing soldiers, while Sue played the piano.

5. How many people were in the family?...................

6. Who had been away?...................................

7. What warmed the room?................................

Draw a line under the right sentences below:

8. The room was warm.
   The room was cold.

9. They were in the dining room.
   They were in the sitting room.

---

"Hurrah!" cried the boys, "Two home runs!  Three cheers for our team!"

Put one word on the line and make the sentence right:

10. The boys were looking at a........................game.

**Scoring these tests.**  Tests in which the pupil responds by writing out answers to questions are generally quite difficult to score.  In the case of the Thorndike–McCall Test, the Manual submits acceptable and unacceptable answers. Even with the help of the Manual the process of scoring in this case is laborious and somewhat lacking in objectivity. As a general thing, teachers in preparing tests will find it desirable, in the interest of both objectivity and ease of scoring, to provide well-controlled responses.  For example, in the Van Wagenen Reading Scale the use of multiple choice reduces the likelihood of guessing.  Since the pupil is asked to underline words already on the page, difficulties over substituted word meanings are eliminated.

### Van Wagenen Reading Scales
*English Literature Scale Beta*
Published by the Public School Publishing Co., Bloomington, Illinois

#### Paragraph 3

"And I must lie here like a bed-ridden monk," exclaimed Ivanhoe, "while the game that gives me freedom or death is played out by the hand of others!  Look from the window again, kind maiden, but beware that you are not marked by the archers beneath. Look out once more, and tell me if they yet advance to the storm."

With patient courage, strengthened by the interval which she had employed in mental devotion, Rebecca again took post at the lattice, sheltering herself however, so as not to be visible from beneath.

"What dost thou see, Rebecca?" again demanded the wounded knight.

"Nothing but the cloud of arrows flying so thick as to dazzle mine eyes, and to hide the bowmen who shoot them."

6. (69) Underline the word or words which describe the character of Rebecca as revealed in this incident.

    selfish   kind   annoying   cowardly   brave

7. (76) Underline the word or words which describe the feelings of Ivanhoe.

    uneasy   calm   impatient   troubled   disdainful

## IV. INDIVIDUAL DIAGNOSIS IN READING

**Importance of recent studies.** A great variety of educational investigations have yielded data, in recent years, which throw light on the great differences which exist among pupils. In fact these differences are so great that even under the most favorable conditions of homogeneous grouping of pupils, wide differences will still exist. This fact lends great importance to individual diagnostic procedures. It is quite obvious that no teacher can secure all the information needed for intelligent teaching by means of group tests alone.

Diagnostic and remedial teaching is based upon a recognition of the importance of finding causes for failure to achieve. Such causes may be quite varied in nature. In fact, the assumption is that the causes in any given case may include factors which have not previously been encountered. Diagnosis becomes therefore a distinctly exploratory process in which the teacher approaches the problem with an open mind and unbiased judgment.

Brooks suggests that diagnosis be guided by three underlying principles:[1]

1. Diagnosis must make as minute an analysis as possible of the

[1] Brooks, F. D. *The Applied Psychology of Reading*, p. 169. New York, D. Appleton and Company.

child's reading habits to find out which ones are not functioning properly.

2. Such an analysis, to be correct, must be based upon all available relevant facts.

3. Open-mindedness is the essence of scientific spirit; it is essential in evaluating all data.   The purpose of diagnosis is not to
bolster up some theory or vindicate some method, but to find
the truth, whatever it may be.

**General fields of diagnosis.**   For the sake of convenience
there may be assumed to be three types of information to be
secured through diagnosis: (1) Deficiencies in motor phases
of reading may be fundamentally responsible for the child's
failure to make satisfactory progress in reading; (2) detailed
studies of the abilities of the pupil in the different specific
reading skills may indicate the types of reading performance in which the pupil needs assistance; and (3) wide
varieties of information concerning the child and his
characteristics may throw light on the causes of reading
deficiencies.

### 1. *Diagnosis in motor phases of reading*

**Recent studies.**   Laboratory studies dealing with the
motor phases of reading are a relatively recent development.[1]
Elaborate apparatus has made possible detailed information
concerning the eye-movements of readers.   In reading, the
eye moves forward along a line in an irregular way.   There
may be many pauses, then a return sweep to the next line.
The pauses are called "fixations."   It has been found that
individuals vary greatly in the number of fixations per line.
The number of fixations is also affected by the fact of reading being silent or oral.   If the forward movements made
by the eye are too great, the eyes make short regressive
or backward movements.   Such movements are called

[1] Judd, C. H.   *Reading; Its Nature and Development.*   Chicago, University of Chicago Press.

"regressions," and the short pauses following them are called "refixations." Contrary to the belief of many, words and letters are not "seen" while the eyes are moving, but only during fixation pauses. The movements of the eye are too rapid to permit of "seeing" during the movements.

**Eye-movements and reading ability.** A complete discussion of the relation between characteristics of eye-movements and reading ability is not possible at this point. The teacher will be interested in the problem to the extent that through studies of eye-movements she is able to make a more effective diagnosis of reading difficulties. In large measure detailed diagnosis in this field is a laboratory problem. This discussion will be confined largely to those aspects of the problem which can be dealt with by the classroom teacher.

**Variations in eye-movements.** Considerable variations are found in the eye-movements of different readers. The eye-movements have a definite relationship to reading ability. For example, good readers have wide recognition spans and make fewer regressions than poor readers. The number of fixations per line often varies from four to thirteen or fourteen, as is shown in Table 29, with six or seven fixations quite common. In oral reading there are more pauses than in silent reading, and the pauses also are longer in oral than in silent reading. At the same time there are great differences in the number of words seen during a particular fixation. In silent reading the number of words seen in fixation is larger than in oral reading.[1]

**Eye-voice span.** In reading orally the eye is traveling forward ahead of the voice. The distance between the word being spoken and the one at which the reader is looking is known as the eye-voice span. A rough way of measuring it

[1] Buswell, G. T. *An Experimental Study of the Eye-Voice Span in Reading.* Supplementary Educational Monograph, no. 17, University of Chicago.

## TABLE 29. GRADE MEDIANS FOR EYE-MOVEMENTS IN SILENT READING

(After Buswell and Judd)

| | IB | IA | II | III | IV | V | VI | VII | F | So | J | Se | Col |
|---|---|---|---|---|---|---|---|---|---|---|---|---|---|
| Average number of fixations per line. | 18.6 | 15.5 | 10.7 | 8.9 | 7.3 | 6.9 | 7.3 | 6.8 | 7.2 | 5.8 | 5.5 | 6.4 | 5.9 |
| Average duration of fixations...... | 16.5 | 10.8 | 9.1 | 7.9 | 6.7 | 6.3 | 5.9 | 6.0 | 6.1 | 6.2 | 5.6 | 6.2 | 6.3 |
| Average number of regressive movements per line........ | 5.1 | 4.0 | 2.3 | 1.8 | 1.4 | 1.3 | 1.6 | 1.5 | 1.0 | 0.7 | 0.7 | 0.7 | 0.5 |

is to slip a piece of cardboard over the reading material as the reader reaches a point in a line, and see how many words he reads after his view has been cut off. The span is wider for good readers than for poor readers. To a certain extent, eye-voice span is necessary in order that the reader may render correct meaning and even pronunciation.

## 2. *Detailed studies of reading abilities*

**Steps in individual diagnosis.** This chapter has already discussed methods of diagnosis in specific reading skills. In any individual diagnosis the results of the various group tests will be taken into account. Often it may be desirable to give other tests. While no rules can be laid down to cover all cases, the following steps may be helpful in planning a diagnosis of an individual child:

1. Consider results of reading tests already given.
2. Give general measures of reading power or ability, as, for example, Thorndike–McCall, and Haggerty Sigma 1, and Sigma 3.
3. Give standardized tests measuring narrower aspects of reading, as, for example, Gates Silent Reading Tests.
4. Prepare informal tests to measure specific skills for which standardized tests are not available.

**Obtaining general information about pupils.** The possible causes for deficiency in reading are so numerous that in cases showing marked deficiencies the teacher will need to secure information of a detailed character concerning the individual child. Such factors as physical condition, mentality, home environment, attitude, interests, and conduct will be given careful consideration. In addition, there will be need of a careful study of the child's reading habits and skills. Such detailed studies in some cases require a high degree of technical skill, and in some instances special apparatus. In a great many cases, however, the skills and knowledges required may be acquired by the teacher and the work may be carried on with the regular school equipment.

**Recording information about pupils.** Since the data secured through diagnostic procedures are to be employed in later remedial teaching, it is very important that there be some organized methods for preserving the data in usable form. The Diagnostic Summary Sheet which follows has been devised with this thought in mind. In its present form, however, it does not make provision for recording all of the data which are likely to accrue from a modern testing program. Such a summary sheet will therefore be supplemented by other types of records.

FORM 4. DIAGNOSTIC SUMMARY SHEET

Name...........School..........Sex......Room......City........
Date of birth........C.A.........M.A.........I.Q.......Grade....
Date of enrollment..............Date of test.....................

*Home history:*
1. Name of father...........Nationality........Occupation........
2. Name of mother..........Nationality.......Occupation........
3. Living with.............Language spoken at home.............
4. Own home........Rented........Condition of home............
5. How many books are in the home?..............................
6. Magazines...................Newspapers.....................
7. How much is read at home?....................................
8. Take books from the library?.............Kind................
9. Do you read to some one?......Does some one read to you?......

*School history:*
1. Schools attended: Where............Number.......Kind.......
2. Grades: Repeated...........Skipped...........Normal........
3. Teacher's estimate: Oral reading.........Silent reading........
   Attitude....................Industry......................
   Intelligence.............Scholarship....................
4. Is home work required?.........Oral..........Silent..........
5. *What difficulty did teacher notice in the reading?*..................
6. How has teacher attempted to remedy difficulty?.................

*Temperament:* (Indicate by underlining)
1. Timid or aggressive
2. Industrious or lazy
3. Careful or careless
4. Independent or dependent
5. Coöperative or individualistic
6. Confident or uncertain
7. Deliberative or impulsive
8. Docile or obstinate
      9. General characteristics.................................

*General difficulties in reading:*
1. Eye-movements:
    Rhythmical...................Smooth.......................
    Regressive...................Periods of confusion...........
    Rapid.......................Slow........................
    Narrow span................,..Wide span...................
    Return sweep: Good.................Poor...................
2. Extraneous movements:
    Pointing with finger..................Pencil.................
    Turning of head....................Wiggling...............
    Fingering hair.....................Fingers.................
3. Vocalization:
    Lip movements: None........Slight........Active...........
    Whispering.......................................
4. Motor deficiencies: Lisping......Stuttering.....Stammering......
5. Language disturbances................................
6. Visual: Dyslexia..............Defective vision................
7. Memory span: Short......Long......Visual......Auditory......
8. Guessing: At words...............At responses...........
9. Mechanics: Word-poor reader........Word-by-word reader.......
    Purposeless reader.................................
    Slow, laborious reader..........Dull, monotonous reader.......
    Over-careful.........Disregard for punctuation............
    Difficulty in phrasing.......................
10. Breathing: Difficult...........Agrees with pauses.............

### DIFFICULTIES IN ORAL NARRATIVE READING

1. Rate per minute
2. Gross mispronunciation
    *a.* Words skipped
    *b.* Guessed at pronunciation
3. Minor mispronunciation
    *a.* Parts of words
    *b.* Wrong accent
    *c.* Wrong syllabication
    *d.* Similar words
    *e.* Confusion of words
    *f.* Words with one vowel, two vowels
    *g.* Words with one syllable
4. Omissions
    *a.* Whole words
    *b.* Syllable
        Beginning of word

    Within the word
    End of the word
    *c.* Words not changing meaning
    *d.* Phrases
    *e.* Words at beginning of sentence
    *f.* Words at end of sentence
    *g.* Possessive nouns
5. Insertion
    *a.* Whole words
    *b.* Syllables
        Beginning of word
        Within the word
        End of word
    *c.* Words not changing meaning
    *d.* Words that change the meaning but make complete sense

e. Phrases
f. Words at beginning of sentence
g. Words at the end of sentence
h. Letters
i. Words erroneous to material read

6. Repetition
   a. Words
      Beginning of sentence
      Within sentence
      End of sentence
   b. Parts of words
   c. Groups of words
   d. Phrases
   e. To correct errors
   f. To improve upon expression

7. Substitutions
   a. Words that look alike
   b. Syllables
   c. Synonyms
   d. Unlike words
   e. Words that do not make sense

8. Skipping
   a. Difficult words
   b. Whole phrases
   c. Whole lines
   d. Parts of sentences

9. Word recognition
   a. Phonic
   b. Sight
   c. Isolated words
   d. Words in context

10. Pronounce words correctly, but does not know meaning
11. Pronounces word ahead in the line
12. Poor phrasing
13. Enunciation

### DIFFICULTIES IN SILENT NARRATIVE READING

1. Rate per minute
2. Difficulty in getting meaning
   a. From whole paragraphs
   b. From whole sentences
   c. By skimming
   d. By getting answers to specific questions
   e. By getting answers to thought questions
   f. By getting answers to puzzle type of questions
3. Difficulty in comparing
   a. Words of same meaning
   b. Statements of same meaning
4. Difficulty
   a. To get particular idea
   b. To take directions
   c. To answer questions
      What pupil reads silently
      What examiner reads orally
   d. To find and verify answers
   e. To reproduce what has been read
5. Difficulty to keep one's place
6. Difficulty in judging the correctness of statements.

## V. REMEDIAL INSTRUCTION IN READING

By means of reading tests two types of need for remedial instruction may be revealed. A study of the results of group tests may indicate the points of strength or weakness in a class, a school, or a school system. On the other hand, tests may be employed in making a detailed diagnosis of the difficulties of an individual pupil. Both types of activity are worth while and will here be discussed separately.

In the same way two lines of activity may be carried on

for remedial purposes. Teachers may organize group activities designed to correct the more common difficulties found in the class. At the same time pupils may be given specific drill or assistance with problems of learning which are largely peculiar to individuals.

**The Gates Silent Reading Tests.** The use of tests for locating class needs is well illustrated through the medium of the Gates Silent Reading Tests.[1] The data in Table 30, taken from the author's book, indicate the extent to which classes in the same grade with nearly equal mental abilities may vary in achievement as measured by any test. By examining this table one can locate the classes which make the lowest score. The results are based upon Gates Silent Reading Tests, Test C. The class in school A reads very rapidly, but shows a very poor score for accuracy. Class F reads correctly nearly four times as much as Class A. Other comparisons can be made.

TABLE 30. VARIATIONS IN CLASS ACHIEVEMENTS, GATES SILENT READING TESTS

| SCHOOL | NUMBER OF PUPILS | AVERAGE NUMBER OF PARAGRAPHS READ | AVERAGE NUMBER CORRECT | AVERAGE PER CENT CORRECT |
|---|---|---|---|---|
| A | 40 | 16. | 4. | 25 |
| B | 35 | 14.2 | 6.4 | 45 |
| C | 33 | 15.4 | 7.7 | 50 |
| D | 38 | 10.4 | 8.4 | 81 |
| E | 40 | 15.9 | 10.6 | 66 |
| F | 40 | 20.5 | 12.9 | 57 |

It not infrequently happens that a class will score higher on some reading abilities than on others. Below are submitted the scores of a fifth-grade class including the Thorndike–McCall Test and the Gates Silent Reading Tests, A,

[1] Gates, Arthur I. *The Improvement of Reading*, p. 199, 1927. By permission of The Macmillan Company, publishers.

B, C, D.    The median scores for the four Gates tests, expressed in reading grades, are as follows:

Test A............6.5
Test B............7.25
Test C............8.25
Test D............5.9

It will be seen that the difference between the score on Reading to Understand Precise Directions (C), and Reading to Note Details (D), is more than two and one-fourth school years.   Since in this case the tests were administered at the end of the school year, the medians are approximately at standard for Tests A and D, and more than one grade above standard for Test B, while the median score for Test C is more than two grades above standard.   It is readily apparent that in terms of group needs this group of children needs further training in Reading to Note Details (D), as well as Reading to Appreciate General Significance (A).

**The McCall-Crabbs Test Lessons in Reading.**    In order to improve Ability to Note Details, Gates suggests the use of the McCall-Crabbs Test Lessons in Reading.   These are prepared in booklets of 94 pages, with a test on each page. Provision is made for converting the scores into grade scores.   It is thus possible to note progress of pupils from time to time.   Since the booklet contains so many tests there is material available for very frequent tests (about every other day) during the school year.   A sample test from these practice materials is given below.   More material, providing training in other specific abilities, is needed.

McCALL–CRABBS TEST LESSONS IN READING [1]

TEST LESSON 2

One spring day Harry saw a bird's nest tucked away in the hedge along the lane.   He tried and tried to see into the little home without disturbing it, but could not.   Suddenly he thought

[1] By permission of Bureau of Publications, Teachers College, Columbia University.

of something. Away he ran to his workshop. Soon he came back carrying a little round mirror, a long narrow piece of tin, and two nails.

Harry pinched the tin around the edge of the mirror. When the ends met, he bent each out. Then he fastened the mirror to the end of a long pole by slipping the pole between the bent ends of the tin and nailing it fast. Harry held his mirror over the hedge, and to his delight, he saw three little blue eggs in a bed of feathers.

1. Harry fastened the mirror to the
    (*a*) hedge;   (*b*) pole;   (*c*) tree;   (*d*) nest.
2. The number of eggs in the nest was (*a*) 2;   (*b*) 4;   (*c*) 5;   (*d*) 3.
3. The bird's nest was in
    (*a*) the hedge;   (*b*) a lane;   (*c*) a tree;   (*d*) the ground.
4. The piece of tin was
    (*a*) square;   (*b*) round;   (*c*) small;   (*d*) long.
5. The tin was pinched around the
    (*a*) hammer;   (*b*) nest;   (*c*) nail;   (*d*) mirror.
6. Harry found nails in the
    (*a*) workshop;   (*b*) lane;   (*c*) hedge;   (*d*) mirror.
7. The hedge was along the
    (*a*) road;   (*b*) lane;   (*c*) creek;   (*d*) garden.
8. The mirror and the tin were fastened to the pole with
    (*a*) three nails;   (*b*) one nail;   (*c*) four nails;   (*d*) two nails.
9. He used the mirror to see into a
    (*a*) hedge;   (*b*) lane;   (*c*) nest;   (*d*) tree.

| Number right... | 0 | 1 | 2 | 3 | 4 | 5 | 6 | 7 | 8 | 9 | 10 |
|---|---|---|---|---|---|---|---|---|---|---|---|
| Grade score..... | 2.5 | 2.9 | 3.2 | 3.5 | 3.9 | 4.3 | 4.7 | 5.4 | 6.1 | 7.1 | —— |

## 1. *Remedial instruction for individual pupils*

**With a fifth-grade class.** Table 31 gives reading **test** data for a fifth-grade class. Reference to this Table will show that there are great variations in the scores made by individual pupils on the four tests. For example, pupil No. 32 received a grade score of 5 on Test A, 6 on Test B, 8 on Test C, and 8.2 on Test D. While the class as a whole made its lowest score on Test D, pupil No. 32 made his best score on this test. A number of other pupils in the list could be studied in the same way. The suggestion of the data is that group remedial exercises, no matter how carefully planned, will not meet the needs of all pupils. Individual difficulties must be located and individual training provided.

TABLE 31. READING TEST RESULTS FOR A FIFTH-GRADE CLASS

| PUPIL | AGE | THORNDIKE-McCALL | | GATES | | | | | | | |
| | | Score | R.Q. | A | | B | | C | | D | |
| | | | | P | G | P | G | P | G | P | G |
|---|---|---|---|---|---|---|---|---|---|---|---|
| 1 | 11.95 | 60 | 116 | 93 | 5.5 | 93 | 6.0 | 94 | 8.0 | 100 | 7.8 |
| 2 | 11.42 | 50 | 109 | 100 | 6.0 | 100 | 6.0 | 79 | 7.5 | 91 | 5.4 |
| 3 | 10.75 | 43 | 100 | 100 | 5.0 | 94 | 7.0 | 94 | 8.5 | 100 | 4.8 |
| 4 | 10.58 | 50 | 118 | 93 | 6.0 | 94 | 7.0 | 100 | 9.5 | 100 | 6.6 |
| 5 | 13 | 48 | 92 | 72 | 6.0 | 46 | 5.0 | 82 | 9.5 | 94 | 4.6 |
| 6 | 11.00 | 45 | 102 | 100 | 6.5 | 95 | 8.5 | 93 | 6.0 | 94 | 5.8 |
| 7 | 10.58 | 50 | 118 | 78 | 5.0 | 94 | 7.0 | 69 | 8.0 | 90 | 7.4 |
| 8 | 11.92 | 50 | 105 | 93 | 6.5 | 100 | 8.0 | 39 | 4.0 | 100 | 5.8 |
| 9 | 10.5 | 54 | 127 | 95 | 9.0 | 100 | 10.0 | 79 | 9.5 | 98 | 11.0 |
| 10 | 10.83 | 40 | 93 | 84 | 7.5 | 81 | 6.0 | 83 | 7.5 | 95 | 7.4 |
| 11 | 10.83 | 45 | 103 | 90 | 4.2 | 100 | 6.5 | 87 | 7.0 | 94 | 4.7 |
| 12 | 11.60 | 38 | 86 | 90 | 4.5 | 85 | 5.0 | 81 | 6.5 | 98 | 4.8 |
| 13 | 11.33 | 46 | 101 | 100 | 9.0 | 100 | 9.5 | 100 | 6.0 | 100 | 5.0 |
| 14 | 12.75 | 48 | 94 | 92 | 5.0 | 90 | 4.5 | 87 | 6.5 | 100 | 4.5 |
| 15 | 11.92 | 36 | 76 | 90 | 4.2 | 90 | 4.5 | 93 | 6.0 | 96 | 4.3 |
| 16 | 9.00 | 51 | 125 | 100 | 9.0 | 95 | 6.0 | 100 | 10.5 | 100 | 4.5 |
| 17 | 11.08 | 43 | 97 | 81 | 6.0 | 100 | 8.5 | 86 | 9.5 | 100 | 8.9 |
| 18 | 10.33 | 43 | 104 | 84 | 7.5 | 67 | 5.5 | 92 | 6.0 | 92 | 6.6 |
| 19 | 11.83 | 50 | 105 | 100 | 9.0 | 100 | 8.0 | 80 | 8.0 | 93 | 8.9 |
| 20 | 10.83 | 54 | 124 | 100 | 8.0 | 100 | 9.5 | 87 | 6.5 | 100 | 9.8 |
| 21 | 13.08 | 42 | 80 | 100 | 6.0 | 71 | 4.5 | 79 | 7.5 | 97 | 5.4 |
| 22 | 10.42 | 45 | 108 | 100 | 6.0 | 100 | 7.5 | 95 | 11.0 | 97 | 6.2 |
| 23 | 12 | 51 | 105 | 93 | 6.5 | 100 | 8.5 | 100 | 9.5 | 100 | 8.6 |
| 24 | 13.10 | 48 | 91 | 93 | 5.5 | 76 | 6.0 | 68 | 8.5 | 82 | 5.5 |
| 25 | 10.5 | 50 | 119 | 87 | 6.5 | 72 | 8.0 | 72 | 10.5 | 94 | 4.7 |
| 26 | 14.42 | 45 | 78 | 100 | 9.0 | 100 | 10.0 | 87 | 10.5 | 100 | 10.1 |
| 27 | 12.33 | 48 | 97 | 72 | 3.9 | 92 | 5.0 | 100 | 9.0 | 97 | 6.2 |
| 28 | 10.75 | 48 | 111 | 93 | 6.0 | 100 | 7.0 | 100 | 9.5 | 100 | 4.9 |
| 29 | 11.83 | 50 | 105 | 73 | 6.5 | 89 | 7.5 | 79 | 9.5 | 92 | 9.5 |
| 30 | 13.42 | 40 | 75 | No data | | | | | | | |
| 31 | 11.5 | 48 | 104 | 100 | 8.0 | 100 | 7.5 | 89 | 8.5 | 97 | 6.2 |
| 32 | 12.75 | 42 | 82 | 78 | 5.0 | 81 | 6.0 | 84 | 8.0 | 89 | 8.2 |
| 33 | 11.5 | 45 | 83 | 95 | 10.0 | 79 | 7.0 | 92 | 11.0 | 92 | 9.5 |
| 34 | 10.08 | 46 | 114 | 100 | 4.5 | 90 | 4.2 | 100 | 6.0 | 100 | 4.1 |
| 35 | 11.25 | 55 | 120 | 100 | 3.9 | 100 | 4.2 | 93 | 6.5 | 100 | 4.1 |
| 36 | 11.58 | 42 | 91 | 100 | 7.0 | 77 | 6.0 | 94 | 7.5 | 94 | 4.9 |
| 37 | 12.42 | 40 | 81 | 60 | 3.0 | 86 | 3.5 | 59 | 4.0 | 93 | 3.4 |
| 38 | 11.17 | 54 | 120 | 100 | 7.0 | 100 | 8.5 | 94 | 8.5 | 97 | 6.6 |

R.Q. = Reading Quotient.    P. = Percentage of Accuracy.    G. = Reading Grade.

**Typical diagnoses.** In the case of the Gates tests the author gives the following suggestions[1] for remedial work in the Manual which accompanies the tests:

[1] By permission of Bureau of Publications, Teachers College, Columbia University.

In the diagnosis of an individual or a class, these scores must be viewed together. A few illustrative diagnoses will indicate how this may be done.

| PUPIL | AGE | M.A. | GRADE | TEST A | | | TEST B | | |
|---|---|---|---|---|---|---|---|---|---|
| | | | | Amount Correct Age | Per Cent Correct | Per Cent Correct Age | Amount Correct Age | Per Cent Correct | Per Cent Correct Age |
| 1 | 11.5 | 11.6 | 5.6 | 11.4 | 85 | 10.9 | 11.4 | 85 | 12.3 |
| 2 | 10.6 | 10.8 | 4.6 | 9.0 | 100 | 19.0 | 8.3 | 100 | 19.0 |
| 3 | 10.8 | 11.0 | 4.8 | 8.6 | 43 | 8.0 | 8.6 | 43 | 8.9 |
| 4 | 10.7 | 10.7 | 4.6 | 12.0 | 93 | 12.9 | 12.0 | 87 | 12.7 |
| 5 | 10.5 | 10.4 | 4.5 | 10.4 | 84 | 10.8 | 10.4 | 77 | 10.6 |
| 6 | 10.8 | 10.6 | 4.7 | 9.0 | 55 | 8.9 | 8.8 | 44 | 8.9 |

| PUPIL | TEST C | | | TEST D | | |
|---|---|---|---|---|---|---|
| | Amount Correct Age | Per Cent Correct | Per Cent Correct Age | Amount Correct Age | Per Cent Correct | Per Cent Correct Age |
| 1 | 11.4 | 65 | 11.4 | 11.7 | 94 | 11.3 |
| 2 | 8.3 | 100 | 19.0 | 8.8 | 100 | 16.0 |
| 3 | 8.3 | 33 | 8.4 | 8.6 | 64 | 8.0 |
| 4 | 12.0 | 85 | 16.0 | 11.7 | 95 | 11.7 |
| 5 | 9.5 | 46 | 9.6 | 10.7 | 92 | 10.7 |
| 6 | 8.9 | 36 | 8.8 | 10.7 | 90 | 10.6 |

Pupil 1, of average intelligence and a trifle more than half through Grade 5, shows in all the tests not far from average ability, both in gross achievement (that is, strictly speaking, in the number of exercises or amount of correct reading) and in the accuracy of comprehension (that is, in the percentage which the number of correct exercises is of the total number attempted by this pupil). What shall we say of such a case? We should say that this is merely a mediocre (or average) attainment. The writer would say that more and better instruction should be given in all types of reading. In types like A, B, and particularly C, special attention should be given to accuracy of interpretation.

Pupil 2 has a perfect score in accuracy; not a single paragraph was misinterpreted. While this is, in one sense, an admirable achievement, this pupil is really in need of remedial instruction.

Note that, while every paragraph attempted counted as correct since no errors were made, this pupil's scores in number correct only equal those of the average pupil of 9.0, 8.3, 8.3, and 8.8 years, for the four tests, respectively. This pupil is, in other words, from 1.6 to 2.3 years behind the average. He is obviously a slow reader; his efforts are painfully laborious. He is over-careful and should be encouraged to grasp the printed lines more rapidly. Training by the use of reading material of the sorts used in the team of tests should produce improvement in rate without loss of accuracy in most cases.

Pupil 3 contrasts with Pupil 2 in that he is nearly up to the average in all tests in the amount he reads correctly in a given time but below average in accuracy in every other type of reading. Unlike Pupil 2, Pupil 3 is a rapid-fire reader. He hurries the pace; if a phrase or sentence is obscure, it is rarely re-read. The procedure is nervously fast; he seems to be satisfied to get what he can as he pushes through. For Pupil 3, the same materials — like those of which these tests are composed — may be used as with Pupil 2, but they should be used in a different way. Pupil 2 should be urged to speed up and his growth of rate should be determined and displayed with special emphasis, whereas Pupil 3 should be encouraged to get the meaning, and his errors in interpretation should be shown and discussed and growth in accuracy especially emphasized.

Case 4 illustrates reading ability that is above the average for the pupil's age and grade. While this pupil's work deserves commendation, it need not be considered that further improvement cannot be achieved. Accuracy is not perfection. With an increase in accuracy should be sought a simultaneous improvement in rate. Both should, in this case, be improved together. Pupils of this type should not be neglected merely because they have done very well; they may still do better with relatively little effort.

Pupil 5, unlike those above, shows unevenness in development among the several types of reading. This pupil is about average in the more general types of reading comprehension but especially weak in the techniques required for exact interpretations. He needs training in thoroughness and precision of comprehension. Materials which, unless exactly read, will lead to apparent errors should be utilized abundantly until this pupil has learned to read accurately with fluency.

Pupil 6 shows an average ability in rate and percentage of

accurate reading of details (Test D) but inferior ability in both respects in the other tests. This pupil apparently lacks the skill to get at the essence of a paragraph, since in Tests A, B, and C some significant upshot of the passage must always be grasped whereas, in D, the details may be correctly handled without a perfect idea of the central meaning of the material. Pupil 6, then, needs instruction in interpreting as a whole such materials in such ways as are presented in Tests A, B, and C.

These cases do not exhaust all the particular instances of difficulties that will be encountered in reading but they picture fairly well several common types. Pupils 5 and 6 are but representative of many different combinations of abilities. Pupils are found with all sorts of combinations of weakness, mediocrity, and strength in the various phases of the four types of reading measured by the tests. With a good understanding of the meaning of the test scores and the age and grade norms, little difficulty will be encountered in properly diagnosing the various types of reading difficulties ordinarily encountered.

## 2. Remedial work in oral reading

**The Gray Oral Reading Check Tests.** The use of oral-reading tests will frequently be of value in the diagnosis of reading difficulties. Such tests may reveal not only causes for poor oral reading, but may also indicate difficulties in the mechanics of reading which are responsible for poor silent reading as well. The Gray Oral Reading Check Tests have been used widely for this purpose. The individual record sheet shown below, which accompanies the test, can be used with any reading material which the teacher uses in giving the test. The pupil must be tested alone. He is asked to read the paragraphs, and the teacher notes the nature and number of errors made. The record sheet makes provision for repetitions of the test. Progress can thus be noted.

**Follow-up remedial instruction; second grade.** In order to illustrate how remedial instruction could be provided as a follow-up of the Gray Test, a complete record is given be-

## GRAY ORAL READING CHECK TESTS [1]

No. of Set Used_____

### INDIVIDUAL RECORD SHEET

#### PROGRESSIVE ANALYSIS OF ERRORS IN ORAL READING

Pupil's Name.................................... Age............ Grade..........

| TYPES OF ERRORS | No.1 | Daily | No.2 | Daily | No.3 | Daily | No.4 | Daily | No.5 | Daily |
|---|---|---|---|---|---|---|---|---|---|---|
| **I. INDIVIDUAL WORDS** | | | | | | | | | | |
| 1. Non recognition........ | | | | | | | | | | |
| 2. Gross mispronunciation | | | | | | | | | | |
| 3. Partial mispronunciation | | | | | | | | | | |
|   *a.* Monosyllabic Words | | | | | | | | | | |
|     1. Consonant........ | | | | | | | | | | |
|     2. Vowel............ | | | | | | | | | | |
|     3. Consonant blends.. | | | | | | | | | | |
|     4. Vowel digraph .... | | | | | | | | | | |
|     5. Pronounce silent letters........ | | | | | | | | | | |
|     6. Insert letters..... | | | | | | | | | | |
|     7. Pronounce backwards........ | | | | | | | | | | |
|     8. Rearrange letters.. | | | | | | | | | | |
|   *b.* Polysyllabic Words | | | | | | | | | | |
|     1. Accent........... | | | | | | | | | | |
|     2. Syllabication...... | | | | | | | | | | |
|     3. Omit syllable .... | | | | | | | | | | |
|     4. Insert syllable .... | | | | | | | | | | |
|     5. Rearrange letters of syllables........ | | | | | | | | | | |
|     6. Incorrect pronunciation of a syllable | | | | | | | | | | |
| 4. Enunciation ............ | | | | | | | | | | |
| 5. Substitutions........... | | | | | | | | | | |
| 6. Insertions............. | | | | | | | | | | |
| 7. Omissions............. | | | | | | | | | | |
| 8. Other types of error { .......... | | | | | | | | | | |
| **II. GROUPS OF WORDS** | | | | | | | | | | |
| 1. Change order......... | | | | | | | | | | |
| 2. Add words to complete meaning according to fancy............. | | | | | | | | | | |
| 3. Omit one or more lines. | | | | | | | | | | |
| 4. Insert two or more words | | | | | | | | | | |
| 5. Omit two or more words | | | | | | | | | | |
| 6. Substitute two or more words............ | | | | | | | | | | |
| 7. Repeat two or more words............. | | | | | | | | | | |
| 8. Other types of error { .......... | | | | | | | | | | |
| Pupil's test record { Rate...... | | | | | | | | | | |
|   { Errors..... | | | | | | | | | | |
| Standard Scores for the | | | | | | | | | | |
|   Grade { Rate............ | | | | | | | | | | |
|     { Errors........... | | | | | | | | | | |
| Date of Each Test.......... | | | | | | | | | | |

[1] By permission of Public School Publishing Company.

low of the remedial instruction provided for a second grade. The remedial exercises followed in this instance are not submitted as models, but rather as suggestions of what is demanded in a second-grade class. No doubt better methods could be developed in many instances.

### REMEDIAL READING WORK, SECOND GRADE [1]

(Follow-up work after Gray Test)

Gray's Oral Reading Test, Form 1, was given to the entire second grade to find what pupils were having great difficulty with their reading. As each child read, a record was kept of the difficulties the child had. Thus all the pupils were listed showing the number of seconds it took them to read the selection, and the number of errors made. On each separate sheet was shown what each child's difficulties were.

A group of eight pupils showing the greatest number of difficulties was given special help for a twenty minute period twice a day. The regular grade teacher was given a list of other pupils showing considerable difficulty with reading. After each child's record, were listed the types of difficulties shown in the test.

The pupils in the special group were given help in the type of thing they showed a need of. Their mental ability as well as physical condition were kept in mind as work progressed so that not too much would be expected of them. The following shows in a brief way the difficulties found and training done to attempt to remedy them.

1. Non-recognition of words
   a. Reviewing their background in phonics showed the type of training they needed to help them to recognize words.
      (1) consonant blends
      (2) vowel sounds
      (3) blending consonants and vowels
      (4) studying words in "families"
      (5) finding words on cards or in books with certain blends in them
      (6) finding certain blends and sounds in words at board
      (7) making lists of words with same sounds in them

[1] This description of procedures has been supplied through the courtesy of Miss Lenore Torgrimson, Remedial Teacher, Barrington Public Schools, Barrington, Illinois.

2. Mispronunciation or partial mispronunciation of words
    a. Same as under 1
    b. Comparing words as to likenesses and differences; as, saw was
        (1) words of this type that were often confused were printed on cards for special study
        (2) as words were substituted in their reading they were made note of so cards could be printed
        (3) as words were missed, they were made note of so that this special type could be drilled upon. In this way, all difficulties with words were checked as the work went on.

3. Substituting words
    a. The type of training on words given under 2b was helpful with this difficulty.
    b. Making the child conscious of the change of meaning, if words were substituted.

4. Inserting words
    a. See under 3b.

5. Omitting words
    a. See under 3b.

6. Word reading
    a. This shows that the child's eye-span needs to be increased as well as word difficulties need to be removed. The previous exercises show how word difficulties were remedied.
    b. Methods used to increase eye-span
        (1) rapid flashing of phrases and short sentences
        (2) silent reading from books of simple material
        (3) reading phrase or sentence silently, then looking up from book and telling what read
        (4) having cards with phrases, short or long sentences posted on. These have been cut from old readers. A card (curtain) is raised and lowered according to a systematic timing so that child has the same length of time in which to read each card of the same length. A record is kept to see if a child can read each phrase with one look. He practices a certain pack until he can. Then a pack of little longer phrases will be given him. The length of sentence will be increased as his ability to see a longer series of words increases.
        (5) reading of very easy material tends to increase eye-span and speed of reading

7. Wrong grouping of words, that is, pausing in wrong places when reading.

   *a.* This shows that what the child needs is study of thought units. He needs work in "phrasing." He needs to learn what words belong together as his pauses will be at end of phrases instead of the middle of a phrase.

     (1) Finding phrases in reading material was one method used.

     (2) Practice in reading phrases of increasing lengths.

     (3) Practice in reading short sentences without pausing.

     (4) Practice in reading sentences where one pause was necessary.

     (5) Practice reading longer sentences where several pauses were necessary.

       (*a*) Sentences cut from old readers were used for this. At first marks were used to show where pauses should occur. Later, pupils read silently to discover where pauses should occur, then read orally showing where to pause.

8. Repeating words

   *a.* This might be due to poor eyesight, carelessness, or too much stress on speed.

     (1) The nervous child should not be made to hurry as he is often the one who makes this mistake.

     (2) The careless child has to learn to look more carefully.

     (3) Keeping thought in mind instead of mechanics of reading would help.

When another form of Gray's Oral Reading Test was given October 21, it was found that three of the special group had made enough improvement to be excused, and some of the regular room group showed more need of special help. In the same manner, each time the grade was tested, the grouping showing the greatest need for help was the group chosen.

**Follow-up remedial instruction; upper grades.** The following outline gives further suggestions for remedial work in the upper grades:

TYPES OF READING EXERCISES USED TO DEVELOP SPECIFIC READING SKILLS — GRADES SEVEN AND EIGHT

I. Exercises to aid in comprehension:

   1. Nonsense tests. A time limit was set and no re-reading

was allowed.  This was a good test for comprehension and concentration.

2. Reading followed by written answers:

 *a.* Answers to questions dictated by teacher.

 *b.* Summarizing what had been read.

 *c.* Underlining the correct word-exercises similar to the ones found on Monroe Silent Reading Test.

3. Reading with oral responses:

 *a.* Answers to questions given by the teacher.

 *b.* Each pupil told part of the story.

4. Reading to act out:

 *a.* Motion picture type.

 *b.* Pupils read about eight selections, then choose one to re-read and to act to the class.  If he leaves out certain parts the other children call his attention to it and show him how it should have been done.

5. Tangled sentences to arrange in order.

6. True-false tests.

7. Yes-no tests.

8. Topsy-turvy sentences.

9. Fact and opinion exercises.  Pupils pick out from a list of twenty statements those which are fact and those which are opinions.

10. Puzzle paragraphs.  Pupils are given a list of words and paragraphs and asked to choose titles for each one.

II. Exercises to aid in organization:

1. Relationship exercises — a long list of words of different relationship are given.  Pupils make other lists having the same relationship.

2. Puzzle paragraphs.  Pupils were given a list of words, each of which might be used as a title for a paragraph. Pupils read a series of paragraphs and choose a title for each one.

III. Exercises to aid in retention:

1. Reading of long stories and then choosing the parts that are most interesting to tell to the class.  Sometimes the most humorous parts are chosen.

2. Reproduce orally the story that has been read.

3. Writing answers to questions dictated by the teacher after the child is through reading.

4. Reading and acting exercise.

IV. Exercises to increase speed of reading:
  1. Drill with flash cards with Yes—No sentences.
  2. Drill with flash card questions. Extra flash card drill may be given to the slow readers while the faster readers are doing silent reading.
  3. Timed reading and re-reading, of the same exercise to note the decrease in time required for successive readings.
  4. Timed reading exercises, noting the number of words read per minute and then comparing this with the rate on other similar drills. A table of the rate may be kept at the board.

### 3. *Case study in remedial reading instruction*

In order to illustrate the application of the various techniques which have been presented as they apply to an individual pupil, a fairly complete case study is described below:

*A fifth-grade boy who was retarded in all phases of reading because of poor language habits, lack of interest in reading, careless habits of work, and poor habits of thinking while reading* [1]

**Introductory statement.** J. E. was twelve years old when the study of his case began in October, 1921. His parents were foreign born, and he heard little English spoken in the home. His own use of English was very poor, and he had difficulty in pronouncing words containing *th*, *w*, and *v*. His teachers reported that he was below the average for his grade in most subjects. He was not interested in his progress in school, and acknowledged that he had always disliked reading and had read very little outside of school. He had few books and no magazines at home, and his parents read nothing except foreign newspapers. He went to the picture show almost every night, and worked as a delivery boy one or two evenings each week.

**Preliminary diagnosis.** A study of his case was made through the use of five standardized tests. The names of the tests, J. E.'s scores, and the standard fifth-grade scores appear in Table 32.

[1] Taken from Gray, W. S. *Remedial Cases in Reading: Their Diagnosis and Treatment.* Supplementary Educational Monograph, no. 22. University of Chicago. Reprinted by permission.

### TABLE 32. A PUPIL'S SCORES ON FIVE TESTS

| TESTS | J. E.'s SCORES | STANDARD FIFTH-GRADE SCORES |
|---|---|---|
| The Illinois Intelligence Test............. | 76. | 100. |
| The Gray Oral Reading Test............ | 28.75 | 48. |
| The Burgess Silent Reading Test........ | 32. | 50. |
| The Courtis Silent Reading Test: | | |
| Rate..................................... | 99. | 168. |
| Comprehension...................... | 77. | 93. |
| The Monroe Silent Reading Test: | | |
| Comprehension...................... | 11. | 17.8 |

The scores indicate that the pupil was distinctly below the average for his grade in general intelligence, and in all phases of reading. An examination of his oral-reading record showed that he read slowly and very inaccurately. His major difficulties in the simple passages were: (*a*) repetitions; (*b*) numerous substitutions of such words as *so* for *as* and *this* for *it*, which did not change the meaning materially; (*c*) occasional substitutions of such words as *home* for *own*, which showed that he did not have the content of the passage clearly in mind; (*d*) slight errors in the pronunciation of such words as *makes* for *made*, *puts* for *put*, and *mass* for *masses*; and (*e*) omissions and insertions of short words. In more difficult passages, he was frequently unable to pronounce polysyllabic words.

**Detailed diagnosis.** In the Jones Vocabulary Test, he made a score of 95 on the sight list and 96 on the phonetic list. These scores indicated that he recognized simple isolated words with a fair degree of accuracy. On the other hand, several informal tests in oral reading showed that he failed to recognize words in context which he recognized accurately when they were isolated. It was very clear that many of these inaccuracies were due to carelessness. When cautioned to read carefully he did noticeably better. When told that he had made three mistakes in a sentence he usually re-read it correctly.

Other significant facts were revealed by informal tests. He read very haltingly, recognizing one word at each fixation. Owing to language difficulties he was able to recognize words individually more rapidly than he was able to pronounce them. In his effort to read fluently he made many errors. For example, he reversed the order of words or substituted words in sentence, as *I shall stay here right* for *I shall stay right here*, or *rode me on my back* for *rode upon my back*, or *This is not a safety place* for *This is not a safe place*. Another characteristic of his reading was that most of his errors in recognizing words were on the final letters of syllables. For example, he read *pussy* for *puss*, *hurry* for *hurrah*, and *come* for *coming*. This seemed to be due to the fact that he saw the beginning of the word and guessed at the ending.

Informal tests of comprehension showed that difficulties in recognition interfered to some extent with accurate interpretation. He was first asked to read two simple paragraphs orally. He then read the next two paragraphs silently. Finally, two paragraphs were read to him. His reproduction scores were 47, 38, and 61, respectively. These and other similar results indicated clearly that when he was freed from the obligations of recognition, he was able to understand the content of passages much better. In still other tests it was found that he was unable to answer thought-provoking questions, or to think independently about the content of passages which he could reproduce in detail. He was seriously handicapped in the interpretation of relatively difficult passages by his narrow background of experience, his limited meaning vocabulary, and his inability to think clearly.

**Summary of diagnosis.** The diagnosis showed that J. E. was below normal in general mental ability, and was considerably retarded in all phases of reading. His oral reading was very poor because of inadequate language habits, inability to recognize familiar words in groups, inaccuracies in the recognition of unfamiliar words, and carelessness due to lack of interest in reading. His rate of silent reading was considerably below standard because of difficulties in recognizing words, a narrow span of recognition, and lack of experience in reading. His interpretation of what he read was poor because of low native intelligence, a limited background of experience, a small meaning of vocabulary, and poor habits of thinking while reading. His difficulties in the mechanics of reading also accentuated his difficulties in interpretation.

**Remedial instruction.** The facts brought out in the diagnosis led to the conclusion that remedial instruction should attempt to accomplish the following purposes: (*a*) to stimulate an interest in reading and a pride in doing his best; (*b*) to develop greater fluency and accuracy in the use of English; (*c*) to overcome difficulties in the mechanics of reading including difficulties in recognition, a narrow span of recognition, ineffective grouping in oral reading, and a slow rate of silent reading; and (*d*) to increase his power of interpretation by directing his attention to the content and by stimulating good habits of thinking while reading. In order to accomplish these aims, he was given individual instruction for twenty-five minutes each day.

**Stimulating an interest in reading.** Most of the time during the first few days was spent in informal discussions in order to study his case more carefully and to discover his interests. He talked freely whenever given an opportunity, but his chief topics of conversation were moving pictures and the games which he played on the street. He said he did not read because he failed to find interesting stories. He remarked one day that he "might" like to read stories about horses or dogs if he could find them. The library was searched for suitable selections. Several stories were read to him at first. When he became interested, the teacher read the difficult parts to him and he was asked to read the simpler passages. He was delighted with "A Story Told by a Donkey" in the *Winston Second Reader*. It was started one day near the end of the period, and he came early the following day, found the book, and read part of it himself. He was later given simple editions of *Black Beauty*, and *The Dog of Flanders*. The more difficult parts were read to him. Many stories about dogs and horses which interested him were found in readers and story-books. Other animal stories were assigned later. He was keenly interested in them, and it was some time before he wanted to read about other things.

After he had read several stories which were suggested to him, he became interested in looking through the books on the reading table and was finally attracted by the pictures in *Ab the Cave Man*, especially the one showing how Ab killed the tiger. The book was begun in class, and for the first time he expressed a desire to take a book home. He came back the following day very much excited about the story. He finished the book in a few days, and said he would take another if it was interesting. *Robinson Crusoe* was suggested. He liked this book even better and read at home each evening. He found that the story of *Robinson Crusoe* was being shown at a moving-picture theater; he went to see it, and he sat up late to complete the book. He read *Gulliver's Travels* (Baldwin's edition), other books of adventure, and short stories of various types before the end of the training period. He occasionally remarked, "I used to hate reading but now I like it." .

**Developing greater fluency and accuracy in the use of English.** During informal conversation periods, opportunity was taken to supply suitable words when he hesitated in talking, to pronounce words correctly when he had difficulty, and to correct errors in sentence structure. He was frequently asked to reproduce stories which he had read for practice in expressing himself freely. Questions were asked to direct his attention to the main points, and to aid him in telling them in correct sequence. He was given definite suggestions for improving these reproductions, and the teacher occasionally told the stories to him. He was also given help in pronouncing words which caused difficulty. The reading of a large amount of carefully selected material increased his background of experience, enlarged his speaking and meaning vocabularies, and supplied him with something interesting to talk about. After considerable progress had been made, he frequently corrected his own errors.

**Overcoming difficulties in the mechanics of reading:**

(a) *By increasing his accuracy of recognition.* The first remedial steps were aimed to direct his attention to the content, to check his rate of reading, and to hold him responsible for accurate recognition. He was assigned very simple selections during the first few weeks, and he was frequently asked to read these selections silently. The content was then discussed in order to insure accurate interpretation, and he was finally asked to read them aloud accurately. If he made careless errors, he was asked to re-read. Such questions as "How far did the boy go?" or "How large was the boy?" sometimes enabled him to correct his errors without additional help. When he read selections at sight, questions or suggestions were given from time to time to direct his attention to the content. In such cases he was usually able to read with a fair degree of accuracy.

Words which caused difficulty during the reading exercises were used in sentences at the end of the period. He frequently made substitutions, such as *run* for *ran*, and *most* for *must*, because he did not recognize the details of the words accurately. Such words were first used in sentences, and then printed on cards and used in quick-perception drills. Sometimes two similar words were presented together in order that he might note their similarities and differences. Furthermore, he repeatedly omitted or changed the ending of a word because he looked at only the beginning. In order to overcome this difficulty, he was encouraged to look at the entire word before attempting to pronounce it. Such endings as *ly*, *ive*, *ing*, *ful*, and *er* were also given special attention.

(b) *By increasing his span of accurate recognition.* His greatest difficulty in recognition was his inability to recognize groups of words accurately. In addition to the help which was given to make him independent in the recognition of individual words, quick-perception exercises were given each day to increase his span of recognition. A record of his errors was kept for several weeks, and he became interested in decreasing the number each day. He entered a contest with a boy who had the same difficulty and, although they did not work together, they compared scores daily.

(c) *By developing ability in effective grouping.* During reading exercises he was encouraged to read words in thought groups. Satisfactory results frequently were secured by directing his attention to the content. Phrases were occasionally underlined in sentences on the blackboard or indicated in a reader by passing a pencil rapidly under the words which belonged together. When he read haltingly, recognizing only one word at a time, a few paragraphs were read to him as he followed the lines with his eyes, and effective grouping was emphasized. After hearing passages read, he usually re-read them better and proceeded with greater fluency.

(d) *By increasing his rate of silent reading.* As he gained in accuracy and span of recognition, his rate of reading increased. Near the end of the period of training emphasis was placed on rapid silent reading. He was encouraged to read as rapidly as he could interpret. The silent reading which he did outside of class also gave a large amount of practice in rapid reading.

**Increasing his power of interpretation.** His attention was directed to the content, and accurate interpretation was required at all times. Selections were discussed at length, thought-provoking questions were asked, and passages of a problematic nature were assigned to encourage independent thinking. By stimulating his interest in reading, extending his experience, and enlarging his meaning vocabulary, his power of interpretation increased noticeably.

**Results.** He was given four of the five tests originally given (Table 32) after eleven weeks of training. The scores which he made before training, his December scores, and the standard scores for his grade are included in Table 33.

TABLE 33. A PUPIL'S REPEAT SCORES, SHOWING PROGRESS

| TESTS | OCTOBER SCORES | DECEMBER SCORES | STANDARD FIFTH-GRADE SCORES |
|---|---|---|---|
| The Gray Oral Reading Test.......... | 28.75 | 33.75 | 48. |
| The Burgess Silent Reading Test...... | 32. | 38. | 50. |
| The Curtis Silent Reading Test: | | | |
| Rate............................. | 99. | 114. | 168. |
| Comprehension.................... | 77. | 91. | 93. |
| The Monroe Silent Reading Test: | | | |
| Comprehension.................... | 11. | 13.3 | 17.8 |

The scores indicate that he had made progress in all phases of reading, but that he was not yet up to the standard for his grade. It was evident that additional training in all phases of reading could be continued to distinct advantage. Because of the large number of ineffective reading habits which he had acquired, it was concluded that a much longer period of remedial training than is usual would be required to develop effective habits.

## QUESTIONS FOR STUDY, DISCUSSION, AND REPORT

1. Enumerate the reasons why rapid developments have taken place in the field of reading instruction.

2. What conditions of modern life increase the importance of reading ability?

3. Develop a series of remedial exercises to help overcome vocabulary deficiencies.

4. You have been requested to make a survey of reading in a city public school system. List the tests you would give, telling what each test measures and your reasons for using it.

5. Make as complete a diagnosis as possible of an individual child who is having difficulty in reading. Report your procedures, findings, and recommendations in detail.

6. Select five of the specific reading abilities listed on pages 250–255. Prepare a list of references to magazine articles or books

which would be helpful to a teacher who is seeking to develop those abilities on the part of her pupils.

7. What reading abilities would you expect to be large factors in success of pupils in arithmetic? Why?

## SELECTED REFERENCES

Anderson, C. J., and Davidson, Isobel. *Reading Objectives.* Laurel Book Company, 1925.

Brooks, F. D. *The Applied Psychology of Reading.* D. Appleton and Company, 1926.

Brueckner, L. J., and Cutright, P. *The Technics and Evaluation of a Supervisory Program in Work Reading.* Educational Bulletin no. 12, Minneapolis Public Schools, 1927.

Buswell, Guy T. *Fundamental Reading Habits.* Supplementary Educational Monograph no. 20; University of Chicago, June, 1922.

Gates, Arthur I. *The Improvement of Reading.* New York, The Macmillan Company, 1927.

Gray, William S. *Remedial Cases in Reading: Their Diagnosis and Treatment.* Supplementary Educational Monograph no. 22; University of Chicago, 1922.

Gray, William S. *Summary of Investigations Relating to Reading.* Supplementary Educational Monograph no. 28; University of Chicago, 1925.

Gray, William S. "Annual Supplements to the Summary of Investigations Relating to Reading"; in *Elementary School Journal,* vols. 26, 27, and 28.

Hilpert, Ruth E. *Reading in the St. Cloud Public Schools.* Board of Education, St. Cloud, Minnesota, 1924.

Stone, Clarence R. *Silent and Oral Reading.* Boston, Houghton Mifflin Company, 1926.

St. Louis Committee of Teachers, *English for Kindergarten and Grades I–IV,* Curriculum Bulletin no. 4, Board of Education, St. Louis, 1926.

*Twenty-Fourth Yearbook, National Society for the Study of Education.* Report of the National Committee on Reading, Part I. Bloomington, Illinois, Public School Publishing Company, 1925.

Zirbes, Laura. *Comparative Studies of Current Practice in Reading, with Techniques for the Improvement of Teaching.* Teachers College Dissertation, 1928.

## READING TESTS CITED IN CHAPTER VIII

| TEST | GRADES | PUBLISHER |
|---|---|---|
| Thorndike–McCall Reading Scale | 2–12 | Bureau of Publications, Teachers College, Columbia University, New York, N.Y. |
| Monroe Standardized Silent Reading Tests | 3–12 | Public School Publishing Company, Bloomington, Ill. |
| Gates Primary Reading Tests | 1–2 | Bureau of Publications, Teachers College, Columbia University, New York, N.Y. |
| Iowa Silent Reading Tests | 3–9 | World Book Company, Publishers, Yonkers-on-Hudson, New York. |
| Chapman–Cook Speed of Reading Test | 4–8 | Educational Test Bureau, Minneapolis, Minnesota. |
| Van Wagenen English Literature Scale | 5–12 | Public School Publishing Co., Bloomington, Illinois |
| Los Angeles Primary Reading Test | 1–3 | Research Service Company, Los Angeles, California. |
| Indiana Recall Test | 2–4 | State Normal School, Indiana, Pennsylvania. |
| Minneapolis Second Grade Reading Test | 2 | Educational Test Bureau, Minneapolis, Minnesota |
| Los Angeles Elementary Reading Test | 3–8 | Research Service Company, Los Angeles, California. |
| McCall–Crabbs Test Lessons in Reading | 2–8 | Bureau of Publications, Teachers College, Columbia University, New York, N.Y. |
| Gray Standardized Oral Reading Check Tests | Elementary | Public School Publishing Company, Bloomington, Ill. |
| Gray, Oral Reading Test | Elementary | Public School Publishing Company, Bloomington, Ill. |
| Burgess Scale for Measuring Ability in Silent Reading | Elementary | Russell Sage Foundation, New York. |
| Courtis Silent Reading Test No. 2 | 2–6 | S. A. Courtis, Detroit, Mich. |
| Haggerty Reading Examination, Sigma 1 | 1–3 | World Book Company, Yonkers, New York. |
| Haggerty Reading Examination, Sigma 3 | 6–12 | World Book Company, Yonkers, New York. |

# CHAPTER IX

## DIAGNOSTIC AND REMEDIAL TEACHING
## IN LANGUAGE

**The functions of language.** Training in language is probably the most fundamental task of the school. Language is one of the many forms of reaction of the individual, and one which has been highly developed by the human race. Speech is a mode of behavior that has been evolved as a means of setting up relations between human beings. Speech makes it possible for individuals to exchange ideas and experience. The school rightly devotes the major portion of its activities to making pupils expert in speech responses to all of the significant elements of their environment.

Language is the individual type of reaction which enables the pupil to establish vital contact with the "vast accumulations of knowledge of the ages." Language also makes it possible to transmit to future generations the important contributions of the present. Without language the human race would descend to the level of behavior typical of that of the lower forms of animal life. Words provide contacts "on which civilization depends for its evolution and present form." The school must provide a form of training that will "connect the pupil with the racial experience involved in words," so that the individual may respond to verbal stimuli in ways that are truly educative. As Overstreet [1] says, "The most powerful approach to the readers is always through that which stirs their emotions. Every word,

[1] Overstreet, H. A. *Influencing Human Behavior*, p. 98. New York, The People's Institute Publishing Company.

therefore, which has an 'emotion' quality has power as over against the word which is emotionally neutral."

**The aim of instruction.** The aim of instruction in oral and written composition is to provide a series of educative experiences which will develop in the pupils the desire and the ability to express their ideas or to relate their experiences in a clear, direct, interesting, and forceful manner. Language should not be considered as the end in itself, but rather as the means of expressing both thought and feeling.

**The complexity of language.** Language ability is very complex, and is made up of many elements. The three major divisions of language ability are rhetorical factors, such as the choice of words, the richness of the vocabulary, the suitability of the materials, and the logical organization of the discussion; grammatical factors, such as errors in speech; and formal factors, such as pronunciation, enunciation, punctuation, and spelling. These three groups of factors are involved in oral speech; likewise all three are involved in written speech. The essentials of effective oral and written language expression are nearly identical. Any sentence, either oral or written, should be made up of words that say plainly and precisely what is meant, should be grammatical, and should be well constructed. Since for most people oral language is practically the only means of verbal expression used, it is deserving of a far greater emphasis than it now receives.

**The socialization of language instruction.** In recent years there has been a marked drift from disciplinary to social values in education. Probably in no subject is this more striking than in language. The necessity of definite consideration of both oral and written composition has been recognized by the school. Increased provision for training in oral expression is provided by such forms of class procedure as the socialized recitation, project work, the topical recitation, and the problem method. In such classes vital expressional situations exist. Grammar is no longer taught in most elementary schools as an end in itself, but rather as a means to an end. Formal grammar has been replaced to a large extent by functional grammar, which stresses those rational phases of grammar that make clear to the pupils the nature of errors and provide an intelligible basis for self-checking and self-correction.

**Language in life situations.** Emphasis is being placed upon the provision of training which will insure increased efficiency in expression in situations in life in which oral and written English functions naturally. To this end surveys have been made of the way in which children use oral or written expression in life, both in and outside the school. The results of these investigations have influenced markedly the procedures in language instruction, and are often made a partial basis for the curriculum. The following list of general life situations in which language is used grew out of a summary of such studies:

I. Life situations in which spoken English is used
    A. Conversations
        At the table, at social gatherings, in discussion groups, at public gatherings, in public places, during introductions, during calls, at interviews, in greetings and partings, in asking directions, in telephoning.
    B. Meetings
        1. Informal proceedings such as classes, auditorium exercises
        2. Formal Proceedings of organizations, clubs, committees
    C. Practical discussions
        1. Speeches of felicitation, dedication, presentation of gifts, acceptance of gifts, introduction of speakers, inauguration speeches, speeches upon retiring from service, substitute or impromptu speeches.
        2. Reports of meetings, conferences, visits, illustrated lectures, demonstration talks.

3. Persuasive talks as in membership drives, political campaigns, school campaigns, for thrift, health, cleanliness; as in applying for the position of office boy or paper carrier; as in selling tickets to school entertainments.
4. Messages and announcements of games, lectures, exhibits, entertainment, meetings.
5. Explanations and directions as to how to make a radio, a cake, or a flower box; how to go to a park or a railway station; how to iron a dress or care for the children.

D. Anecdotes and stories
   1. Telling anecdotes and stories to children in the home, school, or social group.
   2. Telling anecdotes and stories to adults at social functions, on the train, at the dinner table, at informal gatherings of friends, to people who are sick or in trouble, at public meetings.

II. Life situations in which written English is used
   A. Letters
      1. Business letters to firms for information, for supplies.
      2. Social letters to school friends, to parents, to children in other communities.
      3. Informal notes: excuses, invitations.
      4. Formal notes.
   B. Notices of games, lectures, exhibits, entertainments, meetings.
   C. Reports of committee to school or class; of delegate to class or school council; official, president of school council; financial, money saved by class each week; minutes of council or club; reviews, books, articles, speeches, plays; of observations or experiments.
   D. Note-taking for preparation of papers, stories, discussion, and reports.
   E. Filling out forms, mail-order blanks, application for money orders, checks, deposit slips, test forms, telegrams or cablegrams; information blanks or questionnaires, budgets.
   F. Making a bibliography.
   G. Creative writing for papers, clubs, class, newspaper or magazine articles in school or local paper, diaries, imaginative writing, such as stories, poems, plays.[1]

[1] State of Iowa, 1928, *Course of Study for Elementary Schools*, pp. 263–64.

## I. MEASUREMENT IN COMPOSITION

Measurement in composition has been almost wholly confined to the evaluation of written expression. Composition scales, some for measuring general merit and others for diagnostic purposes, have been constructed. Standard tests of technical composition elements, such as grammar and punctuation, have also been devised.

### 1. *General composition scales*

The general principle of a composition scale is the setting up of a series of composition specimens of increasing merit. Each specimen has a fixed value determined by statistical procedures. In grading a composition the teacher compares its general merit with that of the specimens in the scale, and gives it a value equal to that of the specimen which in the judgment of the rater it most nearly resembles.

**The Hillegas and Hudelson Scales.** The best known scales for measuring the general merit of compositions are the Hillegas and the Hudelson scales. Neither of these scales can be used to analyze the merit or the specific defects of the pupil's written work.

The median achievements in English composition by grades, according to the Hillegas scale, are given in Table 34.

TABLE 34. MEDIAN ACHIEVEMENT IN ENGLISH COMPOSITION
BY GRADE
(After Hillegas)

| SCHOOL SYSTEM | GRADES | | | | | |
|---|---|---|---|---|---|---|
| | 4 | 5 | 6 | 7 | 8 | 9 |
| Lead, South Dakota............. | 3.6 | 4.1 | 4.6 | 5.0 | 5.6 | |
| Nassau County, New York....... | 2.8 | 3.4 | 3.8 | 4.2 | 4.6 | 5.0 |
| Mobile County, Alabama........ | 3.2 | 3.9 | 4.3 | 4.2 | .. | 5.6 |
| Tentative Standard Median...... | 3.5 | 4.0 | 4.5 | 5.0 | 5.5 | 6.0 |

The data in Table 34 show that there is only a very small growth in composition ability, in the localities listed, from grade to grade. The interval between the tentative standard medians for the several grades is only one half of a step on the Hillegas scale. The amount of growth in composition ability between grades four and nine is equal to the difference in general merit between the following specimens from the Hillegas scale:

### Specimens from the Hillegas Scale

#### Sample 94

Value 369. Written by a boy in the second year of the high school, aged 14 years.

When Sulla came back from his conquest Marius had put himself consul so sulla with the army he had with him in his conquest seized the government from Marius and put himself in consul and had a list of his enemys printy and the men whoes names were on this list we beheaded.

#### Sample 534

Value 585. Written by a boy in the fourth year of the high school, aged 16 years.

#### Fluellen

The passages given show the following characteristic of Fluellen: his inclination to brag, his professed knowledge of History, his complaining character, his great patriotism, pride of his leader, admired honesty, revengeful, love of fun and punishment of those who deserve it.[1]

The following specimens illustrate the Hudelson Scale: [2]

Value 1.0

a smow roll Fight om slatters hill

the boys wen up there am they had about a 150 smowballs arn Jack Harris hit Mat ames right im the stomict and they had smow balls goming fron side to side am about sunset the boy wer I happy

---

[1] *The Hillegas Composition Scale*, Bureau of Publications, Teachers College, Columbia University, New York City.

[2] From *Hudelson's English Composition Scale*. Copyright, 1923, by World Book Company, publishers, Yonkers-on-Hudson, New York.

am ome with his eye all with a rag aroung it the Gernorl what find soldiers I got they went doun the Hhill playing Yonce doe dolle dod

### Value 4.0
#### A Snowball Fight on Slatter's Hill

The boys that lived in the south end of the town built a snow fort and had three hundred snowballs ready for their attack against their enemies, the boys from the North end of town.  As their enemies passed they hit the leaden the very first one and then started on the rest.   Not more than a dozen reached the fort and they were taken prisoners.  After that when any fight was talked about the boys would always mention the Fight on Slatter's Hill.

### Value 6.0
#### A Snowball Fight on Slatter's Hill

"Slatter's Hill was a rise of ground covering prhaps an acre and quarter of ground, generally termed "No Man's Land.""

"One Night the North Enders under command of Jack Harris quietly took charge of the hill and erected a strong snow fort. Fancy the chagrin of the South Enders next morning when they saw the North Enders in posassion of the stronghold.   News traveled rapidly and soon it was learned that the South Enders under command of Mat Ames would attack the following Saturday."

"Saturday came and there was about thirty of we North Enders in the fort and a pile of about three-hundred snowballs.   About 2 P.M. the South Enders made their attack, fifty strong and charged the fort.   A well directed snowball from the hand of General J. Harris took General M. Ames in the pit of the stomach and the fight was on.   The fight waged fiercely and thrise we were almost driven from the fort.   But the boys fough gamely and we defeated the South Enders who marched away whistling "Yankee Doode," and we jeered them as they wnet."

"After the fight General Harris paying no attention to his black I said "Men I'm proud of you""

After that when any deed of bravery or pluck was mentioned the boys would say, "Golly you ought to have been at Slatter's Hill"

Specific detailed directions to be followed to secure compositions to be rated by these scales have been provided by the authors.   In the Teachers' Manuals standard topics for compositions are suggested and scoring procedures are described. When making measurements for comparative purposes, the directions should be followed carefully by the teacher.

### 2. *Analytical composition scales*

**Scales for different kinds of discourse.** In order to make it possible to determine specifically the factors that may contribute to the lack of general merit of compositions, analytical scales have been devised. One of the first of these analytical scales, namely the Harvard-Newton Composition Scale, was produced by Ballou in 1914. He constructed scales for measuring four forms of discourse — narration, description, exposition, and argument. The scales are especially designed for the upper grades. Each scale consists of six specimens with assigned values. The scales are definitely diagnostic, since following each composition there is a brief and specific summary of its merit and defects, and a discussion of the reasons for its rank in the scale.

The following illustration from the exposition scale will make clear its nature:

THE HARVARD-NEWTON SCALE

*"C" Grade Composition. Value, 71.4 per cent*
(Composition No. 17 in the complete set)

How to Give a Dinner Party

After you have sent out invitations for your dinner the arrangement of the table is the first thing to decide. The center piece may be flowers or anything desired.

After that has been decided upon, the courses are the next thing to decide upon. It depends on the courses what silver and china are used. Always the knives are placed on the right with the spoons, which are arranged in the order of which you use them the first one being nearest the plate. The forks are at the left of the plate in the same order as the spoons. The glasses are at the right above the knife. The napkins are at the left beside the forks. The maid serves the person left of the hostess first.

When the dinner is ready the guests assemble, but before entering the dining-room the men draw from a box or hat, which contains the names of the ladies present, one of the names, the one he draws he escorts into dinner he seats her first then sits at her left.

### Merits

This theme, with the exception of one or two sentences, is arranged in an orderly fashion, and leaves a clear impression on the reader's mind. There is a fair knowledge of paragraph structure. The spelling is accurate.

### Defects

There are, however, numerous faults. Only the third paragraph pertains to the title of the composition: the first and second tell how to prepare for a dinner party. There is room for improvement in paragraph structure: paragraphs one and two should be combined. The first sentence in the second paragraph should be subordinated, and the last sentence does not pertain to the master idea of the paragraph. The use of short sentences is monotonous. There are two "run-on" sentences in the last paragraph. The repetition of the words *decide upon* is unpleasant. The use of pronouns is lax: *you* is used for *one* in lines 1 and 7; and *one* is used ambiguously in line 14. Commas are omitted in lines 1 and 7. The expression *anything desired* is vague, and the expression *always the knives* is awkward.

### Comparison

The theme is ranked higher than No. 4 because it is more coherent, and the sentence structure is better. Because the sentence structure is more monotonous, and because it is not so well punctuated, the theme is placed lower than No. 2.

**Scales for measuring story and form value in compositions.** In 1916, Willing devised a scale for measuring the story and form value of compositions. His scale consists of eight compositions with arbitrarily assigned values in multiples of 10, and ranging from 20 to 90. Each specimen is assigned a double value, namely, a story value and a form value, the latter based on the number of mechanical errors it contains. Each specimen is followed by a note indicating the number of mistakes per one hundred written words in spelling, punctuation, and syntax. The rating of a composition by this scale thus provides a general index of the relative story value and form value of the theme.

No provision is made for the specific analysis of merits or faults due to other factors than spelling, punctuation, and syntax. The following specimen from the Willing scale,[1] value 40, indicates its nature:

My antie had her barn trown down last week and had all her chickens killed from the storm. Whitch happened at twelve oclock at night. She had 30 chickens and one horse the horse was saved he ran over to our house and claped on the dor whit his feet. When we saw him my father took him in the barn where he slepped the night with our horse. When our antie told us about the accident we were very sory the next night all my anties things were frozen. The storm blew terrible the next morning and I could not go to school so I had to stay home the whole week.

---

Number of mistakes in spelling, punctuation, and syntax per hundred words, 17.

**Measuring structure, thought, and mechanics.** The Van Wagenen English Composition Scales consist of a separate scale for each of the three forms of discourse, narration, description, and exposition. The specimens in the scales are each assigned separate values for structure, content, and mechanics, each term being defined for the benefit of the scorer. Van Wagenen [2] recognized the fact that these are

[1] Willing, M. H. *Scale for Measuring English Composition*. Public School Publishing Company, Bloomington, Illinois.

[2] Van Wagenen, M. J. "The Minnesota English Composition Scales: Their Derivation and Validity"; in *Educational Administration and Supervision*, Vol. 7, pp. 481–99. (December, 1921.)

three very different characteristics of a composition. He states:

Each quality ... must be considered as a distinct scale in itself. Only as a matter of accident would 80 in thought content, for instance, be the same distance from the arbitary zero point selected as 80 in mechanics ... Hence, simply adding together the three values assigned for the three qualities of a theme and dividing the sum by three will not be likely to give a measure of the general merit of a theme that is much, if any, more accurate than would be the measure of a liquid obtained by adding together its density, its temperature, and its volume, and then dividing the result by three.

In comparing a composition with the scale the teacher gives it a three-fold score, rating each factor according to the value of the specimen most nearly resembling it. The final composite rating of a composition is arrived at by a quite complicated mathematical formula. These scales are accompanied by a series of sample specimens, with standard ratings given for practice in scoring. The following specimen suggests the general nature of the Van Wagenen scales:[1]

Structure 62          Mechanics 55          Thought Content 54

### WHEN MOTHER WAS AWAY

It was late in the spring when my mother went to the cities. It was so hot the most of the boys did not like to go to school in the afternoon so as no body was home to write my excuses I did not have to bring one and could stay out when ever I want to.

There was a bunch of us boys who were build a spring board and was staying out ever onc in while so we could get it done. Thise went one for about a week and the teacher found that we were staying out for our own good. And so she made us make up our time which was not so much fun as it was very hot and had to stay till six o'clock and then got a poor report card.

[1] *Minnesota English Composition Scales; Narration Scale.* M. J. Van Wagenen, University of Minnesota.

### 3. *Special types of scales*

**Letter-writing scales.** Several scales have been devised for rating special types of writing, such as letters. The Lewis scale, for example, is in five parts — a scale for simple order letters, one for letters of application, one for simple narrative social letters, one for expository social letters, and one for rating simple narratives.

In Minneapolis, informal scales for rating friendly letters have been devised for use in grades three through six. The specimens were selected from a large number of typical letters collected by the teachers throughout the entire system. There are four letters for each grade, ranging from "Poor" through "Excellent." To aid teachers and pupils in the use of the scale an evaluation of each letter is given. The models serve as standards for rating letters. The following scale for grade 5 will explain the nature of the content:

### MINNEAPOLIS LETTER RATING SCALE

#### *Fifth Grade*

*Poor*

603 Tenth Avenue South,
Minneapolis, Minn.
May 28, 1924

Dear Friend:

Oh, say Vincent would you like to come to Minneapolis on your summer vacation? I know you would like to come up here. We can have a good time together. We could go swimming, fishing, hiking. We would visit Longfellows Gardens. We would go to the court house and see the statue of Father of Waters and we would hear the new chimes. Minneapolis is a very interesting city. It has many large buildings. I have a good time in Minneapolis here well good by come as soon as you can

From your loving friend,

The ejaculation in the opening sentence, the faulty sentence structure, monotonous repetition, poor organization, and errors in punctuation and capitalization classify this letter as poor. In content, it is better than the poor for fourth grade, because there is an effort on the part of the writer to interest his friend.

*Fair*

2450 First Av. S.E.
Minneapolis, Minn
May 28, 1924

Dear Max:

Will you come and visit me?  I will be very happy if you do.
All my friends have gone away.  I will let you play with Blackie
and our kittens.  We will play with my bat and ball, and my
football.  I will take you to parks, and we will go for hikes.

We will go swimming and rowing with my boat.  If you do not
know how to swim, I will show you.  It is very easy.

Your loving friend,

This letter is not good  because of the meagre vocabulary, immature sentence structure,
and needless repetition.  The form and mechanics are correct.

*Good*

2738 Bryant Avenue,
Minneapolis, Minn.
May 26, 1924

My dear Friend:

Mother and I would like very much to have you come to Minneapolis and spend the summer with us.  I am sure you would have a
delightful time for you could see the wonderful flour mills for which
Minneapolis is noted.  Also you could see the wonderful lakes.
There are also sports that you would enjoy, such as horseback-
riding, golfing, fishing, and swimming.

Kindly let us know as quickly as possible so we can make the
necessary arrangements.

Your loving chum,

This letter is good because it is a sincere, earnest invitation, correct in form and mechanics.
It is not excellent because the tone is formal and the personal note is lacking.   It is also
weakened by the repetition of "wonderful" and "also."

*Excellent*

909 Oliver Ave. N.
Minneapolis, Minn.
May 26, 1924

Dear Lois:

Mother says I may have any guest I wish to spend the summer
with me.  I choose you from a large group of dear friends and
cousins.  At our summer home near Minneapolis we have a
beautiful lawn which extends to the lake.  On the south side of the

house there is a garden, bordered by many trees, not orange or fig trees as you have in California, but trees which bear nice juicy, red apples which I'm sure you would like. Please, Lois, write at once telling me when you are coming.

Your loving cousin,

The personal touch in this letter, the good descriptive words, and the skillful use made of comparison mark it as excellent. It is also correct as to form and mechanics.

#### 4. *Standard tests in grammar and punctuation*

Standard tests for measuring the ability of pupils with respect to specific elements on written English have been devised. Many of these tests are based on the results of extensive investigations of the most common faults in written and oral speech, and hence give valuable information to teachers regarding the important essentials of English expression. Some of the tests are especially helpful for diagnosing pupil weaknesses. Several typical tests, illustrating varied approaches to the problem, will be briefly described. Other tests are listed in the Appendix.

(1) *Briggs English Form Test, Alpha and Beta.* This test contains twenty sentences of gradually increasing difficulty, based upon seven essentials in punctuation. Illustrations of each essential occur four times in cycles of increasing complexity. Standards are given for grades seven through twelve.

(2) *Charters Diagnostic Language Test.* This test for grades three to twelve is published in four parts each with alternates: a test in pronouns, one on verbs, and two based on miscellaneous errors. Each test consists of forty sentences in which the pupil is to check the correct expressions and to rewrite those that are incorrect.

(3) *Kirby Grammar Tests for Grades Seven through Twelve.* These tests contain two forms, each containing 43 sentences dealing with varied grammatical quotations. For each sentence in the five sections a grammatical rule is given in an accompanying list. The pupils are directed to

underline the correct form out of two that are given and to devise from the list the rule applied.

(4) *Pressey Diagnostic Tests in Capitalization, Punctuation, Grammar, and Sentence Structure.* The Pressey Diagnostic Tests stress vital points in functional grammar. They are accompanied by diagnostic score sheets. The grammar and sentence structure tests consist of three groups of four sentences each. The student is directed to check the incorrect sentence.

(5) *Wilson Language Error Test.* The Wilson test is a proof-reading test. The pupils are directed to correct all mistakes that appear in a printed composition, just as it was written by a student. Three stories for use at intervals throughout the year are provided. Norms are available for grades three through twelve.

(6) *Greene Tests of Linguistic Organization.* This test is designed to measure the ability of pupils to organize subject matter logically. The pupil is required to rearrange jumbled sentences in complete sentences. Norms are provided for grades three through twelve.

## 5. *Reliability of ratings of compositions*

**Difficulty in rating.** As with any tool, skill in the use of composition scales may be developed through practice. This fact has been established through careful experimentation by Hudelson [1] and others. Wide variations in ratings of compositions by various judges were greatly reduced by careful training in the use of the scales. The difficulty of rating compositions is due largely to the fact that not a single, definitely isolated quality or characteristic is to be evaluated, but a composite of an indefinite number of ele-

[1] Hudelson, Earl. "The Effect of Objective Standards upon Composition Teachers' Judgment"; in *Journal of Educational Research*, vol. 12, pp. 329–40. (December, 1925.)

ments all of which contribute to the merits of the material. All of these elements affect different individuals subjectively in different ways. Since the appraisal of the general merit of a composition is wholly subjective, differences in the ratings of several individuals are certain to exist. These differences are much more marked than would be the case, for example, in the measurement of the weight of an object which is a single, definitely isolated element for which definite, objective units of measurement exist. A scale of weights is quantitative and definite; a scale of compositions is qualitative and indefinite. A composition scale enables the teacher to estimate fairly reliably the qualitative features of a theme in rough quantitative terms.

**The value of composition scales.** In the hands of a trained scorer the composition scale is a valuable means of appraising school products. Scales will do much to reduce the variability in teachers' marks and to increase their accuracy. Definite standards of attainment can be suggested for each grade. Pupils may be taught how to score their work, thereby gaining a clearer idea of the objectives toward which they are striving. Scales may also serve as incentives to self-improvement through competition with previous ratings.

**The chief limitations of tests and scales.** The chief limitation of composition scales and other forms of measurement is that they have stressed the mechanical and rhetorical elements, and have neglected such vital factors as the organization of ideas and the originality, freshness, and inventiveness of thought for which teachers of compositions are constantly striving. The fact that the pupils' work on a test shows that he knows when a mark of punctuation is to be used is no guarantee that he will use it properly in his ordinary writing, nor does recognition of incorrect forms of expression insure the use of the correct form in conversation.

The lack of reliability of ratings of compositions by both untrained and trained scorers suggests that at least three persons should rate a composition to secure a reliable measure of its general merit. In such cases the average of the three ratings may be used.

## II. TECHNIQUES OF DIAGNOSIS IN COMPOSITION

**Test deficiencies.** The nature of the defects in certain phases of composition, such as mechanics and grammar, can be readily determined by measurement or by inspection, while in other phases, such as structure, originality, and richness of vocabulary, it is quite difficult to determine with precision what the difficulty or deficiency is. The various composition scales and standard tests on technical aspects of English are valuable tools for general diagnosis. For example, scores based on scales indicate the general level of merit of composition, but in no way indicate the specific nature of the merits or deficiencies of given compositions. A more complete form of diagnosis than is supplied by these general scales and tests is therefore required. Scores on standard tests enable the teacher to determine the relative standing of the class in comparison with other classes; however, a careful analysis must be made of the responses of individual pupils on the various test items to locate specific deficiencies on which remedial work must be undertaken.

**Tests for specific defects.** Most of the standard tests that are now available do not provide for a complete comprehensive diagnosis of deficiencies. For example, tests of punctuation, such as that of Briggs, do not contain examples of many of the detailed and specific uses of the different marks of punctuation; instead they afford a general measure of the pupil's ability to punctuate by testing his ability to apply a few of the uses of each mark. Teachers must, therefore. supplement these tests by means of informal exercises on detailed uses of punctuation marks, such as are found in some textbooks and in other forms of standardized practice exercises. Such an exercise on the uses of the apostrophe from the Brueckner–King Language Drills is given below.

BRUECKNER–KING LANGUAGE DRILLS [1]

*Sixth Grade*

LESSON XXXVIII

*Test on the Use of the Apostrophe*

Underline the words in the following which should be written with an apostrophe. Write in the apostrophe.

1. Its paws were caught in the boys trap.
2. The room isnt large enough for us.
3. Theyve sent us a Christmas present.
4. The childrens books were neatly piled on the table.
5. Im glad to see that the girls are here.
6. They dont know that the boys are throwing stones.
7. Hes the uncle who has two large farms.
8. Mens caps are on that counter.
9. Werent you glad to see us come?
10. When its warmer we may go.
11. He hasnt been here today.
12. These are the ladys handkerchiefs.
13. Youre to go to the store for supplies.
14. The girl doesnt know what to do with the baby robin.
15. His father lives on Mr. Smiths farm.
16. A sheeps wool weighs about seven pounds.
17. The girls hats were made by their mothers.
18. Wasnt that the place where we saw the pigs?
19. This dogs kennel isnt well built, is it?
20. The boys didnt lose the game today.

The inspection of compositions and other written work will of course reveal many deficiencies and errors. Particular errors will be noted in certain compositions, and constructive comments should be made by the teachers in such cases. General errors common to many papers should be recorded

[1] Published by Mentzer Bush, Chicago, Illinois.

in convenient form by the teacher, and discussed at some later meeting of the class.

**An effective technique of diagnosis.** This technique consists in providing for the correction by the class of original compositions written on the blackboard. Pupils in the class may be permitted to comment on the errors that appear. In this way many sources of error may easily be located by the teacher, and defects due to lack of knowledge and ignorance may be eliminated.

In the upper grades, errors due to lack of knowledge of important grammatical principles may be discovered by tests similar to the Kirby Grammar Tests. Similarly the teacher may use tests to locate specific deficiencies in punctuation, verb forms, etc.

Many errors observed in oral and written English are due to such factors as carelessness, unwillingness to appear "highbrow," sheer ignorance of the correct forms to use, and the influence of the quality of speech used by persons in the home, or on the playground.

## III. FACTORS TO BE CONSIDERED IN DIAGNOSIS IN COMPOSITION

The problem of diagnosis in composition may be considered from the point of view of the three factors involved — the rhetorical, the grammatical, and the formal, described briefly on the following pages.

### 1. *Diagnosis of rhetorical factors*

**Pressey's study of errors made.** It is very difficult to diagnose specifically the nature of rhetorical factors in a written composition, although differences in such elements as richness of expression in particular compositions, clarity of style, and the logical organization of the content are quite readily apparent. An important approach to a solution of this problem is that devised by Pressey,[1] who made a statistical study of children's errors in sentence structure. He analyzed 980 papers (182,985 words) written by pupils in grades seven to twelve. He explains the importance of this study as follows:

It seems a fair contention that an error is important in proportion as it makes it difficult for the reader to obtain the writer's meaning. From this point of view many errors in capitalization and in grammar are minor: if a child fails to capitalize in referring to "the Great West" or writes "he don't" for "he doesn't," he may distract the reader by offending the reader's sense for the proprieties, but he does not obscure meaning. Mistakes in sentence structure do often make the meaning obscure. Mistakes in sentence structure are, then, even more important than their frequency would indicate. They are also very important because difficulties in sentence structure frequently lead to errors in punctuation and capitalization.

The comparative frequency of the various types of errors in sentence structure found by Pressey is shown in Table 35.

TABLE 35. FREQUENCY OF ERROR IN SENTENCE STRUCTURE

(After Pressey)

| ERROR | PER CENT |
|---|---|
| Fragments used as sentences | 11 |
| Stringy sentences | 33 |
| Choppy sentences | 4 |
| Lack of parallel construction | 5 |
| Pronoun with no antecedent | 11 |
| Pronoun not near antecedent | 7 |
| Change in tense | 7 |
| Redundancy and repetition | 5 |
| Omitted word or phrase | 5 |
| Generally incoherent sentence | 5 |
| Miscellaneous | 7 |

The data in the table show that errors in sentence structure are due to a few frequently recurring faults. "Stringy sentences," the use of "fragments as sentences," and faulty

[1] Pressey, S. L. "A Statistical Study of Children's Errors in Sentence Structure"; in *The English Journal*, vol. 14, pp. 529–35. (September, 1925.)

reference of pronouns constitute over half of all of the errors
in sentence structure.   The other types of errors occur less
frequently.   However, each of them occurs often enough to
be a matter of definite concern to the teacher.

**Van Wagenen's evaluation guide.**   Several of the analytical composition scales contain general statements by
means of which the teacher may evaluate such characteristics of composition as thought content and structure, but
this appraisal must be made on the basis of personal judgment rather than according to specific prescribed techniques,
such as may be used for example in determining the frequency of misspellings in a composition.   Van Wagenen
listed the following considerations as guides for the individuals who evaluated the specimens of compositions from
which his scales were derived: [1]

*Thought Content*

In grading for thought content, take into consideration:
  For exposition:
    Adherence to subject
    Interest of the treatment
    Continuity of thought
    Clearness of perception
    Discrimination in selection of words
  For description:
    Maintenance of point of view (both physical and mental)
    Vividness of picture
    Emotional reaction
    Vigor and originality of diction
  For narration:
    Sufficient explanation of the situation
    Naturalness and appropriateness of dialogue (if used)
    Clear progress of narrative to a definite conclusion
    Use of suspense or surprise
    Descriptive touches
    Adequacy and variety of diction

[1] From *Van Wagenen's English Composition Scales*.  Copyright, 1923,
by World Book Company, Publishers, Yonkers-on-Hudson, New York.

*Sentence and Paragraph Structure*

In grading for sentence and paragraph structure, take into consideration:

Unity
Coherence
Emphasis
Variety and complexity of sentences

The writer who uses many complex sentences shows a greater maturity of mind than the one who uses very simple or unnecessarily compounded sentences, even though from the very fact of the greater complexity, he may make more actual mistakes in structure.

## 2. *Diagnosis of grammatical factors*

Diagnosis of errors due to grammatical factors is a relatively simple problem, since these errors manifest themselves in both oral and written speech. Numerous studies have been made of the kinds of errors most frequently made in both forms of discourse by both children and adults.

**Errors in oral English.** Lyman has summarized the results of extensive investigations of the kinds of errors made most frequently by pupils in their oral speech. Table 36 contains his summary.

An analysis of the data in Table 36 reveals a striking similarity in the types of errors found most frequently in each of these communities. From 49 to 62 per cent of the errors were in verb forms (items 8, 9, 10, 11, and 12); from 9 to 21 per cent were in syntactical redundancy; from 10 to 14 per cent were in pronouns (items 1 to 7); and from 8 to 14 per cent were in double negatives. It should be noted that in this list of errors in oral English no report is given of errors due to mistakes in sentence structure, incoherent sentences, the misuse of connectives, and similar types of errors. A study of the minute details of each list shows that certain errors may be peculiar to a particular locality.

TABLE 36. PERCENTAGE DISTRIBUTION OF ERRORS IN ORAL ENGLISH IN KANSAS CITY, BONHAM, COLUMBIA, DETROIT, HIBBING, AND PITTSBURGH[1]

| | Kansas City | Bonham | Columbia | Detroit | Hibbing | Pittsburgh |
|---|---|---|---|---|---|---|
| 1. Subject of the verb not in the nominative case | 4 | 5 | 3 | 4 | 3 | 3 |
| 2. Predicate nominative not in the nominative case | 2 | .. | 1 | 1 | 1 | 2 |
| 3. Object of the verb or preposition not in the objective case | 1 | .. | .. | 1 | 1 | 1 |
| 4. Wrong form of pronoun | 2 | .. | 1 | 2 | 3 | 2 |
| 5. First personal pronoun standing first | 2 | 2 | 2 | 1 | 2 | 2 |
| 6. Failure of a pronoun to agree with its antecedent | .. | .. | .. | 1 | 1 | 1 |
| 7. Confusion of demonstrative adjective and personal pronoun | 3 | 3 | 4 | 3 | 2 | 2 |
| 8. Failure of a verb to agree with subject in number & person | 14 | 8 | 9 | 12 | 9 | 13 |
| 9. Confusion of past and present tenses | 2 | 5 | 6 | 12 | 7 | 3 |
| 10. Confusion of past tense and past participle | 24 | 20 | 19 | 14 | 8 | 14 |
| 11. Wrong tense form | 5 | 2 | 4 | 3 | 5 | 5 |
| 12. Wrong verb | 12 | 21 | 24 | 18 | 20 | 18 |
| 13. Incorrect use of the mood | .. | .. | .. | .. | .. | .. |
| 14. Confusion of comparative and superlative | 1 | .. | .. | .. | .. | 1 |
| 15. Confusion of adjective and adverbs | 4 | 1 | 6 | 2 | 2 | 2 |
| 16. Misplaced modifiers | .. | .. | .. | 1 | 1 | .. |
| 17. Double negatives | 11 | 14 | 10 | 9 | 8 | 10 |
| 18. Confusion of preposition and conjunction | .. | .. | 1 | .. | .. | .. |
| 19. Syntactical redundance | 10 | 9 | 9 | 15 | 21 | 16 |
| 20. Wrong part of speech due to similarity of sound | 1 | .. | .. | 1 | .. | .. |
| 21. Confusion of prepositions | .. | .. | .. | .. | .. | .. |
| 22. Pronunciation and enunciation | .. | .. | .. | .. | .. | 2 |
| 23. Adverb instead of negative form of verb | .. | .. | .. | .. | 2 | 3 |
| 24. Words omitted | .. | .. | .. | .. | 2 | .. |
| 25. Miscellaneous | .. | .. | .. | .. | 2 | .. |
| Total number of errors | 5,883 | 500 | 500 | 11,207 | 10,190 | 25,676 |

[1] Lyman, R. L. *Summary of Investigations Relating to Grammar, Language, and Composition,* p. 73. University of Chicago.

This variation suggests the need of making studies to determine the needs of each school community.

Various procedures may be used in collecting the errors made by the members in a single class. The errors may be recorded informally, as they occur during the regular class work in all subjects. A pupil secretary may be appointed to keep the record. The chief difficulty with this procedure is that in many classes there is relatively little opportunity for oral expression by the pupils. Whatever talking is done by them is likely not to be their normal free speech since there is an element of control in the mere presence of the teacher. To overcome this difficulty a survey of errors in oral English was made in Minneapolis by recording the errors that occurred during civic-league periods and free-activity periods, when the pupils were engaged in discussing topics of interest and importance to them and when their speech was free and uncontrolled. It had previously been found by experiment that many errors were made in such free periods by pupils who made practically no English errors in their regular class work.

**Errors in written speech.** Technical errors in grammar and punctuation in written compositions have been treated in a large number of investigations.

One of the most detailed studies of errors in written speech was made in Kansas City by Charters and Miller.[1] The errors were tabulated under twenty-seven headings, as given in Table 37.

A study of this table shows that 38 per cent of all errors were mistakes in punctuation. Three types of errors were reported under this classification: "failure to put period at end of statement," 30 per cent; "failure to put question

[1] Charters, W. W., and Miller, Edith. *A Course of Study in Grammar Based on Language Errors of Children of Kansas City, Missouri.* University of Missouri Bulletins, vol. 26, no. 2, Education Series no. 9, 1915.

TABLE 37. WORKING LIST OF WRITTEN ERRORS USED BY TABULATORS AND THE NUMBER AND PERCENTAGE OF EACH KIND OF ERROR

(Charters and Miller)

| Error | TOTAL | PER CENT | PERCENTAGE OF FIRST TWENTY-ONE ERRORS |
|---|---|---|---|
| 1. Subject of verb not in nominative case..... | 42 | 0 | 1 |
| 2. Predicate nominative not in nominative case | 49 | 0 | 1 |
| 3. Object of verb or preposition not in objective case.................................. | 48 | 0 | 1 |
| 4. Wrong form of noun or pronoun........... | 655 | 5 | 16 |
| 5. First personal pronoun standing first in a series................................ | 25 | 0 | 1 |
| 6. Disagreement of noun and pronoun in number, person, and gender............... | 162 | 1 | 4 |
| 7. Confusion of demonstrative adjective and personal pronoun...................... | 3 | 0 | 0 |
| 8. Failure of verb to agree with its subject in number and person.................... | 753 | 6 | 19 |
| 9. Confusion of past and present tenses....... | 474 | 4 | 12 |
| 10. Confusion of past tense and past participle. | 188 | 2 | 5 |
| 11. Wrong tense forms...................... | 198 | 2 | 5 |
| 12. Wrong verb........................... | 265 | 2 | 7 |
| 13. Incorrect use of mood.................... | 61 | 0 | 2 |
| 14. Incorrect comparison of adjectives......... | 12 | 0 | 0 |
| 15. Confusion of comparatives and superlatives. | 8 | 0 | 0 |
| 16. Confusion of adjectives and adverbs....... | 253 | 2 | 6 |
| 17. Misplaced modifier...................... | 225 | 2 | 6 |
| 18. Double negative........................ | 58 | 0 | 1 |
| 19. Confusion of prepositions and conjunctions. | 53 | 0 | 1 |
| 20. Syntactical redundancy.................. | 467 | 4 | 11 |
| 21. Wrong part of speech due to similarity of sound................................ | 1334 | 11 | .. |
| 22. Failure to put period at end of statement.. | 3600 | 30 | .. |
| 23. Failure to put question mark at end of question.................................. | 208 | 2 | .. |
| 24. Failure to put apostrophe to denote possession................................ | 744 | 6 | .. |
| 25. Omission of subject..................... | 313 | 3 | .. |
| 26. Omission of predicate................... | 297 | 2 | .. |
| 27. Confusion of dependent and independent clauses............................... | 1059 | 9 | .. |

mark at end of question," 2 per cent; "failure to put apostrophe to denote possession," 6 per cent. Sixteen per cent of all errors were verb errors; 11 per cent, use of incorrect part of speech because of similarity in sound; 6 per cent, noun or pronoun errors; 4 per cent, syntactical redundancy; and 2 per cent, errors due to confusion of adjectives and adverbs.

Several other studies revealed approximately the same results. In these studies between 30 per cent and 55 per cent of all errors were found to be due to faulty punctuation. Verb errors uniformly hold the highest ranking when only errors in grammar are considered.

These investigations of errors in the written compositions of elementary-school pupils are deficient in that little consideration is given to such items of importance in written composition as sentence structure, meagerness of vocabulary, and clarity of statement. Nor has any consideration been given to the materials that pupils write in life outside the school. That such information should be secured is self-evident and important.

**Bobbitt's study of letter errors.** Bobbitt,[1] for example,

TABLE 38. FREQUENCY OF GENERAL TYPES OF ERRORS IN
THE FREE WRITTEN ENGLISH OF ADULTS
(Bobbitt)

|  | FREQUENCY |
|---|---|
| 1. Errors in punctuation | 2796 |
| 2. Errors in expression | 2287 |
| 3. Errors in capitalization | 1183 |
| 4. Errors in abbreviation | 192 |
| 5. Errors in spelling | 191 |
| 6. Errors in grammar | 157 |
| 7. Improper margins | 147 |
| 8. Errors in writing numbers | 81 |
| 9. Errors in word-compounding | 76 |
| Total | 7110 |

[1] Bobbitt, Sarah. "Shortcomings of the Written English of Adults"; in *Curriculum Investigations* of F. Bobbitt and others. Supplementary Educational Mimeograph, no. 31, p. 111. Chicago, University of Chicago, 1926.

reported an analysis of the errors found in a random sampling of 362 letters addressed by adults to the "Voice of the People" and printed in *The Chicago Daily News*. In all 7110 errors were found, an average of about twenty errors per letter, or one error to every fourteen words. The errors were classified as shown in Table 38.

The ten most frequent errors reported by Bobbitt were:

1. Commas incorrectly omitted with non-restrictive or parenthetical modifiers.
2. Incorrect punctuation of an abbreviation.
3. Failure to use period to disassociate independent statements.
4. Superfluous punctuation.
5. Failure properly to disassociate the independent clauses in a long compound sentence.
6. Words in series not properly separated by commas.
7. Commas not used where needed to set off appositives.
8. Commas omitted where restrictive modifiers come between other closely related groups of words.
9. Failure to use a question mark after an interrogative sentence.
10. Omission of quotation marks with a direct quotation.

Only 157 errors classified as strictly grammatical were recorded. Of these approximately 33 per cent were errors in the tense of the verb; and 21 per cent were errors in the agreement of the verb and the subject in number; and 10 per cent were incorrect uses of "shall," "will," "should" and "would." These verb-errors constituted 65 per cent of all errors in grammatical usage. The information supplied by such studies as that of Bobbitt should be a valuable guide for teachers in determining the points to stress in their remedial teaching.

**Diagnosis of difficulties in punctuation.** In the summaries of errors in written composition that have been given in the preceding pages, it was shown that from approximately 30 to 55 per cent of all errors were due to faulty punctuation. In no case was a detailed analysis made of the specific uses of each of the marks of punctuation, nor of the number of times that errors were made in each of these specific uses. Such information for any class is essential if the teacher is to be expected to give specific remedial exercises to overcome special difficulties.

Wasserman and Brueckner [1] prepared an exercise in which were contained all of the important uses of eight marks of punctuation commonly taught below the eighth grade, as follows:

### THE IMPORTANT USES OF THE PUNCTUATION MARKS
(Wasserman and Brueckner)

I. Capitalization
   a. The beginning of a sentence
   b. Proper nouns
   c. Insertion in letters; also omission
   d. In a direct quotation

II. Period
   a. At the end of a sentence
   b. In an abbreviation
   c. Insertion in letters

III. Comma
   a. Between the parts of a compound sentence
   b. In nouns of address
   c. After words or phrases of introduction
   d. After clauses of introduction
   e. Words of a series
   f. Appositives
   g. In a non-restrictive clause
   h. Parenthetic expressions
   i. Setting off short direct quotations
   j. Separating the parts of a date
   k. Headings of letters
   l. Salutations

[1] Unpublished study.

> *m.* End of letters
> *n.* After "hello"

IV. Quotation Marks
> *a.* In an unbroken quotation, with the descriptive element preceding the quotation
> *b.* In an unbroken quotation, with the descriptive element following the quotation
> *c.* In a broken quotation

V. Apostrophe
> *a.* In a singular possessive
> *b.* In a plural possessive
> *c.* After a proper noun ending in s
> *d.* In a contraction
> *e.* After a plural possessive that is a proper name
> *f.* In plurals of letters, i.e., A's
> *g.* In possessive of children

VI. Colon
> *a.* Salutation of a letter

VII. Semicolon
> *a.* When the connective in a compound sentence is omitted

VIII. Question Mark
> *a.* In an interrogation

**A proof-reading exercise.** To determine the relative difficulty of each of these specific uses of punctuation marks, 148 sixth-grade pupils were each given a mimeographed copy of the exercise, with all punctuation marks and capitals missing. They were directed to encircle the letters in the exercise that should be capitalized, and to put in the proper punctuation marks. Previous experimental studies showed a correlation of +.83 between the number of mistakes when the material was dictated and when it was given in mimeographed form. Because of this fact, and because of greater ease in scoring the papers, the proof-reading exercise was used. The two parts of the test material used in this investigation were as follows:

## A Proof-Reading Exercise
### (Wasserman and Brueckner)

Name...................... Grade.......... Date..........

*Directions*: 1. Encircle the letters that should be capitalized.
2. Put in the proper punctuation marks.

### Part I: A

1. i must tell you about my friends john and mary
2. one day when they were outside playing mary asked john what would you like to eat
3. i would like a dish of ice cream said john
4. not i said mary id like an apple
5. meanwhile dr jones a rich man passed by
6. a dog who was wagging his tail was following the doctor
7. it was dr jones dog
8. hello children said the doctor as his dog began to play with johns hat which had been blown off by the wind
9. hello said john and mary
10. the doctor who was the childrens best friend asked them what marks they got in school last term
11. we both received all As said the two children
12. we do not however expect to get the same marks this term the two said
13. the doctor said the children had done well therefore he bought them ice cream and apples
14. a week later mary happened to be describing dr jones dog to me
15. he is very good but he chases the boys hats all the time
16. all of the joneses friends have dogs
17. its a pleasure to have a nice dog
18. james dog is big and he likes to be covered with red green blue and yellow ribbons
19. next week i will tell you about another boys friends

PART II

> 2423   clinton   ave   n
> minneapolis   minn
> november   7   1928

mr   john   smith
  chicago   ill
dear   sir
  i   received   your   letter   and   i   was   very   glad   to   hear
from   you   i   expect   to   hear   from   you   again   on   monday
november   18th   1928

> yours   truly
> b   jones

**Results of the study.** The papers of the pupils were then marked and the errors tabulated. Two kinds of errors were found, those due to omission of marks and capitals, and those due to their faulty insertion. Less than eight per cent of the total number of errors was due to insertions. The total number of errors for each mark of punctuation is given in the upper part of Table 39. The total number of errors for each of the specific marks of punctuation is given in the lower part of the table. The table also shows the ranking of each specific use for each mark of punctuation, and for all uses, according to the number of times errors were made in its use in the test exercise. The code letters correspond to the list of marks and their uses given on page 359.

The largest number of errors was due to the faulty uses of the comma — 3940 errors in all. The next largest number of errors was due to incorrect uses of the apostrophe — 1293 errors in all. The specific use of a mark of punctuation in which there was the largest number of errors was type IIIc, the use of the comma after words or phrases of introduction — 726 errors in all. The number of errors on various specific marks of punctuation included in the test ranged from 726 to 58. The average number of errors per pupil

## TABLE 39. NUMBER OF ERRORS AND RANK OF PUNCTUATION MARKS AND THEIR SPECIFIC USES

(Wasserman and Brueckner)

| MARKS OF PUNCTUATION | INSERTION ERRORS | OMISSION ERRORS | TOTAL ERRORS | INSERTION RANK | OMISSION RANK | COMBINED RANK |
|---|---|---|---|---|---|---|
| I. Capitalization..... | 68 | 779 | 847 | 4 | 3 | 4 |
| II. Period........... | 106 | 764 | 870 | 2 | 4 | 3 |
| III. Comma.......... | 239 | 3701 | 3940 | 1 | 1 | 1 |
| IV. Quotation marks... | 87 | 491 | 578 | 3 | 5 | 5 |
| V. Apostrophe....... | 15 | 1278 | 1293 | 7 | 2 | 2 |
| VI. Colon............ | .. | 84 | 84 | 8 | 7 | 7 |
| VII. Semicolon........ | 6 | 148 | 154 | 6 | 6 | 6 |
| VIII. Question mark.... | 29 | 29 | 58 | 5 | 8 | 8 |
| Total.......... | 550 | 7274 | 7824 | | | |

### RANK OF USES

| MARKS OF PUNCTUATION | INSERTION ERRORS | OMISSION ERRORS | TOTAL ERRORS | INSERTION | OMISSION | ALL TYPES | FINAL RANK |
|---|---|---|---|---|---|---|---|
| I. Capitalization | | | | | | | |
| a.................. | 0 | 131 | 131 | 3.5 | 2 | 2 | 22 |
| b.................. | 0 | 466 | 466 | 3.5 | 1 | 1 | 5 |
| c.................. | 64 | 63 | 127 | 1 | 4 | 3 | 23 |
| d.................. | 4 | 119 | 123 | 2 | 3 | 4 | 24 |
| II. Period | | | | | | | |
| a.................. | 22 | 238 | 260 | 2 | 2 | 2 | 11 |
| b.................. | 0 | 526 | 526 | 3 | 1 | 1 | 4 |
| c.................. | 86 | 0 | 86 | 1 | 3 | 3 | 30 |
| III. Comma | | | | | | | |
| a.................. | 45 | 356 | 401 | 2 | 4 | 4 | 6 |
| b.................. | 13 | 126 | 139 | 6 | 10 | 10 | 20 |
| c.................. | 9 | 717 | 726 | 9.5 | 1 | 1 | 1 |
| d.................. | 12 | 128 | 140 | 7 | 9 | 9 | 19 |
| e.................. | 36 | 47 | 83 | 3 | 14 | 13 | 32 |
| f.................. | 8 | 267 | 275 | 11 | 6 | 5 | 9 |
| g.................. | 3 | 673 | 676 | 12 | 2 | 2 | 2 |
| h.................. | 0 | 268 | 268 | 13.5 | 5 | 6 | 10 |
| i.................. | 48 | 574 | 622 | 1 | 3 | 3 | 3 |
| j.................. | 29 | 154 | 183 | 4 | 7 | 7 | 14 |
| k.................. | 16 | 62 | 78 | 5 | 13 | 14 | 32 |
| l.................. | 9 | 89 | 98 | 9.5 | 12 | 12 | 29 |
| m.................. | 11 | 94 | 105 | 8 | 11 | 11 | 27 |
| n.................. | 0 | 146 | 146 | 13.5 | 8 | 8 | 18 |
| IV. Quotation mark | | | | | | | |
| a.................. | 46 | 272 | 318 | 1 | 1 | 1 | 8 |
| b.................. | 36 | 66 | 102 | 2 | 3 | 3 | 28 |
| c.................. | 5 | 153 | 158 | 3 | 2 | 2 | 15 |
| V. Apostrophe | | | | | | | |
| a.................. | 0 | 206 | 206 | 3.5 | 2 | 2 | 12 |
| b.................. | 15 | 135 | 150 | 1 | 5 | 4 | 17 |
| c.................. | 0 | 383 | 383 | 3.5 | 1 | 1 | 7 |
| d.................. | 0 | 184 | 184 | 3.5 | 3 | 3 | 13 |
| e.................. | 0 | 136 | 136 | 3.5 | 4 | 5 | 21 |
| f.................. | 0 | 112 | 112 | 3.5 | 7 | 7 | 26 |
| g.................. | 0 | 122 | 122 | 3.5 | 6 | 6 | 25 |
| VI. Colon | | | | | | | |
| a.................. | 0 | 84 | 84 | | | | 31 |
| VII. Semicolon | | | | | | | |
| a.................. | 6 | 148 | 154 | | | | 16 |
| VIII. Question mark...... | 29 | 29 | 58 | | | | 33 |

was approximately 52. The final rank for each specific item indicates roughly its relative difficulty.

The exercise given on page 361 may be used by any teacher to determine specific deficiencies and faults of individual pupils in punctuation and in the use of capital letters. The test can be given in less than half an hour. It may also be divided into sections and dictated to the pupils. Duplicate forms can easily be prepared by either using new words in the sentences, or by rearranging the order in which they are presented.

## IV. REMEDIAL TEACHING IN COMPOSITION

After the teacher has discovered the general as well as the specific weaknesses of the class and of individuals, the next step is to find the remedies. The teacher must differentiate clearly between those procedures that are intended to inspire in the children a desire to write and an interest in writing, and those techniques used to eradicate errors of a technical or mechanical nature.

### 1. *Stimulating the desire to write*

**Utilizing social situations.** In order to develop an interest in writing the teacher must use all possible means to create and utilize social situations in the class in which there will be a free and easy discussion and interchange of ideas. The value of life situations as a source of language expression is well expressed in the following statement: [1]

A real situation provides many factors essential to good language training:

1. The feeling that he has something worthwhile to say tends to overcome the self-consciousness of the timid child. The knowledge that he knew more than any other child in the room about the machinery used in preparing the ground and planting corn, led

[1] Taken from the *Iowa State Course of Study*, p. 262; published in 1928.

one extremely self-conscious second grade boy to give a very good talk on this subject.

2. Formal language requirements are more forcefully presented in a natural situation than when introduced as exercises. Even primary children can learn the use of an outline in planning an assembly program on "How the Indians Care for their Sick," or in planning a group report on "How We Made Soap." The importance of brevity and clearness in stating a recipe for making a gingerbread boy is apparent to children in first grade.

3. Constructive criticism, with a free exchange of ideas, results when teacher and pupils are equally interested in the outcome, i.e., writing a report for the school paper.

4. The child recognizes the importance of organization when he is telling his classmates something which he feels they should understand and remember, e.g., "How I Taught my Pony to Shake Hands," or "How to Make a Loom." Even a first grade child realizes clearly the importance of sequence in dictating a report, "How We Made Apple Jelly."

5. Greater interest in neatness, appearance, and form of work results from a real situation. A group of children who are making a chart, "Our Winter Bouquet," with a brief paragraph of explanation written and pasted under each specimen, need no reminder from the teacher to interest them in keeping the chart free from blots of ink and splotches of paste.

6. A greater attention to content is secured. A class which is writing to ask a favor from a stranger sees real purpose in making the letter brief, to the point, and courteous.

7. The real "audience situation" created when a child has an audience eager to hear something that he feels is worthwhile, is a great incentive to overcoming mumbling and poor enunciation. The child feels that it is important to speak so as to be clearly understood.

8. The stimulus that comes from real need leads to greater effort on the part of the child. Children who are preparing an assembly program telling how candles are made will work with a zeal that is surprising.

The lessons should be characterized by an atmosphere of appreciation and enjoyment. Pupils should be so stimulated by the discussion that they will be impelled by a strong urge to express their thoughts either orally or in writing.

The teacher should constantly place before children good models by reading well written passages from the best compositions submitted by the class, or selections from suitable pieces of literature. Through carefully guided discussions the teacher should let the pupils discover the excellences of the models.

**Training pupils to organize their ideas.** Before pupils in the grades write a composition there should be a period of preparation. For training purposes pupils in a class may, as a group, study the procedures to follow in writing a composition by going through the various steps under the direction of the teacher. As a basis for this type of exercise the teacher should have in mind the general objectives for the grade, and should select a topic which is of immediate interest to the pupils. Such topics may be selected either from a previously prepared list, or may arise in the course of the work in any school subject. There should first be a general discussion of the topic by the class, so that the purpose will be clear to all of the pupils; the ways in which the topic might be treated should then be considered; the points that might be treated should be listed on the blackboard; with the help of the teacher an outline of the essay should then be prepared; brief oral discussions of each point in the outline should be called for; these comments should be criticized by the teacher and the pupils, and ways of improving or enriching them suggested; vocabulary exercises on words pertinent to the topic should be used to introduce vivid, expressive ideas; and standards for evaluating compositions should be discussed and applied concretely. When these preliminary stages of the preparations have been completed, all of the pupils will be so saturated with ideas that the writing, according to the general outline prepared by the class, is a relatively simple task. The training received through such exercises will be of great value as a means of improving the free written expression of the pupils.

**Class appraisal of compositions.** After the compositions have been written, the teacher should select certain of them for class discussion. Some of them may be read aloud and appraised. Their strong points should first be considered. Some of the compositions illustrating certain defects should be written on the blackboard and discussed. In this way the principles of composition may be presented concretely to the pupils. Suggestions as to how the particular composition can be improved in structure, style, and content may be called for and incorporated in the specimen. The final step is the reading of the revision to show the improvement that has resulted from the class discussion. Such lessons may be used at any time as a means of developing the capacity for self-criticism by the pupils. A growing comprehension of the basic qualities that underlie good composition is also assured.

**Encouraging creative composition.** Not all of the written work of pupils should be done at the direction of the teacher. Every opportunity should be given pupils to write freely on matters of interest to themselves. Such occasions will arise in connection with units of work in reading, the social studies, arithmetic, art, and other subjects. The school paper, the class magazine, and many other avenues of free expression are provided in the modern school. Many magazines publish outstanding contributions written by pupils. The teacher can do much to encourage this creative type of composition. Excellent discussions of the general procedures to use are presented in Hughes Mearns's *Creative Youth*, and in *Creative Power* by the same author.

### 2. Correcting mechanical and technical defects

**Practice tests to reveal pupil difficulties.** Since mechanical and technical defects vary widely from pupil to pupil, it is essential that teaching techniques be used that make it possible to adapt the remedial work to the needs of the individual. This may be accomplished through the use of practice exercises on specific points. It is futile, for example, to give a pupil practice on general punctuation when his difficulty is chiefly due to specific defects in uses of the comma or period, which may be determined by a specific, comprehensive diagnostic test. What he needs is a set of practice exercises which explain the specific items to him, give him models to study, and then provide carefully directed practice in the correct use of the specific items.

Several sets of standardized practice exercises to eliminate mechanical and grammatical defects in English have been designed.

**The Pribble-Brezler Practice Cards in English.**[1] These tests consist of one series of cards, the same cards to be used in all grades. Each card contains an exercise designed to correct one or more faults in language. The materials were chosen on the basis of the relative frequency with which the faults involved were formed in various scientific investigations of pupils' errors in oral and written speech. Models are given and practice in applying the correct form is provided. The Matravers Test, Study, and Practice Exercises in Grammar have a similar purpose.

**The Brueckner-King Language Drills.** These drills are published in four booklets, one for grades 3 and 4, one for grade 5, one for grade 6, and one for grades 7 and 8. The exercises in these drills are graded in difficulty and parallel current courses of study. The materials in the drills were selected on the basis of their cruciality as determined by the frequency with which the items are used incorrectly by pupils in oral and written speech, according to the scientific

[1] Published by Lyons and Carnahan.

studies of defects in English. Those booklets contain standard tests on punctuation, verb forms, sentence structure, and important grammatical principles. They also contain diagnostic tests on the various elements included in the exercises, and provision for cumulative practice on all points considered in the previous exercises. Because of the specific, detailed nature of the lesson units they are very well adapted to individualized, remedial instruction. Provision is made for self-scoring and for an individual progress graph. On the pages which follow is given a typical practice exercise on the use of capital letters, and a typical exercise on verb forms.

### BRUECKNER–KING LANGUAGE DRILLS

#### I. Using Capital Letters

A. Which words in the following sentences should begin with capital letters? Tell why.

1. the boy left friday for chicago.
2. his father, mr. smith, has his vacation in september.
3. mrs. smith visited england last august.
4. i asked, "what am i to do today?"

#### A New Use of Capitals

B. Where are capitals used in this poem?

> Mary had a little lamb,
> Its fleece was white as snow;
> And everywhere that Mary went
> The lamb was sure to go.

Find a poem in your readers. You will see that every line of the poem begins with a capital letter.

C. Draw a line under each word in the following that should begin with a capital letter.

1. mr. jones is to be in new york sunday.
2.  simple simon met a pie man
    going to the fair.
    said simple simon to the pie man,
    "let me taste your ware."

3. chicago is the city in which john jones lives.
4. our teacher, miss smith, lives on first street.
5. the first two days in april were thursday and friday.
6. mrs. arthur is harry's mother.

D. Your teacher will dictate these sentences to you.

## II. *Selecting Correct Forms of Words*

Draw a line through one of the words in each sentence that is not correct. The sentence below is marked correctly.

They haven't (any, ~~no~~) new clothes.

1. The girl (lies, lays) in the swing.
2. The man gave us (them, those) apples.
3. I have (ate, eaten) my dinner.
4. They have (went, gone) to school already.
5. Has he (did, done) his work well.
6. The boy (ran, run) away from the fire.
7. We (ain't had, haven't had) any rain this week.
8. There (is, are) many fish in the lake.
9. His brother (came, come) with him.
10. The big dog (sat, sit) on the sidewalk.
11. You (may, can) go if you wish.
12. The people have (gone, went) home already.
    (Thirteen other items similar to the above follow.)

Other well-known materials in pamphlet form to diagnose difficulties and to provide remedial work are:

Mullen and Lanz. *Exercises and Tests in English.* Boston, Ginn and Company.

Guiler. *Diagnostic Tests in Punctuation and Remedial Exercises.* Chicago, Rand-McNally Company.

Uhl-Hatz. *Practice Lessons in English.* Boston, Ginn and Company.

## 3. *Results of a campaign to eliminate errors in English*

An intensive campaign to eliminate errors in oral English resulted in Minneapolis in a very large improvement throughout the city. It is now possible to give concrete evidence of the value of different methods that can be used to eliminate errors in oral English. The improvement due to the campaigning was measured by means of tests covering the fifty commonest errors found in the survey of errors in oral English in the Minneapolis elementary schools. The tests were so constructed that the children were to mark sentences that had the correct grammatical construction for each error "right," and the incorrect form "wrong." Half of the sentences were right and half of them were wrong. A different error was included in each sentence.

In order that it might be possible to measure the value of different methods of teaching that might be used to eliminate errors in English, the schools of the city were divided into six groups of approximately equal size and ability. The methods used by each of these groups were as follows:

*Group* 1. The list of errors will be given to pupils as in other groups. The plan will be explained to them, but no intensive work is to be done in school.

*Group* 2. The correction of errors in oral speech and in written composition should be intensified, but no other types of attack on correction of speech errors are to be made.

*Group* 3. The work in this group is to take the form of drill games only, with no attempt at emphasis upon the correction of errors in oral speech and written composition.

*Group* 4. These pupils will attempt to dramatize this attack on speech errors by writing short plays, slogans, preparing programs, etc.

*Group* 5. Pupils in this group will work out some plan for reporting and listing speech errors which they have observed. The corrected forms of these reported errors will be listed on the blackboard and kept before the pupils.

*Group* 6. In this group, pupils are to be allowed to plan *their own* projects for accomplishing this work and to work them out in coöperation with the teacher.

On a basis of a tabulation of the results of the first and second tests, the improvement made of each of the groups was determined. The results were as follows:

TABLE 40. IMPROVEMENT BY GROUPS — MEDIAN SCORES —
MINNEAPOLIS

| GROUPS | FIRST TEST | SECOND TEST | PER CENT OF POSSIBLE GAIN |
|---|---|---|---|
| Group I | 73 | 79 | 22 |
| Group II | 72 | 82 | 36 |
| Group III | 73 | 83 | 37 |
| Group IV | 72 | 85 | 46 |
| Group V | 72 | 83 | 39 |
| Group VI | 72 | 86 | 50 |

The smallest per cent of possible gain was made by
schools in Group I. This was to be expected since these
schools took no part in the campaign. Undoubtedly there
were in this group schools which would have made a very
large improvement if they had taken part in the work.
Group VI, in which the pupils in coöperation with the
teachers planned their own activity, made the largest gain.
In Group IV, where slogans and dramatizations were used,
the gain was almost as great. It can be seen from the table
that all groups did equally well on the first test.

It should be clear from these results that wherever work
is attempted which has for its purpose the elimination of
errors in oral English, one of the primary considerations
must be the use that can be made of pupil activities in
bringing about improvement.

A tabulation of the methods submitted, in reply to the
request for the activities found to be most helpful in Group
VI, shows that the following list of activities was most frequently chosen by the children.

| | |
|---|---|
| C or X sentence drills | 50 |
| Language-downs and contests | 42 |
| Listening and reporting on errors | 41 |
| Games | 23 |
| Children illustrating by sentences | 23 |
| Dramatizations | 6 |
| Rimes, jingles, slogans | 6 |
| Blanks to be filled | 6 |

The method most frequently reported was the "right or wrong" drill. There were numerous variations of the method, but the usual procedure was the reading of a sentence by the teacher. The pupil responded by saying "Right" or "Wrong." If the latter, he also gave the correct form. The children often made the test sentences themselves. In one building the rooms made test sentences, each week, for the room next higher up. Often the making of the test sentences rested in the hands of the English Committee. The sentences were also given in written form, either typed or written on the blackboard, to be marked "C" or "X."

One building using drills and contests divided each room into small groups with a leader in each group.

In several instances another variation was used. Each child was given two cards, one containing a "C," the other "X." As a sentence was dictated each pupil indicated his reply by showing the proper card.

"English downs" and contests were next in order. The competitive spirit was prominent, and pupils planned their work to satisfy the desire for winning. The contests were conducted after the manner of spell-downs, using sentences. Pupils retained their places if they knew whether the sentence contained an error or not. The contests were often between groups, between rooms, or, more often, between boys and girls.

A close rival of this method was the plan of reporting errors heard and of correcting them. In one building a leader was chosen for each room. He was given a mallet which he used in tapping every time an error was heard. The correction was made and the recitation proceeded.

A third grade made cardboard buttons four inches in diameter. On one side were the words "I use Correct English." On the other was one of the fifty errors with its corrected form. Whenever an error in speech was made, it was the duty of the child who was wearing that particular button that day to correct the error instantly — or forfeit the button.

A frequently used plan was to have children give illustrations of errors by original sentences. Games, too, played an important part in this group.

It is surprising to find so few dramatic activities reported in Group VI — 2 per cent, especially so in view of the fact that the group (Group IV) assigned to the dramatization method made nearly as great a gain (46 per cent) as did the project group (50 per cent). A room which had just finished reading *Robinson Crusoe* decided to write a short play in which Robinson Crusoe teaches Friday good English.

Another room planned an English tournament in the manner of an athletic meet. Plans for booklets were worked out. Activities were carried over into other work. Many rooms made charts and graphs showing progress.

The results of this study corroborate the investigations by Collings, Meriam, Courtis, and others. In each case the greatest gain was made by the groups in which the pupils had a hand in planning the attack on the work. These findings open up a large field of study of methods of teaching, and suggest that it is most necessary for teachers and supervisors to take into consideration the purposes and interests of children in the organization of class work. There is also apparently great value in intensive periods of work on school subjects.

### 4. *General remedial suggestions based on experimental evidence*

A large number of experimental studies in the teaching of language have been made. A complete analysis of the most significant studies reported from 1900 to 1928 is contained in the monograph by Lyman.[1]  Because of limitations of space only a summary of the findings of the chapter on methods of teaching will be given in this chapter.

In spite of the shortcomings of most of the objective studies in methods of teaching, the investigators have created strong presumption in favor of certain innovations in teaching language and composition.  Among the more important considerations are the following.

1. Regimented group instruction in language is inferior to individual instruction.  To hold a mixed class together with a reasonable minimum of language content and at the same time keep each pupil's efforts focussed on his individual needs is exceedingly difficult.  If adequately determined with reference to language attainments, ability grouping may aid materially in the solution of such difficulty.

2. Gifted pupils at least may be largely thrown on their own responsibility and may become their own critics.  The extent to which an aroused and functioning language conscience among such pupils will improve their expression is at present largely a matter of conjecture.  Moreover, Abbott and Trabue presented evidence to show that 25 per cent of high-school seniors have better literary tastes than 25 per cent of their teachers.[2]  Leonard's studies seem to indicate that capable pupils may be able to criticize their own papers for language errors fully as well as many of their teachers.

3. Coy's study, showing the extent to which challenging topics call forth pupil's best work, suggests further investigation.  In what way and to what extent is excellence in composition, both in content and in quality, conditioned upon the vitality of the expressional situations into which pupils are directed?  Again, granted that "personal-experience topics" are by far the most popular both with pupils and teachers, what particular content values, if any, are found in compositions written on such topics?  Has the loose narrative type of organization, almost inevitable in such discourse, any lasting value in teaching pupils to think?  After all, language experiences are intended to develop habits, and "what is

[1] Lyman, R. L.  *Summary of Investigations Relating to Grammar, Language, and Composition*, pp. 253–55.  University of Chicago.

[2] Abbott, Allan, and Trabue, M. R.  "A Measure of Ability to Judge Poetry"; in *Teachers College Record*, vol. 22, pp. 101–26.  (March, 1921.)

most popular" may not be "what is most opportune." This position is perhaps in contrast with school experiences in literature which ought to develop attitudes; in literature "the opportune" may possibly deserve primary attention.

4. Class time may profitably be used for necessary drill both of individuals and of groups. It is certain that intensive drill will produce immediate results. However, vital questions arise with regard to language drill which are as yet unanswered. (a) To what extent does intensive group drill imply lasting improvement? (b) How shall a teacher know when his class has reached a plateau of language improvement? (c) By what teaching cycles and in what grades are certain language elements best inculcated? (d) What compensating losses are to be considered when classes are subjected to protracted drill? (e) What is the effect of language drill on pupils from cultured homes whose speech habits are natively correct? (f) How are pupils' language habits affected by the speech habits of teachers, especially those who practice the pernicious "and" habit common in the conversation of untrained people with little children? All these and many kindred questions are open for study.

5. The pressure for acceptable writing and speaking, if intelligently and diligently stressed in all subject-matter classes, ought materially to improve the pupils' language habits. Evidence indicates that at present the transfer of training from English classes to other expressional situations is not impressive unless strong administrative pressure is exerted on teachers and pupils alike. Experimentation in methods of teaching English has no more attractive and promising field. What is the effect of slovenly expression in content classes? What is the effect of reasonably guarded expression in content classes?

6. Some of the studies appear to indicate that the class period in language-composition may be profitably devoted to laboratory procedure. Although the experiments in supervised study have in general produced negative results, expression is beyond question a series of activities to be supervised; it is not subject matter to be taught, learned, and recited. "No subject is more truly a 'shop' or 'laboratory subject' than English." [1]

[1] *Reorganization of English in Secondary Schools*, p. 28. United States Bureau of Education, Bulletin no. 2, 1917.

## QUESTIONS FOR STUDY, DISCUSSION, AND REPORT

1. What are the functions of language instruction?

2. In what ways does the typical question-and-answer recitation interfere with the development of good habits of oral speech? A lesson in which the teacher asked two hundred questions in a forty-minute period has been reported.

3. Observe a lesson of any kind in the classroom, and make a record of the kinds of responses made by pupils, as sentences, parts of sentences, phrases, single words, etc.

4. Record the errors in oral English during a class period. Compare this record with the errors observed during some free-activity period or on the playground.

5. Suggest methods that may be used to improve oral English and to extend its use by pupils in recitations.

6. What are the most common types of speech defects?

7. Find out what types of remedial work can be carried on with pupils who have speech defects. What is the possibility of curing them?

8. List typical situations in life outside the school that require the use of written English on the part of pupils. Is the school doing all that it could to help the pupils do better the writing they will do in life outside the school?

9. Get a standard test in English and give it to a class. Analyze the results.

10. Secure specimens of compositions under standard conditions. Have the compositions scored by several judges by means of a scale. Compare the ratings by different judges.

11. Is it easy to diagnose the defects of compositions? Try to apply the diagnostic techniques described in this chapter to a set of compositions.

12. Comment on the value of self-rating of compositions by pupils.

13. Outline a remedial program to eliminate common errors in oral and written speech. Why should a special remedial period be set aside for work on known common errors?

14. Why is it advisable to encourage pupil participation in the planning of a remedial program?

## SELECTED REFERENCES

Blanton, S., and Blanton, M.   *Speech Training for Children.*  New York, Century Company, 1920.

Charters, W. W.   *Curriculum Construction*, pp. 278–96.  New York, The Macmillan Company, 1923.

Courtis, S. A.   *The Gary Public Schools: Measurement of Classroom Products*, pp. 216–62.  New York, General Education Board, 1919.

Hudelson, Earl.   "English Composition: Its Aims, Methods, and Measurement"; in *Twenty-Second Yearbook of the National Society for the Study of Education*, Part I.  Bloomington, Illinois, Public School Publishing Company, 1923.

Johnson, R. I.   *English Expression; A Study of Curriculum Building.*  Bloomington, Illinois, Public School Publishing Company, 1926.

Klapper, Paul.   *Teaching English in Elementary and Junior High Schools.*  New York, D. Appleton and Company, 1925.

Lyman, R.   *Summary of Investigations Relating to Grammar, Language, and Composition.*  Supplementary Educational Monograph, no. 36.  University of Chicago Press, 1929.

Sheridan, B. M.   *Speaking and Writing English.*  Chicago, Sanborn, 1926.

Troxell, E.   *Language and Literature in the Kindergarten and Primary Grades.*  New York, Charles Scribner's Sons, 1927.

Webster, E. H., and Smith, D.   *Teaching English in the Junior High School.*  Yonkers-on-Hudson, New York, World Book Company, 1927.

Willing, M. H.   *Valid Diagnosis in High School Composition.*  Teachers College Contributions to Education, no. 230.  New York, Columbia University, 1926.

# ENGLISH AND LANGUAGE TESTS CITED IN CHAPTER IX

| Test | Grades or Ages | Publisher |
|---|---|---|
| Briggs English Form Test | 7–9 | Bureau of Publications, Teachers College, Columbia University, N.Y. |
| Charters Diagnostic Language Tests | 3–8 | Public School Publishing Co., Bloomington, Ill. |
| Clapp Test for Correct English | 4–8 | Houghton Mifflin Company, Boston |
| Clapp–Young Self-Marking English Test | 5–12 | Houghton Mifflin Company, Boston |
| Hillegas Scale for Measurement of English Composition | Elementary | Bureau of Publications, Teachers College, Columbia University, N.Y. |
| Hudelson English Composition Scale | 4–12 | World Book Company, Yonkers-on-Hudson, N.Y. |
| Kirby Grammar Test | 7–12 | Bureau of Educational Research and Service, University of Iowa, Iowa City, Iowa |
| Lewis English Composition Scales | 3–12 | World Book Company, Yonkers-on-Hudson, N.Y. |
| Nassau County Supplement to the Hillegas Scale | 4–12 | Bureau of Publications, Teachers College, Columbia University, N.Y. |
| Pressy Diagnostic Tests in English Composition | High School | Public School Publishing Co., Bloomington, Ill. |
| Van Wagenen English Composition Scales | 3-through college | World Book Company, Yonkers-on-Hudson, N.Y. |
| Willing Scale for Measuring Written Composition | 4–9 | Public School Publishing Co., Bloomington, Ill. |
| Wilson Language Error Test | 3–12 | World Book Company, Yonkers-on-Hudson, N.Y. |

# CHAPTER X

## DIAGNOSTIC AND REMEDIAL TEACHING IN SPELLING

### 1. *The functions of instruction in spelling*

**Teaching objectives.** The functions of instruction in spelling are: (1) to develop in the child a spelling consciousness — that is, an awareness of correct and incorrect spelling: (2) to develop in the child a desire to use correct spelling in all written work, and a disposition to check all written work for correctness of spelling by means of the dictionary before disposing of it: (3) to help the pupil to acquire effective methods of studying spelling: (4) to insure an understanding and the ability to apply common principles governing capitalization, contractions, abbreviations, and modified forms.

Modern educational theory has shifted the emphasis in spelling instruction from the mere mastery of a set list of words to the development of power in spelling, as defined in the four functions given above. The effectiveness of teaching is no longer measured solely by the scores made by pupils in dictated lists of words. Unless the results of instruction in spelling transfer to other written work the teaching is judged to be relatively ineffective.

As is true in all school subjects, striking individual differences in spelling ability exist in every class. The problem of the teacher is to devise a method of teaching that will take these differences into account. Experiments show that there is no single best way for all pupils to study spelling. "It is found, instead, that each pupil has a choice as to the way to study that is best for him. Each child has a natural rate of growth, and succeeds best when allowed to progress at his own natural rate." It is a further problem of the teacher not only to make certain that the pupils learn a basic list of important words, but also to see to it that there is provision made for the development of an additional vocabulary that varies from individual to individual in ways that are distinctive and significant.

**Life situations in spelling.** To achieve the proper objectives in the creative teaching of spelling, the teacher must select life situations vital to the child in which spelling functions. Such situations arise naturally in many of the activities in which the pupils engage, both in and out of school; as, in letter-writing, preparing book reports, preparing written lessons, outlining topics, and writing compositions. It has been found that in such writing pupils use and misspell many words that are not found in the list of words in the textbook for that grade. To develop power in spelling pupils must be taught in such a way that they acquire a technique for mastering words other than those in the spelling textbook. The degree to which the pupils become "self-active" in developing the ability to spell correctly the words used in all of their written work is an important measure of the success of the teacher's work.

Pupils who are conscious of the need for correct spelling and who wish to grow in spelling power need the help of the teacher. The teacher's problem, instead of being merely "testing," becomes that of helping pupils to acquire effective techniques of study and of helping them to measure the effectiveness of the techniques they are using. She helps the pupils to modify these techniques if they are found to be ineffective. In the case of pupils who do not improve in their ability to spell, the teacher must make a diagnosis of the causes of difficulty and prescribe definite remedial exercises.

## 2. *The measurement of spelling ability*

The teacher of spelling should secure a general measure of the spelling ability of pupils as a basis of educational guidance. Such information should supplement the evaluation of the results of teaching as measured by the tests given, from time to time, on words selected from the spelling curriculum. These more frequent informal tests should help the pupil to discover the words he has not yet mastered, and also enable the teacher to locate the pupils who are having serious spelling difficulty.

There are several excellent standard tests of general spelling ability that may be used for survey purposes. The Morrison–McCall Spelling Scales consist of eight lists of fifty words of equal difficulty. Any one of these tests may be used for an initial survey of spelling. The same test is given to all grades, 3 to 8. Another series of excellent spelling tests is the Monroe Timed Sentence Spelling Tests, which consists of three tests, one test for grades 3 and 4, one test for grades 5 and 6, and one test for grades 7 and 8. All of these tests consist of words that the average person frequently uses in written discourse. The Ayres Measuring Scale for Ability in Spelling is also a useful testing instrument.

The authors of several of the newer textbooks in spelling have prepared standard tests which may be used to measure the efficiency of instruction in schools using the textbooks. Sometimes these tests appear in the textbooks, and in some cases they are supplied by the publishers on request.

## 3. *How to construct a spelling test*

**The number of words to use.** As has been pointed out in Chapter III, any teacher can prepare a standard spelling test by using words selected from a standard spelling scale, such as the Ayres Scale for Ability in Spelling, or the Iowa

Spelling Scales. Both of these scales consist of words that are used frequently in written discourse. The difficulty of these words has been determined by having them spelled by large numbers of children. From the per cent of correct spellings of each word the relative difficulty of the words was calculated. The authors assume that words that are misspelled by equal per cents of pupils in the same grade are of equal difficulty for that group. The words on the scales have been divided into groups. All of the words in each group are of approximately the same difficulty.

After a careful series of investigations, Otis[1] reached the conclusion that the most reliable measure of spelling ability is obtained by using words for which there is an average correct spelling of 50 per cent. If the tests for a grade were made up of words of 100 per cent average correct spelling the test would be too easy, and the class scores would all approximate 100 per cent. If the words were all of from 0 to 10 per cent average correct spelling, they would be so difficult that many of the pupils above average in spelling ability and all of the pupils of lowest ability would score zero on the test. If words of an average 50 per cent correct spelling are selected, it seems that reliable measures will be secured, since the words are so difficult that there will be few perfect scores and yet not so difficult that the most inferior pupils will misspell the entire list. The purpose for which the test is given will determine the number of words to use. For general survey purposes a list of 20 words suffices. Otis and Starch[2] have both shown, however, that a list of only 20 words gives a very poor measure of individual abil-

---

[1] Otis, A. S. "The Reliability of Spelling Scales"; in *School and Society*, vol. 4, p. 753.

[2] Starch, Daniel. "The Measurement of Efficiency in Spelling, and the Overlapping of Grades in Combined Measurements of Reading, Writing, and Spelling"; in *Journal of Educational Psychology*, vol. 6, pp. 167–86. (March, 1915.)

ity.  Otis says that at least 100 words should be used. Starch recommends the use of 200 words.  Morrison and McCall use only 50 words in their tests.  However, their tests are in scaled form, containing words of all degrees of difficulty.  For practical reasons it is recommended that the teacher use a test of not more than 50 words having an average difficulty of 50 per cent for the grade.  On the Ayres and Iowa scales the percentages of accuracy for each grade are indicated at the top of each of the columns of words. In case there are not enough 50 per cent words for a grade, an equal number of needed words should be chosen from the next higher and lower columns.

List *vs.* sentence form.  The words in the test may be given to the pupils either as lists or dictated to them in sentences.  The rate at which the sentences are dictated may be so timed that the pupils are required to write at a speed that is normal for their grade.  Courtis and Monroe both report that the average per cent of accuracy in spelling is between 5 and 10 per cent higher on list tests than on timed dictation exercises.

In most spelling classes words are dictated as lists.  This results in a focussing of attention on the spelling of the particular words.  This creates a more or less unnatural situation, since in life people seldom write mere lists of dictated words.  Spelling functions naturally in writing letters or compositions.  In these situations the attention is focussed on expressing thoughts and not on spelling.  It has frequently been found that pupils whose work in the spelling class is correct misspell the same words in their compositions when they are writing freely and are not attending consciously to spelling.

The writing of timed sentence dictation exercises approximates the conditions under which the child in his everyday activities writes at a normal rate.  The measure thus secured is more likely to yield a correct appraisal of his spelling ability than is secured by list tests.

**Rate of dictation on timed-dictation exercises.** The rate of dictation in each grade is determined by the normal rates at which children write, and the amount of time taken to dictate the sentences. Freeman's standards may be used as a basis for rate of writing. The time to be allowed for dictation may be found either by dividing by 10 the number of letters in the material to be dictated, or as Monroe suggests, by allowing for dictation 10 per cent of the time that is allowed for writing. The rule for finding the amount of time per sentence may be expressed by the formula,

$$T = nt + \frac{n}{10},$$

in which $T$ is the total time, $n$ the number of letters, and $t$ the time per letter.

Table 41 contains both Freeman's standards for rate and Monroe's suggested time, not including dictation, to be allowed per letter in dictation exercises.

TABLE 41. STANDARDS FOR RATE TO BE USED IN PREPARING TIMED-DICTATION EXERCISES

| | GRADE | | | | | | |
|---|---|---|---|---|---|---|---|
| | II | III | IV | V | VI | VII | VIII |
| Freeman's standards (letters per minute) | 36 | 48 | 56 | 65 | 72 | 80 | 90 |
| Monroe suggested time in seconds per letters for dictated exercises | 1.83 | 1.38 | 1.18 | 1.01 | .92 | .83 | .73 |

**To determine time.** To determine the amount of time to be allowed for a sentence, first count the number of letters it contains, and then multiply the number of letters by the number of seconds per letter for the specified grade as given in Table 41. To this add the time for dictation, or $n/10$. For example, the sentence, "Mary is my little sister," contains twenty letters. The time to be allowed for writing in grade V may be found by multiplying 1.01 seconds by 20; the result, 20.2 seconds, is the amount of time to allow for writing. For dictation, $20/10$ or 2 seconds are allowed. Fractions of seconds are counted to the next whole second. The total time is $20.2 + 2$, or 22.2 seconds, or 23 seconds. In the following timed-dictation exercises for grade V the rate at which the sentences are to be dictated is indicated.

### SAMPLE TEST — GRADE V

| SECOND MARK | | | NUMBER OF LETTERS | TIME |
|---|---|---|---|---|
| 1. | (60) | *Stop* the *child outside* the door. | (26) | 29 |
| 2. | (29) | *Four ships* have *gone* to sea. | (22) | 25 |
| 3. | (54) | *Why* did they *kill* the dog? | (20) | 23 |
| 4. | (17) | A *year ago these wells* went dry. | (25) | 28 |
| 5. | (45) | The *other* day I *cut* my finger. | (23) | 26 |
| 6. | (11) | The *sea* is very *far* from here. | (23) | 26 |
| 7. | (37) | *Soon* we *pass* the *camp* on the hill. | (26) | 29 |
| 8. | ( 6) | Did he *ever catch* the dog? | (20) | 23 |
| 9. | (29) | They *must* go *into* the city. | (21) | 24 |
| 10. | (53) | *Now* he has spent all he had. | (21) | 24 |
| | (17) | Stop. | | |

The (60) in parenthesis at the beginning of the first sentence means that the first sentence should be dictated when the second hand of the watch is at the 60-second mark. The (29) before the second sentence shows that the second sentence should be read when the second hand reaches the 29-second mark. The numbers in parenthesis at the beginning of the other sentences indicate the second mark at which each of them is to be dictated.

**How to construct a timed-dictation exercise.** The following simple procedure may be followed in constructing a timed-dictation exercise:

1. From a standard scale or from the regular spelling curriculum, select from 20 to 25 words for the test.

2. Prepare short sentences in which these words are embedded. Try to use at least two of the test words in each sentence. Do not use sentences in which the test words are the last words.

3. Count the number of letters in each of the sentences. Place the numbers in parenthesis at the end of each sentence. In the lower grades sentences containing more than 25 or 30 letters should be avoided, and in the upper grades sentences should not exceed 40 letters. If the sentences are longer the pupils cannot remember the words in them.

4. Use the formula,

$$T = nt + \frac{n}{10}$$

to find the length of time to be allowed for each sentence. Use the number of seconds per letter given in Table 41. Place this result in a second parenthesis on the end of the sentence, as shown in the specimen on page 386.

5. Find the second mark on the face of the watch at which the sentences are to be dictated. If the first sentence is dictated at the 60-second mark, as in the test on page 386, and 29 seconds are allowed for the writing of the first sentence, obviously the second sentence must be dictated at the 29-second mark. Twenty-five seconds are allowed for the second sentence. The second hand will not pass beyond the 60-second mark before this time has elapsed, and will reach the 54-second mark, at which time the third sentence will be read. The fourth sentence is dictated at the 17-second mark. This mark may be found by subtracting 60 from 77, or 54 plus 23 (the time needed to write the third sentence), which will give 17, the number of seconds in the next minute required for the writing of the third sentence. In like manner the second marks at which the other sentences are to be dictated may be determined.

6. Place in parenthesis at the begining of each sentence the second mark at which the sentence is to be dictated.

### 4. *Accuracy of spelling in compositions*

**The Gary Survey results.** Very few studies have been made to determine the accuracy with which pupils spell the

words in written compositions. In the Gary Survey [1] are
reported the results of one such study. In this report mistakes in spelling were divided into two groups, namely, slips
or lapses, and actual misspellings. An example of a lapse is
writing *the* for they, that is, dropping a letter at the end of
the word. In Table 42 are given the city-wide median coefficients of spelling. The spelling coefficient was found by
determining the number of misspellings and lapses per thousand written words. For example, if a pupil misspelled 5
words in a composition of 100 words, his spelling coefficient
was 50; that is, he misspelled words at the rate of 50 in a
thousand. Data are given for slips, misspellings, and total.

TABLE 42. SPELLING COEFFICIENT IN COMPOSITION TESTS,
GARY SCHOOLS

(Courtis)

| GRADE | LAPSES | MISSPELLINGS | TOTAL |
|---|---|---|---|
| 4. | 16.8 | 57.0 | 73.8 |
| 5. | 13.3 | 52.6 | 65.9 |
| 6. | 10.6 | 43.1 | 53.7 |
| 7. | 7.5 | 24.3 | 31.8 |
| 8. | 6.1 | 13.6 | 19.7 |
| 9. | 3.2 | 13.9 | 17.1 |
| 10. | 3.4 | 9.8 | 13.2 |
| 11. | .8 | 8.6 | 9.4 |
| 12. | 3.0 | 6.0 | 9.0 |

The median spelling coefficient for grade 4 was 73.8, which
is equivalent to a misspelling of 7.38 per cent of all words
written. The medians for each grade were successively less.
In grade 12 the coefficient was only 9.0 or less than one per
cent of misspelling on the written compositions. The data
show that in grade 4 lapses accounted for 16.8 mistakes in
writing a thousand words, and that there were 57.0 actual
misspellings per thousand words. In all grades lapses
caused a large per cent of error. The number of misspell-

[1] The Gary Survey. *The Measurement of Classroom Products*, p. 93.

ings was considerably greater than the number of lapses in each grade. These results show that in all grades the pupils of Gary misspelled only a very small per cent of all the words they wrote. No similar data for other schools are available. In discussing these facts, Courtis points out that the pupils used very easy words in their compositions. This may account for the low per cent of misspelling. Pupils probably choose to write only those words that they know how to spell.

The spelling coefficients for pupils in any class can easily be found. The first step is to count the number of written words. This may be done by the pupils after papers have been exchanged. Next the spelling must be checked and the total number of words misspelled found, counting repeated misspellings of the same word. Upper-grade classes may be used for this checking. Then by dividing the number of misspellings by the number of words in the composition the spelling coefficient of each pupil may be computed.

### 5. *The place of tests in the teaching procedure*

**A weekly teaching procedure.** The place of informal weekly list tests and timed-dictation exercises in the teaching routine is indicated in the following analysis of the activities of the weekly teaching procedure [1] to be followed in the study of a basic list of required words:

ANALYSIS OF DAILY ACTIVITIES IN TEACHING SPELLING

(Minneapolis Schools)

*Monday*
1. Teacher reads list of words aloud, enunciating syllables distinctly.
   a. Written on board one word at a time and hard spots pointed out.
   b. Read from textbook.

[1] A pre-test technique, adapted from Horn-Ashbaugh's plan of teaching spelling, used in Minneapolis schools.

2. Pupils read words in concert after teacher from the board or textbook, enunciating syllables distinctly.
3. Pupils ask about meaning and uses of words.
4. Words are used orally in sentences by pupils.
5. Dictionary is used to find meaning when necessary.
6. Words are dictated by teacher.
7. Papers are exchanged and corrected.
8. Difficult words are determined.
9. Pupils write misspelled words in notebook.
10. Construction of graphs is begun.

*Tuesday*
1. The teacher supervises methods of study used by the pupils.
2. Pupils study the words they missed on Monday.
3. Teacher aids pupils to diagnose their own difficulties.
4. Teacher works with special cases or groups.
5. The meaning and use of words is made clear.
6. Teacher supervises activities of pupils who make no errors.

*Wednesday*
1. All pupils are retested on all new words for the week by a list test.
2. Papers are marked by pupils.
3. New errors are determined and recorded.
4. Persistent errors are noted and checked.
5. Graphs to show progress are constructed.
6. Handwriting of test is studied to show its effect on spelling.
7. The spelling of important derivatives is studied and tested. (At intervals.)
8. Words of the week one month previous are retested.
9. Consideration is given to misspellings in other subjects.

*Thursday*
1. Each pupil studies intensively the words he has missed.
2. Special diagnostic and remedial work is done by teacher with deficient pupils.
3. Words with persistent errors and difficulties from previous weeks are given special study.
4. Derivatives that are important are tested.    (At intervals.)
5. Timed-dictation exercises are given for review.

6. Games are used to establish correct spelling habits.
7. Words missed in other school subjects may be studied.
8. Special provision is made for pupils with no misspellings on the tests.

*Friday*
1. The new words of the week are retested in list form or in timed dictation exercises.
2. Papers are scored and the results graphed.
3. Persistent errors are noted by teachers and recorded by pupils.
4. Games.
5. Timed-dictation exercises containing review words are given.
6. The errors in spelling in other subjects are considered.

Briefly summarized, after a careful preliminary study of all new words, list tests are given on Monday to help the pupil to determine the words he does not know how to spell. These words should form the basis for the work in his study period on Tuesday. On Wednesday a re-test is given by a list test. Then the words that have not yet been learned by each pupil are determined. These words are carefully studied on Thursday with the special help of the teacher. Finally on Friday the list test is given for the third time as a final check. On Wednesday and Friday special timed-dictation exercises, in which are included for review selected words of previous weeks, may be used to determine how well the pupils have mastered them.

## 6. *Diagnostic procedures in spelling*

**Scores determine general level only.** Scores on standard spelling scales enable the teacher to determine the general level of the spelling ability of the class as a whole. The scores also serve as a rough index of the spelling ability of individual pupils.

The scores in informal daily or weekly tests enable the teacher to determine the rates at which different pupils master given lists of words, and the words that seem to involve special difficulty. Experiments have shown that pupils know many of the words that are found in the textbooks before the words are studied. The number of words known varies from individual to individual. Pupils do not all learn to spell the words at the same rate. Some pupils learn very quickly the words they do not already know; other pupils labor with a relatively small return for the efforts put forth because their methods of study are faulty and uneconomical. Clearly there is a big difference in the efficiency of the study habits of pupils.

**Specific diagnostic procedure in spelling.** Various techniques for making analytical diagnoses of the causes of pupil difficulty in spelling have been used. Some investigators have attempted to classify errors by analyzing the misspellings, and grouping them according to apparent causes. Other investigators have made careful psychological studies of the work of pupils of inferior spelling ability through a direct observation of and a measurement of the efficiency of their methods of work. Other studies have been made of various incidental factors that may affect spelling, such as the health, mentality, and general attitude of the pupil. Typical studies of each kind will now be described.

**Bock and Harter's study of spelling errors.** Book and Harter [1] secured spelling-test papers from children in grades 2 to 8, on the average 520 test papers to a grade. A careful analysis of the errors appearing on these papers was next made. The errors were then classified into two major groups, one group consisting of errors due to mistakes in expression or inadequate mental control over known words, and the other group consisting of errors on words previously

---

[1] Book, W. F., and Harter, R. S. "Mistakes Which Pupils Make in Spelling"; in *Journal of Educational Research*, vol. 19, pp. 106–18.

not learned. This classification of errors is given in Table 43. Data showing the per cent of error for each cause for grades 2 to 6 only are included in the table. Illustrations of each kind of error are given at the foot of the table.

The data in Table 43 shows that in grade 2 approximately 69 per cent of all errors made were due to mistakes in expression or inadequate control over known words. The two most frequent errors in this group were those due to carelessness and to omission of letters, which together accounted for 38.7 per cent of all errors in this grade. In all grades the omission of letters in known words was a major cause of misspelling. Errors due to phonetic spelling of words not learned seemed to increase from grade to grade. Two other major kinds of errors or words not learned were due to ignorance of the word, or failure to hear or perceive the word correctly. The many types of errors on words not learned show the importance of both correct observation of the word and individual word study.

Hollingsworth's[1] classification of errors due to lack of control over words already known is quite similar to that of Book and Harter. Cornman[2] has made a classification of errors due to motor or sensori incoördination, or to a complication of causes. Gill[3] has shown that 57.9 per cent of the errors he analyzed were due to silent letters.

**Davis's study of pupil difficulties in spelling.** One of the most significant studies of pupil difficulties in spelling was made by the teachers of Richmond, Indiana, under the direction of Miss Georgia Davis.[4] The results of a survey

[1] Hollingsworth, L. S. *The Psychology of Special Disability in Spelling.* Teachers College Contributions, no. 88.

[2] Cornman, O. P. *Spelling in the Elementary School.* Boston, Ginn and Company, 1902.

[3] Gill, E. J. "The Teaching of Spelling"; in *Journal of Experimental Pedagogy,* vol. 1, pp. 310–19.

[4] Davis, G. "Remedial Work in Spelling"; in *Elementary School Journal,* vol. 27, pp. 615–26. (April, 1927.)

### TABLE 43. ANALYSIS OF SPELLING ERRORS

(Book and Harter)

#### (a) Errors Due to Inadequate Mental Control Over Known Words

| | GRADE | | | | |
|---|---|---|---|---|---|
| | 2 | 3 | 4 | 5 | 6 |
| *Mistakes of expression* | | | | | |
| 1. Omission................... | 20.9 | 17.7 | 18.9 | 21.5 | 17.0 |
| 2. Anticipation............... | 1.9 | 1.7 | 4.0 | 2.7 | 3.0 |
| 3. Repeating or adding a letter.. | 7.2 | 6.7 | 8.4 | 8.8 | 6.2 |
| 4. Transposition.............. | 6.9 | 7.1 | 5.9 | 10.4 | 4.1 |
| 5. Carelessness............... | 17.8 | 8.7 | 4.9 | 3.6 | 4.4 |
| 6. Doubling wrong letter....... | .1 | .5 | .4 | .3 | .1 |
| 7. Interference............... | 4.0 | 2.8 | 1.3 | 1.0 | 1.3 |
| 8. Forgetting word............ | 4.6 | 1.5 | 1.1 | 1.3 | 1.9 |
| 9. Substitution............... | 5.6 | 4.6 | 4.2 | 2.3 | .8 |
| | 69.0 | 51.3 | 49.1 | 51.9 | 38.8 |

| TYPE ILLUSTRATION | TYPE ILLUSTRATION |
|---|---|
| 1. the for they | 6. speel for spell |
| 2. converstation for conversation | 7. swap for soap |
| 3. theeth for teeth | 8. Arthur for author |
| 4. esaily for easily | 9. dog, dod |
| 5. surily for surely | |

#### (b) Errors in Words Not Learned

| | GRADE | | | | |
|---|---|---|---|---|---|
| | 2 | 3 | 4 | 5 | 6 |
| *Mistakes of expression* | | | | | |
| 1. Phonetic spelling............ | 13.6 | 19.1 | 32.7 | 26.2 | 34.7 |
| 2. Mispronunciation........... | .4 | .1 | .3 | .1 | .9 |
| 3. Alternatives................ | .1 | .5 | 1.1 | .0 | .8 |
| 4. Doubling................... | .7 | 1.7 | 1.4 | 1.3 | 1.7 |
| 5. Non-doubling .............. | 1.3 | .3 | 2.7 | 3.8 | 7.8 |
| 6. Substitution of similar letters and syllables............... | 1.6 | 1.2 | .1 | .3 | .8 |
| 7. Homonyms.................. | 1.6 | 4.9 | 2.5 | 2.7 | 2.6 |
| 8. Ignorance of word........... | 6.0 | 10.8 | 4.6 | 8.8 | 9.0 |
| 9. Failure to hear or perceive word correctly............ | 5.8 | 10.0 | 5.5 | 5.1 | 2.9 |
| | 31.1 | 48.6 | 50.9 | 48.3 | 61.2 |

| TYPE ILLUSTRATION | TYPE ILLUSTRATION |
|---|---|
| 1. Wensday | 6. goiny for going |
| 2. chimley | 7. bare for bear |
| 3. ei or ie confused | 8. parallel — parell |
| 4. Hellen for Helen | 9. bureau — mural |
| 5. galons for gallon | |

test showed that there were 275 pupils in grades 2 through 6 who were in need of remedial work in spelling. It was decided to do special work with these cases. They were given the Illinois General Intelligence Scale. The results are given in Table 44. It was found that the I.Q.s of this group of pupils varied.

TABLE 44. DISTRIBUTION OF THE 275 POOR SPELLERS ON THE BASIS OF THEIR INTELLIGENCE QUOTIENTS

(Richmond, Indiana, Schools)

| I.Q. | NUMBER OF PUPILS |
|---|---|
| 110 or above........................................ | 15 |
| 90–109............................................ | 106 |
| 80– 89............................................. | 77 |
| 70– 79............................................. | 51 |
| Below 70........................................... | 26 |
| Total.......................................... | 275 |
| Median I.Q............................... | 86 |

On the whole the group was considerably below average. The median I.Q. was 86, and the range in I.Q.s was from below 70 to above 110. Data are presented in Miss Davis's report, showing that these pupils were not only low in spelling ability as measured by the spelling tests, but also profited very little from the work on the words for the week.

**Special individual diagnostic study.** A special individual diagnostic study was then made by the teachers of remedial classes to determine, through observation and interview, the causes of the deficiencies in spelling for each of the pupils. Table 45 contains the list of difficulties encountered by the 275 pupils, and the frequency of each difficulty.

The most common difficulties found were: (1) a poor technique of steps in learning how to spell; (2) poor quality of writing; (3) faulty pronunciation; (4) a faulty attitude toward spelling; (5) failure to associate the sound of the letters or the syllables with the spelling of the words.

**Practice exercises to overcome defects.** After the teacher had made the diagnosis, a careful record was kept of the "practices found helpful in assisting pupils to overcome their particular difficulties." A goodly number of practices were tried out by the teachers, many of them proving to be of little value. At the end of the investigation a list was made of the practices which were considered "most worth while by the teachers in charge of remedial classes." The list of difficulties and practices used to overcome each defect is as follows:

TABLE 45. DIFFICULTIES ENCOUNTERED IN SPELLING BY THE 275 PUPILS, AND THE FREQUENCY OF EACH DIFFICULTY

(Richmond, Indiana, Schools)

| DIFFICULTY | FREQUENCY |
|---|---|
| 1. Has not mastered the steps in learning to spell a word..... | 88 |
| 2. Writes poorly......................................... | 88 |
| 3. Cannot pronounce the words being studied............... | 78 |
| 4. Has bad attitude toward spelling, as shown by (a) failure to apply himself during the study period or by (b) seeming lack of interest........................................... | 71 |
| 5. Does not associate the sound of the letters or the syllables with the spelling of the word........................... | 49 |
| 6. Needs more time than can be devoted to spelling in the regular class............................................ | 21 |
| 7. Is discouraged because he misspelled so many words in the Monday test.......................................... | 20 |
| 8. Has speech defect.................................... | 16 |
| 9. Does not mark paper correctly......................... | 16 |
| 10. Interchanges letters................................. | 10 |
| 11. Copies words incorrectly when studying................. | 7 |
| 12. Is unable to remember a word for any length of time...... | 6 |
| 13. Has poor hearing.................................... | 5 |
| 14. Writes so slowly that he cannot keep up with the class.... | 5 |
| 15. Is irregular in attendance............................ | 4 |
| 16. Has poor vision..................................... | 3 |
| 17. Does not compare while studying...................... | 3 |
| 18. Does not know meaning of words....................... | 3 |
| 19. Adds extra letters................................... | 2 |
| 20. Misses syllables in the middle of words................. | 2 |
| 21. Thinks he cannot spell............................... | 1 |
| 22. Leaves off last letter................................ | 1 |
| 23. Seems to learn only through eye....................... | 1 |
| 24. Seems to learn only through ear....................... | 1 |

### Spelling Difficulties, and Remedial Practices

1. Has not mastered the steps in learning to spell a word.
   a. Teach steps until every child knows them and uses them.
   b. Study each word with the children.
2. Writes poorly.
   a. Discover particular letters or combinations of letters that are difficult and practice on these letters or combinations.
   b. Practice words containing writing difficulties.
3. Cannot pronounce the words being studied.
   a. Go over the words before the children study them so that every child will know what he is studying.
   b. Help the child to unlock words for himself.
4. Has bad attitude toward spelling.
   a. Supervise study closely so that the child will get into the habit of studying words correctly without wasting time.
   b. Try to show need for study.
   c. Give study work under time pressure.
   d. Try to appeal to pride.
   e. Try to work up competition with self.
   f. Give reward.
5. Does not associate the sound of the letters or the syllables with the spelling of the word.
   a. Teach letter sounds.
   b. Listen to careful pronunciation.
   c. Teach the child to syllabify words.
   d. Say words slowly again and again to hear sounds.
6. Needs more time than can be devoted to spelling in the regular class.
   a. Give more time after school or during the day when other work is finished.
7. Is discouraged because he misspelled so many words in the Monday test.
   a. Take a few words at a time.
   b. Study at odd times during the day.
   c. Have the pupil stay longer in the afternoon than the others.
8. Has speech defect.
   a. Listen to pronunciation.
   b. Look at word carefully.
   c. Teach difficult combinations.
9. Does not mark paper correctly.
   a. Teach the child how to check.

  *b.* Insist on rechecking.

  *c.* Always check paper.

10. Interchanges letters.

  *a.* Study words carefully.

  *b.* Underline difficult part.

  *c.* Try to spell by syllables.

11. Copies words incorrectly when studying.

  *a.* Check the child closely during study until he acquires the habit of checking with correct form each time.

  *b.* Give the pupil hectographed copy for comparison during study.

12. Is unable to remember a word for any length of time.

  *a.* Go over words more frequently during study.

  *b.* Review during spare time words previously studied.

13. Has poor hearing.

  *a.* Move the child to the front of the room.

  *b.* Stress steps in study other than those based on hearing.

14. Writes so slowly that he cannot keep up with the class.

  *a.* Write the word being dictated, leaving out the words missed.

  *b.* Encourage the child to write faster.

15. Irregular in attendance.

16. Has poor vision.

  *a.* Move the child to the front of the room.

  *b.* Encourage the child to listen carefully as the teacher pronounces the word carefully.

17. Does not compare while studying.

  *a.* Teach each step with special attention to comparison.

  *b.* Watch study work.

18. Does not know meaning of words.

  *a.* Try to show the child the reason for knowing the meaning.

  *b.* Go over words carefully during introduction.

19. Adds extra letters.

  *a.* Look at word carefully.

  *b.* Spell to self while writing at beginning of study.

20. Misses syllables in the middle of words.

  *a.* Spell by syllables with special attention to part likely to be missed.

21. Thinks he cannot spell.

  *a.* Give simple words to establish the child's confidence, excusing him from the regular spelling for a time.

22. Leaves off last letter.
   *a.* Call the child's attention to difficulty.
23. Seems to learn only through eye.
   *a.* Give special attention to steps involving the use of the eye.
24. Seems to learn only through ear.
   *a.* Give special attention to steps involving the use of the ear.

**Atkin's study of pupil's study-habits.** Investigations have shown that lack of efficient methods of study is one of the chief causes of failure to learn to spell. This fault may be discovered either by measurement or by clinical case-study and interview. Atkin's investigation [1] deals with the study-habits of two types of pupils, one consisting of a group with high learning-indices in spelling, and the other of a group with low learning-indices in spelling. These learning-indices were determined by means of a new type of test, the so-called "learning" tests, which have been devised by Courtis.[2] The procedure used to determine learning-indices consists in giving the pupil a test consisting of a selected list of 50 words. The test is followed by a ten-minute study period in which the pupil studies the words in the test in any way that he chooses. At the end of the study period, the same test is repeated. The learning-index is determined by the number of words the pupil has learned during the short study period. Suppose that each of two pupils misspelled 30 words in the initial test. If one pupil learns to spell many new words during the study period his learning-index is high; if the other learns to spell few new words his learning-index is relatively low. As is stated in the Hamtramck *Course of Study*, "The learning tests provided for... when properly used, measure directly the in-

[1] Atkin, S. *The Learning Indices and Study Methods of School Children in Spelling.* Unpublished master's thesis, University of Minnesota.

[2] These tests are contained in the Hamtramck *Course of Study in Spelling*; Public Schools, Hamtramck, Michigan.

itiative of the pupil and his control over methods of assimilation in spelling."

The variations in spelling-indices found by Atkin for pupils in grades 4 to 6, and 7, are shown in Table 46.

TABLE 46. DISTRIBUTION OF THE LEARNING-INDICES OF
397 PUPILS

(After Atkin)

| LEARNING-INDEX | GRADES | | TOTAL |
| | 4A–5B | 6A–7B | |
| --- | --- | --- | --- |
| 170– 79 | 1 | | 1 |
| 160– 69 | 1 | | 1 |
| 150– 59 | | 1 | 1 |
| 140– 49 | | 2 | 2 |
| 130– 39 | 2 | 3 | 5 |
| 120– 29 | 2 | 1 | 3 |
| 110– 19 | 4 | 3 | 7 |
| 100– 09 | 1 | 1 | 2 |
| 90– 99 | 2 | 4 | 6 |
| 80– 89 | 6 | 7 | 13 |
| 70– 79 | 9 | 5 | 14 |
| 60– 69 | 7 | 12 | 19 |
| 50– 59 | 9 | 10 | 19 |
| 40– 49 | 12 | 32 | 44 |
| 30– 39 | 24 | 43 | 67 |
| 20– 29 | 17 | 39 | 56 |
| 10– 19 | 18 | 55 | 73 |
| 0– 9 | 18 | 27 | 45 |
| (–4)–(–1) | 4 | 15 | 19 |
| Total | 137 | 260 | 397 |
| Median | 34.5 | 27.5 | 30.9 |
| Median I.Q. | 108.0 | 108.0 | 108.0 |

The highest learning-index found was in the 170–179 group. This index was found for a 4A boy whose initial score on the test was 34 words correct, and who made a perfect score of 50 words on the second test. The learning-indices varied from this high level to 19 indices which were negative. This shows that each of these 19 pupils, in fact, made a lower score on the test after a study period than they made in the first test. The median index for the whole group was 30.9. The median index for the 4A–5B pupils was 34.5; the median for the 6A–7B pupils was 27.5. Atkin reports that the median I.Q. for each group was 108.

## 7. *Study traits of good and poor spellers*

The following case which had a high learning-index, will show something of the diagnostic procedure and the remedial measures that must be used to secure spelling improvement with certain types of pupils.

In order to study the work-habits of pupils with either superior or inferior learning ability, Atkin selected cases of pupils with high or with low learning-indices. He secured information of various kinds about these pupils from teachers and from the school records, and then made a careful clinical study of their habits of work. He used the method of careful observation, supplemented by information he could secure from the pupils by careful questioning. The following case-study reported by Atkin describes his findings for a pupil with a very high learning-index:

### Case 1. *A 4A boy with superior work-habits*

History. A boy — grade 4A; learning-index, 178 (34–50); I.Q., 115, median; S.Q., 102, median; spelling grade, A; reading grade, A; attendance, 94½.

Physical condition, good; visual defects, none; auditory defects, none; speech defects, none; other defects, none.

Temperament, very aggressive; very industrious; careful; markedly independent; and outstandingly individualistic.

Miscellaneous factors; careless in speech; a fast writer; very sensitive, strong positive personality; and not much encouragement from home as to scholarship.

**Observation of the examiner.** Very systematic. Looked at word, visualized, vocalized. Wrote down words on paper, looked at printed sheet again, compared word as written on paper with spelling on mimeographed sheet.    Repeated this process for other words.    Concentrated very well.    Was at ease; he did not twist about.    Was consistent in method.    Very anxious to study. While I was questioning him, he would always attempt to break away and return to his studying.    He did not seem to like to be disturbed from study; seemed to enjoy studying.    He impressed me as being very industrious.    Good penman.    Showed signs of being a very systematic personality, unusually so for a child in 4A grade.

**Testimony of the pupil.**    Looked at word, then thought word, let it "sink in"; closed eyes and vocalized, visualized, and then wrote the word down on paper, then checked with printed form, and, if written correctly, wrote it down two more times without recourse to printed sheet.    At this time, he went to next word unless written form did not check with printed form, in which instance he repeated all of the above-mentioned steps.    He did not use syllabication, but he did avail himself of simple transfer.

**Conclusions.**    Atkin's conclusions for all pupils with high learning-indices included in his study are as follows:

The outstanding characteristics of the study methods of children in spelling at the very high learning level are the presence of a very systematic and well-organized plan of study or approach in doing their work.    All of these children used a number of the following techniques in studying their spelling: — visualization, vocalization, transfer, syllabication, writing down the words on paper while looking at the mimeographed form, and writing down the words on paper from memory.    It is true that the children did not use the above-mentioned techniques in the same order, for variation in method was an outstanding characteristic of this group of spellers. Another marked feature of the manner in which these children did their work was the zeal with which most of them studied, and the unusual display of initiative common to both boys and girls and to those in the two grade groups.

### CASE-STUDIES OF PUPILS WITH LOW
#### LEARNING-INDICES

The following case reported by Atkin is a description of the traits and study habits of a pupil with a very low learning-index.

## Case 1.  *A 4A boy with poor work-habits*

**History.**  Sex, boy; grade, 4A; L.I., 19 (44–46); I.Q., 136 — very high; S.Q., 115 — high; spelling grade, C; reading grade, C; attendance, 84.

Physical condition, not very strong; visual defects, none; auditory defects, none; speech defects, none; other defects, none.

Temperament, aggressive; lazy; careless; independent; individualistic.

Other factors, slovenly in speech; very slow writer; very high ability and comprehensive in reading; very rapid reader; very capable, but very lazy — very indifferent — has exceptionally good opinion of his ability; mother helps him very much in writing and in arithmetic.

**Observation and testimony combined.**  First, he took a word that he thought not so hard; wrote it down twice without looking at printed form; then checked with printed form.  With difficult words, he first thought the words; did not vocalize; then wrote them down four times and checked with mimeographed form; did not syllabicate; never thought in terms of transfer; always took whole word at a time.

**Conclusions.**  Atkin summarized his findings for pupils with very low learning-indices as follows:

Analysis of the study methods of children having very low learning-indices reveals many noticeable weaknesses.  There is a marked lack of systematic method, organization, and self-direction in the study of spelling in this group.  Most of the cases show a distinct lack of concentration, lack of organized study, and lack of effective self-direction.  Such devices as vocalization, syllabication, visualization, and transfer were used but seldom, and then not very effectively.

**Gates's** [1] **classification of causes of backwardness in spelling.**  Gates has made what is probably the most complete classification of the *causes* of backwardness in spelling.  These he states as follows:

[1] Gates, Arthur I.  *The Psychology of Reading and Spelling.*  Teachers College Contributions to Education, no. 129, 1922.

I. Defects or deficiencies of training
   a. Lack of training (chiefly in methods of perceiving words)
   b. Inappropriate phonic, phonetic, etc., training
   c. Change of training
   d. Loss of training at critical periods
   e. Early training in foreign language
   f. Unfavorable home training (home spoiling, etc.)

II. Unfavorable behavior; general
   a. Disinclination, inertia, not otherwise accounted for
   b. Emotional or nervous instability

III. Defects of sensory mechanisms (excluding muscular defects)
   a. Visual
   b. Auditory

IV. Defects of motor mechanism
   a. General motor incoördination, etc.
   b. Defective writing
   c. Defective articulation
   d. Defective eye-muscle control
   e. Inappropriate eye-movements in reading
   f. Inappropriate eye-voice span

V. Defects or deficiencies of connecting mechanisms
   a. Inadequate intelligence
   b. Congenital word-blindness, alexia, etc.
   c. Defects of "visual memory," "auditory memory," etc.
   d. Defects of "general visual perception"
   e. Defects of "visual imagery"
   f. "Special disability"

## 8. Suggested remedial measures

**Helpful steps.** As was shown in Miss Davis's study, reported on page 397, in many cases the remedial measures needed to insure improvement in spelling are obvious; in others many different remedial devices must be applied. The following are among the most helpful steps to be taken in remedial work in spelling:

1. An improvement in the quality of the writing of poor spellers, and exercises to increase control over the mechanics of writing, should eliminate one of the chief causes of poor spelling.

2. Efficient methods of study should be taught to all pupils. Pupils should be helped to determine the effectiveness of the techniques of study they use by means of learning tests. The teacher should suggest changes in the study procedures of pupils who do not learn to spell efficiently.

3. Pupils should be taught to recheck all written work to eliminate errors due to lapses. Errors due to lapses may be discovered by simply rechecking the written work as a "proof-reading" exercise. Approximately 50 per cent of the errors in writing are due to lapses.

4. Many misspellings, due to ignorance of the word, would be eliminated if the pupils learned the value of checking by the dictionary the spelling of every word about which they are doubtful. This suggests the need of carefully planned lessons on the use and value of the dictionary.

5. The teacher should look for physical handicaps, such as visual and auditory defects, which interfere with efficient spelling. Many of these faults can be remedied by simple medical measures.

6. An important factor provided for, in the individual-study plan proposed above, is accurate pronunciation and articulation. This fault may be due in part to imperfect visual perception of words. Witty [1] found that "careful drill on hearing, pronouncing, visualizing, and spelling all words in syllabic rhythms" was very helpful. Appropriate phonic or phonetic exercises also are of value in such cases.

7. A factor that should not be overlooked is the meaning of the words being learned. Hollingsworth [2] found a significant relation between spelling difficulty and a knowledge of the meaning of words. The teacher should, therefore, make certain that the pupils know the meanings of the words in the spelling lesson.

8. In cases in which there is a bad attitude toward spelling, the teacher must make every effort to bring about a change. The use of games, progress charts, and other forms of incentives will be found of great value in such cases. Frequently such cases are the result of failure to make any improvement in spelling, due to faulty study habits, failure to concentrate, and similar faults. Often a combination of difficulties and deficiencies will be revealed

[1] Witty, P. A. "Diagnosis and Remedial Treatment of Poor Spellers"; in *Journal of Educational Research*, vol. 13, pp. 39–44. (January, 1926.)

[2] Hollingsworth, L. S. *The Psychology of Special Disability in Spelling*. Teachers College Contributions to Education, no. 88, 1918.

by a careful clinical examination. These weaknesses must be removed by systematic remedial exercises and corrective measures.

**Tidyman's suggested technique.** Tidyman [1] suggests the following technique, which embodies the results of numerous investigations of the psychology of spelling, as the one to be taught to pupils for use in studying individual words:

1. Select from three to five hard words for study, and begin the study of each word by pronouncing it and using it in a sentence, if there is any doubt about its meaning or use.
2. Pronounce and copy it by syllables.
3. Underline the hard part of the word, and compare it with a word having the same difficulty.
4. The pupils close their eyes and try to see the word.
5. Write the word from memory several times, spelling softly to themselves as they write.
6. After each word has been studied in this way, write the whole day's list from memory several times. The order of words should be varied in each repetition.
7. Write in sentences the word that presents difficulty in meaning or use.
8. Check off, on the study list, the words learned.

## QUESTIONS FOR STUDY, DISCUSSION, AND REPORT

1. Make a statement of what you consider to be the functions of instruction in spelling.
2. Prepare a timed-dictation test in spelling and administer it to a class. Tabulate the results, find the class average.
3. Give the same test words as a list test. Tabulate the results, and find the class average. Compare the results for the class and for individuals on both tests.
4. Give a standard spelling test to a class and summarize the results. Compare with standards.
5. Secure a set of composition papers, and find the coefficient of misspelling.

[1] Tidyman, W. F. *The Supervision of Elementary Subjects*, chap. 3. New York, D. Appleton and Company.

6. What is meant by the pre-test technique in teaching spelling?

7. How many words are contained in the textbook for each grade? Compare the number of words in several textbooks.

8. Compare the teaching methods in several spelling textbooks, and point out differences in the methods presented.

9. Secure a set of spelling papers, and attempt to classify the errors in the papers according to Book and Harter's classification.

10. Study the spelling study-habits of a pupil deficient in spelling, using the technique described by Miss Davis. Classify the faults observed, and prescribe a remedial program.

11. Apply the technique of testimony as developed by Atkin to a good speller and to a poor speller. Report your results in writing, and recommend a remedial program.

12. Outline a spelling procedure that you think will develop in the pupil the capacity of self-diagnosis and the ability to discover methods of study that will produce maximum results in his particular case.

13. Would you prescribe the same method of study for all pupils?

14. How do you account for the findings of Atkin regarding the wide variability in the study-habits of good and poor spellers?

## SELECTED REFERENCES

Ashbaugh, E. J. *The Iowa Spelling Scales*, Journal of Educational Research, Monograph no. 3, 1922.

Ayres, L. P. *A Measuring Scale for Ability in Spelling.* New York, Russell Sage Foundation, 1915.

Breed, F. S. *How to Teach Spelling.* Danville, New York, Owen Publishing Company, 1930.

Gates, A. R. *The Psychology of Reading and Spelling with Special Reference to Disability.* Teachers College Contributions to Education, no. 129. New York, Columbia University, 1922.

Hollingsworth, L. S. *The Psychology of Special Disability in Spelling.* Teachers College Contributions to Education, no. 88. New York, Columbia University, 1918.

Horn, E. "Commonwealth List"; in *Fourth Yearbook of the Department of Superintendence*, pp. 143 ff. Washington, D.C., Department of Superintendence, 1926.

Tidyman, W. F. *Teaching of Spelling*. Yonkers-on-Hudson, New York, World Book Company, 1919.

## SPELLING TESTS CITED IN CHAPTER X

| TEST | GRADES OR AGES | PUBLISHER |
|---|---|---|
| Ayres Spelling Scale | Elementary | Russell Sage Foundation, N.Y. |
| Iowa Spelling Scales (Ashbaugh) | 2–8 | Public School Publishing Co., Bloomington, Illinois |
| Monroe Timed Sentence Spelling Tests | 2–8 | Public School Publishing Co., Bloomington, Illinois |
| Morrison–McCall Spelling Scale | 2–8 | World Book Company, Yonkers-on-Hudson, N.Y. |

# CHAPTER XI

## DIAGNOSTIC AND REMEDIAL TEACHING IN HANDWRITING

### 1. *The function of instruction in handwriting*

**A valid measure of the effectiveness of teaching.** The activities of the handwriting period should be devoted not only to practice to develop handwriting skill, but to provision for the carry-over of the training from these drills to the improvement of the daily written work in all subjects. The pupil must see the need of handwriting as a means of written expression. He should realize that as such it should be read with little effort. He should become conscious of and accept ordinary standards of legibility and speed. Thus is developed a sense of consideration for others and an urge to attack actively the illegibility of one's writing, as well as a feeling against eccentric individualization.

The extent to which the pupil attacks actively and purposefully the improvement of his handwriting may be considered to be a valid measure of the effectiveness of the teaching. The pupil should be made familiar with accepted standards; he should learn the common defects of writing, and learn to determine what the defects of his own writing are; he should learn what the causes of these defects are, and how to eliminate them; and with the help of the teacher he should undertake a systematic corrective program, and should measure the effectiveness of his efforts to improve his handwriting.

**Aims and objectives.** The following is an excellent statement [1] prepared by a group of specialists, of the general aims and objectives of handwriting.

[1] *Fourth Yearbook of the Department of Superintendence*, pages 113–14, Washington, D.C., National Education Association, 1926.

### WHAT THE SUBJECT IS FOR

1. To develop sufficient skill to enable pupils to write easily, legibly, and rapidly enough to meet present needs and social requirements.
2. To equip the child with methods of work so that he will attack his writing problems intelligently.
3. To diagnose individual writing difficulties.
4. To aid the child to recognize and make use of his peculiar individual learning capacities.
5. To provide experiences which will tend to develop in the child more power to direct his own practice and more ability to judge whether or not he is succeeding in that practice.
6. To provide the means for each individual to progress at his best rate.
7. To develop an appreciation of the relationship between correct body adjustment and an efficient writing production.
8. To secure acceptable and customary arrangement and form for written work (margins, spacing, etc.).
9. To develop a social urge to use the skill attained in all writing situations.
10. To train pupils to be able at the end of the sixth grade, to write quality 60 (Ayres scale) or better, and at a rate 70 letters per minute or better.

## 2. *The measurement of handwriting*

**Measurement a definite part of teaching procedure.**  Before the introduction of standard handwriting scales, teachers had no definite way of knowing whether or not the pupils were attaining a satisfactory standard, or whether the requirements of the course of study were reasonable.  There was no way of showing the pupil that he was making progress in his efforts to improve his writing.  The teacher thus lacked a valuable device for motivating the practice needed to develop the skills essential to good writing.

At the present time, in many schools, self-measurement of quality of handwriting by the pupils forms a definite part of the teaching procedure, and standards are set up which the pupils are expected to achieve.

Several kinds of handwriting scales have been devised. The Ayres Handwriting Scale (Three Slant Edition), consists of a series of samples of writing, arranged in the order of their legibility. Legibility of the samples was determined by the average of the rates at which they could be read by a number of individuals. The Thorndike Handwriting Scale consists of a series of samples, arranged in the order of their general merit. General merit, defined as beauty, legibility, and character, was determined for each sample on the basis of a combination of the judgments of a large number of individuals. Several other scales have been published which have samples whose values have been arrived at by rating the samples on either the Ayres or Thorndike Scales. For example, the Ayres Scale, Gettysburg Edition, contains a series of samples whose value was determined by comparison with the original Ayres Scale (Three Slant Edition).

**The nature of handwriting scales.** The contents of general handwriting scales have been selected in various ways. The Thorndike Scale contains samples of writing from all levels of the school, mostly, however, from the upper grades. This is also true of the Ayres Scale. Such scales make it possible for a supervisor to use the same instrument for measuring the progress made from grade to grade. Because of differences in size and quality of the writing of pupils in the lower grades and the samples in these scales the rating of the writing of the lower grades has been difficult and unreliable.

**The Minneapolis Handwriting Scale.** Some school systems have therefore developed scales for different levels of the school, such as scales for the primary, the intermediate, and the upper grades. The specimens in these scales consist of selections from the written work of the pupils at each level. The result is that there are variations from scale to scale in the size of the writing and in other characteristics affected by the maturity of the pupils. Successful attempts have been made to assign values to the samples on the scales according to one of the general handwriting scales. This has made it possible to measure progress from grade to grade, although there may be some question as to the equivalence of ratings on the several scales. The chief advantage of scales for each grade or for several grades over the general survey scale lies in the fact that the handwriting of pupils is then measured by a scale consisting of samples quite similar in general style and size.

**Freeman's diagnostic scale.** Freeman has devised a diagnostic scale, which may be used to diagnose the defects in specimens of handwriting. This scale consists of five sets of samples. Each of these five sets serves as a basis for diagnosing deficiencies in one of the following five characteristics of handwriting: uniformity of slant, uniformity of alignment, equality of the line, letter formation, and spacing. In each division of the scale there are given specimens of three degrees of excellence, with scores of 1, 3, and 5 respectively. For example, in the first division of the Freeman scale, the samples represent three degrees of uniformity of slant. Specimens are rated according to the value assigned the sample in the scale which they most nearly resemble.

### 3. Securing the specimens for measuring handwriting

**Methods of securing specimens.** Various methods may be used to secure specimens of handwriting for measurement purposes. Two aspects may be measured, namely, rate and quality. In the days of the copy book the specimens exhibited were the best writing of the individuals. Rate was sacrificed to secure writing of a high degree of general merit as far as appearance was concerned. This method obviously did not provide a valid measure of either the rate or the

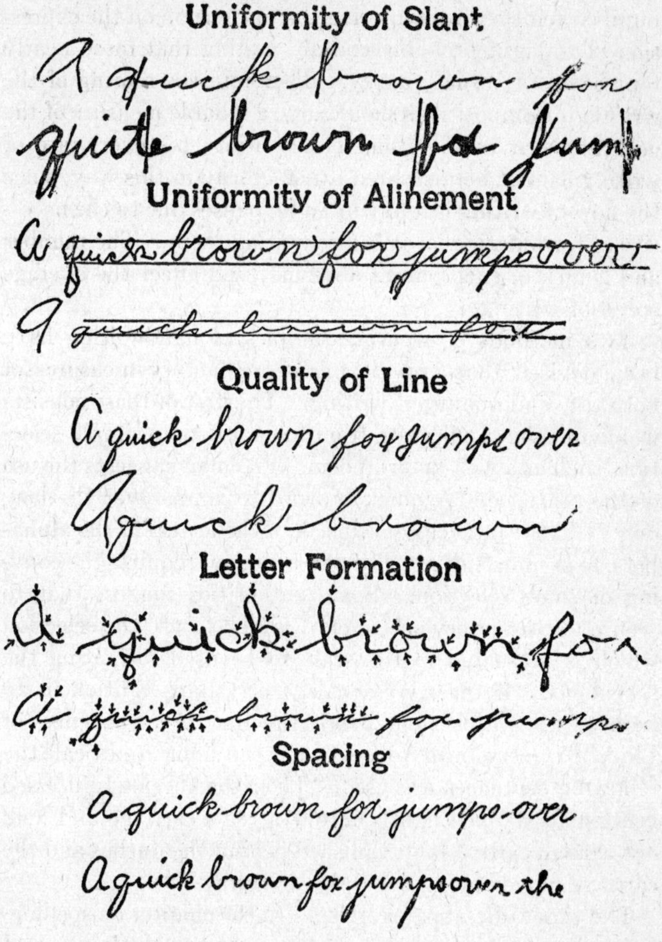

## Uniformity of Slant

*A quick brown fox*

*quite brown fox jump*

## Uniformity of Alinement

*A quick brown fox jumps over*

*A quick brown fox*

## Quality of Line

*A quick brown fox jumps over*

*A quick brown*

## Letter Formation

*A quick brown fox*

*A quick brown fox jumps*

## Spacing

*A quick brown fox jumps over*

*A quick brown fox jumps over the*

FIG. 5

Illustrative Specimens from Freeman's *The Teaching of Handwriting*. Houghton Mifflin Company.

quality of ordinary handwriting. Compositions written by pupils when they are centering their attention on the expression of thought probably contain writing that more nearly represents the usual quality. Therefore the scoring of the writing in compositions should give a reliable measure of the general merit of the usual handwriting; however, rate of writing cannot be measured satisfactorily in this way, since the flow of writing is interrupted by pauses due to the necessity of formulating ideas before writing them. The number and length of such pauses obviously will affect the average speed of writing.

Two methods of securing samples of handwriting have been devised that provide fairly satisfactory measures of both rate and quality of writing. The first of these consists in having the pupil write from memory some simple selection, such as a well-known poem. Freeman suggests the use of the sentence, "A quick brown fox jumps over the lazy dog." This sentence contains all of the letters of the alphabet one or more times. The other method requires the copying of some selection. Some authorities suggest that to secure a satisfactory specimen it is well to use the selection which is presented in the scale to be used for rating the specimens. If the Ayres Scale, Gettysburg Edition, is to be used, the pupils should copy the first three sentences of Lincoln's Gettysburg Address. For the Thorndike Scale the following sentences are used, "Then the carelessly dressed gentleman stepped lightly into Warren's carriage and held out a small card. John vanished behind the bushes and the carriage moved along down the driveway."

**The timed-dictation exercise.** In the chapter on spelling, a timed-dictation exercise was given which may also be used to secure a specimen of the pupils' writing when the rate at which they are to write is controlled by the rate at which the material is dictated. The following statement includes the directions for giving a timed-dictation exercise, used in the Minneapolis schools, and also suitable tests for lower and upper grades.

## TIMED-DICTATION TEST III

In a timed-dictation exercise, the material is dictated in such a way that the children write at a rate which has been found to be a standard when children are writing freely. The method of giving the test is as follows:

1. Read all of the test sentences once before the children begin to write.
2. Dictate the sentences one at a time as a practice test exercise on a day before the test itself. Dictate in the following manner:

   When the second hand of the watch reaches the 60 second mark, dictate the first sentence. The number before the second sentence indicates the point which the second hand should reach before the second sentence is dictated. In grade 3 this is the 31 second mark, and so on for the six sentences. The third sentence should be dictated when the second hand reaches the 21 second mark. Teachers should use the time indicated for their respective grades. Sentences should be dictated only once.
3. On the following day give the test in the same way the practice test was given.
4. When the test is completed, papers should be collected.

## FORM C

Dictate the sentence when the second hand of the watch reaches the mark indicated before each sentence.

| GRADES | 3 | 4 | 5 |
|---|---|---|---|
| 1 | (60) | (60) | (60) |
| 2 | (31) | (27) | (23) |
| 3 | (21) | (11) | ( 1) |
| 4 | (60) | (45) | (30) |
| 5 | (26) | ( 8) | (50) |
| 6 | (57) | (35) | (13) |
| Stop | (45) | (17) | (46) |

Put the book in your bag. (19)
The garden was full of yellow flowers. (31)
Throw the stick into the lake. (24)
I heard the baby cry. (16)
My home is in this block. (19)
We moved into this street yesterday. (30)

| Grades | 6 | 7 | 8–9 |
|--------|------|------|------|
| 1 | (60) | (60) | (60) |
| 2 | (32) | (27) | (24) |
| 3 | (58) | (48) | (43) |
| 4 | (41) | (24) | (15) |
| 5 | (11) | (48) | (42) |
| 6 | (44) | (15) | ( 6) |
| 7 | (19) | (43) | (28) |
| 8 | (45) | ( 4) | (47) |
| 9 | (24) | (36) | (13) |
| 10 | (46) | (54) | (29) |
| Stop | (18) | (21) | (53) |

My sweater was torn at the shoulder.  (29)
Which team will win the game?  (23)
The letter didn't say anything about the picnic.  (30)
I found a quarter near the garage.  (27)
The holiday was a pleasant surprise.  (30)
Whose pattern was used for this apron?  (31)
I waited ten minutes for you.  (23)
The village streets were full of soldiers.  (35)
The cabin had no kitchen.  (20)
My grandfather watched the sunset.  (29)

**Directions to the pupils.**  Great care must be taken in stating the directions which are given to pupils, since they are a very strong influence in determining the rate and quality of writing.  If comparisons are to be made with the results for other groups and with standard scores, the exact formula used in collecting the samples, both as to time and pupil directions, must be followed.  Slight changes in the statement of directions to pupils will produce marked changes in the results.  This will be clear if the following directions, each of which will result in a different kind of response, are considered:

> Write as well as you can.
> Write as rapidly as you can.
> Write as rapidly and as well as you can.
> Write rapidly but do not hurry.
> Copy this selection.
> Write neatly and rapidly.

Freeman thinks that the best single set of specimens can be secured in response to the directions, "Write as well as you can and as rapidly as you can."  In timed-dictation exercises the pupils should merely be told: "You are to write the sentences as I dictate them.  Listen carefully. I shall not re-read the sentences."

**Measuring rate of writing.**  To secure a satisfactory rate of writing pupils should be required to write a simple memory selection. If all write the same selection, the number of letters written can easily be counted. The selection should contain words with which the pupils are familiar, so that there are no spelling difficulties. To guard against lapses of memory the teacher should either write the selection on the blackboard or supply each pupil with a printed or mimeographed copy for reference. If the pupils are required to write unfamiliar or difficult material from a printed copy, the rate of writing will be affected by the pupil's rates of reading and the number of times he must refer to the copy. The criticism that the material in it is too difficult has often been directed against the use of the first three sentences in the Gettysburg Address, as material to be copied by pupils in the lower grades of the elementary school.

The time of writing should be two or three minutes. The labor of counting the number of letters written is unnecessarily increased by having the pupils write for a greater length of time. To avoid error, the teacher should use a stop watch. If an ordinary watch is used, the teacher should direct the pupils to begin writing when the second hand reaches the zero mark, and should record the time when the writing begins and when the pupils are to be told to stop writing. Exactly the time agreed upon should be allowed.

It should be clear that the rate at which the pupil writes in copying material or in writing a selection from memory is a "free choice" on his part. He may choose to write rapidly or he may choose to write slowly. It is obvious therefore that the directions to pupils used in such "free-choice" tests are very important factors to be considered, since they determine his mental set toward the task at hand. This criticism does not apply to the rate of writing on timed-dictation exercises in which the rate is automatically controlled.

**Measuring quality of handwriting.**  The quality of a specimen of handwriting is measured by comparing it with the samples in a standard scale.  The specimen is assigned the rating that is given to the sample in the scale which it most nearly resembles.  Freeman [1] has issued the following directions for using his scale:

The specimen to be judged is graded according to each category separately and given the rank of the specimen in the chart with which it most nearly corresponds in each case.  The total rank is calculated by summing up the five individual ranks.  Thus, if letter formation is given double value, the lowest possible rank is 6 and the highest possible rank is 30 $(5 + 5 + 5 + 10 + 5)$, and the range is 24.

Several precautions are to be observed in making the judgments. The value of the method rests upon the fact that different features of the writing are singled out, one at a time, and graded by being given a rank in one of only three steps.  The differences between the steps are marked, and the ease of placing a specimen should be correspondingly easy.

This method implies, however, that

(1) The attention is fixed on only one characteristic at a time.
(2) The judgment on one point be not allowed to influence the judgment on the other point.
(3) The same fault be counted only once.
(4) General impressions be disregarded.

The record card devised by W. S. Monroe [2] affords a convenient means of tabulating the scores on repeated tests secured by means of Freeman's Scale.  This card is so arranged as to permit the pupil to record his score on each of the five divisions of the Freeman Scale, his total score on that scale, his quality score on the Ayres Scale and his speed of writing in letters per minute.  The score on each of these

[1] Freeman, F. N.  *Experimental Education*, p. 86.  Boston, Houghton Mifflin Company, 1916.
[2] Monroe, W. S.  *Measuring the Results of Teaching*, p. 216.  Boston, Houghton Mifflin Company, 1918.

**eight** items is to be entered on the chart for four consecutive, dated trials, thus showing diagnostically the pupil's development in handwriting.

Investigations have shown that individuals vary considerably in the accuracy with which they can rate samples of handwriting. Standard sets of samples of writing have been assembled by Thorndike and Miss Shaw,[1] which may be used for practice in scoring and for measuring the accuracy with which an individual can score. Usually such practice results in a marked increase in the accuracy of scoring. For example, at the close of an experiment on the effect of practice with instruction in the use of the Ayres Scale, Gray[2] drew the following conclusion:

Accuracy in grading writing by a scale may be produced by careful training in the use of the scale. In the past the assumption has been made that ability to grade expertly in a subject came with an expert knowledge of the subject. While the experiment does not disprove this assumption, it indicates clearly that another avenue of approach to such expert ability is through a period of careful training. This implies that grading may be considered a field more or less by itself, and gives a glimpse of a type of work in education whose chief interest is the accurate use of units of measurement.

Several plans have been suggested to insure greater accuracy in scoring. Ayres[3] suggests that scoring will be considerably more accurate if the scoring is done twice by the same individual. He describes the "sorting method," to be used in such cases, as follows:

The procedure may be as follows: Score samples and distribute them in piles, the 20's in one pile, all the 30's in another and so on.

---

[1] Shaw, Lena. Supervisor of Handwriting, Detroit, Michigan.

[2] Gray, C. T. "The Training of Judgment in the Use of the Ayres Scale of Handwriting"; in *Journal of Educational Psychology*, vol. 6, pp. 85–90.

[3] Ayres, L. P. *A Scale for Measuring the Handwriting of School Children.* New York; Russell Sage Foundation. Bulletin 113.

Mark these values on the backs of the papers, then shuffle the samples and score them a second time. Finally make careful decisions to overcome any disagreements in the two scorings.

If more accurate results are desired, the average of the ratings given by the "sorting method" by three competent judges should be used as the true rating of a specimen.

### 4. *Factors affecting instruction in handwriting*

There is little experimental evidence as to the relative effectiveness of different penmanship systems; however, there is available considerable significant information regarding certain factors that affect instruction in handwriting.

**Movement.** Nutt [1] found that none of the handwriting systems develop any appreciable amount of arm-movement in younger children. He found that arm-movement develops in the ages from ten to fourteen. Nutt also found no correlation between speed and movement in writing for a short period of time. Probably arm or muscular movement may result in greater speed if speed is measured during a long period of time. Nutt also found that well-developed movement did not produce greater speed or better quality of writing than movement in which the arm moved but little.

**Rhythm.** Nutt believes that the pupil's natural rhythm of motion is an important factor in writing. The quality of rhythm increases with age, but has no relation to the amount of arm-movement or to the quality of writing. Nutt found that speed of writing and rhythm mature together. These findings have tended to discredit penmanship systems in which stress is placed on uniformity of movement, rather than upon the development of rhythm similar to that needed in writing letters involving different kinds of strokes in various combinations.

[1] Nutt, H. W. "Rhythm in Handwriting"; in *Elementary School Journal*, vol. 17, pp. 432–45.

Freeman [1] points out that the good writer, as contrasted with the poor writer, breaks the entire writing movement into units or strokes. These units are not broken into separate parts by complete pauses, in most cases, but by a slowing down of the movement. Thus the flow of writing proceeds by a "succession of alternate flights and rests." "The poor writer either does not slow down at the places where there is a radical change in the direction of the stroke, or he slows down at those places where it is not appropriate."

**Speed.** Investigations show that, in general, motor speed increases with age until maturity. Therefore speed of counting in handwriting exercises should be determined by the level of maturity of the pupils who are practicing, as well as by their control over the writing activity. In some of the earlier systems no differentiation was made in the speed of counting from grade to grade. Pupils in all grades were required to perform the same exercises at the same rate of speed. This practice has practically been eliminated in more modern systems of penmanship. Nutt shows that speed is increased by an increase in the rhythmic character of the movement. Therefore special attention should be given to exercises which develop rhythm in writing.

**Writing in other school subjects.** While tests should be used to secure specimens to be used to measure the status of writing in a school system, there must be a systematic plan for developing a satisfactory level of writing in all school subjects. The teacher should therefore from time to time rate, or require the pupils to rate, the writing on compositions submitted in the English or social science classes, the written work in arithmetic classes, and such other written work as may be required of pupils. The work in the handwriting period should be organized in such a way that due

[1] Freeman, F. N., and Dougherty, M. L. *How to Teach Handwriting,* p. 15. Boston, Houghton Mifflin Company, 1923.

consideration is given to the improvement of all writing. The chief criticism of the "copy-book" systems was that there was no transfer from the work of the handwriting period to the writing done at other times. In some schools handwriting scales are placed in a convenient space on a bulletin board. A certain standard for quality is agreed upon, and no written work is accepted which does not meet this standard. The steady insistence on a satisfactory quality of writing at all times will do much to develop an appreciation on the part of the pupils that slovenly, illegible writing is socially not acceptable.

## 5. Norms of progress

**The Freeman and Ayres norms.** Norms of progress for both rate and quality of writing indicate the degree of handwriting ability which should exist at each grade level. Freeman [1] and Ayres [2] have proposed the norms of progress given in Table 47. The norm that they propose for grade 8, the end of the training period for ability in handwriting, implies the level of attainment that should be reached by that time.

TABLE 47. NORMS OF PROGRESS PROPOSED BY FREEMAN
AND AYRES

| RATE | GRADE | | | | | | |
|---|---|---|---|---|---|---|---|
| | 2 | 3 | 4 | 5 | 6 | 7 | 8 |
| Freeman (number of letters)........ | 36 | 48 | 56 | 65 | 72 | 80 | 90 |
| Freeman (quality)................. | 44 | 47 | 50 | 55 | 59 | 64 | 70 |
| Ayres (number of letters)........... | 31 | 44 | 55 | 64 | 71 | 76 | 79 |
| Ayres (quality).................... | 38 | 42 | 46 | 50 | 54 | 58 | 62 |

[1] Freeman, F. N. *Fourteenth Yearbook of the National Society for the Study of Education*, Part 1, pp. 61–77.

[2] Ayres, L. P. *A Scale for Measuring the Handwriting of School Children.* New York, Russell Sage Foundation. Bulletin 113.

Ayres' norms were based on median performances of large numbers of children. Freeman's norms were not based on median scores, but were determined by the medians of the upper half of the scores on about five thousand specimens for each grade from fifty-six cities. The norms for each grade have been found to be somewhat higher than the median scores for many schools found by Ayres. However, the norms proposed by Freeman should not be modified, since they are consistent with the results of studies of the demands of life outside the school and in high school, made by such investigators as Lewis,[1] and Koos.[2]

### 6. *Diagnosis in handwriting*

**The most common defects.** Investigations have shown that an inferior quality of handwriting may be due to a number of causes. Freeman's scale, for example, enables the teacher or pupil to determine the degree of merit of a particular sample on such characteristics as alignment, spacing, slant, equality of line, and letter formation. Gray[3] has prepared a score card for measuring a larger number of characteristics as shown in Form 5.

Miss Nystrom, supervisor of handwriting in Minneapolis, has made a series of investigations of defects that may reduce the legibility of handwriting. Seven different kinds of defects have been isolated. In Table 48 are given the frequencies with which the various defects were found in five hundred specimens of the best, the median, and the poorest handwriting, from grades six to nine.

[1] Lewis, E. E. "The Present Standard of Handwriting in Iowa Normal Training High Schools"; in *Educational Administration and Supervision*, vol. 1, pp. 663-71.

[2] Koos, L. V. "The Determination of Ultimate Standards of Quality in Handwriting for the Public Schools"; in *Elementary School Journal*, vol. 18, pp. 423-46.

[3] Gray, C. T. *A Score Card for the Measurement of Handwriting*. Bulletin of the University of Texas, no. 37, July, 1915.

FORM 5. STANDARD SCORE CARD FOR MEASURING HANDWRITING

(Devised by C. T. Gray)

Pupil. . . . . . . . . . . . . . . . . . . . . . . . . . . .Age. . . . . . . . . . . . . . . .Date. . . . . . . .

Grade. . . . . . . . . . . . . . . . . . . . . . . . . . . . . . . . . . .School. . . . . . . . . . . . . . . .

Sample Number. . . . . . . . . . . . . . . . .Teacher. . . . . . . . . . . . . . . . . . . . . . . . .

| SAMPLE | PERFECT SCORE | SCORE 1 2 3 4 5 6 7 8 9 10 11 12 13 14 |
|---|---|---|
| 1. Heaviness. . . . . . . . . . . . . . | 3 | . . . . . . . . . . . . . . . . . . . . . . . . . . . . |
| 2. Slant. . . . . . . . . . . . . . . . . .<br>    Uniformity<br>    Mixed | 5 | . . . . . . . . . . . . . . . . . . . . . . . . . . . . |
| 3. Size. . . . . . . . . . . . . . . . . . .<br>    Uniformity<br>    Too large<br>    Too small | 7 | . . . . . . . . . . . . . . . . . . . . . . . . . . . . |
| 4. Alignment. . . . . . . . . . . . . . . | 8 | . . . . . . . . . . . . . . . . . . . . . . . . . . . . |
| 5. Spacing of lines. . . . . . . . . .<br>    Uniformity<br>    Too close<br>    Too far apart | 9 | . . . . . . . . . . . . . . . . . . . . . . . . . . . . |
| 6. Spacing of words. . . . . . . . . | 11 | . . . . . . . . . . . . . . . . . . . . . . . . . . . . |
|     Uniformity<br>    Too close<br>    Too far apart | | |
| 7. Spacing of letters. . . . . . . . . | 18 | . . . . . . . . . . . . . . . . . . . . . . . . . . . . |
|     Uniformity<br>    Too close<br>    Too far apart | | |
| 8. Neatness. . . . . . . . . . . . . . . .<br>    Blotches<br>    Carelessness | 13 | . . . . . . . . . . . . . . . . . . . . . . . . . . . . |
| 9. Formation of letters. . . . . . . | 26 | . . . . . . . . . . . . . . . . . . . . . . . . . . . . |
|     General form. . . . . . . . . . | 8 | . . . . . . . . . . . . . . . . . . . . . . . . . . . . |
|     Smoothness. . . . . . . . . . . | 6 | . . . . . . . . . . . . . . . . . . . . . . . . . . . . |
|     Letters not closed. . . . . . | 5 | . . . . . . . . . . . . . . . . . . . . . . . . . . . . |
|     Parts omitted. . . . . . . . . | 5 | . . . . . . . . . . . . . . . . . . . . . . . . . . . . |
|     Parts added. . . . . . . . . . | 2 | . . . . . . . . . . . . . . . . . . . . . . . . . . . . |
|         Total Score. . . . . . . . . | . . | . . . . . . . . . . . . . . . . . . . . . . . . . . . . |

TABLE 48. DEFECTS IN HANDWRITING AFFECTING ITS
LEGIBILITY

(After Nystrom)

| | KIND OF DEFECT | FREQUENCY OF OCCURRENCE | TOTAL BY TYPES |
|---|---|---|---|
| 1. Color | (a) Irregular color | 177 | 177 |
| 2. Size | (a) Irregular size | 200 | 319 |
| | (b) Too large size | 62 | |
| | (c) Too small size | 57 | |
| 3. Slant | (a) Irregular slant | 240 | 326 |
| | (b) Too much slant | 61 | |
| | (c) Lack of slant | 25 | |
| 4. Letter spacing | (a) Irregular letter spacing | 267 | 331 |
| | (b) Crowded letter spacing | 62 | |
| | (c) Scattered letter spacing | 2 | |
| 5. Beginning and ending strokes | (a) Irregular beginning and ending strokes | 270 | 381 |
| | (b) Long beginning and ending strokes | 63 | |
| | (c) Short beginning and ending strokes | 48 | |
| 6. Word spacing | (a) Irregular word spacing | 171 | 415 |
| | (b) Scattered word spacing | 177 | |
| | (c) Crowded word spacing | 67 | |
| 7. Alignment | (a) Irregular alignment | 300 | 374 |
| | (b) Writing below the line | 58 | |
| | (c) Writing above the line | 16 | |

The largest single group of defects, it will be seen, was due to faulty word spacing. Faulty beginning and ending strokes, which are directly related to faulty word spacing, were the next most frequent defects. Irregular alignment of writing, irregular letter spacing, faulty slant, and defects due to size contributed greatly to decreasing the legibility of specimens.

Miss Nystrom has devised an individual record blank on

which the defects of a particular pupil may be indicated. This record is kept by the pupil himself. It gives him an opportunity to analyze his writing in eight different timed-dictation tests. The analysis is based on seven major qualities — color, size, slant, letter spacing, beginning and ending strokes, word spacing, and alignment. Each of these qualities is analyzed, as follows:

    I. Color
       Correct — Too light — Shaded curves — Heavy down strokes — Too heavy
   II. Size
       Correct — Irregular — Too large — Too small
 III. Slant
       Correct — Irregular — Too slanting — Lacking **slant**
  IV. Letter spacing
       Correct — Irregular — Crowded — Scattered
   V. Beginning and ending strokes
       Correct — Irregular — Too long — Too short
  VI. Word spacing
       Correct — Irregular — Crowded — Scattered
 VII. Alignment
       Correct — Irregular — Under line — Over line

The pupil diagnoses the defects in his own writing by checking the various items which most nearly describe it. To aid him in making the diagnosis of his defects, diagnostic charts[1] have been devised for each of the seven major qualities. In the "Slant Chart," for instance, four specimens of writing are given, each representing a type of slant: correct slant, which sets the standard, irregular slant, too slanting, and lacking slant. The cause of each defect is indicated above the specimen containing it. Questions are given which insure an intelligent pupil approach to the diagnosis. Investigations have shown that almost any combination of the seven general kinds of defects may occur

[1] Nystrom, E. C.  *Self-Corrective Handwriting Charts*, Farnham Press, Minneapolis.

in specimens of handwriting. This shows that special provision must be made for some form of remedial work adapted to the needs of each individual.

**Diagnosis of difficulties.** Miss Nystrom has prepared the following statement as to the cause of each difficulty, with remedial suggestions: [1]

1. *Color.* Further study to determine the causes for these defects has resulted in a rather definite diagnosis. For instance, too light a line is caused by holding the pen too nearly vertical, too far from the point, or turned so that the eye is underneath. Shaded curves are caused by holding the pen so that the eye of the pen is toward the left or right. Heavy downstrokes are caused by pressing upon the pen with the forefinger. Very heavy writing is caused by holding the pen so near the point that there is not room enough for the nails of the two little fingers to carry the hand comfortably. This places the weight of the whole hand upon the pen. Correct color can be secured by bending the thumb so sharply that the tip of it lifts the pen in the hand, and by holding the pen far enough from the point to give the nails of the two little fingers room enough to carry the hand comfortably.

2. *Size.* Irregular size of writing is the result of an unsteady movement, usually caused by holding the pen with the thumb straight. Too large writing is the result of using only arm movement, usually caused by holding the pen too far from the point. Too small writing is the result of using only finger movement, usually caused by holding the pen too near the point. Correct size is the result of writing letters in the standard size for the grade by using the correct combination of finger and arm movement. This can be done by "digging" the thumb nail into the pen, a position of the thumb which lifts the pen in the hand and allows the right degree of finger movement, and by holding the pen back from the point far enough to let the nails of the two little fingers carry the hand comfortably, which allows the right degree of arm movement.

3. *Slant.* Irregular slant is usually caused by not shifting the paper to the right often enough to keep the writing directly within the line of vision. Sometimes, however, with the paper held correctly, irregularity of slant is caused by a writing motion toward the right elbow instead of toward the center of the body. Too

[1] By permission of the author.

slanting a writing is usually caused by slanting the paper too much. Lack of slant in writing is usually caused by holding the paper so that the lines are horizontal. Correct slant can be secured by holding the paper so that the lines on the paper slant in the same direction as the fingers of the left hand when the hand is extended diagonally across the desk and by directing the writing motion toward the center of the body.

Experiments have shown an involuntary tendency toward this direction of motion, and also that this motion is most easy to control with regard to uniformity of performance. This is true as well for the left-handed person as for the right-handed person, and is the reason for the tendency to backhand slant in left-handed writing. This slant does not adapt itself easily to the modern alphabet, nor does it help in the matter of legibility.

4. *Handedness.* It is of most importance for the teacher to know all the reliable findings available concerning handedness. The old philosophy of method held that this is a right-handed world, that the left-handed person was socially misfit, and that for this reason he should be trained to use his right hand. This was largely a matter of opinion. Now we know from scientific research that two-thirds of such changes can be made successfully, but that one-third suffers many types of serious nervous reactions. The real danger lies in the fact that as yet we have no way of determining whether the outcome will be successful or not.

The teacher's problem with regard to handedness, especially with the very young children, becomes one of determining whether or not the child is left-handed. Some very definite helps in this matter have resulted from work carried on by Dr. Travis of the University of Iowa. These include, particularly, an induction test, as well as simultaneous writing tests, mirror tracing tests, and tests for determining whether or not vision is "left-handed."

5. *Letter spacing.* Irregular letter spacing is usually the result of irregular slant. Crowded letter spacing is usually the result of too much slant. Scattered letter spacing is usually the result of a lack of slant. Correct letter spacing can be secured by making the upward curves of the letters in the standard slant. When this is done the curve will be that of a two space oval of correct slant.

6. *Beginning and ending strokes.* Irregular beginning and ending strokes occur when the letters are irregular in size. Long beginning and ending strokes are usually caused by writing the letters too

large in size. Sometimes, however, they are caused by too much slant in the letters. Short beginning and ending strokes are usually caused by writing the letters too small in size. Sometimes, however, they are caused by a lack of slant in the letters. Correct beginning and ending strokes depend upon correct size of the letters. Correct beginning strokes can be secured by starting them on the line and curving them in correct slant for all the letters except *a*, *o*, *d*, *g*, *q*, and *c*. The beginning strokes for these letters should start at the top of the letter and curve down to the line. Correct ending strokes should be the same in height as the low letters.

7. *Word spacing.* Irregular word spacing is caused by irregular beginning and ending strokes. Crowded word spacing is usually caused by long beginning and ending strokes. Scattered word spacing is usually caused by short beginning and ending strokes. Correct word spacing depends upon correct beginning and ending strokes. The beginning strokes of a word should start just under the tip of the ending stroke of the preceding word. When words begin with *a*, *o*, *d*, *g*, *q*, and *c*, space enough for a beginning stroke should be allowed.

8. *Alignment.* Irregular alignment is caused by not shifting the paper to the left often enough to keep the writing directly within the line of vision. Writing below the line is usually caused by slanting the paper too much. Writing above the line is usually caused by holding the paper so that the lines on the paper are horizontal. Correct alignment can be secured if the paper is held correctly and shifted to the left often enough to keep the writing directly within the line of vision.

9. *Form of letters.* Correct form of the letters depends upon a sensing of the units of rhythm which control the writing motion, as well as upon the elements of size, slant and spacing. Counting, which is descriptive enough to keep the writer keenly conscious of the vital or difficult strokes of letters, and which allows pauses for retracings, helps to control the rhythm of motion. Counting, both descriptive and numerical, however, has been much overdone. The count should be used only until a word is learned. Prolonging its use beyond this point hinders rather than helps. A very simple count which controls all possible combinations of strokes follows.

The dash (–) indicates a decided pause in the writing motion, and the accent mark (ı) indicates the difficult strokes.

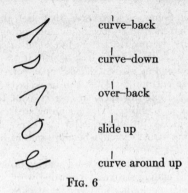

curve–back

curve–down

over–back

slide up

curve around up

Fig. 6

## 7. *Remedial work in writing*

**Group methods.** When the causes of lack of legibility have been determined, the next step is to provide for the right kind of corrective work. In the past certain hand-writing systems have stressed the development of "move-ment" by means of a set of exercises, designed to develop the "large muscles" and to establish coördination of the motor activities of writing. Classes as a whole were all given the same exercise. No attempt, however, was made to adapt the instruction to the needs of individual pupils. Freeman and Dougherty [1] have devised a graded set of exercises which stress the concept of rhythm as well as movement in writing. In addition to this these exercises made special provision for the elimination of defects due to the factors included in the Freeman Diagnostic Scale. These exercises are intended for group work, and no method is provided for adapting the instruction to individual needs.

**Individualizing practice in handwriting.** Several plans for the teaching of handwriting provide for the complete in-dividualization of the practice. These plans may be classi-

[1] Freeman, F. N., and Dougherty, M. D. *How to Teach Handwriting.* Boston, Houghton Mifflin Company, 1923.

fied into two groups. One group consists of exercises so administered that the pupils may progress at various rates through the whole series of lessons. The Courtis–Shaw Standard Practice Tests in Handwriting are of this type. The other group consists of organized sets of exercises intended to eliminate specific faults and defects in the writing of individual pupils. The Self-Corrective Handwriting Charts of Miss Nystrom are of the second type.

**The Courtis Standard Practice Tests in Handwriting.** The Courtis Standard Practice Tests in Handwriting consist of two series of graded exercises, one for grades 3 through 5, and one for grades 6 through 8. Each series begins with the writing of simple words, and progresses through units of increasing difficulty until the pupils are required to write complete paragraphs. For each unit there are standard rates for each grade at which pupils are expected to write. For each grade there is also given a standard for quality. There is an increase in both rate and quality of writing from grade to grade. In each grade the whole class begins with lesson 1, at the beginning of the year. On the next day those pupils who meet the standards for rate and quality on the first exercise take the second lesson. Those whose rate and quality were not satisfactory are required to repeat the same exercise. Provision is made for self-measurement of quality by the pupils. Each day throughout the year pupils who meet the standard set for the grade in particular lessons proceed to the next lesson, until all lessons in the series are completed. Some pupils progress rapidly through the whole set of exercises; some pupils do not make such satisfactory progress. The data in Table 49 show the expected variations in progress, based on a study by Miss Shaw, that may be found at the end of a semester's work in typical classes in grades 3 to 8.

These practice tests are an excellent device for motivating

## TABLE 49. RATE OF PROGRESS OF ANY CLASS AT THE END OF EIGHTEEN WEEKS

| LESSON | 3B | 3A | 4B | 4A | 5B | 5A | 6B | 6A | 7B | 7A | 8B | 8A |
|---|---|---|---|---|---|---|---|---|---|---|---|---|
| 1 | | | | | | | | | | | | |
| 2 | | | | | | | | | | | | |
| 3 | | | | | | | | | | | | |
| 4 | 3 | | | | | | | | | | | |
| 5 | 4 | | 2 | | | | | | | | | |
| 6 | 4 | | 2 | 2 | | | | | | | | |
| 7 | 6 | 1 | 2 | | | | 1 | | | | 3 | |
| 8 | 4 | 1 | 4 | 2 | | 1 | | | | | 1 | |
| 9 | 6 | 4 | 2 | | 1 | | | | | | | |
| 10 | 4 | 5 | 3 | 2 | 1 | 2 | 2 | | | 2 | | |
| 11 | 3 | 4 | 6 | 2 | 1 | | 1 | | 1 | | 2 | 2 |
| 12 | 10 | 2 | 5 | | 1 | 2 | 3 | | 1 | 2 | | 1 |
| 13 | 3 | 6 | 3 | | 4 | 2 | 3 | 2 | 1 | | 1 | 3 |
| 14 | 3 | 4 | 6 | 1 | 2 | 1 | 1 | 1 | 2 | | 4 | |
| 15 | 6 | 3 | 4 | 1 | 3 | 5 | 2 | 3 | 5 | 3 | 4 | 6 |
| 16 | | | | | 3 | 2 | 3 | 3 | 2 | 5 | 1 | 2 |
| 17 | | | | | 4 | 1 | 2 | 2 | | | 4 | 2 |
| 18 | | | | | | 2 | 4 | 3 | 3 | 3 | 1 | 4 |
| 19 | | | | | 4 | 6 | 1 | 1 | 4 | 2 | 5 | 5 |
| 20 | | | | | 4 | 1 | 1 | 0 | 1 | 5 | 2 | 3 |
| Per cent finished | 44 | 70 | 61 | 90 | 72 | 75 | 76 | 85 | 80 | 78 | 72 | 72 |

This table is to be read as follows:

In a 3B grade at the end of eighteen weeks 3 per cent of the children were on lesson 4, 4 per cent on lesson 5, 4 per cent on lesson 6, etc.

The last row of figures shows the number of pupils who had completed the entire set of drill exercises.

practice in handwriting. Provision is made for group competition, and for competition with one's own records. Some provision is made for diagnosis of defects, but no diagnostic charts such as those devised by Miss Nystrom are included in the plan. Pupils who complete the series of exercises for their grade are excused from further practice, provided that all of their written work is up to the standard set for their grade.

The Practice Sentences in Handwriting devised by Leamer provide for individual progress, through a series of graded lessons, in a way quite similar to the plan employed by Courtis.

**Self-Corrective Handwriting Charts.** The Self-Corrective Handwriting Charts, devised by Miss Nystrom,[1] provide an excellent means of individualizing instruction. The plan is not based on the idea of progress through a set of exercises, but on the idea of helping pupils to overcome defects that affect the legibility of any of their writing. Her plan is the result of a long series of carefully conducted investigations in which consideration has also been given to the results of scientific studies by other workers in this field. The principles which underlie this plan are stated as follows:

a. Individualization of instruction to meet individual needs, through diagnosis of difficulties and provision of specific remedies for these difficulties.

b. Socialization of instruction through problems requiring coöperative group activity, and through provision of goals to be reached.

c. Vitalization of instruction for the child by considering as handwriting, not formal penmanship drill, but the daily written work in all subjects.

The results of the experimental investigations of Miss Nystrom are summarized in the following statement:

[1] Published by the Farnham Press, Minneapolis.

Experiments have shown that legibility, or excellence in handwriting, does not depend upon a special type of movement, but upon the proper combination of shoulder, forearm, and finger movements. This combination of movements differs in individuals as their length of fingers and arms differs, and as their ages and degrees of physical control differ.

Furthermore, these experiments have shown that this combination of shoulder, forearm, and finger movements depends upon the correct holding of the pen and paper. Problems of color, size, beginning and ending strokes, as well as the individual letter forms controlled by these, depend upon the posture of the pen. Problems of slant, letter spacing, and alignment, with the letter forms controlled by these, depend upon the posture of the paper. The diagram in Figure 7 shows the relationships among the several factors.

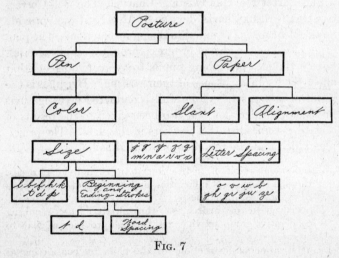

Fig. 7

This close dependence of the elements of legibility upon the posture of the pen and paper is most important in its effect on the correction of defects in legibility. For instance, the correction of defects in color tends to correct defects in size. Correction of defects in slant tends to correct defects in letter spacing. Correction of defects in slant also tends to correct defects in alignment.

It is on account of this close dependence of the elements of legibility upon the posture of the pen and paper, that the correction of defects in legibility is considered in the order that is followed in this series of exercises.

With each of the diagnostic charts there is a specific set of printed directions and exercises for overcoming the defects revealed by the diagnosis. The handwriting specimens to be considered for diagnosis during the class period may be selected from any of the written work of the pupils and are not limited to the material written during the time allotted to handwriting. In this way the time devoted to special practice is made to function directly in the improvement of all writing.

Sets of exercises for correcting defects in slant have been prepared by Miss Nystrom, which are obtainable in printed form from the Board of Education, Minneapolis. These exercises have been worked out for each of the elements in good handwriting, and give detailed directions for overcoming defects, but are too detailed for reproduction here.

## QUESTIONS FOR STUDY, DISCUSSION, AND REPORT

1. Outline a procedure for making a survey of handwriting. Prepare specific directions for securing the samples to be scored.
2. Give a handwriting test according to accepted procedures.
3. Score the set of papers for some handwriting test for general merit. Score the papers at some subsequent time, and compare the results of both scorings. Account for differences found. Compare the results with standards.
4. Secure a set of thirty papers. Have them scored independently by at least five scorers, and compare the results.
5. Compare the rating of handwriting specimens for individual pupils secured by the test method, and from typical written work not secured under test conditions.
6. Compare the quality of handwriting secured when different sets of directions, such as are described on page 416, are used.
7. Try to make a diagnosis of the defects in handwriting specimens, using a diagnostic handwriting chart.
8. Observe a handwriting lesson. Can you suggest ways of im-

proving the teaching procedure in the light of the discussion in this chapter?

9. Describe a method by which a teacher might develop an informal handwriting scale from specimens secured from the pupils.

10. Why is it desirable to help pupils to diagnose their difficulties in handwriting?

11. If possible, observe the writing posture of some pupil who is left-handed. Some of them have very bad posture. If no cases are available, describe cases that you have observed in the past.

## SELECTED REFERENCES

Freeman, F. N. *The Teaching of Handwriting*. Boston, Houghton Mifflin Company, 1914.

Freeman, F. N., and Dougherty, M. L. *How to Teach Handwriting*. Boston, Houghton Mifflin Company, 1923.

Taylor, J. S. *The Supervision and Teaching of Handwriting*. Richmond, Johnson Publishing Company, 1926.

West, P. V. *Changing Practices in the Teaching of Handwriting*. Bloomington, Illinois, Public School Publishing Company, 1927.

Wise, Marjorie. *On the Techniques of Manuscript Writing*. New York, Charles Scribner's Sons, 1924.

## HANDWRITING TESTS CITED IN CHAPTER XI

| Test | Grades or Ages | Publisher |
| --- | --- | --- |
| Ayres Measuring Scale for Handwriting (Gettysburg Edition) | Elementary | Russell Sage Foundation, New York |
| Courtis Standard Practice Tests in Handwriting (Courtis–Shaw) | 3–8 | World Book Company, Yonkers-on-Hudson, New York |
| Freeman Chart for Diagnosing Faults in Handwriting | All | Houghton Mifflin Company, Boston |
| Nystrom Self-Corrective Handwriting Charts | 2–12 | Farnham Press, Minneapolis |
| Thorndike Handwriting Scale | 2–8 | Bureau of Publication, Teachers College, Columbia University, New York |

# CHAPTER XII
## DIAGNOSTIC AND REMEDIAL TEACHING IN THE SOCIAL STUDIES

**Content of this subject.** In no subject is the teacher of to-day being charged with heavier responsibilities than in the social studies. The separate subjects from which social-science materials are largely drawn, such as geography, history and civics have, of course, been taught for years. In recent years, however, much greater emphasis has come to be placed upon a functional interpretation of these subjects. The burden of educating for citizenship is being placed upon the social studies. The schools are being called upon to "produce a generation of informed, thinking, and socially disposed citizens."[1] It no longer suffices to teach the facts of geography and history. Complex and varied outcomes are set up which demand radical variations in materials and teaching methods.

While problems of method, content, and measurement are closely related in all subjects, the social studies offer a particularly good example of the manner in which the factors are interdependent. For this reason it has been thought best to discuss some of the problems of determining the curriculum in the social studies, and at the same time to point out the various problems of method and measurement which arise.

[1] Rugg, Harold O., and Hockett, John. *Objective Studies in Map Location*, p. 8. Social Science Monographs, no. 1. The Lincoln School of Teachers College, Columbia University, New York.

### I. OBJECTIVES AND OUTCOMES IN THE SOCIAL STUDIES

**Complexity of the outcomes.**    Some conception of the complexity of the outcomes sought in social-studies teaching may be obtained from the following very general objectives developed by the Superintendent's Yearbook Committee:[1]

I. To help pupils to acquire information and skill which will be of value to them in continuing their education.

II. To help pupils to explore vocational interests through the materials of the social studies.

III. To help pupils to enjoy the materials and methods of the social studies for their own sake.

IV. To help pupils protect their own interests while respecting the interests of others.

V. To help pupils become generous and efficient contributors to the solution of common problems of school life, and of civic, economic and social life.

It is obvious that all of the above objectives could be subjected to an analysis which would yield a long list of more specific objectives.

In subjects such as spelling and writing, skills are the principal outcomes sought.    The teacher does seek other outcomes.    She may believe that learning never takes place singly.[2]    Yet the materials employed are relatively simple.

In social studies not only the objectives sought but the materials employed are almost infinitely complex.    The task of the curriculum maker here involves at least four definite problems.    It is desired that pupils acquire information, develop habits of thinking, acquire right social attitudes, and engage in socially desirable behavior.    Each of

---

[1] *Fourth Yearbook, Department of Superintendence*, p. 347.

[2] Kilpatrick, William Heard.    *The Foundations of Method*, chapters 1–6.

these desired outcomes presents a different problem in method and measurement.

**Selection of content.** One of the very difficult problems in the social studies is the selection of the facts to be learned. In a subject such as geography the amount of available information is amazingly large. Five commonly used geographies mention from 500 to 600 cities.[1] "Forty New England cities are mentioned in a running account of only 545 words. Twenty-two Southern cities are mentioned on one page; 13 more on the following page; 22 North Atlantic cities on one page and 17 on the following. The same geography treats 43 cities in South America in the same 'lick-and-a-promise' manner. Among these are Oroya, Jujuy, Tucuman, Narraquilla, LaGuaria, Paita, Potosi. How many of them do you know? How many of them should children be expected to learn?"[2] The problem here raised applies perhaps with equal force to both history and geography. Dates, cities, names of persons, battles, movements, mountain ranges, rivers, and islands pass before the child in what must seem to him a never-ending panorama.

It is obvious that the child cannot be expected to learn all of these numerous and rapidly increasing facts. A selection must be made. Who is to make the selection, and how is it to be made? The teacher in practice probably follows the textbook, but even here a further selection must be made. What seems important to one teacher will not seem important to another. What receives emphasis in one city or school may not receive emphasis in another.

## 1. *Objective studies*

Numerous studies are available the purpose of which has been to apply certain criteria to the selection of the facts to

[1] Rugg, Harold O., and Hockett, John. *Op. cit.*, p. 4.
[2] *Ibid.*, p. 5.

be taught in the social studies. Reference can be made here to only a few of these, and the reader should consult the studies which are included in the bibliography at the end of the chapter.

**The study of Rugg and Hockett.** One of the most comprehensive studies in the selection of facts to be taught is that of Rugg and Hockett.[1] The purpose of this investigation was to determine the relative importance of map locations in contemporary life. The following types of locations were studied:

1. Cities of the United States
2. Cities of the world
3. Countries
4. Sections and regions within or overlapping countries
5. Rivers
6. Mountains
7. Islands
8. Bodies of water
9. States of the United States
10. Railroads, steamship routes, industrial areas, agricultural areas

In selecting the location-facts in each group the following criteria were used:

1. Population
2. Foreign trade
3. Bank clearings
4. Area
5. Frequency of use by frontier thinkers in critical magazines
6. Frequency of use by frontier thinkers in critical books
7. Number of articles in all important magazines
8. Washburne's rank-order list

The results of the study appear in rank-order lists of the various types of location facts, such as cities and rivers.

---

[1] Rugg, Harold O., and Hockett, John. *Objective Studies in Map Location.* Social Science Monographs, no. 1. The Lincoln School of Teachers College, Columbia University, New York City.

Many other studies could be listed if space were available. At first thought these studies might appear to offer a solution to the problem. While they are no doubt valuable, it is found that certain developments in teaching method are complicating even these more or less objective methods of approach.

**Changes in educational philosophy.** Modern educational philosophy emphasizes pupil growth as the principal outcome of education. It is contended that growth takes place most rapidly and effectively when learning grows out of the "felt needs" of children. If schools are to be organized so as to utilize this principle they should make definite provision for pupil participation in the selection, planning, and execution of learning activities. The teacher becomes a leader of children, not a taskmaster. One way to describe the changes taking place would be to say that the tendency is toward "pupil-activity" schools rather than "teacher-domination" schools. The two types of schools can best be made clear by means of concrete descriptions [1] of actual lessons taught in accordance with the two procedures:

*Teacher D (a teacher-dominated school)* was a rigid disciplinarian. Every child was compelled to keep in perfect order, to sit rigidly in the standard position, to pay absolute attention to everything that was said, and to strive to achieve perfection in all his work. Papers were marked with care, every i not dotted, and every t not crossed being noted and later corrected by the pupil. Answers to questions which were not in the exact language of the book were counted wrong, and there were no supplementary readings or discussions. On the other hand, the lessons assigned were short so that it was possible to learn them. Any child could ask any normal questions he wished about anything he did not understand, but the questions had to be asked during the study period, not during the recitation. The teacher was absolutely fair and impartial, knew every child's weakness and success, and held herself

[1] Taken from L. J. Brueckner, *Scales for the Rating of Teaching Skill.* University of Minnesota Press, Minneapolis, 1927.

up to the standards she had set for the class.   Deliberate misbe-
havior was sure to receive swift and vigorous corporal punishment;
failure to learn meant additional tasks.   There was much drill and
review.   Class questioning was vigorous and snappy, and was
enjoyed by those who had their lessons.   At the end of the work on
France, every child who was marked satisfactory had a large mass
of exact information at his tongue's end and had put in many days
of concentrated vigorous study.

*Teacher F* (*a pupil-activity school*) began more than a week before
the subject of France was reached to bring material about France
into the classroom.   Pictures of the cities of France were hung on
the walls.   References to France and illustrations from French life
began to turn up in other classes.   During her spare time before
and after school the children found the teacher at work upon what,
in response to questions, she called her travel book, which she was
making for her own pleasure as a present to a friend.   Finally a
group of pupils came and asked if they, too, couldn't make a travel
book as their geography work.   The teacher raised her objections,
but finally gave permission to the group to try to persuade the rest
of the class to adopt the idea, stipulating only that the class must
present a workable plan whereby all could cover the required work
in the course of study.   The next day, at class time, a committee
appointed by the class presented a good plan.   The teacher again
raised certain objections which were met by the class as soon as
they saw the problems.   The teacher accepted the revised plan,
and the class promptly organized itself into committees and went
to work.   They either bought the material needed themselves or
asked the teacher to get it for them.   In four weeks' time they
had covered the whole French geography and much more besides.
They had interested other teachers in their project, so that in literature, art, music, and other subjects the influence of their interest was apparent.   Every child in the class had a travel book and,
while some were better than others, there was not one which did
not show creditable standards of workmanship.   The teacher
was kept busy supplying materials, answering questions, helping
children achieve their plan, but except for an occasional taking
of the class discussion to bring some problem of discipline, workmanship, or understanding before the class for their solution, had
no direct hand in the control or direction of the class.   The work
on France closed with an exhibit of the travel books and the visit
of two French friends of the teacher, who were traveling through

the city. There was no drill, no recitation of things learned, no work in the usual sense, but every child acquired a very thorough and vital knowledge of French life and ways, and valued his Travel Book highly.

Under the first of these two methods, the facts learned are readily subject to control. Under the second method the exact facts learned by any two students may not be the same. Moreover, the proponents of the methods might take the position that the exact facts learned are of only secondary importance so long as the pupils have been engaged in useful activities and have formed useful purposes. Whether these methods must be supplemented by formal drill activities on the desired facts is an open question.

Another tendency in the field of method is toward an extension in the variety and amount of material covered by the pupil in the social studies. An illustration can be found in the "Morrison Mastery Technique." [1] Under this method the pupils spend a large proportion of their time in the classroom in actual reading and study. The materials are not confined to the text, but include a great variety of sources. It is entirely likely that different pupils will learn different sets of facts. The same materials will not necessarily be read by all pupils. Pupils with wide interests, good reading ability, and exceptional industry will read far more than pupils of limited ability. The result is that wide differences in curriculum and materials obtain within the same class.

**Nature of development in methods.** The changes taking place in methods of teaching have been more or less gradual. They have probably passed through several stages or levels. A survey of social-studies instruction in a large number of schools would be likely to reveal the existence of many levels or stages of development. In order to show in a more detailed way the nature of the developments which are taking

[1] Morrison, H. C. *The Practice of Teaching in Secondary Schools.* University of Chicago Press.

place, the following levels of teaching in the social sciences [1] have been prepared. It should be kept in mind that these levels as described are tentative, and merely approximate the types of procedure which might be found by analysis of actual teaching procedures followed. The descriptions serve, however, to give a more concrete and concise presentation of developments in teaching procedure.

It is quite obvious that the problems of measurement, for example, will be quite different in Level 1 than in Level 6. The same can be said for materials of instruction.

## 2. Tentative levels for teaching of social science

*Level 1.* The social-science subjects are taught without relationship to each other. History is a memorizing of historical events in chronological order; geography is a study of locations and products; citizenship is abstract teaching not related in any way to the child's activities or environment; man's relation to nature or the study of life in nature (elementary biology) is practically untaught. There is complete teacher control; no diagnostic or remedial work; no provisions for individual differences; no correlation with other subjects; no applications are made. The textbook is the sole source of content and children are discouraged from making contributions from their experiences and outside readings. The text is the basis of organization; assignments are pages in the textbook.

*Level 2.* The social-science subjects are still taught without relationship to each other but they are now taught by means of the *topical method.* The topics, however, are assigned to the class as a whole, and no attempt is made to provide for individual differences. The teacher uses various devices to *interest* the pupils in their work. The teacher emphasizes the need of obedience to rules, tries to inculcate in the child the ideals of home responsibility and respect for parents. She teaches elementary health habits. There is still complete teacher control but this teacher provides for some directed pupil activities. Informal tests are given occasionally, usually at stated intervals without regard to a specific need, and

---

[1] Prepared by group of graduate students at the University of Minnesota as the basis for a discussion of problems in the supervision of social science. Similar levels are available for the separate social studies.

she fails to follow up by systematical, pertinent remedial work whatever errors or difficulties the tests may reveal. Correlation with other subjects is incidental; textbook problems, maps, globes, graphs, and pictures are used; there is logical textbook organization. The test, *supplemented by meager assignments to reference material*, is the source of content. The teacher herself is more interested in her work and is better prepared than the teacher in Level 1. She encourages pupils having difficulty to come to her for help which she willingly gives; she realizes the value of good textbooks and does what she can to provide them for the school. Applications are largely limited to the teaching of citizenship, and much of this is done through precept rather than activities in a practical situation.

*Level* 3. On this level the social-science subjects are no longer isolated subjects, but *they are correlated* rather than integrated. That is, the subjects as such are taught, but they are related to each other. There is also a correlation with other subjects of the curriculum, but this is incidental. The teacher, through pupil participation, devices, provides for activities which will cultivate responsibility, self-appraisal, initiative, cleanliness, kindness, service, patriotism, etc. She approaches the study of geography from the psychological point of view by giving the pupils topics to study, about which they are familiar and interested. This she correlates with interesting items about the growth, habitation, and habits of the plants and animals that may tie-up with the topics being studied. She still stresses sequential, and factual learning, but she shows more and more skill in relating facts and presenting the causes and effects of natural, political, and social developments. In this relation she brings in the political, economic, and social institutions of importance to the child's knowledge. Informal tests are given and the teacher pays special attention to *general* diagnosis and attempts remedial work but with the idea of making up a deficiency rather than getting at the cause of the difficulty and working out a solution from that point of view. The textbook is supplemented by problems prepared by the teacher with the help of the pupils.

*Level* 4. The main difference in this level and that of Level 3 is degree rather than new factors added. There is a general enrichment of the curriculum. Coöperation and activities are present but they do not grow out of large units of work. The pupils now not only participate in the government of the school, for example, as monitors, yard policemen, etc., but they originate some of the rules of the government. They have some school organization that they conduct themselves, *including* the teacher rather than participating with her. The pupils may in their organization discuss school conditions and make suggestions; and they may initiate programs containing dramatization of historical events, nature stories, and topics of geographical interest, and other inter-correlations, but this work is quite apart from the regular social-science curricula *provided* for *semi-socialized classes*, while great freedom is allowed the pupil in expression, initiative, suggestions; group activity is provided for; but the recitation is in charge of the teacher. Topical recitations are given, discussions encouraged, cues of pupil interest utilized. The teacher makes a definite effort to develop skill in the use of sources of information. Interest in current events, use of newspapers, magazines, and books is developed by reference to them in a constructive way, and through using them as supplemental reading material. We find at this level a *breakdown of separate subjects in two respects*. Geography becomes a study of the relationships which exist between human life and the natural environment, and it is difficult to tell whether the work is one on geography or nature study. The same can be said about the study of history and citizenship. Correlation between Geography and History is still largely incidental, as for instance, use of maps to locate historical events. With this new approach the dependence of men and races upon each other and upon nature is developed, and the pupils are taught to judge between the wise and unwise use of land and other natural resources.

*Level 5.* At this level we see a general breakdown of *compartmental subject organization in the social-science subjects* although in a given recitation one phase of the work may be emphasized and another phase not be present. Skills and knowledge are not neglected but the emphasis is on the development of points of view, interests, attitudes and ideals. The teacher attempts to cultivate historical and locational mindedness, and the ability to form sound generalizations. Physical efficiency and the proper use of leisure time are stressed. The individual is trained to take his proper place among his fellow men by allowing him to use his initiative, practice self-control, and coöperate with the other pupils and the teacher in carrying out the school program. Pupils are encouraged to participate also in social activities. In diagnosing cases, the teacher goes beyond tests and individual drill materials, and uses school records, the child's case history, family background, if need be, and the child's personality and characteristics are considered in the remedial program. Pupils whose work is satisfactory assist the teacher in helping the deficient pupil.

Intercorrelation is used when possible, and a variety of applications are made. *The activities grow out of large units of work organized by the teacher with the coöperation of the pupils.* Excursions, dramatizations, and experiments are carried on by the children. The textbook is richly supplemented by actual problems, projects, and excursions. References are widely used.

The teacher anticipates difficulties that may arise and provides a constructive and preventive program. She also shows more discretion in her selection and use of diagnostic and remedial materials and drill exercises when they are needed. She also arranges her work so as to provide for individual needs. Faulty, inefficient methods of work are corrected and pupils are taught to appraise their own work and keep charts and graphs of their individual and class progress. Responsive activities, such as taking part in dramatization, making outlines, writing themes, making notebooks, drawing maps, charts and graphs, and collecting materials are carried on. The textbook is supplemented by the use of charts, maps, pictures, and the use of problems suggested by the teacher and carried out by the pupils. An increase in the use of reference material is made.

*Level* 6. At this level *compartmentalized subject organization breaks down.* The work is organized about large fields of endeavor which have been found socially valuable through studies of experts in the field, and through needs revealed by contributions made to social, economic, and industrial life, through experience in those fields. To a greater degree than before, the teacher is awake to incidents that arise in the class, she makes use of them and adapts them to life situations. The teacher and pupils coöperate in planning the work, and as far as is practical the *school activities grow out of purposeful situations. Class periods are socialized. Drills and learning exercises* are necessary, but this work is *motivated and vitalized through the need that is found for the skill or information* in the socializing activities. The work is highly supplemented by a large variety of reliable and pertinent instruction materials.

A few additional objectives desired at this level are to train the pupil to think about social questions and institutions; develop concern for the improvement of the common welfare; racial, religious, national, and social tolerance. Memory of events and factual knowledge is incidental to the major objectives of developing high ideals, right attitudes, and desirable habits. *Community interests and projects are utilized.* The textbook is a source of information supplemented by a rich variety of other readings, teacher and pupil experience, excursions, and other sources of information. Diagnostic and remedial work is provided as needed and the individual is cared for by the use of individualized materials, provisions for consideration of topics of interest to him, and distribution of opportunity for participation in school and community projects.

### 3. *Problems of content, method, and measurement*

**Relation to teaching and measurement.** It is evident from the foregoing discussion that the social studies present some serious problems in the selection of content. These problems, also, have a definite relation to teaching method and measurement. If methods of fact selection can be found whereby it would be possible to determine what facts the pupil should learn, it might be assumed to be a relatively simple matter to provide for the teaching of these facts. However, there are those who would insist that the social studies be taught with greater regard for method than for content. Such persons may suggest that the teaching methods employed be similar to the procedure used by Teacher F, just described. In the event that such methods are used, how shall the facts to be learned be controlled? The pupil may learn a large number of facts, but they may not be the ones which objective studies would suggest that he should learn.

Not infrequently mention is made of the relatively small number of measuring devices in the social studies. It is readily apparent that the test-maker faces a more or less baffling situation in this field. In the first place there is not complete agreement on the facts to be learned. He cannot make tests to meet all conditions, though occasionally he tries. In some cases the solution of the problem is sought through making the tests as comprehensive as possible in the hope that by this method different pupils and schools will have an equal chance. This plan, however, tends to encourage teachers and pupils to emphasize memorization of great numbers of facts in an effort to make high test scores. It tends also to prevent pupils from evaluating the relative importance of facts, since they seek to learn as many as possible rather than to select.

## II. THE PROBLEM OF DIAGNOSIS IN THE SOCIAL STUDIES

As has been pointed out previously, the purpose of diagnosis is to secure facts concerning the instructional needs of pupils. The teacher wants to know the respects in which pupils are deficient, and if possible she wants to know why they are deficient. Assuming that we know what facts children should learn in social-studies instruction, it would be a relatively simple matter to take inventory of the facts which have been learned. It is not difficult to discover whether or not a given child knows the areas in the United States which produce lumber; it is not so easy, however, to determine whether the pupil has obtained a proper point of view with reference to the responsibilities of citizenship in the conservation of lumber as a natural resource. Will the pupil as a citizen continue to give thought to the problem of conservation, and will such thought contribute to socially desirable attitude and civic behavior?

There is first, then, the problem of diagnosing deficiencies in those knowledges and attitudes which constitute the desired outcomes in the social studies. In the second place, if a pupil does not succeed in the social studies his failure may be due to deficiencies in the skills which he needs for effective study, e.g., reading, vocabulary, and knowledge of and ability to use various sources of material.

**Measurement difficulties.**  It is obvious from the fore-going discussion that measuring instruments are not available for taking inventory of all the outcomes which teachers hope to secure through instruction in the social studies. Only a few of the more significant approaches to the problem can be considered.  It must be readily admitted that many outcomes are not sufficiently well defined at present to permit of even an attempt at the construction of tests.  In other instances, measurement seems to be a baffling problem.

Many of the tests which have thus far been devised in the social studies are probably of doubtful value for diagnostic purposes.  At the same time the differences in the objectives and outcomes sought in different schools may force each teacher to prepare her own tests.  In spite of these conditions many of the tests which have been published have value for specific purposes.  In some instances the tests suggest to the teacher methods by which she can prepare other tests, more or less informal in character, but designed to fit the particular needs of the teacher in making a diagnosis of pupils in the social studies.  In most cases it has been possible to reproduce only a small section of any test.

**Types of tests.**  The tests to be considered here may be roughly classified as follows:

1. Background tests
2. Information tests
3. Thought tests
4. Tests of understanding
5. Attitude tests

We shall consider each of these types of tests in order.

### 1. *Background tests*

**The Kepner Background Tests.**  One form of diagnosis is to determine, in advance of teaching, what pupils already know about the subjects to be taught. The theory back of this procedure is the same as that back of all diagnosis, namely, the orientation of teaching effort. Much valuable time is lost teaching what pupils already know. As a result there is not time for pupils to learn what they do not know. One of the few background tests is that prepared by Kepner and known as the Kepner Background Tests in Social Science. This test is noteworthy also because it is one of the few attempts that have been made at the preparation of tests in the field of general social science. There has been much discussion of unifying the social studies.[1] Thus far, however, little progress has been made in preparing tests for the new type of organization of material. The Kepner Tests are designed for high school use, and deal largely with factual material.

The tests are largely historical. This limits their use for diagnosis in other social-study fields. The fact also that they measure largely fact knowledge means that other outcomes cannot be measured. It would nevertheless appear that many more tests of this general sort are needed. If such a background test could be prepared, covering the various fields of social studies as well as different types of desired outcomes, it would constitute a considerable advancement in measurement in the social studies. Teachers may find it to their advantage to prepare "background" tests of many different kinds in terms of the materials used and the outcomes desired in a particular course.

## 2. Tests of information

The most common type of test. More tests are available which measure information in the social studies than of any other type. It is but natural that this should be true. It is

---

[1] "The Nation at Work on the Public School Curriculum"; *Fourth Yearbook, Department of Superintendence*, p. 324.

relatively easy to determine whether or not a pupil knows a given date or fact.   At the same time, teaching of the social studies has probably emphasized fact knowledge to a great extent.   Not only the new-type objective tests but also the old-type examinations stressed knowledge.   The typical textbook has been encyclopedic in character.   It has given meager treatment to great numbers of facts, and has placed a premium upon memory work.

There are also those who contend that standardized as well as informal new-type examinations have increased the emphasis which has been placed upon fact knowledge in teaching.   Whatever the truth may be in this connection, the teacher will be interested in so planning her measuring procedures as to avoid overemphasis on any particular type of outcome.   This attitude on the part of the teacher will mean that information tests will not be discarded.   A test will not be overlooked merely because it measures only knowledge of facts.   Such a test will be used with a knowledge of its purpose and limitations.

From a diagnostic standpoint most of the information tests available are disappointing.   These tests will help the teacher to determine whether or not children know certain facts.   There is generally, however, no way of knowing why children do not know these facts.   In other words, if a lack of a knowledge of given facts constitutes a failure on the part of the pupil, we do not know *why* he fails.   The problem is made more difficult by the fact that there is not agreement as to the rôle which fact knowledge should play in the social studies.   The relative importance of different facts is not known.   In addition, the value of fact knowledge as a whole is sometimes questioned.   If, then, a teacher discovers that fact knowledge of pupils is small, that discovery has only slight diagnostic value.   The teacher would probably be safe in assuming, however, that marked deficiency in fact knowledge would suggest deficiencies in teaching, especially if such lack of a knowledge of facts is coupled with deficiency in ability to "think" in the field of the social studies. The tests of information are therefore valuable to the teacher as a general diagnostic device. There may also be those teachers who would insist that pupils should learn certain facts as lists of minimum essentials. In this case the tests would be valuable for the purpose of determining whether or not such facts have been learned.

The number of available information tests is large, and only a few will be described here. In selecting the tests here described no effort has been made to apply criteria of reliability in the statistical sense. The tests included have been chosen because they are suggestive to teachers.

**Van Wagenen History Scales.** Perhaps the best known history scale is that of Van Wagenen. Only the information scale is described here, since other parts of the scale are described under "thought tests." The Van Wagenen Test has been very carefully prepared, and elaborate scoring and statistical treatment have been provided. The questions have been arranged in the order of increasing difficulty. While the scoring is carefully worked out, its objectivity in the hands of many teachers may be questioned because of the plan of half credit for half correct answers. It may perhaps be questioned whether tests of this type will have wide application for diagnostic purposes in the hands of classroom teachers. The intricate scoring plan will probably keep many teachers from using the tests.

VAN WAGENEN AMERICAN HISTORY SCALES [1]

Information Scale S1.    General.    Grades 5 and 6.

DIRECTIONS. Begin with question 1 and answer as many of the questions as you can. Answer them in order. If you can-

[1] Teachers College, Columbia University.

not answer all the parts of any question, answer as many of the parts as you can. Start.

---

GROUP 1 (Average value 58.5)

1. (54) **Of** these occupations — fishing, raising of tobacco, raising of rice, ship-building — (*a*) which two were most extensively carried on in the New England colonies?

1.

2.

*b.* Which two were most extensively carried on in the Southern colonies?

1.

2.

As has been pointed out in a previous chapter, the value of certain statistical scores for diagnostic purposes may be questioned. Thus scores reduced to subject ages, reading ages, spelling ages, and so on, together with B scores and T scores, tell something of the level of achievement which a pupil has reached. They do not, however, tell us anything about the reasons for failure to achieve. It would therefore appear that such tests have their greatest value for survey or administrative, rather than for teaching uses.

**The Burton Civics Test.** Among the more recently developed information tests is that by the Burtons. This test makes no pretense of measuring anything but information. The test is easily scored. A few sample items from the test are given below. Some of the most interesting items in the test are those which deal with the meaning of terms. In one sense these items perhaps belong under the category of a vocabulary test. The use of complete sentences as alternate answers to the questions probably makes for accuracy of discrimination.

## BURTON CIVICS TEST [1]

### Form A. For Grades 5 to 9

1. What is a plain-clothes man? . . . . . . . . . . . . . . . . . . . . . . ☐
   1. A man who buys and sells old clothes
   2. A policeman who does not wear a uniform
   3. A tailor who makes men's suits and coats

2. What is a precinct? . . . . . . . . . . . . . . . . . . . . . . . . . . . . ☐
   1. A city law
   2. A city officer
   3. A part of a city or county

**The Brown-Woody Civics Test.** These tests, which have already been referred to under the measurement of vocabulary, also include a section on information. The sample items below are illustrative. The use of the yes-no response probably encourages guessing on the part of the pupils. The reliability coefficients for this test are very high. In spite of this fact one is inclined to question the plan of stating the questions in many instances in such form as to suggest the answers. The scoring is, of course, objective and simple. The items have been selected because of their appearance in a number of different texts. Including the various parts of the tests it becomes sufficiently comprehensive to give considerable reliability.

### BROWN–WOODY CIVICS TEST [2]

### Form A. For Grades 7 to 12

### PART II. CIVIC INFORMATION

DIRECTIONS. Draw a line under the right answer to each question.

---

[1] From Burton Civics Test. Copyright, 1928, by World Book Company, publishers, Yonkers-on-Hudson, New York.

[2] From Brown–Woody Civics Test. Copyright, 1926, by World Book Company, publishers, Yonkers-on-Hudson, New York.

*Begin here.*

1. Is the United States a democracy?      Yes    No    1
2. Is the Constitution of the United States
   the highest law of the land?      Yes    No    2
3. May any adult become a candidate for
   office, local or national?      Yes    No    3

**The Hill Civics Tests.**   Hill calls one of his tests a "Civic Action Test," and the other "Information Test."   Many of the items in the information tests would probably be called vocabulary tests.   While the "Action" tests deal with activities, the basis of each item seems to be knowledge of "what to do," or "how."   The test does not give a measure of "civic action" meaning conduct or behavior.   Rather it tells the teacher whether or not a child knows what to do in a given situation.   The tests seem very suggestive to teachers. The number of situations in actual life is of course much greater than the ones included in the test.   It would seem possible to make much greater use of this form of test, not only for civics in the field of community government, but also within the school community.

In recent years much emphasis has been placed upon organizing the school as a community in which citizenship is to be practiced *now*.   Do pupils know what to do in various school situations which arise?   If the school and the community are to be looked upon as places in which citizenship is to be practiced, it is clear that certain knowledges will be necessary.   Tests measuring such knowledges might be employed in helpful ways.   Particularly would such tests be helpful in promoting self-appraisal on the part of children.

### HILL CIVIC ACTION TEST[1]

(   ) 1. You have a pet dog for which you must secure a license.

---

[1] *Hill Civics Tests.*   Public School Publishing Company, Bloomington, Illinois.

To get the license you would apply to:

*a.* The coroner or his assistants.

*b.* A policeman or the sheriff.

*c.* The county clerk or the city clerk.

*d.* An officer of the health department.

### 3. *Thought tests*

The term "thought tests" is loosely used. Probably there is little agreement on what is meant by "thinking." Teachers speak of training pupils to "think," but the exact meaning is a different matter. There seems to be agreement on the position that social-studies instruction should not consist entirely of fact knowledge. Many other outcomes are desired. The exact nature of the outcomes is not always clear. It is not surprising, therefore, to find that a study of tests so far prepared in the field of "civic thinking" should reveal considerable variation in test construction. Perhaps it should be stated that some of the tests are not "thought tests" at all. Teachers appreciate the need of tests which measure something besides fact knowledge. For this reason, every new test is received with cordial interest in the hope that it may suggest practicable techniques for measuring some of the more intangible outcomes of social-studies instruction.

**The Brown-Woody Civics Test.** This test has a section called "Civic Thinking." The section from the test given on page 458 will make clear the principle upon which the test is based. Examination of the test will also suggest how easily the various factors, such as thought and attitude, may be confused. If the pupil marks the items below correctly shall we conclude that his processes of thought or reasoning are such that by means of them he arrives at the real reason why a citizen should give information about the whereabouts of a criminal to the police? Or are we to conclude that a correct answer merely indicates that the pupil knows what the correct answer should be? What evidence have we, if any, as to the motive which would actually move the pupil to notify the police, or even as to whether or not the pupil would notify the police? These questions are not raised in disparagement of the test. This test has been and will continue to be useful. Without doubt it is a measure of certain types of civic knowledge. Whether and to what extent it is a measure of "thinking" is perhaps another question.

BROWN–WOODY CIVICS TEST [1]

Form A. For Grades 7 to 12

PART III. CIVIC THINKING

SECTION 2

DIRECTIONS. Read this paragraph and the five statements under it. Then draw a circle around the number of the statement that gives the best answer to the question asked in the paragraph. Proceed with the other paragraphs in the same manner.

---

*Begin here.*

1. Suppose that a sensational hold-up has been staged by three masked bandits in which $10,000 worth of stocks, bonds, and valuable papers have been stolen from a bank in the heart of the city. In the chase that ensued after the discovery of the robbery, one policeman was fatally wounded and another seriously injured by bullets from the guns of the bandits. Suppose that you know that the bandits have taken refuge in a house in your neighborhood. As a citizen, why should you give this information to the police?

1. Your own life is in danger.
2. Your home may be robbed of valuables.
3. You have always feared bandits.
4. Criminals against society should be restrained.
5. You may receive a large reward.

**The Barr Diagnostic Test.** The Barr Diagnostic Test has a section which may be said to measure certain aspects of "thinking." For example, in the sample item given, the pupil is asked to select the statement which he considers most difficult to prove or to disprove. Without doubt certain forms of reflective thinking are involved here; that is, unless the pupil answers by mere guess. The pupil might seek to classify the statements as to facts or mere opinions. There may be efforts at evaluation. It would appear that this type of test is suggestive to teachers in the development of informal tests measuring the pupil's ability to evaluate material.

Test V probably measures ability to interpret facts. If great emphasis is to be placed in the social studies upon intelligent interpretation of facts, movements, and events, it would appear that the type of measurement illustrated in this section of the Barr Test would take on great importance. Teachers will readily think of other sets of facts which can be subjected to similar treatment in test construction.

BARR DIAGNOSTIC TEST IN AMERICAN HISTORY [1]

TEST III

2. Put a cross (X) before two of the following statements that you consider the most difficult to prove or disprove.

(a) The battle of Gettysburg was fought July, 1863.

(b) The Spanish-American War resulted in the growth of imperialism in the United States.

(c) Secretary Chase was ambitious to be nominated for president in the place of Lincoln in 1864.

(d) Taft was elected president in 1908.

---

[1] *Barr Diagnostic Test in American History*, by A. S. Barr, Public School Publishing Company, Bloomington, Illinois.

TEST V

1. The United States was at war in 1863, 1898 and 1917. In 1840, 90,000 immigrants came to America; in 1855, 430,000 immigrants came; in 1863, 100,000 immigrants came; in 1867, 350,000; in 1882, 788,000 came; in 1898, 225,000 came; in 1913, 1,200,000; in 1917, 200,000.

   Put a cross (X) before two of the following conclusions that might be drawn from the above facts.

   (a) Immigration into the United States increases during periods of war.

   (b) There has been a general increase in the immigration into the United States during the period 1840–1917.

   (c) War reduces immigration.

   (d) Immigration into the United States decreased during the period of 1840–1917.

   (e) The greater majority of the immigrants to the United States since 1900 came from southern and eastern Europe.

**Posey-Van Wagenen Geography Scales.** The Posey–Van Wagenen Tests in geography constitute another attempt to measure "thinking." A section from Thought Scale S is reproduced below. Perhaps the abilities measured in the different items are not always exactly alike. As an illustration an answer to the first item given involves a knowledge of the hemisphere in which Southern South America is located as well as the hemisphere in which our own continent is located. Perhaps knowledge plus application of knowledge is measured in this instance. In the third item given below it is difficult to see that anything beyond mere comprehension in reading is measured. In the case of the second item the pupil might give the correct answer from memory, that is, instead of reasoning from the facts given he might know what animals Kansas raises in large numbers.

It should be remembered, however, that this test does, in many of its items at least, measure the ability of pupils to see relationships between facts of geography. As such it is superior to tests which merely determine whether or not a pupil knows a given fact. There is need of more tests of this type which measure the ability of pupils to appreciate factual relationships.

### POSEY–VAN WAGENEN GEOGRAPHY SCALES[1]

#### THOUGHT S, DIVISION I

1. (55)

When it is winter here in the northern hemisphere it is summer in the southern hemisphere.

When it is winter here what season is it in the southern part of South America?

2. (56)

Kansas is one of the leading corn-producing states of the United States. Which of these animals would you expect to be raised in large numbers: sheep, hogs or goats?

3. (57)

The farther poleward we go from any place the colder it is likely to be. Petrograd is farther north than Moscow, and Moscow is farther north than Athens.

(a) Will a traveler be likely to find it coldest in winter in Moscow, Petrograd, or Athens?

### 4. Tests of "understanding"

The Pressey-Richards Tests on Understanding of American History. These tests represent a somewhat different example of efforts to measure "thinking." In the case of the test item shown here for illustrative purposes it is clear that the test seeks to measure the extent to which pupils have correctly appraised historical characters. It is true, of course, that a pupil might mark William Penn as *diplomatic* merely because of bare fact knowledge, rather than because of an actual appraisal. It is hardly likely, however, that this would be true for all children. It should also be kept in mind that the method of teaching would have an important

[1] *Posey–Van Wagenen Geography Scales.* Public School Publishing Company, Bloomington, Illinois.

effect on the value of this test. If teaching has emphasized mere knowledge of facts pupils might be expected to be more likely to answer the questions in terms of memory than if the emphasis has been upon providing a rich background of information about the characters. Coupled with the appropriate type of teaching this test would therefore seem to be of considerable value.

### PRESSEY–RICHARDS TEST ON UNDERSTANDING OF AMERICAN HISTORY

#### TEST 1: CHARACTER JUDGMENT [1]

DIRECTIONS: In each of the lines below there is the name of some man prominent in American History. This name is printed in capitals at the beginning of the line. Following the name there are four adjectives printed in small letters. You are to draw a line under the adjective that you think BEST describes the man whose name appears at the beginning of the list. The first list has been correctly marked; "courageous" gives the best description of Columbus of any of the adjectives after his name, so it has been underlined. Do not underline more than one adjective in any list.

1. COLUMBUS: cowardly   proud   <u>courageous</u>   rich

2. WILLIAM PENN: tricky   hesitant   carefree   diplomatic
3. ROGER WILLIAMS: self-seeking   suspicious   fearless   bad
4. BENJAMIN FRANKLIN: emotional   retiring
    prudent       blunt
5. PATRICK HENRY: hesitant   fiery   profound   dignified

### 5. Attitude tests

The measurement of attitudes presents serious difficulties. Examination of some of the tests of this type which have appeared will make clear some of the difficulties involved.

**The Hill Civic Attitudes Test.** This test is an example of this type. In the second item of the test shown on page 463

[1] *Pressey–Richards Test on Understanding of American History.* Public School Publishing Company, Bloomington, Illinois.

is one to conclude that a correct answer means that the pupil actually has the correct attitude, or merely that he knows what the correct attitude is? Will the boy in actual practice "knock at the door and offer to pay for the window," or does he merely know that this is what he should do? While this may be true it must still be admitted that the tests have value, if nothing else, as measures of knowledge.

### Hill Civic Attitudes Test[1]

1. In using public property, the good citizen should:
   a. Handle it carelessly because he does not own it.
   b. Take as good care of it as if it were his own.
   c. Use it so as to get the greatest amount of fun and enjoyment out of it.
   d. Take better care of it than if he owned it because it belongs to others.
2. You are playing ball with two friends. When you are "at bat," you knock the ball through a window. In this case:
   a. Knock at the door and offer to pay for the window.
   b. Run away as fast as you can so that no one will see you.
   c. Tell the owner that one of your comrades hit the ball.
   d. Tell the owner to call your father on the phone and talk to him.

**The Northwestern University Citizenship Tests.** Those who have prepared tests measuring attitude or traits of character have recognized the difficulty of getting reactions which actually represented pupil attitudes. Among the efforts of this type may be mentioned the Northwestern University Citizenship Tests. As is apparent from the sample which follows these tests tend to throw the pupil off his guard in two ways. In the first place, he is told that some of the items are probably of little importance. In the second place, "blinds" having no significance whatever are interspersed with the items actually used for measurement. Thus the pupil may not be conscious of just what is being measured by the test.

[1] *Hill Civics Tests.* Public School Publishing Company, Bloomington, Illinois.

## SAMPLE SECTIONS FROM NORTHWESTERN UNIVERSITY CITIZENSHIP TESTS

### I THINK IT IS —

| | very, very important | quite important | of some importance | quite unimportant | of no importance |
|---|---|---|---|---|---|
| 1. To wear colors in your clothing that match well | ........ | ........ | ........ | ........ | ........ |
| 2. To avoid coarse, incorrect speech and bad manners | ........ | ........ | ........ | ........ | ........ |

### I WOULD —

| | feel very, very much pleased | feel pleased | not care one way or the other | feel sorry | feel very, very sorry |
|---|---|---|---|---|---|
| If my best friend — | | | | | |
| 1. when his problems were too hard for him handed in as his own some his sister did for him. | ........ | ........ | ........ | ........ | ........ |
| 2. one day when he got home from the store found he was five cents short on change; the next day at the school cafeteria the cashier gave him five cents too much change; he thought a little of keeping it, but returned it to the cashier. | ........ | ........ | ........ | ........ | ........ |

One of the problems in connection with tests of this type is their subjectivity. Mature, superior adults would probably not rank the items in the same way. It is difficult to appraise the importance of the items correctly.

### B. DIAGNOSIS IN ACQUIRING SKILLS

**Demands made on the acquiring skills.** Social-studies instruction as it is being conducted in many schools makes heavy demands upon the skills and abilities of pupils. A large amount of varied reading is required. The reading material is varied not only in subject-matter, but in style and difficulty as well. Pupils are asked to read maps, graphs, diagrams, tables, and charts of many kinds. They must also be able to get the thought from the reading materials. They are called upon to interpret and evaluate materials. Only a few of the demands made upon pupils by social-studies instruction have been mentioned. It would seem obvious that if the pupil is to succeed in the social studies he must be in possession of an adequate series of *acquiring* skills. Diagnosis should take account of measurement of such skills. A pupil may fail in the social studies, not because of factors in the material or presentation of the social-studies subject-matter, but because he is unable to read or interpret the materials provided.

It was pointed out in the chapter on Diagnosis and Remedial Work in Reading that an effective reading program would make of every teacher a teacher of reading. It seems reasonable to expect that among the skills necessary for achievement in the social studies, reading skills will occupy a prominent place. At the present time scientific data are not available as to the importance of any single reading skill in achievement in any social-science subject. However, if in the preparation of a history lesson a pupil is forced to use, let us say, the table of contents, and if at the same time he does not know how to use a table of contents, difficulties are almost certain to arise. The pupil must know how to do the things he is asked to do, or if not he must learn how before he can succeed in the larger enterprise of learning in which he is engaged. To many persons this may seem a platitude. The facts are, however, that even high-school students often lack ability to use a table of contents or an index, as well as other skills frequently demanded in social-studies instruction.[1]

**Relation to reading tests.** To describe completely all methods of diagnosis in the *acquiring skills* would involve a repetition of much material in other chapters. For this reason only a few illustrative materials will be given here, and the reader is referred especially to the chapter on Diagnostic and Remedial Teaching in Reading.

## 1. *Diagnosis of vocabulary difficulties*

**The vocabulary-load.** Inability to succeed in the social studies might be due to lack of knowledge of the technical vocabulary employed in the social studies. To whatever extent pupils are called upon to secure information in social studies from printed materials, it might be assumed that vocabulary would be an important factor in success. From a teaching point of view the vocabulary problem takes at least two forms. In the first place, it is desirable that the vocabulary-load of the materials of instruction be within the comprehension of the pupils for whom the materials are intended. In the second place, the teacher faces the problem of helping pupils to acquire the vocabulary needed for success in any field. Studies of the vocabulary-loads of various textbooks

---

[1] Leavitt, Charles E. *The Relation Between Certain Reading Skills and Achievement in European History.* Unpublished master's thesis. Northwestern University Library.

indicate that there is much variation in the terminology used in different books.[1]

The variations in the vocabularies of different types of materials serve to make the task of the teacher more difficult. Especially is this true under the more modern methods of teaching where pupils consult a large variety of materials in the preparation of their assignments.[2] It would appear that increase in the use of these methods would make larger demands upon the pupil's vocabulary. Probably the complex problem of diagnosing the pupil's difficulties in vocabulary will never be solved by standardized tests. There are, however, some standardized tests which employ techniques of test construction which are suggestive of further work along this line.

**The Pressey-Richards Test.** An illustration of a vocabulary test is that included in the Pressey–Richards Test on Understanding of American History. Unlike the Brown–Woody Test, the Pressey–Richards Test includes the words to be defined in questions. Several alternate answers are supplied in phrase form from which the child is asked to choose. This form of test response would seem to be of value in testing children on the meaning of words for which synonyms are not readily available. An illustration is available in the section from the test shown below. For example, the word *stockade* might be said to be a barrier. It is, however, a barrier for a particular purpose. The form of the test makes it possible to include the purpose.

There is need of other tests based upon different aspects of the vocabulary problem and calling for different types of responses. Teachers will find it desirable to develop techniques whereby such tests may be constructed in terms of the needs of local teaching procedures.

---

[1] Pressey, Luella. *The Technical Vocabularies of the Public School Subjects: History.* Public School Publishing Company, 1924.

[2] Morrison, H. C. *The Practice of Teaching in Secondary Schools.* University of Chicago Press.

DIRECTIONS: On the page below there are some questions. Each question is followed by four answers; only one of these answers is right. You are to find the right answer and draw a line under it. The first question has been correctly answered.

1. What is a stockade?
   A part of a gun          A supply of ammunition
   A public punishment      <u>A barrier for defense</u>

2. What is an envoy?
   A transport    Spy     Diplomatic Agent     Bill

3. What is a dynasty?
   A ruling family          An earthquake
   An electrical appliance  A league of nations

## 2. Tests on the reading of social-studies materials

It is conceded that different reading skills and abilities are required for reading different types of materials.[2] Recognition of this fact has led test makers to prepare reading tests in terms of particular types of materials.

**The Barr Diagnostic Test in American History.** The test is designed to determine the extent to which the pupil is able to get the thought from reading of historical material. As would be expected the abilities which the tests attempt to measure are very complex. The author evidently recognized this fact since he provided several types of response for each paragraph read.

**The Van Wagenen Reading Scale in History.** The Van Wagenen Reading Scale in History measures somewhat different abilities from those measured by the Barr Diagnostic Test. The type of response provided for would indicate

[1] *Pressey–Richards Test on Understanding of American History.* Public School Publishing Company, Bloomington, Illinois.

[2] O'Brien, John A. *Reading, Its Psychology and Pedagogy,* chapter 5.

that the Van Wagenen tests measure accuracy of interpretation in detailed aspects of reading. They do not measure the general idea brought out in the paragraph, but rather ability to note details.

### 3. *Study of pupil difficulties*

**McCallister's list.** Another approach to the problem of diagnosis and remedial instruction has been made through a study of the reading difficulties which pupils encounter in the social studies.[1] It is only recently that such investigations have been carried on in the social studies, although in arithmetic a great many such studies have been made. By observation of the pupil's study procedures McCallister developed a list of reading difficulties in American History on the high-school level. At the same time he also made the analysis for mathematics and general science. The list of difficulties quoted below, however, contains only those which are typical of the work in American History.

While McCallister does not suggest specific remedial devices, he does indicate certain general lines along which such work may be carried on:

1. Pupils may be trained in the methods of attack required by the reading activities.
2. Pupils may be trained to recognize relations and to perform the various forms of thinking required by the activities.
3. Pupils may be led to recognize shortcomings in their previous training and to adopt practices of review in order to secure information requisite to the understanding of new materials.
4. Pupils may be taught to overcome difficulties with the vocabulary when they are encountered.
5. Pupils may be led to sense the necessity for accurate interpretation.

[1] McCallister, James M. "Reading Difficulties in Studying Content Subjects"; in *The Elementary School Journal*, vol. 31, pp. 191–202. (November, 1930.)

This study emphasizes the need for a direct approach to the solution of reading difficulties through effective guidance of the study activities of pupils.  McCallister lists three steps in this process:

1. Analysis of the techniques of teaching and of the materials assigned for the purpose of determining the reading activities required.
2. Identification of the pupil's difficulties in performing the reading activities.
3. Organization of a procedure of guidance adapted to the needs of the class.

The approach suggested in this study is significant in that it is concerned only with the actual reading which the pupil does in his study activities.  No special exercises are set up. The plan is to attack the difficulties as they arise in the regular study activities.  It may perhaps be assumed that this plan would hardly be effective unless provision is made for some time spent in study in the classroom under teacher guidance.  Specific methods of remedying the difficulties must also be developed.  It remains to be seen whether a similar study in lower grades would show that the difficulties are the same for lower-grade pupils.  McCallister's approach, however, is very suggestive of methods which could be used by teachers for the purpose of securing an inventory of the difficulties faced by pupils in studying any content subject.

### READING DIFFICULTIES ENCOUNTERED BY PUPILS IN STUDYING AMERICAN HISTORY
#### (McCallister)

1. Reading difficulties growing out of pupils' methods of attack:
   Comprehension of only part of passage shown by omission of points of major importance
   Failure to use given references in locating materials

Failure to use statement of minimal essentials as a guide to reading

Copying material from textbook without interpreting it

Failure to recognize problem caused by careless reading

Failure to select materials pertinent to problem caused by partial reading of assigned passage

Use of previous knowledge instead of assigned passage in reacting to problem

2. Reading difficulties caused by inability to recognize relations:

Failure to recognize relation of reference materials to problem

Failure to discriminate between relevant and irrelevant material

Inability to recognize relations among items in statement of minimal essentials

Inability to interpret mimeographed statement of minimal essentials in light of major problem of unit

Failure to recognize relative values shown by substitution of a general statement for specific points of importance

Lack of critical reading shown by failure to discriminate between historical facts and mere probabilities

3. Reading difficulties arising from lack of knowledge of subject-matter: (none listed for American History)

4. Reading difficulties caused by deficiencies in vocabulary:

Misunderstanding of instructional materials caused by misinterpretation of vocabulary

Inability to interpret instructional materials caused by lack of understanding of vocabulary

5. Reading difficulties caused by inaccuracies:

Misunderstanding of essential point in unit caused by inaccuracy in interpreting reference materials

Misreading technical words shown by errors in spelling

6. Reading difficulties arising from lack of clearness in directions given to pupils:

Misinterpretation of problem caused by arrangement of directions

### 4. *Problems in measuring ability to read social-studies material*

**Importance of the reading skills.** The illustrations drawn from the tests just described bring out some of the problems of diagnosis in ability to read particular types of material. While the Barr test does, for example, attempt to measure specific abilities, the number of different abilities tested is probably entirely too limited. Unless measuring instruments are provided which sample a considerable number of the abilities demanded in reading a given selection, the teacher has no way of knowing *why* the pupil failed to make a satisfactory score on the test. In fact the real reason for failure may not be included in the test at all.

The work which has thus far been done in reading indicates that reading is dependent upon a large number of specific skills and abilities. One list of such skills (see page 250) includes 42 specific items. While such lists of abilities have been prepared for work-type reading in general, it is probably a safe assumption that the skills required for successful study through reading in the social studies are no less complex.

**Abilities involved in social-studies mastery.** For example, there is given on the pages which follow a list of abilities which may be involved in successful achievement in the social studies. No doubt many other abilities are important. The list is presented without any data as to the relative importance of the different items. If teachers believe that these abilities are of importance to pupils in studying social-studies materials they may prepare tests to cover them.

SOME ABILITIES WHICH MAY BE INVOLVED IN ACHIEVEMENT
IN THE SOCIAL STUDIES

**A.** Ability to locate material quickly
   1. Knowledge of and ability to use an index
   2. Ability to use a table of contents
   3. Ability to use a dictionary
   4. Ability to use library files

5. Ability to use reference materials
6. Ability to use maps, tables, graphs, charts
7. Ability to skim

B. Ability to comprehend quickly what is read
1. A vocabulary of accurate meanings in the various social-studies fields
2. Ability to grasp the meaning of sentences

C. Ability to select and evaluate materials
1. Judging the validity of information
2. Finding data on a single subject from a variety of sources
3. Ability to determine whether or not certain materials answer a given question
4. Ability to select essential and non-essential material
5. Ability to find solutions to problems with the help of reading materials

D. Ability to organize what is read
1. Ability to outline
2. Ability to summarize

E. Ability to remember what is read

F. A knowledge of the best sources of materials

**An illustrative test.** To illustrate the skills demanded, a test is given herewith that may be used to locate specific skills, and to determine how effectively the pupils can use these skills in their social-science studies.

### ABILITY TO USE INDEX

Test: *Essentials of Geography,* Books I and II, Brigham and McFarlane

1. Ability to locate information when key word is stated as main topic in index:
   Which of the topics listed below do you find in your text? Draw a line under the topics that are discussed.

   Montana   Black Hills   sponges   weather bureau   rubber
      almonds   marble   sardines   ocean cables

2. Ability to locate information when key word is stated as subtopic in index:

On what pages will you find information on the following topics?

> Middle Atlantic cities, pages ......
> navigation of Great Lakes, pages ......
> climate of state of Washington, pages ......
> shape of earth, pages ......
> forests of South America, pages ......

3. Ability to locate information when main and sub-topics are specifically stated:

In questions listed below underline the key word which you find in the index:

Draw two lines under the important key word.

Draw one line under the less important key word or subtopic.

1. What are the important industries of Europe?

2. Describe the coast line of Maine.

3. Shall we find summer resorts in the New England States?

4. Is coal mined in Great Britain?

5. Give an account of the early history of California.

4. Ability to locate information when main and sub-topics are not specifically stated:

On what pages will you find information to answer the following questions?

1. Who helps to protect the trees from fire? pages ......

2. To what extent does New Jersey contribute to the food supply of the nation? pages ......

3. Describe the advance of civilization among the people of Asia, pages ......

4. To what extent does the Mississippi River aid in the growth of industries? pages ......

5. Does the United States export any of its products to other countries? pages ......

## III. REMEDIAL WORK IN THE SOCIAL STUDIES

It is evident from the foregoing discussion that remedial work in the social studies becomes a more difficult and less exact procedure than would be the case in a subject such as arithmetic. In the four fundamental operations in arithmetic it is possible to inventory the pupil's ability and to prescribe needed practice with a measure of specificity. Social-studies outcomes are difficult to inventory, and even when measured we do not know what procedures to follow in order to overcome deficiencies in all cases. Some progress has been made, however, and it will be the purpose of this section to illustrate some of the more promising techniques. Perhaps the following lines of activity are most suggestive:

A. Motivation through purposeful activities.
B. Specific remedial teaching designed to overcome deficiencies in the skills necessary to do successful work in the social studies, e.g., reading.
C. Methods for overcoming deficiencies in such outcomes as fact knowledge, understanding or attitudes.
D. Procedures for stimulating and directing the reading of social-studies materials.

### A. MOTIVATION THROUGH PURPOSEFUL ACTIVITIES

Without doubt a great many of the difficulties encountered by pupils would be readily overcome if proper motivation were provided. Recent educational philosophy assumes motivation to be most effective when learning activity proceeds as a "purposeful life experience." [1] In this case the felt needs of children become the principal motivating influence in learning. On page 442 an example of such a teaching procedure is given. The following list of activities of teachers in carrying on purposeful activities is supplied merely because it may be helpful to teachers.

[1] Kilpatrick, William Heard. *The Foundations of Method.*

I. *Preparation for the project*
   A. By the teacher
      1. Study of children's interest and needs
      2. Survey of subject-matter and abilities to be developed
   B. By pupils and teacher together
      1. Possible projects growing out of this survey
      2. Anticipation of procedure and establishment of goal
      3. Gathering materials, books, and other necessary equipment
   C. Stimulation of pupils to purposeful activity

II. *Discovering the present status of the pupils*
   A. Attempts by the teacher to measure
      1. Abilities and purposes
      2. Attitudes and ideals
   B. Informal or standard tests of knowledge and information
   C. Use of the results in guiding emphasis in teaching

III. *Assignment of work through planning by teacher and pupils*
   A. By children themselves because of stimulation of purposes
   B. By teacher, through assisting pupils to select tasks by
      1. Questions
      2. Problems
   C. By using a course of study planned to show the ultimate outcomes of the projects

IV. *Supervision of activities of the pupils*
   A. Provision for purposing throughout the whole unit
   B. Help in planning
   C. Guidance in execution of plans
   D. Guidance in formulation of judgments
   E. Help in generalization
   F. Elimination of undesirable conditions in the learning situation
   G. Provision for further purposing growing out of activity

V. *Supervision of study*

    A. Assistance in solution of problems or carrying out assignments by

        1. Answering questions

        2. Helping to find material

        3. Suggestions as to methods of study

        4. Specific training in how to study

        5. Discovering difficulties in studying

        6. Training children to help each other

VI. *Remedial assistance*

    A. Interpretation of the results of tests

    B. Study of individual differences

    C. Analysis of specific difficulties

    D. Individual assistance

    E. Assistance in groups

    F. Training children to help each other

VII. *Activities at the close of the project*

    A. Discovering the amount of growth by

        1. Standard tests of knowledge and skills

        2. Teacher's tests

        3. Attempts to determine growth in attitudes, ideals, and in the power to purpose

    B. Comparison of results with initial tests

    C. Interpretations of results to determine evidences of growth

    D. Use of results in building future plans

    E. Conservation of results of the work through generalizations

    F. Evidences of the effect on the life of the child outside the school

VIII. Report of results of projects to conserve progress made and suggest the use of similar projects by other teachers

### B. SPECIFIC INSTRUCTION IN ACQUIRING SKILLS

**How to teach the necessary skills.** Assuming that a number of the skills necessary to successful work in the social studies are known, the next step would be to develop means whereby such skills may be taught to pupils. In the studies reviewed below an attempt has been made to carry out this procedure. The studies are presented because of their suggestive character.

### 1. *Teaching pupils to outline*

**Barton's study.**    Barton undertook to evaluate outlining as a study procedure.[1]   He raises the question, "Does a pupil learn more facts if he systematically and thoroughly outlines the subject-matter assigned for study?"   In five experimental groups ninety-four pupils in high schools were taught to study portions of the textbook by careful outlining procedures, while an equal number of pupils in control groups did not use these outlining procedures.   The achievements of the two groups were compared, and the experimental groups which had followed the outlining procedure showed a significant superiority.   In view of the fact that the outlining methods followed in the experiment appeared to be effective it seems worth while to describe them more fully.

**What does outlining involve?**   Barton points out that any job analysis of the process of outlining would probably suggest the following activities as essential in teaching outlining:

1. A study of the methods of notation used in outlining.
2. The acquiring of the concepts major, subordinate, or minor, coördinate, and irrelevant.
3. A study of "sentence" and "topical" outlines.
4. A study of the different means employed by a writer to indicate the "core" or "central" idea of a single paragraph or that of a series of paragraphs, for example:
    a. Topic sentence
    b. Topic phrase

[1] Barton, William Alexander.   *Outlining as a Study Procedure.*   Teachers College Contributions to Education, no. 411.

    *c.* Topic suggested or implied in the content of the paragraph

    *d.* "Key" sentence, or phrase, embodied in a paragraph which develops a paragraph topic which is itself a subdivision of a big topic in the whole selection

    *e.* Introductory paragraph

    *f.* Summary paragraph

5. A study of the kinds of "guideposts" used by a writer to indicate the plan or structure of his thinking:

    *a.* Numerical

    *b.* Verbal

    *c.* Typographical (italics, capitals, etc.)

It seems well to offer at this point the suggestion, " Do not let the search for 'guideposts' draw attention away from, or actually conceal, the writer's thought."

**Specific exercises suggested.** The preceding list of activities seems to suggest the following specific exercises as basic to the acquirement of skill in making an outline.

1. Exercises in identifying only the major points or ideas in the material read.

2. Exercises in identifying only the topic of the paragraph.

3. Exercises in observing digressions from the main point of a paragraph or a big topic in an extended unit of reading. (Some digressions are relevant; some, however, are irrelevant and unwarranted. The ability to identify digressions will assist in the identification of major points and overcome the tendency to include irrelevant ideas in the outline.)

4. Exercises in determining the method or the combination of methods by which a paragraph is developed, for example, by

    *a.* Proof

    *b.* Repetition

    *c.* Explanation

    *d.* Details

    *e.* Illustration

    *f.* Cause and result

5. Exercises in identifying the ways in which an author indicates the structure of his thought, for example:

    *a.* Topic sentence

    *b.* Topic phrase

    *c.* Introductory paragraph
    *d.* Summarizing paragraph

6. Exercises in identifying the topic sentence or the topic phrase which, although it is included in the paragraph, serves solely to indicate a big topic, or a major point, of which the paragraph topic is a subdivision.

7. Exercises in abstracting the topic of a paragraph which is only suggested or implied by the content of the paragraph.

8. Exercises in identifying the "guideposts" frequently used to indicate the structure of a writer's thought, for example:
    *a.* Numerical
    *b.* Verbal
    *c.* Typographical

9. Exercises in comparing ready-made outlines with the subject-matter which they represent. The purpose of this exercise is the identification of the thought-bases of the outline.

10. Exercises in completing skeleton outlines placed in the hands of pupils. The completion should give practice in
    *a.* Supplying a generalized topic or statement appropriate to a major division, or a minor subdivision of thought.
    *b.* Supplying the missing subordinate elements for indicated divisions of thought.

11. Exercises in which the pupil is guided in discovering specific thought-relationships of ideas.

12. Exercises in which the pupil discovers thought-relationships independently.

13. Practice in evaluating ideas according to clearly defined and easily understood criteria. (It is the use of an idea that determines its value in the thought-structure. Ideas used in the same way should be treated identically in the outline.)

14. Exercises in discovering thought-relationships revealed by the structure of a sentence.

15. Practice in organizing, in a meaningful outline, the subject-matter of disconnectedly written textbooks.

16. Practice in using the table of contents to get a meaningful and unified impression of the whole or of a part of a textbook.

17. Examination with new-type tests to discover the pupil's understanding of the principles of outlining as revealed by his ability to apply them to subject-matter included in the tests.

18. Practice in condensing the successive paragraphs of a chapter or a magazine article, each in a single sentence, without attempting to organize them into an outline.

19. Practice in condensing successive paragraphs each in a single sentence, underscoring the important items, and putting the subsidiary items in parentheses.
20. Practice in marking in some appropriate chapter, or magazine article, all the transitional phrases or sentences that introduce important divisions.
21. Practice, with the help of the text, in restoring the original organization of the thought, the elements of the organization being totally confused in materials supplied to the pupil. That is, using a well-organized set of notes as material, have the items mimeographed in uniform succession (for example, with the same indentation or without any indentation) thus obliterating all evidence of any organization. Distribute copies to the class and have the pupils rewrite the notes, restoring the original organization as far as possible from evidence of the text.

**Elements in teaching pupils to outline.** The above list of studies and exercises in outlining indicates that many elements are involved in developing ability to outline. Barton also describes, in considerable detail, the teaching methods employed. Several types of lessons were used, including the following:

1. Finding the main point of a paragraph
2. Matching main points with paragraphs
3. Making an outline
4. Making outlines for paragraphs
5. Making a detailed outline of a paragraph
6. Finding the supporting details for the main point of a paragraph
7. Using an outline in a problem assignment
8. Finding the facts to support an opinion
9. Filling in an outline
10. Making notes for a report
11. Finding the big topics or ideas in what you read

Lack of space prevents complete presentation of these illustrative lessons.

## 2. *Teaching pupils to summarize*

**Newlun's experiment.**    Newlun sought to determine whether "ability to summarize the important facts in lessons, chapters, phases, etc., of history increases achievement of fifth-grade pupils in history or in reading." [1]    He states the results of his experiment as follows:

### TEACHING PUPILS TO SUMMARIZE

1. Most children typified by the subjects in this experiment can be taught to summarize in history by devoting a portion of their class period to this training for a period of twelve weeks or less.
2. The effect of teaching children to summarize in history varies.
3. Summarizing in history, if properly developed and used, can improve the achievement in history more than ordinary study to prepare for topical or question-answer recitations of the kinds used by teachers in this experiment.
4. Summarizing used as a method of study in history does not guarantee an increase of achievement in history over ordinary study procedure, if the skill is not developed to a sufficient degree, even though the children have a significant amount of skill.
5. A moderate degree of skill in summarizing in history used regularly in studying history will probably increase achievement in the mastery of facts and information in history over ordinary study procedure.
6. A fairly high degree of skill in summarizing in history used regularly as a study procedure seems sure to increase achievement in the mastery of facts and information in history over ordinary ways of studying.
7. The use of summarizing as a method of study in history will not be likely to affect achievement in reading to any significant extent.
8. The use of a portion of the class time in history to teach children to summarize historical information offers no hazard to the achievement of the children in other respects.
9. The effect of a cessation of practice seems to be the same in summarizing as in other skills.

[1] Newlun, Chester Otto.    *Teaching Children to Summarize in Fifth-Grade History*.    Teachers College Contributions to Education, no. 404.

SUMMARIZING A STUDY SKILL

1. Summarizing is a desirable study skill.
2. Children in a grade as low as the fifth can be successfully taught to summarize in history by using only a portion of their class time.
3. The most important skill in summarizing is the ability to distinguish between the important and the less important for the purpose in mind.
4. Summarizing can under certain circumstances readily become a mechanical process in which children may depend upon such props as remembering lists of important points selected by others, certain keys of the author such as questions at the end of chapters, marginal headings, and the like. The result is that their training is only in skill required to put such items together in the order in which they have been memorized.
5. Summarizing done as described in 4 above will probably not cause any appreciable improvement over ordinary study.
6. Summarizing is most effective when it is entirely the result of the pupils' own thinking, provided the pupils are guided in such a way as to develop the ability to do the kind of thinking necessary.
7. Children develop the skill to summarize more quickly and more effectively if the process challenges them; i.e., the greater their interest or readiness for the training the more rapidly and the more effectively will the skill be attained.
8. It is probably more difficult to attain skill in making oral summaries than in making written summaries. This may be due to an oral-English difficulty.
9. Best ways of training children to summarize effectively need to be found by experimentation.

**Methods used.** In carrying on the experiment the co-operating teachers were supplied with an outline for a tentative procedure for teaching pupils to summarize. This outline is given below:

OUTLINE FOR TENTATIVE PROCEDURE FOR TEACHING PUPILS TO SUMMARIZE

1. Require pupils to prepare for a selected portion of subject-matter (this will be dominantly, but possibly not entirely,

selected portions of reading material), during the first two weeks.

    *a.* A good title or the name of the subject covered.

    *b.* A required number of principal or most important facts in their proper order.

    *c.* A written summary based on (*a*) and (*b*).

2. Use the ten-minute period in making sure that the pupils know what is meant by a summary, and in pupil and teacher discussion of the summaries prepared to evaluate their merit and worth. Teach pupils how to make a good summary.

3. During the second two weeks, the assignment will call for preparation of written summaries without designating the number of facts to be included.

4. During the next two or three weeks, the assignment will call for preparation of oral summaries.

5. During the remainder of the twelve-week period, the procedure will follow a plan agreed upon in conference between the teacher and me.

6. Use with the experimental group, in teaching summaries, the test-teach-test technique. It might well follow the procedure of having pupils develop a summary on one day and write this summary the next day. The following day a new summary can be developed and the next day the pupils should be again required to make this summary and so on. The giving of oral summaries can take the place of written ones after facility in written summaries has been achieved.

7. Require the summaries to be based on larger units of work, a chapter, a period, or a movement, etc., as soon as possible.

8. This tentative procedure may be varied at any time by conferring with me.

9. At the end of the twelve-week period the pupils should be able:

    *a.* To tell concisely and clearly how to make a summary.

    *b.* To write a good summary of any portion of historical subject-matter with which they are familiar.

    *c.* To give a concise and accurate oral summary of such material.

**The study of other skills.** While the studies in outlining and summarizing just referred to do not give teachers as specific assistance as many would desire, yet they suggest what might be done in many skills or abilities which enter into successful achievement in the social studies. Enterprising teachers will be interested in studying the problem experimentally to determine the importance of the several abilities and the ways in which they function.

### C. REMEDYING DEFICIENCIES IN FACT KNOWLEDGE

**Teaching difficulties.** Thus far attention has been given to the problem of remedial work only as it concerns the skills or tools by which pupils carry on their work in the social studies. It is unfortunate that no well-developed procedures are available for remedying deficiencies in the various outcomes of the social studies. For example, if it is learned by means of a test that the pupil lacks a knowledge of facts no clear-cut procedure for remedying the difficulty is available. The traditional practice of teachers has been to ask such pupils to "study some more." Without doubt this is a makeshift. It is likely that the pupils' failure grows out of a lack of ability to "study," or some other cause which is frequently unknown. Attention has already been called to the great number of facts to be learned, and the difficulty of selecting the facts which are most important. When general fact-knowledge tests are given there is no way of knowing whether the pupil's lack of knowledge as shown by these tests is significant or not. There is no certainty that the tests include the facts which the pupil should know, or even the ones which have been taught in class. The pupil may thus fail merely because the teaching and testing have not covered the same ground.

### 1. *Workbooks to accompany texts*

The situation described above would seem to argue for measuring instruments developed in the classroom to fit the instructional process and materials followed. Essentially such tests would be curriculum tests, developed in terms of the curriculum followed by the teacher. If the teacher believes that the facts included in such tests are vital to success in the social studies she can hold pupils to mastery of such facts. Pupils who fail on the tests may be asked to re-read the materials, during which process the teacher may give attention to the reading or study difficulties of pupils.

**Rugg's Pupil's Workbook.** One of the best examples of this type of procedure is that found in the *Pupil's Workbook* to accompany *An Introduction to American Civilization.*[1] The textbook in this case is organized in large units. In the workbook each chapter in the text has been paralleled by a problem. The problem is developed in such a way that it includes instructions to the pupil, exercises, and texts.

If tests of this type are carefully prepared, covering the facts and other outcomes which the teacher desires to develop, it would appear that they can be made a very helpful device in diagnostic and remedial teaching. It must of course be remembered that many outcomes can as yet not be measured by these or any other known tests. In so far, however, as fact knowledge is a desired outcome these devices are helpful.

## 2. *Testing and drill devices*

**The Brueckner-Cutright Essential Location Exercises in Geography.** These test and drill devices illustrate an attempt to combine testing and drill materials. The tests are arranged on a card on one side of which is placed a test, and on the other side the drill exercise. The pupil looks at the name of the first city listed on the card. He then locates the city on the map, and writes the number marking the location

[1] Rugg, Harold O., and Mendenhall, James E. *Pupil's Workbook* to accompany *An Introduction to American Civilization.* Ginn and Company.

of the city on a piece of paper. He then places the numbers of the locations on his paper in the order in which they appear on the card. Having completed the test the pupil turns the card over and checks his answers with the key on the opposite side of the test.

He is now supplied with a study map on which the locations with both numbers and names are given. He has discovered with the help of the test what locations he does not know. He is provided with the means whereby he can learn the facts he did not know. The test can be repeated as often as necessary until the locations have been learned.

The preparation of the tests in their present form means that the cards can be used over and over again, since no marks are placed upon them. Since the cards are available covering a variety of location facts over wide geographic areas, their application is rather general.

From a diagnostic standpoint, the development of testing materials whereby the pupil can discover his own weaknesses is a highly desirable development. If, in addition, remedial exercises can be provided whereby the pupil's weaknesses can be overcome the teacher is supplied with much-needed assistance. There is need of development of many types of information tests which will be diagnostic in character. At the present time the teacher cannot depend very largely upon commercial tests. Very few of them are adapted to diagnostic purposes. At best they are suggestive of tests which can be prepared by the teacher himself.

## QUESTIONS FOR STUDY, DISCUSSION, AND REPORT

1. Why is it more difficult to make inventory tests in the social studies than in arithmetic?
2. What are some of the methods which have been used for determining the facts which should be taught in the social studies?
3. What relationship exists between knowledge of facts and ability to "think"?

4. What is the influence of the teacher's philosophy of education upon the problems of measurement in the social studies?
5. Many schools are employing methods which utilize a wide range of materials in books and magazines. How shall the pupils be tested on this reading? Is it always desirable to test them on such reading? Why?
6. How could a teacher determine the reading abilities and skills necessary to successful achievement in the social studies?
7. The measurement of attitudes is considered very difficult. Explain why this is true.
8. Have recent developments in teaching method increased or decreased the emphasis upon fact knowledge as an outcome? Give reasons for your answer.

## SELECTED REFERENCES

Ayer, Adelaide. *Some Difficulties in Elementary School History.* Columbia University Contributions to Education, no. 212. Teachers College, Columbia University, New York.

Barton, William Alexander. *Outlining as a Study Procedure.* Columbia University Contributions to Education, no. 411. Teachers College, Columbia University, New York.

Burton, William H., *The Supervision of Elementary School Subjects*, Chapters 7, 8, and 9. New York, D. Appleton and Company, 1929.

Gold, Mary S. "Testing Vocabulary in History"; in *The Historical Outlook*, vol. 17, pp. 285–91. (October, 1926.)

Kimmel, William Glenn. *The Management of the Reading Program in the Social Studies.* Bulletin of the Board of Education, New York City.

McCallister, James M. "Reading Difficulties in Studying Content Subjects"; in *The Elementary School Journal*, vol. 31, pp. 191–202. (November, 1930.)

McCallister, James M. "Guiding Pupils' Reading Activities in the Study of Content Subjects"; in *The Elementary School Journal*, vol. 31, pp. 271–85. (December, 1930.)

Mathews, C. O. *Grade Placement of Curriculum Materials in the Social Studies.* Columbia University Contributions to Education, no. 241. Teachers College, Columbia University, New York.

O'Dell, C. W. *Scales for Rating Pupil's Answers to Nine Types of*

*Thought Questions in American History.* Bureau of Educational Research, University of Illinois, April, 1927.

Newlun, Chester Otto. *Teaching Children to Summarize in Fifth-Grade History.* Columbia University Contributions to Education, no. 404. Teachers College, Columbia University, New York.

Ruch, G. M., and others. *Objective Examination Methods in the Social Studies.* Chicago, Scott, Foresman and Company, 1926.

Rugg, Harold O., and Hockett, John A. *Objective Studies in Map Location.* Social Science Monographs no. 1; Lincoln School, Teachers College, Columbia University, New York.

*Third Yearbook, Department of Superintendence, National Education Association,* Chapter VII.

## SOCIAL STUDIES TESTS CITED IN CHAPTER XII

| TEST | GRADES | PUBLISHER |
|---|---|---|
| Kepner Background Tests in Social Science | High School | Ginn & Co., New York. |
| Van Wagenen American History Scales | 5–6 | Public School Publishing Company, Bloomington, Ill. |
| Burton Civics Test | 5–9 | World Book Company, Yonkers-on-Hudson, N.Y. |
| Brown–Woody Civics Test | 7–12 | World Book Company, Yonkers-on-Hudson, N.Y. |
| Hill Civics Tests | 6–12 | Public School Publishing Company, Bloomington, Ill. |
| Barr Diagnostic Test in American History | 8–12 | Public School Publishing Company, Bloomington, Ill. |
| Posey–Van Wagenen Geography Scales | 5–8 | Public School Publishing Company, Bloomington, Ill. |
| Pressey–Richards Test of Understanding of American History | 6–12 | Public School Publishing Company, Bloomington, Ill. |
| Northwestern University Citizenship Tests | High school and College | Division of Research, School of Education Northwestern University, Evanston, Illinois. |
| Brueckner–Cutright Essential Location Exercises in Geography | 4–8 | Educational Test Bureau, Minneapolis, Minn. |

# CHAPTER XIII

## DIAGNOSIS AND REMEDIAL WORK IN CHARACTER EDUCATION

**New importance in recent years.** While character has always been one of the desired outcomes of education, the movement for effective character education has recently received greatly renewed emphasis.[1] There are probably many reasons for this renewed emphasis. There has recently been much concern about the so-called crime wave, especially as it involves young people.[2] While there seems to be considerable uncertainty in regard to actual conditions as to the prevalence of juvenile crime, still the widespread discussion of the problem has without doubt heightened interest in the general problem of preventing crime through more effective education for character.

There are those who believe that because of the decreasing influence of the home that the school must assume a larger residual function in character education. At the same time current educational philosophy stresses as basic the development of good character.[3] The development of character traits is one of the important concomitants of educational effort. The net result of the newer educational philosophy is to make the so-called character-education outcomes primary in any learning situation. The more traditional outcomes, such as the skills and knowledges acquired, come to be secondary. Without doubt these modifications in

[1] Bagley, W. C., and Kyte, C. C. *The California Curriculum Study*, pp. 240, 260–61, 269, 277.

[2] Vollmer, August. "The Prevention and Detection of Crime as Viewed by a Police Officer"; in *Annals, American Academy of Political and Social Science*, May, 1926, p. 149.

[3] Kilpatrick, William Heard. *The Foundations of Method.*

current educational philosophy are having much to do with the greater attention now being given to character education.

## I. OBJECTIVES OF CHARACTER EDUCATION

Perhaps no field of education is more intangible than that of character education. It is intangible because we do not know what kinds of teaching or life experiences make for good character. It is intangible further because we do not agree on what constitutes good character. We are further confused by a lack of generally accepted terminology, with the result that while on paper two schools may have the same character-education program, in reality the two may be very different.

**Meaning of character education.** The term *character* is given many meanings. Charters maintains that the term character should be applied only to the more fundamental of traits.[1] In this way *accuracy* would be termed a trait of personality, but not of character. A man may have good character and yet not be accurate. Accuracy is not a sufficiently fundamental trait. It follows, however, that the exact line of demarcation between traits of character and personality is difficult to draw.

Germane and Germane[2] define character education as follows:

Character education is a process through which the child learns to make wholesome social adjustments to his many perplexing life situations. Perplexing life situations are all those occasions in daily life which vex, disturb, and annoy because there is a conflict between what one impulsively wishes to do and what one is obligated to do. Wholesome social adjustments are those happy and successful ways and habits of responding which are beneficial both to oneself and to others.

[1] Charters, W. W. *The Teaching of Ideals*, 1927, p. 41.
[2] Germane, Chas. E., and Germane, Edith. *Character Education*, p. x. Silver, Burdett and Company, New York, 1929.

These authors also define character "as the sum total of one's ways of responding that have become fairly well established or set."

In the absence of objective or scientific data in regard to the objectives of character education, it is not unnatural that we have found it necessary to resort to personal opinion. In this way a variety of *codes* has arisen. The Hutchins, Boy Scout, and Stephens College Codes are examples.[1] While these various codes have their points of excellence, no one knows whether or not they are "right," or inclusive.

**Curriculum projects in character education.** Perhaps the best known of the efforts to set up objectives for character education is the Denver project directed by L. Thomas Hopkins. This list of traits is expressed in the form of ideals which underly "major activities of life." Each ideal is defined by synonyms or statements of clarification. The list follows:

THIRTY IDEALS UNDERLYING THE MAJOR ACTIVITIES OF LIFE[2]

1. Appreciation of beauty, people, humor
2. Adaptability — Ability to adjust, to alter so as to fit for new use; alertness; ability to respond to changing conditions
3. Courtesy — An act of kindness performed with politeness; affability; refinement
4. Coöperation — Concurrence in action; acting or operating jointly with others
5. Courage — That quality which enables one to encounter difficulties with firmness; pluck; valor
6. Desire for improvement — Pride in doing things well
7. Foresight — Act of looking forward; action in reference to the future; prudence
8. Generosity — Liberality in spirit or act
9. Good health, correct posture; cleanliness
10. Gratitude — Kindness awakened by favor received; thankfulness

[1] Hutchins, William J.  *Children's Code of Morals for Elementary Schools.* National Capitol Press, Washington, D.C.

[2] Charters, W. W.  *The Teaching of Ideals*, pp. 61–63.  By permission of The Macmillan Company, publishers.

11. Honesty — Fairness and straightforwardness of conduct, speech, etc.; integrity; sincerity; truthfulness; sense of honor
12. Happiness — The enjoyment or pleasurable satisfaction attendant upon welfare of any kind; mental and moral health and freedom from irksome care; cheerfulness; harmony
13. Industry — Habitual diligence in any employment or pursuit; concentration; steady attention to business; application
14. Initiative — Energy or aptitude displayed in the action that tends to develop new fields; self-reliance; originality; enterprise; resourcefulness; self-confidence
15. Judgment — The operation of the mind involving comparison; discrimination; sense of relative values; ability to decide rightly, justly, wisely; sense of proportion; deliberation
16. Morality — Conforming to the standard of right; righteousness; justice; virtue
17. Neatness — Orderliness; tidiness; systematic arrangement
18. Open-mindedness — Willingness to see two sides of a proposition; tentative judgment
19. Punctuality — Habit of keeping one's engagements at right time; promptness
20. Reponsibility — Ability to respond or answer for one's conduct or obligations; trustworthiness; accountability; dependability
21. Reverence — Deep respect for worthy accomplishment
22. Self-judgment — Self-improvement based on self-analysis
23. Self-control — Restraint exercised over one's self; modesty; calmness; temperance, self-command; inhibition
24. Sympathy — Fellow-feeling; tenderness; compassion; tolerance
25. Sociability — Companionability; friendliness; loyalty; desire for the company of others
26. Service to society — Civic consciousness; appreciation of existing institutions; respect for property of others
27. Tact — Discerning sense of what is right, proper; peculiar ability to deal with others without giving offense
28. Thoroughness — Determination to carry plans through every obstacle; perseverance; exactness
29. Thrift — Economy; frugality
30. Unselfishness

**Scientific studies.** In some curriculum fields efforts have been made to determine the content by activity analysis.

Thus far no organized efforts have been made to apply such techniques to the field of character education. As a result teachers must in the main rely on such lists as that prepared in Denver, or one of their own making. In other words, we must rely mainly on individual or group opinion.

**Complexity of outcomes.** The Denver list of ideals just given includes thirty which were selected from an original list of seventy-four. Merely a casual examination of the list of thirty suggests the complexity of the various outcomes in character education. Each of the ideals listed is a very complex concept which probably is affected, in any individual, by a great number of factors. For example, *appreciation* is probably dependent upon a large number of factors of native abilities, personal experiences, or emotional characteristics. Over many of these factors the school has as yet exercised little control.

Teachers who are confronted with these lists of ideals are likely to ask first how these ideals can be developed in the classroom. Few courses of study have thus far suggested very definitely means whereby the various outcomes in character education can be furthered. In part this is due to the fact that we do not know in detail what should be done to develop the various ideals. Moreover, there is great difference of opinion as to what means should be employed. These differences of opinion can perhaps best be considered in the next section, dealing with current practices in character education.

## II. CURRENT PRACTICES IN TRAINING FOR CHARACTER

### 1. *Direct moral instruction*

In a general way two types of character-education programs have been carried on in the schools — direct and indirect.

**Charters' statement.** Charters gives the following by way of explanation as to the meaning of the two terms:

By direct moral instruction we mean that form of instruction in morals which begins with the consideration of traits. This is in contradistinction to indirect moral instruction in which we begin with a consideration of situations. I use indirect instruction when I am teaching penmanship and urging the ideal of speed as a supplementing trait. In this case the topic of instruction is penmanship and in making an excellent penman I develop the trait of speed as a by-product. If, however, I begin with the boy who lacks speed and concentrate upon this trait in a variety of situations (one of which may be penmanship), I am using direct moral instruction: my attention to penmanship is indirect and supplemental.[1]

Each of the plans has its supporters. At the present time there is little scientific evidence in support of the relative effectiveness of the two procedures. The weakness of indirect moral instruction is held to be lack of definiteness or system. Under this plan it is argued that moral instruction is largely accidental. It may be overlooked either entirely or in part. Furthermore, it may be inadequate to meet the needs of the more serious individual cases.

The greatest weakness of direct moral instruction is that it may not meet the needs of children. It is possible that such instruction often fails to grow out of the felt needs of children. If it does not come into their experience at a time when their level of experience is such that they appreciate the meaning and significance of the instruction offered, the work of the teacher may be without significant results. Thus it is evident that both of the plans have their weaknesses.

Perhaps the position taken by the Committee on Charac-

[1] Charters, W. W. *The Teaching of Ideals*, p. 184. By permission of The Macmillan Company, publishers. 1927.

ter Education of the National Education Association is the one most acceptable to teachers at present: [1]

Direct moral instruction is, to be sure, but one phase of moral education in the schools; it may be a minor phase, yet of sufficient importance to make its omission a serious handicap. In order to realize all the objectives of character or moral education it seems that all the available means and methods must be utilized — home, school, church, state, vocations, and general social life of the community — with such methods as may be employed in each case. Some of the methods available to the school are:

(a) The example and personal influence of teachers and other school officers

(b) Indirect moral instruction through each and all of the school studies

(c) Direct moral instruction by groups and on some occasions through personal conferences

(d) Student participation in the management of the school community — sometimes called student participation in government

(e) All other varieties of extracurricular activities of the school: e.g., assembly periods, debating, musical and dramatical performances, athletic contests, parties, etc.

**Advantages of the direct method.** The use of the above plan, it is maintained, will make available to teachers the advantages of both the direct and indirect methods. Charters [2] sets forth the advantages of the direct method, as follows:

The advantages of direct moral instruction are at least two in number. First, it provides conditions favorable for enthusiastic work so that through sustained attention it produces a powerful momentum. The attention is centered upon the trait and its method of development rather than upon the subject and the course of study. The learner concentrates upon the trait action, and if the exercise is continued until habits are formed, the curve

[1] *Character Education*, p. 67. Report of the Committee on Character Education of the National Education Association.

[2] Charters, W. W. *The Teaching of Ideals*, pp. 186–87. By permission of The Macmillan Company.

of attainment in the trait may not fall after the drive is past. Often, indeed, the drive puts a failing habit "over the top" and projects it upon its way to a permanent place in the nervous system. Without the drive this safety point might not be reached.

In the second place, direct moral instruction gives teachers and pupils the opportunity to systematize and summarize the trait in a number of ways. For instance, a child may have learned incidentally some of the forms of courtesy in some situations and may not have encountered other situations. In such a case when direct moral instruction is resorted to, it is possible to teach all important situations to which the trait applies. The mere listing of all the situations governed by the trait is the simplest form of systematization. For example, when we ask where courage or neatness can be shown, a long list of items can be found, and in all probability no attention has been paid to some of them. Such a system of checking is not possible by the use of indirect moral instruction; yet it is a necessary device. We need reviews, summaries, and drills in moral instructions just as in any other field of experience, and these are provided in part by supplementary direct moral instruction where the trait becomes avowedly and frankly the topic for discussion and instruction in the class.

## 2. *Indirect moral instruction*

**Charters on the indirect method.** Commenting on the indirect method, Charters [1] says:

Because instruction is carried on at the moment when it is needed, the desire for the trait is present or can be aroused with relative ease. For example, when the child has been inaccurate in arithmetic and has felt the force of the appropriate penalties, he is naturally by the laws of probability more interested in the trait of accuracy than he would be if the topic of accuracy applied to arithmetic situations were scheduled months in advance for 9:15 A.M. on Friday, February 24. Another advantage of giving instruction as needed is that it is then easy to secure the use of reason and discussion in arriving at the best methods for controlling situations. The trait of openmindedness, for example, is best applied to social science problems when social science discussions are taking place. The specific trait actions — the things one must

[1] Charters, W. W. *The Teaching of Ideals*, pp. 163–64. By permission of The Macmillan Company, publishers.

do to be openminded — can be most effectively developed "on the ground" in those specific situations which arise from day to day. When the visiting opponents have arrived, children learn best just what to do to make the visitors feel that the pupils of the local school are courteous to opponents. Moreover, under these conditions practice in the exercise of the trait actions can be immediately secured because the situations are directly at hand. By this means we can at once proceed to apply accuracy to arithmetic situations, maintain openmindedness in regard to social problems, and use courtesy in entertaining visiting teams. Further than this, the resulting evaluations and satisfactions, or dissatisfactions, that come from plans carried into action are within easy reach because the plan can actually be put into operation.

## 3. *Typical programs*

**The Elgin program.** The program of character education employed at Elgin, Illinois, under Superintendent R. W. Fairchild, is an example of a program based largely upon direct methods. The brief description of the plan given below is taken from the *Fourth Yearbook* (pages 394–95) of the Department of Superintendence of the National Educational Association.

### THE ELGIN PLAN

The superintendent of schools of Elgin outlined a course in character education in his annual report of 1924–25. The course is divided into the following sections: Morals, Manners, Respect for Property, Safety, Thrift, Patriotism. The plan is to present the work of Morals on Mondays, Manners on Tuesdays, Respect for Property on Wednesdays, Safety on Thursdays and Thrift and Patriotism on Fridays. Fifteen minutes is devoted each morning to the presentation of this work throughout grades one to eight.

The superintendent of schools reports that it has been found impressive to use a key-word each day. Upon entering the building, regardless of the entrance used, the pupil is confronted with a placard, approximately $6 \times 12$ inches in size, suspended in the corridor. Upon the placard is the key-word for the day. It may be "honesty," "gentleness," or some other word. This key-word likewise appears upon the blackboard of each school room on that day. Oftentimes, in addition to the key-word, there is an outline helping the child to think of its meaning and its applications.

The following methods are reported as effective in carrying out the plan: Class discussion led by the teacher, class discussion led by some pupil who has prepared himself well, the chain question method among pupils, reports on specially assigned topics, debates especially in the upper grades, composition work, dramatization, clippings mounted upon the bulletin board, reporting and discussing experiences, and the use of four-minute speakers. It will be observed that the outline is not differentiated by grades. The differences in teachers are relied upon to introduce the necessary variety from grade to grade.

The section on morals carries these major headings in the outline: Sense of Justice, Truthfulness, Honesty, Reliability and Fidelity, Self-Reliance, Obedience and Respect for Authority, Forgiveness, Unselfishness, Coöperation and Loyalty, Punctuality, Kindness and Generosity, Perseverance, Industry, Humility, Associations, Self-Control, Habit Formation, the Law of the Kingdom. It will be observed that there are a total of eighteen major headings. The points outlined under punctuality are typical. This outline is as follows:

*Punctuality.* If there is any virtue at which we should aim, it is that of being prompt.

A. Necessary for success in life.
  1. Procrastination a very bad habit.
  2. One must be ready and quick to act.
  3. Promptness in keeping appointments.
  4. Promptness in getting work done.
B. A virtue to be cultivated in youth.
  1. Avoidance of dawdling over school work.
  2. Avoid putting things off.

**The inductive method.** Gregg has emphasized a method which is called the inductive method. It is part way between the direct and the indirect methods, being looked upon as indirect by the pupil but clearly direct in the mind of the teacher.[1] The several steps in this method are given below:

[1] Gregg, F. M. "Inductive Method of Character Education"; in *American Educational Digest*, vol. 48, pp. 222, 224 (January, 1929.)

### GREGG'S INDUCTIVE METHOD PLAN

1. Indirect stimulation of trait actions as the basis of trait percepts in the classroom. The teacher builds a realization of punctuality by creating school situations which demand punctual behavior.

2. Vicarious introduction through story and so forth to non-school trait percepts and to school traits in non-school situations. In Step 1 punctuality is only associated in the pupil's mind with school situations. How can the concept be associated with life situations? Largely by bringing these life activities into the classroom through story and drama.

3. Development of trait concepts by using the direct method in regular weekly lessons. This step brings together the background experiences developed by Steps 1 and 2. The meaning and application of the trait punctuality is approached rather directly through discussion, dramatization and so forth. The concept punctuality is approached rather directly through discussion, dramatization and so forth. The concept punctuality is emotionalized by exercising the idea in connection with the inner urges. These urges include the tendencies toward self-assertion, self-subjection and others.

4. Provision for motivating the proposed character trait through the stimulation of a "social gallery," such as a school club. In the previous steps the individual has been led to understand, accept and strive for punctuality. Now this trait is accepted by the group and the individual finds himself subjected to the approval or disapproval of his fellows. Conscience will then develop, for it is the nature of conscience to cause one to be elated if his "social gallery" or group approves a moral act, or to feel dejected if the social group disapproves an immoral act.

5. Conversion of the concept into an ideal (an emotionalized concept) through the influence of motivating forces. The idea of punctuality becomes associated with the feelings. The individual "falls in love" with punctuality because the group approves an[d] punctual behavior brings satisfaction.

6. Conversion of the idea into a concept or generalized conduct response through frequent opportunities for habituation in such a way that they will transfer to life situations outside of the classroom. This step involves the generalization of the concept punctuality until the individual readily and habitually manifests the

trait. The manifestation is a conduct response to peripheral, verbal or often subtle stimuli. Readiness to respond depends upon how well the habit has been established and whether the necessity for punctuality provokes a favorable attitude.

**The Iowa Plan.**[1] This well-known plan, developed under the leadership of Professor Edwin D. Starbuck, has received so much attention that it deserves mention in any consideration of the teaching of character. Those who are interested in this problem should examine carefully a copy of the plan. Only a few quotations from it can be given here. The foundation principles of the plan are as follows:

### THE IOWA PLAN

#### I. FOUNDATION PRINCIPLES

1. *Have a Goal.* Character education must keep before parents and instructors an end as distinct as that before a traveler who would take a journey or a factory manager who would turn out a finished product or an artist who would create a work of art. It should be consciously purposeful, not haphazard. The methods herein outlined move towards a definite goal.

2. *Measure the Progress and the Product.* The flower of moral culture eludes scales and measuring sticks. But there are fundamental attitudes that are as measurable as are the "points" in stock judging, or the "skills" in arithmetic, writing and music. Character development promises to be able to know where it is going and what progress it is making. This outline presents a fairly successful scale for character-rating.

3. *The End is Personal.* The school is made for the child and not the child for the school. The kingdom of Character Education is in the hearts, minds, and muscles of children, not in general precepts or abstract principles. Cultivate *persons who* live gracefully and helpfully, not *virtues that* seem desirable. The virtues are the flowers of the good life. Its roots, trunk, twigs and fruits are made out of deeds, including thought-deeds.

4. *The End is Social.* Organize the school as a whole and in every part as a *democratic community of persons.* "To socialize, to

---

[1] Published by The Character Education Institution, Chevy Chase, Washington, D.C.

citizenize and to moralize are the same." Societies and democracies of the future will be safe and wholesome if the thoughts, sympathies and activities of children are socially re-centered.

5. *The End is Practical.* The moral person is not simply abstractly good but good for something. He is part of a busy, constructive, creative program. He works, plays, studies, loves and worships. The center of gravity of moral values has shifted once and for all and finally away from the favored ones of wealth and prestige whose virtues are just humanity's adornments, to the mass of busy, common folk who are doing the work of the world. The virtues are not treasures to be won but attitudes towards the actual situations men and women have to face. Not virtue for virtue's sake but rightness and righteousness for life's sake — the growing, self-realizing life of individuals and societies.

6. *The Sure Foundations of Character Life in Conduct.* The school throughout must be a personally acquiring, socially adjusting, mutually achieving society, not a conversation club or a lecture bureau. Its problems must be real. One actual ethical situation met and solved is worth more to the child than a dozen imaginary moral questions selected as topics of discussion. *Practice* the good life rather than entertain thoughts *about* it.

7. *Vitalize Conduct Through the Sympathies.* The likes, the desires, the longings, the loves are springs of action. Build up bodies of specific dislikes and hatreds of ugliness in conduct and sets of tastes and prejudices in favor of that which is clean, kindly, courageous and noble. The moral feelings should be instruments of the real self in the act of meeting actual situations.

8. *Furnish the Mind Richly with Imagery and Symbols of Right Living.* Conduct moves surely in the direction of its dominant imagery. Its mental pictures are its pillar of cloud and pillar of fire. See that the mind of every child is attracted to the best pieces of art; is entangled in the plot of wholesome novels, plays and movies; is resonant with proverbs, poetry, precepts and wise sayings; is vibrant with the rhythm and melody of the best music; is inspired with admiration of great personalities and is self-hypnotized by the thought of noble deeds. Every false brooding is the link of a prisoner's chain or the stone of a prison wall. A clean imagination is the true deliverer. An ideal is a conscious image made personal.

9. *Develop Progressive Skill in Moral Thoughtfulness.* During the early years reduce self-conscious goodness and reasoned con-

duct to a minimum. Don't tempt the child to analyze the moral life until he has one; first, conduct; then the sympathies; next, the imagination, and finally, reasoned behavior. Cultivate the power on occasion, to face real moral situations thoughtfully, to criticize conduct, to form clear and accurate judgments of right behavior, to organize the feelings into higher ethical sentiments, to attain conscious self-control and to help direct wisely the life of the group.

10. *Translate Duty into Beauty.* Like all worth-while games the game of living is difficult to learn. The sign of mastery is joy in the performance. Cultivate habits of living out gracefully the clean and kindly life. The good character is full of harmony within and without, the harmony of music. The good in character is like the good in manners, but more. Transform sheer duty into an impelling and inviting sense of beauty.

11. *Familiarize Children with the Best of the Racial Traditions.* The life of humanity is a sort of racial organism with unitary being. Its future is created out of its past. The children are its living, growing present. Their characters will be whole and sound in proportion as they draw from the total heritage. They need to live over again some of its myth and legend, its poetry and drama, its work and play, its customs and history. They need to learn its wisdom, respect its great personalities and revere its ideals.

12. *Awaken Loyalty to a Cause.* Character is a by-product of a worthy cause made personal. The cause should usually be a real situation, always capable of being carried over into a completed and alleviating thought or act, not an imaginary one that ends in a sentiment. It must always be within the child's grasp — a flower to a sick child, help to a tired mother, food to a famine-stricken country, completion of a school project. It should summon the child's own discriminating thought and effort and stand out as an end *desired* and *sought after.* Character consists in thoughtful selection of a cause together with personal loyalty to that cause.

13. *Stimulate the Spirit of Reverence.* Feel after, with the child, the Life that is more than meat, the Truth that is more than fact, the Law that is more than event. Don't preach; don't pretend. Be simple, direct, genuine. Admiration of comely objects is schooling in the highest act of worship. Respect for laws of nature and of the state are elements in the truest reverence. To feel the fascination of the quest for fuller knowledge is not different in kind from hunger and thirst after righteousness. Love of noble personalities is not unlike devotion to the Spirit of Life. The person is morally safe who has reverence within his inner parts.

**Steps in teaching for character.** In the last analysis the problem of character education is reduced to the problems of the individual pupils. No two pupils are exactly alike in instructional needs, either in character education or any other field. For this reason there appears to be much merit in the approach recommended by Charters.[1] He lists five principles which are basic to effective work in modifying the behavior of individuals. They are:

1. Diagnosing the situation
2. Creating desire
3. Developing a plan of action
4. Requiring practice
5. Integrating personality

It is impractical to cover all these phases of a character-education program in this chapter. For this reason the remainder of the chapter will be devoted to two aspects of the problem. The first of these is concerned with methods of measurement and diagnosis which are available; the second will be concerned with remedial measures.

## III. DIAGNOSIS IN CHARACTER EDUCATION

### 1. *The problem*

**The importance of careful diagnosis.** As a basis for character-education procedure the value of careful diagnosis is attested in several ways. In the first place, the differences between individuals are very great. Not only do individual pupils present different problems, but the causes back of an undesirable trait may be very different in these individuals. The force of this statement can be better appreciated through the study of a single trait. Perhaps the trait which has been subjected to the most careful study is that of *deceit*. Hartshorne and May [2] give the following analysis of deception:

[1] Charters, W. W. *Loc. cit.*, pp. 5–13.

[2] Hartshorne, Hugh, and May, Mark A. *Studies in Deceit*, pp. 402–05. By permission of The Macmillan Company, publishers.

## Analysis of Deceit

A complete act of deception involves at least the following factors: (1) the person, persons, or institution deceived, (2) the motive for doing it, (3) the thing about which the deceiver deceives, (4) the way in which it is done, (5) the consequences to the deceiver, the deceived, and others.

I. Persons or institutions deceived

    A. Persons to whom the deceiver is or pretends to be loyal, such as members of the immediate family and friends

    B. Institutions or organizations to which the deceiver is or pretends to be loyal, such as his church (if he is a member), his school, his clubs, his teams

    C. Persons to whom the deceiver owes no special allegiance, such as acquaintances, strangers, merchants, plumbers

    D. Institutions or organizations to which he owes no special allegiance, such as the railroad company, the gas company

    E. Enemies of the deceiver

II. General motives for deceiving

The number of specific motives for deception is very great, and no detailed analysis is here attempted, but most of them may be classified as follows:

    A. The desire to do positive harm to the deceived and cause suffering and hardships (Motive: e.g., revenge)

    B. The desire to cause inconvenience or embarrassment or perhaps dishonor to the deceived (Motive: e.g., jealousy or envy)

    C. The desire to gain something in the way of money, objects, property, or advantage, prestige, applause, approval, etc. (Motive: e.g., aggressive greed)

    D. The desire to protect or defend oneself against reproof, embarrassment, physical pain, punishment, dishonor, loss of property, etc. (Motive: defense tendencies)

    E. The desire to compensate oneself for some loss or some handicap (Motive: compensatory tendencies)

    F. The desire to promote or defend the interests and welfare of a person or persons to whom the deceiver owes allegiance (A. of section I above) (Motive: loyalty to friends)

    G. The desire to promote or defend the welfare and interests of B. of section I above (Motive: loyalty to a cause)

    H. The desire to promote or defend the welfare and happiness of C. of section I above (Motive: social justice)

    I. The desire to promote or defend the welfare of D. of section I above (Motive: community welfare)

    J. The desire to promote or defend the welfare of E. of section I above (Motive: coöperative respect)

III. The things about which the deceiver deceives

    A. Social values, such as the importance of events

    B. Economic values, the worth of goods

    C. Acts of conduct, his own or others'

    D. Motives for conduct, his own or others'

    E. Inventions

    F. Knowledge or information, possessed by himself or others

    G. Skills and abilities

    H. Physical events, such as storms, or facts of time and place

    I. Beliefs, his own or others'

    J. Feelings, his own or others'

IV. How the deception is accomplished

    A. By giving the deceived actual false information either oral or written but communicated by language; such things as fabrications, invention of stories, reporting events that never happened

    B. By distorting true information so that the deceived will be misled as to conclusions. This is done by overstatements, exaggerations, etc., or by understatements or by otherwise twisting the truth.

    C. By concealing information, by silence, evasions, denials, etc.

    D. By acting in such a way as to mislead the deceived concerning the true intentions, motives, beliefs, or feelings of the deceiver or others

    E. By supplying the deceived with inadequate sensory data, so that the total situation will appear different from what it really is. Sleight-of-hand tricks, fake advertisements, etc., are illustrations.

V. Possible undesirable consequences to the deceiver, if caught, or to the deceived or others
   A. Severe punishment or suffering
   B. Imprisonment and deprivations
   C. Loss of all social standing, social ostracism
   D. Loss of membership in some organization
   E. Loss of friends
   F. Loss of confidence of others
   G. Loss of property, fines
   H. Severe reprimand
   I. Mild rebuke or reproval
   J. Temporary embarrassment

From the above analysis of deception it is clear that perhaps no two cases will have the same setting. The situation, the motive, the method, or the consequences may vary. In fact the authors point out that there are, on a conservative estimate, twenty-five thousand combinations of these factors. If now it is kept in mind that only one trait has been taken account of in this analysis, and that equally complex problems are encountered in numerous other traits, one comes to realize the great probabilities for variations from individual to individual. In fact, it would appear that individual diagnosis and remedial teaching is inescapable if real progress is to be made.

**What are behavior problems?** A diagnostic procedure is necessary in character education from another point of view. There is an impression among some teachers that pupils may be divided into two types — "good" and "bad." Often such teachers feel that only a few pupils present conduct problems. Recent studies of children's behavior suggest that such a conception is unsound. Wickman reaches the conclusion that behavior must be viewed in the "active definition." [1] Any behavior may become a problem if it is so regarded by the adult who deals with the child.   There is thus no absolute line between "desirable" and "undesirable behavior."   For example, a child may be a problem to one teacher, and not to another.

Studies of children's behavior also reveal the fact that large proportions of the children in the schools present what teachers regard as "behavior problems."   Table 50, taken from Wickman's study,[2] is illustrative of this fact.

TABLE 50. TOTAL INCIDENCE OF BEHAVIOR PROBLEMS IN 874 CHILDREN, REPORTED BY TEACHERS OF AN ELEMENTARY PUBLIC SCHOOL, CLEVELAND, 1926

| TYPE OF PROBLEM | PER CENT OF 874 PUPILS | TYPE OF PROBLEM | PER CENT OF 874 PUPILS |
|---|---|---|---|
| Whispering | 74.7 | Fearful | 9.3 |
| Inattentive | 59.0 | Physical coward | 8.8 |
| Careless in work | 44.4 | Nervous | 8.7 |
| Tattling | 42.0 | Willfully Disobedient | 8.2 |
| Disorderly in class | 38.8 | Destroying property | 8.2 |
| Interrupting | 38.7 | Unhappy, Depressed | 8.0 |
| Failure to Study | 36.2 | Quarrelsome | 7.9 |
| Shy, Withdrawing | 35.2 | Stubborn in group | 7.5 |
| Day Dreaming | 33.4 | Rude, Impudent | 6.7 |
| Lack of interest | 31.8 | Impertinent, Defiant | 5.6 |
| Overactive | 30.9 | Carrying grudges | 4.9 |
| Cheating | 29.5 | Stealing articles | 4.0 |
| Oversensitive | 25.5 | Masturbation | 3.9 |
| Neglectful | 25.4 | Enuresis | 3.9 |
| Physically lazy | 20.8 | Sissy (Or Tomboy) | 3.6 |
| Lying, Untruthful | 19.6 | Suspicious | 2.1 |
| Unnecessary tardiness | 17.6 | Cruel, Bullying | 1.7 |
| Acting "Smart" | 14.6 | Profanity | 1.7 |
| Overcritical | 14.2 | Truancy | 1.6 |
| Imaginative Tales | 13.3 | Temper Outbursts | 1.5 |
| Meddlesome | 12.6 | Stealing money | 0.7 |
| Sullen, Sulky | 12.5 | Stealing food, sweets | 0.7 |
| Domineering | 12.1 | Obscene notes, talk | 0.3 |
| Slovenly appearance | 11.8 | Smoking | 0.2 |
| Suggestible | 9.4 | | |

[1] Wickman, E. K.   *Children's Behavior and Teachers' Attitudes*, chapters 1 and 3.   Division of Publications, The Commonwealth Fund.
[2] *Ibid.*, p. 30.

**The nature of behavior problems.** Not only are behavior problems widely distributed among children, but the problems themselves are varied in nature. The following list, submitted by Wickman,[1] is illustrative:

### THE NATURE OF BEHAVIOR PROBLEMS

*Group I. Violations of general standards of morality and integrity* (76)
Stealing, 11: stealing, 9; theft, 2.
Dishonesties, 44: lying, 7; untruthfulness, 7; dishonesty, 3; deceitfulness, 6; evasion of truth, 2; cheating, 7; falsehood, 1; bluffing, 2; untrustworthiness, 2; pretense, 1; fabrication, 1; exaggeration, 1; copying from others' papers, 1; hypocrisy, 1; lack of honor, 1; forgery, 1.
"Immorality," 12: bad physical habits, 3; immorality, 4; obscenity, 2; unclean thoughts, glances, notes, 1; vulgarity, 1; sex problems, 1.
Profanity, 4: swearing, 2; profanity, 2.
Smoking, 2.
Miscellany, 3: unlawfulness, lack of ideals, unjustness.

*Group II. Transgressions against authority* (27)
Disobedience, 14: disrespect to authority, 4; defiance, 4; impertinence, 1; slowness in obeying instructions, 1; refusal to do things when asked, 1; willful misconstruction, 1; refusal to do anything that is right unless forced, 1; insubordination, 1.

*Group III. Violations of general school regulations* (30)
Truancy, 16; tardiness, 11; irregularity in attendance, 1; taking articles home, 1; destroying materials, 1.

*Group IV. Violations of Classroom Rules* (70)
Disorderliness, 33. (Many individual descriptions of petty behavior annoyances or failure to comply with school routine, e.g., playing with pencil, disorderly lines, unnecessary noise, etc.)
Restlessness, 4; interruptions, 16; too social, 9; whispering, 6; lack of supplies, 2; miscellaneous, 6.

*Group V. Violations of school work requirements* (41)
Inattention, 13: inattention-inattentiveness, 11; lack of concentration, 2.

[1] *Op. cit.*, pp. 151–57.

Lack of interest, 4: indifference, 3; lack of interest, 1.

Carelessness, 11: carelessness, 6; irresponsibility, 2; unreliability, 1; lack of pride in work, 1; inaccuracy, 1.

Laziness, 13: laziness, 4; lack of effort, 1; idleness, 1; dawdling, 1; procrastination, 1; refusing to form habit of preparedness, 1.

Indolence, 1: lack of initiative, 1; shirking, 1; evades duties, 1.

*Group VI. Difficulties with other children* (38)

Annoying other children, 24: annoying, 11; cruelty, 3; roughness, 3; fighting, 4; bullying, 2; punching, 1.

Tattling, 6.

Miscellany, 8: disregard of rights of others, 2; getting others into trouble, 1; quarrelsomeness, 1; colored and whites fighting, 1; laughing at others' mistakes, 1; imposing on others, 1; interfering with work of others, 1.

*Group VII. Undesirable personality traits* (136)

Negativisms, 27: stubbornness, 16; sulkiness, 3; sullenness, 1; contrariness, 2; obstinacy, 2; disposition to argue, 1; hectoring, 1; persistency, 1.

Unacceptable social manners, 19: impudence, 6; impoliteness, 5; rudeness, 3; discourtesy, 3; uncivil, 1; sarcastic, 1.

Self-indulgences, 15: selfishness, 9; unsportsmanship, 2; jealousy, 1; greediness, 1; not altruistic, 1; lack of loyalty, 1.

Arrogance, 14: overbearing, 2; forwardness, 2; overconfidence, 2; domineering, 1; feeling of superiority, 1; boastfulness, 1; dictatorialness, 1; always wants to lead, 1; pride, 1; conceited, 1; too independent, 1.

Diffidence, 14: bashfulness, 4; shyness, 3; sensitiveness, 2; too dependent, 2; self-conscious, 1; too timid, 1; failure to join group, 1.

Evasions, 11: evasiveness, 1; lack of forthrightness, 1; insincere, 1; sneakiness, 1; failure to confess fault, 1; overcritical of others to hide faults, 2; evades punishments, 1; thoughtlessness, 2; forgetting, 1.

Interferences, 12: destructiveness, 5; curiosity, 2; meddlesomeness, 2; gossiping, 2; inquisitiveness, 1.

Lack of emotional control, 13: temper, 6; lack of self-control, 5; crying, 2.

Undesirable mental states, 3; dissatisfied, 1; unhappy, 1; resentful, 1.

Miscellany, 8: uncleanliness of habits and personal appearance, 2; lack of pride in self, 2; listlessness, 1; silliness, 3.

Such a widespread prevalence of "behavior problems" suggests that pupils cannot be classified as "good" and "bad." Behavior problems arise in the teaching of large proportions of the children. For this reason behavior is a matter of degree rather than kind. Any child may become at some time or other a "behavior problem." Diagnosis is thus not a field of activity for a few problem cases only, but a vital part of the approach to the teaching of all children in character education.

**Teachers' attitude toward behavior.** In the foregoing discussion no account has been taken of the manner in which teachers locate pupils who present behavior problems. It has been found that teachers tend to emphasize most of these overt types of behavior which interfere with the conduct of school work. There is a suggestion in the results of Wickman's studies that teachers fail to identify many important behavior problems which are rated as very serious by mental hygienists. The following summary is descriptive: [1]

### TEACHER ANALYSIS OF BEHAVIOR ACTS

According to the reports obtained in the one Cleveland school, the lines along which the teachers distinguished between the problem child and the well-adjusted child are rather clearly drawn. We may summarize the analysis of our data on the teachers' reactions to the behavior adjustments of their pupils as follows:

1. Though teachers find distressing behavior to occur in a majority of their pupils, in evaluating the total behavior adjustments of the children they consider that the majority are "exceptionally well-adjusted."

2. Teachers fail to interpret many problems in child behavior as symptomatic of educational, social, or emotional maladjustment. Only when the behavior of a child is of a certain distressing

[1] Wickman, E. K. *Op. cit.*, pp. 77–79.

kind and exhibited to an extreme degree is significance attached to the behavior disorder.

3. In estimating the total behavior adjustments of their pupils, the teachers took mainly into account whether or not the child was obedient, truthful, docile, amenable to the imposed requirements of study and classroom order.

4. Entirely desirable or ideal behavior is recognized by the teachers only in the exceptional child and is characterized by the absence of any behavior expressions which frustrate the teachers' desires for orderliness and their immediate purposes in teaching, or which violate their standards of moral values.

5. The teachers prefer the less active, more compliant behavior of girls to the more aggressive, independent behavior of boys. Desirable conduct for teachers, thus, takes on the distinguishing characteristics of girl behavior.

6. The problem child in school is identified by the teachers as one who is antagonistic to authority, does not conform to classroom order and routine, does not make the expected application to prescribed school work, violates the teachers' standards of integrity. But it is to be observed that these behavior tendencies are generally multiplied or exhibited in an extreme degree before the pupil is recognized as an important case of maladjustment.

7. The purely personal problems of children which do not frustrate or affect the immediate purposes of the teachers are not identified as symptomatic of significant maladjustment.

8. Children who exhibit problems of stealing, lying, and disobedience, frequently or habitually, are associated in the minds of teachers with many other problems of a directly irritating and frustrating type.

9. Teachers associate problems of disobedience and disorderliness with children whom they report frequently or habitually to show lack of interest in their school work.

10. Children who are reported for being frequently or habitually shy and retiring are regarded by the teachers as free from any of the extravagant overt types of behavior that are considered serious problems.

11. The frequency with which various problems in behavior occur in combination in the individual child precludes the treatment of any one of them as an adequate means for remedying the underlying social or emotional maladjustment of which the particular form of undesirable behavior is only a symptom.

**The development of positive traits.** So far the discussion has concerned itself with the prevalence of undesirable forms of behavior. Without doubt many pupils who present no serious difficulties to the teacher need attention in various ways. Such pupils may exhibit many positive traits which need to be strengthened. There must be opportunity for practice in the development of the desirable traits which the child exhibits to more or less varying degrees. Careful diagnosis may reveal the needs of the child for such practice.

## IV. MEASUREMENT IN CHARACTER-EDUCATION DIAGNOSIS

**Difficulty due to complexity.** The complexity of the problems of training for character makes obvious the difficulty of measurement in this field. It is of course true that certain forms of overt behavior may be observed objectively and recorded. For example, the teacher may observe the number of times a child whispers to the boy across the aisle. The measurement of traits, however, becomes a far more complex problem. Let us suppose that honesty is to be measured. The teacher finds that Johnny has stolen a pencil from the desk of a fellow pupil. What significance shall be attached to this one overt act? Is the child dishonest? If so, what degree of dishonesty is presented?

It should perhaps be stated at the outset that a complete diagnosis cannot be made by so-called "paper and pencil" tests. A comprehensive diagnosis will include studies of considerable variety touching upon the many factors which may influence character. Charters lists the following factors to be considered in making a diagnosis, following the methods used by juvenile delinquency agencies:

1. Family history
2. Home and neighborhood conditions and influences
3. Companions

4. Habits
5. Interests
6. School-and-work history
7. Delinquencies
8. Physical characteristics
9. Psychological examinations
10. Mental balance
11. Personality traits
12. Delinquents' own story
13. Staff conference summary
14. Subsequent history

It is apparent that only a small part of the diagnostic work involving all of the above factors can be accomplished by means of tests. Nevertheless there has recently been much interest in testing in the field of character education. The work which has been done in the measurement of intelligence and of achievement in school subjects has no doubt stimulated much of the activity in the measurement field in character education.

**Types of tests.** The efforts which have been made at measurement in character education may be classified into the following types:

1. Tests of knowledge
2. Attitude tests
3. Conduct or behavior scales
4. Measures of individual traits of character
5. Measures of personality

### 1. *Tests of moral knowledge*

**Difficulties faced.** In nearly all fields of educational measurement, it has been found that factual knowledge is one of the easiest outcomes to measure. In history we can easily determine whether a given child knows the date of the Battle of Gettysburg. Likewise in the field of moral knowledge it is a relatively simple matter to determine whether or not a child knows that he should not pick flowers in a public park. It is perhaps not as simple to find out whether or not this same child refrains from picking flowers in the public park. Such questions as this complicate what might appear to be a relatively simple process of measurement. There are thus controversies over fields actually measured by moral-knowledge tests. There is likewise difference of opinion concerning the effectiveness of moral knowledge as a control in conduct. There is some evidence, however, to indicate that moral knowledge has a certain consistency. Fairly high correlations exist between comparable forms of the same test. This suggests that moral knowledge has a certain stability which may be a factor of some importance in conduct.

**Specificity of moral knowledge.** Widespread and complete transfer of training would, from some points of view, be of great value in teaching moral knowledge. If one could be assured that having taught, let us say, the decalogue, children would be able to discriminate between desirable and undesirable conduct in specific instances, the teaching of moral knowledge would be relatively simple. There are several reasons, however, why the teacher cannot depend too much on transfer of training.

In the first place, the correlations between various types of conduct are very low. Individuals may be honest in one situation, and not in another. In the second place, the sources of our moral codes are such that there is not complete agreement as to what constitutes socially desirable conduct. For instance, the child's knowledge of moral codes has probably been picked up in home, school, Boy Scouts, street, or gang. It is probably too much to expect that these various sources are in agreement. The pupil will probably have difficulty under these conditions in tracing any specific act of conduct back to a basic principle of "right" or "wrong." As an example, a boy gives the conductor on the street car three cents, when the fare for a twelve-year-old boy is seven cents. When questioned he replies that the boys in his group follow this practice. The same boy returns a dime to a storekeeper which he could keep without being detected. In either case it appears that specific codes, rather than general principles, motivate his conduct.

**Growing complexity of the problem.** The measurement of moral knowledge is made even more difficult by its growing complexity. As social organization becomes more complicated, types of situations multiply, while the amount of specific moral knowledge required grows steadily. Even among adults of the highest moral standards problems arise concerning which there is considerable disagreement. The arguments over the ethics of stock market manipulations are illustrative. The complexity of ethical behavior is made evident by the following outline taken from the study by Hartshorne and May.[1]

BRIEF OUTLINE OF CERTAIN MENTAL CONTENTS AND SKILLS
INVOLVED IN ETHICAL BEHAVIOR

A. Certain tools needed for the intelligent consideration of problems of social adjustment
   1. Adequate social-ethical vocabulary
   2. Adequate control of language — the ability to say the right thing and to understand the more subtle nuances of delicate social adjustment
   3. Assimilation of the fundamental ideas or generalizations in terms of which life is coming increasingly to be understood, such as:

     The idea of sex
     The idea of God
     The idea of right and wrong
     The idea of natural law

[1] Hartshorne, Hugh, and May, Mark A., *Studies in the Organization of Character*, pp. 34–37. By permission of The Macmillan Company, publishers.

The idea of growth
The idea of evolution
The idea of coöperation
The idea of personality
The idea of custom
The idea of design
The idea of legislation
The idea of education
The idea of work
The idea of fun
The idea of the machine
The idea of self-forgetting service

B. Particular knowledge and skills needed for making social adjustments

1. Knowledge of natural law, physical and biological, and the limitations and possibilities of experience

2. Knowledge of body and mind in general and of oneself in particular: to understand the causes and consequences of certain kinds of behavior in oneself and others, the nature of temptation, reasons for social and legal requirements and desiderata, to control self for growth

3. Knowledge of how people behave toward one another in all sorts of situations: home, school, church, public meetings, committee meetings, discussion groups, play groups, emergencies, studying, visiting, etc.; the significance of this behavior for the life of the groups concerned

4. Knowledge of race experience in solving problems of social adjustment, as recorded in history, folklore, fiction, biography, poetry; particularly, knowledge of motives and purposes and their consequences

5. Knowledge of moral principles held by different groups and their implications and applications in concrete situations

6. Knowledge of constitutional rights and obligations, legislative enactments, and sanctions affecting oneself and one's groups

7. Knowledge of institutions and other coöperative bodies and movements affecting oneself or needed as instruments of social adjustment, such as the church, the school, the home, the state, the town or city or community or block or neighborhood and its government, community agencies

of welfare and safety, such as the police department, fire department, health department, national associations, such as the Child Labor Committee and Red Cross, the movie, the playground, the library, the museum, local industries, the jail, the hospital, the court, the clinic; what they do, their history, their value, their address, how to coöperate

8. Knowledge of how the work of the world is carried on in mining, agriculture, industry, commerce, finance, transportation, communication, the trades and professions; mechanical and social aspects

9. Knowledge of contemporary peoples, races, nations, their contacts, conflicting interests, efforts toward peaceful settlement of disputes and world organization, effects of war and armament, historical and current utopias

10. Knowledge of the trend of evolution, theories of the universe, and the place of man in the universe

11. Knowledge of how men have experienced God in connection with nature and in the control and development of self and society; prayer, reflection, retrospect, valuation, foresight, repentance, forgiveness, aspiration, unification

12. Knowledge of causes and consequences of social behavior, the habit of foresight and valuation, the recognition of personal and social responsibility, the habit of moral thoughtfulness

13. Knowledge of how to think with the materials of social action, the habit of inhibition, abstraction from prejudice, gathering and weighing of evidence, use of past experience, willingness to experiment, discipline of group thinking, open-minded consideration of differences, respect for self and others, freedom from social suggestion, social perception and imagination

14. Knowledge of the sources of information needed and the habit of making constant reference to them

It is obvious that to measure all the specific ethical knowledges suggested by the above list is a formidable project, yet it is very likely that the list is far from complete. A further problem arises because of the fact that not all of the questions involve facts only. Some are in the realm of opinion largely, if not only. Perhaps, therefore, the classification of knowledge tests into two groups, information and opinion, as followed by Hartshorne and May, is desirable. We shall follow this classification in our further consideration of the subject.

## 2. Information tests

Only a few of the tests so far devised can be reproduced here, and the ones reproduced have been selected because it is believed that they will be suggestive to teachers.

**Recognitions test.** This test aims to measure the extent to which an individual can classify situations. For example, is "using street-car transfers that are out of date" cheating, lying, stealing, "wrong," or "not wrong"? The test is based upon the assumption that regardless of whether or not the individual acts differently because of his ability to classify the situations, he cannot be successfully subjected to intelligent social control unless he can classify his own conduct. A sample from the test [1] is given below:

### A RECOGNITIONS TEST

After each statement are five letters: C, L, S, X, J. If the deed is a case of cheating, draw a circle around the C; if it is lying, around the L; if it is stealing, around the S. If it is something wrong, but not either cheating, lying, or stealing, put a circle around the X. If it is not wrong at all, put a circle around the J. If the thing is both cheating and lying or stealing and lying or all three, encircle all the letters you need to in order to express your opinion. (A sample is given, which is here omitted.)

Bullying younger children . . . . . . . . . . . . . . . . . C L S X J
Using street car transfers that are out of date C L S X J
Riding on the back of a truck without the
    driver's knowing it . . . . . . . . . . . . . . . . . . . . . C L S X J
Apologizing for a misdeed when you are not
    really sorry . . . . . . . . . . . . . . . . . . . . . . . . . . . C L S X J

[1] Hartshorne and May. *Loc. cit.*, p. 40.

Forgetting to brush your teeth for a day .... C   L   S   X   J
Talking loudly in the hallways when classes
    are in session ........................... C   L   S   X   J
Picking flowers in a public park ............ C   L   S   X   J
When you don't want to go somewhere,
    making up an excuse so as not to hurt any-
    one's feelings ........................... C   L   S   X   J

## Social-ethical vocabulary.

It has been contended that a vocabulary of social-ethical terms was necessary to acceptable social conduct, since communication with others about the complex situations involved would be impossible without such a vocabulary.[1] The test given below, taken again from the study of Hartshorne and May,[2] is an example.

### A SOCIAL-ETHICAL VOCABULARY TEST

The directions require that the number of the word that means the same or most nearly the same as the first word in the line shall be entered in the space at the right.

1. BRAVERY.   1–folly, 2–courage, 3–livery, 4–impertinence, 5–humanity   .... 1

2. SCOFF.   1–cold, 2–angry, 3–make fun of, 4–extol, 5–expound   .... 2

3. MALICE.   1–spite, 2–poison, 3–glass, 4–character, 5–hammer   .... 3

4. SLUGGARD.   1–snail, 2–lazy person, 3–lax, 4–shot, 5–regard   .... 4

5. REPROACH.   1–come near, 2–insect, 3–scold, 4–steal game, 5–nerve   .... 5

6. JUDICIOUS.   1–punch, 2–spoken, 3–jury, 4–wise, 5–learned   .... 6

7. SUMPTUOUS.   1–conceited, 2–expensive, 3–repast, 4–meager, 5–fairylike   .... 7

8. INTROSPECTIVE.   1–lookover, 2–inspection, 3–self-examination, 4–inward, 5–sight   .... 8

[1] Schwesinger, Gladys.   *The Social-Ethical Significance of Vocabulary.* Teachers College Contributions to Education, no. 211, 1926.

[2] Hartshorne and May.   *Op. cit.,* p. 43.

**Foreseeing of consequences.** In the judgment of Hartshorne and May, foresight is a conspicuous factor in intelligence. It is also an outgrowth of experience. One of the tests in this field seeks to measure "probability." The sample item from the test given on page 522 is illustrative. There is probably some question about what is measured by tests such as these. It would appear, however, that the knowledge needed for making correct answers to these test items is important in the field of social knowledge. Certainly some ability to predict the various possible outcomes of a given social action is one of the desirable results to be secured in character education.[1] The authors find a rather high reliability for this particular test.

**Opinion ballots.** Not all the knowledge expected of children in the field of character education is factual or objective. Is it one's duty to read a newspaper every day? There is obviously no objective final answer to such a question. Much of the knowledge in morals which children are expected to acquire is of this subjective nature. Tests of this type of knowledge were prepared in such a way that the child may vote by underlining "No," "Yes," or "S," the latter meaning "sometimes." The "Duties" test from which a sample item is given on page 523 [2] is an example. The difficulty with this type of test is that of securing a criterion. If adults' answers are taken as "correct" we are not sure that they are the answers to be expected from children. The plan followed by Hartshorne and May was to allow a score of 2 if the item was marked in line with the predominant vote of the class, and a score of 1 if the answer corresponded with the next most frequent reply. Any other reply was 0. Thus on each single item a child could score 2, 1, or 0.

[1] Hartshorne and May, *op. cit.*, pp. 44–45.
[2] From Hartshorne and May, *op. cit.*, p. 47.

## FORESEEING CONSEQUENCES TEST

| This is likely to happen. | This might happen, but not likely | This would not happen. | |
|---|---|---|---|
| | | | John started across the street without looking both ways. |
| ........ | ........ | ........ | 1. He got hit with an automobile. |
| ........ | ........ | ........ | 2. He caused an accident to other people. |
| ........ | ........ | ........ | 3. The traffic laws were changed so that boys could cross more safely. |
| ........ | ........ | ........ | 4. It scared the automobile drivers who saw him. |
| ........ | ........ | ........ | 5. He was the cause of an automobile driver being put in jail. |
| ........ | ........ | ........ | 6. Two cars collided trying to avoid him. |
| ........ | ........ | ........ | 7. He got across as safely as any one. |
| ........ | ........ | ........ | 8. He got confused when he looked up and saw a car coming. |

### A Duties Test

1. To help a slow or dull child with his lessons    Yes   S   No
2. To read the newspapers every day    Yes   S   No
3. To call your teacher's attention to the fact if you received a higher grade than you deserved    Yes   S   No
4. To keep a diary    Yes   S   No
5. To sneeze when you feel like it    Yes   S   No
6. To jeer at a child who has just been punished    Yes   S   No
7. To smile when things go wrong    Yes   S   No
8. To report another pupil if you see him cheating    Yes   S   No

**The Provocations Test.** Another type of opinion-ballot is the Provocations Test.[1] The test is called by this name because it tends to call forth a response which conflicts with ideal responses. The theory of this test is that since the pupil is asked to pass judgment on the particular responses which are listed in the test, the examiner learns something of the level of moral judgment which has been attained by the pupil. The test is interesting as an illustration of the difficulty of securing standards for answers. The authors give an interesting illustration: "The neighbors had been kept awake at night by two cats fighting; so Fred set his bulldog on them." Of a class of graduate students, 19 per cent said this was right conduct, 53 per cent said it was excusable, and 28 per cent said it was wrong. The division of opinion is suggestive of the difficulty of securing a standard.

### A Provocations Test

Here are some little stories of what some children did. You are to decide whether they did right or wrong. If what they did was not quite right, perhaps it was at least excusable in view of the circumstances. Look at the sample first.

Sample: Jane's family were too poor to buy fruit for her sick brother. So every now and then Jane took an apple or an orange from a fruit stand and brought it home to him.

[1] From Hartshorne and May, *op. cit.*, p. 50.

Now if you think she was absolutely wrong in taking
the fruit, put a circle around the Wr, like this.... R  Ex  (Wr)

But if she did exactly right, encircle the R, like this.. (R)  Ex  Wr

If you think she was wrong but excusable in view of
her desire to bring it to her sick brother, encircle the
Ex, like this................................... R  (Ex)  W

Begin here and do the rest in the same way:

   1. Helen noticed that nearly everyone in the class
      was cheating on a test; so she cheated too..... R  Ex  Wr

   2. Harry was a Christian boy.  One day a Jewish
      boy called Harry a "dirty Christian."  Harry
      knocked him down........................ R  Ex  Wr

   3. Charles did not want to play marbles for keeps,
      but the boys called him a "sissy"; so he went
      ahead and played for keeps anyway.......... R  Ex  Wr

   4. On the way to Sunday school Jack matched
      pennies with the other boys in order to get some
      money for the Sunday-school collection....... R  Ex  Wr

### 3. Attitude tests

The term *attitude test* is no doubt somewhat vague, due
partially to the many meanings attached to the word
"attitude."  Charters makes a distinction between attitudes
and "ideals," in which "ideals" refers to objects of desire or
goals and "attitudes" means *mind set*.[1]  According to this
distinction, which will be accepted here, any trait good or
bad may be set up as an object of desire, as an *ideal*.  One
may then speak of an *attitude* toward any ideal, such as
honesty or punctuality.

**The Northwestern University Citizenship Tests.**  These
tests, prepared by Dr. G. H. Betts, are one example of an
effort to measure attitudes.  In these tests the pupil is
asked to indicate his judgment of the seriousness of a series

[1] Charters, W. W.  *The Teaching of Ideals*, p. 34.

## BALLOT 1. HOW SERIOUS (WRONG) IS IT?

Theodore Roosevelt once scornfully called some men who had done things he thought were wrong, "undesirable citizens." What is it that makes one a good or a bad citizen in his home? Would you not say that it is his acts, the way he conducts himself?

Some of the items (acts) listed below are probably more important than others in making good citizens in the home. You may think some of the acts are serious, or wrong, and that others are not. Vote in the proper column for each item to show how serious or wrong the act is. Vote but once for each item.

Think carefully, vote as you think. Make the best score you can.

| HOW SERIOUS (WRONG) IS THE ACT? I THINK IT IS — | very, very serious | very serious | some-what serious | not very serious | not serious at all |
|---|---|---|---|---|---|
| 1. Joyce has the habit of coming late to her meals quite often. | ...... | ...... | ...... | ...... | ...... |
| 2. William tells his mother he has forgotten to do her errand when he really has not forgotten, but has spent the time practicing baseball with his team. | ...... | ...... | ...... | ...... | ...... |
| 3. Finding ten cents on the bureau, Elsie takes it without asking anybody and buys a pencil which she needs. | ...... | ...... | ...... | ...... | ...... |
| 4. When getting ready for bed, Lloyd lets his shoes drop to the floor as he takes them off, rather than placing them quietly on the floor. | ...... | ...... | ...... | ...... | ...... |
| 5. Tom's father gave him a half-dollar for his school bank. On his way to school Tom sees in a store window a baseball marked down from one dollar to fifty cents, so he buys the ball with the half-dollar, meaning to earn money soon and then put the half-dollar in the bank. | ...... | ...... | ...... | ...... | ...... |

of trait actions.   A copy of one portion of the test known as
"The Citizen at Home" is shown on page 525.   In the second
part of this test the pupil is asked how he would "feel if
your best friend did" the things mentioned in the several
items.

Tests of this type raise a number of interesting problems.
If a pupil marks the test correctly, does this mean that his
marking actually represents his attitude, or does it merely
mean that he knows what his attitude should be and marks
the test accordingly?   Probably there is no answer to this
question at the present time.   If the teacher could be assured that if a child knows he should be punctual he will be
punctual the problem would be greatly simplified.   In that
case it would be possible to measure the trait in terms of the
pupil's knowledge of its importance or significance.   As has
already been pointed out, there is slight evidence to justify
the teacher in such an assumption.

As in other tests of this type, the Northwestern University
Citizenship Tests seek to overcome this difficulty by the insertion of "blinds" (items which have no significance in the
scoring of the test, and which tend to throw the pupil off his
guard concerning what is being measured).   It is probably
too early to appraise the value of tests of this kind.   They
are, however, suggestive to teachers.   For instance, the
trait actions included, together with the effort to rank
them, would without doubt provoke thought and discussion regarding the importance of the various traits represented.   In this way the tests may be a form of motivation quite regardless of their effectiveness as measures of
attitudes.

**Punishments Tests.**   Hartshorne and May present an interesting attitudes test under this title.   The response to
the test is based on the assumption that there is a relationship in untrained minds between the seriousness of an of-

## An Attitudes Test

Boys and girls are sometimes punished when they deserve it, and sometimes they do not deserve it. Below are some things for which they might be punished. If you think the thing does not deserve punishment put a check mark in the column which says, "Do not punish." If you think it does deserve punishment, then put a check mark in the column which tells how easy or hard the punishment should be.

| | Do not punish | Punish | | | | | | |
|---|---|---|---|---|---|---|---|---|
| | | Very lightly | Lightly | Rather strictly | Hard | Very severely | | |
| (a) Taking a few apples from a fruit stand | ... | ... | ... | ... | ... | ... | (a) |
| (b) Shining your shoes every morning | ... | ... | | ... | ... | ... | (b) |
| (c) Robbing a house and then burning it | ... | ... | ... | ... | ... | ... | (c) |
| **Part I** | | | | | | | |
| 1 Looking up answers in a book during an examination | ... | ... | ... | ... | ... | ... | 1 |
| 2. Peeping in a game of blind man's buff at a party | ... | ... | | ... | ... | ... | 2 |
| 3. Tripping and dirty play in a basket-ball game | ... | ... | ... | ... | | ... | 3 |
| 4. Taking some candy from the teacher's desk | ... | ... | ... | ... | | ... | 4 |
| 8. Copying from another pupil's paper on an examination | ... | ... | ... | ... | | ... | 8 |
| 12. Pretending not to hear when someone calls | ... | ... | ... | ... | ... | | 12 |
| 13. Refusing to help buy a radio for the class | ... | ... | ... | ... | ... | ... | 13 |
| 14. Reading a story during study period | ... | ... | ... | ... | ... | ... | 14 |
| 20. Refusing to help make toys for sick children | ... | ... | ... | ... | ... | ... | 20 |
| 25. Keeping an article you found when the owner's name is on it | ... | ... | ... | ... | ... | ... | 25 |
| **Part II** | | | | | | | |
| Do you think a boy or girl should be punished for lying | | | | | | | |
| 61. if it meant keeping out of trouble? | ... | ... | ... | ... | ... | ... | 61 |
| 62. if it made him seem like a "regular fellow"? | ... | ... | ... | ... | ... | ... | 62 |
| 63. if it were done just in fun? | ... | ... | ... | ... | ... | ... | 63 |
| 64. if telling the truth hurt somebody's feelings? | ... | ... | ... | ... | ... | ... | 64 |
| 65. if telling the truth would disgrace his parents? | ... | ... | ... | ... | ... | ... | 65 |

fense and the punishment to be inflicted.   Thus it was believed that a test which selected degrees of punishment for various specific offenses might reveal certain social attitudes. The directions to pupils and a sample test-item [1] are given on page 527.

**Expletives test.**   Hartshorne and May point out that feelings are usually expressed by some form of ejaculation or expletive.   It therefore seemed reasonable that a multiple-choice test listing certain word-responses descriptive of the situation presented would constitute a promising form of test.   The sample which follows [2] suggests the method used. While the authors present no data in regard to these tests, they appear to suggest ways in which teachers might construct tests measuring attitudes as evidenced in specific situations.

### EXPLETIVES TEST

Here are some stories about what some children of your age did. Read each story carefully and do what it tells you to do.

1. On the way to school Harold stopped to help an old woman shovel the snow from her sidewalk.
   Check the two words or phrases that best fit this story.
   Check *only two.*
   (  ) Good scout          (  ) What of it?
   (  ) Time wasted         (  ) Why shouldn't he?
   (  ) Splendid thing to do (  ) Goody-goody

2. When the teacher gave out answer sheets and asked each pupil to correct his own paper, John changed a lot of the answers on his paper so they would match the answer sheet.
   Remember to check the *two* words or phrases that best fit the story.
   (  ) Low down trick      (  ) Good for him
   (  ) Foolish             (  ) Why not?
   (  ) Clever stunt        (  ) Unfair to others

3. At a party Grace saw a chance to win easily by playing un-

[1] From Hartshorne and May, *op. cit.*, p. 67.          [2] *Ibid.*, p. 69.

fairly. But she didn't because she was afraid she would be put out of the game.

( ) Right spirit       ( ) Silly
( ) Cowardly       ( ) Of course she didn't
( ) Foolish       ( ) Good girl

4. While the teacher was out of the room Ruth took a few pieces of candy from her desk.

( ) A fine idea       ( ) Crooked
( ) What of it?       ( ) Clever stunt
( ) The mean thing       ( ) Served the teacher right

### 4. *Tests of conduct or behavior*

In reality most of the devices for measuring conduct are not tests; they are rating scales to be used by some person other than the one who is being rated. In some cases devices provide for self-rating on the part of pupils. The Health Chores of the National Tuberculosis Association are an example. The pupil records each day certain items of behavior conducive to health. This procedure has been criticized because of the contention that it encourages pupils to falsify their record in order to win awards or merit ratings. The real facts in this regard are probably not known. At the same time the fact that many teachers have the impression that the practice is undesirable limits its use. The examples of rating devices given here are largely of the type to be used by the teacher in rating the pupil.

**Rating scales for behavior problems.** Another type of conduct scale is that shown by Wickman,[1] which follows. The teacher is asked to rate the seriousness of a considerable list of behavior problems as they occur in a particular child. Four degrees of seriousness are provided for in the scale. This type of measurement has many advantages from the point of view of the teacher. The check marks on the scale, connected by a line, present a graphic view of the

[1] Wickman, E. K. *Children's Behavior and Teachers' Attitudes*, p. 207. Division of Publications, The Commonwealth Fund.

A Conduct Scale

Schedule B–4

How serious (or undesirable) is this behavior in *any* child?

| (Partial list only) | Of no consequence ↓ | Of only slight consequence ↓ | Makes for considerable difficulty ↓ | An extremely grave problem ↓ |
|---|---|---|---|---|
| Tardiness | ...... | ...... | ...... | ...... |
| Truancy | ...... | ...... | ...... | ...... |
| Destroying school materials | ...... | ...... | ...... | ...... |
| Untruthfulness (lying) | ...... | ...... | ...... | ...... |
| Imaginative lying | ...... | ...... | ...... | ...... |
| Cheating | ...... | ...... | ...... | ...... |
| Stealing | ...... | ...... | ...... | ...... |
| Profanity | ...... | ...... | ...... | ...... |
| Smoking | ...... | ...... | ...... | ...... |
| Obscene notes, pictures, talk | ...... | ...... | ...... | ...... |
| Masturbation | ...... | ...... | ...... | ...... |
| Heterosexual activity (with opposite sex) | ...... | ...... | ...... | ...... |
| Disorderliness (violations of classroom discipline) | ...... | ...... | ...... | ...... |
| Whispering and note-writing | ...... | ...... | ...... | ...... |
| Interrupting (talkativeness) | ...... | ...... | ...... | ...... |
| Restlessness (overactivity) | ...... | ...... | ...... | ...... |
| Inattention | ...... | ...... | ...... | ...... |
| Lack of interest in work | ...... | ...... | ...... | ...... |
| Carelessness in work | ...... | ...... | ...... | ...... |
| Laziness | ...... | ...... | ...... | ...... |
| Unreliableness (irresponsible) (evasion of duties) | ...... | ...... | ...... | ...... |
| Disobedience | ...... | ...... | ...... | ...... |
| Impertinence (insubordination and defiance) | ...... | ...... | ...... | ...... |
| Cruelty and bullying | ...... | ...... | ...... | ...... |
| Quarrelsomeness (annoying other children) | ...... | ...... | ...... | ...... |
| Tattling | ...... | ...... | ...... | ...... |

(Be sure you have rated each item)

child's behavior problems. Second ratings can be made by the teacher to note progress. Without doubt the use of such scales by the teacher will make her more observing of the behavior of children, as well as more discriminating in regard to behavior problems.

**Purchasing-errand test.** This test, devised by Voelker, is more than a knowledge test.[1] It seeks to place the pupil in an actual situation and to measure his conduct in that situation. Series L of these tests seeks to answer the following questions in regard to a pupil: Can he be trusted to refuse credit which is not due him? to stick to a point when he knows he is right; to refuse help in the solution of a puzzle when he has been instructed to solve it independently; to return borrowed money according to promise; not to accept overchange; not to accept a tip for a trifling courtesy; to do a given task exactly as it was given him to do; to work faithfully at an assigned task when there are other interests that distract him; not to peek when he is placed on his honor to keep his eyes closed; and not to cheat on an examination?

The item, "Can the subject be trusted not to accept overchange?" which is illustrative, is given herewith.

### PURCHASING-ERRAND TEST

Can the subject be trusted not to accept overchange?

*Directions:* The subject is handed a card on which is written his own name and the words: "One copy of opposites test, nine cents." The examiner hands him a twenty-five cent piece and requests him to go to the neighboring stationery store to purchase a copy of the test.

When the subject arrives at the store, the examiner's confederate takes the card, hands out an envelope containing the test and says, "Nine cents, please." When the subject hands her the twenty-five-cent piece, she carelessly hands him two dimes, one nickel and one cent.

If the subject immediately returns the ten cents overchange to

[1] Voelker, Paul F. *The Function of Ideals and Attitudes in Social Education*, pp. 74–75. Teachers College Contributions to Education, no. 112, 1921.

the clerk she thanks him and records the fact on the card.   If he brings twenty-six cents to the examiner, the latter says: "Did I not give you twenty-five cents?"   If the subject says "yes" the examiner says: "Did you put some of your own money in with this?"

*Scoring*: If the subject returns the change to the clerk, or if on returning all the money to the examiner he insists that none of it is his own, he is scored 10.   If he keeps the over-change he is scored zero.

**The Olson Scale.**   A very interesting type of Personal Characteristic Rating Scale has been devised by Olson.[1] Five descriptions of children have been prepared, and these have been arranged like a penmanship scale.   In each description have been included those traits or characteristics which have high correlations — that is those which usually "go together."   The scale is prepared with a graphic provision for marking on the basis of a nine-point scale.   The descriptions are arranged in order from least desirable to most desirable.   In the use of the scale the teacher can read the various descriptions and select the one which most nearly describes the child in question.   Perhaps the teacher may decide that the child is better than No. 1, but not as good as No. 2; in this case the child would be rated with 2 on the nine point scale or halfway between No. 1 and No. 2.   To illustrate the scale, descriptions 3 and 5 are here reproduced, side by side.

3

This child makes an unfavorable impression on people with his physique and bearing.   He is rather negligent of his personal appearance.   He may be either exceptionally strong or have some physical defects.   He is apt to be over-active in his physical output of energy, but is not easily fatigued.   He talks

5

This child is fastidious in his personal appearance.   His physique and bearing are generally unnoticed.   He has some physical difficulties; he is slow in action and does not seem to have ordinary endurance.   He talks more than his share.   His behavior is acceptable to ordinary social standards.   He follows

[1] Olson, Willard C.   *A Scale for Rating Personal Characteristics*, University of Michigan, Ann Arbor, Michigan.   1930.

more than his share. There are occasional violations of ordinary social standards. He prefers social activities to all else, but is bold and insensitive in his social relationships. He is apt to be critical of authority and often is very stubborn. He is rude and freely criticizes others. He is unsympathetic, disobliging and cold. He has strong and frequent changes of mood. He is not easily discouraged. He is impatient in unpleasant situations. As a rule he is cheerful to the point of hilarity. He is inclined to be easygoing with no apparent worries. When his problems are discussed with him, he is entirely uninhibited. He spills everything and seems to enjoy it. He complies very slowly with suggestions. He is apt to act impulsively.

very few social activities, but is confident of himself in social relationships. He is ordinarily obedient to authority. He treats others with ordinary civility and respect and often yields to others rather than assert himself. He seldom criticizes. He is very sympathetic. He is rather stolid with rare changes of mood. He is easily discouraged and is inclined to give up before giving a thing an adequate trial. He is sometimes dejected, melancholy, and in the dumps. He is very submissive and long suffering in unpleasant situations. He is often apprehensive and worries unduly. He does not volunteer information in a discussion of himself or his problems. He is somewhat suspicious and has to be reassured. He seems to be very cautious and calculating in his actions.

It will be noted that this scale seeks a measure of personality in its totality, rather than in terms of its details. Most rating scales seek to inventory personal characteristics and to rate each individual characteristic. In this respect the Olson Scale is similar to the Brueckner Scale for Rating Teaching Skill.[1] Scales of this type facilitate rating, since the individual being rated can be compared with concrete descriptions of individuals of varying characteristics.

Thus far, the Olson Scale has not been used sufficiently to justify predictions as to its utility. It represents, however, an interesting departure from the traditional rating devices in the field of personality characteristics.

[1] Brueckner, L. J. *A Scale for Rating Teaching Skill.* University of Minnesota Press, Minneapolis. 1927.

### 5. *Measures of individual traits*

**Complexity of measurement of traits.**  One of the reasons for slow progress in the measurement of traits is the complexity of these traits as evidenced in human behavior.  For example, punctuality is not a general characteristic of all the behavior of an individual.  One may be punctual in arriving at his office, but habitually late for dinner.  One may likewise be honest in paying his debts, but may cheat in an examination.  It is thus impossible to make sweeping classifications of persons into "honest" and "dishonest" groups.  Perfect and complete honesty rarely if ever exists.  Letter-perfect punctuality perhaps is equally difficult to find.

The complexity of the measurement of traits has led experimenters to seek to measure traits with a variety of procedures.  The best example is the Character Education Inquiry made under the direction of Hartshorne and May.[1]  These investigators undertook the measurement of deceit by an elaborate battery of tests which would measure deception under different conditions.  Deceptive behavior was divided into three types — cheating, stealing, and lying.  Appropriate measures were then devised for measuring each of the three types.  The aim was to construct the tests in such a way that not only the existence of deception, but the amount of deception would be shown.  The number of different tests is so large that space forbids the discussion of more than a few illustrative test forms.

**Measuring cheating.**  Cheating may be exhibited in the classroom, at home, in athletic contests, or in parlor games.  Cheating in the classroom is one of the commonest forms with which the teacher has to deal.  For this reason the sample test devices given deal with this form of cheating.

**The copying technique.**  In this plan of procedure two

[1] Hartshorne, Hugh, and May, Mark A.  *Studies in Deceit*, and *Studies in the Organization of Character.*

test-forms of some simple exercise are prepared in such a manner that while they are very similar, there are enough differences in arrangement so that if a pupil working on one form copies from a pupil working on another form that fact will immediately be evident to the scorer. In giving the test the papers of the two forms are distributed alternately and "staggered" in order that pupils side by side or back to front will not have the same form. The sample item below, taken from the tests,[1] is illustrative: It is an *opposites* test. The pupil is asked to find the word which has an opposite meaning to the word in capitals, and to write its number on the dotted line at the right.

### Form A

1. GIVE 1 present 2 accept 3 take 4 wish 5 absent............ 1
2. FRIEND 1 soldier 2 true 3 false 4 enemy 5 fight............ 2
3. HELP 1 hinder 2 assist 3 someone 4 need 5 chantey........ 3
4. BORROW 1 steal 2 return 3 book 4 loan 5 debt............ 4
5. KIND 1 sweet 2 cruel 3 sort 4 sympathy 5 always......... 5

### Form B

1. GIVE 1 present 2 accept 3 wish 4 take 5 absent............ 1
2. FRIEND 1 soldier 2 false 3 true 4 enemy 5 fight............ 2
3. HELP 1 hinder 2 need 3 someone 4 assist 5 chantey........ 3
4. BORROW 1 steal 2 book 3 return 4 loan 5 debt............. 4
5. KIND 1 sweet 2 sort 3 cruel 4 sympathy 5 always.......... 5

In the above items the same words are contained in both forms, but they are arranged so that the correct answers will not have the same numbers in the two forms. Thus if a pupil copies from someone sitting beside him his answers will be wrong. In the opinion of the authors this test is not a satisfactory measure of cheating, since one cannot tell from the pupil's paper whether he has copied or merely made mistakes. The test is included here merely to illustrate the difficulties arising in attempting to prepare tests of this type.

[1] Hartshorne, Hugh, and May, Mark A. *Studies in Deceit*, p. 50.

**The duplicating technique.** This procedure in the judgment of the authors has been quite successful. The plan is to give any short answer test. The papers are then collected and removed from the schoolroom, where duplicates are made of them with great care, showing exactly how the pupils marked the tests. At a later class period the papers are returned together with keys, and pupils are asked to score them. The papers scored by the pupils are then compared with the duplicates. Deception consists in raising one's score by copying answers from the key. A sample of the Information Test of this type is given below:[1]

1. Bombay is a city in China    France    Japan    India
2. Pongee is a dance    food    fabric    drink
3. Hannibal is the name of a general    king    prize fighter    river
4. One horse power equals 746 watts    1000 watts    16⅔ watts    2.45 watts
5. Brahmaputra is the name of a    flower    goddess    language    river

In order to cheat the pupil has to erase the circles made around his original answers and draw others.

**The improbable-achievement technique.** This is a method of requiring a pupil to perform a feat so difficult that if he succeeds in it beyond a certain level the likelihood is that he has cheated. Several types of these tests have been developed, employing both puzzles and paper and pencil techniques. The Squares Test shown on page 537[2] is an example of the paper and pencil type. From the sample it will be evident that cheating consists in opening one's eyes so as to make a better score. The principal weakness of the test lies in the difficulty of determining what level of achievement can be expected without cheating.

[1] Hartshorne, Hugh, and May, Mark A.    *Studies in Deceit*, p. 50.
[2] *Ibid.*, p. 61.

### SQUARES PUZZLE TEST

Put your pencil point on the cross in Square No. 1. When the signal is given, shut your eyes and move the pencil in the direction of the arrow around the center and back to the cross, without touching the sides of the lane. Wait for the signal for each trial.

After each trial if you succeeded in doing that square correctly, put a check mark on the line after the number of the square you have just tried. If you touched the side once you lose the square, and get no score for it. After the last trial enter the total score using the table at the right for finding the score. The maximum score is 100.

| Record of Trials | | Score Values Table | |
|---|---|---|---|
| Square 1 . . . . . . . . . . . | | Any one right is | 5 |
| Square 2 . . . . . . . . . . . | | Any two right is | 15 |
| Square 3 . . . . . . . . . . . | Total Score . . . . . . | Any three right is | 30 |
| Square 4 . . . . . . . . . . . | | Any four right is | 60 |
| Square 5 . . . . . . . . . . . | | Any five right is | 100 |

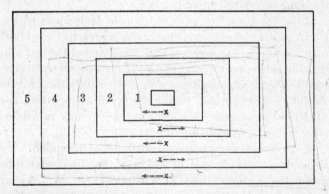

**Method for measuring the stealing type of deception.** Hartshorne and May set forth five general criteria [1] for measuring the stealing type of deception. They are:

1. It must be a group situation.
2. Money must be used in a natural way or appear as a natural part of the situation.

[1] Hartshorne, Hugh, and May, Mark A. *Studies in Deceit*, p. 90.

3. There must be an opportunity to take all or some known part of the money apparently without being detected in the act.
4. The subject must feel that he is not merely being clever in getting away with the money but that he is actually stealing it from a particular person or institution.
5. It must be possible to check exactly what the subject does.

**The planted-dime test.**    The plan used in this test is to distribute some boxes to pupils according to seating plan of the class, each box being numbered.    Each box contains some puzzles, not all of which are used.    In each box is a dime supposedly belonging to another puzzle which is not used.    The examiner shows the dime puzzle to the children but does not ask them to solve it.    Each pupil returns his box to a large receptacle in the front of the room.    The purpose of the test is to see whether or not the pupils would take the dime before returning the box.

Many teachers feel reluctant to use techniques of this kind, since they feel that it constitutes a breach of good faith with the pupils.    Others feel that the giving of the test may actually encourage dishonesty.    Probably the real truth in regard to these problems is unknown.    Certainly the methods should be very carefully and scientifically employed, and used only in sincere efforts for helping pupils to achieve greater ideals of conduct.[1]

**Methods for measuring the lying types of deception.**    For measuring the lying type of deception, the Character Education Inquiry used the CEI Attitudes Test SA.    As can be seen from the sample reproduced, the test lists a large number of specific conduct-acts which have widespread social approval.    Many of these are rarely done.    A child who answers correctly all of these items is probably not truthful in his replies.    A statistical method was used in arriving at the norms for the test.    It is quite difficult to see how this type of measure can be used to test the truthfulness of indi-

[1] Hartshorne, Hugh, and May, Mark A.    *Studies in Deceit*, p. 90.

vidual pupils. It would appear that its application is largely limited to the testing of large groups, followed by statistical treatment of the results. As the authors point out, there is not complete certainty about what is measured by the test.

CEI ATTITUDES TEST, SA[1]

FORM ONE

Name............................Date............................

School..........................Grade............................

Answer the following questions by underlining YES or NO. If your answer is YES, draw a line under YES. If your answer is NO, draw a line under NO. Please answer every question.

1. Did you ever accept the credit or honor for anything when you knew the credit or honor belonged to some one else?....................................... YES  NO  1

2. Did you ever act greedily by taking more than your share of anything?............................. YES  NO  2

3. Did you ever blame another for something you had done when you knew all the time it was your fault? YES  NO  3

4. Do you usually report the number of a car you see speeding?...................................... YES  NO  4

5. Do you always preserve order when the teacher is out of the room?.................................. YES  NO  5

6. Do you report other pupils whom you see cheating? YES  NO  6

7. Did you ever pretend to understand a thing when you really did not understand it?..................... YES  NO  7

8. Have you ever disobeyed any law of your country or rule of your school?............................. YES  NO  8

[1] Character Education Institution, Chevy Chase, Washington, D.C.

9. Do you speak to all the people you are acquainted
with, even the ones you do not like?.............   YES   NO   9

10. Do you usually call the attention of people to the fact
that you have on new shoes or a new suit or dress?.   YES   NO   10

**Conclusions from the use of the foregoing tests.**    The
tests illustrated above practically all deal with the single
trait of honesty.   At their present stage of development the
use of these techniques in the classroom by the teacher presents considerable difficulty.   It is believed, however, that a
study of the tests by teachers may be suggestive of ways in
which teachers may become more observing in regard to the
character traits of pupils.    Tests must be made covering
other traits before anything like a comprehensive trait
measurement can be made.    At the present time the
greatest significance of the tests and their use grows
out of the conclusions which the authors reach following
their studies.    Many of these conclusions are of interest to
the teacher in planning an effective program to promote
honesty as a trait in children.    Concerning the results of
the use of the tests, the authors [1] say:

1. No one is honest or dishonest by "nature."   Where conflict
arises between a child and his environment, deception is a natural
mode of adjustment, having in itself no "moral" significance.   If
indirect ways of gaining his ends are successful, they will be continued unless definite training is undertaken through which direct
and honest methods may also become successful.

2. Apart from the actual practice of direct or honest methods of
gaining ends where a conflict of wills is actually involved, the mere
urging of honest behavior by teachers or the discussion of standards
and ideals of honesty, no matter how much such general ideas may
be "emotionalized," has no necessary relation to the control of
conduct.   The extent to which individuals may be affected, either
for better or for worse, is not known, but there seems to be evidence

[1] Hartshorne, H., and May, M. *Studies in deceit*, 412–14.

that such effects as may result are not generally good and are some-times unwholesome.

3. This does not imply that the teaching of general ideas, stand-ards, and ideals is not desirable and necessary, but only that the prevailing ways of inculcating ideals probably do little good and may do some harm.

4. The large place occupied by the "situation" in the suggestion and control of conduct, not only in its larger aspects, such as the example of other pupils, the personality of the teacher, etc., but also in its more subtle aspects, such as the nature of the opportunity to deceive, the kind of material or test on which it is possible, the relation of the child to this material, and so on, points to the need of a careful educational analysis of all such situations for the purpose of making explicit the nature of the direct or honest mode of re-sponse in detail, so that when a child is placed in these situations there may be a genuine opportunity for him to practice direct methods of adjustment.

5. Along with such practice of direct or honest responses there should go a careful study of them in terms of the personal relations involved, so that in the child's imagination the honest mode of pro-cedure may be clearly distinguished from the dishonest mode as a way of social interaction, and the consequences of either method may be observed and used in evaluating the relative desirability of direct versus indirect procedures. Such analyses would provide the foundation for the understanding of social ideals and laws and the basis for an intelligent allegiance to such ideals as proved consonant with social welfare.

6. The association of deceit with sundry handicaps in social background, home conditions, companions, personal limitations, and so on indicates the need for understanding particular examples of dishonest practice before undertaking to "judge" the blame-worthiness of the individual. As far as possible, such social and personal limitations should be removed, not only for the sake of getting more honest behavior, but for the sake of the child's whole development. But obviously the widespread practice of deceit makes the application of radical environmental changes an absurd-ity. There is no evidence for supposing that children who are more likely to resort to deceptive methods than others would not use honorable methods with equal satisfaction if the situation in which dishonesty is practiced were sufficiently controlled by those who are responsible for their behavior. That is, the main atten-

tion of educators should be placed not so much on devices for teaching honesty or any other "trait" as on the reconstruction of school practices in such a way as to provide not occasional but consistent and regular opportunities for the successful use by both teachers and pupils of such forms of conduct as make for the common good.

**Factors in deceit.** Probably studies have not gone far enough in the field to warrant any far-reaching conclusions in regard to the various factors in the development of traits of character. Nevertheless the results from the studies of Hartshorne and May are interesting and thought-provoking. Their general summary [1] is as follows:

### RESULTS OF THE STUDY OF DECEIT

1. *The relation of deceit to age.* The older pupils in any given school group are slightly more deceptive than the younger children. The differences vary with the test situation and the group tested.

2. *Sex differences.* Sex seems to make no difference. On some tests and in some groups, the boys are more deceptive; on other tests and in other groups the girls are more deceptive. In the home situation the girls usually cheat more than the boys, but the cause is presumably a difference in interest rather than in honor.

3. *Relation of deception to intelligence.* Honesty is positively related to intelligence. In almost any group of children of approximately the same age, those of higher levels of intelligence deceive definitely less than those of lower levels. The child who scores above the average for his age in intelligence will, other things being equal, score below the average for his age in deception.

4. *Emotional instability.* Children who show symptoms of emotional instability or maladjustment (as measured by one standard test) are more likely to deceive than those with fewer such symptoms.

5. *Physical condition.* This, as measured by our tests, is unassociated with deceit even in athletic contests.

6. *Socio-economic background.* Deceit is definitely associated with the economic level of the home. Children whose fathers are engaged in occupations yielding the higher incomes are less decep-

[1] Hartshorne and May, *op. cit.*, pp. 408–12.

tive than children of day laborers. When the occupations of fathers are classified in four levels, the children from the higher levels deceive the least, those from the second higher next, and so on to those of the lowest level, who cheat the most. When more detailed studies of the economic and social conditions of the home are made, the results show again that children from the higher socio-economic levels deceive less than children from lower socio-economic levels.

7. *Cultural background.* Children who have better manners, who are better acquainted with art and music and the influences that indicate culture and refinement, and whose parents treat them decently are less deceptive than others who do not show these refinements.

8. *Other home conditions.* Deceit is associated with such factors as parental discord, parental example, bad discipline, unsocial attitude toward the children, impoverished type of community, and changing social or economic situation; and certain combinations of these "handicaps" with personal handicaps tend to distinguish the group of most dishonest from the group of most honest children.

9. *Nationality of parents.* Children of parents who were born in Northern Europe or America are less deceptive in classroom cheating situations than children of parents born in South Europe. Colored children cheat more than most of the white groups. Certain racial and national differences persist even when allowance is made for differences in intelligence and socio-economic level.

10. *Religious affiliations.* Between children reporting affiliations with the three main religious groups, Catholics, Jews, and Protestants, and between various Protestant groups, there are no *general* differences which are not attributable to differences in intelligence and social level; but on certain tests the particular groups measured show real differences not thus entirely accounted for.

11. *Kinship.* Deception runs in families to about the same extent as eye color, length of forearm, and other inherited structures. This does not prove that it is inherited. But the general drift of the evidence inclines one to believe that, if all children received identical nurture, they would still vary in deception.

12. *Grade.* In most tests there are no grade differences. In the I.E.R. school tests, there is a steady increase in deception from grades six to eight, but grade five is the most deceptive.

13. *Grade retardation.* Children who are over-age for their grade tend to cheat more than those who are under the average age for

their grade. The more intelligent in the grade or in the class group cheat less, and the less intelligent cheat more. It is probably not the fact of being over-age for one's grade that matters, but of being both older and also less intelligent.

14. *School achievement*. Those who get high marks cheat slightly less than those who get low marks; but where their achievement is stated in terms of their mental age, there is no evidence of any relation between their academic status and their tendency to deceive.

15. *Deportment*. Deportment marks vary with the school and teacher, but on the whole high deportment marks are associated with less cheating in school and low marks with more cheating in school. Pupils who receive A in deportment cheat definitely less than those who receive C.

16. *Associates*. There is considerable resemblance in amount of cheating between classmates. That is, a pupil's cheating score on certain of the classroom tests is very much like that of his associates. There is a slight resemblance between friends even when they are not in the same class.

17. *Suggestibility*. Greater resistance to the sort of suggestion found in the Otis suggestibility tests is associated with less cheating.

18. *Movie attendance*. Children who attend the movies more than once a week tend to cheat slightly more than children who attend occasionally but less than once a week.

19. *Teacher Influence*. The general relations that exist between the teacher and the class influence cheating. On the whole, there is less cheating when these relations are free and cordial and there is a spirit of good will and coöperation.

20. *Progressive methods and morale*. The progressive schools tested do not cheat as much as most of the conventional schools tested. This seems to be due to the factor of school or classroom morale, for which the teacher is largely responsible but which also characterizes the whole school or class group from year to year.

21. *Sunday-School enrollment and attendance*. Those enrolled in Protestant Sunday Schools cheat less than those not enrolled. There is no relation, however, between Sunday-School attendance and deception. Children who attend regularly cheat in day school about the same as those who rarely or never attend.

22. *Membership in organizations purporting to teach honesty*. Children who belong to certain organizations purporting to teach honesty deceive about the same as (and in one case more than) children who do not belong. Furthermore, in one organization

length of membership and rank achieved were positively correlated with deceptiveness.

23. *Deceit not a unified trait.* The results of these studies show that neither deceit nor its opposite, "honesty," are unified character traits, but rather specific functions of life situations. Most children will deceive in certain situations and not in others. Lying, cheating, and stealing as measured by the test situations used in these studies are only very loosely related. Even cheating in the classroom is rather highly specific, for a child may cheat on an arithmetic test and not on a spelling test, etc. Whether a child will practice deceit in any given situation depends in part on his intelligence, age, home background, and the like and in part on the nature of the situation itself and his particular relation to it.

24. *The motivation of deceit.* The motives for cheating, lying, or stealing are complex and inhere for the most part in the general situations themselves. The most common motive for cheating on classroom exercises is the desire to do well.

*Summary.* The concomitants of deceit are, in order of their importance, (1) classroom association; (2) general personal handicaps, such as relatively low I.Q., poor resistance to suggestion, and emotional instability; (3) cultural and social limitations in the home background; and (4) such other miscellaneous facts as are loosely correlated with deception.

## V. REMEDIAL TEACHING IN CHARACTER EDUCATION

It is unfortunate that devices for remedial teaching in this field are not more specific. In the preceding pages several methods for measuring traits or characteristics have been described. If it be assumed that the teacher can determine, let us say, degree of honesty in a child, there is still not available to the teacher any specific procedure which will help to correct any deficiencies in honesty. In the chapter on arithmetic specific devices for correcting various deficiencies were shown. Thus far no similar materials are available in character education. Most of the character-education procedures thus far devised are general teaching procedures which certain persons believe are effective. There are even doubts about their general effectiveness, let alone their specific effects in a given situation.

### 1. *Character education through correlation*

**An indirect method.** One of the more significant movements in character education has been the effort to correlate it with other subjects. This plan is essentially an indirect method of approach. It is based on the assumption that in the teaching of the various school subjects, certain habits or traits are developed. Thus, arithmetic may develop accuracy, neatness, honesty in treatment of answers, and perhaps many other traits. Those who advocate this method believe that there is at least some transfer from these school-subject situations to their situations in everyday life. The methods suggested in the *Fourth Yearbook* of the Department of Superintendence [1] for teaching character-outcomes through spelling and school assemblies are suggestive of this indirect method of approach. These are:

*Character education through the teaching of spelling.* There is a right way to spell a word. All other ways are wrong. The teacher makes provision — manages and controls circumstances and conditions so that every learner can spell every word correctly and most surely and carefully expresses hearty approval when this is accomplished and just as certainly and heartily expresses disapproval of every mistake. Under normal conditions — under conditions that practically every teacher can provide — it is possible for every pupil to spell every word correctly. If this is not done, the teacher has failed in achieving the maximum character results. If there has been any failure, then two supplementary lessons must be learned. First, the mistakes must be corrected — corrected where they happened — that is, in the conduct of the learner himself. The second lesson, so very important for character results, is the development of appropriate amount and kind of shame that should accompany such a procedure. There are three essential means for accomplishing this latter result. This

[1] Pages 405–06.

wrong spelling separates the wrong spellers from those who spelled correctly; second, their conduct meets the disapproval of the teacher and their own disapproval; third, extra time is required to correct the mistakes.

Another fundamental principle of character education is well illustrated by spelling. If the time and attention that are often used in correcting wrong spelling were given to preventing wrong spelling — and this can be done — there would be fewer mistakes to correct.

A first principle in character education is thus well illustrated by spelling — doing the best that can be done under the circumstances and providing the conditions for correct spelling.

A second principle is the development of what may be properly termed "a spelling conscience." A vital and enlightened spelling conscience involves the three factors in an enlightened conscience — first, the abiding desire and decision to spell correctly — the decision not to guess at spelling; second, an appropriate remorse — a sense of shame if words are misspelled; third, a successful way of learning to spell involving the right use of the dictionary. All this procedure means the right use of approval and disapproval of teacher, class and self.

*School Assemblies*

To develop leadership through leading and directing companions

To develop citizenship through graceful coöperation

To develop proper school spirit and unity

To provide for self-expression

To teach pupils proper conduct at public gatherings — that is, to develop audience training

To inspire a spirit of service

To develop social coherence, school unity

To widen and deepen the interest of teachers and pupils in school life

To add dignity to service in student organizations by appropriate public recognition of their work through the installation of officers and presentation of insignia

To release motives for better work and higher standards

The assembly is an extracurricular activity conducted by the pupils and teachers, and recognized by the school as a means of training in that phase of constructive, democratic citizenship which has to do with mass instruction through public meetings.

*Club Activities*

To train the citizens of a school to perform better those desirable activities they are going to perform anyway

To afford an opportunity for developing leadership

To create and intensify interest in things worth while

To aid in the formation of friendships based on a mutual interest in worth-while things

To develop freedom of the individual, respect for law, coöperation, and service

To satisfy the adolescent's craving for sociability

To give ethical training

To develop spontaneity

To arouse the desire for self-government and the sense of responsibility for the selection of leaders on the basis of worth

To develop initiative

**Use of concrete situations.**    An excellent example of this type of procedure is that suggested by Horn.[1]    To quote the author:

An illustration of what is meant by concrete situations will serve to make clear as well as to illustrate the most important principles which should be observed in teaching.    In a middle western city the children in going to school cut across lots.    Lawns were damaged, shrubbery broken down, and flower beds ruined.    The first grade teacher saw in this situation a need for moral instruction. She could have lectured her pupils on that point and laid down rules, but having been trained to give a different type of moral instruction she did not do that.    Rather, she went about the job frankly and directly.    She took her pupils out to see some of these lots with the damaged lawns, shrubbery, and flower beds.    She asked them if they saw anything there that they would not like if they owned the property.    She asked the pupils how they thought the householders felt about the damage.    The children saw very readily that the householders, of course, would not like to have their property harmed.

She might have stopped at that point by saying, "Let's not do that any more."    Instead, she asked, "How can we be sure that we stop cutting across these lots?"

[1] Horn, Ernest, "Teaching a Lesson in Moral Education"; in *Minnesota Journal of Education*, vol. 8, pp. 177–79.    (September, 1927.)

The pupils discussed a plan for stopping this trespass and they did stop it. They soon observed, however, that the pupils of the other grades were cutting across the lawns. They asked whether they ought not to try to get the rest of the pupils to stop damaging these properties. Again they formulated their plan of action. They went to the householders and apologized to them, explaining that they really had not meant to do any damage. They asked the owners' permission to put up signs opposite the places where most of the damage had been done. The pupils made these signs themselves and put them up. Then they planned short speeches and chose representatives to go to the other grades in the school to make an appeal to them to stop cutting across lots. They also posted little girls and boys opposite these corners near the school to remind boys and girls that they should not cut across the lots.

Now the teacher could have let the matter stop there. She had obtained results in terms of conduct. Instead she led her pupils to apply what they had learned to other situations. She asked them if they could think of other instances where they had, without thinking, damaged the property of others. Two children suggested that they remembered sliding down a neighbor's hay stack; others that they had been playing in an empty building without the permission of the owner, and so on, until the blackboard was full of a variety of cases of trespass.

Then, working sympathetically, she led the children to state the general principles or ideals that they should keep in mind in all these situations. Each child who had been trespassing was led to plan how not to trespass in the future.

Notice the essential steps in this teaching. First, it started with a concrete situation that could be readily understood by the children. Second, the pupils themselves were allowed to sense what was wrong in that situation. Third, the pupils were allowed to formulate for themselves a plan for right conduct. Fourth, they were allowed to carry it out, and they were left with the feeling that they had not done their job until it was carried out. Mere talking was seen not to be enough. Fifth, they were encouraged to plan for transferring what they had learned in this situation to other situations of a similar type; and sixth, they were guided in formulating in their own words and for themselves principles of conduct to govern them in the future. Finally, provision should be made for an occasional checking up of the number of times that each child has responded correctly in similar situations.

## 2. Suggested projects

**The Iowa Plan suggestions, by grades.** Teachers often find it difficult to find the exact situations in which character-education outcomes may be realized. The Iowa Plan lists, in chart form, a variety of projects for each grade. Those interested may secure a copy of the bulletin in which the plan was described from Character Education Institution, Chevy Chase, Washington, D.C.

## QUESTIONS FOR STUDY, DISCUSSION, AND REPORT

1. Compare the Iowa Plan and the Denver List of objectives in character education.
2. Prepare a rating of a pupil by means of the Haggerty–Olson–Wickman Scale.
3. Distinguish between the direct and indirect plans of character education.
4. Read carefully and evaluate the Iowa Plan. List its strong and its weak points.
5. Prepare a list of activities whereby a teacher may secure outcomes in character education. Indicate the grade for which your list is prepared.
6. Make a study of a class of pupils, with the assistance of such character measures as you can secure. Can you use your test results as a basis for recommendations to the teacher regarding remedial work?
7. Prepare a list of suggestions whereby a teacher might correlate character education with arithmetic.
8. Make a case study of an individual child who is a disciplinary problem in the schools. Prepare recommendations to the child's teacher.

## SELECTED REFERENCES

Charters, W. W. *The Teaching of Ideals.* New York, The Macmillan Company, 1928. 372 p.

Chicago Association for Child Study and Parent Education. *Intelligent Parenthood.* University of Chicago Press, 1926. 326 p.

Fairchild, R. W., and Kilcullen, Mae T.  *A Course in Character Education*.  Elgin, Illinois, News Printing Company, 1930. 35 pp.

Germane, Charles E., and Gayton, Edith.  *Character Education*.  New York, Silver, Burdett and Company, 1929.  259 and 224 pp.

Gregg, Fred M.  *A Course of Study in Character Education*.  Nebraska State Department of Instruction, Lincoln, Nebraska, 1927.  205 p.

Hartshorne, Hugh, and May, Mark A.  *Studies in Deceit*.  New York, The Macmillan Company, 1928.  720 p.

Hartshorne, Hugh, and May, Mark A.  *Studies in the Organization of Character*.  New York, The Macmillan Company, 1930. 503 pp.

Maryland Department of Education.  *The Teaching of Citizenship in the Elementary School*.  Maryland School Bulletin, August, 1926.  262 p.

National Education Association, Committee on Character Education, Milton Bennion, Chairman.  *Character Education*.  United States Bureau of Education, Bulletin, 1926, no. 7.  89 p. Washington, D.C., Government Printing Office.

National Education Association, Department of Superintendence. *Fourth Yearbook*, National Education Association.  Washington, D.C.  520 p.

Neumann, Henry.  *Education for Moral Growth*.  New York, D. Appleton and Company, 1923.  383 p.

Norfolk City Schools.  *Character Education in the Norfolk Elementary Schools*.  Bulletin no. 1, 1928.  207 p.

Oakland Public Schools.  *Building Character Through Activities*. Oakland, California.  121 p.

Olson, Willard C.  *Problem Tendencies in Children*.  A Method for their Measurement and Description.  Minneapolis, Minnesota, The University of Minnesota Press.  1930.  90 pp.

Starbuck, Edwin D., and others.  *Character Education Methods*. The Iowa Plan.  $20,000 Award, 1922.  Character Education Institution, Chevy Chase, Washington, D.C.

Starbuck, Edwin D., and Shuttleworth, Frank K.  *A Guide for Literature for Character Training*, vol. 1.  New York, The Macmillan Company, 1928.  389 p.

## LIST OF TESTS IN CHARACTER EDUCATION

| Test | Publisher |
|---|---|
| Haggerty–Olson–Wickman Conduct Scale | World Book Company, Yonkers, New York. |
| Northwestern University Citizenship Test | Division of Research, School of Education, Northwestern University, Evanston, Ill. |
| Olson Personal Characteristics Rating Scale | W. C. Olson, School of Education, University of Michigan, Ann Arbor, Michigan. |
| CEI Tests | Association Press, 347 Madison Avenue, New York, N.Y. |

Those who wish further information in regard to these tests should write the Association Press (above address). The various tests are also discussed in the reports of the Character Education Inquiry:

| | |
|---|---|
| Hartshorne, Hugh A., and May, Mark A., *Studies in Deceit* | The Macmillan Company, New York, 1928. 306 pp. |
| Hartshorne, Hugh A., and May, Mark A., *Studies in the Organization of Character* | The Macmillan Company, New York, 1930. 503 pp. |
| Hartshorne, Hugh A., and May, Mark A., *Studies in Service and Self-Control* | The Macmillan Company, New York, 1929. 559 pp. |

The above volumes are especially helpful to all who wish to emphasize work in the field of measurement in character education.

# CHAPTER XIV

## DIAGNOSTIC AND REMEDIAL TEACHING IN HEALTH EDUCATION

**Importance of the health problem.** The importance of health education has been increasingly recognized during the last three decades. More accurate data in regard to the ravages of disease and ill health have given emphasis to the economic losses involved, and the relationship of health to happiness and general social welfare has been recognized. Along with a greater recognition of the importance of health have come great strides in medical science which have contributed richly to our control over health. Medical men and teachers alike have come to recognize the strategic place of the school in furthering the health-education movement.

The improvements which have been made in health during the last fifty years are a measure of the effectiveness of the techniques which have been employed. Merely to mention the lines along which improvement has taken place, we have the following:

1. Elimination of scourges like typhoid and cholera
2. Reduction in death rates
3. Lengthening of life
4. Decline in infant mortality
5. Progress made in treating and preventing such diseases as tuberculosis and diphtheria

While measurable progress has been made, the movement has only begun. Staggering losses still occur from the ravages of disease. Dr. Dublin, of the Metropolitan Life Insurance Company, estimates that it costs $7200 to rear a child in an average family to the age of eighteen. In case of premature death, there is an economic loss, not only of this amount, but also of the future income of the individual, which he estimates to be $29,000. Dr. Haven Emerson estimates that the cost of tuberculosis was $800,000,000 in 1921, while the cost of nursing and medical care for the heart patients in the United States in 1927 was placed at $90,000,-000.

The above discussion takes no account of the many undetected diseases which cause loss of achievement even though the child remains in school, nor of the losses in efficiency suffered by many apparently healthy children due to malnutrition or other factors in health.

## I. OBJECTIVES OF HEALTH EDUCATION

A recognition of the many factors which operate in problems of health has led to a broader conception of health education in the schools. The following statement of aims is illustrative:

### THE AIMS OF HEALTH EDUCATION [1]

The aims of health education may be briefly stated as follows:

1. To instruct children and youth so that they may conserve and improve their own health.
2. To establish in them the habits and principles of living which throughout their school life, and in later years, will assure that abundant vigor and vitality which provide the basis for the greatest possible happiness and service in personal, family, and community life.
3. To influence parents and other adults, through the health-education program for children, to better habits and attitudes, so that the school may become an effective agency for the promotion of the social aspects of health education in the family and community as well as in the school itself.
4. To improve the individual and community life of the future; to insure a better second generation, and a still better third generation; a healthier and fitter nation and race.

[1] *Report of the Joint Committee on Health Problems in Education*, p. 13.

**Specific objectives.** At the same time that a more comprehensive program of health education is desired there has also been a tendency to develop the health-education curriculum in terms of the more specific skills or abilities to be developed. The following quotation from Bobbitt [1] is an example. While this list contains a considerable number of abilities, it is probably far from comprehensive, yet a perusal of the list suggests the complex nature of the problems to be faced by the teacher in carrying on a program of health education.

## HEALTH OBJECTIVES

Ability to control one's dietary in such ways as to make one's food contribute in maximum measure to one's physical well-being.

Ability to keep the body mechanism properly oxygenated.

Ability to utilize muscular exercise as a lifelong means of maintaining a high level of physical vitality.

Ability and disposition throughout life to engage with pleasure and profit in a varied repertory of games, sports, athletics, such as swimming, skating, hiking, rowing, riding, tennis, golf, ball games of various kinds, running games, dancing, fishing, hunting, canoeing, motoring, camping, athletic events, etc.

Ability to carry one's self and to move and act with ease, grace, and precision.

Ability to maintain postures conducive to the best physical functioning.

Ability to make one's sleep contribute in maximum measure to the development and maintenance of a high level of physical vitality.

Ability to relax physically and mentally at proper times and in proper ways.

Ability to protect one's self from micro-organisms; and to deal with them and their products effectively in case of attack.

Ability to take proper precautions against the spread of disease.

Ability to dress in ways that promote the physical well-being to a maximum degree.

Ability and disposition to maintain personal cleanliness.

[1] Bobbitt, Franklin. *How to Make a Curriculum*, pp. 165–77. Boston, Houghton Mifflin Company, 1924.

Ability to secure that variety or diversity of physical experiences necessary for maximum well-being.

Ability to draw up an individual program of work, play, rest, sleep, meals, etc., best suited to one's physical nature and capacity.

Ability to avoid preventable accidents.

Ability to deal with conditions produced by many kinds of common accidents.

Ability to care for the teeth, eyes, nose, ears, throat, skin, hair and scalp, nails, and feet.

Ability to keep reasonably well-informed, in the degree to be expected of the layman, as to the discoveries of science in the fields of health conservation and promotion.

Ability to take the protective, precautionary, or remedial steps necessary to protect one's self or family from common ailments.

Ability wisely to utilize the services of physicians, nurses, dentists, and other specialists in health and physical up-building and maintenance.

Ability to make one's various mental and emotional states and activities contribute in maximum degree to one's physical functioning.

## II. CURRENT PROGRAMS IN HEALTH EDUCATION

Modern health programs in the schools include at least three phases: (1) health service, (2) physical education, and (3) health education.[1] It is perhaps unfortunate that these phases of health education have developed more or less independently, creating difficult problems of coördination. The importance of a unified program of health education becomes evident when the complex character of health education is recalled. Good health depends upon a large number of closely interrelated factors.

It would appear obvious that no problem so complex and far-reaching in its nature can be effectively solved without a well-coördinated program of work. It is important, there-

[1] Wood, Thomas D. *Health Education; Report of the Joint Committee on Health Problems in Education*, p. 31.

fore, that those individuals in charge of the various phases of health education must work in close coöperation. School systems in which there is a director of health education who coördinates the various aspects of the work will probably find the problem somewhat simpler. In the last analysis, however, the health-education program becomes the responsibility of the classroom teacher. In fact, some parts of all of the three major phases of health education must reach the pupil through the teacher. The responsibility of the teacher for health education has been well set forth by Wootten: [1]

The classroom teacher is strategically situated to accept the responsibility for health education. There are many reasons why the classroom teacher should have the major responsibility for health work in the schools. (1) A successful health education program necessitates a thorough study of each child. The classroom teacher has more hours of close association with the school child than any one except the child's mother. This gives her an opportunity for a careful and sympathetic study of each child's needs that is not offered to any other person outside the home. (2) Since health is a new subject in our schools and a subject that is closely interwoven with the child's home life, it should be in the hands of trained leaders. The teacher's position carries with it the possibility of this type of leadership and her tact and persistence are invariably responsible for the necessary coöperation of the parents. (3) The development of healthful behavior is the chief aim of health education. The occasional health talks from outside lecturers, no matter how interesting, are not sufficient stimuli for the formation of health habits. Habits of any kind are a matter of repeated action, and it is only through a carefully planned hour to hour schedule that the teacher is able to drill the children in the many health habits that are essential to their best development. (4) Some of the most valuable health instruction is given in correlation with other subjects in the curriculum. The teacher is usually dictator in her schoolroom procedure. This gives her a chance to

[1] Wootten, Kathleen Wilkinson, *A Health Education Procedure*, pp. 11–12. New York, The National Tuberculosis Association, 1926.

use every available opportunity for health work.   (5) The other members of the health supervision corps, the medical inspector and the school nurse, are dependent upon the teacher's intelligent coöperation for the success of their work.   Especially important is her coöperation in detection and exclusion of communicable diseases, and the detection of remedial defects and the follow-up work for their correction.   (6) Janitors are rarely trained and the cleaning as well as the ventilation, heating, seating, lighting and water supply of every school needs intelligent supervision.  Again the classroom teacher's position makes her the natural sanitary inspector and supervisor of school hygiene.  If she is trained to meet this responsibility along with that of the hygiene of the school child she has a limitless fund of first hand material that will interest the children because of its direct connection with their daily lives.

### A. HEALTH SERVICE

A thoroughgoing health-service program in the schools has many phases, the more important among which are:

1. Detection, treatment or correction of defects and diseases and immunization against the latter.
2. Healthful location, construction, equipment, safety, care and use of the school plant.
3. Maintenance of health in teachers.

All of these phases are closely related.   In this discussion they have been separated merely for convenience in treatment.   It is obvious that diseases may spread from teachers to pupils, or vice versa.   It is also true that poor hygienic conditions of the school plan may adversely affect the health of both teachers and pupils.

### 1. Detection, treatment or correction of defects and diseases and immunization against the latter

With the coming of school nurses and physicians it has sometimes erroneously been assumed by teachers that it is not their function to detect defects and diseases.   This theory is no doubt unsound, and is productive of much harm. In the first place, nurses and physicians are not always immediately at hand, and perhaps by the time they arrive all the pupils of a classroom and even of a school may have been exposed to a contagious disease. In some States, Pennsylvania, for example, the teacher in practice becomes a member of the local board of health. She becomes under this law responsible for the exclusion of children who show signs of illness from infectious diseases and those children who have been exposed to such diseases. The law is evidently based on the assumption that if children are to be compelled to go to school the law must also protect them while they are in school.

While not all States place this legal responsibility on the teacher, health authorities recognize the strategic position of the teacher in any health program, and in many cases the local organization and administration of the schools places similar responsibility on the teacher. If the teacher is to discharge this responsibility she must have knowledge of the symptoms of disease. In this work a careful outline of the signs and symptoms of disease will be helpful to the teacher. Such an outline is given by Wootten.[1]

Wood has given us a valuable outline, which is reproduced here.

### SIGNS OF HEALTH DISORDERS AND PHYSICAL DEFECTS IN SCHOOL CHILDREN [2]

The following signs of disorder have been arranged in three groups for the use of teachers in detecting possible health and physical defects in children under their care.

Group I contains signs of disorder which teachers should be trained to notice and report to constituted authorities. Group II

[1] Wootten, Kathleen Wilkinson. *A Health Education Procedure*, pp. 66–97.

[2] Arranged for teachers by Thomas D. Wood, M.D., Teachers College, Columbia University, New York City.

names signs of abnormality pointing to more chronic disorders which should be remedied early.   Group III contains indications of disturbances which are important in connection with other signs of physical disorder.

*Group I.    Indications of Health Disorders in Children Which Teachers should be Trained to Notice and to Report to Constituted Authorities*

Signs
   Nausea or vomiting
   Chill, convulsions (fits)
   Dizziness, faintness, or unusual pallor (alarming paleness of the face)
   Eruption (rash) of any kind
   Fever
   Running nose
   Red or running eyes
   Sore or inflamed throat
   Acutely swollen glands
   New cough
   Any distinct or disturbing change from usual appearance or conduct of child

The foregoing signs should be used by teachers as a basis for excluding pupils from school for the day or until the signs have disappeared or until the proper health officer has authorized the return of the pupil to school.

*Group II.    Signs of Abnormality Pointing to More Chronic Disorders Which should be Remedied Early*

.Signs
   Mouth-breathing
   Loud breathing
   Nasal voice
   Catarrh
   Frequent colds          Disorders of nose, throat, ear, and organs of
   Offensive breath           respiration
   Chronic cough
   Deafness
   Twitching of lips
   Headache

Headache
Crossed eye
Squinting
Holding book too near face
} Eye disorders and defects

Decayed teeth
Crooked teeth
Discoloration of teeth
Offensive breath
} Teeth defects

Inability to hold objects well
Spasmodic movements
Twitching of eye, face, or any part of body
Nail-biting
Perverted tastes
Sex disturbances
} Nervous disorders

Pain in feet
Toeing out markedly
Flatfoot gait
Swelling, puffiness of feet
Excessive perspiration of feet
} Defects of feet

Unequal height of shoulders
Flat chest
Round neck and shoulders
Stooping
} Incorrect posture

*Group III. Indications of Disturbance Which are Important in Connection with Other Signs of Physical Disorder*

Signs
Deficient weight
Pallor
Lassitude
Perverted tastes (food)
Slow mentality
Peculiar or faulty postures
Underdevelopment
Excessive fat
Low endurance
Disinclination to play
Fatigue
} Nutritional and general disorders

Pigeon-toed gait  
Shuffling, inelastic walk  
Exaggerated knee action in walking  
Shifting from foot to foot  
Standing on outer edge of feet  
Standing on inner side of feet, heels  
    turned out  
Locking knee  
Leaning against wall or desk  
Shoes run over at either side  
Wearing out soles asymmetrically  
Twitching of foot muscles  

} Defects of feet and legs, and defective movements

**Immunization.** The problems arising in connection with immunization are illustrative of the interdependence of the various phases of the health program. While it is important, as part of the health-service program, to promote campaigns for vaccination against smallpox or typhoid fever, it is generally recognized that the program of health education is a vital element in the prevention of the spread of disease. For example, it is generally conceded that good health in some measure prevents disease. Thus the enterprise of educating children and adults to the importance of maintaining a high level of bodily vitality becomes an important aspect of health supervision. In the same way, to the extent that participation in physical activities promotes good health, physical education assumes an important relationship to the health program.

It is important that teachers recognize the basic facts in regard to immunization. It is now recognized that while general good health probably reduces the likelihood of contagious disease, it is not in itself a complete preventive. For this reason it becomes desirable to develop immunity through the use of such means as vaccination and diphtheria toxin-anti-toxin. In this work the schools can do much to educate both children and adults. In the case of many diseases there are as yet no reliable means of immunization. In these cases reliance must be placed upon isolation of infected or supposedly infected persons, and the exclusion from school of children affected with colds, coughs, fever, or sore throat. It is important that teachers with these ailments also be excluded from school.

**Health surveys.** It has been estimated by Hoag that ninety per cent of the ordinary defects of school children can be detected by teachers. In the making of a health survey school physicians and nurses can be of excellent assistance. However, the making of such a survey should not be omitted merely because nurses and physicians are not at hand. Frequently the coöperation of local physicians may be secured, if their assistance is enlisted by the principal or teacher.

The equipment needed by the teacher for a health survey is simple and inexpensive. Wootten [1] suggests the following:

One record form for each child.
One pair of scales.
Two tape measures.
One height and weight table for boys.
One height and weight table for girls.
One classroom weight record.
One Snellen's vision chart for vision test.
One loud ticking or stop watch for hearing test.
One curtain pole for posture test.
One tongue depressor for each child (broken and burned immediately after use).

**Weight as a measure of growth and health.** Weight has been widely used as a diagnostic index of health. While growth is a sign of health, it is probable that too much emphasis has been placed upon the importance of weight as a means of diagnosis. In recent years it has been found that

[1] Wootten, Kathleen Wilkinson. *A Health Education Procedure*, p. 62.

many factors influence weight, such as height and form or size of bony framework. Even height-weight tables probably cannot be relied upon entirely. For these reasons it is important that the interpretation of the significance of data in regard to the weight of any child be interpreted in the light of other information concerning health. Overweight or underweight may mean little in itself.

Weight is nevertheless an important factor in health. It is more important to know that a child is making gains in weight than to know how his weight compares with the standard for his age and height. It is also believed that weighing and measuring may be important in an educational way. Charts of increases in weight may encourage children to form good health habits. The child's desire to grow big and tall thus becomes a motivating factor.

**Health examinations.** It is generally recommended that each child be given a thorough health examination each year by a competent physician. The purpose of this examination is not only to detect possible defects and to single out pupils in need of remedial treatment, but also to prevent the development of serious difficulties in apparently healthy children. Many defects can be overcome if detected in the early stages. These same defects may be very serious if overlooked until they become readily apparent. It is important that examinations be made in the school, and that the resulting data be placed in the hands of teachers.

**Recording health data.** If proper use is to be made by teachers and health workers of the data accruing from health examinations, proper record-forms must be provided. Preferably such records should make provision for several recordings, in order that progress may be noted during any one year or from year to year. It is also desirable that the records be made in duplicate, so that both teachers and health supervisors may be in possession of copies.

**Preventable diseases.** Many ailments though not communicable must be given early and effective attention if their ravages are to be stopped or reduced. Among these are heart diseases, diabetes, rickets, and obesity. In these cases correct habits of living are important. There is accumulating evidence that nutritional defects have a relationship to many disorders, such as defects of the teeth, headache, indigestion, nervousness, and fatigue. More attention is given to these problems under the head of nutrition.

**Personality disorders.** The importance of mental health is being increasingly recognized. Moreover it is being found that various nervous and mental disturbances of adult life have their origin in unhygienic childhood habits. It therefore becomes important that the school be organized so as to provide a healthful happy experience for children. In this way the methods of teaching and discipline employed may take on great importance in the specific field of character education. Arithmetic may be taught in such a manner as to promote emotional instability, fear, or worry. A child who is constantly confronted with tasks which are too difficult for him may develop traits of personality which later become serious.

**The follow-up program in the correction of remediable health defects.** It has long been the practice of examining physicians and nurses to notify parents of the defects which examinations reveal. Unless such cases are followed up effectively it often happens that the defects go uncorrected. In some cases this failure on the part of parents to provide for the correction of defects is merely negligence, in other cases it is financial inability. In either case it is important that school authorities follow up the case to protect the child from the negligence or poverty of the parents. The organization of clinics has done much to provide medical attention for needy children. Physicians and dentists in many communities have coöperated generously in many cases to provide such clinical services.

**Coöperation between home and school.** The importance of coöperation between home and school in health education is being increasingly recognized. Much work has been done along this line by nurses and teachers through home calls, parent-teacher organizations, and various forms of adult education.

### 2. Health and the school plant

Great strides have been made in recent years in the effective planning and construction of school buildings.[1] The progress made has been especially notable in such respects as lighting, ventilation, and sanitary facilities. In spite of the progress which has been made there are still many poorly lighted buildings with unsatisfactory equipment. While such buildings should be replaced as rapidly as possible, it is likely that many teachers will face the problem for many years to come of promoting satisfactory health conditions in such buildings. Even excellent building design and construction are not substitutes for a knowledge of school hygiene on the part of the teacher.

**Air and ventilation.** While the importance of ventilation has long been stressed, scientific investigations have somewhat modified the theory in regard to it.[2] Formerly it was held that in crowded rooms discomfort and injury resulted from a depletion of the oxygen in the air, or an increase in carbon dioxide. It has been found that such depletion in oxygen or increase in carbon dioxide is very unlikely. On the other hand the discomfort is found to be due largely to too high temperatures, excessive humidity, or absence of

[1] Strayer, G. D., and Engelhardt, N. L. *Standards for Elementary School Buildings.*

[2] New York State Commission on Ventilation Report.

motion in the air. In other words the discomfort is thermal and physical, rather than chemical.

The new theories have somewhat upset earlier opinions in regard to the effectiveness or desirability of certain types of mechanical ventilation. Some schools have been built which depend entirely on window ventilation. The use of such methods places the problems of ventilation squarely up to the teacher, since she cannot depend on mechanical means which are remotely controlled. In any case the teacher cannot escape responsibility for proper ventilation and temperature in the schoolroom. The subject is too inclusive for treatment here, but the suggestions made in the *Report of the Joint Committee on Health Problems in Education* may be helpful. This *Report* (pages 38–39) offers the following suggestions:

1. *Temperature.* During the colder seasons of the year the most desirable schoolroom temperatures are from 65 to 70 degrees, averaging around 68. A fluctuating or changing temperature within the limits stated above is preferable to unchanging uniformity.

2. *Humidity.* Excessively moist or dry atmospheres, particularly when combined with temperatures around 70 degrees or above, are less comfortable and may be less favorable for health. Practically, within the temperature range of 65 degrees to 70 degrees in climates where the winter temperature does not approach zero weather for continued periods of time, it is not apparent that humidity makes much difference.

3. *Air motion.* Within the temperature range of 65 to 70 degrees it is more comfortable to have a slight fluctuating air motion such as would naturally occur with window ventilation and gravity exhaust. Air motion should not be in such amounts as to cause draughts.

4. *Air change.* Some air change is necessary and there should be provision for circulation of air through the room. Expressed in quantitative terms this need not be more than 10 cubic feet per minute per occupant. There is reason to believe that the common legal standard of 30 cubic feet per minute per occupant is excessive and unnecessary.

Despite the difficulties of proving it, a belief persists among scientific groups that outdoor air possesses certain properties imparted to it by sunlight which are favorable to health.   In line with this assumption it is believed that it is better to admit air directly to the schoolroom from out of doors than to send air to the classroom over heating coils and through metal ducts.

5. Air should be as clean as practicable and free from obnoxious gases and offending odors not because in the amounts that would ordinarily occur these factors are directly inimical to health but because they are annoying and uncomfortable.

6. The manner of obtaining favorable air conditions is dependent on structural provisions and maintenance. Without going into detail it is necessary that there be means for favoring air circulation through the room.   Practically favorable conditions can be obtained with window ventilation and gravity exhaust.   While types of mechanical ventilation are capable of producing comfortable air conditions it has not been demonstrated that they possess superior advantages from the standpoint of health.

**Hygiene of instruction.**   Hygiene of instruction relates to management of the school with reference to length of school day, order of subjects in the program, length of periods for recitation and study, recess periods, rest periods, forms of discipline, hygiene of the eye, fatigue, and many other factors.   A comprehensive discussion of all of these problems is impossible at this point.   The importance of hygiene of instruction is being increasingly recognized.   Particularly is this true as regards the control of emotional factors and the hygiene of the eye.   A detailed discussion is found in Terman and Almack's *Hygiene of the School Child.*[1]

**Hygiene of the eye.**   There is a general impression that sight is our most important sense, and recent efforts at sight conservation have emphasized the importance of conserving sight in various ways.   In many instances children whose vision is defective would probably lose what vision remains

[1] Terman, L. M., and Almack, J. C.   *The Hygiene of the School Child.* Revised and enlarged edition.   Boston, Houghton Mifflin Company, 1929.

if they were subjected to the regular routine of the school. For these pupils special classes have been developed which are conducted in such a manner as to make as little demand upon the children's eyesight as possible. In this way the child may protect what little vision he has, which, although it may be impaired, is still a priceless asset.

It is not only for pupils with seriously impaired vision, however, that sight conservation is important. Unhygienic methods of instruction may impair the vision of pupils who for the moment have no visual difficulties. It is therefore of greatest importance that teachers recognize the importance of controlling schoolroom conditions and practices in the interest of the conservation of eyesight. The suggestions offered for maintaining hygiene of the eye in the *Report of the Joint Committee on Health Problems in Education* [1] are very helpful.

### 3. *The health of teachers and other school employees*

The health of teachers is an important problem in two ways. In the first place the health of the teacher has an important bearing on the health of children. Not only is this true with reference to the possible spread of infectious diseases, but also because the teacher's state of health may be an important factor in her mental and emotional influence in the school. It is not to be expected that a teacher who is discouraged and fatigued by poor health can radiate good cheer and enthusiasm in the schoolroom. In the second place, the teacher's health is an important factor in her own efficiency in instruction. Serious losses occur in every school system through absences of teachers caused by illness. According to a report from Gary, Indiana, teachers lose on an average four school days from illness during each school

[1] Series of reports published by National Education Association, 1201 Sixteenth Street, Washington, D.C.

year. These figures were taken from averages over a period of six years. About 70 per cent of the teachers lost some time from illness, with an average of 1.5 cases of illness for every teacher. Nearly $17,000 was paid from the sick-benefit fund for 871 cases during the school year of 1928–29. These data suggest the economic importance of health among teachers.

**Teacher-health programs.** Teacher-training institutions have undertaken teacher-health programs, which have at least three important aspects:

1. Complete health examination of every student, with follow-up.
2. A healthful program of living.
3. Direct instruction in personal hygiene.

The teaching profession, as most others, carries with it certain conditions which are probably not favorable to health. These conditions must be offset where possible. Among them are:

1. Indifference or ignorance of teachers in regard to their own personal hygiene, and the hygiene of the school.
2. Long hours of sedentary occupation.
3. Overwork caused by large classes and endless paper work, and over-detailed reports.
4. Nervous strain of over-strenuous training for the profession, followed by exhaustive school discipline, excessive standing, and constant use of voice and eyes.
5. The monotonous repetition of the average school program.
6. The dwarfing tendency of dealing constantly with immature minds.
7. Insufficiency of salary.
8. Lack of wholesome recreation.[1]

While there is disagreement about the extent to which many of the above factors operate with reference to teacher health, it is probably also a safe assumption that these and many other factors operate in individual schools or with individual teachers.

[1] Wootten, Kathleen Wilkinson. *A Health Education Procedure*, p. 16.

## B. HEALTH INSTRUCTION

No extensive treatment of the problems of health instruction can be given here. The teacher should avail herself of the many excellent discussions of this work found in the references at the end of the chapter. Attention will therefore be given here to three aspects of the problem only; namely, nutrition, safety education, and health instruction through correlation. Many aspects of health instruction are indirectly touched upon in other parts of this chapter. It is important that the teacher should recognize the complexity of the outcomes in health instruction, as well as the potentialities of the various school activities for health instruction; therefore the activities discussed here should be looked upon as being merely illustrative, and not at all comprehensive.

**Nutrition and health.** Accumulating facts in regard to the relation between nutrition and health are so striking that the school cannot afford to overlook them. There is space here only to refer to one or two instances which emphasize the importance of instruction in nutrition.

The Joint Committee on Health Problems in Education reports studies by Bunting, as follows:

In the University of Michigan a group of dentists working under the leadership of Dr. R. W. Bunting has made a survey of a number of orphanages and children's homes, and finds that dental caries is much less prevalent where diet is good. A carefully controlled study conducted for two years with two large groups of children has furnished a more conclusive demonstration of the relationship between diet and tooth decay. Over three hundred children were kept on a prescribed diet which afforded each child a quart of milk and some green vegetables and fruit each day, but eliminated sugar and white flour as far as possible. The result was a very definite arrest of dental caries in a large proportion of the children.[1]

[1] *Report of the Joint Committee on Health Problems in Education*, pp. 50–51.

At the University of Iowa, Drs. J. D. Boyd and C. L. Grain found that a number of children showed actual hardening of certain tooth areas subject to decay. Careful study showed that these children were diabetics whose diet had been carefully controlled to include a large amount of milk, cream, butter, eggs, cod liver oil, meat, bulky vegetables, and fruit. Such a diet is high in minerals and vitamins. They next undertook to supply this type of diet to children in the orthopedic ward of a hospital. In every instance caries was arrested and no new decay resulted.[1]

Many other illustrations could be supplied testifying to the importance of nutrition. The problem of instruction in nutrition is complicated by the fact that teachers have generally not had sufficient training in the field to do really effective work. In part this is due to the fact that the importance of the subject has only recently been fully recognized. In any case it is fairly certain that if teachers are to do effective work in this field they must give careful study to the problem. We may expect that in future teacher-training programs much emphasis will be placed upon knowledge of the relation between nutrition and health.

**Health education through correlation.** While the importance of correlating health instruction with other subjects has been realized for some time, it is only recently that scientific studies have revealed the true nature of the opportunities of this procedure. It is being found that many subjects in the school curriculum have much material in them which has a bearing on health education. Chappelear's findings are summarized in Table 51.[2]

While Chappelear's data concern high-school sciences, yet they are suggestive of the manner in which other subjects

---

[1] *Report of the Joint Committee on Health Problems in Education*, p. 51.

[2] Chappelear, Claude S. *Health Subject-Matter in Natural Sciences.* Teachers College, Columbia University.

TABLE 51. SUMMARY OF ALL ANALYSES OF THE HEALTH CONTENT IN THE SUBJECT-MATTER OF NATURAL SCIENCES

| | PERCENTAGE OF TOTAL SUBJECT-MATTER DEVOTED TO HEALTH IN EACH SCIENCE | | | |
| --- | --- | --- | --- | --- |
| | General Science | Biology | Chemistry | Physics |
| Page analysis of 5 textbooks.. | 30.78 | 36.99 | 9.16 | 3.05 |
| Topical analysis of 5 state courses of study........... | 39.49 | 42.80 | 16.65 | 2.76 |
| Topical analysis of 5 city courses of study........... | 34.91 | 32.23 | 14.45 | 6.13 |
| Credit point analysis of 13 college entrance examinations | | 33.23 | 5.79 | 2.82 |
| Credit point analysis of 20 New York State Regent's examinations............. | | 31.93 | 7.77 | 1.03 |
| Average.............. | 33.36 | 35.44 | 10.76 | 3.16 |

may contribute to health education. If general or elementary sciences are offered in the lower grades the likelihood is that they offer opportunities to teach many important facts in connection with health.

**Safety education.** Death and injury from accidents have assumed such proportions in our country that the prevention of accidents takes on great importance as an activity in the promotion of health. There are no doubt many reasons for the increase in number of accidents. Among the more important are the increased use of automobiles and high-speed machinery. A large proportion of the accidents fall in the preventable class. Some conception of the seriousness of the problem may be secured from an examination of Table 52.[1] Data in the table apply to victims of all ages. Further information in regard to accidents among children is given by Table 53.

The principal causes of accidents are carelessness, indif-

[1] Table 52 is from the *Report of the Joint Committee on Health Problems in Education*, p. 96.

TABLE 52. CAUSES OF ACCIDENTAL DEATH IN CONTINENTAL
UNITED STATES BY AGES — 1927 *

| CAUSES | UNDER 5 | 5–9 | 10–14 | ABOVE | | TOTALS |
| | | | | 15–19 | 20 | |
|---|---|---|---|---|---|---|
| Automobile accidents......... | 1,294 | 2,240 | 1,026 | 1,461 | 15,673 | 20,704 |
| Drowning.................. | 599 | 653 | 865 | 1,111 | 4,018 | 7,246 |
| Burns (conflagration excepted) | 2,223 | 691 | 213 | 196 | 2,614 | 5,937 |
| Falls..................... | 533 | 313 | 224 | 257 | 13,583 | 14,913 |
| Railroad.................. | 131 | 163 | 217 | 514 | 5,769 | 6,794 |
| Conflagration.............. | 345 | 145 | 62 | 52 | 892 | 1,496 |
| Firearms.................. | 112 | 171 | 384 | 552 | 1,428 | 2,647 |
| Poisoning................. | 808 | 111 | 42 | 70 | 1,413 | 2,444 |
| All other Causes †.......... | 2,105 | 639 | 614 | 1,624 | 15,718 | 20,987 |
| Total................ | 8,150 | 5,126 | 3,647 | 5,377 | 61,108 | 83,408 |

* Data in this table are from registration states only including 89.8 per cent of the total
population.
† Includes asphyxiation, suffocation, machines, electricity, excessive heat or cold, etc.

School accidents................. 669
Home accidents.................. 499
Public accidents................. 398
Industrial accidents............. 6
Total..................... 1572

TABLE 53. DEATH AND INJURIES TO CHILDREN, 6 TO 16, FROM
MARCH 1 TO DECEMBER 31, 1923 *

| CAUSES OR CONTRIBUTING FACTORS | KILLED | INJURED |
|---|---|---|
| Crossing streets not at crossing............... | 184 | 3,583 |
| Playing games in the roadway................ | 56 | 1,865 |
| Crossing streets at street crossing............ | 40 | 1,274 |
| Running off sidewalk into street.............. | 31 | 677 |
| Collisions of vehicles....................... | 3 | 622 |
| Bicycle riding carelessly..................... | 10 | 522 |
| Stealing rides on vehicles.................... | 19 | 431 |
| Climbing trees, poles, fences, etc............. | 66 | 227 |
| Roller skating, coasting, etc., in roadway...... | 11 | 207 |
| While at play.............................. | 7 | 155 |
| Jumping on or off cars, etc., in motion........ | 1 | 147 |
| Falling over obstacles or into excavations...... | 1 | 145 |
| Other causes.............................. | 321 | 10,929 |
| Total.............................. | 750 | 20,784 |

* Wood, Thomas D. (Chairman), *Health Education*, p. 67.

ference, and ignorance. Care to prevent accidents must not only be a matter of knowledge, but must become a habit. Children must be taught to recognize dangerous situations, and to respond quickly with appropriate actions. Such precautions as looking both ways before crossing a street, and picking up banana peels, glass, and nails should be automatic. Some individuals guard themselves against losing their fountain pens by always replacing them in their pockets after use. After a time this practice becomes a habit and there is no forgetting to replace the pen. In the same way pupils can be trained to respect certain rules of safety as a matter of habit. Forgetting will thus play a smaller part.

Indifference usually results from a lack of knowledge of the seriousness of many types of situations in which accidents occur. It is important that the school eliminate this cause of indifference as much as possible by providing constant information in regard to the various causes of accidents.

Recently, many types of activities for education in safety have been developed. Among them are:

1. Dramatization of traffic courts, imaginary accidents, and desirable conduct in the interest of safety
2. Stories of accidents
3. Motion pictures on safety
4. Safety clubs
5. Junior Police Organizations
6. Safety themes in English classes
7. Safety mottoes

The *Report of the Joint Committee on Health Problems in Education* outlines a series of suggestions for organizing a program of safety education, as follows: [1]

[1] *Report of the Joint Committee on Health Problems in Education*, pp. 100–01.

### The Organization of a Safety Program for a School

From studies that have been made of the methods of organizing safety in various school systems the following program is suggested.

1. Prevention of traffic accidents about the school buildings
   a. Dangerous crossings near schools
   b. Organizing safety patrols and councils
   c. Provision for parking cars about the school
   d. Supervision of school bus transportation
2. Prevention of traffic accidents within the building
   a. Provisions for a traffic squad to control traffic
   b. Providing for adequate lighting and protection of stairways
3. Prevention of accidents in the gymnasium or playgrounds, and in athletics
   a. Leaders corps to prevent accidents in gymnasium
   b. Adequate supervision of play spaces by patrols
   c. Reducing accidents on the athletic field — condition of the playing field, protection of players, conditioning of players
   d. Supervision of athletics by trained physical education directors
4. Prevention of accidents in shops and laboratories
   a. Safeguarding dangerous machinery
   b. Instruction in the proper use of hand tools
   c. Supervision over operation of machinery
5. Fire prevention and fire drills
   a. Cleanliness in school classrooms and storage rooms
   b. Provisions for fighting fires
   c. Regular fire drills
   d. Coöperation with fire department or other local organizations in home inspection work
6. First aid
   a. Providing first aid cabinet for school
   b. Responsible persons for administering first aid
7. Teaching safety in the classroom
   A course of study in safety providing for instruction at various age levels. Safety may be taught in correlation with many different subjects, particularly with civics, health and physical education, science, chemistry, biology, language, etc. Many schools devote from 5 to 15 minutes a day to a definite safety lesson.
8. Other valuable safety work

*a.* The use of the school assembly for plays, pageants, motion pictures, etc.
*b.* Making of safety posters
*c.* Using posters from national safety organizations
*d.* Safety activities for various clubs — life-saving, Boy Scouts, first aid, swimming, etc.
*e.* Safety programs in home rooms

### C. PHYSICAL EDUCATION

No comprehensive discussion of physical education can be attempted here. Only those aspects which are more or less directly related to health education can be considered. While physical education concerns itself largely with opportunities for big-muscle development and activities, it is impossible to separate these activities from the larger program of health education. Probably the healthy organism is not achieved through isolated activities, but rather by means of a well-rounded control of the child's environment including activities, hygienic living, correction of defects, and promotion of mental health. When objectives are set forth for physical education it will readily be recognized that other aspects of the health program also contribute to these objectives. Among the generally accepted objectives for physical education are the following:

1. To improve general health
2. To obtain good posture
3. To make pupils alert, accurate, vigorous, and able to endure
4. To cultivate a spirit of fair play
5. To develop initiative and leadership
6. To teach a love of outdoor recreation

In order to realize these objectives physical-education programs in schools have included three main types of activities:

1. Gymnastics, both formal and informal
2. Recreational activities, games, clubs, etc.
3. Relief drills

**Measurement and diagnosis in physical education.** In some aspects of physical education, measures of proficiency are easily secured. For example, one can readily measure the distance which a boy can jump. Many athletic activities are of this type. On the other hand there are certain respects in which measurement in physical education is exceedingly difficult. We have practically no diagnostic measures in physical education at the present time. A pupil's achievement in the high jump is easily measured, but if his achievement is low we have almost no way of finding out why it is low. Some progress has been made in developing tests which are somewhat analytical, as for example the Rogers tests.[1] The tests include the following:

1. Forced lung capacity, measured with the wet spirometer in cubic inches.
2 and 3. Strength of grip (of forearm) (flexion) of each hand, measured by grasping the elliptical monometer or hand-dynamometer, in pounds.
4. Strength of back (extension) measured by lifting, with knees straight, using the back and leg dynamometer in pounds.
5. Strength of legs (extension) measured by lifting, carrying the weight on the thighs, with the back and leg dynamometer.
6. Strength of arms (shoulder girdle) (extension) by "push-ups" from straight-arm hang on the parallel bars, as many times as possible.
7. Strength of arms (and shoulder girdle) (flexion) by "chinning" or "pull-ups" using eight inch rings attached to an overhead ladder.

The scores on these tests are combined into a "Strength Index." The greatest value of such measures has been held to be that of their adaptability for classification purposes in physical education. It is perhaps obvious that pupils will vary greatly in physical fitness for participation in various

[1] Rogers, Frederick Rand. *Rogers Physical Capacity Tests in the Administration of Physical Education.* Bureau of Publications, Teachers College, Columbia University.

types of activities. If through the use of such measures it would be possible accurately to select pupils for different types of activities such measures would have great value. At the present time little is known concerning the adaptabilities of these measures to the actual classroom situation.

**Diagnostic tests.** Some efforts have been made to secure diagnostic measures in the fields of physical activities. For example, if one is unable to play tennis effectively, what are the reasons for failure? If the various elements in tennis can be singled out it may be possible to provide better assistance on the part of the instructor. An example is the Tennis Test shown below. While not entirely objective, it is evident that such a device makes possible attention to specific elements in the activity which might be overlooked if no such device is at hand.

TENNIS TEST 3s, 1929 [1]

I. *Forehand Drive* . . . . . . . . . . . . . . . . . . . . . . . . . . . . . 15 points
   *Accuracy* . . . . . . . . . . . . . . . . . . . . . . . . . . 10
   Ball to be played from behind the base line and driven into opposite court between service and base line.

        3 out of 4 . . . . . . . . 10
        2 out of 4 . . . . . . . . 5
        1 out of 4 . . . . . . . . 3

   *Form* . . . . . . . . . . . . . . . . . . . . . . . . . . . . . **5**
        Grip . . . . . . . . . . . . 1
        Side to net . . . . . . . . 1
        Trans. of weight . . . 1
        Straight arm . . . . . . 1
        Follow through . . . . 1

II. *Backhand Drive* . . . . . . . . . . . . . . . . . . . . . . . . . . . . **15**
   *Accuracy* . . . . . . . . . . . . . . . . . . . . . . . . . . 10
        Same as forehand.
   *Form* . . . . . . . . . . . . . . . . . . . . . . . . . . . . . 5
        Same as forehand.

[1] Unpublished material used in Department of Physical Education, University of Minnesota.

III. *Service*........................................ 10
    *Accuracy*............................ 6
        2 balls to be served from L court
        2 balls to be served from R court
            3 out of 4..... 6
            2 out of 4..... 3
            1 out of 4..... 1
    *Form*................................ 4
        Side to net........ 1
        Straight arm...... 1
        Trans. of weight... 1
        Follow through.... 1
IV. *Written Quiz*................................ 10

                                    Total    50 points

### III. DIAGNOSIS IN HEALTH EDUCATION

It would appear to be obvious that the problems of measurement in health education are very complex. Such measurement is not merely concerned with a few simple skills or knowledges but with attitudes, ideals, habits, and more or less complex conduct patterns. Paper and pencil tests can never become adequate. They will always have to be supplemented by various types of observational procedure.

Complete diagnosis in the field of health education will not be possible for the teacher in many instances without the assistance of the physician and psychologist. Yet, even these specialists will always welcome the assistance of the teacher who through her intimate and constant contact with the pupil is in position to discover much valuable information about the child.

**Types of measurement.** The *Report of the Joint Committee on Health Problems in Education* (pages 33–34), lists six types of measurement in health education:

1. Anatomical and physiological measures of health status
2. Paper and pencil tests of health knowledge

3. Paper and pencil tests of health attitude
4. Observation of health activities
5. Self-checking on health practices
6. Rating of others on health practices

For the sake of convenience each of these types of measurement will be discussed separately.

**Measures of health status.** Many of the measures of health status are only available to the physician. At the same time there are a number of aspects in which teachers may observe the pupil's state of health with considerable accuracy. Height and weight can be readily determined. Abnormalities in many cases may be noted. Appetite, regularity of hours of sleep and many other items may be noted. Teachers will be helped by lists of the characteristics of a healthy individual. The one which appears below is suggestive: [1]

### THE HEALTHY ORGANISM: PHYSIOLOGIC HEALTH

Physiologic health implies the well-being of each cell and organ, and their harmonious coöperation. Indications of this are:

1. Proper growth in height, weight, structural and functional development. This includes more than mere freedom from malformation, abnormal growth, or structural defects.
2. Full efficiency of functions: muscular, nervous, mental, glandular, nutritive, circulatory, respiratory, excretory, and reproductive. This means that there is a feeling of abundant energy for all the ordinary activities of life, and some reserve for unusual strains.

It may require a careful physical examination to discover in detail the condition of the child on all points mentioned above. But there are certain simple evidences of bodily health which any one may easily observe.

1. The healthy child is largely unconscious of his body. He has a general sense of well-being, a feeling of muscular power and of pleasure in movement. He is not conscious of the vital organs. When a child is in pain, or in ill health, on the other hand, he becomes conscious of parts of his body, which in so far as he knew before might have been non-existent.

[1] From *Report of the Joint Committee on Health Problems in Education.*

2. He possesses sufficient vigor so that a reasonable amount of work and play is more stimulating than fatiguing.

3. His appetite is steady, wholesome, and not capricious.

4. His weight does not vary widely from the average weight for his age and skeletal structure.

5. He sleeps well, and during the normal regular hours of sleep, he recovers satisfactorily from fatigue.

6. He is able to adapt himself to new conditions of environment, climate, or modes of life without undue physiological disturbances.

## The Healthy Personality: Mental, Emotional, Moral and Social Health

The healthy personality may be said to be one which enables the individual to make successful, happy, or effective adjustments to his environment.

It is not to be expected or desired that all persons should conform to one pattern of personality, but it may be useful to name some of the characteristics found, in varying degrees and combinations, in personalities of a healthy child.

1. The child possesses intelligence adequate to meet the demands of life.

2. He is able to concentrate his attention upon the matter before him, and to perceive the important elements of the situation with accuracy and alertness.

3. He is interested in the world about him, and curious to understand it.

4. He is generally self-confident; he expects success and achieves it with reasonable frequency.

5. He is active in overcoming difficulties; he does not "daydream" so much that he fails to meet the actual situation.

6. His predominating emotional qualities are happiness, cheerfulness, courageousness. He is not troubled by unnecessary fears, shyness, or timidity. His emotional responses are those that are appropriate and useful for the occasion.

7. He does not ordinarily brood or sulk, or indulge in morbid introspection.

8. He has many objective interests: friends, hobbies, games in which he finds adequate self-expression.

9. He is companionable and mingles easily with other children.

He adapts himself easily to coöperative enterprises; to leadership or followship.

10. The child's relationships with children of the opposite sex are wholesome.
11. He has a sense of responsibility for the happiness and well-being of his friends, schoolmates, and members of his family.

**Health-knowledge tests.** Health is dependent upon many factors besides knowledge. Among these are attitudes and habits. At the same time knowledge of facts in regard to health is no doubt of considerable importance in promoting the right attitudes and habits. There is, however, no complete agreement on the importance of knowledge in health education. Perhaps it is safe to say that health knowledge is at least one of the factors in health which the teacher will wish to take account of in attempting diagnostic measurement in health education.

**The Gates-Strang Health Knowledge Test.** The Gates–Strang is one of the best-known health-knowledge tests. Its content has been determined by an analysis of twenty courses of study in health in rural and city schools. In addition the original 754 items were organized in a test and criticized by a group of experts. Finally the test was reduced to 520 items. These items were organized into standardized tests containing 64 items. The total number of items is distributed as follows:

| Topic | Number of Item |
| --- | --- |
| Food | 98 |
| Disease prevention | 78 |
| Physiology | 33 |
| Exercise and posture | 30 |
| Cleanliness | 27 |
| Fresh air and sunshine | 21 |
| Mental hygiene | 18 |
| Care of the eyes | 17 |
| Safety | 15 |

| Topic | Number of Item |
|---|---|
| Defects including malnutrition | 14 |
| Clothing | 14 |
| Care of the teeth | 14 |
| Water | 13 |
| Industrial hygiene | 12 |
| Values of health | 12 |
| First aid | 11 |
| Elimination of bodily wastes | 10 |
| Care of the hair | 10 |
| Rest and sleep | 10 |
| Disposal of garbage and waste | 10 |
| Child care | 9 |
| Names of scientists and miscellaneous items | 8 |
| Alcohol | 7 |
| Care of ears, nose, and throat | 6 |
| Care of feet | 6 |
| Patent medicine and drugs | 5 |
| Tobacco | 4 |
| Health laws | 3 |
| Public health administration | 3 |
| Health organizations | 2 |

The Public School Achievement Tests, by Orleans and Sealy, include a section on health knowledge. The test is in four parts, one provided with a true-false response, one with completion response, one with multiple-choice response, and one with a matching exercise. This test is not so comprehensive as the Gates–Strang Test, but differs in that four types of response are used.

**Tests of health attitude.** The problems of attitude testing are discussed in the chapter on character education. It is the feeling of some that there is little correlation between what one believes or prefers and one's conduct. If this is true, tests of attitude can probably be given little attention as measures of conduct. Little has thus far been done to prepare tests which measure health attitudes.

**Observation of health activities.** It would appear that this is one of the most fruitful directions in which measurement in health education might be extended. It is desired that health education eventuate in good conduct and wholesome health activities. Such conduct and activities can be observed and distinguished from unhealthful behavior. This method of measurement has, however, one drawback; it is very time-consuming. A further weakness is that unless the teacher has some definite list of items to check against, many important aspects of health may be forgotten. *Health Behavior*, by Wood and Lerrigo, contains many such lists which may be effectively used by the teacher in checking on the health behavior of the child.[1]

**Self-checking on health practices.** One of the best examples of this method is the Health-Chores scheme of the National Anti-Tuberculosis Association. The pupil records on a chart the performance of certain acts tending to promote health, such as brushing of teeth, drinking ample amounts of water, and regular hours of sleep. This method places the recording responsibility on the pupil, and since the records are posted it is maintained that it stimulates pupils to make good records. Thus it is held to be an effective motivating device. On the other hand it is criticized because pupil ratings of their own conduct are open to error. In addition it is claimed that it promotes dishonesty, since the pupil may falsify the record to make a good showing.

The report of the Joint Committee on Health Problems in Education suggests that the shortcomings of the method may be less pronounced if suitable forms are used, and if the device is not used too frequently or checked by the teacher as a rating device. Reference to the character-education

---

[1] Wood, Thomas D., and Lerrigo, Marion O. *Health Behavior*. Public School Publishing Company, Bloomington, Illinois. 1927.

problems involved is also made in the chapter on character education.

The Payne Health-Conduct Scale is another example of the practice of self-checking. Perhaps parts of this scale could also be used by the teacher in checking on the health conduct of pupils.

**Teacher rating of health practices.** Thus far little has been done to develop scales by which the teacher can rate the health behavior of the child. In the field of character education some interesting devices are now being developed which are shown in Chapter XIII. Such scales as those included in *Health Behavior*, by Wood and Lerrigo, are of some value. There is, however, no provision for rating the child on the various items. It is thus difficult to use the scales for measuring progress made by children.

It would appear that some of the devices used in measuring other aspects of children's behavior might be employed in the field of health behavior. The Behavior Rating Schedule by Haggerty, Olson, and Wickman is an example. Some of the items already in the scale lie definitely in the field of health. No doubt others could be found. It would appear that the rating method used could also be employed.

**Ratings by other pupils.** In the field of character tests, Hartshorne and May developed what is known as a "guess who" test. A number of brief descriptions of children are listed on a sheet of paper. The pupils are told that each of these descriptions applies to some member of the class. They are asked to guess who the pupil is who corresponds to the description. The *Report of the Joint Committee on Health Problems in Education* suggests that this device could be used by assembling brief descriptions, such as the following:

He always comes to school with dirty hands.

He never goes out to play in the afternoon but stays in the house.

He acts sleepy most of the time.

Pupils would be asked to guess who the individual is who corresponds to these descriptions.

**Securing composite health ratings.** Considerable progress in the rating field has been made with tests which give composite ratings. The Brueckner Scales for Rating Teaching Skill are an example. In the rating of personality characteristics, the Olson scale already shown in the chapter on character education is illustrative. No doubt similar scales could be prepared covering the field of health. Such scales could be used for self-rating by pupils. The teacher may say to a pupil, "Here are some descriptions of children. Read them, and see which child is most like yourself. Which one of the children described would you want to be like?" In this way such devices may become effective for motivation purposes.

## IV. ILLUSTRATIVE TEACHING PROCEDURES

It is not feasible in this chapter to give any comprehensive discussion of teaching methods or procedures in health education. A few illustrative procedures are given below which it has been thought might be suggestive to teachers. Much help can be secured by teachers from the many excellent references which are given at the end of the chapter. The materials which follow are intended merely to introduce the various types or approaches.

**Organizing a teaching outline.** Teachers often find difficulty in organizing their work for a relatively new field, such as health education. This difficulty has been recognized in the *Detroit Course of Study in Health Instruction*. Teachers have been provided in this course with illustrative procedures for organizing outlines for the several units.

A sample outline for teaching a unit on "Energy and Vitality" is given here.

### ENERGY AND VITALITY, TEACHING OUTLINE

Alertness, pep, enthusiasm and endurance are qualities upon which the schools should place a premium. These qualities are definite measures of health. Normal girls and boys whose daily habits are organized in a healthful way, display these qualities in everything they do. Every child should discover the laws that govern the building up and conserving of a full reservoir of energy and vitality.

The problems of *leisure time* and *qualities of mind* are directly related to this problem of *"Energy and Vitality"* and these three problems should be developed concurrently.

Before beginning these problems the teacher should read carefully the pages relating to health clubs, plays, posters, scrapbooks and problems.

The following outline indicates the steps that may be taken in developing the problem of *energy* and *vitality*. A detailed discussion of methods will be found in the text.

| I The problem introduced | Selected readings | Stories of great men and women. What qualities did they possess? Story of Roosevelt, etc. |
| | Class discussion | What qualities make for failure? What qualities make for success? Which of these qualities depend upon health? |
| | Summarizing | How can we attack this problem? What is energy? vitality? What is their relation? |
| II Discovery of the field | Comparison of people and animals | Are these qualities found in animals? Differences in pupils and people we know. List those qualities denoting absence of energy and vitality. |
| | Class discussion | Discovery that right habits of living are the true foundation and source of energy and vitality. Which habits are good? Which bad? |

| | | |
|---|---|---|
| **III**<br>Search for facts | Bad qualities | What causes lack of energy and vitality?<br>No endurance, pep, enthusiasm, etc.<br>What are results of this lack? Page 110. |
| | Good qualities | What builds up energy and vitality?<br>Why have we endurance, drive, etc?<br>Are these qualities valuable? Why? Page 112. |
| | Classify causes | Relate the nine factors to energy and vitality.<br>Group all causes. Page 115.<br>See leisure time and qualities of mind. Pages 119–26.<br>Read about body systems. |
| **IV**<br>Investigations and activities | Supplementary Reading | See bibliography. Page 118.<br>See textbook analysis. Page 18.<br>Find stories of people illustrating energy and vitality. |
| | Health Club | Form health club. Page 162. |
| | Class Activities | Each pupil rate self on good qualities.<br>Make rating card for above. Basis of 100 per cent.<br>Assign special topics to pupils.<br>Slogans — A "pep" song. Posters.<br>Dramatize each quality — good and bad.<br>Give play.<br>See chapter on problems. Page 139. |
| **V**<br>A health program outlined | | Summarize class activities and the information gained.<br>Formulate health laws. Page 174.<br>Check health habits. Page 169. |

**Plays and pageantry.** Dramatization is one of the best means of arousing interest in any subject. It not only appeals to children and speaks to them in their own language of picture and action, but it catches the attention of parents and adults in the community as well. The health play thus becomes a means of bringing school and community to a joint realization of the importance of the problems of health. One of the most recent movements in the field of dramatization provides for the use of plays written by the children themselves. In many schools the materials or properties used in the plays are constructed by the pupils. This provides excellent opportunities for correlating the work of the various departments — home economics and industrial training, for examples.

Teachers who wish to carry on dramatic work in the field of health education should write the bureau of Educational Dramatics, Community Service, 315 Fourth Avenue, New York City, for lists of materials. Many of these materials deal with other subjects, but they can be adapted to health-education purposes.

**Graphic methods.** The value of graphic materials is being recognized by all sorts of publicity and educational agencies. Newspapers, magazines, and advertising carry increasingly large amounts of graphic material. One of the best attempts to utilize graphic materials is found in the *Detroit Course of Study in Health Instruction*.

## QUESTIONS FOR STUDY, DISCUSSION, AND REPORT

1. Trace the origins and development of health education in the schools.
2. Indicate the respects in which character education and health education present similar problems.
3. Why would it be unwise to classify a child as in poor health because he is slightly underweight?

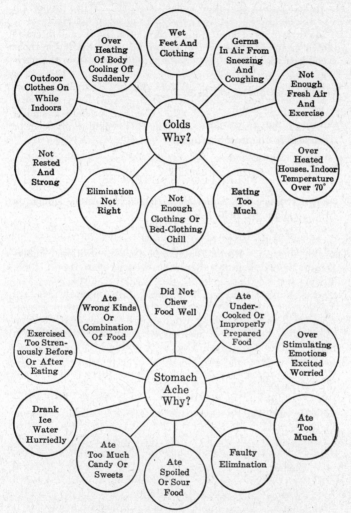

FIG. 8. POSSIBLE CAUSES OF COMMON AILMENTS

From *Detroit Course of Study in Health Institution*

4. Make a health survey of a class of pupils. What proportion of the children are entirely free from physical defects?

5. Make an observational study of the play activities and interests of a group of children. What would you suggest for those children who do not participate in any activities on the playground?

6. What elementary-school subjects supply the greatest opportunities for health education? Give reasons for your views.

7. Examine Fig. 8 on page 591. Can you prepare a similar diagram for other ailments? What help could a physician or nurse give you in this project?

## SELECTED REFERENCES

Averill, Lawrence A. *Educational Hygiene*. Boston, Houghton Mifflin Company, 1926. 546 p.

Commonwealth Fund, Division of Publications. *Serving the Child in Fargo*. New York, 1928. 127 p.

Dansdill, Theresa. *Health Training in Schools*. National Tuberculosis Association, 370 Seventh Avenue, New York, 1928. 405 p.

National Education Association, and the American Medical Association. Joint Committee on Health Problems in Education, Dr. Thomas D. Wood, Chairman. A series of Reports on sale by the National Education Association, 1201 Sixteenth Street, N.W., Washington, D.C.

(a) *Health Education*. 1924. 164 p.

(b) *Conserving the Sight of School Children*. 1925. 46 p.

(c) *The Deafened School Child*. 1928. 38 p.

National Society for the Study of Education. *Twenty-Fifth Yearbook*, Part I: "The Present Status of Safety Education." Bloomington, Illinois, Public School Publishing Company, 1926. 410 p.

Whitcomb, Charlotte T., and Beveridge, John H. *Our Health Habits*. Chicago, Rand McNally and Company, 1926. 608 p.

Wood, Thomas D., and Cassidy, Rosalind R. *The New Physical Education*. New York, The Macmillan Company, 1927. 457 p.

Wood, Thomas D., and Lerrigo, Marion O. *Health Behavior*. Bloomington, Illinois, Public School Publishing Company, 1927. 150 p.

Wood, Thomas D., and Rowell, H. G. *Health Through the Preven-*

*tion and Control of Disease.*   Yonkers, New York, World Book
Company, 1925.   122 p.

Wood, Thomas D., and Rowell, H. G.   *Health Supervision and
Medical Inspection of Schools.*   Philadelphia, Pennsylvania,
W. B. Saunders Company, 1927.   367 p.

Wootten, Kathleen Wilkinson.   *A Health Education Procedure.*
New York, The National Tuberculosis Association, 1926.   420 p.

## HEALTH EDUCATION TESTS

| Test | Publisher |
| --- | --- |
| Rogers Physical Ability Tests | Bureau of Publications, Teachers College, Columbia University, New York, N.Y. |
| Gates–Strang Health Knowledge Test | Bureau of Publications, Teachers College, Columbia University, New York, N.Y. |
| Public School Achievement Tests Health Knowledge | Public School Publishing Company, Bloomington, Illinois. |
| Payne Health Conduct Sale | Public School Publishing Company, Bloomington, Illinois. |

# INDEX

8
367
1941